Macmillan Law Masters

Housing Law and Policy

MACMILLAN LAW MASTERS

Series Editor **Marise Cremona**

Business Law (2nd edn)   Stephen Judge
Company Law (3rd edn)   Janet Dine
Constitutional and Administrative Law (3rd edn)   John Alder
Contract Law (3rd edn)   Ewan McKendrick
Conveyancing (3rd edn)   Priscilla Sarton
Criminal Law (2nd edn)   Marise Cremona
Employment Law (3rd edn)   Deborah J. Lockton
Environmental Law and Ethics   John Alder and David Wilkinson
Evidence   Raymond Emson
Family Law (2nd edn)   Kate Standley
Housing Law and Policy   David Cowan
Intellectual Property Law   Tina Hart and Linda Fazzani
Land Law (3rd edn)   Kate Green
Landlord and Tenant Law (3rd edn)   Margaret Wilkie and Godfrey Cole
Law of the European Union (2nd edn)   Jo Shaw
Law of Succession   Catherine Rendell
Law of Trusts   Patrick McLoughlin and Catherine Rendell
Legal Method (3rd edn)   Ian McLeod
Legal Theory   Ian McLeod
Social Security Law   Robert East
Torts (2nd edn)   Alastair Mullis and Ken Oliphant

Housing Law and Policy

David Cowan
Lecturer, University of Bristol

Law series editor: Marise Cremona
Senior Fellow, Centre for Commercial Law Studies
Queen Mary and Westfield College, University of London

MACMILLAN

First published 1999 by
MACMILLAN PRESS LTD
Houndmills, Basingstoke, Hampshire RG21 6XS
and London
Companies and representatives
throughout the world

ISBN 0-333-71846-1

A catalogue record for this book is available
from the British Library.

This book is printed on paper suitable for recycling and
made from fully managed and sustained forest sources.

10   9   8   7   6   5   4   3   2   1
08   07   06   05   04   03   02   01   00   99

Copy-edited and typeset by Povey–Edmondson
Tavistock and Rochdale, England

Printed and bound in Great Britain by
Creative Print & Design (Wales) Ebbw Vale

Coventry University

Contents

Preface

The bookshelves of academic housing lawyers, at least in the United Kingdom, have been weighed down in the 1990s, not so much by legislation, as by encyclopaedias, textbooks, books of law cases (commonly combined with other legal commentary), and other materials usually aimed at legal practitioners. In order to make themselves distinctive, texts aimed at the student market commonly proclaim themselves as being interdisciplinary or, at the least, taking into account literature from non-legal sources.

The usual word adopted by such authors to describe their texts is 'contextual', but the inclusion of this word, often, hardly detracts from the weight of doctrinal law stuffed into these texts. What the reader is usually offered is a well-written exposition of legal principles basically relating to the law of landlord and tenant (which includes the right to buy) and homelessness. Housing law is usually portrayed as a politically neutral arbiter of relationships between landlords and tenants, as well as of homelessness duties. The wealth of socio-legal and similar housing policy research is ignored, despite its importance to undergraduate study. The legal principles are complex – this must be admitted – but complexity on its own does not, or should not, make a degree course textbook. It certainly does not justify the existence of more books than can be counted on two hands. Theory, and its relevance to housing law, is ignored; and housing law is portrayed as a subject without any structure. For example, homelessness (again, as with all other similar books) is confined to chapters at the end of the book without explanation as to why it is considered at all, let alone at that point.

The approach adopted in this book is different. I have treated housing 'law' as problematic, structured and political. Rather than resort to legal doctrine and the usual legal textbook style, this book is more interested in what I describe as the *contexts of law* and their policy frame. In so doing, rather than draw upon cases, statutes, etc., I have preferred to draw upon housing studies and socio-legal literature which amplify and illustrate the fundamental dilemmas in housing. My style is uncompromisingly political (old Labour), but I take the view that housing *is* political and consequently should be portrayed as such.

The book is divided into three related, themed parts, which can be viewed as building-blocks. The overriding arguments relate to the use of tenure, and the shift towards what is termed 'responsibility'. The first part discusses the regulatory crisis affecting each housing tenure. Particular attention is paid to the methods through which tenures are financed and boundaries between tenures breached. To what extent is central regulation responsible for this crisis? Second, access to housing is discussed, providing a critique of the concepts of 'housing need' and 'affordability'.

Is the use of these concepts defensible, or do we simply pay lip-service to them? How is housing tenure affected by access issues? Third, individual housing rights are discussed in the context of a shift towards individual responsibility, drawing particularly upon criminological and criminal justice theory. What are the rationales for this shift away from due process rights to a more penal regime? What does this shift tell us about our use of tenure?

As with any study of this nature, I have drawn upon and abused my friendships and acquaintances. Indeed, people who didn't know me at all offered advice and assistance, and in some cases read chapters for me. The generosity of academic colleagues constantly amazes me, particularly as we are all faced with considerable resource pressures from within institutions and outside them. Indeed, as Bristol offered me a sabbatical for the academic year 1997–8 (after only having been here for two years) to write this book, my colleagues were saddled with doing my teaching.

The Socio-Legal Studies Association Conference has provided an important forum for discussion of housing issues. It has become gratifyingly easy to organize the housing stream, mainly because of the wealth of socio-legal housing research currently being conducted. I have gained much from listening to the insights of those who have contributed to sessions and debate within the housing stream. Many of those insights have been included in this book, referenced accordingly.

Some people should be mentioned individually. In no particular order, the following have all read and commented upon (at length usually) at least one chapter: Andrew Sanders, Rod Edmunds, Caroline Hunter, Rose Gilroy, Christina Pantazis, Paddy Hilyard, Matthew Waddington, Gwynn Davis, Nick Dearden, Lisa Whitehouse, Martin Partington, Lois Bibbings, Andrew Cowan. Caroline Hunter, Sarah Blandy, Martin Loughlin, Alex Marsh, Andrew Sanders and Carolyn Hoyle provided me with their as yet unpublished work; also, many have let me use their conference contributions. Lois Bibbings made attempts to stop me seeing binary divides everywhere and Christina Pantazis was a fantastic co-worker at the same time I was writing this book. Martin Partington listened to the ramblings of a confused person in early 1997 and helped mould them into something more coherent.

Three people have considerably influenced the shape of this book as it developed. Andrew Sanders and Paddy Hillyard may find that most of the better ideas in this book owe a considerable amount to our discussions. Andrew's office, being next door to mine, made him an easy target. I have particularly drawn upon my lunchtime discussions with Paddy about postmodern social policy, panopticism and synopticism in Chapter 10. My great friend and former colleague, Rod Edmunds, has read and commented on virtually every chapter whilst sustaining his many other commitments.

The usual caveats apply.

I began writing in December 1997 and finished in February 1999. The series editor, Marise Cremona, the anonymous external reviewer, and the publishers have been most accommodating during this period to a book which is rather different from most others in the series.

During the writing period, Jake Cowan has come into the world. This book is dedicated to my loves, Jake and Helen.

June 1999   DAVID COWAN

Table of Cases

Table of Statutes

Abbreviations

AST	Assured Shorthold Tenancy
BCA	Basic Credit Approval
BES	Business Expansion Scheme
BSA	Building Societies Association
CHR	Common Housing Register
CCT	Compulsory Competitive Tendering
CML	Council of Mortgage Lenders
DETR	Department of Environment, Transport and the Regions (from 1996)
DoE	Department of Environment (until 1996)
DoH	Department of Health
DSS	Department of Social Security
EHO	Environmental Health Officer
GIA	General Improvement Area
HAA	Housing Action Area
HAG	Housing Association Grant
HAMA	Housing Association as Managing Agent
HAT	Housing Action Trust
HIP	Housing Investment Programme
HIT	Housing Investment Trust
HMO	House in Multiple Occupation
HPU	Homeless Persons Unit
HRA	Housing Revenue Account
LSVT	Large Scale Voluntary Transfer
MIRAS	Mortgage Interest Relief at Source
NSP	Notice of Seeking Possession
PEP	Priority Estates Project
PRS	Private Rented Sector
RDG	Revenue Deficit Grant
RSL	Registered Social Landlord
RTIA	Receipts Taken Into Account
SCA	Supplementary Credit Approval
SHG	Social Housing Grant
TCI	Total Cost Indicators
TMO	Tenant Management Organization

For Helen and Jake, with love

Introduction

This is a book about the interrelation and interaction between housing 'law' and housing policy. Housing 'law' is given a particular meaning. The book does not stop at a discussion of the cases, statutes, quasi-legislation and other aspects of legalism which litter the arena of housing law. Indeed, much of what is traditionally regarded as housing law has been marginalized within this text. Neither is the approach adopted one of 'law in context(s)'. Rather, the approach is generally to analyse, consider and extrapolate upon *the contexts of law*. Drawing on studies in different subjects – sociology, social policy, economics and their diffusion within the housing studies movement – I have attempted to map out these contexts whilst adapting the framework usually adopted within housing law. My objectives are fourfold: first, to place housing within the rapidly developing sphere of socio-legal studies; second, to attempt to provide some broad structure to housing law studies; third, to map out key directions in housing; and fourth, to politicize our discussions of housing.

My writing style is 'heart-on-sleeve' political, left of centre (and certainly left of New Labour), and occasionally impish. It is readily accepted that this style will not appeal to everyone, but hopefully this is a question of style and not content. Throughout, I have tried to be innovative, to raise ideas for discussion, and most of all to be thought-provoking within the constraints of a declamatory style. My personal aims for this book are that it should start housing lawyers discussing their subject in more meaningful ways than has been the case hitherto; and for those within the housing studies movement to appreciate the role and importance of housing law.

For far too long housing law has been dominated by constricting its involvement to a narrow base of legislation and case law. Of course, there is a mass of such material (more than enough to teach several modular units), but what does it illustrate about housing? Such discussion is commonly also circular: 'decisions refer to rules and rules to decisions' (Teubner, 1984, p. 295). Constricting its parameters in this way has also constricted the development of academic housing law studies. Put simply, housing law has been left without a conceptual core. Why, for example, is homelessness commonly left to the end of a course (and most housing law books)? Indeed, why is it taught at all in a course about *housing*? The answer is that it forms a critical part of the housing system: access to, and allocation of, housing. It also provides an important example of the way in which law is often subrogated to more practical demands (such as the lack of supply of accommodation), organizational imperatives (the avoidance of obligations to house certain persons such as those who are bad payers) as well as moral and political beliefs (see Cowan, 1997).

Within studies of housing policy, the law has commonly been avoided or ignored. This is not an error in itself, simply an omission, for, as we see throughout this book, the law itself is commonly avoided or ignored in practice. Nevertheless, the law forms a significant backdrop to the operation of the housing system, and forms one of the key tools of housing policy-makers. In fact, housing law and academic housing lawyers have a distinct and important role to play within both housing policy and housing studies (the latter being a broader formulation). Academic housing lawyers have, rather, marginalized themselves by strict adherence to doctrinal approaches which cannot 'speak to' housing experiences.

In thinking about what we mean by housing 'policy', I take as my starting point the definition adopted by Donnison in his classic text: 'To study "housing policy" is to examine, from a particular standpoint, the functions, capacities and responsibilities of government, and its relations with the governed' (1967, p. 9). The primary focus, then, is upon government and the way it constructs its relationships with the governed. The law is, as I have said, a key tool, although policy analysts have also concentrated upon the development of the law through various Consultation Papers. However, the process of analysing policy development is, as Marsh argues, 'a considerably more subtle and demanding task' (1998, p. 8) because policy development is usually shrouded by obfuscation. A clear example of this was the method used by the Major government to reform the homelessness legislation. The discourse was dominated by concerns over fraud and abuse, particularly by a category of persons referred to as 'single mothers', which enabled that government to introduce swingeing cuts to the system (see Cowan, 1998). In various chapters of this book, I have drawn attention to this obfuscation of policy as the social construction of a sub-category of persons who are 'inappropriate' recipients of state largesse, which justifies penalising legislation affecting a broader category. Housing benefit recipients, asylum-seekers, other 'persons from abroad' and the homeless have all been affected in this way.

Housing policy has at least two other foci. First, there is an apparent expectation that changing housing policy will effect change in the housing system. By contrast, as Partington observes, 'there are some who regard it as surprising that any of the prescribed objectives of legislation are ever actually achieved' (1990, p. 71). This is what socio-legal studies refer to as the 'gap' problem, and what, more positively, is referred to elsewhere as 'the implementation of housing policy'. Implementation is problematic (I am writing this the day the 'Stephen Lawrence Report', which provides the most vivid examples of the failure of policy, is published), which compels a consideration of micro responses to policy development. There are plenty of examples in this book of implementation issues and problems (particularly in relation to discrimination). The most germane example relates to the gap between the security of tenure legislation and the (lack of) application of those rules in the County Court. Second, there are issues around the 'appraisal or evaluation of the success of the policy' (Malpass

& Murie, 1994, p. 6), and this can lead to policy renewal and/or stagnation. Once again, there are plenty of examples in this book, and the Stephen Lawrence Report also provides evidence of this pattern.

In the rest of this introduction, I want to draw attention, first, to the structure of this book, and, second, to a number of issues that dominate the book itself and (my) thinking about housing 'law'.

The Structure of this Book

The book has three parts and two introductory chapters (including this one). In the next chapter, an outline is given of the approach to housing law adopted in this book in the form of a critique of other approaches to housing law and locating housing law as a distinct subject albeit one related to other aspects within the law curriculum. To a certain extent this is a personal exegesis and one which some students may wish to avoid (although non-law students may find it useful as an introduction to different law subjects).

The three parts of the book discuss the following issues: the regulation of the housing system (which I take to include house building and mortgage lending); access to housing; and individual rights in housing. In each, there has been an appreciation, and response to, discrete issues. However, it is also important to appreciate that these parts also have intersections and overlaps. Thus, there is a complex interaction between each part. A pertinent, current example relates to the suggestion that 'problem estates' are caused by allocation policies which allocate 'problem families' to those estates causing a spiral of decline. This is shown to affect not only the way in which we allocate accommodation (including the persons to whom we *do not* allocate accommodation) but also the types of rights we give to those allocatees. It is also true to say that they are cumulative – rights in housing are affected by the regulatory system and who accesses what.

Each of the three parts is located within a separate theoretical structure. This is outlined in a short section at the beginning of each chapter, which also provides a brief consideration of the way that structure impacts upon the chapters discussed in the part. For convenience's sake, the rest of this section will set out this theoretical structure.

Part I Housing and Regulatory Failure

Drawing upon socio-legal theory, particularly that of Teubner, this part considers the operation of the system of housing regulation, in terms of the relationship between the state, on the one hand, and the development of housing tenures (as to which, see below), on the other. It is argued that there is a crisis caused by regulatory failure in the housing system. This crisis has compounded itself, and caused the rise of what Teubner refers to as the 'regulatory trilemma': 'the law is ineffective because it creates no change in behaviour'; the law has 'disintegrating effects in the regulated field'; or the law 'overstrains' itself and is 'captured' by the regulated system (1985, p. 311). We can see these effects occurring in relation to each housing sector, but they are particularly apparent when we consider the private rented sector.

Part II   Access to Housing: Need, Affordability, and Tenure Neutrality

Our thinking about access to housing has been dominated by two concepts, need and affordability. It is commonly argued that access to social-sector accommodation is based upon a household's 'housing need', whereas access to private-sector accommodation is based upon affordability. Successive governments, of whatever hue, have argued that a decent home should be available for all at a price within their means. Both need and affordability are ill thought out. I have argued that they are manipulated by central government, not only through indirect pricing mechanisms such as Housing Benefit, but also as a result of direct policies. Indeed, I regard housing need as a concept to which lip service is commonly paid but, when required, it is neatly sidestepped and ignored. The clearest example of this is in relation to the series of controls placed on asylum seekers and 'other persons from abroad'.

Part III   Rights and Responsibilities: From Due Process to Crime Control

In the final part of the book, we consider the individual rights that households have in housing. The argument is that there has been a shift in the way that we think about these rights so that, rather than concentrating on rights, our focus is upon the responsibility of households to their housing as well as to their 'community' (a word which is rarely defined). Drawing explicitly on models of criminal justice, I have argued that this shift has occurred in part because of the failure of the state to control crime (Garland, 1996). It is a shift away from 'due process' towards 'crime control'. In the process, our thinking about individual rights has shifted away from their development, and towards 'the repression of criminal conduct' (Packer, 1969, p. 158). It is because of this that 'the law-abiding citizen then becomes the victim of all sorts of unjustifiable invasions of his interests' (Packer, 1969, p. 158). The adoption of the introductory tenancy regimes, use of zero tolerance housing management strategies, and other measures against 'anti-social behaviour' provide the sharpest examples of this trend.

Questions of Housing Law and Policy

The Tenure Question

Tenure as Sorting Concept

The first set of questions, which permeates through the whole of this book, relate to *tenure*. Tenure is used as the sorting concept for many of the ideas in this book, although it is not used in the way familiar to lawyers through study of the law of real property (which refers to a system of landholding with the monarch as its figurehead). Using tenure is controversial, however. I accept that it is a concept which has 'great analytical limitations' (Malpass & Murie, 1994, p. 8). It is these limitations which have ultimately made it a suitable sorting concept. The difficulties apparent in the concept of tenure can be shown to affect the progression of both housing law and housing policy. The concept raises sets of dilemmas which are regularly confused. Embracing that confusion enables us to re-evaluate the relationship between the different subjects which concern themselves with housing.

This work has already been begun by Sarah Blandy and Barry Goodchild in their important work on tenure (forthcoming). They separate tenure into a series of discourses to which they refer as: A) the legal discourse; B) the housing discourse; and C) housing law. Their work enables us to rethink housing status. In the next chapter, I have broadly engaged in a consideration of the relationship between categories A) and C) in the context of a critique of the development of housing law thinking. Tenure is framed in the rest of this book in the broad terms of the housing discourse, which broadly divides housing occupation into four 'quasi-scientific' categories, as Barlow and Duncan put it (1989, p. 220): owner-occupation (or home ownership); private renting; local authority renting; and renting from a Registered Social Landlord (referred to throughout this book as 'RSLs'). This is because government regulation and policy thinking is, and has been, determined within these broad categorizations throughout this century.

There are some conceptual inadequacies in adopting these four categories, however. These inadequacies can generally be traced back to the fact that, as organizing concepts, they are blunt tools. They refer to 'a whole range of financial, social, political and economic relations surrounding housing' (Barlow & Duncan, 1989, p. 220). Malpass and Murie, for example, refer to the fact that the categories are 'far more heterogeneous than the labels imply' (1994, p. 8). In other words, each tenure 'has become highly differentiated' (Murie, 1997, p. 448) and caters for wide ranges of groups within wide ranges of accommodation types.

Equally, they do not respect contract and property models of the legal relationships involved. Home ownership appears to include some leaseholds (a rental agreement by another name), for example, but it is unclear where it can be cut off from other tenures. Does holding a lease for

17 years make a person a home owner, for example? Property lawyers might, in answering this question, refer to the fact that only leases of more than 21 years can be registered in the land registry with the tenant as proprietor. To a certain extent, though, this and similar legal questions reflect the divisions between Blandy and Goodchild's A) and B) categories. It tells us that the legal discourse and housing policy are, paradoxically, incompatible. This is a paradox because of the relationship between policy-makers and legislation, the former supposedly driving the latter. It is a problem which appears time and time again in our consideration of housing law. So, for example, certain obligations are implied into leases for less than seven years by statute. Why choose seven? It seems that this was an arbitrary choice so as to include all those 'short-term tenants . . . who deserve protection' (Law Commission, 1996, para. 8.16). The important point, though, is that there is no *common* discourse of housing tenure. Property lawyers see it differently from, as I argue, housing lawyers, who see it differently from housing policy-makers. In many ways, we should then lose this discourse, which is debilitating and stifles interdisciplinarity, and adopt more neutral language. Although admittedly inconsistent, I have sought to use the word 'sector' where possible instead of tenure.

Blandy and Goodchild would not necessarily accept my categorization. So, for example, they view the housing discourse broadly as mirroring the legal discourse and involving categorizations based upon housing relationships. From this perspective, they view owner-occupation as separated from *all* leasehold-based relationships and non-proprietary relationships; leasehold relationships are then sub-divided further into more familiar relationships depending upon sectors of the housing market. They accept that B) 'represents an intermediate level of abstraction . . . [which is] sometimes an oversimplification or a misstatement from a legal viewpoint' and can only be understood in relation to categories A) and C). However, they suggest that this is the focus of much of the housing research (which lends credence to the problems in interdisciplinarity).

I accept these limitations inherent in my division of tenure. Indeed, in this book, I have extrapolated upon the limitations. Neither am I wedded to tenure (having described another book as adopting an 'overly rigid approach to tenure', nor could I be). However, as a starting point, sorting through tenure enables a number of important – actually, critical – points to be made.

Hitherto, housing policy has been constructed upon tenure lines (in the sense adopted in this book). This was most apparent during the Thatcher–Major years in the documents produced by those governments in relation to the 'progression' of housing policy. A short White Paper issued in 1987 heralded several dramatic changes – limiting local authorities role in the provision of housing and deregulation of the private rented sector, to name just two – but was constructed upon tenure lines (DoE, 1987). The same is true of the 1995 White Paper which has been scathingly referred to as 'a revealing document for it shows quite clearly the lack of policies designed to address current problems in the housing market' (Malpass, 1996, p. 468; DoE, 1995).

The tenure issue is adequately embraced in a short document, 'Principles for a New Housing Policy', written by Hilary Armstrong, the Housing Minister (1997). In 'Principles', Armstrong's positions is as follows: 'Housing policy is too often regarded tenure-by-tenure. I want to see a more comprehensive and integrated approach applied at both the national and the local level' (para. 4). So far so good, one might say. Extrapolating upon this, Armstrong clearly sees a central role for local authorities in developing 'real comprehensive housing strategies' developing a broad public–private approach to housing, with a focus upon the 'long-term needs of residents'. Subsequently, though, housing is discussed tenure-by-tenure (para. 10). My principal cause for complaint, though, lies with the following:

> 'I am agnostic about the ownership of housing – local authorities or housing associations; public or private sector – and want to move away from the ideological baggage that comes with that issue. What is important is not, primarily, who delivers. It is what works that counts. By that I do not mean short-termism and opportunism, which can masquerade as pragmatism. We need housing which works and goes on working.' (para. 5)

My complaint arises because you *cannot* be agnostic about the ownership of housing, and who delivers *is* important. The problem is that tenure has developed to the extent that each has its own defined issues and dilemmas.

My complaint can best be approached through the three parts of this book. Broadly, it can be said that tenure is being 'put up to be knocked down'. In the first part, there is a rigid tenure separation, enforced by the approaches of successive governments to regulation. As we have seen, this has been tenurially based. So, for example, the so-called 'social sector', which I take to mean local authority and RSL provision, has differential regulation; and it goes without saying that exactly the same applies to private renting and owner-occupation. What this means is that different regulatory issues and dilemmas are forced. The 'ideological baggage', as Armstrong puts it, must be opened if one is to do anything about it. In this part, I have drawn attention to the cross-tenurial interests that have been created through several schemes; and the 'ideological baggage' has been reflected in the development of some of these, particularly those that are to be influenced by the tenants themselves (Blandy and Goodchild refer to these as 'tenure conversion rights' which adequately conveys the message).

In the second part of the book, which considers access to housing, I argue that for some people, access to housing is determined by their point of access. Local authorities can use the private rented sector in satisfaction of their obligations to the homeless; they can use RSLs to provide accommodation to the homeless and those on the housing register (colloquially known as 'the waiting list'. The development of RSLs, in terms of their relationships with the local authority as well as the level of knowledge of them within their catchment area, influences who will be allocated their accommodation. The level, cost, and quality of the private rented sector has similar influence. Access to home ownership is either impossible or restricted. Tenure conversion rights, such as the right to buy, are other examples of the convergence of tenure. The point is that access to housing is not tenure-specific any more, if it ever was.

In the third part, though, the effects of all of this are played out. Housing law operates differentially between tenures and the people affected by this agnosticism about ownership are the occupants of property. This is true in terms of the rights which people have in their properties. Their level of security depends upon who their landlord or lender happens to be and when they began their occupation. Thus, in this part of the book, the tenures are considered side-by-side, as opposed to meriting separate chapters, for it is important that what I have described as the 'conflicts and manifest absurdities' should generate concern. Indeed, the shift away from due process has made this all the more apparent.

That shift, however, together with other aspects such as the possession process through which occupation is terminated, also teach us something else. Tenure is important in the way we conceptualize housing. Access rights, occupation rights, and termination rights are driven by a discourse that ascribes different characteristics to different tenures. This is both explicit and implicit within the structure of housing law, and has been driven by the direction of post-war housing policy. This exploration of the discourse of housing tenure is, as yet, at an early stage (see Jacobs & Manzi, 1996). Caroline Hunter and Judy Nixon's work has been most valuable here for it has begun the process of considering the ways that judges (1998a), the media (specifically, the *London Evening Standard* (1998b)), and politicians (1999) reflect upon housing debt. Their starting point is that people get into debt for similar reasons, but the portrayal of housing debt is tenured:

> '[I]ndividual owner-occupiers defaulting on mortgage payments are characterised as victims of forces beyond their control who should be helped out of the quagmire of debt. Tenants with rent arrears, on the other hand, have traditionally been portrayed as feckless and anti-social, either deliberately withholding payments or incapable of financial management. Local authority landlords are similarly portrayed in a negative way as inefficient at best and corrupt at worst.' (1998b)

Furthermore, housing debt discourse reveals 'a pattern of rewards and punishments inherent in the policy process that accords with our understanding of the relative power and powerlessness of the different groups, with local authorities characterised as the deviants, owner-occupiers the advantaged and lending institutions framed as [powerful groups with negative images]' (1999). Local authority tenure is stigmatized within this discourse, in images of empty rundown estates and tower blocks (Jacobs & Manzi, 1998).

To summarize: tenure is the sorting concept used in this book because it is a central driver within housing law and policy; tenure is defined as consisting of four separate categories – home ownership, private renting, RSLs, and local authority; tenure does, however, have considerable limitations which must be recognised; nevertheless, tenure can teach us much about problems and issues arising in the direction of housing law and policy, as well as the way we think about housing.

Tenure as an Excluding Structural Concept

Using tenure in the way outlined in the previous section has two unfortunate consequences in terms of the structure of this book. First, a concentration upon tenure requires a concentration upon methods of consumption of housing. This has very much been the focus of most of housing law, which has concerned itself with the modes of consumption and rights of occupants but hardly at all with broader housing market processes. This means that a discussion of the methods and vagaries of the production of housing are marginalized in this book (although some aspects are covered in Chapter 3). In this sense, this book provides a rather traditional approach to housing law studies but my primary focus is a restructuring of the thinking behind housing law.

Equally traditional is the general exclusion of squatting from the discussion in this book. Squatting itself is a tenure – it is a method of holding land – in which there is limited security (unless the squatter lives unimpeded in the property for 12 or more years, thus extinguishing the claims of the owner), but it is not readily included within the quadumvirate of tenures. There are issues of regulation, access, and due process/crime control for squatters, which would fit neatly into this book. However, their lack of appearance in this book partly reflects their general exclusion from discussions about tenure, partly the limited research that exists, to my knowledge, about this tenure, and partly a desire to keep the book to a manageable length in order to keep the publishers on my side.

The Finance Question

The changing regulatory matrix within each tenure has created a number of different dilemmas for government and individual occupants because of the ways in which each tenure is being financed. The move away from 'bricks and mortar' subsidy in the 'social' sector, the move away from rent control/regulation in the private rented sector, and the deregulation of lending have had a concomitant effect on individual payments for housing. This has caused a huge rise in the mechanism adopted by government to 'take the strain' of increased individual costs for rented housing – Housing Benefit – and welfare benefits for home owners struggling to meet housing costs – Income Support. Both Conservative and New Labour governments have sought to solve the cost problem in two separate ways. First, and contrary to the rhetoric of broader policy, the Major and Blair governments have sought to *control* the individual levels of rents. Second, they have sought to reduce the number of claimants by, in some cases, literally cutting off entitlements to 'inappropriate applicants' and, in other cases, by reducing allowable amounts. The recent concentration upon welfare fraud (see DSS, 1998) provides one example of the second approach.

The dilemmas reflect the following financial (im-)balances: how to maintain the semblance of deregulation, when regulation has proved necessary; how to maintain the profitability for housing providers and lenders, whilst reducing the cost of welfare; how to balance profitability against casualization within the labour market; how to reduce welfare spending and increase incentives towards paid employment; how to balance the housing programme against the Treasury's concerns about the national economy; how to reduce public spending and lever greater levels of private-sector finance into social housing, whilst nevertheless maintaining sustainable rent levels. These dilemmas are being worked out under different nomenclatures, such as 'sustainability' and 'afford-ability'. Much attention has been given to determining the meaning of these words, but the questions remain and the answers are, as yet, incomplete.

Related to this are questions about the 'social sector' (see Murie, 1997), and what we mean by 'social' housing. The questions about the 'social sector' are caused by its lack of expansion – indeed, its contraction – and the inability of governments to finance it, because any level of public subsidy affects broader public expenditure and borrowing. For the Conservative government, one solution to this dilemma was to transfer local authority housing into the hands of private, profit-making companies; indeed, there were reports that, had the Conservatives won the 1996 general election, local authorities would have been required to transfer their stock to such companies. New Labour has adopted the Conservative government's modified version of local housing companies – modified in the sense that they cannot be profit-making entities (particularly for Scottish social housing (Hetherington, 1998)). The transfer of the social housing stock into the hands of such entities, including other privately funded RSLs, has proceeded apace but there are concerns that financial institutions will only be interested in that part of the stock which has resale value (Murie, 1997, pp. 456–7).

The Human Rights Question

The Human Rights Act received Royal Assent in 1998. This incorporates into UK law the European Convention on Human Rights, to which the UK has been a signatory since its inception. Neither the Act nor the Convention provide a right to housing *per se*, but the 1998 Act may well affect the way we conceptualize and operationalize housing law. I have not drawn upon it generally in this book because so far the Act has had no effect on this branch of law. Equally, the Convention has had no effect on housing law's development. It is for this reason that it has been mostly excluded from the text. It is raised here though, because the 1998 Act may well galvanize us into a reconsideration of the role of human rights in housing law and policy. Indeed, all law and law-making processes are being reconfigured within the human rights agenda.

In this book, the Human Rights Act has been specifically drawn upon in the analysis of the existing discrimination against gay and lesbian succession to tenancies under the security of tenure legislation. Its influence will extend beyond this, but it is difficult to pinpoint the challenges to which it will inexorably lead. For example, it is unlikely to affect the laws of access to housing because the UK already meets the requirements. All proposed legislation is now given a certificate by the relevant Secretary of State that it complies with the 1998 Act – the Asylum and Immigration Bill, which affects access rights of the affected persons, has been given such a certificate. Arguably, this Bill would have been required to remedy the human rights deficiencies of the previous law. Individual local authorities must comply with the 1998 Act, and this may well lead to a scrutiny of individual policies.

As to the broader effect on housing law and policy, two leading legal practitioners make the following point:

'It is to be hoped that human rights legislation will, directly or indirectly, have an appreciable effect on the serious problems which exist as to the availability and quality of housing. What is certain is that the content, application and practice of housing law will move forward with a renewed vigour. As professionals concerned with people's homes, we should struggle to ensure that the law actually achieves as much as it promises.' (Arden & Baker, 1998, p. 9)

Bibliography

Arden, A. and Baker, C. (1998), 'Housing and the Human Rights Bill', March, *Legal Action*, 8

Armstrong, H. (1998), *Principles for a New Housing Policy*, London: DETR

Barlow, J. and Duncan, S. (1989), 'The use and abuse of housing tenure', vol 3, *Housing Studies*, 219

Blandy, S. and Goodchild, B. (forthcoming), 'From tenure to rights: conceptualising the changing focus of housing law in England', vol 16, *Housing, Theory and Society*

Cowan, D. (1997), *Homelessness: The (In-)Appropriate Applicant*, Aldershot: Dartmouth

Cowan, D. (1998), 'Reforming the homelessness legislation', vol 57, *Critical Social Policy*, 433

Department of Environment (1987), *Housing: The Government's Proposals*, Cm 214, London: HMSO

Department of Environment (1995), *Our Future Homes*, Cm 2901, London: HMSO

Department of Social Security (DSS) (1998), *Beating Fraud is Everyone's Business*, Cm 4012, London: DSS

Donnison, D. (1967), *The Government of Housing*, London: Penguin

Garland, D. (1996), 'The limits of the sovereign state', vol 36, *British Journal of Criminology*, 445

Hetherington, P. (1998), 'Council houses unloved, unlettable', *The Guardian*, 10 November

Hunter, C. and Nixon, J. (1998a), 'Better a public tenant than a private borrower be: the possession process and the threat of eviction', in D. Cowan (ed.), *Housing: Participation and Exclusion*, Aldershot: Dartmouth

Hunter, C. and Nixon, J. (1998b), 'Tenure preference, discourse and debt: language's role in tenure stigmatisation', vol 11, *Journal of Habitat International*, 421

Jacobs, K. and Manzi, T. (1996), 'Discourse and policy change: the significance of language for housing research', vol 11, *Housing Studies*, 543

Jacobs, K. and Manzi, T. (1998), 'Urban renewal and the culture of conservatism: changing perceptions of the tower block and implications for contemporary renewal initiatives', vol 55, *Critical Social Policy*, 157

Law Commission (1996), *Landlord and Tenant: Responsibility for State and Condition of Property*, Law Com No 238, London: HMSO

Malpass, P. (1996), 'The unravelling of housing policy in Britain', vol 11, *Housing Studies*, 459

Malpass, P. and Murie, A. (1994), *Housing Policy and Practice*, London: Macmillan

Marsh, A. (1998), 'Processes of change in housing policy', in A. Marsh and D. Mullins (eds), *Housing and Public Policy*, Buckingham: Open University Press

Murie, A. (1997), 'The social rented sector, housing and the welfare state in the UK', vol 12, *Housing Studies*, 437

Nixon, J. and Hunter, C. (1999), 'Tenure preference, housing policy and debt: the role of language in creating and transmitting tenure stigmatisation', paper presented at the European Network for Housing Research Conference, Cardiff, 7–11 September

Packer, H. (1969), *The Limits of the Criminal Sanction*, California: Stanford University Press

Partington, M. (1990), 'Rethinking British housing law: the failure of the Housing Act 1988', in M. Freeman (ed), *Critical Issues in Welfare Law*, London: Stevens & Sons

Teubner, G. (1984), 'Autopoiesis in law and society: a rejoinder to Blankenburg', vol 18, *Law & Society Review*, 292

Teubner, G. (1985), 'After legal instrumentalism? Strategic models of post-regulatory law', in G. Teubner (ed), *Dilemmas of Law in the Welfare State*, Berlin: de Gruyter

1 Some Assumptions of Housing Lawyers: A Critique

'Throughout [the development of the subject], the emphasis has been on "practice" rather than theory, even though academics have been as involved in the development of the subject as have practitioners. *Housing Law* is pre-eminently practical: it is about the rules and regulations governing the occupation of *homes*.' (Arden, 1997, p. 1)

This book eschews the dominant belief that housing law is 'all the law about housing', for I argue that this gets us into all sorts of problems. It is necessary for me to outline, albeit briefly, some of these problems so that the reader may become aware of the limits of this approach as well as appreciate the limits of that which appears in the rest of this book. This critique can be summarized in the following way: the 'all the law about housing' school tell us nothing about the everyday reality of housing law. Perhaps it tells us how housing should work (from one perspective) but it does not speak to our reality. In fleshing out this point, four central issues will briefly be considered.

First, we avoid asking the really difficult questions, such as what we mean by 'housing',[1] and, for that matter, what we mean by 'law' in this context. The certainty of Arden that housing law is 'pre-eminently practical' suggests one conception of 'law' but, as is shown below, the law of housing often owes little to the law which is practised. Furthermore, Arden's equalizing of housing law and the 'rules and regulations governing the occupation of homes' makes a fundamental error, for the distinction between 'house' and 'home' is critical to the appreciation of the limits of housing law.

Second, it leads to housing law textbooks in which issues such as homelessness appear, seemingly without appreciation of the fact that this significantly widens the scope of the phrase 'all the law about housing'. The homelessness chapter often appears at the end of the text and with no acknowledged reason for its inclusion; in these texts it seems that housing law has no apparent central, governing structure. Recently, housing law books have started to include a discussion of owner-occupation law but, once again, there has been no rhyme nor reason as to why it should or should not appear (other than it is an essential part of the law about housing) or indeed as to where it should be located in the scheme of that law. We housing law academics have been conceptually naive.

One explanation of this conceptual naivety may well be that housing law is only a recent invitee into the law school domain. Prior to this, texts would concentrate on one particular aspect of housing law, such as landlord and tenant, housing welfare law, homelessness or housing discrimination. It was the achievement of one academic and one practitioner to put these and other diverse areas together under the overarching banner of housing law (Arden & Partington, 1983). Their approach was based on the types of legal status given to occupiers: 'They explain the classes of occupation known to the common law and then the classes of protection created by statute which are based on the common law classification' (Stewart, 1996, p. 11). For the academic, the classes of occupation approach, in my view, represents too narrow a focus.

Take, for example, the lease – an undoubtedly difficult legal concept upon which a proportion of housing law depends for its efficacy. The lease, in fact, infiltrates every aspect of housing law to the extent that it does not even begin the enquiry required in housing law. A proportion of occupiers are owners by virtue of having been granted a lease; RSLs and local authorities mostly grant leases (or versions thereof); the private rented sector uses the concept of a lease. Yet, each sector uses the concept of a lease in a different way and relies on different protective mechanisms. In fact, all we can really say through this classification approach is that housing law is a variant of property law.

The approach does not even assist with the analysis of more modern uses which have cleverly crafted the classification so as to create cross-tenurial interests such as rent-to-mortgage or DIYSO (Do-It-Yourself Shared Ownership). For, if the classification scheme is the necessary prerequisite for plucking out the relevant protective mechanism, which protective mechanism applies to the analysis of these interests? It is precisely because housing lawyers have had to cope with outdated methods of land holding that such innovations exist. Furthermore, in adopting this approach, we are endorsing the view that 'the language of housing law with its talk of "protection" and "security" effectively makes the point that the law is the protector of the weak' (Nelken, 1983, p. 24). All I am saying here is that these texts should not form the basis for the study of housing law in law schools; no doubt they are useful tools for the practitioner.

In 1996, Stewart's *Rethinking Housing Law* adopted an approach based upon housing tenure in the sense in which housing policy texts tend to use it (see Malpass & Murie, 1994, Ch. 1) through a consideration of the regulation of owner-occupation, private sector tenancies, RSLs, and local authorities. This liberating text does have difficulties (into which tenure does DIYSO fit? is homelessness relevant?) but it is also an approach adopted in part in this text because, however we might wish to perceive it, this is the approach adopted by government in manipulating the law about the way housing is provided.

Third, the 'all the law about housing' approach means that housing law is contrived to be a straight application of legislation, cases, and (if we are lucky) some commentary. In other words, housing law has been dismantled from its base so that, in the same way as Megarry and Wade's

The Law of Real Property (1984), it fits within the positivist tradition of legal study; that is, the basic legal rules are divined without much appreciation of the values which gave rise to them. Doubtless, this is of use to the legal practitioner. Issues such as the relationship between housing law and gender, housing law and the study of housing policy, housing law and economics/finance (indeed, everything that is interesting about housing law), however, have most commonly been ignored. Most surprisingly given its current dominance, housing law has been divorced from the sociological approach to law.

Thus, housing law has often been ignored by those working in other disciplines related to housing, including sociology. The single benefit of this approach, however, has been the increasing awareness of the incomprehensibility of housing law which has led to calls for a more consumerist, codified approach (see, for example, Partington, 1993; Whitehouse, 1998). On its own, though, complexity does not, or should not, make a degree course topic. What is required is a challenging conceptual core around which it is possible to place the role of housing law in terms of where it fits within the continuum of legal studies as well as (perhaps controversially) its role in society.

The final, consequential point, is that the 'all the law about housing' approach has led to housing law becoming divorced from its disciplinary accompanists in the social sciences. This is like Blur without Damon Albarn, Oasis without Liam Gallagher, even the Spice Girls without Geri – it can operate, but it is not nearly as good. Furthermore, the stagnation of academic housing law has meant that it is totally out of kilter with these accompanists. This appears to have been to the extent that an attempt to mix social housing law with policy ended up keeping them rigidly separated (Hughes & Lowe, 1995; Cowan, 1995; Menski, 1996; Hunter, 1997). It has been argued that the study of housing is conceptually underdeveloped. Kemeny (1992, p. 5) argues that '[housing] is neither a discipline in the sense that it abstracts out a dimension of society, nor is it an established "subject-based discipline" in university power structures, even if it is rapidly becoming so.' (for a similar contribution to the debate about law see Thomas, 1997) Kemeny suggests that

> 'The end-result of this subject-fixated approach is that abstracting "housing" out of social structure and focusing upon it leads to a failure to integrate it into the wider social processes of which it is a part. Housing studies therefore tends to become a specialism, divorced from wider social issues. It becomes a sterile and limited empirical focus, concentrating on analysing the housing market and housing policy.' (p. 13)

A mix of housing law with housing policy can provide a relevant analytical structure, a starting point from which a limited conceptual exploration might begin. If this highlights the inadequacies of the legalistic approach (as it will be argued that it does), then all good and well for its challenge to the orthodoxy.

The process of reconstructing housing law must, therefore, begin with a re-evaluation of the sources of law and the influences upon them. This is the first stage in developing a conceptual structure for this book. It will be argued that the notion of equality before the law, as encapsulated within the 'rule of law', is obviously fallacious and that there are cleavages within and between diverse sources of law. Currently, so-called law is being interpreted and applied in a wide number of administrative institutions. There is a further, much more important point which is that the application and interpretation of housing law often reflects the dominant legal ideology of individualism and the supposed notion of contractual freedom. I will be arguing that housing law is a process through which society's structural inequalities are made all the more apparent.

The following section attempts to re-orientate the debate about housing law by arguing that, classically, its focus on housing rather than 'home' is a mechanism which has obscured the distinction between public and private. From this perspective, it will be argued that housing law has traditionally been dominated by masculine approaches and, in this way, has ignored gendered discussion. The housing experience can, in no sense, be described as gender neutral but this is most often the assumption of housing law.

The next stage is to orientate the notion of housing law. This is done by contrasting the approach taken in housing law to that in other legal subjects upon which the former draws (property law, contract law, and public law). Here I will be adopting a rather narrow, legalistic conception of these other subjects but this should provide guidance for those not acquainted with law topics. A further rationale for this approach is that it seems to be the appropriate method for drawing out what is meant (at least in my own conception) by housing law. My concern in this section will be to provide an approach to housing law, rooted in housing studies analyses, that operates as a critique of those other legal subjects as well as of itself. In other words, my approach to housing law can be regarded as an opportunist's critique of the limits of law and legal process.

1.1   Sources of Housing Law

So far, it has been argued that current housing law texts offer a view of law which is far too narrow. For them, it seems that housing law exists only in the Statutes passed by Parliament, the various pieces of quasi-legislation (such as Statutory Instruments, Circulars, and Codes of Guidance of dubious legal status) and the law as decided by judges in individual cases. To a certain extent this is a caricature, although it is one which serves to show that housing law texts are more often for the practitioner, who needs this information, than for the academic for whom, in my view, this is a starting point.

The approach adopted in this text is a challenge to these ideas as well as, implicitly, a challenge to the idea of the 'rule of law'. Dicey described the rule of law as embodying three principles (Dicey, 1902, Ch. 4): Parliamentary supremacy; 'no man is above the law; but [also] that here every man, whatever be his rank or condition, is subject to the ordinary law of the realm and amenable to the jurisdiction of the ordinary tribunals' (p. 189); rights are determined by the courts. The sociological tradition in legal studies has emphasized that these three principles are deficient in almost every respect, particularly in their application to modern law (see Cotterell, 1992, pp. 157–79).

The association in the title of this book of housing law *and* policy is not coincidental. It represents not a rejection of the past approach but a willingness to extend it into areas outside the traditional preserves and domination of the law school. The association with policy is an attempt to extricate housing law from its self-imposed constriction. It enables a more rounded consideration to be adopted. So, for example, the relationship between central and local government has, according to one author, been the subject of intense juridification during the past twenty or so years (Loughlin, 1996). The character of that law has depended upon the way(s) in which the central–local axis has been perceived by the legislatively predominant power (central government). The perception of local government by those controlling central government has seriously affected the general financing, allocation, and provision of housing. These connections are important for appreciating the role of housing organizations, the power differential between organizations and the effect on the individual. If housing law is about the construction of individual rights (between the provider and purchaser), it is therefore critical for us to have this background information as it provides the context for the construction of these rights.

This is not just an extrapolation of an ideological approach to law. The ever-expanding dominion of law actually requires this approach in certain instances, albeit these are presently limited. In *Pepper* v. *Hart* [1993] AC 625, the House of Lords argued that where a statutory provision was unclear, reference might be made to Parliamentary debates in order to gauge what the provision was intended to mean. In other words, government policy as expressed in Consultation Papers, Parliamentary debates, public statements of Ministers – all of which influence the shape of the law – might now be considered to be part of law in certain circumstances. If, as housing law texts without fail tell us, housing law is complex and not readily understandable, then it follows that these extra sources are as critical as any others.

Further, though, the sources of housing law reflect the broader societal requirements of organizational accountability as well as different regulatory models (for example, see the approach to accountability adopted by Loughlin, 1992; or evident in the *Citizen's Charter* (Cabinet Office, 1991); or in the Housing Act 1996 in relation to 'social' housing providers). It is glib to say that housing law takes place in a variety of different arenas but this glibness obscures the fact that housing law rarely takes place in the courts. Sometimes this is because the courts simply abdicate their responsibility, using the circular argument that regulation is the responsibility of the housing provider (see, for example, the comments of Lord Brightman in *R* v. *Hillingdon LBC ex parte Puhlhofer* [1986] AC 484);[2] sometimes, it is because the issue is 'political' or raises questions of a financial nature that the courts are not equipped to answer; or sometimes, there is simply an alternative, cheaper forum for dispute resolution (such as the Commission for Local Administration, the District Auditor, or even an internal review by the body responsible for the original decision).

It is the last form which has proved most popular in the latter half of the twentieth century (after the Franks Committee, 1957) and also at times most controversial. The District Auditor's report into alleged gerrymandering in Westminster City Council provides a case study in itself: the auditor enquired into the way Westminster City Council 'targeted' certain areas for sale of its accommodation under the so-called 'homes for votes' policy, described by the council under the euphemism 'Building Stable Communities'. The auditor's five volume report contains more housing law than any other single document of its type, despite the auditor's difficulties in retrieving relevant information (Magill, 1996, Vol. 1, pp. 7–8). It also presents one view of the practice of administration in local government. The report recommended that certain officers and councillors should repay £31,677,064 to the Council, subject to any appeal.[3]

Other forms of regulatory accountability are less public but more prevalent. In particular, the rise and rise of tribunals (such as the rent assessment committee – see Farmer, 1974, Ch. 5; Street, 1975, Ch. 2), internal reviews of individual decisions (that is, reconsidering original decisions – see Sainsbury & Eardley, 1992; Cowan, 1998a), or ombudsmen (James, 1997), are part of the attempt to widen the regulatory network in order to cheapen and thus widen access to justice. The Housing Act 1996 contained the following provisions in this mould: Schedule 2 (ombudsman); section 115 (leasehold valuation tribunal); section 129 (internal review); sections 164–5 (internal review); sections 202–3 (internal review). Considerable concerns have been raised about the quality of 'justice' applied by those who conduct such a review or appeal (the two are slightly different – see Sainsbury, 1994).

Developing an American perspective, it has been argued that an internal review needs to be assessed against criteria designed to analyse judicial proceedings, precisely because these are quasi-judicial proceedings. They are the first rung of the ladder – often, no further steps are taken by those aggrieved by decisions – and thus should be judged as quasi-adjudicatory mechanisms. Results of empirical research into these reviews/appeals, almost uniformly have shown that considerable concerns exist when they are judged against the relevant criteria of accuracy and fairness (see Sainsbury, 1992 for an important discussion of the meaning of these concepts). My own research into homelessness appeals suggests that many procedures used would 'make the walls of Jericho look sound' (Cowan, 1998a). In other words, it may well be that cheap justice is no justice. Research into the application of the new internal review in homelessness cases has startlingly found that hitherto the process is hardly ever used by persons who have been unsuccessful in their application (Cowan & Hunter, 1998)

An equally important point is that housing law takes place in arenas in which housing law authors fear to tread. Furthermore, whilst considerable concerns are raised from a legal perspective, it can be argued that this perspective is itself too narrow. The (sometimes unspoken) assumption of many lawyers is that the application and interpretation of law takes place in an orderly environment, governed by the doctrine of precedent (like cases should be treated alike). If it is not, then it should be. That it is not, and will not be, comes as something of a shock. The application and interpretation of law in these fora takes place in a totally alien (to lawyers anyway) environment which often emphasizes administrative expediency and alegalism.

Adopting a broader conception of law, exemplified by that adopted in the socio-legal studies movement, often can uncover a mismatch between positivist law and actual practice. For example, Loveland's work uncovered what might be termed a 'local law' (Mashaw, 1983) in three local authority homeless persons units, which interpret and apply homelessness law (Loveland, 1995). These administrative practices, created by administrative expediency, can be regarded as sources of law themselves for they are formed and operate in accordance with the doctrine of precedent. One reason why that might be necessary is that the law does not and could not possibly lay down rules governing every housing circumstance. Often, it lays down broad discretionary rules which are then filled in by administrative practice, either with or without knowledge of the 'usual' sources of law. Sometimes, administrators are unaware even of the broad discretionary rules but regard their practice as the primary source of law.

There are plenty of examples of this type of legal research which challenge the foundations of legal positivism and the so-called 'rule of law'. It might therefore be argued that 'all pigs are equal before the law, but some pigs are more equal than others'. This might refer to differential access to justice (for example, as a result of legal aid limits and the willingness to fund certain types of action; access to quality advice; access to proceedings); different fora of justice (it is noticeable that the wealth differential carries with it differential fora – owner-occupiers, including private renters, generally are deemed capable of using the courts; housing association tenants have a specific ombudsman scheme; local authority tenants, and those seeking access to local authority tenancies, generally must seek justice from the authority itself initially); and different quality of justice provided by each fora.

Furthermore, it can be argued that law is more commonly identified with the protection of interests which, at any given time, appear to be dominant. Consider the following passage from Nelken's study of the implementation of the harassment and unlawful eviction provisions in the Rent Act 1965:

'Legislation is a creature of political action and a product of a particular historical set of events and forces; it is therefore framed and implemented in terms of the concerns and purposes of law-makers and law-enforcement agencies. . . . Legislation is, in a sense, an experiment in controlled social change. . . . Legislative outcomes can be influenced by constraints which shape the ambitions of those who make and enforce the law, and the opportunities open to them to effect their purposes.' (1983, p. 21)

Nelken's concern was to argue that generalist analyses of legislation and its effects, in Marxist or liberal terms, explained nothing. Thus, the harassment and unlawful eviction rules which might have been seen as working class gains or as an attack on the landlord class ignored the existence of very different types of landlords (from large commercial landlords through to resident landlords). Larger landlords tend to use 'business-orientated' methods which are classed as commercial, not criminal. Less sophisticated resident landlords, who themselves were often working class, more commonly fell foul of the law. Thus, the main conclusion to the study was that the legislative response 'reflected and reinforced established boundaries of propriety and impropriety in the use and abuse of property rights' (p. 27).

Nelken's critique provides an important counterbalance to many knee-jerk reactions to legislation, as well as more thoughtful studies (for example, he is critical of much of the academic work conducted on the Rent Act 1977). The process of legislative law-making is not susceptible to any narrow analyses. Indeed, its complexity is mirrored by many of the analyses which inform the academic appreciation of the processes of this 'experiment in social change'. So, for example, one approach might be that legislative law-making is influenced by the role of the media, the self-proclaimed arbiters of moral opinion. As, an article in *The Guardian* observed about the relationship between the *Daily Mail* and the Major government:

'And when the *Daily Mail* campaigns, a weak government falters, fudges and becomes far less keen on no-fault divorce and foreigners. Trace the latest Major lurch to the right and you will trace the push and shove of the *Daily Mail* . . . that famous and growing constituency, Middle England, from the Essex provisionals to the Wilts officials, casts around for that confirmation and reinforcement of dearly held prejudices which produces a good stripe on the lawn and the bracing spasm of fury which get it to the train on time in the morning. Increasingly, they pick up the *Daily Mail*.' (Nevin, 1997)

Much recent housing legislation has been influenced by the media, which has itself provided representations of its own notion of *consensus* (for discussion, see Cohen & Young, 1973; Hall *et al.*, 1978; Fowler, 1991). In turn, that is dependent upon its assumed readership as well as those who own and/or edit the newspapers, television, and radio. So, the relationship between the media's adoption and adaption of the single mother myth in relation to homelessness ('single mothers become pregnant to get a council house through the homelessness legislation') fed a moral panic[4] and seemed to provide the principal rationale for reforming that legislation (although the situation was more complex – see Cowan, 1998b).

At the same time, the media has devoted considerable column inches and minutes of airtime to a discussion of that supposed bastion of dominant ideology – the judiciary. The usual claim has been that the judiciary have usurped Parliament's will and have thus disturbed the will of the majority, particularly on issues such as homelessness (Doran, 1996), as well as asylum and immigration policy (Cohen, 1996). Nevertheless, analysis of these judicial decisions might suggest that the judges were simply applying the usual principles. Discussion of these decisions usually takes place under the preconceived belief in the rise of judicial radicalism or liberalism (whichever epithet is preferred), although this is the subject of some dispute (see Cowan, 1997b, pp. 141 *et seq*). It can be argued that such representations are induced by judicial decisions which deny the (say) newspaper's own perception of consensus. Those judicial decisions which accord with that perception are therefore ignored. Thus, an article in the *Daily Mail* has (re-)constructed the attack on the judiciary in the following way:

'What should worry us most about a privacy law is the way in which a frequently servile judiciary might choose to interpret it. On the best construction, the judiciary allows its celebrated independence to lead it inevitably towards the most liberal, and politically correct, adjudications in any issue, placing the rights of minorities all too frequently above those of the majority' (Heffer, 6 February 1998)

The supposed realignment of the judiciary with the 'left' covers up the fact that Heffer is more disgusted by the way the judiciary do not support the New Right crusade.

Academic attacks on the judiciary have generally focussed upon the way judges interpret the law. This tends to be strongly individualistic, in accordance with their own ideologies influenced by their 'strikingly homogeneous' backgrounds and their having been imbued during the process of climbing up the legal ladder, from student, to practitioner, to judge (Cotterell, 1992, pp. 232–6, drawing upon Griffiths, 1991). It appears, for example, that certain District Judges are imbued with the stereotypical characterizations of local authority tenants as opposed to owner-occupiers, which is reflected in the procedures attributed to repossession within each sector of the housing market (see the contribution of Hunter & Nixon, 1998; as well as the authors' more general collaboration: Nixon *et al.*, 1996).

Perhaps it should come as no surprise that the judicial experience of housing welfare law has been essentially one of *laissez-faire* individualism (see James, 1974). The most notorious example of this ideological approach has been in the judicialization of the homelessness legislation in which pronouncements of the House of Lords have tended to be based upon Conservative ideology rather than the policy upon which that legislation was originally based (Loveland, 1996a; Cowan, 1997a; Hunter & Miles, 1997). Hunt argues that the way the law 'marks out its own self-limitations' is the critical issue:

> 'The ideological core of the modern state lies in the varieties of the idea of a state based on law (Rechtsstaat) epitomised by the constitutional doctrine of the rule of law. This powerful ideological motif coexists with legal renunciation, the self-conscious recognition of arenas of state action with which the courts will not interfere.' (Hunt, 1991, p. 119).

To summarize: an approach to housing law based upon legislation, quasi-legislation, and case law has its place but it also has limitations. It does not speak of the 'real' differential experience of the various different legal and quasi-legal fora, the relationship between individuals and law, nor the very different types of law being applied by administrative agencies charged with the delivery of housing law, nor the forces that lead to the creation of law and the responses of the judiciary. In other words, the important relationship between housing law and society is most commonly ignored and thus the ability to argue that housing law in some way mirrors a dominant ideology is also lost. Housing law, in other words, represents a classic example of the following theses:

> '1) The aggregate effects of law in modern democratic societies work to the systematic disadvantage of the least advantaged social classes and groups.
> 2) The content, procedures and practice of law constitute an *arena of struggle* within which the relative positions and advantages of social classes are changed over time as a result of the interplay of struggles within the legal arena and those outside it.' (Hunt, 1991, p. 125)

1.2   Housing and Home

In any attempt to extrapolate upon notions of housing law (of whatever variety), a moment should be taken to dwell upon what is meant by 'housing' for this word is being deliberately used to define the limits of this legal study. There is little doubt that the word was initially chosen as one of convenience for it described what was being discussed – housing rights.

In other words, the initial focus of housing law was the rights of the housed. Housing was being conceptualized as a series of external rights exercised by the occupier against some other person or organisation. As these rights often depend(-ed) upon an object being called a 'dwelling house', it was not surprising that the neater reductionist term of 'housing' was used.

The concept, however, must be regarded as a term of convenience for otherwise it limits the field of enquiry to such an extent that housing law becomes an excursus of 'all the law about the dwelling or structure'. No doubt for this reason, only recently have housing lawyers discovered the importance of 'home', although their concerns have generally revolved around the redistribution of occupation rights after relationship break-down. The housing–home relationship is important because each is concerned with overlapping but different spheres of study. So, Watson argues as follows:

'A "house" is generally taken to be synonymous with a dwelling or a physical structure, whereas a "home" is not. A "home" implies a set of social relations, or a set of activities within a physical structure, whereas a "house" does not. The home as a social concept is strongly linked with a notion of family – the parental home, the marital home, the ancestral home. The word "home" conjures up such images as personal warmth, comfort, stability, and security, it carries a meaning beyond the simple notion of shelter.' (1983, p. 60)

Tomas & Dittmar's study suggested that housed women drew the distinction in the following terms:

'A house is just a house – four walls and a roof.
A home is a place of warmth and belonging among friends and family.'

On the other hand, in their study, homeless women drew the distinction in the following way

'. . . a house is someone else's house where other people live with you (dependence). Home is a place of your own where you can be alone (independence). With the exception of "somewhere nice", expressions such as "warmth" and "belonging" were not mentioned at all by homeless women.' (1995, pp. 504–5)

However, the 'home' can generally be portrayed in terms of the reflection of oneself. This was a central point of Watson's thesis in her 1983 article, carried into her future work, for the 'sexual division of labour within the household has implications for different members of the household's relation to the "home" and hence to "homelessness" . . . one individual in a household may be potentially homeless, according to a broad definition of the term whilst another is not.' (1983, p. 63).

Use of the term 'housing' in this context therefore implies that law does not enter the private sphere of 'home'. In this way, it limits its field of enquiry to issues that a supposedly dominant masculine culture can cope with. It is not without significance that the phrase 'an English*man's* home is his castle' should involve a gendered distinction between house (an arena for legal regulation) and home (as castle, enabling the male to repel the borders of regulation). Remnants of this dichotomy came to the fore during debates over what the law should prescribe to be the effects of domestic violence and, more critically, whether these effects should differ depending upon whether the relationship involved a married couple or a cohabiting couple. The principal cause of this debate was over whether cohabitees could be required to transfer property interests (and thus their public rights to housing) when one had committed an act of 'domestic violence' (the domestic signifying the private realm) to the other. The domestic violence Bill was initially scuppered (although it has subsequently been enacted) by right wing politicians, goaded on by the media (in particular, the *Daily Mail* and one of its guest writers, William Oddie, who espoused an explicitly moralist New Right agenda). It was occasionally argued at different times and for different purposes that domestic violence was not a proper subject for the legal regulation of occupation rights, thus reinforcing the public/private dichotomy.

Although controversial, it also appears that the term 'home' can itself be gendered (compare Saunders, 1990, Ch. 5 (in the context of a distinct project of theorizing urban sociological perspectives), on the one hand, with Darke, 1994; Watson, 1988; Morris & Winn, 1990, Ch. 4; Somerville, 1994). Thus, the home is seen as the location where structural inequalities are played out in relation to (for example) the labour market, caring for relatives, male–female power differential (the literature is huge in this area, but is developed in Pascall, 1997; see also Darke's personalized excursus, 1994). However, the individual experience is equally translated into an individual conception of home, and, thus, 'home for each individual is shaped to some extent by that person's ideal understanding of the concept, or by their beliefs about what constitutes a home' (Neale, 1997, p. 45; see also Somervill, 1992). A further aspect to this structural inequality is reflected in the design of accommodation – 'the shape of the "standard family" is suggested by the shape of the "standard dwelling"'; 'even at student level, only 25 per cent of architects are women' (Pascall, 1997, p. 138; see also Darke, 1997, pp. 88–100).

The house–home spheres tell us much about the limits of our subject and enables a warning about gender neutrality to be made. The externalized approach, however, has never been enforced with any rigour by authors. Indeed, precisely the opposite seems to have been the case – housing law texts have breached the public/private divide at every opportunity (after the law has breached it). Almost ubiquitously, housing law texts have chapters covering relationship breakdown in some form or other. In other words, housing law is also interpreted by most as 'much of the law about the home' (compare Stewart's contribution which does adopt a housing perspective, 1996). It does not cover 'all the law' simply because this is dealt with in other areas of legal study designed specifically for this purpose (a distinction adopted in this book, albeit with reference to the broader approach offered by feminist housing scholars). Housing law academics have proved equally willing to enter into the more general debate about structural inequalities in accessing accommodation.

So far, discussion has centred around gendered constructions of housing and home. However, a further dimension often afforded discussion in housing texts has been the issue of racial discrimination (although not the equally important current issue of immigration: see Waddington, 1998) in housing allocation, as well as racial discrimination/harassment occurring inside the home. Here, it might be argued that the distinction between house and home has been more prominent. For example, the local authority response to the enforcement of anti-racial harassment clauses in tenancy agreements has generally been minimal, despite central government pressure (see Bridges & Forbes, 1990; Department of Environment, 1994; see generally, Cowan, 1997b, Ch. 5).[5]

A further limit caused by the house–home distinction is that the design and production of accommodation is rarely, if ever, discussed by housing lawyers who are far keener to discuss rights of occupation. Texts are keen to discuss the structural inequalities (within the law) of occupation rights (consumption); however, they have proved less keen to discuss a more furtive, initial form of structural inequality in the construction process (production). Here, there is a vast difference between housing law and housing studies where the construction issue is considered as crucial as any rights that may exist in the accommodation (see, for example, Ball, 1983).

1.3   Housing Law – A Distinctive Arena

This section attempts to draw a distinction between the approach of housing law and those areas of law with which it is usually associated (property law, contract law, public law). Housing law is based upon these subjects but there is a divergence of approach and emphasis between them and housing. This does not make housing peculiar or particular but, as with (say) employment law, it makes it distinctive and, for me, critical. In one sense, I am providing a critique of a caricature of these subjects, for many academics neither think about their subject nor teach it in the way in which they are presented here. Nevertheless, this approach provides a method of distinguishing the contexts of housing law from the morass and helps us to identify the housing law reflex. So, whilst courts strive for solutions to housing problems based upon the precepts of their knowledge of property, contract, or public law (whichever appears relevant), it can be argued that housing law itself could provide its own solution. Such a version of housing law is rooted in an alternative concept of housing studies, which stresses the relevance of inequalities based on class, discrimination, affordability, prejudice, as well as the broader issues created by the politics of housing.

For the purposes of this discussion, the way in which a 'lease' is created will be used as an example. The question that will be asked is as follows: what does the lease mean in contract, property and public law? It can be argued that each of these subjects has a mutually exclusive response to the creation of a lease which exposes the thinking behind that subject. Housing law, in fact, has an answer to each permutation. Indeed, it can be argued rather boldly that housing law thinking can explain the problems encountered by each subject with the lease.

The Lease in Contract Law – The San(ct)ity of Bargain

The form of the lease is a contract between the landlord(s) and the tenant(s). It is made up of an *offer* of property made by the landlord to the tenant who subsequently *accepts* and agrees to make a payment of rent at certain set times, known in contract law as *consideration*. The assumption made in the form of the law of contract is an equality of bargaining power, evident in an ability to negotiate the terms of the contract such as the amount of the rent. This is a simple extension of the 'rule of law' principle that, in the eyes of the law, we are all equal. Thus, the assumption made in contract law is that most of us[6] are free of any constraints imposed upon our contract-making power. This results in the law of contract becoming a blind, blunt, individualistic tool, satisfying the so-called capitalist 'need' to engage in bargaining relationships.

The substance of contract law is different and, in many ways, a contradiction of its form (see further Kennedy, 1976). The assumption of equality means that the law has considerable problems with the apparent fact that contractual relationships represent an inequality of bargaining power. Although there have been fluctuations, it is not surprising that there is no contractual doctrine of inequality of bargaining power for such a doctrine ultimately would explicitly contradict the form. However, there are limited, paternalistic exceptions for avoiding the contract such as duress, undue influence, or inability to contract due to lacking 'legal capacity' (for discussion see Beale, 1983). There are other empirical problems with the notion as well (discussed plentifully in the literature, a sample of which can be found in Beale *et al.*, 1995; Wheeler & Shaw, 1994; see also Trebilcock, 1993), in particular the indeterminacy of power (for a sustained, powerful appreciation of power see the collection of Foucault's contributions to the debate: Gordon, 1980; also Hunt & Wickham, 1994).

Neither do these notions of sanctity and equality adequately explain the housing relationship. For example, housing contracts are most usually standard form (either that of the landlord, the Law Society, the local authority, mortgage company[7]) including terms prescribed by statute. These are non-negotiable and so an element of coercion pre-exists in the 'bargain' (see Beale, 1983, pp. 130–1). Inequalities in housing are both individual (for example, the case of race and housing – the classic text here is Henderson & Karn, 1987) and systemic (for example, the production of housing tends, for various reasons, to favour the owner–occupation axis: Ball, 1983).[8] There is also a more basic inequality – a mismatch between supply and demand. One of the final documents produced by the Conservative government on housing issues made this dramatic admission of inequality:

'The most recent set of household projections, published by the government last year, indicate that there could be 4.4 million more households in England between 1991 and 2016. *This is almost one million more than the figures for which we are currently planning.*' (Department of Environment, 1996, para. 1.1)

Even at the time of writing, whilst it can truly be said that there is a crude surplus of residential accommodation, it can be premised that there is 'a substantial shortage of housing, approaching three million' units of accommodation (Balchin, 1995, p. 3).[9]

These inequalities infiltrate into every part of the housing process, from housing production[10] to individual access, rights, and security. Equally, government intervention in the housing market has sought to affect the bargaining position on both levels, often through the use of direct and indirect subsidies (see generally Gibb & Munro, 1990; Hills, 1991). One of the most distressing examples of government intervention in recent years has been with the mortgage contract (in which the assumption is of equality). This intervention, which might have been to imply certain terms in the contract guaranteeing freedom from repossession for a certain period, simply ensured that mortgage companies included the following statement in their publicity:

'Your home is at risk if you do not keep up repayments on a mortgage or other loan secured on it.' (by virtue of the Consumer Credit (Advertisements) Regulations 1989, SI 1989/1125, Sch 1, Part II, para. 2)

A number of other examples might further assist: mortgage interest tax relief at source (MIRAS) was a crucial method used by the state to bolster home ownership and increase the individual's purchase power. In 1996–1997, the average tax relief given to individual home owners through MIRAS was about £220 (compared to £800 in 1990–1991: Wilcox, 1997, p. 179). The ability of landlords to charge market rents was to be assured by the concomitant increase in availability of Housing Benefit ('Housing Benefit will take the strain'). In May 1996, the average weekly Housing Benefit given to housing association tenants was £46.27 and to private tenants £53.15 (Wilcox, 1997, p. 190). A staggering 68 per cent of housing association tenants are in receipt of benefit. Table 1.1 shows how, since

1981, the government has influenced housing costs in Great Britain through general subsidies and means-tested assistance.

Government constraints on local authority and housing association house building have radically altered the terrain, causing a quasi-market to develop (Bartlett & Le Grand, 1993). The various attempts at making provision for the homeless have radically affected the ability of the appropriately needy[11] in seeking accommodation. In other words, the supposedly level-playing field of market provision is already so affected by the individual and systemic inequalities in housing provision and consumption as to make the contractual notion of equality rather fickle. In no sense can the creation of a lease be regarded as the contract of two equal parties. Subtle forces are at play involving government subsidy, the nature of the landlord, the nature of the tenant, the availability of accommodation in the area, and the choice of tenure. Part of the task of housing law is to consider how these inequalities are presented *in order for a response to be provided to it.*

It should not be supposed that, once the derivation of the inequality is uncovered, government intervention has sought to plaster over the crack.[12] Such an opinion is far too simplistic for it neither takes account of the policy process, the political process nor the process of implementation. Indeed as we shall see, if anything, the approach of government has often been to heighten the inequality. So, for example, the amount of public money available to housing has always been subject to the party political prerogative of tax cuts.

Even those aspects of housing law which are supposed directly to benefit those unable to take part in the contractual process, often operate more to benefit those able to take part. A classic example concerns the

Table 1.1   Assistance with housing costs for home owners, council and private tenants (£million)

Assistance	1980/81	1988/89	1991/92	1997/98
General Subsidies				
Home owners	4294	7452	6717	2245
Council tenants	4751	1317	1003	(685)
Private tenants		181	151	
Total	9045	8951	7870	1560
Means-tested assistance				
Home owners	158	399	1034	761
Council tenants	1876	3793	4547	5371
Private tenants	302	1090	1979	3542
Total	2336	5282	7560	9675

Source: Wilcox, 1997, p. 195

allocation of council housing which, until recently, enabled the 'better-off' working class to access council housing (see Cole & Furbey, 1994, pp. 138–47). Popular prejudices were reinforced through home visits which assessed '. . . housing standards and "suitability" [of the applicants] for different standards of housing' (Central Housing Advisory Committee (CHAC), 1969, para. 88). Furthermore, inequalities due to policies and their effects can be localized. Consider the following admonition from the CHAC:

> 'We were surprised to find some housing authorities [which] took a moralistic attitude towards applicants: the underlying philosophy seemed to be that council tenancies were to be given only to those who "deserved" them and that the "most deserving" should get the best houses. Thus unmarried mothers, cohabitees, "dirty" families, and "transients" tended to be grouped together as "undesirable". Moral rectitude, social conformity, clean living and a "clear" rent book on occasion seemed to be essential qualifications for eligibility – at least for new houses.' (CHAC, 1969, para. 96)

If we now return to our lease, it is impossibly bland to say that it is based, as contract law doctrine would have it, upon equality of bargaining power. The housing market is quite simply littered with examples of inequality. We must also be careful not to generalize. First, the individualizing notion of contract law means that each individual instance must be considered to build up a true picture. Second, this individualization must be conceptualized in spatial and temporal terms, for at different times and in different places the location of inequalities will itself be localized. Third, this individualization is subject to the exigencies of government involvement with housing costs. Fourth, the lease may also carry with it certain rights which will affect the type of person to whom it is granted. An example of this is the affixation to certain council leases of the right to buy the home.

The effect of that policy of selling council houses to individual tenants provides an example of all four of these issues. Geographically, the results were often quite different depending upon a number of discrete factors, such as the value of home ownership as against renting (see Forrest & Murie, 1991). There are now large divisions between sectors of the housing market (in 1995, 67.5 per cent were owner occupiers in England, compared with 57.9 per cent in Scotland). It would also be a distinct failure to see the relationship between different sectors as historically static. In fact, during the twentieth century there has almost been a revolution in property occupation by sector as Table 1.2 shows.

Table 1.2 does not show the way that tenures have developed geographically (or spatially), however. So, for example, some areas had high levels of home ownership before 1914 (see Forrest *et al.*, 1990, pp. 56–64).

Table 1.2   Housing tenure[13] in England and Wales

Year	Owner-occupation *(per cent)*	Private renting *(per cent)*	RSLs *(per cent)*	Local authority *(per cent)*
1914	10	90*		n/a
1951	31	52*		17
1971	52	19*		29
1981	60	10	2	28
1996	69	9	4	17

* relates to both private renting and RSLs
Source: Malpass & Murie, 1994; DETR

With these warnings in mind, an admonition about the use of contract in the housing context might be expressed in this way:

'The legal relations of [housing] exhibit the characteristics of a distinctive form of law which, on the one hand, embodies the general features of contract doctrine (universality and individuali[z]ation) and, on the other, comprises a significant specialisation which in most legal systems marks off the contract of [housing] as distinct from other contractual forms. The individuali[z]ing element of general contract doctrine represents the presupposition of a voluntary relation between formally legal subjects, whereas the specialisation of the contract of [housing] allocates distinctive sets of rights and duties to [landlord] and [tenant]. It is this combination of identity and difference which demonstrates the practical and ideological significance of the legal relation of [housing]. It constructs an apparent coherence within a framework which both denies and confirms the underlying inequality of the [housing] relation.' (Hunt, 1991, p. 123 – the words in square brackets have been substituted for terms associated with employment process).

The Lease in Property Law – The Tenure Question

The lease has formed part of the law of real property (broadly 'exclusive rights over land') since the end of the fifteenth century, before which it was classed as personal property (exclusive rights over other types of property). It is this 'conceptual ambivalence' (Gray, 1993, p. 674) that marks it out within the law of property. Were it a mere personal right, it would be subject to the rules of contract law but as it is now also a property right, it forms a mix of both. The critical dividing point is whether a third party who buys the property is bound by the lease. So, if L grants a lease to T and a further person, X, purchases the landlord's interest, the question would be whether X is bound by T's lease. A property lawyer's answer would be that, provided it is a lease and not a personal right, X would be so bound (subject to certain exceptions).

The critical question is then what distinguishes the lease from a personal right (usually termed a licence or a lodging arrangement). A property lawyer's clear answer is that a lease is 'exclusive possession for a term at a rent' (*Street* v. *Mountford* [1985] 1 AC 809; *cf Ashburn Anstalt* v. *Arnold* [1988] where the requirement of rent is questioned (correctly)). For reasons which will subsequently become clear, many landlords attempted to avoid granting leases or exclusive possession and instead attempted to grant licences. This caused real problems for property lawyers because, whilst the requirement of a term is easy to satisfy (for example, rent being paid weekly or monthly), the notion of exclusive possession seems to be incapable of definition other than the broad one of being able to keep the landlord out of the premises.[14] In other words, the distinction held so dear by property lawyers between property and personal rights was threatened. As with all knee-jerk responses to threats, the property lawyer merely reimposed the barrier by restating the norm.

So, the House of Lords in *Street* were adamant that the position and intention of the parties (the contractual solution) was irrelevant. The only thing that mattered was whether the landlord had granted exclusive possession for a term at a rent. Whether the landlord had called the agreement a 'licence' or a 'lease' did not matter. All that was relevant was whether exclusive possession for a term had been granted. So, the contractual belief in the sanctity of bargain was jettisoned by the courts in these cases in favour of a broader property-based approach. In doing so, one might assume that the House of Lords took into account the fact that there is a declining amount of residential accommodation (see Table 1.2 above) and that any security is based upon the grant of a lease or exclusive possession. But this was not the case, for Lord Templeman (who has been the major judicial player in the development of this doctrine) was absolutely clear that this was as irrelevant as the label the parties had given to the arrangement. This is entirely in keeping with the notion of equality within the rule of law. After all, it does not matter who grants the lease (Roger Street was a solicitor who should have known better: see Street, 1985) or what the purpose of the arrangement is for the rule of law. Templeman states this quite explicitly:

'If Mr Street has succeeded, where owners have failed these past 70 years, in driving a coach and horses through the Rent Acts, he must be left to enjoy the benefit of his ingenuity unless and until Parliament intervenes. I accept that the Rent Acts are irrelevant to the problem of determining the legal effect of the rights granted by the agreement. Like the professed intentions of the parties, the Rent Acts cannot alter the effect of the agreement.' (at, p. 820)

Whilst the issue became less apparent after the security given to tenants was severely weakened in 1988, several questions have subsequently arisen about the relevance of intention and the nature of the bargain. Part of the problem has been that these discrepancies have emanated from the pen of Lord Templeman himself, which suggest that the distinction (that he created) masks a more fundamental protection of the relational and transactional inequality. So, in later cases, Templeman explicitly located his reasoning on the basis of comments by the occupants as well as the landlord's position. In other words, such matters became important when they suited the purpose. So in *Antoniades* v. *Villiers*, the following is used:

> 'He [the landlord] kept going on about it being a licence and not in the Rent Act. I didn't know either but was pleased to have a place after three or four months of chasing.
> I didn't understand what was meant by exclusive possession or licence. Signed because so glad to move in. Had been looking for three months.' (comments by occupants, [1990] 1 AC 417, 462).

Of course, when dealing with a local authority landlord in *Westminster City Council* v. *Clarke*, the local authority position had to be taken into account (after all, we don't want local authorities being forced to house 'undesirables'):

> 'In reaching this conclusion I take into account the object of the council, namely the provision of accommodation for vulnerable homeless persons . . ..
> This is a very special case which depends on the peculiar nature of the hostel maintained by the council, the use of the hostel by the council, the totality, immediacy and objectives of the powers exercisable by the council and the restrictions imposed upon Mr. Clarke.' [1992] 1 All ER 695, 703

It is apparent that the property law approach, based on the rule of law, is as simplistic as the contractual approach, for the complexity of the arrangements and situational inequalities are not susceptible to general solutions – a fact with which few would disagree. An approach steeped in the tradition of housing law thinking would, however, provide a solution as well as highlighting a problem. The solution is simple. Housing studies often divide the occupation of accommodation into a number of different tenures. Part of the original study by Rex and Moore (1967) was concerned to provide an explanatory theory of urban class relations based on 'strength in the housing market or, more generally, in the system of housing allocation'. The study has proved problematic (see the summary of these problems in Morris & Winn, 1990, pp. 214–15) but highly influential as a starting point for the development of urban sociological perspectives. Occupation of property is divided into a number of different tenures in the following way:

'1. The outright owners of large houses in desirable areas.
2. Mortgage payers who 'own' whole houses in desirable areas.
3. Council tenants in Council-built houses.
4. Council tenants in slum houses awaiting demolition.
5. Tenants of private house-owners, usually in the inner ring.
6. House owners who must take lodgers to meet loan repayments.
7. Lodgers in rooms.' (Rex & Moore, 1967, p. 274)

This tenurial basis does not assist us with our legal analysis of the difference between a lease and a licence until we reduce it, as Stewart (1996) and others do, to four basic tenures: owner-occupation; private renting; housing association; local authority.

Splitting it up in this way enables us to concentrate our analysis and change it between each sector depending upon the nature of accessing the lease in each. For example, accessing local authority tenure is now essentially through a queuing system – once at the head of the queue, the local authority comes under an obligation to house the person.[15] In the private renting sector, it is often the case that people will have been looking for accommodation for a considerable period so that landlords might exploit the situation in terms of the amount of rent charged or seeking to evict a tenant (in other words, rachmanism). Some RSLs have agreements with local authorities to house a certain proportion of people and are thus obliged to do so. In other words, the inequalities are different in each sector and will depend, even within each sector, on individual circumstance.

Certainly, Lord Templeman appeared to have appreciated these distinctions after *Street* but nonetheless stuck to the principles outlined in that case. The point here is that in this situation, as in all others, the judiciary should come clean and tell us the basis for their decision. Carr essentially makes the same point:

'Apparently, in nine cases out of ten the intentions of the parties are not going to be relevant. In those cases, however, where a definite accommodating purpose is served by the arrangement and exclusive possession is not granted to the occupier (because of the degree of control retained by the landlord), then an examination of the purpose should be undertaken in order to check the validity of the arrangement and whether the non-transfer of the property interest is genuine. That examination of purpose inevitably involves social policy considerations.' (Carr, 1998, p. 119)

That examination of purpose inevitably divides the issue along the concept of tenure used in housing studies because any other analysis is too general and simple. This was why Templeman consistently contradicted himself.

Our answer – that housing tenures are more complex than property lawyers care to consider – causes certain problems. First, there is the problem caused by the mindset of property lawyers who cannot divide tenure in this way because tenure has a particular meaning to them (all land is owned by the crown). An impasse develops, which disables the lawyer from accessing the important relationship between housing tenures. The lease is used in each form of housing tenure. Yet, when the government seeks to influence the housing market, it does not do so through the blunt concept of a lease but through a review of priorities between and within each housing tenure. Housing (as distinct from property) lawyers, more by instinct than design, have been forced to re-evaluate the notion of tenure along housing policy lines. As this has been done, it might be argued, so the courts have followed suit – explaining Templeman's apparent contradiction.

Secondly, cross-tenurial interests are being created which affect the nature of tenure (even if they do not affect the law). For example, the Leasehold Reform, Housing and Urban Development Act 1993 set up the rents-to-mortgage scheme. Even though take-up of this scheme has been minimal (only 25 cases), it nevertheless forms part of a much broader development to increase home ownership through schemes which, in housing terminology, are called 'shared ownership' (see Bramley *et al.*, 1995). We need to be aware of the limits of the tenurial basis, even though it best suits an analysis of law and policy. The catch-22 for authors of housing law texts is that, whilst a tenurial approach can assist with the explanation of contradictions in judicial approaches, tenure is too general to explain the individual housing relationship. Defining tenures is an important step but even within the tenures the power differential can be radically altered on an individual level. This really is the same point as Nelken (1983) makes, that landlords are not a class in themselves.

We need to go further, however, for there is an inelegance in regarding 'private renting' as a discrete tenure. A person who has a 99-year lease, in property law, would be regarded as renting, but in the sub-division employed here, such a lease would fall within the home ownership category; a person who does not rent at all but has a licence to occupy would probably be regarded as falling within the category of private renting but clearly this is inaccurate as a matter of law. *The point is that each of our categories has a number of hidden assumptions and each is heterogeneous.* 'Ownership', for example, does not describe the mortgage relationship under which the lender takes the ownership interest and the borrower simply has the right to repay the loan. When local authority tenants take the right to manage their estates, does this change the tenure? Tenure is an organising concept with limitations:

> '. . . while some social relations of housing provision and consumption *may* have a substantive link with the legal rights and responsibilities of occupancy, 'tenure' has become 'shorthand' to describe broad categories which very often do not have substantive, binding attributes.'
> (Barlow & Duncan, 1989, p. 229; original emphasis)

The authors argue that we should abandon 'this single, uniform housing shorthand'.

Nevertheless, it is the shorthand used in this book, because the operation both of housing provision and housing consumption tends to reflect its dominance. Regulatory interventions usually occur on the basis that they affect particular tenures or tenures generally. Of course, regulation might affect only part of the sector (for example, it is only since 1974 that rent regulation and security of tenure has affected the *furnished* part of the private rented sector) but this makes the important point that regulatory cleavages occur within the sector (as well as implementation problems as, for example, landlords used to put a few pieces of poor quality furniture in the property and rent it out furnished). Furthermore, if as the housing Minister, Hilary Armstrong, says, it does not matter who provides housing, 'it is what works that counts', we need to be alive to the distinctions between the tenures. For example, if a regime is created in which people are allocated to tenures willy-nilly, it would be iniquitous if the rights in each tenure are different. Yet, this is precisely what is happening as tenants are being transferred from council housing into other tenures (home ownership, housing association, private renting) in which they have less, or at the least different types of, security. A tenure analysis allows us to grapple this important disadvantage of current policy and allows us to argue for a move to a new type of tenancy (a 'social housing' tenancy).

In short, tenure is a concept which does have limitations. However, it also has advantages. These advantages are particularly relevant in (re)considering the role of regulation.

The final point that we need to make in this section is that the divide between property and personal rights is a divide which does not (or should not) exist in housing law because it is largely irrelevant. Protection is an important concept in housing law but rather than the narrow protection offered by property law against third parties, our concern is with the security of the individual within the context of the housing market. So, the protection of rights against third parties is considered from a totally different perspective in housing law. For example, our concern with short-term private-sector renting is the security offered to the renter through the medium of legislation and the effect that has on the housing market. So, housing law is inherently and explicitly political. There is, thus, a more preliminary concern, rarely covered in property law courses other than in oblique terms, with access to housing. Cowan and Fionda put the matter this way in arguing that homelessness should at the least feature as one of the subjects covered in property law:

'[Property] lawyers concern themselves with the 'included' and not the 'excluded'. [Property] law is a subject where we consider the rights of the included, as consumers, but those unable to consume do not feature. The challenging notion of 'citizenship', which might be defined in this context as 'the ability to consume',[16] assists us in our appreciation of a more radical approach. This preoccupation with consumerism is at odds with the more traditional socialist view of citizenship as social inclusion – a preoccupation with the welfare of the most marginalised and poverty-stricken in society in order to ensure their inclusion in the mainstream of society; that is, empowerment through social unity.' (1998, p. 265)[17]

Public Law and Private Politics: The Case of the Lease

Public law governs part of the relationships in which public authorities are engaged, either with other public authorities or with individuals. So, for example, the enquiry duties and housing obligations contained in the homelessness legislation are almost uniformly subject to public law. The enforcement of public law rights in the courts is by special judicial proceedings taken in the High Court, known as judicial review.

> 'Broadly stated, the modern form of judicial review is designed to uphold a certain interpretation of the rule of law and the separation of powers – its function is to *ensure that executive bodies remain within the limits of the powers that the legislature has granted.*' (Loveland, 1996b, p. 81)

Supposedly, this process is speedy as an application to the court has to be made within three months of the decision which is being challenged. A preliminary stage to the process is inserted in which a judge must grant leave before an application may proceed to a full hearing. Other than these two diverting factors, there are other theoretical limits to the court's consideration and the decision. First, the process is not supposed to consider the merits of the public authority's decision (that is, whether the decision is right or wrong on its facts), only to consider whether that decision was 'illegal', 'unreasonable or irrational', 'procedurally unfair'. Unreasonableness (sometimes known as *Wednesbury* unreasonableness) has a particular meaning; a decision can only be successfully challenged *if it is so unreasonable that no reasonable person would have made the decision – a sort of double unreasonableness.*

Second, the courts cannot substitute their own decision for that of the public authority. If the applicant is successful by way of judicial review, as opposed to 'normal' procedures, the result is that the public authority must reconsider its decision. It can make exactly the same decision again (unless it is illegal or unreasonable). Third, only certain decisions of public bodies are subject to the process. It may come as a surprise that there is no convincing answer to which decisions, and for that matter which bodies, are subject to the process. However, getting it wrong can have disastrous effects. This is considered below, for there is a particular resonance in all subjects which touch upon the 'welfare state' as that state now contains a mix of public and private elements, sometimes known as quasi-markets, or, rather more controversially, as part of the 'post-Fordist state'.[18]

Before we attempt to answer these questions, we need to consider the justification for limiting the jurisdiction in these cases (for limitation it obviously is). In the context of the rule of law and its critique, it does not come as much of a surprise that the rationale depends upon a particular view of the public body and that the procedures involved actually favour that body (there is an enormous literature, but see (conventionally) Wade & Forsyth, 1996, or (unconventionally) Birkinshaw, 1994, Ch. 6). In certain areas of housing law, the judiciary have furthered the imbalance by arguing, almost as a knee-jerk reaction, that the courts should be wary of opening judicial review too widely. Consider the following:

> 'My Lords, I am troubled at the prolific use of judicial review for the purpose of challenging the performance by local authorities of their functions under the [homelessness legislation]. Parliament intended the local authority to be the judge of fact . . .. Although the action or inaction of a local authority is clearly susceptible to judicial review where they have misconstrued the Act, or abused their powers or otherwise acted perversely, I think that great judicial restraint should be exercised in giving leave to proceed by judicial review. . . . [I]t is not, in my opinion, appropriate that the remedy of judicial review, which is a discretionary remedy, should be made use of to monitor the actions of local authorities under the Act save in the exceptional case.' (*Puhlhofer* v. *Hillingdon LBC* [1986] 1 All ER 467, 474, *per* Lord Brightman)

This is probably the most widely cited comment by a judge in homelessness cases. Any belief in the rule of law after such a comment should surely be shattered. However, it is also inaccurate in a number of respects. The so-called prolific use of judicial review consisted of 84 applications for leave to seek judicial review in 1987, 105 in 1988, and 176 in 1989. When compared to the number of unsuccessful homelessness applications, these are tiny proportions (less than 0.0005 per cent). Nevertheless, a direct result of the *Puhlhofer* decision was that, in 1987, 74.2 per cent of applications for leave in homelessness cases were rejected. However, the year after the figure was 56.2 per cent, and it appeared to decline further in the following years. The compilers of this quantitative data make the following point, suggesting that it may not be the applicant who wishes to abuse the judicial process:

> 'While the frequent use of judicial review in this area is perfectly understandable from the perspective of the applicants, the way in which some local authorities use the procedure as a substitute for tighter internal scrutiny of decisions and as an additional hurdle into accommodation requires much more critical attention from judicial and legal commentators that it has so far received.' (Sunkin *et al.*, 1993, p. 15)

Finally, if one believes that the number of homelessness applications is low, consider Table 1.3.

Of the questions posed earlier (what is a public body? what decisions are subject to judicial review?), it must be conceded that no definitive answer can be given to cover each and every case: 'A quest for a single definition of public which can provide such a global and final categorisation is inapposite and leads only to confusion and contradiction' (Black, 1996, p. 52). These are important questions which simply cannot, and should not, be coherently answered. The classic examples are RSLs and the Housing Corporation. The latter is almost certainly a public body subject to judicial review. This can be gleaned from the following information: it is a statutory creation; it is funded by the government; it takes decisions, for example, whether a housing association is entitled to register with it or how much money might be available to an association; members of the Corporation are appointed by the government; it has power to make regulations which bind and affect RSLs (for a more general discussion see Baldwin & McCrudden, 1990).

On the other hand, whether RSLs are public bodies for this purpose is unclear (in addition to the following discussion see Handy, 1997). In favour of them being so are the following factors: they receive public money through the housing corporation; they usually have agreements with local authorities under which they will house certain persons at the top of the local authority's waiting list (this might be termed a public function); they are sometimes partly funded by local authorities; it is usual for RSLs to operate waiting lists for applicants in the same way as local authorities; their status, to a certain extent, depends upon registration with the Corporation which, itself, is governed by statute. Furthermore, judicial guidance here tends to be rather broad:

Table 1.3   Applications for leave to seek Judicial Review in housing cases by type, 1987–1989 (excluding homelessness) – actual numbers

	1987	1988	1989
Housing Benefits	9	11	13
Compulsory Purchase Order	6	5	4
Rates	7	5	3
Repairs	8	2	1
Possession	–	1	5
Grants	2	1	8
Transfers	1	2	4
Squatting	1	12	6
Other/Unclassified	23	17	12

Source: Sunkin *et al.*, 1993

'Possibly the only essential elements are what can be described as a public element, which can take many different forms, and the exclusion from the jurisdiction of bodies whose sole source of power is a consensual submission to their jurisdiction.' (*R* v. *Panel on Take-overs and Mergers ex parte Datafin PLC* [1987] QB 815, *per* Donaldson MR)

The take-over panel was held to be subject to judicial review because 'but for' their involvement in regulation, the government itself would have to do so. An ideological application of this test might suggest that, given the current penchant for self-regulation, limited government involvement and general governmental desire to avoid as much public expenditure as possible, government ideally would do nothing. As another judge has said, 'there is a difference between what may affect the public and what amounts to a public duty' – only the latter would be subject to judicial review (*R* v. *Disciplinary Committee of the Jockey Club ex parte Aga Khan* [1993] 2 All ER 853, *per* Farquharson LJ).

Judged from this perspective, RSLs' joint allocations schemes with local authorities are simply matters of agreement and not duty; as is the point about their funding from local authorities. Indeed, the fact that the tenancies they offer form part of the private sector suggests that they are essentially private bodies. Registration with the Corporation is irrelevant because that only shows a willingness to submit to their control and not an assumption of publicness. And receipt of public monies from the Corporation is equally irrelevant because there is no public duty attached to it; more particularly because this is usually, if not always, mixed with private-sector finance. A slightly different approach would be to look at the purpose of the housing association. For example, those associations which have been set up to take over and manage the whole of a local authority's stock of housing might well be subject to public law on the basis that they are *in loco parentis* (see Handy, 1997, p. 13 for this distinction).

Other parts of housing law, such as the contractual approach to housing management currently in operation through 'Best Value' or compulsory competitive tendering, raise similarly intractable questions (see Harden, 1992; Birkinshaw, 1994, Vincent-Jones, 1994; Vincent-Jones and Harries, 1998). One suggested answer is to let the second question determine the answer to the first. There is clearly a high degree of overlap between the two in any event. For example, in *Datafin*, the Court suggested that there were narrow limits to its powers on certain issues reflecting the fact that the take-over panel was only marginally within its jurisdiction.

In the early cases, a distinction was drawn between the decision-making functions of a public authority (subject to judicial review) and the executive functions (not subject to judicial review but susceptible to challenge in private law). In other words, decisions required to be made on the basis of a discretionary exercise were subject to judicial review, others were not. Such a distinction seems reasonable until one appreciates that even 'executive functions', where no discretion seems to be involved, can, in fact, operate in a discretionary fashion – for example, in terms of getting in the relevant facts (Sainsbury, 1992). It seems to be established that matters that are conducted in the housing association's position as landlord (or tenant) are usually part of the private law. So, for example, enforcement of the terms of the tenancy is a private law matter as is the seeking of eviction (although a policy of when to seek eviction might be subject to judicial review).

The question is that when one of these public bodies grants a lease to a tenant, is this a decision-making function (we have decided to grant you a lease) or an executive function (we grant you a lease)? To say that the answer depends upon the context does not help. Equally, however, Donaldson's comment in *Datafin* shows a political naivety for, in the housing context, the very nature of government has been stripped back to the extent that government has attempted to avoid building new units of accommodation, cut back its housing expenditure dramatically, and largely adopted a *laissez-faire* market policy on issues such as welfare housing.

Once again, the legal approach seems to have been to discuss whether the issue is regulated by public or private law and not the *a priori* question of the relationship between government and housing tenure. Local government, for example, is now a bare shell with little in the way of obligations other than as a means of regulating the contracts into which it enters – contracts affect housing management, homelessness enquiry duties, Housing Benefit processing, the allocation and provision of community care and children services, etc. It might be suggested that the only difference between local government and other privatised industries is that there is no 'OFLA' (or some such body) regulating local government. On the other hand, RSLs, which may well be private organisations (at least, on one view), have taken over much local authority accommodation, if not all of it in some areas, and are now the major providers of housing. Does this tip the balance in favour of them being public bodies or does the existence of significant private finance continue to ensure private status?

It is difficult to be more helpful than this on these issues. They remain crucial to the implementation and application of housing law. Their vagueness no doubt assists the judiciary in ensuring its status as ultimate arbiter. However, this assistance does no more than eat up the available legal aid budget and, in itself, undermines the principles of equal access to justice.

Conclusion

The approach adopted in all of the subsequent chapters is an attempt at providing an analysis which builds upon a vision of housing law. That vision of housing law is critical. It does not depend upon the existence of legislation and cases. Often the most critical developments in housing law occur without reference to either. As housing law has grown up, it has also presented challenges to the legal orthodoxy. For example, shared ownership schemes were a clever manipulation of pre-existing law into a genuine tenurial advance.

Subsequent chapters adopt the use of 'tenure' which is most commonly found in the housing studies literature. This is a concept with limitations – at times, for example, it is frustratingly vague – but it nevertheless allows us to pose important questions throughout this text about the regulatory schema adopted within housing law as well as questioning the role and value of tenure (and, more broadly, of categorization generally). At times, it is difficult to appreciate where certain facets of the housing regulatory system 'belong' in the book's structure. For this, one can only apologise and restate the problems of organizing concepts.

Finally, in this chapter I have sought to outline the approach taken in this book for in no sense does it fit within the textbook tradition of legal studies. It is opinionated and presents not so much a study of law 'in context' but a study of the *contexts of law*. The aim is to show the tensions that exist in the housing system between different actors with greater emphasis on certain of these – the impact of central government upon the housing system provides one such focus as do those who (attempt to) consume housing. You are invited to disagree with the opinions expressed here, as well as the structure of this book – that is what academic debate is about. What is undeniable, however, is that having set out the terrain of housing law, one finds that it is desperately in need of 'intensive care' (to borrow David Hoath's expressive phrase). The succeeding chapters of this book underline how much reform is required.

Further Reading

There are a number of important texts dealing with housing law, housing policy and the sociology of housing. For the rationale of the approach adopted by the early housing law texts, see the preface in A. Arden & M. Partington (1983), *Housing Law*, London: Sweet & Maxwell; see also Arden's editorial in the *Journal of Housing Law*, issue 1 in 1997. The classic urban sociology text – J. Rex & R. Moore (1967), *Race, Community and Conflict: A Study of Sparkbrook*, Oxford: OUP – developed a theory based upon the proposition that 'people are distinguished from one another by their strength in the housing market, or, more generally, in the system of housing allocations'. They then set out different tenure types in the context of 'a class struggle between groups differentially placed with regard to the means of housing . . .'

This approach, together with others, has been developed and questioned in the following texts: P. Saunders (1986), *Social Theory and the Urban Question*, London: Hutchinson; (1990), *A Nation of Home Owners*, London: Unwin Hyman – for a specific critique of Saunders' approach see R. Forrest, A. Murie & P. Williams (1990), *Home Ownership: Differentiation and Fragmentation*, London: Unwin

Hyman; P. Somerville (1990), 'Home sweet home', vol 4, *Housing Studies*, 113–18. A brief selection of the broader literature includes R. Pahl (1968), *Readings in Urban Sociology*, London: Pergamon; M. Castells (1977), *The Urban Question: a Marxist Approach*, London: Edward Arnold; J. Lambert, C. Paris, & B. Blackaby (1978), *Housing Policy and the State*, London: Macmillan; J. Morris & M. Winn (1990), *Housing and Social Inequality*, London: Hilary Shipman; J. Kemeny (1980), *The Myth of Home Ownership*, London: Routledge; J. Kemeny (1992), *Housing and Social Theory*, London: Routledge.

The significant exception to the dearth of theoretical/conceptual analyses comes from within the feminist movement – see S. Watson (1988), *Accommodating Inequality*, Sydney: Allen & Unwin; and two edited collections: R. Gilroy & R. Woods (1994), *Housing Women*, London: Routledge; C. Booth, J. Darke & S. Yeandle (1997), *Changing Places: Women's Lives in the City*, London: Paul Chapman.

A recent, more depressing strand of thought in housing policy reflects the belief that housing policy has become a neglected (and underfunded) part of social welfare, at the same time as housing policy has become an accepted field of study within educational institutions: A. Murie (1997), 'The social rented sector, housing and the welfare state in the UK', vol 12, *Housing Studies*, 437; G. Bramley (1997), 'Housing policy: a case of terminal decline?', vol 25, *Policy and Politics*, 387; P. Malpass (1996), 'The unravelling of housing policy in Britain', vol 11, *Housing Studies*, 459.

For a broader approach to 'sources of law' see C. Harlow & R. Rawlings (1997), *Law and Administration*, London: Butterworths; G. Richardson (1993), *Law, Process and Custody: Prisoners and Patients*, London: Weidenfeld & Nicolson; P. Birkinshaw (1994), *Grievances, Remedies and the State*, London: Sweet & Maxwell; also, H. Genn & G. Richardson (1994), *Administrative Law & Government Action*, Oxford: Oxford University Press. On the operation of tribunals and informal reviews/appeals, see R. Baldwin, N. Wikeley & R. Young (1992), *Judging Social Security*, Oxford: Oxford University Press. On leases, an interesting contextual approach is attempted (with varying degrees of success) in S. Bright & G. Gilbert (1994), *Landlord and Tenant*, Oxford: Oxford University Press; M. Partington (1980), *Landlord and Tenant*, London: Weidenfeld & Nicolson (this is now rather dated). Other texts on the same subject are notable by their inability to contextualize it.

The only other attempt made to conceptualize housing law is in A. Stewart (1996), *Rethinking Housing Law*, London: Sweet & Maxwell, Ch. 1. This is an important text which sets out an approach to the systems of *regulation* used in housing law from three different perspectives: individual property relations; individual statutory relationships; the sphere of regulatory relationships. Whilst this provides a structure for analysis, I have argued it causes confusion as to the reach of housing law. Indeed, the concentration on law as regulation overly limits the analysis (see Cowan, (1997) vol 24, *Journal of Law and Society*, 459–61).

Endnotes

1. As shown below, Arden's conjunction of 'house' with 'home' is a classic example of the confusion exhibited in housing law texts.
2. This trusting approach ensures that housing providers often go without being subject to judicial regulation.

3. The District Auditor's report has recently been criticised by the Court of Appeal, and is considered further in chapter 12 below.

4. The concept of a moral panic involves a situation when 'a condition, episode, person, or group of persons emerges to become defined as a threat to societal values or interests' (Cohen, 1972, p. 28). The *locus classicus* was Cohen's study of the construction of the moral panic around the mods and rockers. See also the study of 'welfare scroungerphobia' conducted by Golding & Middleton, 1982.

5. There is some evidence to suggest that local authorities use such clauses as attempts at social change, but, because of the legal problems caused by definitions of racial harassment as well as other legal issues, they will usually evict racial harassers on other grounds such as rent arrears or anti-nuisance clauses (Fitzgerald, 1989).

6. Excluded are those the law holds to be without the requisite mental capacity, for example minors or the 'mentally disordered or drunkards' (Goff & Jones, 1986, p. 424), who can only make valid contracts for certain things. The most vivid application of this doctrine was by the House of Lords in *R* v. *Bexley LBC ex parte B, Oldham MBC ex parte G* [1993] 25 HLR 319.

7. Strictly, a mortgage is a lease. The more commonly used form of security is a charge.

8. For a brilliant, sustained analysis, as well as discussion of the definition of inequality, see Murie, 1983.

9. This takes into account the number of unfit dwellings; hidden households; second homes; those undergoing significant conversion or improvement.

10. A few days after the White Paper, the Conservative budget (once again) cut the amount available to housing!

11. These are difficult terms: see Cowan, 1997b, Chs 1 and 2.

12. The mortgage intervention above is an example of the Major government's plaster skimming.

13. Compare with the unnecessary concept of tenure used by landlords, derived from the feudal notion that all land belongs to the monarch.

14. See the circular point that, where a landlord has reserved a right to re-enter the property in the agreement, this is suggestive of a lease being granted because if a personal right had been granted then there would have been no need to retain that right in the agreement.

15. As we shall see, though, historically 'undesirables' have been housed in the worst accommodation. It is an unfortunate fact that in some areas, the homeless are uniformly considered to be 'undesirable'.

16. This might be derived from, for example, the approach of *The Citizen's Charter* (1991, HMSO) – note the individualization of the Citizen through the apostrophe – which discussed citizenship in the context of the relationship between the individual and the State by reference to the quality of public services, choice between competing providers of public services, expected minimum standards of public services, and efficiency in their provision.

17. Peter Mandelson touched on this idea when he outlined New Labour's plans to eradicate social exclusion: 'Our vision is to end social exclusion. Our priority is to redirect and reform social programmes and the welfare state towards that goal. Our strategy is to build a broad ranging political consensus for action' (in *Labour's next steps: tackling social exclusion*, unpublished lecture to the Fabian Society, August 14 1997).

18. Post-Fordism derives from the mass production by Henry Ford of cars ('you can have any car you want as long as it is black'): 'Crudely, it has been suggested

that if Fordism is represented by a homology between mass production, mass consumption, modernist cultural forms and the mass provision of welfare then post-Fordism is characterised by an emerging coalition between flexible production, differentiated and segmented consumption patterns, post-modernist cultural forms and a restructured welfare state.' (Loader & Burrows, 1994, p. 1; see also, Williams, 1994).

Bibliography

Arden, A. (1997), 'Editorial', vol 1, *Journal of Housing Law*, 1–2

Arden, A. and Partington, M. (1983), *Housing Law*, London: Sweet & Maxwell

Balchin, P. (1995), *Housing Policy: An Introduction*, London: Routledge

Baldwin, J. and McCrudden, C. (1990), *Regulation and Public Law*, London: Weidenfeld & Nicolson

Ball, M. (1983), *Housing Policy and Economic Power: the Political Economy of Owner Occupation*, London: Methuen

Barlow, J. and Duncan, S. (1989), 'The use and abuse of housing tenure', vol 3, *Housing Studies*, 219

Beale, H. (1983), 'Inequality of bargaining power', vol 3, *Oxford Journal of Legal Studies*, 123

Beale, H., Bishop, M. and Furmston, M. (1995), *Contract Law Cases and Materials*, London: Butterworths

Birkinshaw, P. (1994), *Grievances, Remedies and the State*, London: Sweet & Maxwell

Black, J. (1996), 'Constitutionalising self-regulation', vol 59, *Modern Law Review*, 24

Bramley, G., Dunmore, K., Durrant, C. and Smart, G. (1995), *Do-it-yourself Shared Ownership: an Evaluation*, London: Housing Corporation

Bridges, L. and Forbes, D. (1990), *Making the Law Work on Racial Harassment*, London: Legal Action Group

Cabinet Office (1991), *The Citizen's Charter*, London: HMSO

Carr, H. (1998), 'The sorting of the forks from the spades', in D. Cowan (ed.), *Housing: Participation and Exclusion*, Aldershot: Dartmouth

Central Housing Advisory Committee (CHAC) (1969), *Council Housing: Purposes, Procedures and Priorities*, London: HMSO

Cohen, N. (1996), 'The long arm of the law', *The Independent on Sunday*, 5 November

Cohen, S. (1972), *Folk Devils and Moral Panics*, London: McKee & Gibbon

Cohen, S. and Young, J. (eds) (1973), *The Manufacture of News: Deviance, Social Problems and the Mass Media*, London: Constable

Cole, I. and Furbey, R. (1994), *The Eclipse of Council Housing*, London: Routledge

Cotterell, R. (1992), *The Sociology of Law*, London: Butterworths

Cowan, D. (1995), Review of Hughes, D. and Lowe, S. (1995), *Social Housing Law and Policy*, Public Law, 668

Cowan, D. (1997a), 'Doing the government's work', vol 60, *Modern Law Review*, 275

Cowan, D. (1997b), *Homelessness: The (In-)Appropriate Applicant*, Aldershot: Dartmouth

Cowan, D. (1998a), 'Homelessness internal appeals mechanisms: serving the administrative process?', vol 27 *Anglo-American Law Review*, 66 (Pt 1), 169 (Pt 2)

Cowan, D. (1998b), 'Reforming the homelessness legislation', vol 57, *Critical Social Policy*, 435

Cowan, D. and Fionda, J. (1998), 'Homelessness', in S. Bright and J. Dewar (eds), *Land Law: Themes and Perspectives*, Oxford: Oxford University Press

Cowan, D. and Hunter, C. (1998), 'Internal reviews in homelessness cases', paper presented to the European Network of Housing, University of Wales, Cardiff, 1998

Darke, J. (1994), 'Women and the meaning of home', in R. Gilroy and R. Woods (eds), *Housing Women*, London: Routledge

Darke, J. (1997), 'Challenges for planning', in C. Booth, J. Darke and S. Yeandle (eds), *Changing Places: Women's Lives in the City*, London: Paul Chapman

Department of the Environment (DoE) (1994), *Racial Incidents in Council Housing: The Local Authority Response*, London: HMSO

Department of the Environment (DoE) (1996), *Household Growth: Where Shall we Live?*, London: Stationery Office

Dicey, A. (1902), *The Law of the Constitution*, London: Macmillan

Doran, A. (1996), 'Tenant's £20,000 worth of cheek', *Daily Mail*, 19 February

Farmer, J. (1974), *Tribunals and Government*, London: Weidenfeld & Nicolson

Fitzgerald, M. (1989), 'Legal approaches to racial harassment in council housing: the case for reassessment', vol 16, *New Community*, 93

Forrest, R. and Murie, A. (1991), *Selling the Welfare State: The Privatization of Public Housing*, London: Routledge

Forrest, R., Murie, A. and Williams, P. (1990), *Home Ownership: Differentiation and Fragmentation*, London: Unwin Hyman

Fowler, R. (1991), *Language in the News: Discourse and Ideology in the Press*, London: Routledge

Franks Committee, The, (1957), *Administrative Tribunals and Enquiries*, London: HMSO

Gibb, K. and Munro, M. (1990), *Housing Finance in the UK*, London: Macmillan

Goff, R. and Jones, G. (1986), *The Law of Restitution*, London: Sweet & Maxwell

Golding, P. and Middleton, S. (1982), *Images of Welfare*, Oxford: Martin Robertson

Gordon, C. (1980), *Power/Knowledge: Selected Interviews and Other Writings 1972–1977*, Brighton: Harvester

Gray, K. (1993), *Elements of Property Law*, London: Butterworths

Griffiths, J. (1991), *The Politics of the Judiciary*, London: Fontana

Hall, S., Critcher, C., Jefferson, T., Clarke, J. and Roberts, B. (1978), *Policing the Crisis: Mugging, the State, and Law and Order*, London: Macmillan

Handy, C. (1997), 'Housing associations: public or private law?', vol 1, *Journal of Housing Law*, 12

Harden, I. (1992), *The Contracting State*, Buckingham: Open University Press

Heffer, S. (1998), 'An insidious arrogance', *Daily Mail*, 6 February

Henderson. J and Karn, V. (1987), *Race, Class and State Housing: Inequality and the Allocation of Public Housing in Britain*, Aldershot: Gower

Hills, J. (1991), *Unravelling Housing Finance*, Oxford: Oxford University Press

Hughes, D. and Lowe, S. (1995), *Social Housing Law and Policy*, London: Butterworths

Hunt, A. (1991), 'Marxism, law, legal theory and jurisprudence', in P. Fitzpatrick (ed.), *Dangerous Supplements: Resistance and Renewal in Jurisprudence*, London: Pluto

Hunt, A. and Wickham, G. (1994), *Foucault and Law: Towards a Sociology of Law as Governance*, London: Pluto

Hunter, C. (1997), Review of Hughes, D. and Lowe, S. (1995), *Social Housing Law and Policy*, Journal of Housing Law, vol 1, pp. 47

Hunter, C. and Miles, J. (1997), 'The unsettling of settled law on 'settled accommodation': the House of Lords and the homelessness legislation old and new', vol 19, *Journal of Social Welfare and Family Law*, 267

Hunter, C. and Nixon, J. (1998), 'Better a public tenant than a private borrower be: the possession process and threat of eviction', in D. Cowan (ed.), *Housing: Participation and Exclusion*, Aldershot: Dartmouth

James, D. (1974), 'Homelessness: can the courts contribute?', vol 1, *British Journal of Law and Society*, 195

James, R. (1997), *Private Ombudsmen and Public Law*, Aldershot: Dartmouth

Kemeny, J. (1992), *Housing and Social Theory*, London: Routledge

Kennedy, D. (1976), 'Form and substance in private law adjudication', *Harvard Law Review*, 89

Loader, B. and Burrows, R. (1994), 'Introduction', in R. Burrows and B. Loader (eds), *Towards a Post-Fordist Welfare State*, London: Routledge

Loughlin, M. (1992), *Administrative Accountability in Local Government*, York: Joseph Rowntree Foundation

Loughlin, M. (1996), *Legality and Locality*, Oxford: Oxford University Press

Loveland, I. (1995), *Housing Homeless Persons*, Oxford: Oxford University Press

Loveland, I. (1996a), 'The status of children as applicants under the homelessness legislation – judicial subversion of legislative intent', vol 8, *Child and Family Law Quarterly*, 89

Loveland, I. (1996b), *Constitutional Law: A Critical Introduction*, London: Butterworths

Magill, J. (1996), *Westminster City Council Audit of Accounts 1987/88 to 1994/95: Designated Sales*, London: Deloitte & Touche

Malpass, P. and Murie, A. (1994), *Housing Policy and Practice*, London: Macmillan

Mashaw, J. (1983), *Bureaucratic Justice*, New York: New Haven

Megarry, R. and Wade, H. (1984), *The Law of Real Property*, London: Stevens

Menski, W. (1996), Review of Hughes, D. and Lowe, S. (1995), vol 10, *Social Housing Law and Policy, Immigration and Nationality Law and Practice*, 116

Morris, J. and Winn, M. (1990), *Housing and Social Inequality*, London: Hilary Shipman

Murie, A. (1983), *Housing Inequality and Deprivation*, London: Heinemann

Neale, J. (1997) 'Theorising homelessness: contemporary sociological and feminist perspectives', in R. Burrows, N. Pleace, and D. Quilgars (eds), *Homelessness and Social Policy*, London: Routledge

Nelken, D. (1983), *The Limits of Legal Process: A Study of Landlords, Law and Crime*, London: Academic Books

Nevin, C. (1997), 'The mail order biz', *The Guardian*, 12 February

Nixon, J., Smith, Y., Wishart, B. and Hunter C. (1996), *Housing Cases in County Courts*, Bristol: The Policy Press

Pascall, G. (1997), *Social Policy: A New Feminist Analysis*, London: Routledge

Partington, M. (1993), 'Citizenship and housing', in R. Blackburn (ed.), *Rights of Citizenship*, London: Mansell

Rex, J. & Moore, R. (1967), *Race, Community and Conflict: A Study of Sparkbrook*, Oxford: Oxford University Press

Sainsbury, R. (1992), 'Administrative justice: discretion and procedure in social security decision-making', in K. Hawkins (ed.), *The Uses of Discretion*, Oxford: Clarendon

Sainsbury, R. (1994), 'Internal reviews and the weakening of social security claimants' rights of appeal', in H. Genn and G. Richardson (eds), *Administrative Law and Government Action*, Oxford: Oxford University Press

Sainsbury, R. and Eardley, T. (1992), *Housing Benefit Reviews*, London: HMSO

Saunders, P. (1990), *A Nation of Home Owners*, London: Unwin Hyman

Somerville, P. (1992), 'Homelessness and the meaning of home: rooflessness or rootlessness?', vol 16, *International Journal of Urban and Regional Research*, 529

Somerville, P. (1994), 'Tenure, gender and household structure', vol 9, *Housing Studies*, 329

Stewart, A. (1996), *Rethinking Housing Law*, London: Sweet & Maxwell

Street, H. (1975), *Justice in the Welfare State*, London: Stevens

Street, R. (1985), 'Coach and horses trip cancelled?: Rent Act avoidance after *Street v. Mountford*', *Conveyancer*, 328

Sunkin, M, Bridges. L and Meszaros, G. (1993), *Judicial Review in Perspective*, London: The Public Law Project

Thomas, P. (1997), 'Socio-legal studies: the case of disappearing fleas and bustards', in P. Thomas (ed.), *Socio-Legal Studies*, Dartmouth, Aldershot

Tomas, A. and Dittmar, H. (1995), 'The experience of homeless women: an exploration of housing histories and the meaning of home', vol 10, *Housing Studies*, 493

Trebilcock, M. (1993), *The Limits of Freedom of Contract*, Mass: Harvard University Press

Vincent-Jones, P. (1994), 'The limits of near contractual governance: local authority internal trading under compulsory competitive tendering', vol 21, *Journal of Law and Society*, 214

Vincent-Jones, P. and Harries, A. (1998), 'Compulsory competitive tendering of housing management: a case study', in D. Cowan (ed.), *Housing: Participation and Exclusion*, Aldershot: Dartmouth

Waddington, M. (1998), 'Too poor to stay here: 'illegal immigrants' and homelessness', in D. Cowan, *Housing: Participation and Exclusion*, Aldershot: Dartmouth

Wade, H. and Forsyth, C. (1996), *Administrative Law*, Oxford: Oxford University Press

Watson, S. (1983), 'Definitions of homelessness: a feminist perspective', vol 2, *Critical Social Policy*, 60

Watson, S. (1988), *Accommodating Inequality: Gender and Housing*, Sydney: Allen & Unwin

Wheeler, S. and Shaw, J. (1994), *Contract Law: Cases, Materials and Commentary*, Oxford: Oxford University Press

Whitehouse, L. (1998), 'The home owner: citizen or consumer?', in S. Bright and J. Dewar, *Land Law: Themes and Perspectives*, Oxford: Oxford University Press

Wilcox, S. (1997), *Housing Finance Review 1997/98*, York: Joseph Rowntree Foundation

Williams, F. (1994), 'Social relations, welfare and the post-Fordism debate', in R. Burrows and B. Loader (eds), *Towards a Post-Fordist Welfare State*, London: Routledge

Part I

Housing and Regulatory Failure

'In order to achieve the[ir] policy objectives . . . successive governments have, for well over a century, created a vast body of what is now described as housing law. Despite its volume, however, there is clear evidence that the law fails to deliver its policy objectives. Too many people still live in accommodation that is in disgraceful condition, for which very high rent must be paid and in relation to which there is inadequate security of tenure . . . The continuing failure of housing law to deliver its policy objectives – particularly in parts of the private rented sector – must at least raise the question as to whether a new approach to the regulation of the housing market might now be required. The traditional reliance on the use of law and legal procedures does not seem to be an adequate basis for the delivery of fundamental housing rights.' (Partington, 1998, p. 65)

Introduction to Part I

In Part I, we consider the ways in which each of the housing providers in the identified tenures – local authority, RSL, private renting, and home ownership – have been and are regulated. 'Housing providers' in this context means not only those who are actually responsible for the provision of housing but also those who facilitate it. For example, public and private finance plays a crucial role in the regulation of all housing providers and this is reflected in the succeeding chapters. In fact, public finance has since the 1970s been gradually drying up and the housing system has begun to draw upon private finance in increasingly innovative ways. As that market has been deregulated, the provision of finance has become more complex, and financiers have (for example) sought to impose 'private-sector disciplines' on the provision of social housing. The marketization of social housing is reflected both in the regulation of its development and consumption. To take one example, the importation of 'direct line' methods into social housing ('one call does it all') is a by-product of these changing structures. The marketization of private housing has been reflected in changing regulatory and institutional structures. This complexity is important, for it shows the critical role that central government has had in influencing the development and/or regression of each tenure. Nevertheless, central government's preferences have to be transferred into actual practice and this leads us directly into considerations of the role and value of regulation.

The basic argument through part I is actually of *regulatory failure in housing* and we will need to draw on the broader socio-legal literature which concerns itself with 'regulatory crisis' here, in order to illustrate the problems encountered in each housing sector. Drawing upon the 'somewhat obscure theory' of *autopoiesis* (Teubner, 1984, p. 291), it is argued that systems (such as the legal system) are *self referential* and *self-generating*: 'The self-referential closure of the legal system can be found in the circular relation between legal decisions and normative rules: decisions refer to rules and rules to decisions'; or 'external changes . . . are selectively filtered into legal structures and adapted in accordance with a logic of normative development' (Teubner, 1983, p. 249). In this sense, law is *normatively closed*, although it is *cognitively open* 'in that [the legal system] can observe other systems and their environment, and be indirectly affected by them' (Black, 1996, p. 44). The legal system regulates complex social and political worlds but it can only view those worlds from its own perspective. In responding to the ever-increasing complexity of these other worlds, regulation becomes more complex and purposive (that is, law tries to impose structures on other systems):

> '[Law's] function is now political intervention and societal guidance, not conflict resolution; its legitimacy is contingent not on its autonomy but on its success in achieving purposive goals; and its norm structure changes from generality to particularity, with increasing emphasis on purposive interpretation.' (Black, 1996, p. 47; drawing on Teubner, 1983; 1987)

This leads to the creation of what Teubner refers to as the 'regulatory trilemma': 'either "incongruence" of law and society, or "over-legalization" of society, or "over-socialization" of law' (1985, p. 309). In other words, 'the law is ineffective because it creates no change in behaviour'; the law has 'disintegrating effects in the regulated field'; or the law 'overstrains' itself and is 'captured' by the regulated system (*ibid*, p. 311)

On one level, this is an agenda for *de*regulation for, on this view, regulation will never hit its mark. However, Teubner has argued that, whilst regulatory law will fail because it cannot 'speak to' different systems (which will observe the law and be indirectly affected by it, but interpret it from their own system's perspective), we should move to a *reflexive law* (1983), 'a complex interweaving of autonomous discourses' (Teubner, 1992, p. 465). This requires a 'structural coupling' between the different systems of law, politics and society (Teubner, 1985, pp. 310–1; 1988).

This rationale of regulatory failure fits neatly within the confines of the regulatory systems developed for housing. Regulation is a blunt tool that encourages those it affects to seek out its limits – thus, local authorities consistently sought to break free of the financial constrictions of the Local Government and Finance Act 1980 (what Stewart (1996) describes as a game of cat and mouse between the authorities and the government) and building societies found themselves increasingly marginalized within the financial services industry because of the restrictions of their governing legislation. The cat and mouse game between central and local government was being played out against a changing relationship between them, in which central government gradually came to use the power of economic regulation to phase out the local authority role in housing and radically shifted the balance away from partnership to a more domineering role. This occurred through the increasingly tightened controls over local authority finance in the Local Government Finance Act 1989 which restricted authorities' freedom of movement through central prescription of the minutiae – purposive legislation to control and delegitimize the role of local authorities as housing providers.

The system of regulating the private rented sector has led to each of the aspects of the trilemma occurring, most notably through many landlords *de facto* deregulating the industry through avoidance techniques (attempting to avoid the legislation through, for example, granting licences rather than leases) and, on one view (which is not shared by this author), being primarily responsible for the decline of the sector. In 1988, the Conservative government deregulated the industry and attempted to impose 'market disciplines' upon it. However, it can be argued that this legislation simply changed the formal relations, the sector already having been deregulated by those landlords wishing to do so. As Teubner puts it, 'where jurists get infuriated over violations and circumventions of the law, economists praise what they see as economically efficient behaviour' (1992, p. 466). It can also be argued that the 'market' does not operate in the sector (or, at least, the sector is subject to cleavages) because parts of it are determined by the availability of government subsidy (this is actually discussed in Chapter 11 in Part II).

As regards the housebuilding industry, it can be shown that regulation solely through the 'market' causes regulatory failure because profit-maximization creates fissures in the level of production at inappropriate times. There are, in fact, considerable analytical links between the structures outlined in the chapters' and readers may wish to draw analogies between these structures. So, for example, the largest house-builders have sought to increase their profit margins through takeovers (and gaining the land which the other firms have in their 'bank'); building societies have increasingly diversified in the search for surpluses to justify the salaries and bonuses of their bosses; RSLs, similarly, have merged and developed in order to increase their surpluses. On another level, both the Housing Corporation and the Building Societies Association and Commission have sought to *protect* their movements by covering up many RSL or society's failures by finding other members willing to merge with them. In this way, the industry protects itself and the regulator becomes an intermediate organization.

Regulatory failures in each sector are partially responsible for the development of innovative mechanisms *linking the sectors*. Part I begins to show how inter- and intra-tenurial relationships have begun to be created. So, for example, the decline of private renting, partly due to regulation, has meant that the sector has had to be redeveloped; the decline of local authorities has meant that they have had to seek out alternative sources of accommodation; the rise of RSLs has provided one method of mediating between these organizations. So, one method used has been the creation of a multi-tenurial relationship between local authorities, RSLs, and private landlords. One version of this relationship – known as HAMA (Housing Associations as Managing Agents) – ensures that the landlord has a constant flow of income, the RSL receives a limited surplus, and the local authority has a provider outlet for those in housing need (who would otherwise be accommodated in local authority stock, were it sufficient to do so). Thus, this section also links with the developing notions of housing governance through which we are able to appreciate the *diffusion* of the housing system amongst various bodies. One definition of governance neatly summarizes many of the themes which are developed in Part I:

'A baseline definition of governance is that it refers to the action, manner or system of governing in which the boundary between organisations and public and private sectors has become permeable. Governance recognises the interdependence of organisations. The essence of governance is the interactive relationship between and within governmental and non-governmental forces.' (Stoker, 1995; cited in Malpass, 1997, p. 3)

It may be felt that the chapters in this part do not facilitate an appreciation of the links between different sectors because each chapter discusses a separate sector without much conjunction (although see Chapter 6 which discusses the various inter-sectoral transfers). This is, however, deliberate for the regulatory structure is determinedly sectoral. As we see in Part III, this has caused and will cause problems (each sector, for example, gives different levels of security). Only when our regulators are able to transcend sectoral analysis can housing truly develop in this way without disadvantage. The Housing Minister, Hilary Armstrong, went some way to crossing these boundaries in the mission statement *Principles for a New Housing Policy*:

'I am agnostic about the ownership of housing – local authorities or [RSLs]; public or private sector – and want to move away from the ideological baggage that comes with that issue. What is important is not, primarily, who delivers. It is what works that counts. By that I do not mean short-termism and opportunism, which can masquerade as pragmatism. We need housing which works and which goes on working.' (Armstrong, 1998, para 5)

How far the New Labour government is able to change the ideological principles upon which the housing system has been founded in the twentieth century is open to doubt. The home ownership system and all that entails now dominates and is a considerable interest group.

What seems to be the case, though, is that cross-tenurial interests will develop in ways similar to those developed by, or because of, the Conservative governments. Generally, this involved mechanisms which transferred council housing to other sectors. For the Conservatives, this was all about giving council tenants 'choice', within certain constraints. One aspect of choice which has begun to take centre stage is the *participation* of social housing tenants in the management of their homes. This is clearly reflected in Armstrong's mission statement and public statements (see also Hetherington, 1998 a report of Armstrong's speech and comments at a Chartered Institute of Housing Conference). Under the Conservatives, these mechanisms could plausibly be presented as examples of regulatory failure – both the government had no understanding of popular feeling amongst council tenants, who voted against the implementation of government policies; and council officers developed their own ways of breaking free of the stranglehold on their finances imposed by central government by engineering the large scale transfer of their housing to the RSL sector. The eventual success of these moves could hardly be portrayed as Conservative successes for they have involved councils taking advantage of the regulatory environment for their own benefit. Indeed, the central plank of Conservative regulation – 'tenant's choice' which enabled council tenants to transfer from council control – proved a damp squib. Government regulation imposed its *own* views and opinions of council housing upon a largely unwilling audience, rather than finding out that audience's opinion. These issues are considered in Chapter 6, as well as the rise of tenants' associations and management rights. This is explored through the concept of 'voice' – methods of enabling participation amongst tenants – which might be regarded as the true focus of social housing. This move to concentrate on the tenant as participator, particularly in the local development of New Labour's concept of 'Tenant Participation Compacts', suggest the development of a reflexive law in this arena for this reflects a changing power dynamic between tenants as 'passive recipients of landlord bounty' and tenants as policy-makers.

Whilst regulatory failure is endemic within the regulatory system, it is more difficult to pose an alternative which might be successful. Teubner's ideal is for strategic intervention of law by intermediate institutions and indirect regulation (see also Harlow & Rawlings, 1997, Ch. 10; Black, 1996 considers this in the context of self-regulation). Such institutions are able to breach the gap between law and the systems it regulates. One intermediate institution operating in respect of one housing tenure is the Housing Corporation, which is responsible for the RSL industry. Its responsibility is partly to dish out public funds and partly to regulate the industry. Its success, in regulatory terms, lies in its ability to mould itself to the industry's needs at any particular time (although it is often slow in doing so, leading to loss of funds: Langstaff, 1992). However, its role is being marginalized by the regulatory impact of private finance in the movement, which has underlined the Corporation's essentially weak status.

A further angle which is not considered in the chapters in Part I (because our focus is on what is happening as opposed to what might happen) is whether the housing systems should (or could) develop an industry-wide regulator. For example, Martin Partington has begun to do this. Partington's foci are on the complexity and lack of coherence in individual housing rights – a view from which it would be difficult to dissent (see Part III) – as well as the need for a more politically neutral, sustainable approach to housing policy, and the recognition that housing services are 'another branch of the service economy' (1990, pp 74–5). In consequence, he has begun to develop a consumerization thesis (see, for example, Partington, 1990; 1993), through which he has argued that we should concentrate our attention not on housing rights but on developing a model of housing regulator together with the adoption of a consumer perspective (thus, adopting a similar model to the privatized industries, on which Partington explicitly draws: 1998):

> 'A "consumerist" perspective on housing would encourage the bringing together of the provisions that currently exist and their expansion with a view to ensuring that all citizens are guaranteed proper standards of housing service. Such a view, in the housing context, would involve a reanalysis of the roles of the three main actors in the housing market: the Government, the consumers of housing services and the providers of those services.' (1993, p. 133)

Partington's consumerist model has yet to be developed in any meaningful way, and it may well be that it can be manipulated to meet the challenge of reflexive law. The development of a consumerist approach may well involve a redistribution of power. However, regarding 'citizens' as 'consumers' of housing services is problematic because housing, in itself, is not an item of consumption like (say) a television. If housing develops a fault, it cannot be returned to the vendor like some consumer durable. Equally, a concentration on 'citizens' as 'consumers' marginalizes those unable or unwilling to consume. Even so, the nature of the occupant as consumer must differ depending upon their occupation rights. For example, the assured shorthold tenant has what I have termed a 'status of moveability' which weakens their bargaining position (particularly when it comes to repairs and complaining about unlawful eviction). As we discover in Part I, the regulation of housing tenures have developed separately, based upon different regulatory paradigms, and bringing them within the umbrella of consumerism distorts their rationales.

Bibliography

Armstrong, H. (1998), *'Principles for a New Housing Policy'*, London: DETR

Black, J. (1996), 'Constitutionalising self-regulation', vol 59, *Modern Law Review*, 24

Harlow, C. and Rawlings, R. (1997), *Law and Administration*, London: Butterworths

Hetherington, P. (1998), 'Home truths', *The Guardian*, 24 June

Langstaff, M. (1992), 'Housing associations: a move to centre stage', in J. Birchall (ed), *Housing Policy in the 1990s*, London: Routledge

Malpass, P. (1997), 'Introduction', in P. Malpass (ed.), *Ownership Control and Accountability: The New Governance of Housing*, Coventry: Chartered Institute of Housing

Partington, M. (1990), 'Rethinking British housing law: the failure of the Housing Act 1988', in M Freeman (ed.), *Critical Issues in Welfare Law*, London: Stevens & Sons

Partington, M. (1993), 'Citizenship and housing', in R. Blackburn (ed.), *Rights of Citizenship*, London: Mansell

Partington, M. (1998), 'Regulating the housing market: a new approach?', vol 1, *Journal of Housing Law*, 65

Stewart, A. (1996), *Rethinking Housing Law*, London: Sweet & Maxwell

Stoker, G. (1995), 'Public-private partnerships in urban governance', paper presented to the Housing Studies Association Conference, University of Edinburgh, September 1995

Teubner, G. (1983), 'Substantive and reflexive elements in modern law', vol 17, *Law & Society Review*, 240

Teubner, G. (1984), 'Autopoiesis in law and society: a rejoinder to Blankenburg', vol 18, *Law & Society Review*, 292

Teubner, G. (1985), 'After legal instrumentalism? Strategic models of post-regulatory law', in G. Teubner (ed.), *Dilemmas of Law in the Welfare State*, Berlin: de Gruyter

Teubner, G. (1987), 'Juridification: Concepts, aspects, limits, solutions', in G. Teubner (ed.), *Juridification of the Social Spheres*, Berlin: de Gruter

Teubner, G. (1988), 'Evolution of autopoietic law', in G. Teubner (ed.), *Autopoietic Law: A New Approach to Law and Society*, Berlin: de Gruyter

Teubner, G. (1992), 'Regulatory law: chronicle of a death foretold', vol 1, *Social & Legal Studies*, 451

2 Regulatory Failure in the Private Rented Sector

A sea-change has occurred during the twentieth century in the tenure of property. At the start of the century, around 90 per cent of the population rented privately. In 1995, this had fallen to around just 10 per cent. Most of this decline has occurred in the latter part of this century. Indeed, only around 600,000 properties were lost to the sector between the start of the two wars (from 7.2 million to 6.6 million). In the 1930s, new building for private renting was as high 'as it had been in the two decades before 1914' other than during the boom at the turn of the century (Holmans, 1987, p. 407). The sector currently makes up just over 2 million properties. This has not coincided with a period of benign neglect – indeed, at times, attempts to revive the sector have engaged wide debate, a considerable number of official committees, as well as disparate legislation. It is the failure of such legislation which concerns us in this chapter.

For most of this century, debate has been polarized along party political lines, broadly reflecting a belief in the market, on the one hand, or a need to control market tendencies on the other. In the 1990s, however, this debate has been radically altered as a new cross-party consensus has developed, the central tenet of which is to stem the decline through *de*regulation. For the first time this century, it is commonly believed that a healthy private rented sector is required partly for the 'good of the economy' and partly because it is recognized that there must be limits to the level of sustainable home ownership (for discussion, see House of Commons Environment Committee, 1996, paras 87–97; *cf* Department of Environment, 1995a, where 1.5 million new home owners are promised): 'it is possible that we are witnessing structural rather than cyclical change in the owner-occupied sector, i.e., that if the future is characterised by lower inflation, greater job insecurity and high real interest rates, household preferences as between renting and owning may be shifting towards the former' (Kleinman *et al.*, 1996, p. 7). This move towards tenure neutrality is reflected in the policy statement issued by the Housing Minister, Hilary Armstrong: 'I am agnostic about the ownership of housing . . . and want to move away from the ideological baggage that comes with that issue' (Armstrong, 1998).

Nevertheless, the new policies – 'a bewildering display of projects and acronyms' (Carter & Ginsburg, 1994, p. 106) – may well be regarded as being too little and too late. One proposition is that whilst the system of leasehold was an appropriate method of landholding in feudal and post-feudal capitalism, it has become outmoded as we reach the end of the twentieth century. Its demise should be welcomed. Indeed, this is recognized in discussions about the future (or lack of it) for long leaseholds (for the debate on commonhold as a new legal tenure for flats, see Clarke, 1995; on leasehold enfranchisement – the right of long leaseholders to buy the freehold – see Stewart, 1996, pp. 110–116; for background, see Stewart, 1981). When we talk about reviving private renting today, this is often code for needing a form of occupation right which will cater for short-term housing, so encouraging mobility for employment purposes or between periods of home ownership.

The system of landholding where one person lets property to another is an invention enabling capital to be made effectively for a small outlay. This is an important characteristic of private renting. Rent bears no relation to the cost of building the property. Rather it is broadly based upon the current *capital value* of the property (Kemeny, 1981, pp. 27–8). If it is not so based, then sale becomes the most attractive option for landlords. Houses bought a long time before they are rented are therefore most profitable because building or buying costs are minimal by the renting stage. Paradoxically, capital values are based upon the state of the market of properties for sale and are therefore unrelated to the private rented market. The level of rent paid is related to values unrelated to the rental market but to the completely different market of home ownership. This means that the faster capital prices rise, the less attractive renting is for landlords because rental receipts do not reflect the true value of the property. If the landlord decides not to rent, they can sell the property and may also take an increase in the capital value of the property.

Nevertheless, the crucial underlying question concerns the *profitability* of private renting for landlords (on the assumptions in the previous paragraph). The 'central dilemma' is that the current market situation does not provide adequate returns for landlords, who can obtain 'higher returns and lower risk investments elsewhere in the economy' (House of Commons Environment Committee, 1981, para. 14). Institutional investors will, apparently, require a higher return from private renting than they will from commercial property and other less risky investments (Crook *et al.*, 1995, p. 29). For private renting to be as profitable as other investments (such as commerical property or stock market investments), rents would need to be set at levels which those seeking accommodation in this sector would not be able to afford. Furthermore, given that institutions rarely become involved in the market, some would require a *higher* return on their investment initially so as to make their investment reflect the degree of novelty involved (*ibid*). Such rents, though, would be more than the market itself could bear because the ratio of earnings to rent would simply require too high a proportion of earnings (or Housing Benefit) to glean the requisite level of profit. Thus, institutional investors have been slow to return to the rented market place (although certain building societies do have rental offshoots).

This 'central dilemma' assumes that the major reason for entering the private rental market as a supplier is to make a profit. However, research on landlords themselves has generally found that landlords are a heterogeneous group. They range from large organizations with huge tracts of land under their belts (such as the crown, church or government departments) to individuals renting a room in their house. The sector includes accommodation tied to employment and private individuals. This range is consistently shifting over time away from institutional and corporate investment towards individuals, reflecting the level of profit, movement(s) in the owner-occupier market, as well as the different demands of occupiers. It is this differentiation which makes the categorization of 'private renting' the catch-all tenure. Assumptions that all landlords want profit at a particular level are misjudged, for different landlords want different things. For example, those landlords entering the market as a result of difficulties paying-off their mortgage are commonly found simply to want assistance with their mortgage and not a particular rate of return (see Bevan *et al.*, 1995, p. 22). By contrast, institutional investors clearly require a more formalized approach together with appropriate profit-making levels.

Indeed, the 'private renting' label itself is also inaccurate for it includes agreements which strictly do not concern renting, but rather are about licencing the use of accommodation for residential purposes. In over 10 per cent of cases, accommodation is rent free and, thus on one view, cannot be a tenancy (for example, as an adjunct to employment) (Carey, 1995, Figure 1.3). The label is frustratingly inadequate and often even in housing texts it is left undefined (presumably because it is impossible to define). We are never sure whether, for example, long leases[1] are included and, if not, where the cut-off point is. Would a seven-year lease at low rent be included? This and similar questions are critical for the lawyer and legislator who attach different rights and responsibilities to different types of agreement. So, an informal licence to occupy conveys no rights from owner to occupier, whereas complex repairing obligations are conveyed in informal tenancy agreements partly implied into agreements by statute and common law. When, as here, our quest is to discover how the sector is regulated, our frustration can only be compounded by the lack of definition.

There are two related points. First, it is only comparatively recently that a comprehensive code covering both furnished and unfurnished rented accommodation has existed (since 1974). Prior to that, regulation of each of these operated on different bases, which initially reflected the supposed intentions of the occupiers but subsequently was justified from an anti-regulatory bias (see Francis, 1971, p. 203). Second, the regulation under consideration later in this chapter (as well as Ch. 13 below) generally does not cover licences to occupy. Although this is not completely accurate, broadly those occupying rooms with a resident landlord, those in hostels where services are provided (such as the bed and breakfast 'hotels') are licensees and outside the scope of the security provided by the legislation. Consequently, swathes of occupants are within sectors unregulated by the broad body of security legislation covering 'private renting'. These two aspects of intra-sectoral differentiation provide a contrast to the agenda affecting the more 'mainstream' private rented sector.

In trying to answer the key question of whether regulation has caused the decline of the sector (as the Conservatives appear to have believed in 1987), this chapter proceeds in the following way. The first two sections are concerned with rationalizing the decline in the sector. In the first section, we look at two crucial contextual factors: supply and demand, and the notion of 'political risk'. It is argued that both supply and demand were wavering at the turn of the century, *even before the first set of statutory rights were given to tenants*. The twentieth century has been the century of home ownership and this has clearly affected the supply and demand of houses for rent. Furthermore, at least since the 1950s, the notion of 'political risk' has caused investors to be wary of the market. During this period, the term 'rachmanism' was coined to describe a set of landlords which was in the business of abusing the system in order to make large(r) profits from private renting. Political risk partly refers to being tarnished with this reputation. It also refers to the situation caused by the vicissitudes of party politics. Until recently the different political parties had different views of the private rented sector which fed into differences in the ways in which they believed it should be regulated (if at all). Governments change and, in the process, so did the regulation of the private rented sector. It is argued that the regulatory provisions governing this sector have been formed until recently, by way of contrast, on the basis of a narrow view of the decline in turn based upon the prejudice of the relevant party in government. So, those who are anti-regulation have sought to remove regulation and open up the sector to market principles. Those who believe that the market cannot deliver what is required have espoused regulatory principles.

This links in to the following section, which is directly concerned with the impact of regulation and its effects on the market for private renting. In this section, we discuss the different ways and types of controlling and regulating the private rental market. We look at the rationale(s) behind the first controlling legislation in 1915, and also the different parts of the market affected by regulation throughout the century. A word of warning follows: concentration on the merits and demerits of regulation places too much faith in the power of regulation. Socio-legal analysis of this type of regulation and lack of it (unsurprisingly) shows that regulation itself is merely a symptom (at best) of a broader decline – when regulation is in place, it is commonly avoided or unused; when the sector is subject to market principles, not much changes (as we see in Ch. 11 below, the current period of formal deregulation has been matched by informal regulation of parts of the sector through lower levels of Housing Benefit).

Our attention also turns to the pivotal role currently foreseen for this sector. Against a backdrop of lowering investment in social housing and the reaching of potential limits to the level of home ownership, the stimulation of private renting has become a key part of national housing policy. A further aspect relates to the changing levels of security in the workplace and the movement towards the casualization of employment structures. Simply, the workforce is required to be more mobile and there is a need for more flexible ranges of accommodation to match employment mobility. There are now considerable numbers of schemes available apparently seeking to stimulate the market for private renting, both in terms of demand and supply. These schemes involve links being made *across tenures*, so that it may well be that the tenures themselves are beginning to be broken down in order to meet the apparent need for short-term accommodation. We will analyse the success (and otherwise) of these schemes.

The regulation–market debate forms a link with the final section which considers the controls in place as regards 'houses in multiple occupation' ("HMOs"). HMOs are a specific part of the private rental market, deserving of special protection because of the risks to occupiers that are inherent in them. The occupiers of these properties are often the most marginalized in society. The debate about their regulation is also a microcosm of the debate about private renting more generally: will too much regulation stifle their provision? These properties are regarded as an important cause of fire death, as well as raising considerable anxiety amongst the population more generally. However, they also are the source of a considerable proportion of the private rented sector without which the sector would hardly exist. Here the contrast is between the different levels of regulation required to sustain the market: '. . . the conundrum between ensuring a vigorous and thriving sector of the housing market catering for, inter alia, a large and growing student market, and the wish not to overburden the owners of persons letting these properties' (Smith, 1998, p. 168).

2.1   Rationalizing the Decline I: Context

Supply and Demand Factors

In the nineteenth century, private rented housing was commonly built for that purpose. Landowners would sell their properties to housebuilders under 'building leases' through which the housebuilders would develop the land. The housebuilders then commonly sold their lease on to landlords who would rent the property out. Before 1914, rent rises, suggesting market demand, were related to housebuilding periods and satisfaction of that demand (Ball, 1983, p. 27). In the decade prior to 1914 (and the first controlling legislation), the sector's collapse was *'quite spectacular'* because, even at this stage, developing property for rent proved unprofitable (*ibid*, p. 26; my emphasis). During the early part of this century, building societies began to take a more active role in lending money for house purchase. Thus, the lack of profitability of the private rented sector occurred at the same time as building societies began to become developed institutions capable of lending the vast sums of money required to develop tenure switches. Even so:

'. . . during the 1930s private housebuilding boom builders and building societies had to engage in a considerable amount of advertising to persuade people that they should buy rather than rent their home. 'Buy your home with the rent' was one prominent advertising slogan at this time.' (Kemp, 1988a, p. 2)

In this critical inter-war period, the focus of housebuilding changed to the provision of property for home ownership.

As home ownership became the favoured tenure (see Chs 3 & 12), so taxation benefits went with those who entered the tenure. Mortgage payments attracted tax relief; home owners potentially can make gains on property (sometimes spectacularly so); those gains have not been subject to capital gains tax (provided the property is their only or main residence); mortgage repayments reduce over time (as the capital borrowed is reduced and/or inflation effectively reduces the capital borrowed) whereas rent payments only rise (known as the 'rent ratchet'). By contrast, private landlords were taxed on their rental income, received no depreciation allowances, and for much of this century neither landlord nor tenant received subsidy (other than improvement grants).

As capital gains became possible (due to increased demand for home ownership), so many 'landlords' bought rented property for the sole purpose of making capital gains: 'They might, therefore, be better described as 'property dealers' rather than as landlords with long term interests in residential letting' (Crook & Martin, 1988, p. 48). Such practices were particularly prevalent during the 1970s and 1980s, although this has occurred throughout this century on a substantial scale. 'Asset switching' was based upon the unfavourable rate of return from rented property compared with the selling price of the dwelling (Merrett with Gray, 1982, pp. 134–5). At the same time, many tenants purchased the properties they were occupying at below market levels – because the landlord could not have granted vacant possession to any other purchaser, market prices could not be gained (known as the 'value gap': Doling & Davies, 1984).

Properties built for renting in the Victorian era had to cater for a variety of different classes. The quality of property built to let for working classes reflected their lack of bargaining power as well as the limited revenue that might be gleaned by landlords from this client group. Consequently, it was of the worst quality and subjected to the slum clearance provisions since the 1930s. Slum clearance has been responsible for a considerable part of the decline of the sector, which particularly occurred between 1961–1975 when around 64,000 properties were demolished annually. Apparently, 80 per cent of these properties were previously privately rented and were subsequently lost to the sector (House of Commons Environment Committee, 1982, para. 10; Balchin, 1995, p. 92). The rump of the sector is also currently characterized by its level of unfitness; that is, the quality of the current private rented sector is poor (as to which, see below and Ch 14).

Finally, at the same time as the owner occupied sector began to take off, so did local authority housing. Indeed, in the early part of this century, the municipalization of housing tended to cater for that portion of the working class which earlier were the staple tenants. This cut out a profitable part of the demand for the sector. Subsidies to councils were considerable. By contrast, private renting attracted no subsidy.

'Political Risk': Rachmanism and the Perils of the Market

The question of whether to control or regulate the private rented market, and (if so) the level of such control or regulation, has been dominated by political perceptions of the value of the market as well as contrasting intentions as regards municipalization. Consequently, the regime governing the sector has been in a consistent state of flux since the imposition of regulation in 1915. Political debates have been 'at times intense and emotionally charged' affairs and this polarization of views has also added an element of 'political risk' to the equation:

'For the Conservatives . . . the private provision of rented housing has often been portrayed as self-evidently beneficial; the problem is merely that the governments have imposed rent controls on the sector which have made it unprofitable and which only need to be removed for the sector to revive. In contrast, for Labour, the private provision of rented housing is just as obviously pernicious; and rent regulation is needed to curb the worst excesses of the market and in particular to prevent unscrupulous private landlords from exploiting their tenants.' (Kemp, 1997a, p. 82–3)

It follows that political risk, in this sense, related to an uncertain legislative environment affecting private renting. Writing in the era of the New Labour government, which appears to share the Conservative deregulationary values, such sentiments potentially are no longer relevant (although residual concern, no doubt, exists over the views of the Department of the Environment, Transport and the Regions (DETR) towards the sector).

There is, however, an equally salient alternative notion of 'political risk' and this particularly relates to the rise and fall of Peter Rachman in London in the 1950s and early 1960s. Indeed, such was the intensity of the debate caused by 'rachmanism' that all subsequent political debates have been shrouded by his persona (see Kemp, 1997b). Basically, Rachman took advantage of the lack of controls on the *furnished* rental property market at that time – as opposed to the legislative controls over unfurnished property. In London in 1954, he began his operation by cheaply buying property let unfurnished (this could be done because controlled rents were low and capital values were low because he was able to buy the short end of long leases). Initially, he offered money to the tenants to move out and their vacated properties were sub-divided and turned into furnished dwellings.

Tenants of furnished dwellings had fewer rights and hardly any control over their rents (see below). The scarcity of property meant that he could charge considerable sums for it. Furthermore, 'at best, he was 'not particular' about whom he accepted as tenants': prostitutes and black people for whom alternative accommodation was difficult to find (Nelken, 1983, p. 4). Subsequently, rather than paying people to leave (a practice known as 'winkling'), Rachman began to harass indirectly those tenants of unfurnished parts into leaving the accommodation: 'what perhaps began naturally Rachman began to exploit, seeing, perhaps, no point in paying controlled tenants to go if they could be persuaded to do so by other means' (Milner Holland, 1965, p. 252). The properties went unrepaired ('One ex-employee was reported as saying: "One way or another we reckoned we could keep a defective drain going for four or five months without the legal penalties becoming uneconomic"': Nelken, 1983, p. 4). Despite the circulation of stories concerning Rachman in the late 1950s and early 1960s, his property management only became the subject of controversy after it was linked to the Profumo affair (call girls with whom Profumo, the War Minister, had associated lived in Rachman-run properties). For two weeks in 1963, after Rachman's death, considerable political debate about the private rented sector dominated all discussion. It is important to the discussion below about the relevance of regulation to the decline of rental property, that Rachman's property management straddled two different regimes, one based on controlled rents and security for tenants of unfurnished property, the other based upon market principles (at least in part). Neither hindered his progress because he was able to avoid the regulatory structures anyway.

Rachmanism – the charging of exorbitant rents for poor quality housing – represents political risk. It symbolises the *image problems* of the sector and operates as a considerable disincentive against institutions being involved in private renting. It was this which the Conservatives partly sought to address in the 1980s, particularly as part of the package of reforms to the sector presented in the 1987 White Paper.

2.2   Rationalizing the Decline II: Control and Regulation

Since 1915, the private rented sector has been subject to controls of varying levels of stringency affecting its different constituent parts in different ways. The only serious attempt at total deregulation – in the Rent Act 1957 – was followed the year after by further legislation 'designed to "cushion" the full impact [of deregulation]' (Francis, 1971, p. 249; Donnison, 1967, p. 175), so it was never completely brought into force. The control/regulation has taken two forms: first, there has been control/regulation of rent levels; second, there has been restrictions on the common law rights of landlords to possession of the property after notice.

The former would have been ineffective without the latter (as is clearly shown by the Rachman affair).

Rent control/regulation and security of tenure are commonly cited as the reason, or two of the reasons, for the decline of the private rented sector (see, for example, Kemp, 1992, p. 60; Crook, 1992). Sometimes, the critique has adopted rabid proportions – the following comment being an excellent example: 'Wherever rent control has been imposed the effects have been at best adverse, and at worst, catastrophic' (Albon & Stafford, 1987, p. i; see also Institute of Economic Affairs, 1972). Certain facts must, however, be borne in mind:

- First, the level of decline in the sector was lowest during the period of greatest control between 1914–45 and highest after the decontrolling Rent Act 1957. It is commonly forgotten (or deliberately ignored) that during periods of rent control, controls were also applied to mortgage interest levels on the same properties. Therefore, those landlords whose rented property was mortgaged were also protected by central controls.
- Second, the crucial point is that private renting is unprofitable (or, more precisely lacks profitability compared to other investment opportunities) *whatever the controls or regulation applied.* So, at the time of writing when landlords are entitled to *market rents* and most tenants have *limited security,*[2] private renting is not as profitable as other investments. Thus, private renting is quite simply unprofitable whatever scheme is used because the market is unprepared to pay the required level of return.
- Third, the decline of the supply of accommodation in the private renting market, and the level of demand (particularly from low income households), means that, ironically, either controls are required on the level of acceptable rent or the state must subsidise the sector. The current method of market rents has been counterbalanced by state subsidy to tenants through *Housing Benefit.* Controls on the level of Housing Benefit, however, also operate as controls on the level of acceptable rent.

The first part of this section makes an all important distinction between regulation and control of rents, as well as defining security of tenure. We discuss the way the law has been constructed in relation to different sub-sectors of the private rented sector. This is important because the differentiation in regulation provides an argument in itself against the theory that regulation/control has caused the decline of the sector. One needs to reconsider in the context of the different parts of the sector that were subjected to differential regulation/control during this century. The reality is rather more complex than initially meets the eye.

In the second part, an examination of the context of the 1915 legislation yields the important factor that needs adding to our discussion: class. The

1915 legislation can be analysed as a working class gain, although such an approach is 'fraught with dangers' (Watchman, 1980, p. 23; *cf* Damer, 1980). For example, one must add that landlords were also protected by the mortgage controls and that rent control was a result of the 'contradiction between industrial capital's needs for cheap and reliable labour, and the desire of private landlords for market rents' (Balchin, 1995, p. 95). It is also true that the 1915 Act was bound up with the development and rise of the labour and women's movement in Britain (which may also explain subsequent antipathy towards the controls).

In the third part, we will consider the methods used to *avoid* the regulation and control. It will be argued that, should landlords so decide, it was perfectly simple to avoid the regulation provided they had the relevant knowledge and/or muscle. Furthermore, avoidance was an extremely well-known technique. The following description of Rachman's activities from the Milner Holland Committee provides an excellent preface to this analysis:

> 'One of our witnesses told us of an effort to counter Rachman's activities in April 1959. Some 25 of his tenants occupying furnished rooms were encouraged to apply to the Rent Tribunal for a reduction in rent. When 18 of them withdrew their applications, police help was sought. A very thorough investigation was made but the evidence that the applicants had been intimidated was not sufficient to warrant the bringing of charges.' (1965, p. 252)

It will be argued that by the time Conservative legislation enabled landlords to impose widespread market rents on the sector in the Housing Act 1988, the sector was already *de facto* doing so. The fourth section then analyses the 1987 White Paper and the 1988 Act, and examines the claim often made by Conservative Ministers that these alone were responsible for the recent slight rise in the numbers of rented properties in the sector. It will be argued that the evidence points to the fact that most of the rise can be attributed to other contextual factors, such as the decline in the home ownership market as well as the increase in repossessions as a result of the recession which began in the late 1980s. A further contextual factor is the gathering insecurity of the labour market – the move to short-term contracts, greater flexibility and mobility amongst the workforce, and the move to part-time work, all increase the need for flexible accommodation which might be offered by the private rented sector.

Regulation and Control

Meanings
Rent regulation and control: Legislation has shifted, uncomfortably at times, between control, on the one hand, and regulation on the other. Rent control was the first type used in the 1915 legislation and continued through to 1957. The control was through central government, which set

the level of permissible rent rises. The rents of properties let in 1914 were kept at 1914 levels and subject to occasional uplifts after the war (40 per cent in the Rent Restrictions Act 1920, for example). In 1957, the Conservatives' Rent Act opted for market levels – that is, the removal of controls on most properties and regulation through the market. Between 1965–1977, a different regime was operated. During this period, there was regulation of rents by regarding them as 'fair'. In other words, rents were to be fair both to landlords and to tenants. The (classic) distinction between rent control and rent regulation is as follows:

'Unlike rent *control*, which was designed to freeze a market, thus eventually depriving its prices of any systematic or constructive meaning, rent *regulation* is designed to recreate a market in which the over-all pattern of prices responds to changes in supply and demand, while the local impact of severe and abnormal scarcities is kept within bounds.' (Donnison, 1967, p. 266)

Security of tenure: This is the necessary concomitant of some form of rent restriction, whether on the basis of market principles or control. Without it, 'fear of dispossession would in practice nullify any legal rights' (Holmans, 1987, p. 386). 'Security of tenure' is the form of regulation which amends the landlords common law right to possession. Under this system, a landlord cannot gain possession of the property *without a court order*. Such a court order can only be made on the basis of certain pre-defined statutory grounds.

Differentiation within the Sector

The current position is that the security of tenure provisions (which are limited) and rent regulation provisions (based upon what the market will bear) apply to *tenancies only*. However, they do apply to *both* furnished and unfurnished accommodation with exceptions covering *inter alia* resident landlords, holiday lettings, and company lettings. These exceptions have existed since 1974.

Prior to 1974, a distinction was drawn between furnished and unfurnished accommodation. This was partly based upon historical fact (rent control was introduced at a time when most rented property was unfurnished and catered for long-term lets) and subsequently due to spurious reasoning. The Francis committee seemed to believe that the primary reason for the decline in private renting was rent control/regulation. If the systems were assimilated, the furnished sector would decline (it had previously been increasing as landlords switched from unfurnished to furnished). The report fatuously reasons as follows:

'But the nub of the matter, as it seems to us, is this: what would the extension of full security to furnished tenants have on the availability of private accommodation for letting? Of course, there is no 'evidence' – in the sense of facts based on actual experience – that such a reform would reduce the supply. But equally there is no evidence that it would not. . . . After giving the matter anxious consideration, we take the view that complete assimilation of the codes in the manner proposed would, in all probability, result in a serious reduction in the supply of furnished accommodation for letting, without any compensatory addition to the supply of unfurnished accommodation for letting.' (1971, p. 203)

Just three years later, though, the Labour government assimilated the regulatory systems because in the early 1970s the supply of furnished accommodation dried up. This was partly because of the rise of hotels/bed and breakfast accommodation and partly because house prices rose considerably at this time leading to sales.

A further differential has been that the control/regulation to which tenancies have been subjected has depended upon when the tenancy was created. This has meant that different regimes, different rent structures and different relationships will affect similar properties in the same street, suggesting, at best, a lack of coherence to the regulation. The first rent control legislation in 1915 only applied to properties then rented. It did not apply to property built after the Act came into force. Furthermore, after 1923, once tenants left their controlled property, the property ceased to be subject to control. This process was known as 'creeping decontrol' and was on the recommendation of the Onslow committee that controls 'prolong[ed] the shortage of accommodation that rendered them necessary' (1923, p. 8). In 1933, by contrast, property at the top end of the market was immediately decontrolled; the mid-range was subjected to 'creeping decontrol'; and the low range remained controlled (unless between 1923–33, it had been decontrolled). This was on the basis that controls affected the sector according to the value of the property (Marley, 1931). In 1938, on the basis of a further official committee, the mid-range accommodation was split according to value, the more expensive being subject to creeping decontrol. However, in 1939, all property then rented became controlled at the rents being charged at that time. This brief summary suggests that, by 1945, the rental differentiation depended upon when the property was let and which controls it had been subject to prior to the war as opposed to rational central pricing mechanisms (see generally, Bowley, 1948, pp. 205–8).

These controls have attempted to balance scarcity of accommodation (which, in rational markets would require massive increases in rents) against the bargain made between landlord and tenant. An essential element to the debate was context. Rent controls in 1915 and 1939 can be justified on the basis of national emergency and the need to avoid riots caused by rent rises. In the period between the wars, creeping decontrol and deregulation was based upon the belief that retaining controls would stifle the element of private enterprise which brought property onto the rental market.

In 1965, the Labour government introduced 'fair rents' – fair both to landlords and tenants – which effectively were market rents less scarcity value (s. 70(2), Rent Act 1977). This was codified into the Rent Act 1977, which codified the rent legislation also in the 1974 Act. Other than minor schemes introduced in the Housing Act 1980, the next major legislation was the Housing Act 1988. Tenancies created under the Rent Act regime remain subject to that regime but we now have a situation of 'creeping deregulation' under which all properties let post-1989 are subjected to the deregulatory regime of the 1988 Act. Broadly, this retains security of tenure, albeit in modified and limited forms, and creates rent regulation through the market. The current situation is an awkward mix of fair and market rents, regulated and partly regulated tenancies.

The Increase in Rent and Mortgage (War Restrictions) Act 1915

The 1915 Act was a product of market failure, or rather the failure of the market to provide decent housing at a reasonable price. The clamour for reform began in, and was centred around, Glasgow, where before the war accommodation shortages had existed. These were only exacerbated by the arrival of around 16,000 workers into the city's munitions factories at the start of the war. Shortages meant that rents were continually increased and non-payers evicted. Such was the inexorable rises in rent that, even at the outbreak of war, there were 13,000 empty houses in the city (Damar, 1980, p. 90). Rent strikes occurred throughout 1915, together with the ambushing of officials conducting the evictions. The government was inactive on the rents issue, and was more concerned with munitions output (legislating to outlaw strikes and regulate working conditions: see Watchman, 1980, pp. 27–30). In mid-1915, about 20,000 tenants were withholding their rent and when the Sherrif stayed an eviction after a demonstration of between 10–15,000 workers, a telegram was sent to the Prime Minister:

> 'That this meeting of Clyde munitions workers requests the government to state, not later than Saturday first, that it forbids any increase of rent during the period of the war; and that, this failing, a general strike will be declared on 22 November.'

The government then indicated that it would legislate and the Bill became law within four weeks of being presented to Parliament. The power of the organized labour movement was clearly apparent (Damer, 1997).

Whilst the 1915 Act was a product of its own time, its lasting effect has been the realization that regulation is required to balance the needs of labour against the landlord's profit margin. During wartime, such balancing is clearly essential for the so-called war effort. However, in the post-war period, such balancing has tended to come unstuck as the principles of 'private property' and *laissez-faire* have come unstuck. In other words, the 1915 Act provided the structure of rent legislation for more than 40 years, but its force primarily relates to its own peculiar period. For example, inter-war rent strikes in Glasgow were equally well supported but much less potent (see, for example, Melling, 1980).

Avoidance and Evasion

Tax law draws a neat distinction between tax avoidance (acceptable) and tax evasion (unacceptable). Rational tax planning results in reductions of tax payable through *legitimate* techniques – this is avoidance. However, when *illegitimate* techniques are used, this is regarded as evasion. The line between the two is slim (to say the least). In this section, our discussion will centre around methods used by landlords to avoid the fair rent and security provisions in the 1965 Act. These avoidance techniques occasionally merge into evasionary methods, although the point is that those with the requisite knowledge and power are more likely to use the law rather than abuse it; the same is true the other way round. My concentration here is on avoidance techniques because they are slightly more subtle than the brawn used for evasion. However, an important point is that the success of landlords in avoiding the security and rent regulation provisions depended, to a certain, extent, upon their sophistication; or, rather, their ability to enter into, and take advantage of, the legal 'loopholes' that were available. Those who were unaware no doubt opted for alternative techniques although, as I will show, this number must have been small.

Legitimate processes of avoidance included the grant of licences rather than tenancies; avoidance of the mechanism used to determine 'fair rents'; granting of 'company lets', 'agricultural lets', or 'holiday lets'; moving from unfurnished to furnished lettings (before 1974); moving to bed and breakfast type accommodation (Watchman, 1988, pp. 154–5). Changes in common law distinctions between licence and tenancy actually facilitated the process of granting licences (until *Street* v. *Mountford* in 1985 re-established the principle that the fact of exclusive possession was the key criterion and not the label given by the parties to the agreement). The point is that those who complained about rent regulation were also those who were best placed to avoid that regulation (and did so as a matter of course):

> 'The Small Landlords Association in their evidence said that their advice to any landlord contemplating a new let would be "Avoid at all costs creating a fully protected tenancy", while the British Property Federation argued that "there is no reason at all why anyone should structure his affairs in such a way that he gives more security of tenure . . . or anything else than he has to". Some witnesses argued that in parts of the country, particularly Central London, virtually all new lettings were outside the Rent Act.' (House of Commons Environment Committee, 1982, para. 23)

The grant of company, agricultural, or holiday lets were often a sham specifically designed to enable the landlord to avoid giving the tenant the protection of security of tenure and regulation of rent: 'The reasons for adopting such [avoidance] schemes varied from the desire to retain autonomy in dealing with tenants to more complex financial considerations for which these methods were a preliminary' (Nelken, 1983, p. 44). Court judgments have, however, generally found these techniques to be *legitimate*. Indeed, in the only case where the tenant was successful in disowning an 'agricultural let', Gibson LJ in the Court of Appeal registered a strong dissent. In this dissent, the clearest possible expression of the notion of sanctity of contract, and *laissez faire*, is apparent: '. . . the courts have never claimed the power to treat a transaction in private law between private individuals as something other than it really is merely because the social purpose of some legislation would be served by so treating it' (*Gisbourne* v. *Burton* [1988] 3 WLR 921).

In the Rent Act 1965, Richard Crossman MP, then Housing Minister, wanted to take 'rent out of politics' (see Crossman, 1975, p. 627; Banting, 1979, p. 47). The system he devised was to enable the landlord and the tenant to agree the rent between themselves. In default of agreement, either or both could apply to an impartial individual, the Rent Officer, to determine a 'fair rent'. The fair rent was to be based upon the characteristics of the property without taking into account its scarcity. The Rent Officer's judgment as to the fair rent became the contractual rent for three years (although it could be appealed against). The idea of a fair rent came from the Milner Holland Committee, the members of which formed part of Crossman's 'kitchen cabinet' (Nelken, 1983, pp. 34, 39–40). The idea was that the interests of both landlord and tenant should be balanced.

Most often, it appears that Rent Officers actually put up rents, rather than reduced them, which is contrary to what one might suspect. Furthermore, Rent Officers themselves often disagreed, leading to different rents registered on properties in the same streets. One reason for this was that scarcity was a difficult concept to 'unpack'. The Francis committee provided one obvious reason for this: '. . . scarcity is incapable of measurement except by way of an intelligent guess' (1971, p. 58); at the same time, they criticized those who complained that rent officers were not reducing rents as 'plainly involv[ing] a misconception of the purpose of rent regulation' (p. 93). Nelken has shown, on the other hand, how commercial landlords used the fair rent provisions to their own interest – for example, appropriate 'comparables' could be engineered by these landlords as well as joint applications from both landlord and tenant which would then be registered at higher rents (1983, pp. 54–5). Thus, business landlords were able to manipulate the fair rent system so that it suited their own interests; the term 'legal rachmanism' aptly covers this type of conduct. Further, even though fair rents were registered, business landlords still seem to have overcharged, banking on their tenants' ignorance of the law (which allowed tenants to recover any over-payments).

The most serious failing (even recognised by the Francis committee) was that people simply were not using the system. At the end of 1969, the number of applications to Rent Officers for registration of a fair rent represented just 14 per cent of the number of tenancies granted (p. 11). The witnesses to that committee suggested six possible reasons: ignorance; fear of landlord; sense of moral obligation to stand by one's agreement; fear that the rent officer will put up the rent; overriding concern of the tenant to have repairs carried out by the landlord; satisfaction with the existing rent (pp. 14–17). As for 'ignorance', one might suspect that this would be phased out over time as the system became better known. The point made by Partington, though, is that what matters is not what *actually* happens but that the 'landlord's and tenant's perceptions of how they think the scheme works may be more important in determining their attitudes to rent regulation than detailed knowledge of how it actually works in practice' (1980, p. 292). Furthermore, a survey conducted in 1984 found that only 10 per cent of agreements had a registered rent (Todd, 1988, p. 28).

Even before the introduction of market rents in the 1988 Act, landlords were routinely charging them. Even before the weakening of security of tenure in the 1988 Act, landlords were routinely avoiding and evading it. Against the argument that creeping decontrol might encourage rachmanism, Kemp made the following point:

'What this argument ignores is that . . . most relettings have a market rent. Hence the incentive to evict sitting tenants with registered rents already exists and would not be substantially increased if creeping decontrol were to be introduced. This situation contrasts with that which existed in 1957, for at that time most private sector lets were controlled tenancies with restricted rents.' (1988b, p. 181)

What began as a working class gain in 1915 had been whittled down by 1988 to a mere illusion.

Marketization

The New (de)Regulation
Despite the fact that, by 1988 if not before, research had shown how few rents had been referred to Rent Officers for consideration on the fair rent basis, as well as showing how easy it was for landlords to evade the security of tenure provisions, these factors were given prominence in the government's 1987 housing White Paper as the reasons for the decline in the sector: '*As a result of statutory restrictions*, there is now very little private investment in providing new rented housing' (Department of Environment, 1987, p. 9):

'Rent controls have prevented property owners from getting an adequate return on their investment. People who might have been prepared to grant a temporary letting have also been deterred by laws on security of tenure which make it impossible to regain possession of their property when necessary.' (p. 2)

The White Paper proposed that schemes introduced in 1980, which affected only part of the market at that time, should be expanded to cover the whole private rented market. It was proposed that landlords should be entitled to let properties either on a short-term basis (assured shorthold tenancy; hereafter 'AST') or on a long-term basis (assured tenancy).

One of the key aims of the new provisions was to make renting an 'economic proposition' in order to entice institutional investors back onto the market. John Patten, the Housing Minister, was trying to create a legion of 'new model' landlords, 'it's like motherhood and apple pie' (cited in Kemp, 1992, p. 66). We shall consider in the final section of this chapter how successful these provisions have been in achieving this purpose.

In the Housing Act 1988, both types of tenancy were introduced. For both market rents were to be the norm, supplemented by the right of tenants to appeal to the Rent Assessment Committee (although with the AST the Committee could only entertain the appeal if the rent was considered excessive and there were other comparable ASTs in the area). ASTs were to last for a minimum period of six months and could be determined on two months notice. Assured tenancies could only be terminated by court order on slightly modified Rent Act grounds. In order to create an AST rather than an assured tenancy, a landlord would have to serve a notice on the tenant to that effect. The notice procedure has since been changed (in the Housing Act 1996) so that now a notice must be served if an assured tenancy is to be granted. This seems to have been because some *landlords* might not have intended to create anything other than a short-term contract but 'accidentally create full assured tenancies through inexperience (Department of Environment, 1995b, para. 2.7; *cf* Vincent-Jones, 1987). The DoE suggested that the right of an assured tenant to refer the rent for consideration should be abolished because it was little used (about 1500 cases out of 826,000 tenancies) (para. 2.12). No explanation for this tiny proportion was given but one might suspect that the limited security given to the tenant in the 1988 Act would be uppermost in any such explanation. This proposal did not, however, reach the statute book.

Fair *v* Market Rents

A determination of 'fair rent' is based upon all the circumstances (except personal) but in particular to the age, condition, and location of the property, any furniture provided, and any premium charged by the landlord (s. 70(1), Rent Act 1977). From that figure is deducted the amount which represents scarcity value of the property, based on the numbers of regulated tenancies in the locality (s. 70(2)). Rent officers have developed certain techniques for determining fair rents, based for example upon comparable properties (see Francis, 1971), although it is generally accepted that such determinations are based on a 'feel for the market' as opposed to an exact science (which explains why different determinations can be made of the same property by different officers). From rent officer determinations, there is a right of appeal to a Rent Assessment Committee and thereafter through the courts (see *Curtis* v. *London Rent Assessment Committee* [1997] 4 All ER 842).

It has commonly been suggested in the courts that a fair rent is a market rent less scarcity value (and other disregards): *Metropolitan Property Holdings* v. *Finegold* [1975] 1 All ER 389. Nevertheless, one might assume that a 'fair rent' would be a rather different level from the market rent which can be charged for tenancies under the 1988 Act. Indeed, as market rents relate to properties with different types of landlord under different social obligations (if any), such as RSLs, a market rent is difficult to gauge for it might not be charged. Furthermore, as the 1988 Act system postdates the 1977 Act system of rent determination, as well as providing different levels of security of tenure, it cannot have been intended that this would be so. Nevertheless, two Court of Appeal decisions have now established the veracity of this proposition: *Spath Holme* v. *Chairman of the Greater Manchester and Lancashire Rent Assessment Committee* (1996) 28 HLR 107; *Curtis* v. *London Rent Assessment Committee*. In *Curtis*, Auld LJ argued

'Before the introduction of assured tenancies by the 1988 Act the best evidence available was usually fair rent comparables. Now with the advent and growing volume of assured tenancy market rent comparables, they are most commonly relied on as the best evidence of the starting point for determining a fair rent. The 1988 Act has not changed the law as to the assessment of fair rents. But, [the 1988 Act] set in train the progressive diminution in numbers of fair rent comparables and brought into being an ever increasing supply of market rent comparables. Market rents are thus the natural successor to the declining regime of registered fair rents.' (p. 863)

The assumption inherent in this is that the 1988 Act created a market. However, it can be argued that it created *different* sub-markets. For example, there are markets which relies partially or totally on Housing Benefit; or those which rely on students or seasonal lettings. Suggestions of market perfection are misjudged and Housing Benefit, particularly, skews the post-1988 Act system. It has not yet been suggested that assured shorthold tenancies provide an appropriate comparable.

A direct consequence of *Spath Holme* and *Curtis* has, perhaps unsurprisingly, been a significant increase in levels of 'fair rent' on redetermination. Between April and September 1997, 86 per cent of Rent

Officer determinations were more than 5 per cent above RPI; 56 per cent were more than 10 per cent above RPI:

> 'Most of these tenants, and indeed their landlords, could never have anticipated increases of this magnitude under a fair rent system. Many regulated tenants are elderly and on fixed incomes. . . . Landlords have generally acquired regulated tenancies in anticipation of substantial capital gains when the tenancies come to an end. These tenancies have always traded at a discount to vacant possession value . . . [Regulated properties] have been bought in the knowledge that the rents were subject to fair rent controls and that rental yields would be lower than those obtainable from assured tenancies.' (DETR, 1998, para. 2.5)

Fair rent rises have now been restricted to the RPI+ formula used for RSLs (The Rent Acts (Maximum Fair Rent) Order 1999, SI 1999/6). The formula allows for a 7.5 per cent jump over RPI on the first registration and 5 per cent thereafter (subject to any repairs and improvements carried out by the landlord showing in higher rent levels: DETR, 1998, para. 2.11).

Revival or Bubble?

The decline of the sector was halted in the early part of the 1990s and the sector has stabilized. The government believed that the major contributory factor to this was the changes to the regulatory schema in the 1988 Act: 'The key element in achieving this has been the removal of controls over new private rented lettings' (Department of Environment, 1995a, p. 21). What is certainly true is that most lettings in the sector use the AST. However, rises in the numbers of students in higher and further education have created ready markets for the sector. Furthermore, the sector has been bolstered by the slump in the home ownership market (although this has been spatially distributed). Crook *et al.* estimated that one-tenth of landlords in their sample rented because of the slump (1995, p. 11; see also Crook and Kemp, 1996), although the figure is greater if account is taken solely of managing agents (about 20 per cent: Rhodes, 1993). Consequently, when the home ownership market picks up, many of these properties will return into that sector as well as others seeking to shift their capital asset into ownership. On this basis, the sector's stabilization has simply been a bubble which will burst at the first opportunity.

Be that as it may, certain factors have changed the landscape considerably over a much longer term. First, there has been the decline in subsidy to social housing since the mid-1970s. Second, the incentives of home ownership have been reduced by the withdrawal of mortgage interest tax relief as well as the considerable reduction of Income Support mortgage payments if the home owner is entitled to them. Third, whilst all indications from 'customer surveys' are that most still favour home ownership, workforce insecurity, the move to part-time work and short-term contracts all raise questions about the future viability (or 'sustainability') of the home ownership sector. Fourth, in the Housing Act 1996, the Major government sought to create demand for private renting by requiring local authorities to consider whether there is any accommodation in the private rented sector which might be suitable for successful *homelessness* applicants (the duty formerly belonged entirely to the local authority, although they could house homeless applicants in the private rented sector). Fifth, considerable amounts of public money have been given over in tax reliefs or inducements to institutional investors and RSLs to take part in the private rented sector. These are considered in the next section of this chapter.

2.3 'A Bewildering Display of Projects and Acronyms': Schemes to Revive the Sector

In the 1980s and 1990s, the Thatcher/Major governments attempted to show the viability of the private rented sector through a series of demonstration projects. These were explicitly designed to appeal to institutional investors who were guaranteed considerable taxation advantages if they entered the market for a minimum period. The first schemes under the Housing Act 1980 provided no new investment (Kemp, 1988c). However, in 1987, the government announced that it was going to enlarge the Business Expansion Scheme (BES) so as to include private renting property among its objects. Under this scheme, public companies would be set up to take part in the private renting market, letting on assured tenancies. Shareholders would not be subject to capital gains tax if they kept their shares for a minimum of five years. Companies set up broadly fell into two quite different segments: first, there were entrepreneurial companies which hoped to make capital gains through 'astute property purchases . . . and efficient management'; then there were the companies which sought to take advantage of the property slump or University markets which arranged for investors to take a guaranteed capital gain at the end of the BES period (Crook & Kemp, 1996, pp. 60–1).

The schemes seem to have had three effects: first, they proved that commercial rates of return were not possible in the sector, even with the generous capital reliefs granted to investors. Second, company directors' salaries ate into the profit margin ('A significant element of BES operating costs is directors' fees. Deducting these payments reduces the operating costs per dwelling by about £600 per annum on average': Crook *et al.*, 1995, p. 26). Third, whilst over £3 billion was invested in the sector which might not have come in otherwise, most companies were planning to fold at the end of the five-year period.

The failure of the BES did not mean the end of attempts to woo the institutional sector into the market. Indeed, quite the contrary occurred. The 1995 White Paper announced that what was lacking was a 'suitable investment vehicle':

'Most financial institutions do not wish to own property directly, with
the obligations for management that involves. We therefore propose to
allow housing investment trusts to be formed. . . . It will be for the
market to judge whether the opportunity is right and if the return from
renting, as compared with alternative investment, is attractive.'
(Department of Environment, 1995a, p. 22)

Housing investment trusts (HITs) were to benefit from income tax at
corporation levels and capital gains tax exemptions. They would be
entitled to use assured tenancies *or* ASTs. The first HIT failed to reach its
investment target and was not due to be relaunched – one economist was
reported as saying: '[The failure of the first HIT] points out the underlying
difficulties of the mechanism. The game just doesn't seem worth the
candle' (Dobson, 1998). No further attempts were being made at the time
of writing.

These demonstration schemes seeking to attract new investors should be
contrasted with cross-tenurial initiatives, such as the 'Housing Associations as Managing Agents' ("HAMA") programme and the closely related
duty of local authorities to consider whether there are suitable private
rented properties in the area in which they might house certain homeless
households. In HAMA schemes, the RSL acts as an intermediary between
the landlord and the tenant. The RSL guarantees the landlord a certain
sum by way of rent. Sometimes, the RSL contracts with a local authority
so that the authority guarantees the RSL the required level of
nominations. In their earliest form, landlords granted the tenancies
although, as they developed, the RSL took on this responsibility. Over
time, the original objectives have needed to be rationalized because
local authorities often regard them as expensive and unnecessary
accessories. They have withdrawn their support 'and at times have
promoted fierce competition between associations to reduce fees to win
contracts' (Carr *et al.*, 1998). HAMA, therefore, has had to change
direction (although the Housing Corporation has been accused of
responding too slowly to this: see London Research Centre, 1995, para.
2.18). Broader RSL involvement in the sector has been widely canvassed
(Kleinman *et al.*, 1996). Additionally, some local authorities have sought
to involve the private rented sector directly (without the RSL
intermediary).

What these developments suggest is that the age of the institutional
investor is now well and truly over. It needs to be accepted that the main
growth area in the sector comes from small, 'sideline' landlords. New
schemes seeking to enhance the development of these types of landlords,
such as the current 'buy to let' scheme, appear to recognize this. However,
in certain areas, this may cause over-provision compared to the demand
and new landlords may be forced out of the market in some areas. This is a
shifting market and sometimes movement is rapid, but it is the market
segment which perhaps has greatest potential for development (particularly for low-income tenants).

2.4   Houses in Multiple Occupation ('HMOs')

A survey of HMOs in England and Wales in 1986 found that 80 per cent had defective, poor or no means of fire escape. They are considered extremely unsafe by the fire services. The most marginalized groups tend to be housed in them. Management often 'fails to maintain [fire] precautions, despite regular inspections' (ENTEC, 1997, para. 3.3.6). Nevertheless, the regulatory framework is complex, overlaps between different organizations, and is unclear and confusing. Further, there is some support for the proposition that landlords tend to be able to avoid the various controls fairly easily. Together with the concerns about the physical and management standards of HMOs, there was also 'a concern in many resort areas that there is an increasing proliferation of hotels being converted to hostels which cater primarily for benefit recipients and which, it is suggested, are having an adverse effect on local tourism' (Department of Environment, 1995c, para. 1.2).

These concerns might have been assuaged by imposing a mandatory licensing scheme on HMOs (although this is unlikely as landlords are usually able to avoid falling within the definition of HMO). Apparently, 76 per cent of respondents to a Department of Environment (DoE) Consultation Paper were in favour of such a scheme (Department of Environment, 1994; Department of Environment, 1995c, para. 1.4 noting that 'fire authorities and landlords' interests were opposed to licensing.'). The DoE, in line with the deregulation initiative, unfortunately did not agree 'because of the inherent danger that it would lead to excessive cost and bureaucracy by forcing every local authority to follow a standard licensing approach' (Department of Environment, 1995, para. 2.1; there is also a suggestion that increases in HMO rents would also result: para. 3.16). The problem is that however unsafe, however poor the conditions and/or the management, HMOs are a necessary part of the housing 'culture' in which 'many young people, for example, begin their independent lives in a bedsitter or a shared house or a flat' (Department of Environment, 1995a, p. 24). Mandatory licensing schemes are therefore thrown out because it is feared that HMOs would simply be withdrawn from the market. Such a questionable position (as the Francis Committee might have said, 'there is no evidence to prove it, but then again there is no evidence to disprove it') needs to be counterbalanced by the safety issue.

Local authorities have powers to set up registration schemes, take measures to control certain matters, as well as take enforcement action against HMOs which are unfit in some way (s. 352, Housing Act 1985). However, these provisions only apply when the property falls within the definition of an HMO: 'a house which is occupied by persons who do not form a single household' (s. 345(1), 1985 Act). Broadly, the courts have said that whether a house falls within the category of HMO is a question of 'fact and law', and it is clear that whilst one lot of occupants may not be a household, another lot may be, even if they occupy the same house. Thus, with shifting bands of occupants, such as students, difficult questions arise and what may be a valid exercise of local authority power one day may be rendered invalid the following day.

Barnes v. *Sheffield CC* (1995) 27 HLR 719 is a good example of the problems that arise in determining whether students, some of whom, in the beginning, hardly know each other by contrast to those who come as a group. In the latter, it may truly be said that they form part of the same household, although the question is more difficult in the former situation. The Court of Appeal outlined a series of factors which might be taken into consideration in determining whether a group formed a 'household': the origin of the tenancy; whether facilities are shared; responsibility for the whole house or individual rooms; door locks; who is responsible for filling vacancies; allocation of rooms; size of the accommodation; stability of the group; the mode of living. Everton suggests that the court was influenced by 'the need to protect HMO owners from the imposition of possibly undue burdens' (1997, p. 64; although this is unclear in the text of the judgment). Smith suggests that well-advised landlords 'may insist on new residents signing a single agreement, indicate occupiers are responsible for filling vacancies and allocating rooms, refuse to provide locks and ensure facilities are shared' (1997, p. 401). However, in *Barnes*, it was one of the student's parents who suggested that the authority might consider that the accommodation was unsafe.

In truth, there are considerable disincentives for taking this action based upon the occupant's insecurity of tenure (either as licensee, with a 'resident landlord', or because only an assured shorthold tenancy has been granted). Furthermore, there are considerable difficulties in local authorities taking effective action. In one survey, it was found that 'by the time the end of this process had been reached, individuals living 'essentially independent lives', had evolved into people living in a more communal arrangement' (Smith, 1998, p. 173). Local authorities have adopted different approaches in these cases across a spectrum from issuing a notice to the landlord to conduct certain works to not considering student houses as HMOs at all (*ibid*). Such diversity is, one might argue, a response to regulatory failure – a judicial desire not to commit to a specific definition, combined with the weakness of the statutory precondition, suggests that diversity of response in terms of implementation will be natural. The response may reflect the superior bargaining relationship of landlords to the situation of regulatory failure.

New Labour have now issued a Consultation Paper which appears to have learned from this regulatory failure (DETR, 1999). It argues that local authorities are wary of using their powers in shared houses, particularly those occupied by students, after Barnes (see Section 2, paras 23 *et seq.*). The government propose to introduce a mandatory licensing scheme for all HMOs, operated by the local authority, which should also keep any resultant burdens on business to a minimum (section 1, para. 6). The scheme would have a wide but precise definition of HMO, related to the number of persons living in the property at any time, and have a number of broad exclusions from the licensing regulation. An HMO would only be licensed if it reached acceptable standards in three main areas: physical standards, management, and fitness of the person being licensed (section 3). How far this scheme will succeed in its objectives will depend upon the construction placed upon the exclusions from the scheme and the construction of the obligations on licencees.

Conclusion

In this chapter, we have seen how the private rented sector has declined during this century. It has been argued that the reasons for this decline must be seen in the context of housing policy more generally, and the promotion of alternative tenures. The theory that considers rent control and security of tenure as the sole reason for the decline is, at best, unlikely partly because methods of avoiding such control could be seen as the legitimate use of law by landlords. Illegitimate uses of law may have been criticized but these were more likely to have been adopted by landlords without the necessary knowledge or resources.

By the time the Conservatives got around to dealing with the sector in 1988, much of the sector had already deregulated itself. What could plausibly be presented as a working class gain (rent control and security of tenure) had become manipulated by the processes of capital and income accretion so that the gain had been nullified. The sector may have revived since the introduction of the 1988 Act, although the central reason for that revival is more likely to have been the recession than the impact of the Act. The future is more likely to see this sector becoming the (short-term) pivot between the other tenures and recent advances have so positioned it. At the end, though, it can be argued that in achieving this new role it is hampered by its past. If we can forget this past and (re-)mould the sector, this would provide an effective stop-gap. At present, the sector is overladen with past motifs and regulatory failure.

Further Reading

Various texts cover the law relating to security of tenure and rent control/regulation. The most concise of these is Arden and C. Hunter (1996), *Manual of Housing Law*, London: Sweet & Maxwell; covering the changes made in the 1988 legislation, see D. Hoath, 'The Housing Act 1988: a new regime for the private rented sector' (1989) *Journal of Social Welfare Law* 339 (Pt 1), (199) 18 (Pt 2); also J. Martin (1995), *Residential Security*, London: Sweet & Maxwell. An excellent analysis of the 1988 Act can be found in A. Murie, R. Forrest, M. Partington & P. Leather, *The Consumer Implications of the Housing Act 1988*, SAUS Working Paper 77, Bristol: School for Advanced Urban Studies, University of Bristol. For an analysis of rent control from the Marxian perspective, see P. Beirne (1977), *Fair Rent and Legal Fiction*, London: Macmillan. Comparative material can be gleaned from V. Karn and H. Wolman (1992), *Comparing Housing Systems*, Oxford: Clarendon; see also Niebanck (1985), *The Rent Control Debate*, Chapel Hill: University of North Carolina Press.

On reform of the sector, see (for example) S. Merrett (1992), *Towards the Renaissance of Private Rental Housing*, London: Institute of Public Policy Research; R. Best *et al.* (1992), *The Future of Private Renting: Consensus and Action*, York: Joseph Rowntree Foundation. On pre-Rent Act, see J. Cullingworth (1979), *Essays on Housing Policy*, London: Allen & Unwin; see also J. Short (1982), *Housing in Britain*, London: Methuen, pp. 174–188. For early research on HMOs, see A. Thomas with A. Hedges (1986), *The 1985 Physical and Social Survey of Houses in Multiple Occupation in England and Wales*, London: HMSO. For a discussion of collective action against rent rises, see P. Piratin (1978), *Our Flag Stays Red*, London: Lawrence & Wishart, Ch. 4; M. Partington (1981), 'Collective bargaining', in A. Neal (ed), *Law and the Weaker Party*, London: Professional Books.

Endnotes

1. That is, leases for more than 21 years.
2. This applies in respect of property let after 1 January 1989 under the Housing Act 1988's assured shorthold tenancy scheme (as to which, see below).

Bibliography

Albon, R. and Stafford, D. (1987), *Rent Control*, London: Croom Helm

Armstrong, H. (1998) Principles for a New Housing Policy London: DETR

Balchin, P. (1995), *Housing Policy – An Introduction*, London: Routledge

Ball, M. (1983), *Housing Policy and Economic Power*, London: Methuen

Banting, K. (1979), *Poverty, Politics and Policy: Britain in the 1960s*, London: Macmillan

Bevan, M., Kemp, P. and Rhodes, D. (1995), *Private Landlords and Housing Benefit*, York: Centre for Housing Policy, University of York

Bowley, M. (1945), *Housing and the State*, London: Allen & Unwin

Carey, S. (1995), *Private Renting in England 1993/94*, London: OPCS

Carr, H., Sefton-Green, D. and Sharp, C. (1998), 'Managing the landlord-tenant relationship', paper to the Socio-Legal Studies Association Conference, 15–17 April 1998

Carter, M. and Ginsburg, N. (1994) 'New government housing policies', vol 41, *Critical Social Policy*, 100

Clarke, D. (1995), 'Commonhold – a prospect of promise', vol 58, *Modern Law Review*, 486

Crook, A. (1992), 'Private rented housing and the impact of deregulation', in J. Birchall (ed.), *Housing Policy in the 1990s*, London: Routledge

Crook, A., Hughes, J. and Kemp, P. (1995), *The Supply of Privately Rented Homes: Today and Tomorrow*, York: Joseph Rowntree Foundation

Crook, A. and Kemp, P. (1996), 'The revival of private rented housing in Britain', vol 11, *Housing Studies*, 51

Crook, A. and Martin, G. (1988), 'Property speculation, local authority policy and the decline of privately rented housing in the 1980s: an overview', in P. Kemp (ed.), *The Private Provision of Rented Housing: Current Trends and Future Prospects*, Aldershot: Gower

Crossman, R. (1975), *Diaries of a Cabinet Minister*, London: Cape

Damer, S. (1980), 'State, class and housing: Glasgow 1885–1919', in J. Melling (ed.), *Housing, Social Policy and the State*, London: Croom Helm

Department of Environment (1987), *Housing: The Government's Proposals*, Cm 214, London: HMSO

Department of Environment (1994), *Houses in Multiple Occupation – Consultation Paper on the Case for Licensing*, London: DoE

Department of Environment (1995a), *Our Future Homes: Opportunity, Choice, Responsibility*, Cm 2901, London: HMSO

Department of Environment (1995b), *The Legislative Framework for Private Renting*, Consultation Paper linked to the Housing White Paper 'Our Future Homes', London: DoE

Department of Environment (1995c), *Improving Standards in Houses in Multiple Occupation*, Consultation Paper linked to the Housing White Paper 'Our Future Homes', London: DoE

Department of Environment, Transport and the Regions (1998), *Limiting Fair Rent Increases: A Consultation Paper*, London: DETR

Department of Environment, Transport and the Regions (1999), *Licensing of Houses in Multiple Occupation in England*, Consultation Paper, London: DETR

Dobson, J. (1998), 'HITs 'are dead', *Inside Housing*, 30 January

Doling, J. and Davies, M. (1984), *Public Control of Privately Rented Housing*, Aldershot: Gower

Donnison, D. (1967), *The Government of Housing*, London: Pelican

ENTEC (1997), *Fire Risk in HMOs: A Summary Report*, London: DETR

Everton, A. (1997), 'Fire precautions – legal controls in houses in multiple occupation: safe havens . . . or . . . any port in a storm?', vol 19, *Journal of Social Welfare and Family Law*, 61

Francis, H. (1971), *Report of the Committee on the Rent Acts*, Cmnd 4601, London: HMSO

Holmans, A. (1987), *Housing Policy in Britain*, London: Croom Helm

House of Commons Environment Committee (1982), *The Private Rented Housing Sector*, HC 40–I, London: HMSO

House of Commons Environment Committee (1996), *Housing Need*, London: HMSO

Institute of Economic Affairs (1972), *Verdict on Rent Control*, IEA Readings No 7, London: IEA

Kemeny, J. (1981), *The Myth of Home Ownership*, London: Routledge

Kemp, P. (1988a), 'Private renting: an overview', in P. Kemp (ed.), *The Private Provision of Rented Housing: Current Trends and Future Prospects*, Aldershot: Gower

Kemp, P. (1988b), 'New proposals for private renting: creating a commercially viable climate for investment in rented housing?', in P. Kemp (ed.), *The Private Provision of Rented Housing: Current Trends and Future Prospects*, Aldershot: Gower

Kemp, P. (1988c), 'The impact of the assured tenancy scheme, 1980–1986', in P. Kemp (ed.), *The Private Provision of Rented Housing: Current Trends and Future Prospects*, Aldershot: Gower

Kemp, P. (1992), 'Rebuilding the private rented sector?', in P. Malpass & R. Means (eds), *Implementing Housing Policy*, Buckingham: Open University Press

Kemp, P. (1997a), 'Ideology, public policy and private rental housing since the war', in P. Williams (ed.), *Directions in Housing Policy*, London: Paul Chapman

Kemp, P. (1997b), 'Burying Rachman', in J. Goodwin and C. Grant (eds), *Built to Last*, London: Roof

Kleinman, M., Whitehead, C. with Scanlon, K. (1996), *Private Rented Sector*, London: NFHA

London Research Centre (1995), *The Use of the Private Rented Sector to Meet Housing Need: The First Year of the HAMA Initiative*, London: Housing Corporation

Marley, X. (1931), *Final Report of the Inter-Departmental Committee on the Rent Acts*, Cmd 3911, London: HMSO

Melling, J. (1980), 'Clydeside housing and the evolution of state rent control, 1900–1939', in J. Melling (ed.), *Housing, Social Policy and the State*, London: Croom Helm

Merrett, S. with Gray, F. (1982), *Owner Occupation in Britain*, London: Routledge

Milner Holland (1965), *Report of the Committee on Housing in Greater London*, Cmnd 2605, London: HMSO

Nelken, D. (1983), *The Limits of the Legal Process*, London: Academic Press

Partington, M. (1980), *Landlord and Tenant*, London: Weidenfeld & Nicolson

Rhodes, D. (1993), *The State of the Private Rented Sector, Findings No 90*, York: Joseph Rowntree Foundation

Smith, N. (1997), 'Determining a household for the purposes of Part XI of the Housing Act 1985', *Conveyancer*, 395

Smith, N. (1998), 'Bureaucracy or death? Safeguarding lives in houses in multiple occupation', in D. Cowan (ed.), *Housing: Participation and Exclusion*, Aldershot: Dartmouth

Stewart, A. (1981), *Housing Action in an Industrial Suburb*, London: Academic Press

Stewart, A. (1996), *Rethinking Housing Law*, London; Sweet & Maxwell

Todd, J. (1988), 'Recent private lettings', in P. Kemp (ed.), *The Private Provision of Rented Housing: Current Trends and Future Prospects*, Aldershot: Gower

Vincent-Jones, P. (1987), 'Exclusive possession and exclusive control of private rented housing: a socio-legal critique of the lease-licence distinction', vol 14, *Journal of Law and Society*, 445

Watchman, P. (1980), 'The origin of the 1915 Rent Act', vol 5, *Law and State*, 20

Watchman, P. (1988), 'Heartbreak hotel', *Journal of Social Welfare Law*, 147

3 Regulating Home Ownership: Building Societies and the Housebuilding Industry

'What a magnificent contradiction! The construction of houses is fundamentally necessary for the survival of the species and the reproduction of the capacity to labour yet those who labour do not receive wages and salaries sufficient to purchase those dwellings unless the physical attributes of the houses are so primitive as to constitute a threat in the short of long run to health and to diligent labour.' (Merrett, 1982, p. 72)

At the turn of the twenty-first century, the home ownership sector has become so dominant that over 70 per cent of the population form part of the 'property-owning democracy'. Home ownership has almost the same tenure share as did private renting at the turn of the century. In the previous chapter we charted the decline of private renting, considering (amongst other matters) rent control/regulation, the lack of profitability of renting and tax reliefs to landlords. However, other factors have made home ownership more attractive both to individuals as well as to governments.

Whilst ownership is a legal construct, governmental policies have regarded it as the 'natural' tenure (a view explored by Saunders, 1990, pp. 69–84) and sought to give benefits to home owners that increased the tenure's desirability (see Chapter 12 below). These benefits have included, for example, significant advantages built into the taxation system, particularly when compared to the taxation problems of private renting. For the inter-war governments, home ownership was variously seen as a 'bulwark against bolshevism', so that "every spadeful of manure dug in, every fruit tree planted' converted a potential revolutionary into a citizen' (Merrett, 1982, p. 6). However, the role of the state in the inter-war boom in home ownership can be exaggerated for it 'did little to create it' (Ball, 1983, p. 40: 'policy was restricted to one of a guardian angel'). In the 1980s and 1990s, by contrast, the state has been proactive in creating more home owners through giving council tenants the right to buy their homes and broadening the scope of such policies to include most post-1996 housing development by RSLs. The Conservative government expected an additional 1.5 million new home owners to join the throng before 2005 (Department of the Environment, 1995, p. 9).[1]

In the inter-war period, whilst government policy was partly concerned with subsidizing local authorities and creating 'homes fit for heroes', home ownership expanded its net. This was partly because speculative[2] housebuilding for home ownership took off as a result of lower building costs (see Bowley, 1948, pp. 74–83). Partly, it was because building societies had a surfeit of credit which they needed to part with, and did so cheaply. During this crucial period, building societies began to lend for home ownership, as opposed to lending to landlords, and weighted their terms accordingly (Craig, 1986, p. 93). Further, building societies and housebuilders formed a cabal of interests.

In this chapter, our concerns lie with the development of the credit market for home ownership, in particular the role of building societies and with the way in which the housebuilding industry operates. Whilst the taxation system has been levelled out between tenures now, opinion polls continue to suggest a high degree of demand – around 80 per cent of the population – for home ownership. This climate had to be created (in saying this, I am explicitly disagreeing with those who believe that home ownership is the 'natural' tenure); and it is the success of the housebuilding and building society 'movements' in creating this climate that we will analyse in this chapter. Nevertheless, there are signs of regulatory failure in both industries – building societies have sought to break out of the straitjacket of their status in the 1980s and 1990s against a backdrop of increased competition for market share from other parts of the financial services industry. The deregulation initiatives of the Thatcher governments effectively ended the monopoly enjoyed by the societies. Conversely, the housebuilding industry has undergone a decline because market regulation has proved unsuccessful.

Both industries have been assisted by successive governments who have created the necessary conditions for the expansion of home ownership. This has been expressed not only in favourable taxation practices – home owners are not taxed on the imputed rental income from their home as they were before 1962[3] and they received generous tax relief on mortgage interest payments until recently; but also, for example, governments have sought to redefine the regulatory regime at appropriate moments to suit the societies. The most recent examples of changing the climate to suit home ownership have occurred through giving council tenants the right to buy their homes in addition to the deregulation of the building societies in 1986 and 1997. Other methods, such as restraining council house building in the 1930s or credit policies in the early 1970s, have been equally effective. These measures have been responsible for the home ownership booms that occurred at the same time as their introduction.

Home ownership has also served the interests of government well (other than in the early 1990s). At a time when society itself was concerned about revolution, home ownership was regarded as giving people a stake in society – home ownership was 'a bulwark against bolshevism and all that bolshevism stands for' (see generally, Balchin, 1995, pp. 194–197; Clarke & Ginsburg, 1975). Building societies emphasized 'thrift and mutual self-help' (Boddy, 1980, p. 5) and therefore fitted neatly within the Thatcherite duologue of self-reliance and personal responsibility. Additionally, they were largely responsible for funding the Thatcherite home ownership drive, exemplified by their lending to those tenants wishing to purchase their council homes in the 1980s.

Building society lending practices have collaborated in the tenurial climate change during this century, and have facilitated the growth of the housebuilding industry which has gorged itself on the various credit booms. Thus, the rise of each industry was dependent on the other. During the 1930s, private-sector landlords seeking mortgages would find the terms offered unsuitable and relatively unprofitable, as these terms were gauged to home owners' rather different requirements. For example, the term of the mortgage was too short to enable landlords to glean the necessary profit. The shorter the term of the mortgage, the greater the outgoings (that is, the money lent and interest on it): 'private landlords can only profitably use building society loans if rents are charged in excess of what a borrower would pay on comparable property acquired for owner-occupation' (Craig, 1986, p. 93). Furthermore, if the rent charged was sufficiently in excess of the mortgage payments, tenants would find home ownership more attractive as their potential mortgage payments would be less than their rent.

This sea-change in the mortgage market was supplemented with complex collaborative arrangements between building societies and builders in the 1930s. Under these schemes, building societies entered into agreements with housebuilders as a result of which the societies agreed to lend more than their usual 75 per cent of the capital value of the property and, in return, housebuilders deposited cash with the society representing the remaining portion of the loan above the 75 per cent threshold. The housebuilders' cash deposit acted as collateral for the loan and protected the building societies (insurance does this job today). The housebuilders were able to expand the potential breadth of their market because more people could afford to purchase. These schemes (known as the 'builders' pool') produced poorly built accommodation because the builders cut corners to make a profit. In 1939, the schemes were effectively curtailed by legislation after an unsuccessful, but highly publicized, court action brought against this cartel type arrangment. Nevertheless, such schemes, and the development of private insurance guarantess to the same effect, broadened demand and were partly responsible for the rise in home ownership during this period (Craig, 1986). Not surprisingly, booms in home ownership throughout the twentieth century have coincided with periods of building society growth because societies have been the primary providers of capital for house purchase.

The first section of this chapter charts the regulatory matrix of the building societies, from rather simple organizations to the massive conglomerates of today. Until recently this regulatory matrix largely preserved their status and granted them considerable advantages in the marketplace. Societies and government have intertwined their interests at convenient moments during the twentieth century, enabling societies to have considerable power as well as to determine their own regulatory development. Nevertheless, this regulatory development has failed to provide appropriate structures and strictures for the industry, which, in turn, has caused the shift in status away from mutuality towards publicly-owned banking companies (giving rise to windfall profits for ex-society members, together with speculation by members of the public in search of such windfalls). Essentially, though, the 1980s and 1990s have been a time of regulatory crisis for societies because they have found themselves unable to compete with other organizations.

The second section considers the speculative housebuilding industry and its decline. The decline in housebuilding has caused a supply-side failure in the home ownership market that needs to be set against the current and future demand for housing. The focus of studies on housebuilding is the complex interaction of different relationships in the 'structure of housing provision' (Ball 1986b); this is beyond the scope of this book (see, generally, Ball, 1983). However, a broad appreciation of the role, functions and market regulation[4] of housebuilding provides an important aspect of the housing relation together with an example of the failure of market regulation in housing.

3.1   (De-)Regulating Building Societies

The contradiction between the capital values of property and labour wages has meant that 'an essential precondition' in the rise of home ownership has been a concomitant rise in institutions willing and able to lend money to individuals for the purchase of property. At the turn of the century, the single type of institution best placed to do that was the building society (partly because it was already involved in lending within the nascent property market as well as to landlords). The twentieth century story of the rise of home ownership is therefore incomplete without considering the role and regulation of the building society movement that has been partly responsible for the rise in the proportion of home owners.

Building societies have filled the gap between house prices and individual incomes. They have been extremely successful in doing so, having been responsible for the majority of home loans during this century. The scale of their success can be measured in terms of their growth over the same period: in 1920, the sector's total assets, at 1994 prices, were about £2 billion; by 1994, this had increased to £301 billion (Treasury, 1996, Table 1). This staggering growth has been accompanied by the growth of building societies in the personal savings market over the same period. They have made a success out of the supposed recipe for disaster of 'borrowing short and lending long' – that is, until 1986 at any rate, they operated upon the simple proposition that whatever was deposited with them by individuals on a short-term basis was lent out to mortgagors on a long-term basis. Mortgagors were charged levels of interest on the capital they borrowed; depositors were paid interest on the money they deposited. The difference between the two represented the surplus due to the building society itself after deducting the costs of servicing the loans, personnel, etc.

This simple proposition no longer holds true to the extent that it did until the 1980s. Building societies and the broader credit industry were subjected to deregulation during the 1980s and 1990s. This has revolutionized the financial services industry. The current pressures on building societies are whether their status as mutual societies, together with their regulatory structure, provides them with enough scope to remain *competitive* in the future considering the array of other lenders in the marketplace. In 1986, the Building Societies Act began deregulating the industry. The Act enabled building societies to play a more significant role in the developing financial markets. It also increased the ease and willingness of the sector to grant mortgages. The Building Societies Act 1997 further widened their powers and deregulated the sector so as to enable societies to diversify further. These deregulatory moves have been necessary to sustain the industry against increasing competition from banks and other financial institutions in both the savings and mortgage markets.

In this section, our analysis begins with a brief consideration of the historical foundations of the industry. We then turn to look at the reasons why building societies might (and might not) have been favourable locations for personal savings, for this affected the level of mortgage lending, contributing to mortgage 'feasts' as well as mortgage 'famines' (most notably in the 1970s). We then consider why the building societies essentially were able to corner the mortgage market. Their power stemmed from the fact that they tended to work together through powerful trade organizations. This created a cartel and a near monopoly of mortgage lending for them. It was only in the early 1980s that competition from other sectors on both the personal savings and mortgage sides of the balance sheet created a demand from *within* the industry for greater regulatory freedom, which a grateful government willingly proffered. Societies believed that legislative boundaries, broadly formed around 100 years previously, overly restricted their freedom to compete and diversify in an expanding credit market. Contradicting the Conservative government's beliefs, deregulation was pursued by the building societies during the 1980s and 1990s partly because the home ownership market, it was believed, had reached its natural limit. Thus, increased competition within the credit and savings markets was not matched by an increasing demand for loans at that time. Legislation in 1986 and 1997 enabled the societies to break free from the restrictions imposed as a consequence of their history. In the final part of this section, we will consider the fiction of building societies' status as 'mutual' organizations. Mutuality means that depositors and borrowers are members, who are entitled to a say in the direction of the society, and that the societies themselves are non-profit-making organizations (although they are entitled to make a surplus).[5]

Mutuality was recognized as the guiding principle in the earliest legislation but, with the apparent need for competitiveness, it has largely been shed. In short, mutuality may well have been a principle that guided their initial development but societies' practices have shown that this ideology has long been shaken off.

Historical Foundations

The first building societies grew out of the processes of urbanization during the early industrial revolution. The first records relate to a society set up at the Golden Cross Inn in 1775 (Boddy, 1980, p. 5). That they should have been related to inns reflected the fact that they tended to be working class organizations based on a particular locality. Basically, a number of people agreed to pay a fixed sum of money every month to a member of the organization. The money which accrued was then used to buy a plot of land and to build a house on it (and so on until all the members were housed). The organization terminated when the last member was housed. Such associations soon became anachronistic and only the very first actually involved the members in *building*. Associations subsequently took in funds from those simply requiring interest rather than accommodation and this money was used to fund the property side. Depositors were paid their interest out of the sums paid by borrowers. In this way the cycle of deposit and lending was built up, with each financing the other. Between 1845–1873, these associations gradually came to be permanent, as opposed to terminating, societies.

The mutually reinforcing obligations of the agreements have been retained throughout in their status as mutual, non-profit-making societies which worked together as a 'movement' (*cf* the RSL 'movement'). Their distinctive operation came from the fact that their instincts were not entirely commercial: 'Instead the working principle (however difficult to apply in practice) was that of an equitable balance between the interests of borrowers and investors' who were the members of the society (Holmans, 1987, p. 219). In practice, this non-commercial ethos became most valuable in their concerns to keep mortgage interest rates at an affordable level during the severe fluctuations in interest rates in the 1970s (*ibid*, p. 266).

Under the Building Societies Act 1874, societies became subject to the same regulatory structure as friendly societies because their shares were based upon membership as opposed to capital (they thus avoided regulation through company status: Boddy, 1980, p. 9). That Act permitted societies to loan money only by way of mortgage. They were able to take short-term deposits, to invest a specified proportion in mortgages (up to two-thirds) and the remainder was to be placed in 'safe' securities. The Act remained in place, subject to minor amendments, until 1986 and provided the foundations for the twentieth century expansion of the permanent building societies.

The 'Sheltered Circuit' I: Income Stream

In the early part of the century, competition for personal savings through deposits was broadly from government bonds (consols) and bank deposits. Societies had a central advantage over each of these because they were favoured by the taxation system and continued to be so even when government developed its own National Savings and other similar schemes. Until the early 1980s, building societies were entitled to deduct income tax at source on interest payments *at a special rate*. This rate reflected the balance between those investors who paid tax and those who did not ('the composite rate'). The composite rate of tax was less than the standard rate because of this adjustment. Investors were not able to reclaim income tax paid in this way even if those individuals were not liable to pay it.

This system was both convenient to the Inland Revenue and built in an advantage to building societies in the search for recyclable funds. For example, in 1979–80, the composite rate of tax was 21 per cent compared to the basic rate of 30 per cent. This clearly favoured basic rate taxpayers who would pay tax on their interest at a lower rate than if they paid tax direct, although non-taxpayers suffered in the process (Ball, 1983, p. 306). Societies were also able to advertise their interest rates for depositors as both net of *basic rate* tax and grossed-up on the basis of *basic rate* tax. In the late 1920s and early 1930s, the interest rate levels, together with the alternative investment possibilities, became less advantageous to investors than building society rates. Not surprisingly, societies began to receive deposits of large amounts which were then recycled into loans for property purchase, thus fueling the home ownership boom. At other times, alternative investments have proved to yield greater amounts and have thus been more attractive to investors. During these periods, societies had less money available for recycling into mortgages – mortgage rationing and mortgage queues formed (particularly during the 1970s).

In addition to deposits, a society's income stream also comes from mortgage interest payments. The rate of interest on mortgage payments is *variable* and determines the rate of interest paid to depositors. In the early 1930s, the mortgage interest rate was reduced at a slower rate than market interest rates. This enabled building societies to offer higher interest rates to depositors than could be gained elsewhere. Thus, borrowers were subsidizing the higher rates paid to investors. However, during the 1970s, when interest rates became unstable and rose considerably, societies generally kept their mortgage interest rates below inflation, which meant that the interest they were able to offer potential investors was uncompetitive compared with alternative investments. In order to compete for funds, societies began to offer differential interest rates to depositors at this time, with larger interest rates being offered to larger depositors. Competition had earlier been stimulated by societies attempting to increase their market exposure by developing branch offices. Ball characterized these developments as 'a progression through three alternative approaches open to a market monopolist': charge high prices; branch out; charge/pay differential rates (1983, pp. 304–5).

Between 1939–83, the societies' trade organization (the Building Societies Association (BSA)) set the interest rates for both deposits and mortgages. From 1973, societies protected their market monopoly by operating a cartel under which the largest societies accepted those rates (although smaller societies oscillated within and around them: Boddy & Lambert, 1988). The basis for setting the rates appears to have reflected 'the requirements of the housing market, the general level of interest rates, the conflicting interests of investors and borrowers and the societies' need to maintain adequate operating margins and liquid assets' (Boddy, 1980, p. 87; although it was often inaccurate: Boddy & Lambert, 1988). A significant factor was the involvement of central government, particularly when market interest rates rose rapidly in the 1970s. During the early 1970s, governments paid bridging loans to societies in order to keep mortgage interest rates at acceptable levels (which contrasts with the exhortatory tactics used in the 1950s and 1960s) (Holmans, 1987, pp. 278–282). This government involvement made for cheaper, but less, mortgages (see, for example, Stewart, 1996, p. 69).

High interest rates in the 1970s effectively ended the cosy monopoly enjoyed by the building societies, as the advantages of the composite rate of tax were gradually eroded (and withdrawn in 1982) and the banks began to compete more effectively for mortgage and savings business as restrictions on their doing so were gradually whittled away. Higher interest yielding accounts became a major new source of deposit but this led to 'a squeeze on margins and evidence of a reduced rate of growth' (Boddy, 1989, p. 94). At the same time, the increased competition between societies spelt the demise of the cartel, particularly given that the broader financial marketplace was rapidly being deregulated. The knock-on effect of the competition for investors, through increasing interest paid on deposits, was higher mortgage rates to offset these increased costs (Ball, 1986b, p. 36), this provided an incentive to other organizations to join the mortgage market. Finally, when interest rates began to fall, the money (or wholesale) markets became more competitive and provided an alternative, higher-yielding outlet for personal savings.

The 'Sheltered Circuit' II: Mortgage Lending

The mortgage market has been dominated for most of this century by the building societies. The die was cast by the huge level of personal savings deposited with them in the late 1920s and early 1930s which enabled the home ownership expansion to take place. Indeed, this caused societies to liberalize the terms they offered to borrowers. For example, they increased mortgage terms (and therefore lowered interest payments), which widened the potential numbers who could gain mortgages, and they reduced the initial deposit that the potential home owner had to provide. The latter was achieved with the connivance of the housebuilding movement, through a system known as 'pooling' under which the building societies would essentially be guaranteed against loss over a certain loan-to-value ratio (the disastrous consequences of this scheme for the buyers are considered in Craig, 1986; Piratin, 1978, pp. 41–2).

The building societies' main competitors for mortgage lending – local authorities, insurance companies and banks – either could not or did not want to enter the market to the same extent (see Niner, 1975; Holmans, 1987, pp. 230–1; Ball, 1983, pp. 300–1). So, for example, local authorities were subjected to periodic restraints (and they tended to fund the market for second-hand properties as opposed to new builds). The traditional role of clearing banks was in lending to institutional borrowers as opposed to loans to individuals secured against private property. However, at different times the clearing banks were subjected to credit control by the Bank of England, which was able to direct their lending patterns. These controls were overhauled in 1971 but re-imposed in the mid-1970s during a period of exchange control. Known as the 'corset', it basically penalized banks' involvement in the mortgage market. Thus, until the 1980s, the building societies enjoyed a near monopoly of mortgage lending as a result of structural controls placed on their potential competitors.

The election of the first Thatcher government changed all this (although many of the factors which enabled the downfall of this monopoly were already in place). The Thatcher government's central housing policy was the enlargement of home ownership (a policy which had guided previous Conservative administrations) and the stimulation of the mortgage market was essential to the success of that policy. The building society movement (through the BSA) wanted to take part in this expansion and, in the early 1980s, consistently agitated for extensions to their powers (Boddy, 1989, pp. 93–7; see below).

The key moment, however, was when the banks broke free of the corset (and exchange controls) and were able to enter the mortgage market in 1981. Pent-up demand amongst those who were unable to gain mortgages during the 1970s, together with demand from those wishing to buy their council house under the right to buy, caused a lending boom which was dominated by the competitive instincts of the various organizations, with clearing banks gaining more than a quarter of the mortgage market between 1981–3. This competition to the building societies' dominance was all the more significant because of their reliance on personal savings. Banks and other institutions, in contrast, were not so reliant and were able to finance their lending partly through the wholesale markets. Entry into mortgage lending was given added appeal by the fact that in the early 1980s mortgage rates moved closer to the costs of wholesale finance: 'By the mid-1980s a new lending rate pattern had emerged. UK mortgage rates became pegged, not to retail funding, but to a level higher than the marginal cost of wholesale funds, . . .' (Pryke & Whitehead, 1994, p. 75). More institutions began to enter the mortgage market, particularly foreign banks, some of which were totally reliant on raising their income streams through the wholesale market, a practice which became particularly prevalent and innovative after the 'big bang' deregulated the financial services industry within the city in 1986 (*ibid*; Stephens, 1993).

1986–present : The Effect of Deregulation

Whilst the Building Societies Act 1986 provided a new regulatory regime, enabling societies to expand and diversify their enterprises, the deregulation of the markets in the early 1980s and the levelling of the financial playing field meant that the 1986 Act was required to enable the societies to compete effectively. The 1874 legislation had provided the means by which they had prospered but that was in a situation of near market monopoly. The competition of the early 1980s left societies at a disadvantage because of their reliance on personal savings in a market in which better returns could be gained elsewhere on alternative investments. Additionally, the technological revolution affecting the major clearing banks enabled those institutions to become more efficient and cost-effective.

Increasing competition from other financial enterprises in the mortgage market also revolutionized the previously cautious lending practices of societies (Dwelly, 1997). This was manifested by higher loans-to-income and loans-to-value ratios than had previously been available (Doling & Ford, 1991, pp. 112–3). Applicants became able to borrow close to three-and-a-half times their income and up to 100 per cent of the value of their properties. In other words, competition brought greater risk of individual borrower's default to the mortgage lending market (although not completely, as societies relied on mortgage indemnity guarantees to limit their losses).[6] A further factor which caused building societies to crave a new regulatory regime, and thus break out of the 1874 Act's straitjacket, was a belief that the home ownership market was reaching its natural limit. Whilst the market could be sustained by movements within it, new business was diminishing, particularly after the first right-to-buy sales had occurred. Societies therefore wished to take advantage of different markets, such as insurance, estate agency, and conventional banking services.

Building societies agitation for reform in the early 1980s, raised the issue of their separate regulatory status. As mutual societies, they were supposed to act in the interests of their members – borrowers and depositors – but they tended to 'be closed oligarchies subject to little control by the membership . . ., so [their] objectives became closely linked to the importance for senior management of high salaries, status, perks and power: all of which are associated with increasing size in terms of turnover, branches, etc' (Ball, 1983, p. 296). This partly explains the declining number of societies holding a greater proportion of the movement's assets. The search for 'surplus' effectively contradicted their status (*cf* RSLs). In seeking new markets, it was natural that they called into question their mutual status. The BSA itself attempted to resolve this issue by eventually focusing on expanding their role in the housing market in a series of inward-looking reports in the early 1980s:

> 'In emphasising a distinctive role for the societies in housing [the 1984 report] also attempted to head off concerns that diversification into the realm of financial services, combined with common fiscal treatment for all financial institutions, called into question the societies' mutual status and different and separate system of regulation.' (Boddy, 1989, p. 97)

This housing role became apparent only after considerable internal discussion (Building Societies Association 1983; 1984) and formed the bedrock of the approach to government for reform.

It is hardly surprising that the doors of government were willingly opened for the very institutions which were acting to fulfill the Thatcherite dream. The 1986 Act was a result of a close working relationship between the government, the BSA, and the individual societies, which determined the shape of the Act throughout (Boddy & Lambert, 1988; Boddy, 1989). The strength of the BSA lay in its ability to represent and negotiate within its membership (as different societies had different interests, depending (for example) on their size). Indeed, the bargaining strength of the BSA contrasts markedly with the lack until recently, of landlord trade associations. Even in 1986, societies were part of the 'new model landlords' which John Patten had talked about (see Ch. 2) and were hoped to become *providers* of low-cost private rented and social housing (see, for example, Smallwood, 1992). To adapt an expression, the government scratched the building societies' collective back and vice versa.

The division between the traditional role of the societies and the expansion they craved was formally catered for by drawing a distinction between principal purpose, other purposes and powers. Their principal purpose had to be 'that of raising, primarily by the subscriptions of the members, a stock or fund for making to them advances secured on land for their residential use . . .' (s. 5(1), 1986 Act). They were given powers to make loans on overseas land, lend on overdraft (i.e. unsecured loans), act as landlords and/or developers, and invest in subsidiaries (which, importantly, enabled them to set up estate agencies, asset management, personal equity plans, and other financial services) (ss. 16–18). These were divided into three classes: Class 1 was secured loans on residential property, Class 2 was other loans, and Class 3 was the other assets. The relevance of class was that each class could not exceed a specified proportion of the societies' total assets (see Gibb & Munro, 1991). Initially, Class 2 and 3 assets could not exceed 20 per cent, but this was increased to 40 per cent in 1988 to enable societies to take part in the consumer boom to a greater extent than they had been able. Were this regulatory structure felt to be too tight, societies were given the power to change to corporate status on the basis of a 20 per cent vote in favour of doing so.

In exchange for these wider powers, societies had to accept a new form of regulator – the Building Societies Commission. The Commission has various powers, for example, to set levels of capital adequacy before societies were allowed to diversify into other investments, together with certain obligations to investigate. Societies were willing to accept this slight intrusion as a *quid pro quo* of their broader powers, partly because they recognized that there was a gap between their management and members (Mabey & Tillet, 1980; Hawes, 1986) and partly because of high profile scandals in the late 1970s. In fact, the movement has been beset by scandals (for example, with money stolen by directors) and societies have encountered problems leading, or potentially leading to their winding up (the most famous, for trust lawyers anyway, was the collapse of the Birkbeck in 1911). In the past, when societies have been in trouble, the BSA or Chief Registrar, and after 1986 the Commission, have simply required amalgamation and takeover. Thus, regulation is usually conducted by conversation within the less than exacting strictures of the requirement on societies to exercise 'prudent management' (see further Black, 1998).

The Building Societies Ombudsman was also foisted upon the societies in Part IX of the 1986 Act, suggesting that the societies influence was limited on certain issues. Subsequently, societies have challenged the extent of the Ombudsman's jurisdiction and their general attitude towards the right of individuals to have complaints dealt with by the Ombudsman has been poor ('a lack of enthusiasm . . . at its mildest': James, 1997, p. 121).

Since the 1986 Act, societies have diversified considerably, buying into the life insurance market (for example) and essentially joining the consumer market for financial services. In so doing, they place themselves at the mercy of the market and must retain low-risk ratings, maintained by city institutions, in order to continue their movements into the wholesale market. They have been considerably assisted by a regulatory environment which has jumped when they have wanted it to jump. Statutory Instruments and other regulatory guidance, for example from the Commission, have facilitated this movement. The benefits for members of mutual societies have had to be put on hold in order for the societies to keep faith within the 'market' (Kearns & Stephens, 1997, p. 26). Instead of expanding their branch networks, mergers are now sought as part of a movement, paradoxically, towards 'efficiency gains' so that 'where branch networks overlap the combined assets of two societies can be serviced by less than the combined branch network' (*ibid*). Thus, the branches which facilitated the expansion of the movement have been cut back in attempts to 'downsize'.

The most significant effect of the 1986 Act has been the gradual movement to demutualization either through takeover (by banks) or through members' vote. In 1989, the Abbey National was the first building society to vote in favour of taking corporate status and in 1997 the Halifax joined them together with the Alliance & Leicester, Woolwich and

Northern Rock. Conversion reflects the decline in the mortgage market (particularly during the recession of the late 1980s and early 1990s) and consequently the desire to expand into other markets beyond the limits allowed by the 1986 Act. Additionally:

'The most compelling reason for conversion is that it will allow the larger societies to gain access to equity finance to allow them to take over other financial institutions. In this case, conversion can be seen as part of a wider consolidation in the financial services industry, combined with the move towards generic financial institutions offering the complete range of personal finance products.' (Stephens, 1997, p. 199)

The by-product of this has been a pay out to members of about £30 billion by way of windfall payments.

Ironically, demutualization took place at the same time as the Conservative government's deregulation initiative had begun to roll back the legislative barriers created in the 1986 Act. Further deregulation gave societies the power to extend their role in the wholesale market and, for example, own a general insurance company. The government's review of the industry, published in 1996, made it clear that further legislation was still required:

'The government understands the frustration of societies having to wait for the implementation of secondary legislation before they can take advantage of a new business opportunity. This makes it difficult for them to meet the changing needs of their customers and draw up their long-term business plans. . . .
Building societies have an important role to play in maintaining a competitive market in financial services. That market will continue to change and develop. The government believes that societies should be able to diversify, and compete as efficiently and effectively as anyone else in the marketplace without giving up their mutual status. . . .
Building societies are popular with their customers and evidence suggests that in many cases members of the public prefer doing business with building societies than with banks.' (Treasury, 1996, section 3, paras 7 & 10)

The Building Societies Act 1997, given Royal Assent on the day Parliament was dissolved for the general election, therefore broadened considerably the ability of societies to engage in the marketplace. A new principal purpose provision included the ability to own residential property to let, and borrowers no longer needed to be society members (s. 1). Loans secured on land must account for at least 75 per cent of the societies' assets (this can be reduced by quasi-legislation to 60 per cent) but there are few controls over the destination of the other 25 per cent. Just 50 per cent of the societies' funds must come from deposits, the rest may come from the wholesale markets. However, their powers to act as a market-maker are restricted, suggesting that these limits to diversification will eventually either have to be lifted or the larger remaining societies will demutualize.

The Fiction of Mutuality

The market share of the present building societies now accounts for about 38 per cent of the new mortgage market (its share of the retail deposit market oscillates according to news of demutualizations so that individuals can take advantage of windfalls offered to members). This is a far cry from their market share even in the 1980s (which ran at about 70 per cent of the market) and reflects the loss of the biggest lenders from mutual to corporate status. Whilst mutuality is firmly defended by trade organizations such as the BSA (as a visit to its web site proves), it is difficult to see precisely what benefits can come from it, as societies are drawn further into the web of the marketplace and away from their traditional roles. Indeed, one can argue that throughout the twentieth century societies have been more concerned about their collective and individual market share than about the principles of mutuality. Whilst their concerns about keeping mortgage rates at affordable levels during the 1970s might have partly reflected their mutual background (although they were no doubt heavily influenced by government policy during the same period), these concerns were not replicated during the bust cycle in the late 1980s and 1990s, at which point societies were rather more concerned with efficient collection of arrears and repossessions. Market share was equally important to societies during the lending boom in the 1930s when the 'builders' pool' arrangements effectively protected their surpluses and signalled a decline in the quality of building standards. The 1980s deregulation simply made apparent what was already the case.

3.2 Housebuilding and the Pursuit of Profit[7]

One consequence of the deregulation initiatives of the early and mid-1980s was that there was a mass of credit available for house purchase. The majority of the market was 'second hand' – that is, houses which had already been in the sector – and involved households moving (usually upmarket). At the same time the structure of the new housebuilding industry proved to be inefficient in that it was unable to respond to the increase in prices: '. . . a 1% increase in real house prices only led to a 0.16% increase in [building] starts' (Ball, 1996, p. 38). In fact, the construction industry has been broadly declining in the post-war era, with periods of 'feast and famine'. This provides an example of a comparatively unregulated part of the housing market, which supposedly is subject to the principles of the 'market', but which here occupies our attention as a regulatory failure. The dominance of the profit motive, together with the cycles in the house purchase industry, have combined to create this failure. Ball's pessimistic prognosis should be borne in mind:

'The *core argument* is that a combination of characteristics associated with the exceptionally low current level of demand, its extreme volatility and the internal organisation of the industry have created a supply system that invests relatively little in production and training, and hence produces unsophisticated products at comparatively high cost. Housing construction is trapped in a low productivity vicious circle. This unfortunate situation can be neither simply nor quickly remedied.' (1996, p. 2)

Home ownership had its first major increase in tenure share during the 1920s and 1930s. This was due to a peculiar combination of factors: strong demand for housing; cheap labour due to mass unemployment; falling land prices; and cheap building inputs (such as bricks, roof tiles, and cement) (Ball, 1983, pp. 30–1). Housebuilding at this time was *speculative*, in that property was built for the general housing market rather than particular client(s). This structure of housing provision has been the dominant mode of production throughout the post-war era. The housebuilding cycle depends upon construction costs: 'When building costs race ahead of house prices, profitability falls, and vice versa' (Ball, 1986a, p. 19); and when profitability falls, housebuilding also falls (*ibid*).

In the post-war era, construction costs have grown faster than house prices, which generally explains why it is not profitable to build more houses (*ibid*, p. 20). Crucially, profits lie elsewhere. It is suggested that there are three major profit-making opportunities in the construction industry: building profits; land development gain; and extra profits (Duncan, 1986, p. 17). It is the latter two which have dominated the profit-making within the industry. This has been the reason why the industry has contracted so that it is now dominated by the largest firms and the smallest firms. The largest firms bought up the medium-sized firms in order to make a profit out of the land held by those firms (Ball, 1983).

Land development gain occurs when, for example, the infrastructure develops so as to make the site a 'good market proposition' (Duncan, 1986, p. 17). So, for example, 'It would be interesting to know how many millionaires have been made out of people owning land near the new M25' (Ball, 1986a, p. 20).

Extra profits occur when housebuilders are able to sell their houses at above normal prices so generating greater profits (Duncan, 1986, p. 18). This happens, for example, when there is a mass of available credit (during boom periods) or when tax relief enables higher prices to be charged (during the 1980s, for example, tax relief on mortgage payments at marginal taxation levels meant that higher prices could be charged). With building societies and other lenders more wary of lending in the 1990s, after the collapse of the housing market in the late 1980s, and with mortgage tax relief abolished, the extra profits which the industry might generate have become more limited (although salary increases and bonuses paid to certain employees suggest that the top end of the market should continue to generate such profits).

The housebuilding market is now dominated by the volume builders, who are able to spread their risks geographically and between different niches of the market (between, say, starter homes and retirement homes). Over the last 15 years or so, the largest volume builders have increased their market share from 39 per cent to 51 per cent; 14 firms, building more than 2,000 homes per annum, occupy a third of the market, although these firms were worst hit by the recession (Ball, 1996, pp. 30–32). Individual firms have grown over the years through takeovers and mergers with other firms aimed primarily at capturing more land.

The industry's need for development land causes the industry to build-up land banks. During the periodic 'bust' parts of the housing cycle, land is generally cheaper and the industry tends to buy its land then (although this can also inflate the price of land and during this part of the cycle landowners may not put their land on the market). Buying land during 'boom' years is more expensive and thus increases the costs of the development. Thus, most housebuilders tend to have land banks which also minimize their exposure to poor sales (see Ball, 1996, Ch. 5).

The periodic highs and lows of the market mean that subcontracting plays an important role in the industry. Machinery is hired-out rather than owned by housebuilders, and they generally opt for building materials which do not require overly skilled labour. Subcontracting creates problems in its own right, for it can be expensive, the labour force can be of poor quality and untrained ('casualization'), can deliver late (particularly in times of market pressure when the subcontractors are busy on different projects), and makes the housebuilding process less easy to manage. When the Department of the Environment, Transport and the Regions (DETR) calls for the construction process to operate in a 'sustainable' way (DETR, 1998), it must compete against the industry's required profit margin and normal *modus operandi*. The market is notoriously volatile, and this makes housebuilders conservative: 'If the risk of not selling a completed house is high, housebuilders are likely to compound their risk assessment of new building techniques and products. This means that innovations are even less likely to be introduced' (Ball, 1996, p. 29).

In 1996, the Department of the Environment (DoE) was finally forced to take account of the imbalance in the supply of, and demand for, housing. For a considerable number of years, the supply of housing has not kept pace with the demand for housing (although this is politically contentious) (see, for example, House of Commons Environment Committee, 1981). The extent of housing need is unclear, partly because its method of assessment 'can be challenged because there is not a 'neutral' method of calculating it' (House of Commons Environment Committee, 1996, para. 51). However, it now seems to be generally accepted that there will be an additional 4.4 million households before the year 2016 (DoE,

1996; DETR, 1998, para. 16). In 1998, the 'March for the Countryside' collectively expressed the concern of many that housebuilding on 'greenfield' – broadly, rural – sites should be kept to a minimum and that 'brownfield' – or urban – sites should be redeveloped. Responsibility for deciding whether any particular development may go ahead or not belongs to the local authority planning regime, which is closely governed by central 'guidance'.

In the post-war period this guidance has steadily become more favourable to developers. The problem, simply stated, is that brownfield, rehabilitation schemes are expensive and the costs are difficult to estimate with any certainty at the outset. Thus, risk assessment – that is, assessment of the risk to the company's profits of developing the site – is difficult. New developments on greenfield sites are cheaper and can be costed reasonably precisely. The DoE's aim in 1995 was 'to ensure half of all new housing is built on reused sites' (DoE, 1995, p. 47); this has since been updated to 60 per cent (DETR, 1998, para. 39). However, Ball argues that most redevelopment has been of commercial properties (the 'warehouse' flat, for example, so ubiquitous in 1980s London): 'New supply of such land will be very limited in the future, and the easiest pieces of derelict land have generally been developed first so that conversion of what still exists will probably become more difficult and expensive' (1996, p. 39). Thus, the market may well not deliver what the government needs it to deliver on this issue.

Conclusion

This chapter has considered two separate parts of the home ownership system, providing two contrasting examples of regulation. On the one hand, the building societies have been fairly tightly regulated for most of this century, but compensation for that structure came through various privileges that gave them a head start in the marketplace. When other organizations found themselves in a position in which they might compete (as well as building societies beginning to compete in others' traditional business areas), the regulatory structure of the societies was conveniently altered largely in line with their wishes. This legislation, however, misjudged the demands of the marketplace and societies have adopted differing responses to its challenges (for example, changing their status and/or campaigning for new legislation). In 1996, the legislation was changed again to coincide with the interests of the societies. The point here is that the principle legislative provisions (on their allowable purposes) have been designed to allow societies to expand – under the aegis of so-called deregulation initiatives (or rather rule substitution) – and in so doing the relationship between societies and legislators (i.e. government) has reflected concomitant interests. Even so, the failure of different legislative regulatory structures is not surprising, for its fits neatly into the regulatory failure category.

Similarly, regulatory failure of the marketplace has been exposed through the analysis of the mechanisms of production of houses for the market. This has particular resonance in considering the poignant question, 'where shall we live?' The problem is that we shall live wherever the housebuilding industry is able to achieve profit maximization and not where government wishes to set as targets (however, relevant these may be). We have strayed here onto the patch of planning lawyers, but there is considerable overlap as the production of housing is one of the critical issues in housing law and one which housing law has ignored with monotonous regularity.

Further Reading:

On building society law, see A. Arora (1997), *Practical Banking and Building Society Law*, Oxford: Hart. Various loose-leaf collections cover building societies and the construction process. Various texts cover environmental law (and the planning system). However, analytical accounts of law in this area are generally hard to find. Policy studies tend to be more accessible: see, for example, A. Murie *et al.* (1976), *Housing Policy and the Housing System*, London: Allen & Unwin, pp. 148–170. On building societies, the following provide useful points of reference from varying perspectives: M. Boleat (1983), *The Building Society Industry*, London: Allen & Unwin; T. Gough, (1982), *The Economics of the Building Societies*, London: Macmillan; D. Hawes (1986), *Building Societies – The Way Forward*, SAUS Occasional Paper 26, Bristol: School for Advanced Urban Studies, University of Bristol. The BSA also has a useful web site which contains details of its various activities, together with summaries of recent legislation. For an empirical study of new build, see R. Forrest & A. Murie (1993), *New Homes for Home Owners: A Study of New Building and Vacancy Chains in Southern England*, London: HMSO; see also J. Short (1982), *Housing in Britain: The Post War Experience*, London: Methuen, Ch. 5. On the relationship between planning and housing, see especially G. Bramley & C. Watkins (1996), *Steering the Housing Market*, Bristol: Policy Press. On problems created by the housebuilding industry, see V. Karn & L. Sheridan (1994), *New Homes in the 1990s – A Study of Design, Space and Amenity in Housing Association and Private Sector Production*, York: Joseph Rowntree Foundation; in the context of the New Labour government's emphasis on 'sustainability', see DETR (1998), *Sustainable Development: Opportunities for Change, Sustainable Construction*, London: DETR; also the government is currently consulting on regulating certain aspects of the building industry: DETR (1998), *Combating Cowboy Builders*, London: DETR. Chapter 12 below deals with the regulatory structures of the right to buy and the right to buy respectively in the council and RSL sectors.

Endnotes

1. At the same time, concerns have developed that the current levels of home ownership are unsustainable, particularly in the context of the casualization of

the labour market (see, for example, Williams, 1997; Dwelly, 1997; Ch. 12 below).

2. The word 'speculative' refers to the fact that houses built by such companies are commonly built with no particular market in mind. Thus, they are speculative in terms of the potential purchaser.

3. This policy was 'anomalous' in the tax system for it charged tax on 'assets that yielded no cash income' (Holmans, 1987, pp. 271–274).

4. As opposed to in-depth analysis of building regulations, construction contracts, and the planning system.

5. Note that when we discuss non-profit-making organizations, we say that they make 'surpluses' although those same surpluses are the profits of openly capitalistic companies. The difference is simply semantic.

6. Under these schemes, insurance companies insured societies against a proportion of losses from bad debts, i.e. outstanding mortgage less repossession value. The cost of purchasing these schemes was passed on to borrowers who, nevertheless, also retain(ed) their contractual obligations to repay the lender on default. Thus, societies were *doubly* insured. It was this factor which bolstered lenders during the recession (Stephens, 1993, p. 309).

7. The following is a summary of the important work of Michael Ball: 1983; 1986a; 1986b; 1996.

Bibliography

Balchin, P. (1995), *Housing Policy: An Introduction*, London: Routledge

Ball, M. (1983), *Housing Policy and Economic Power: The Political Economy of Owner Occupation*, London: Methuen

Ball, M. (1986a), *Home Ownership: A Suitable Case for Reform*, London: Shelter

Ball, M. (1986b), 'Housing analysis: time for a theoretical refocus?', vol 1, *Housing Studies*, 147

Ball, M. (1996), *Housing and Construction: A Troubled Relationship?*, Bristol: Policy Press

Black, J. (1998), 'Talking about Regulation', *Public Law*, 77

Boddy, M. (1980), *The Building Societies*, London: Macmillan

Boddy, M. (1989), 'Financial deregulation and UK housing finance: government–building society relations and the Building Societies Act, 1986', vol 4, *Housing Studies*, 92

Boddy, M. and Lambert, C. (1988), *The Government–Building Society Connection: From Mortgage Regulation to the Big Bang*, SAUS Working Paper 75, Bristol: School for Advanced Urban Studies, University of Bristol

Bowley, E. (1948), *Housing and the State*, London: Allen & Unwin

Building Societies Association (BSA) (1983), *The Future Constitution of Building Societies*, London: BSA

Building Societies Association (BSA) (1984), *New Legislation for Building Societies*, London: BSA

Clarke, S. and Ginsburg, N. (1975), 'The political economy of housing', in *Political Economy and the Housing Question*, London: London School of Economics

Craig, P. (1986), 'The house that jerry built? Building societies, the State and the politics of owner-occupation', vol 1, *Housing Studies*, 87

Department of the Environment (DoE) (1995), *Our Future Homes: Opportunity, Choice, Responsibility*, Cm 2901, London: HMSO

Department of the Environment (DoE) (1996), *Household Growth: Where Shall we Live?*, Cm 3471, London: HMSO

Department of the Environment, Transport and the Regions (DETR) (1998), *Planning for the Communities of the Future*, London: DETR

Doling, J. and Ford, J. (1991), 'The changing face of home ownership: building societies and household investment strategies', vol 19, *Policy and Politics*, 109

Duncan, S. (1986), 'House building, profits and social efficiency in Sweden and Britain', vol 1, *Housing Studies*, 11

Dwelly, T. (ed.) (1997), *Sustainable Home Ownership: The Debate*, Coventry: Chartered Institute of Housing

Gibb, K. and Munro, M. (1991), *Housing Finance in the UK: An Introduction*, London: Macmillan

Hawes, D. (1986), *Building Societies – The Way Forward*, SAUS Occasional Paper 26, Bristol: School for Advanced Urban Studies, University of Bristol

HM Treasury (1996), *Proposals for a New Building Societies Bill*, London: Treasury

Holmans, A. (1987), *Housing Policy in Britain*, London: Croom Helm

House of Commons Environment Committee (1981), *Department of Environment's Housing Policies*, HC 383, London: HMSO

House of Commons Environment Committee (1996), *Housing Need*, HC 22-I, London: HMSO

James, R. (1997), *Private Ombudsman and Public Law*, Aldershot: Dartmouth

Kearns, A. and Stephens, M. (1997), 'Building societies: changing markets, changing governance', in P. Malpass (ed), *Ownership, Control and Accountability: The New Governance of Housing*, Coventry: Chartered Institute of Housing

Mabey, S. and Tillet, P. (1980), *Building Societies: The Need for Reform*, London: Bow Group

Merrett, S. (1982), *Owner Occupation in Britain*, London: Routledge

Niner, P. (1975), *Local Authority Housing Policy and Practice – A Case Study Approach*, Occasional Paper No 31, Birmingham: Centre for Urban and Regional Studies, University of Birmingham

Piratin, P. (1978), *Our Flag Stays Red*, London: Lawrence & Wishart

Pryke, M. and Whitehead, C. (1994), 'An overview of mortgage-backed securitisation in the UK', vol 9, *Housing Studies*, 75

Saunders, P. (1990), *A Nation of Home Owners*, London: Unwin Hyman

Smallwood, D. (1992), 'Building societies: builders or financiers?', in J. Birchall (ed.), *Housing Policy in the 1990s*, London: Routledge

Stephens, M. (1993), 'Finance for owner occupation in the UK: the sick man of Europe?', vol 21, *Policy and Politics*, 307

Stephens, M. (1997), 'Windfall wars', in J. Goodwin and C. Grant (eds), *Built to Last?*, London: Roof

Stewart, A. (1996), *Rethinking Housing Law*, London: Sweet & Maxwell

4   Regulating the 'Voluntary Housing Movement': The Effect of Private Finance on 'Social' Housing

'In a sense it's incidental that we build houses because it is now about finance and not about housing'. (Pryke, 1994, p. 249)

For centuries, the voluntary housing movement has plugged gaps in the provision of low-cost housing, for example, through alms houses and those engaged in what became known as 'five per cent philanthropy' (the provision of accommodation at below market rents). The last quarter of the twentieth century provided challenges to the core ideals of the sector as providers of low-cost housing. The generic term for this so-called voluntary housing movement, housing associations, was also changed to reflect the different environment of provision of social housing, for after the Housing Act 1996 they became known as 'registered social landlords' (hereafter RSLs).[1]

The central reason for these challenges came in the late 1980s when RSLs were the vehicle chosen by Nicholas Ridley, the then Secretary of State for the Environment, to replace the role of local authorities in the provision of accommodation for those in housing need. The move to 'enabling' within local government, was supposed to be matched by a competitive quasi-market amongst RSLs who were to become the providers of such accommodation (see Bramley, 1993; Goodlad, 1993). Breaking the near-monopoly of state housing provision was meant also to open up the sector, and, in the process, to increase the efficiency and effectiveness of the 'market' for social renting – even though it had never been shown that RSLs were more efficient and effective than local authorities (Centre for Housing Research, 1989).

In the 1980s, RSLs moved from the margins to centre stage (Langstaff, 1992). One can illustrate this by considering their market share in England from 1981 to 1996: in 1981, RSLs accounted for 2.3 per cent of the housing market – around 7.5 per cent of the social housing sector[2] – and managed around 422,000 properties; in 1996, RSLs had a 4.6 per cent market share – accounting for around 20.8 per cent of the social housing sector – and managed around 946,000 properties. Such development is phenomenal and was facilitated by considerable manipulation of the social housing market.

RSLs largely develop property for rent and act as landlords. However, many also build properties for sale, either outright or on terms commonly referred to as shared ownership (although this actually is misleading for it simply refers, most commonly, to long leaseholds: see Ch. 12 for analysis). Consequently, they also take part in the government's programme to increase the number of home owners in the country (this might also be justified by reference to the need to develop 'balanced estates': see Page, 1993).

The 'social' element of RSLs can be found in statements that they are non-profit-making bodies which provide housing at low-cost for those who need it. The central criteria for registration are that the RSL is non-profit-making as well as having among its objects or powers, 'the provision, construction, improvement or management' of housing for letting or to be used as hostels or as part of a co-operative (s. 1(2), Housing Act 1996). Non-profit-making is defined as not trading for profit or not to pay interest or dividends above a rate of 5 per cent (s 1(3); see also Alder & Handy, 1997, p. 22).

Registration is with a body known as the Housing Corporation. This brings the benefits of being able to access public finance with the concomitant obligation to submit to the Corporation's regulatory powers. Currently, over 2,000 RSLs are registered (and many more are not).[3] The benefits of registration are palpable: in 1996/97, RSLs spent £1.078 billion of public money mixed with £900 million of private finance; the pinnacle of the movement was reached in 1992/93 when £2.369 billion of public money was spent together with £950 million of private finance (the reason for the increase was that RSLs were chosen as the government's vehicle to assist with the revitalization of the home ownership market).

It can be argued that registration and the (nominal, as we shall argue) notion of non-profit-making are all that binds a disparate group of different organizations together. Historically, their roots come from different periods, reflecting the ideas and ideals of charity and housing management from those periods. So, thirteenth century alms houses are mixed up, in the legal definition of RSLs, with philanthropic organizations founded by Rowntree and Cadbury, as well as organizations set up to meet the Rachman-induced crisis in private renting in the 1960s (of which the Notting Hill Housing Trust is a prominent member). One might, therefore, argue that the notion of a 'movement', implying common aims and objectives, is stretched even at this level (and quite apart from current dilemmas).

Indeed, the Conservative government threatened to consign any notion of commonality to a bygone, supposedly golden era when it announced that it wished to allow profit-making companies to be able to register on the basis that:

'This will bring the benefits of increased competition, improved value for money in the building programme, wider choice and improved efficiency in housing management.' (DoE, 1995a, p. 30)

Almost the entire consultation process in 1995 was conducted on the basis that profit-making companies would be allowed to register with the Housing Corporation. For example, a linked Consultation Document placed consumerism at the forefront by attempting to define the 'social housing *product*' (DoE, 1995b). However, the profit-making proposal was dropped after careful lobbying. Its last vestiges remain in the ability of registered companies to register with the Corporation also. Whilst this was always the case, its significance lay in a new agenda, the 'local housing company' (see Ch. 6). Copious mentions in policy documentation belie its lack of legal definition. It is merely the label given to a housing association which contains local authority councillors together with tenant representatives and government placepersons, which takes over local authority property. Generous public finance can be levered in through the Estates Renewal Challenge Fund (see Wheal, 1998). In other words, these companies form part of the privatization programme which has altered the tenure of a considerable amount of housing since 1980 and before. Alder is more sanguine:

'The purpose of the local housing company concept appears to be to create an illusion of innovation so as to disadvantage traditional housing associations. . . . Indeed any housing association could structure its governing body to include local and tenant representatives. As in the case of other housing associations the primary legal quality of a local housing company is that it is regulated and its policies set by central government.' (Alder, 1997, p. 37)

In this comment, Alder is also drawing attention to a further discourse, affected by the increasingly politicized context of social housing: the problem of regulation.

Regulation is conducted by the principal funders, central government, through its intermediary the Housing Corporation. However, the Corporation's roots lie in the promotion of voluntary housing (as it was originally conceived in the Housing Act 1964). There is, thus, plenty of room for the well-worn (in socio-legal literature) assertion of 'regulatory capture' (see, for example, Hawkins, 1984); that is, the regulator serves the interests of the regulatee as opposed to broader 'public interest regulatory goals, no matter how vague, ill-defined or contradictory they may be' (Black, 1998, p. 95). Much of the rest of this chapter will be given over to considering the influences on, and of, this form of regulation.

A final prefatory comment is that the current financial regime has encouraged the development of low-cost housing with costs being moved on to tenants who have borne the brunt of the changed funding environment. Paradoxically, then, the concentration on securing finance has often forced RSLs to seem to forget their mission, the provision of low-cost housing to those in need:

'The financial pressures on them have made them increasingly unpopular with tenants and applicants. They have been driven towards amalgamation and rationalisation. They have continued to experience periodic scandals associated with financial management, and their role in rehousing those in the most need has begun to identify them as landlords catering for poor people.' (Murie, 1997, p. 453)

The potential for merger has particularly affected black and ethnic minority RSLs because, despite a five-year funding programme introduced by the Corporation in 1986 and extended to 1996, most such RSLs were small and not best placed in the new financial environment: 'can it be a coincidence that at the very time the housing establishment is finally opening its doors to the black community the financial rules of the game are being turned on their head?' (Chandran, 1990, cited in Mullins, 1992, p. 408).

The first part of this chapter sets the scene for these regulatory developments in considering briefly the history and drawing out some of the key current concerns within the RSL organization(s). Our historical examination begins in 1974 with the significant publicly funded expansion of the RSL movement, although it is readily accepted that the roots of this expansion lie before this period (see Best, 1991). The key date for an appreciation of the current context, though, is 1987, when the DoE issued its White Paper on housing together with a Consultation Document on the future funding of housing associations (as they were then called). This historical analysis is premised on the basis that 'nothing's inevitable', for I will argue that the Conservative's predilection for RSLs was certainly not inevitable. They were simply in the right place at the right time (although it is also true to say that they formed a powerful pressure group) – to adopt a worn phrase used elsewhere, they were 'plannable instruments'.

The second section considers the way the Corporation has responded to the post-1987 environment. Considerable discussion is given over to the way the Corporation's funding and regulatory tactics are determined by central government and private finance. This centres on the critical regulatory document for RSLs: *Performance Standards* (Housing Corporation, 1997a).

The third section outlines and analyses the RSL response to the new funding environment. Of course, many have simply chosen to opt out and are classified as 'non-developing RSLs'. Concerns exist on a number of levels over those that are taking part in the development process as well as over the effect of a somewhat different regulatory environment. The concerns of the developing RSL may well be to keep in line with shifting Housing Corporation regulation, but equally they have to satisfy a multitude of different interests, whilst at the same time concentrating on their financial viability. We will consider the effect on 'voluntariness' of three connected facets of the modern-day existence of many RSLs: professionalization of their governing committees; the move to 'new public management' techniques; as well as risk assessment and risk management.

4.1 Developmental Issues and Future Concerns

Development since 1974

We have already considered the phenomenal growth of the RSL movement during the 1980s and 1990s. This development was, however, never inevitable. The major spurts occurred after the Housing Act 1974 – which introduced a favourable funding regime – and the Housing Act 1988 – which introduced a mixed (public and private) funding regime. The Housing Act 1974 was a Labour government measure, although it was initially promoted by the previous Conservative administration to provide for the rehabilitation of property (Back & Hamnett, 1985, p. 402). That the Act survived at all was significant;[4] that it survived in similar form, with public funding aplenty, led to considerable development within the sector until 1980. This cross-party support was significant, although based upon different rationales. The Conservative administration preferred RSLs 'as semi-private supplements to, covert competitors with, or even potential replacements for local authority housing'; on the other hand, the Labour administration saw the opportunity to create a 'centrally controlled housing service' in contrast to 'the relative autonomy of local authorities' (Noble, 1981, p. 173). Indeed, the rehabilitation of private property would mean that RSLs would take control of some of the privately rented stock, and as such was 'an astute method of achieving social ownership' (Back & Hamnett, 1985, p. 402). It has also been noted that many prominent members of the Labour Party were also supporters of the RSL movement (for example, through one of its arms, the housing cooperative) (see Best, 1991, p. 154).

The 1974 Act contained two major innovations of which, as already mentioned, the most prominent was the new funding mechanism. A treasury-based capital grant, called Housing Association Grant or HAG, was made available to RSLs to cover the difference between the costs of a scheme and the available revenue stream (mostly through rents charged). Additionally, a treasury-based income grant, known as Revenue Deficit Grant or RDG, shored up any subsequent revenue gap. RSLs were, in other words, totally protected within the public sector. A prerequisite of this financial protection was that RSLs were required to register with the Housing Corporation.

The second major innovation of the 1974 Act was that the Housing Corporation – created by the Housing Act 1964 to promote RSLs – gained the power to act as mediator between the RSL and the DoE in the provision of finance (although it had been empowered to provide loans in the Finance Act 1972) as well as gaining powers of monitoring and supervision of RSLs. The subsequent registration process appears to have been chaotic, both in the application and interpretation of registration criteria, as well as a certain bifocalism between promotion and registration models ('. . . the existence of dual functions ensures administrative failure': Noble, 1981, p. 179; see also Lewis & Harden, 1982).

It was the strong level of *public* funding through HAG which ensured that the first Thatcher government lumped RSLs together with local authorities. This was clearly signalled by that government's evident desire to include all RSL properties in their right to buy legislation. Only a House of Lords amendment to that legislation enabled *charitable* RSLs to avoid this consequence of their public-sector funding. The favourable funding regime was also reined in at this time, leading to fewer completions (much to the chagrin of the movement itself).

Nevertheless, by the mid-1980s, RSLs became regarded as key players in the provision of social housing. One problem with the provision of housing by local authorities – for a cost-conscious government – was that any spending by them would count as 'public sector' spending within the treasury conventions. On the other hand, it was possible for RSLs to raise private finance and spend it without it being regarded as public expenditure under the same conventions; only the level of HAG paid out would be regarded as public sector expenditure. This was possible because of the membership of RSLs, which was and remains predominantly within the private sector. Thus, it was the 'voluntarism' of RSLs which enabled the Conservative's to break its self-imposed shackles and begin a significant development programme.

The move towards 'mixed funding' arrangements (that is, a mix of both public and private funding) was justified in a Consultation Paper as creating 'new incentives to associations to deliver their service in the most cost-effective manner, bringing to bear the disciplines of the private sector and strengthening the machinery of public support' (DoE, 1987a, para. 2). The housing White Paper in 1987 praised pre-existing mixed funding arrangements as facilitating 'improved efficiency and allow[ing] public resources to be used more effectively' (DoE, 1987b, para. 4.5). Obtaining private finance was to be made easier by bringing RSLs within the definition of bodies able to grant *private-sector* tenancies in the Housing Act 1988, as a result of which rents could be charged up to market levels, thus ensuring a rate of return on investment. So, tenants would bear the burden of the new market involvement and, realistically in the new regime of providing housing at increased rental costs to low income tenants, it followed that reliance would be placed upon the individual subsidy of Housing Benefit.

A number of ends were served by these reforms, much of which took place outside the strictures of legislation and within the regulatory powers of the Housing Corporation and its funding from the DoE. Huge benefits could be foreseen by those able and willing to enter into development.

The Changed Environment

The changed environment can be considered by looking at five aspects of the new regime: risk; reliance on Housing Benefit; central control; the role of the Housing Corporation; and the effect on the voluntary housing organization(s). These five aspects form the bedrock of the analysis of RSLs in the rest of this chapter.

Risk

HAG had previously been paid at the end of the project and thus bore the brunt of increases in development costs. After the 1988 Act, HAG became 'frontloaded' – that is, paid at the outset on the basis of assumed costs and calculated against figures set by the DoE through the Housing Corporation (these are termed Total Cost Indicators, or TCIs)[5]. Any unforeseen increases in development costs would be the responsibility of the RSL. RDG was abandoned together with contributions to major repairs (see, generally, Randolph, 1993; Langstaff, 1992).

Private finance brings its own risks. For example, the 1987 White Paper assumed that finance would be gained on the basis of low-start payments (i.e. low payments at the beginning, increasing over time). However, developing RSLs have found that low-start finance makes any subsequent development more difficult. A conventional interest-rate-based package enables RSLs to use properties developed earlier as security against further loans (see Chaplin *et al.*, 1995, p. 13).

Added to these developmental risks, the most significant risk is the threat of insolvency and repossession (although increased competition has also led to mergers and takeovers, see below). The level of risk will also differ depending on the exposure of the RSL to the market. What is perhaps less obvious is that the level of risk will also differ depending upon the size of the association prior to the move to mixed funding. RSLs with larger portfolios are able to use their asset wealth as security to gain greater loans and increase their own portfolios at a rate unavailable to smaller RSLs. Thus, larger RSLs, often operating on a national basis, have been able to capture most of the available funding. They have thus increased their proportion of total RSL stock. In 1983, RSLs with more than 2,500 dwellings owned 47 per cent of the total stock in the sector. By 1995/96, 105 RSLs with more than 2,500 dwellings (or five per cent of the total number of RSLs) owned 70 per cent of the total stock (Housing Corporation, 1997b, Table 2.2).

Reliance on Housing Benefit or 'Political Risk'

A basic policy preference of the Conservative Party was to reduce capital grants and increase individual subsidies, such as Housing Benefit. In so doing, rent levels were bound to rise; more so in a mixed funding environment involving higher levels of income repayment by RSLs to their lenders. At first, it was argued that Housing Benefit would 'take the strain' of the higher rents. As an increasing number of their tenants have become reliant on Housing Benefit, so too have RSLs and their funders. Governments being notoriously fickle, this was a dangerous policy option embraced by RSLs; and one which may well be unravelling as the allowable rent for Housing Benefit has begun to be challenged within the Housing Benefit administrative system.

Central government's concern at increases in the Housing Benefit budget have caused benefit levels to be reduced. As 68 per cent of RSL tenants were in receipt of Housing Benefit in 1996 (compared with 53 per cent in 1991: Wilcox, 1997, Table 111b), any limits on the Housing Benefit budget will presumably have a deleterious effect on RSLs (particularly smaller ones which are less able to pool rents). RSL rents were rarely challenged for Housing Benefit purposes until recently (through referral by the local authority to the rent officer – see Ch. 11). This seems to have been because, quite simply, local authorities (which are in charge of the distribution and adjudication of the Housing Benefit system) and RSLs (major recipients of Housing Benefit) have relied on each other to an increasing extent. It would not have been in the interest of the former to restrict the latter's rental stream. Furthermore:

'. . . Housing Benefit officers felt that, if an [RSL] could justify its rents in terms of its costs, then the rent had effectively been sanctioned by central government. The fact that the rent was above the prevailing private sector level did not matter. The Housing Benefit service did not generally attempt to compare association rents with private sector rents because of the different markets in which each operated . . .' (Chaplin *et al.*, 1995, p. 36)

The new requirement that rent officers must consider rent levels against a 'local reference rent' (see Ch. 11) does not apply to RSLs yet as, in most cases, local authorities are not under a duty to refer RSL rents to the rent officer.[6] Nevertheless, local authorities can refer RSL rent to the rent officer for Housing Benefit purposes where the rent is considered to be unreasonably high or the property too large for the claimant. There were about 3–4,000 referrals on this basis in 1995 (Bramley, 1995, p. 29). The sketchy evidence available is that of those referred to the rent officer 'the average property-specific rents . . . were further below the level of local reference rents than in the average private landlord case' (Wilcox, 1997, p. 13). Limits on Housing Benefit therefore mean that the RSL's rental stream is at risk (which may well impact upon allocations policies and practices).

Private funders want RSLs to charge below-market rents so that they have greater leverage on rents if the landlord gets into financial difficulty. If rents are already at market levels, they cannot be put up any further. Rent levels have, however, risen considerably. Part of the problem was that, in the crucial early period after the introduction of mixed funding, the Corporation stressed the need for RSLs to charge 'affordable' rents without defining the term (leading to frustration that brims over in some publications – see, for example, Randolph, 1993, p. 44 – 'Rents were at the same time to be both deregulated but restrained!'). Only recently has the Corporation stepped in to control rent rises at the same time as the government is reviewing its commitment to welfarism and Housing Benefit (see DSS, 1998, Ch. 9 concerning fraud and Ch. 11 below).

'Rolling back the frontiers of the State'
The philosophy of the 1980s was increasing central control over local institutions. As McAuslan put it, 'The dominant political-cum-constitutional issue is centralisation and authoritarianism. The dominant administrative-cum-economic perspective is public choice, . . .' (1989, p. 403). The Thatcher administration's interest in RSLs mirrored, to a certain extent, the motivations of the previous Labour administration. Central government could control RSLs' local provision and development of housing at the same time as withdrawing funding for local authorities. This control could be exercised through the purse strings – the amount of money given to the Housing Corporation for development. The government was (and remains) able to set the priorities for the development programme and, in this way, to influence who is allocated capital grants through the Corporation. Furthermore, the government is able to set the average total cost that it is prepared to fund through HAG (under the pre-Housing Act 1996 scheme) and Social Housing Grant or 'SHG' (under the post-Housing Act 1996 scheme), as well as fixing the complete scheme costs through Total Cost Indicators ('TCIs') which relate to acquisition costs, work costs, and on-costs (see Housing Corporation 1998 for explanation). Thus, it is able to influence who gets funding, as well as the level of that funding. Initially, the level of funding was fixed at 75 per cent, but this has gradually declined to the current level of 54 per cent (HC Circ F2 – 26/97 sets out the levels for 1998–9). The remainder is required to be raised through private finance or other sources (sometimes involving local authority assistance). If the key to obtaining private finance is the promise of a level of public funding, as is often the case, then RSLs must also play the government's game.

Sometimes, the level of government involvement has unforeseen consequences which affect wider policy. A classic example of this has been the move away from rehabilitation (a key foundation of the post-1974 expansion). Rehabilitation work is, quite simply too risky in the 'frontloaded' funding environment. At the beginning of a rehabilitation project, estimations of capital costs are not always clear and easy to budget, because it is not always possible to predict how much work is required to a building. On the other hand, the development of new sites is much easier to budget and, consequently, less risky (see Best, 1997, pp. 115–16; Randolph, 1993, pp. 50–1; Harrison, 1992, pp. 22–3). In the context of the debate about brownfield *v.* greenfield planning policy, this element is commonly forgotten (see DoE, 1997).

The Role of the Housing Corporation
The Housing Corporation's role has similarly changed with the impact of mixed funding. Previously, the Corporation had adopted a 'bottom-up'

process of regulation, 'which emphasised consultation and a combined approach of the Corporation and associations working together' (Harrison, 1992, p. 28; also Mullins, 1997, pp. 307–8). A former Chief Executive of the Housing Corporation has argued that '[the Corporation] now sees its role as an executive, for government policy, whether or not that policy is perceived to promote and assist [housing] associations' (House of Commons Environment Committee, 1993, para. 21). Part of the old role of the Corporation – promotion of the interests of the RSLs – seemed to have been subordinated by the new role – promoting the success of the government's programme:

> 'Undoubtedly as the co-ordinator of the new providers of social housing, there is a pressure on the Corporation to deliver success to the government in terms of measurable achievements as a result of the changes brought about by the Act. However, exactly what this means in detail does not yet seem to have been addressed within the Housing Corporation.' (*ibid*)

This obligation to central government reflects only one of the sometimes conflicting interests which the Corporation has to satisfy in fulfilling its regulatory role. A reflection of the dominance of central government interests came with the release of a Housing Corporation Circular effectively instructing RSLs not to house asylum-seekers and illegal immigrants in line with central government's policy (HC Circ R3 – 04/97). The New Labour government 'intend[ed] to invite the Housing Corporation to consider relaxing its guidance' (DETR press release 529, 18 December 1997), suggesting that the relationship between government and the Corporation is based upon exhortations (as to which, see Black, 1998); whereas the regulatory muscle clearly lies with the government who set up, fund, and appoint members of the Corporation (and can just as easily close it down).

A further set of interests of increasing import are those of private lenders. Whilst private lenders protect their own interests through, for example, setting out their contractual security rights, the Corporation also needs to satisfy private lenders that it provides extra security. This is to attract (conservative) private lenders into a novel market in the first place as well as to retain confidence. Increasingly, this is the interest which is most obviously protected within the regulatory scheme (see below).

Finally, the RSLs interest must also be balanced within the regulatory arrangements. It might be expected that the consideration for receipt of public funding would be the loss of control of certain matters, such as financial accountability. However, the Housing Corporation's statement of its regulatory powers threatens the diversity of the 'movement'. (There is, of course, an irony here: at once, we regard RSLs as forming part of a movement but, at the same time, we are saying we value their diversity.) There is some truth in this, although the Corporation has recently made some attempt to diversify its regulation through providing different regulatory schema for different types of RSL (small/large, for example). However, in many respects, such a change obfuscates the problem that, for some, regulation is anathema, for it overly constricts their entrepreneurialism. Indeed, if one word captures the current spirit of the RSLs movement, it is entrepreneurialism.

Clashing Cultures
The level of control exerted by central government, the Housing Corporation, and private finance finds its ultimate impact in the RSLs' level and type of service provision. RSLs are voluntary organizations. People become involved in them primarily because of a desire 'to contribute to society and/or help the needy' (82.2 per cent in one survey said this was their motivation: Kearns, 1990, p. 44). Such idealism is gradually eroding in favour of professionalization together with the 'new public management ethos' (Walker, 1998). Indeed, the derivation of the quotation beginning this chapter proclaims the centrality of finance in this approach. Allegations that RSL management structures operate like 'self-perpetuating oligarchies' – something like the 'old boy' network – which contrast sharply with housing officers' move towards the new ethos, have been made persistently.

At the same time, this new ethos is also leading to expanding competition between RSLs. In what has been described as the era of 'comfort' – 1974–1981 – RSLs often worked together and respected each other's 'territory', a process known as pepperpotting (see Bramley, 1993, p. 164). Locally based RSLs remained firmly local. The new environment is one of competition for reduced funds. Larger RSLs are best placed because they are able to pool the capital costs of development across their whole stock and are therefore able to build more for less – they can often reduce their development costs below the level prescribed by government in their TCIs. If the major criterion for the receipt of public funds is cost-effectiveness – or building as many properties as possible for less public money – then such RSLs are in the best position to 'win' public funding by 'selling the family silver' (Best, 1997, p. 116).

Locally based RSLs lose out in this competitive process because their limitation is that they are local. In this context, it is perhaps no surprise that many of the former local RSLs have changed their names to reflect broader spatial interests (for example, North Housing Association became Home Housing Association). Malpass' consideration of RSLs' involvement in Bristol showed that, whilst large national RSLs actually had relatively few dwellings in Bristol, five such landlords nevertheless gained potentially important status by being included in the 'Bristol Housing Partnership' with the local authority, and thus were frontrunners for public funding. Informed speculation suggested that their involvement was due to the influence of the Housing Corporation (Malpass, 1997).

The removal of the element of HAG relating to repairs equally threatens the non-profit element of the RSL's business. In order to provide for maintenance services as well as to demonstrate their solvency to private financiers, RSLs must operate at a level of surplus (known as the 'rent surplus fund'). Costs are passed onto the landlord's tenants in the form of increased rents. Further, in order to maintain operational efficiency, the level of void properties and rent arrears must be kept at a minimum at a time when housing management has been 'downsized': 'housing officers are now more concerned with collecting rents and letting homes to ensure that the resources are available to repay mortgages and to satisfy financial institutions that they are efficient and effective organisations such that they can command further loans' (Walker, 1998, p. 78).

The final element of 'clashing cultures' is the extent to which RSLs' developments and allocations are controlled, not by themselves, but by the power of other agencies, such as the local authority. The move by local authorities towards an 'enabling' role has meant that they have stopped developing. They have, however, been able to control the level of RSL development through, for example, having partner RSLs (which the Housing Corporation takes into account in considering whether to fund development) and/or the provision of cheap land with planning permission in return for allocation rights (which therefore reduces the RSL's development costs). Thus, local authorities have found new ways of influencing not only the level of new building in their area, but also *who does it*.

These major tensions appear throughout the rest of the discussion in this chapter, which concentrates on the role of the Housing Corporation in funding and regulating RSLs as well as the ways in which RSLs manage and finance themselves. They form the essential backdrop to the difficult changes under way within the sector. Their global manifestation in practice relates to the loss of *autonomy* – who runs the RSL?

However, these tensions also give rise to a paradox which claws open the treasury-led housing policy of the Thatcher/Major era. An essential part of the argument for putting a halt to local authority housing was that local authorities had become monolithic bureaucracies, unresponsive to their tenants and unable to manage efficiently, effectively, and economically. In short, local authorities were not value for money (in the language of what has been termed 'the blue rinse' of administration: Harlow and Rawlings, 1997, Ch. 5). There have also been concerns about the design and build quality of some local authority developments.

The Thatcher/Major axis used RSLs to break the local authority monopoly (although not completely) but, in the process, also effectively encouraged RSLs, through the mixed funding regime, to become large-scale organizations which are characterized by similar attributes to the local government regime. There are, however, two differences: RSLs' membership is unelected and larger RSLs are nationally based. Many RSLs are finding it difficult to justify even their primary mission of allocation according to need: 'By the mid-1990s, rents for new homes were likely to require those working as a bus driver, postman, clerical officer or bricklayer all to become reliant on Housing Benefit' (Best, 1997, p. 115). Equally, the importance given to finance has had an impact on the output of RSLs in terms of build and design quality. Karn and Sheridan have noted 'a continuing decline in the standards of homes built by housing associations' (1994, p. 93); in 1991/2 68 per cent of newly built general needs accommodation was built 5 per cent or more below the Parker Morris space standards (see further Goodchild & Karn, 1997).

We may not have quite reached the stage of the predatory RSL, looking to monopolize its position through takeovers, mergers and the like (in similar vein to housebuilders), however we cannot be far off it.

4.2   Mixed Funding, Regulation and The Housing Corporation

The Housing Corporation is the provider of public funding to RSLs, as well as being the principal regulator. Despite concerns about this dual role – on the basis that the type of information required for each purpose may intersect but, nevertheless, require different emphases – the Corporation retained both in the Housing Act 1996. Indeed, the regulatory arm was further empowered in cases of, for example, insolvency (although the original clauses in the Bill had to be redefined to take account of the interests of private finance). It is certainly true that the Corporation has taken some time to evolve satisfactorily into the current mixed-funding regime (see Harrison, 1992, pp. 28–31). For example, the move from backdated HAG to frontloaded HAG caught out the Corporation in its first year of operation (which involved spending two times the usual grant level) because RSLs required grants to be paid rather speedier than before. As a consequence the Corporation 'literally ran out of money' and had to save face by drawing funding from its agreed programme for the following year (see, for example, Randolph, 1993, pp. 43–4).

In the following discussion the structure splits the mixed-funding mechanism from the discussion about regulation. This is principally a matter of convenience. Readers should note that the two are inextricably linked – the Corporation's ultimate regulatory weapon is the withdrawal of financial support (see Day *et al.*, 1993, p. 14). Furthermore, current regulation also has funding (both public and private) at its heart, for it concerns the *protection* of the funding.

Whilst regulation is, on its face, primarily premised upon RSLs' receipt of, and dependence upon, public funds, the regulatory mechanisms employed also need to satisfy private finance interests. Furthermore, it can be argued that the Corporation is so directed towards the influx of private finance that the concept of 'regulatory capture' is currently more true in respect of the interests of private finance than the RSLs (the opposite of, it has been argued, the earlier position: Mullins, 1997). Thus, even though the regulatory powers were increased in the 1996 Act, it can be argued that this extension has occurred at the same time as the Corporation's role has become weakened.

The Funding Regime

Receipt of Public Funding
Every year, central government makes a capital allocation to the Corporation through a mechanism called the Approved Development Plan. The TCIs are also fixed by the Treasury at the same time as the capital allocation. Central government bases this capital allocation upon treasury calculations, as influenced by the DETR. In turn, the DETR draws upon various documents, such as the Development Plan submitted by the Corporation (which remains secret: see House of Commons Environment Committee, 1993, paras 55–60). However, the impression one gets is that the decision-making power lies with the Treasury, which both sets the level of capital allocation as well as the percentage of public funding in mixed funded-schemes. This is then announced in the budget statement. The weakness of the DoE in the public spending round under the Conservative regime perhaps explains the relative weakness of general housing expenditure. However, be that as it may, it is clear that the Treasury has exerted downward pressure on the public funding available in mixed-funded projects – the proportion began at 75:25 (public:private) and is currently 54:46. Initially, the government's argument for reducing its input was 'falling construction costs and land values' (House of Commons Environment Committee, 1993, para. 81), but this argument has been difficult to sustain as those costs have increased. Treasury involvement has undoubtedly led to a general decline in available public resources together with increasing proportions of private finance being required.

When the Corporation receives its capital allocation (which also covers other projects, such as shared ownership), it distributes it to its regional offices against a set of criteria that have often appeared to be highly misleading. The principles governing this distribution have been suggested as:

'1. The allocations will reflect the distribution of housing need across the country, and
2. The allocations will recognise that in certain inner city areas housing need is further compounded by other forms of social deprivation, e.g. poor environment, low income and high unemployment.' (Alder & Handy, 1996, p. 270)

In order to assist with this capital distribution, the Corporation employs indicators of housing need. Most notoriously, in 1990, the Housing Needs Index used by the Corporation meant that funding shifted away from London (Harrison, 1992, p. 26). Furthermore, one RSL director has referred to a 'north *versus* south' debate in the context of reduced programmes and the inclination of government to avoid implementing the conclusions of its Housing Needs Index in order to focus investment on lower-cost northern regions and thus increase the number of approvals.' (Langstaff, 1992, p. 39) Since this period, local authorities' Housing Investment Programme statements have been taken into account as well.

Allocations to developing RSLs are thereafter made on a discretionary basis, supposedly in accordance with the criteria specified by the Corporation in a General Determination.[7] The current Determination provides the following criteria:

> '(a) the housing needs to be met, their priority within the housing strategy of the local authority, and their priority within the resources available to the Corporation; and
> (b) the value for money and effectiveness of the expenditure taking into account the location, type and standards of dwellings, amenities and services to be provided; and
> (c) the length of the interest in the dwellings held by the [RSL]; and
> (d) the economy, efficiency and effectiveness of the [RSL] concerned; and
> (e) the rents which the [RSL] may charge when the dwellings are let.' (Housing Corporation, 1997a, para. 8)

No definitions are provided of key words such as economy, efficiency and effectiveness. This is to be expected, partly because such words are hardly susceptible to precise definition; partly because they enable the Corporation to have room to manoeuvre in negotiating with RSLs; partly also (no doubt) because an aggrieved applicant for funding would have difficulty in subsequent proceedings in proving that the Corporation exercised its discretion incorrectly.

The Determination provides the bare bones of the scheme and nothing more. It provides no rules about how to apply for funding or, indeed, what limits there might be to any single application (if any). This can be put down to the previous cosy relationship between the Corporation and the RSLs. Equally, the weight given to each factor is difficult to assess. However, it may be noted that, on their face, more criteria are concerned with the value provided by the RSL than with housing need. Translated into actual practice, it may well be that these criteria are consequently weighted in favour of the larger RSLs which have proportionately lower management costs and can afford to cross-subsidize (from earlier developments) in their bids for capital allocations. Such practice appears to have been endorsed by central government in their 1995 Consultation Paper:

> 'The principle underlying the competition for capital grants will be that, other things being equal, the Government should select schemes which produce the lowest overall Exchequer cost, taking account of both the capital and revenue (Housing Benefit and Special Needs Management

Allowance) consequences. This is best for both tenants and taxpayers.' (DoE, 1995b, para. 4.2)

Thus, it may well be that the move from HAG to SHG will also highlight further incentives to the larger RSLs.

A considerable innovation in the Determination lies in the final criterion, the levels of rent payable. This should be linked to the discussion about affordability for tenants and the level of Housing Benefit required to sustain the RSL (see below). On the question of rent-pooling (i.e. spreading the costs of new development amongst all the RSL's tenants, not just those in the new development), the government said that this would be taken into account in the bidding process but also would 'continue to [be] encourage[d]' (DoE, 1995b, para. 4.3 and Appendix C to that document). The confusion about the merits of rent-pooling – encouragement *v* cost-effectiveness – underlines the Treasury's concern that reductions in capital allocations were simply being offset by increases in Housing Benefit. The White Paper exhibits this same concern:

> 'We need to strike the right balance between getting more homes by keeping grant down and the risks of benefit dependency and the benefit costs of higher rent levels. We recognise there are limits to the reductions in grant which can be achieved. If grant is too low and rents rise too far, this can increase public expenditure in the long term.' (DoE, 1995a, p. 27)

In many ways, the capital/revenue dilemma is the fulfilment of the policy option taken in 1987. The confident assertion that Housing Benefit would 'take the strain' appears, in retrospect, to have been somewhat misguided; it was also compounded by the steadfast refusal of both central government and the Housing Corporation to provide any indication of what was meant by the concept of rent 'affordability'.

Private Finance
Without doubt, the major innovation of the 1987 reforms has been the introduction of significant levels of private finance into RSLs. This has also raised significant questions, as we have seen, about the role and nature of RSLs, together with issues concerning their revenue streams. The available research suggests that RSLs were not particularly inventive when it came to raising private loan finance. So, Chaplin *et al.* found that most RSLs (including the larger ones) tended to opt for fairly simple conventional repayment-based loans (1995, pp. 12–13). Furthermore, few had 'active portfolio management policies'. Indeed, RSLs were not so concerned by the 'formal financial conditions' as the level of information required by the lenders (suggesting an underdeveloped level of regulation) (*ibid*, p. 14). More recent evidence, albeit anecdotal, is of a far more sophisticated and creative level of borrowing; for example, RSLs have sought private finance through Eurobond issues (*cf* local authorities'

involvement in the financial futures market to bolster their Housing Revenue Account). Equally, initial concerns at the number of private lenders willing to enter into the RSL market (see for example, House of Commons Environment Committee, 1993, para. 100, referring to 'just two banks and three building societies contributing the bulk of the money so far raised') seem to have been assuaged by the rising number of willing lenders (in a less risky property market).

The factors which private lenders consider in determining the level of risk of development schemes have been defined more by reference to the type of information available. However,

> 'In general terms, the factors looked for by banks and building societies range across the strength of balance sheet, the amount of cash reserves, the association's ability to break even on the property revenue account, the HAG level on the state programme, the association's level of rent arrears (which is a good reflection of a scheme's projected cash flow) and its timing, to the type of funding facility demanded and the type of security offered.' (Pryke, 1994, p. 253)

Subsequently, the Corporation's required production of regulatory material from RSLs has tended to reflect the needs and demands of private lenders. Indeed, more generally in 'social housing' the interests of private lenders have, in many respects, come to dominate. Two classic examples of this trend are the regulation of RSLs and the day-to-day management practices of many RSLs.

Regulatory Strategies: Standards and Influences

From the late 1980s, there has been a general concern about over-regulation, which has led to programmes such as the deregulation initiative. These general concerns about the level of regulation have been mirrored in the changes affecting the regulation of RSLs. Indeed, this regulation might be viewed as a microcosm of many of the issues arising in the modern state.

It is possible to analyse the processes influencing the regulation of RSLs to assess the extent to which the Corporation is influenced by the various interest groups. Nevertheless, these various interest groups, as well as their members, have their own agendas which can hardly be described as one dimensional. For example, it is commonly argued that the Corporation exercises its regulatory powers to protect the public purse – the public/ governmental interest. However, the government interest can equally be protected by increased powers of RSLs to gain private finance (more development at less cost to the public purse). Thus, regulatory standards might be manipulated so as to make RSLs' structures more amenable to review by private funders. Mullins argues that 'The increasing sophistication of financial monitoring [by the Corporation] has undoubtedly been associated with the growth of private finance' (1997, p. 309).

Two examples evidence this shift. First, there has been a move towards requiring RSLs to provide annual accounts similar to those provided by Public Limited Companies (PLCs). This is most convenient to private funders to whom PLC accounts are familiar. Second, there has been a move towards the simplification of performance review reports. Formerly, these were based on a grading (with five grades), with the Corporation providing information about how the RSL might improve (even if the RSL was in the top grading). RSLs criticized these reports, *inter alia*, on the basis that they could not be shown to potential funders (Day *et al.*, 1993, p. 22). The new system involves a grading (with three grades), with 'sanitising performance reports so that [RSLs] can make them available to their funders' (Mullins,1997, p. 309).

The publication of the Housing Corporation's *Performance Standards* (1997a; hereafter '*Standards*'), which also includes housing management guidance, represents a major progression in the regulation of the RSL movement. It has marked out a new dimension to the process. Formerly, regulation was a combination of inspection visits (most commonly to larger RSLs) and provision of documentation. *Standards*, on the other hand, places far greater emphasis on what has become known as 'desk-top monitoring', which broadly requires RSLs to self-certify themselves against governing criteria. This requires governing criteria to be reasonably tightly developed, although this has not been done in *Standards*. Take, for example, the first two sentences of the first Standard (A): 'The governing bodies of RSLs should be properly constituted and independent. They should be suitably skilled, experienced and accountable.' It would be difficult to identify precisely what the Corporation was looking for without any further information. The Corporation does, it is readily admitted, provide interpretations of each standard, however these simply compound the uncertainty. So, for example, the interpretation of this part of Standard A, requires that governing bodies have 'clear terms of reference'. Day and Klein make the same point when they call performance indicators 'tin-openers rather than dials' (1995, para. 3.13).

A further important point about self-certification is that it can become an anodyne exercise:

'As with all systems based on the self-completion of standard questionnaires, it raises questions both about the extent to which it assesses skill in filling in forms as distinct from performance, and about the criteria used by reviewers to identify possible danger signals.' (Day & Klein, 1995, para. 3.10)

The risk of *Standards* becoming anodyne is probably enhanced by the further move to concentrate on 'outputs' rather than 'processes', whilst nevertheless admitting that 'in some cases, the process itself is the key to compliance' (p. 4). Indeed, it is difficult to envisage a difference between the two (a distinction without a difference?).

However, the major concern lies with the *quality or level* of regulation exerted by the Corporation. Whereas much research pierces the divide between law and practice, highlighting the mismatch between the two, it seems extremely unlikely that questionnaires and self-certification will perform a similar task. Thus, it might be argued that the nature and level of regulation exerted by the Corporation is remarkably low, adding to the perception that the operation of RSLs is kept from view (which is compounded by the lack of recent research upon their practices).

In fact, this move towards self-certification reflects the frustration felt at the previous system by both RSLs and Corporation, both in the level of time commitment as well as in the fact that there were limits to the cost-effectiveness of the process. Cost-effectiveness has become one of the guiding principles of the new process (p. 3); indeed, it might be argued that the other guiding principles are so badly drafted that they undermine the *Standards* themselves, suggesting that cost-effectiveness is the primary criterion.

A further guiding principle of the process is supposedly the need to recognise the autonomy of individual RSLs. Increasing regulation almost inevitably involves RSLs relinquishing their individuality and organizational control (see Day *et al.*'s study of RSLs' concerns about the previous system, Ch. 5). Take, for example, the requirement to allocate according to 'greatest housing need' (Standard F). This transpires to be, with one exception, the requirement to allocate in accordance with exactly the same priorities as *local authorities* in the Housing Act 1996, Part VI (Standard F2.1), about which further comment is made in Chapter 9 below. For now, it is necessary to note that this standardization can hardly facilitate autonomy (more particularly the case when it is recalled that RSLs often have clearly defined priorities which may conflict with this).

Perhaps the greatest incursion into the RSLs' autonomy lies in the entirely new control of rent rises. Comment has already been made upon the government's need to control the levels of both capital (grant) and revenue (Housing Benefit) expenditure. Further stacked against the RSLs are other interest groups which have a common interest in rent levels – tenants (including prospective tenants, who might be charged higher rents) and private funders. The latter's interest arises because of the need for flexibility, where necessary. The lower the rent, the higher it will be able to rise before it affects tenants as well as Housing Benefit (which will assist in cases of impending insolvency). In fact, the initial emphasis for greater regulation of rents came from the proposal to allow profit-making companies to take part in the 'social' sector (DoE, 1995b, para. 5.19) and consequently only related to new stock. However, the formula suggested by the DoE – Retail Price Index $+/- X$, or the 'X Factor' (para. 5.20–5.26) – has now appeared in *Standards*, applying to all RSLs. This is defined with a certain amount of precision although the notion of 'affordability to those in low-paid employment' remains as the centrepiece of the Standard (D). Affordability is, to a certain extent, undermined by the fact that the Corporation assesses this, *inter alia*, in the light of 'the need of the RSL to meet its financial obligations, including in particular the need to service outstanding loan debt' (p. 26). Nowhere did the DoE appreciate that controlling rent rises involves controlling the (quasi-)market and, thus, runs contrary to one of the fundamental principles of the tenancies which RSLs now hand out: *rent deregulation* (see further, Ch. 11 below).

The difficulty with the Corporation's incursion into rent-setting policy is that this has the potential to put it in conflict with private lenders if it is too specific and/or mandatory in its requirement. In fact, the Corporation has phrased this Standard as 'advice' and, equally tentatively, that RSLs 'should endeavour' to keep their rent rises within set levels (Standard D 1.3). These set levels are interpreted in the following way:

'We will compare [the rent per home] increase against a set guideline imit. This will be the percentage increase in the Retail Price Index (all items) plus 1%. In year 1 the comparison will be:

Average rental income per home 1997/98 against *RPI as at September 1996*
Average rental income per home 1996/97   RPI as at September 1995

If the rate of increase in the average rental income per home is higher than RPI + 1%, this will be open to investigation. . . . Where investigation takes place, the RSL will be asked to justify the excess. If there is no adequate explanation, the RSL will have to adjust its rent increases to meet the regulatory requirement. If the RSL fails to do so, the Corporation will take appropriate regulatory action.'

The RPI + /− 1% formula is clearly lifted from the 1995 Consultation and White Papers, reflecting the fact that this incursion was implicitly forced upon the Corporation (it is also the calculation used in gauging allowable price increases by regulators of privatized industries: for discussion, see Prosser, 1997). Alternatively, it might be suggested that the introduction of this regulation has foreshadowed the introduction of profit-making landlords. The toughness of the regulation is, however, mitigated by the fact that a justification will lie in either pre-arranged agreements with tenants as to the level of rents and/or the need to raise rents in line with interest payments (where, for example, these have increased dramatically) (see, for example, DTZ Pieda Consulting, 1998, para. 4.14). In other words, the fear with which the proposals were initially met might prove to be somewhat hasty. This particular regulation may prove to be a damp squib because it changes the basis upon which RSLs have taken mixed funding in the past and the most recent evidence suggests that the RPI formula has less effect than controls on local authority rents (DTZ Pieda Consulting, 1998, paras 4.12–4.17).

The final guiding principle raises considerable uncertainty. Mysteriously termed 'materiality', this apparently means that 'we shall pay proper regard to the relative importance of each requirement within the overall regulatory regime, and to the extent of any shortfall in meeting each requirement' (p. 3). Presumably this means something like 'all standards are equal but some are more equal than others. However, we're not going to tell you, at this stage, which standards are more equal'. Materiality, in other words, enables the Corporation to hedge its bets.

Materiality, in combination with the lack of definitions given in *Standards*, also enables the Corporation to retain one important role: *regulatory supremacy*. In order to comply with the Standards, RSLs are required to discuss with the Corporation their interpretations, which parts are more important than others, and the method of enforcement ('our preference would be to work with the RSL': p. 3). Consequently, *Standards* places the Corporation in the centre of the regulatory relationship. The Corporation is willing to waive certain obligations as well as exempt some RSLs from some Standards, but only after discussion with the Corporation. In a more general survey of such regulatory 'conversations', Black elegantly summarizes their benefits as well as the issues they present:

> 'Conversations ameliorate the limits of rules; they meet the perennial problem of how to resolve the tension between certainty and flexibility; they allow for more general rules to be written which serve as better, because more comprehensible, guides to behaviour, whilst allowing for adjustment to individual circumstances: a form of 'acoustic separation' of law. Conversations have the postmodern credentials of flexibility, communication, responsiveness, and enable individual regulatees to participate in the decision as to the rule's application in their case.
> . . . [Conversations also] raise issues of consistent, fair and objective treatment, of access, participation and accountability.' (1998, pp. 77–8)

By way of conclusion to this section on regulation, one final point needs to be made. Regulation does not necessarily only occur through the Corporation. RSLs are also explicitly and implicitly regulated by private finance when they apply for, are granted, and throughout the period of, a loan. Private finance then provides a key addition to the regulatory matrix – indeed, in many respects, it provides a far more meticulous form of regulation. Being refused a loan, or being unable to make interest payments, suggests problems in the management and regulatory structure of the RSL itself. Furthermore, loan agreements frequently include *restrictive covenants*. For example, they might restrict the types of tenant the RSL can place in their developments (depending on the level of rent control applicable to different tenants whose tenancies take place under different statutory regimes relating to 'fair rent' or market-based rent). Alternatively, there are covenants against indulging in major stock reinvestment for a period. Once again, the interpretation and enforcement of these covenants are a matter of conversations, but this time the success depends upon the source of the loan: 'Lenders have an on-going relationship with [RSLs] and are usually prepared to be flexible to allow an association to achieve its objectives. . . . Where finance has been raised from the capital market the same flexibility does not exist to alter covenant terms.' (National Housing Federation, 1997, p. 24)

4.3 New RSL Management

In this section, I want to draw attention to three relatively new aspects of the 'sharp end' of RSL practice: the developing professionalization of management committees; the 'new public management ethos' of RSLs' housing management; risk assessment and management. The notion of a 'voluntary housing movement' has been challenged by the developments examined in the previous sections of this chapter. This has been brought into particular focus by the incoming level of private finance into the provision of low-cost social housing and is reflected by a multitude of different factors exhibited within the RSL movement, although centred around those RSLs which have been developing since the introduction of the new regime. Each of the matters under consideration reflects these developments within the RSL structures.

First, the ripple effect of the value for money requirement can be witnessed in the development of RSL management committees, particularly in the context of a move towards their professionalization. Here, once again, the issue of private finance is critical, for lenders look at the management committee as one factor affecting their lending decision. In the organizational hierarchy of an RSL, it is the management committee which supposedly sets the agenda: 'RSLs' governing bodies should direct and control all aspects of the RSLs' work in an effective and accountable way' (*Standards*, A3.2).

In the 1990s, concern with issues of 'governance' and 'accountability' (see, for example, Cadbury Report, 1992) equally raised a challenge to the essential element of such committees: *voluntariness*. The concerns that the committees are 'self-perpetuating oligarchies' are mirrored in the range of reports which have concerned themselves with them in the 1990s – from the Nolan Committee on Standards in Public Life (1996) to quangocracy debates (Plummer, 1994) to internal issues of 'competence and accountability' (National Federation of Housing Associations (NFHA), 1995; see also Ashby, 1997 for background information). In 1990, Kearns found that the majority of these volunteers were invited to become members of the committee by members of the board or the RSL's director: 'the new committee members are from similar social backgrounds to existing committee members and are likely to hold similar views and values, and are therefore unlikely to upset any consensus on the committee' (Kearns, 1990, pp. 42–3; see further Kearns, 1994a). These concerns are also reflected in the NFHA report, which also called for greater openness in appointment (NFHA, 1995, para. 6.2).

There is a crucial link to private finance: 'The main concern of reformers seems to be to convince the private financial sector that [RSLs] are efficiently and competently managed' (Kearns, 1994b, p. 19). Such concerns may be putting the cart before the horse for, as Malpass and Murie observe, the management committee can only do what it is asked to do; in other words, its meetings are structured by an agenda for which the chief officers are responsible for preparing (1994, p. 248). Whilst the NFHA report shirked from suggesting that RSLs conduct a 'skills audit' of their management committees, they nevertheless argued that a 'selection committee should identify what would be needed to fill any gaps and address issues of balance' (1995, para. 6.2). The NFHA's approach rather stole the thunder of the Nolan committee (para. 295), although they also drew attention to the requirements of 'experience and expertise'. The bottom line, however, is that the professionalism of management committees is one of the keys to private finance, even though this 'crowd[s] out the other socio-economic groups and women' (Kearns, 1997, p. 56).

The second consideration in this section relates to the influence of 'new public management' techniques. Whilst such generalized terminology hides diverse approaches, its golden thread is a mix of market-based and public sector ideologies (see further Harlow & Rawlings, 1997, pp. 131 *et seq*). We have seen that the Corporation focuses upon both of these in grant allocation, although it appears to give preference to market-based approaches.

New management techniques have begun to influence RSL housing management. Drawing on an empirical study of changes in management styles in one RSL that operated on a national basis, Walker notes how the board and management teams moved towards top-down change, enforcing 'team-based pay' (a collective form of performance-related pay) and renegotiated pay scales – reflecting aspects of 'excellence' (1998, p. 79). Furthermore, the RSL had moved towards significantly decentralizing its operations, for example, leaving policy issues to regional development.

A pilot project was set-up aimed at establishing new organizational cultures in the management of 1,000 homes in inner city Liverpool. The projects aims were 'to (a) reduce operational service delivery and centralised costs by 20%; (b) increase levels of tenant satisfaction; (c) improve performance against key indicators (rent arrears, lettings and empty homes); and (d) improve staff morale' (p. 80). Essentially, the estate was managed through services provided by telephone, employing the schemes, common amongst private-sector organizations, of direct-dial services. Walker's evaluation is important. Drawing on typologies of new public management (Ferlie *et al.*, 1996), he argues that factors associated with private-sector organizations, such as 'efficiency drive', 'in search of excellence', 'downsizing and decentralisation', have gained ascendancy over 'public service orientation' (pp. 82–4). Thus, one of the findings of the study lies in the chameleon-like change in RSL management, the adoption of private-sector corporatist values to the detriment of what might be termed the 'social need' model of housing management. If one is looking for reason(s) for this alteration, one need not look much further than the funding regime which has established the supremacy of value for money and 'crude efficiency' (p. 82).

Finally, we draw attention to the increasing requirement of 'risk assessment' and 'risk management' (see generally, 6, 1998). These reflect the new concerns of management, which needs to focus on 'business strategies' (see, for example, NHF, 1997, Ch. 2). The new language is exhibited in the following, taken from an NHF finance document:

> 'The development of an [RSL's] business strategy must be carried out within the risk management framework. Risks are not limited to direct and immediate financial loss. They include events which may affect the [RSL's] ability to survive and compete in its markets, as well as to maintain its financial strength and positive public image, and the overall quality of its people and services.' (*ibid*, p. 7)

Thus, we end where we began, with the centrality of finance and the question which underlies much of the discussion in this chapter: is the RSL movement about 'social housing' or about securing finance for social housing? It might be argued that the notion and culture of 'social housing' outside the local authority sector has been so underdeveloped that it has proved fertile ground for the speedy impact of the ethos of private finance.

Conclusion

In this chapter, I have steadfastly avoided the more traditional lawyers' question about the RSL movement – whether they are public or private organizations. This is partly because such 'binarization' (the is it or isn't it? approach) is one dimensional and presupposes that such neat definitions exist. It also serves the purpose of fuelling the current divide between public and private law, for we are seeking neat patterns of decision-making practices that we can pigeonhole. In fact, as this chapter has shown, such pigeonholing cannot be done. RSLs have become a complex mixture of different types of interest; this has been reflected in the way they are funded, they way they are regulated, and the way they are managed. Neither can they be regarded as quasi-public or quasi-private, for this simply extends the boundaries of each category, retaining the binarization.

Instead, I have sought to provide the tools to contextualize the development of RSLs, so that the reader might appreciate how they fit within the strategies endorsed by successive Conservative governments throughout the 1980s and 1990s. In the process, one can appreciate how their mix of public and private finance, public bodies (Housing Corporation) and voluntary (largely) private-sector structures, together with their apparent mission of providing low-cost housing to those who need it, has been manipulated to suit essentially public policy aims. These aims began from the premise that local authority housing was 'bad' and that other bodies needed to fill the void created by the disabling of local authorities. RSLs have certainly been able partly to fill this void, but at considerable cost.

These tools suggest the complexity of the regulatory relationships on offer to RSLs. The often-heard complaint of centralization is manifest within our analysis, from the relationship between government funding and priority setting to Corporation management guidance. Reductions in government funding have meant that RSLs have entered the era of competitiveness, which, in turn, has led to regulatory relationships being entered into outside the narrow central government–Housing Corporation–RSL equation. These regulatory relationships have been based upon the influx of different sources of funding. So, for example, local authorities extract nomination rights over stock developed on property sold to RSLs at knock-down prices (see Ch. 9 below). Furthermore, and more concretely in terms of a regulatory schema, private lenders have influenced the way RSLs have run as well as (in rather concentric patterns) affecting the regulatory relationships designed by the Corporation to appease central government. By no means do these actors complete the regulatory matrix of RSLs (as we shall see in Ch. 9 below). Everyone now has a piece of the action.

Further Reading

Discussion of the law relating to RSLs can be found in greater depth in J. Alder & C. Handy (1997), *Housing Associations: the Law of Social Landlords*, London: Sweet & Maxwell; additionally, A. Stewart (1996), *Rethinking Housing Law*, London: Sweet & Maxwell, Ch. 5 provides a useful discussion of the regulation of RSLs.

For a perspective on the RSL movement which considers its accountability in the light of principles of public law, see P. Birkinshaw, I. Harden & N. Lewis (1990), *Government by Moonlight*, London: Unwin Hyman; for the broader context of administration, see C. Harlow & R. Rawlings (1997), *Law and Administration*, London: Butterworths, esp Chs 5–7 & 10.

The housing policy perspective can be found in P. Balchin (1995), *Housing Policy – An Introduction*, London: Routledge, Ch. 7; for an economic approach, see J. Hills (1991), *Unravelling Housing Finance*, Oxford: Oxford University Press, Ch. 8 (although it should be remembered that RSL finance is an area which is continually evolving); see also S. Wilcox & G. Meen (1995), *The Costs of Higher Rents*, London: National Federation of Housing Associations.

Endnotes

1. I have chosen to use this terminology throughout this book whenever referring to the voluntary housing movement. However, readers should be aware that this terminology is relatively recent, since the Housing Act 1996. Before that, RSLs were routinely referred to as 'housing associations', and much of the literature is also to that effect (indeed, some retains this old name).
2. I am defining social sector rather narrowly here to include just RSL and local authority tenures.
3. Little is known about those which are not registered with the Corporation. This lack of knowledge means that they are studiously ignored within this book even though they account for a proportion of the housing market.
4. One of the possible reasons why it survived was that the Chair of the Housing Corporation was Lord Goodman, whose qualities appealed to both political parties. Hew was therefore a powerful manipulator of policy.
5. TCIs 'include acquisition costs, work and VAT, and all additional on-costs. On-costs include professional and legal fees, the association's own development administration costs and capitalized interest accrued on loans during the development period' (Cope, 1990, p. 89). Thus, the TCI represents a key mechanism through which central government can influence the management and other costs of RSLs.
6. Housing Benefit (General) Regulations 1987, SI 1987/1971, Sch 1A, para. 3. However, if this does have a downward effect on private sector rents, this will affect the available comparables for considering the RSL rent. Furthermore, speculation about future Housing Benefit reductions may well affect the ability of RSLs to gain private finance.
7. The legal status of such Determinations is unclear. The governing legislation, in this case 18(2), 1996 Act, regards them as 'such principles as [the Corporation] may from time to time determine', which does not provide much of a clue as to their enforceability, other than through the doctrine of 'legitimate expectations' (although the delimitations of this doctrine are equally unclear).

Bibliography

Alder, J. (1997), 'Social landlords and housing associations – a distinction without a difference', vol 1, *Journal of Housing Law*, 35

Alder, J. and Handy, C. (1997), *Housing Associations: The Law of Social Landlords*, London: Sweet & Maxwell

Ashby, J. (1997), 'The inquiry into housing association governance', in P. Malpass (ed.), *Ownership, Control and Accountability: The New Governance of Housing*, Coventry: Chartered Institute of Housing

Back, G. and Hamnett, C. (1985), 'State housing policy formation and the changing role of housing associations in Britain', vol 13, *Policy and Politics*, 397

Best, R. (1991), 'Housing associations 1890–1990', in S. Lowe and D. Hughes (eds), *A New Century of Social Housing*, Leicester: Leicester University Press

Best, R. (1997), 'Housing associations: a sustainable solution?', in P. Williams (ed), *Directions in Housing Policy*, London: Paul Chapman

Black, J. (1998), 'Talking about regulation', *Public Law*, 77

Bramley, G. (1993), 'Quasi-markets and social housing', in J. Le Grand and W. Bartlett (eds), *Quasi-Markets and Social Policy*, London: Macmillan

Bramley, G. (1995), *Too High a Price*, London: Shelter

Cadbury Report (1992), *Committee on the Financial Aspects of Corporate Governance*, London: Financial Reporting Council

Centre for Housing Research, University of Glasgow (1989), *The Nature and Effectiveness of Housing Management*, London: HMSO

Chaplin, R., Jones, M., Martin, S., Pryke, M., Royce, C., Saw, P., Whitehead, C. and Yang, J. (1995), *Rents and Risks – Investing in Housing Associations*, York: Joseph Rowntree Foundation

Cope, H. (1990), *Housing Associations Policy and Practice*, London: Macmillan

Day, P., Henderson, D. and Klein, R. (1993), *Home Rules: Regulation and Accountability in Social Housing*, York: Joseph Rowntree Foundation

Day, P. and Klein, R. (1995), *The Regulation of Social Housing*, London: National Housing Federation

Department of the Environment (DoE) (1987a), *Finance for Housing Associations: The Government's Proposals*, London: DoE

Department of the Environment (DoE) (1987b), *Housing: the Government's Proposals*, Cm 214, London: HMSO

Department of the Environment (DoE) (1995a), *Our Future Homes – Opportunity, Choice and Responsibility*, Cm 2901, London: HMSO

Department of the Environment (DoE) (1995b), *More Choice in the Social Rented Sector*, Consultation Paper Linked to the Housing White Paper, London: DoE

Department of the Environment (1997), *Household Growth: Where Shall we Live?*, Cm 3471, London: HMSO

Department of Social Security (DSS) (1998), *A New Contract for Welfare*, Cm 3805, London: HMSO

DTZ Piede Consulting (1998), *Rents in Local Authority and Registered Social Landlord Sectors*, London: NHF

Ferlie, E., Ashburner, L., Fitzgerald, L. and Pettigrew, A. (1996), *The New Public management in Action*, Oxford: Oxford University Press

Goodchild, B. and Karn, V. (1997), 'Standards, quality control and house building in the UK', in P. Williams (ed.), *Directions in Housing Policy*, London: Paul Chapman

Goodlad, R. (1993), *The Housing Authority as Enabler*, Coventry: Institute of Housing & London, Longman

Harlow, C. and Rawlings, R. (1997), *Law and Administration*, London: Butterworths

Harrison, J. (1992), *Housing Associations after the 1988 Housing Act*, SAUS Working Paper 108, Bristol: School for Advanced Urban Studies, University of Bristol

Hawkins, K. (1984), *Environment and Enforcement, Regulation and the Social Definition of Pollution*, Oxford: Oxford University Press

House of Commons Environment Committee (1993), *The Housing Corporation*, HC 466, London: HMSO

Housing Corporation (1997a), *Performance Standards*, London: Housing Corporation

Housing Corporation (1997b), *Registered Social Landlords in 1996: General Report*, London: Housing Corporation

Housing Corporation (1997c) 'Lettings to certain persons from abroad', Circ R3 04/97, Housing Corporation

Housing Corporation (1997d) 'Total Cost Indicators, Grant Rates, Value limiting and discount amounts for 1998/99', Circ F2 26/97, Housing Corporation.

Housing Corporation (1998), *Total Cost Indicators 1998/99*, London: Housing Corporation

Karn, V. and Sheridan, L. (1994), *New Homes in the 1990s*, Manchester: University of Manchester and York: Joseph Rowntree Foundation

Kearns, A. (1990), *Voluntarism Management and Accountability*, Glasgow: Housing Associations Research Unit, University of Glasgow

Kearns, A. (1994a), *Going by the Board*, Glasgow: Centre for Housing Research and Urban Studies, University of Glasgow

Kearns, A. (1994b), *On Considering the Governance of Social Housing*, Glasgow: Centre for Housing Research and Urban Studies, University of Glasgow

Kearns, A. (1997), 'Housing association committees: dilemmas of composition', in P. Malpass (ed.), *Ownership, Control and Accountability: The New Governance of Housing*, Coventry: Chartered Institute of Housing

Langstaff, M. (1992), 'Housing associations: a move to centre stage', in J. Birchall (ed), *Housing Policy in the 1990s*, London: Routledge

Lewis, N. and Harden, I. (1982), 'The Housing Corporation and 'voluntary housing', in A. Barker (ed), *Quangos in Britain*, London: Macmillan

McAuslan, P. (1989), 'Administrative Justice – a necessary report?', *Public Law*, 402

Malpass, P. (1997), 'The local governance of housing', in P. Malpass (ed.), *Ownership, Control and Accountability: The New Governance of Housing*, Coventry: Chartered Institute of Housing

Malpass, R. and Murie, A. (1994), *Housing Policy and Practice*, London: Macmillan

Mullins, D. (1992), 'From local politics to state regulation: the legislation and policy on race equality in housing', vol 18, *New Community*, 401

Mullins, D. (1997), 'From regulatory capture to regulated competition: an interest group analysis of the regulation of housing associations in England', vol 12, *Housing Studies*, 301

Murie, A. (1997), 'The social rented sector, housing and the welfare state in the UK', vol 12, *Housing Studies*, 437

National Federation of Housing Associations (NFHA) (1995), *Competence and Accountability: the Report of the Inquiry into Housing Association Governance*, London: NFHA

National Housing Federation (NHF) (1997), *Rents, Resources and Risks – The New Balancing Act*, London: NHF

Noble, D. (1981), 'From rules to discretion: the Housing Corporation', in M. Adler and S. Asquith (eds), *Discretion and Welfare*, London: Heinemann

Nolan Committee on Standards in Public Life (1996), *Local Public Spending Bodies*, London: HMSO

Page, D. (1993), *Building for Communities*, York: Joseph Rowntree Foundation

Perri, 6. (1998), 'Housing policy in the risk archipelago: toward anticipatory and holistic government', vol 13, *Housing Studies*, 347

Plummer, J. (1994), *The Governance Gap: Quangos and Accountability*, York: Joseph Rowntree Foundation

Prosser, T. (1997), *Law and the Regulators*, Oxford: Oxford University Press

Pryke, M. (1994), 'Coping with some of the new risks of social housing in England', in W. Bartlett and G. Bramley (eds), *European Housing Finance – Single Market or Mosaic*, Bristol: School for Advanced Urban Studies, University of Bristol

Randolph, B. (1993), 'The re-privatization of housing associations', in P. Malpass and R. Means (eds), *Implementing Housing Policy*, Buckingham: Open University Press

Walker, R. (1998), 'New public management and housing associations: from comfort to competition', vol 26, *Policy and Politics*, 71

Wheal, C. (1998), 'A tonic for Eastenders', *The Guardian*, 25 March

Wilcox, S. (1997), *Housing Finance Review* 1997/98, York: Joseph Rowntree Foundation

5 Purposive Regulation: The Case of Local Government

In 1979, local authorities provided 32 per cent of the total number of dwellings in Great Britain. In 1995, they provided just 18.9 per cent (Wilcox, 1997, Table 16d). These percentages represent a crude loss of *around two million dwellings* in this tenure. Over the same period, central government subsidy to local authority housing has been slashed by more than 50 per cent and capital investment by around 70 per cent. These various cuts have brought about a repositioning of the sector in line with central government policy. Local government, in other words, increasingly became controlled by central government through regulatory processes which have specified with ever-increasing precision what was required (see, generally, Loughlin, 1996).

This does not imply that local government generally was a willing tool in an overweening, centrally co-ordinated, ideologically driven, coherent campaign which led to the demise of council housing. Indeed, each part of this statement is inaccurate (see Cole & Furbey, 1994). In 1979, the first Thatcher government was partly elected on a platform of de-bureaucratization and increasing marketization. But the campaign against council housing was based more on populism than ideology. Furthermore, those who speak of the demise of council housing forget that the sector still accounts for more than three-and-a-half million dwellings in England alone. This represents a considerable increase in its tenure share from the beginning of the century (which was negligible).

The campaign against council housing actually began much earlier than 1979, when home ownership was promoted as 'the natural tenure' and council housing was delegitimized by being regarded as the residual tenure. So, for example, the Ministry of Housing and Local Government (MHLG) in 1965 (during a Labour administration), argued that:

'The expansion of the public programme now proposed is to meet exceptional needs; it is born partly of a short-term necessity, partly of the conditions inherent in modern urban life. The expansion of building for owner-occupation on the other hand is normal; it reflects a long-term social advance which should gradually pervade every region.' (MHLG, 1965, cited in Murie, 1997a, p. 89)

It can also be posited that council housing's periods of major expansion – after the two world wars of the twentieth century – were products of necessity rather than 'to erect one of the pillars of socialism' (Cole &

Furbey, 1994, p. 61). Council housing was not part of the welfare nationalization hastened in by Beveridge's report. Indeed, it has been suggested that 'Adolf Hitler proved a more decisive influence than William Beveridge in shaping the housing requirements of post-war Britain' (*ibid*, 60; *cf* Murie, 1997b, where the relationship between council housing and the emerging welfare state is regarded as underdeveloped). Local authorities were chosen for this task, it appears, because private speculative housebuilders were not 'plannable instruments' (Aneurin Bevan, quoted in Donnison, 1967, p. 164; see Ch. 3 above) – meaning that the exigencies of the market were inadequate for the required mass housebuilding programme.

This does not mean that the Thatcher/Major axis represented an inevitable, historical transition from public to private provision. In no way can this be argued, for the programme implemented from 1979 was radical (although, in part, derived from the previous Labour government) and involved a considerably different philosophy towards both council housing as well as councils themselves. The 1974–9 Labour government's adoption of an awkward monetarism had set the scene, although the considerable support for council housing (and the autonomy of local government) had been shown by the reaction towards the previous Conservative administration's Housing Finance Act in 1972 (described as an 'abattoir for the slaughter of council house tenants': Skinner & Langdon, 1972, p. 39). The Thatcher governments had learnt from the 1972 Act, as well as other successful and abortive attempts at reform. They had learnt, for example, that overt attempts at constraining local autonomy (such as requiring 'fair rents' to be set as under the 1972 Act) would be resisted. Instead, they resorted to a programme of providing a loose assortment of *incentives* to tenants, local councillors, housing managers, private-sector organizations and RSLs. These ranged from imposing personal financial penalties on elected councillors who refuse to implement legislation ('When your pocket's threatened, your politics change': Cooper, 1996, p. 264) through to practical requirements to raise council tenants' rents to near-market levels, as well as turning housing management into big business. It has been these incentives, not direct action, which have led to the massive withdrawal of state provision of housing.

The main method used to implement these incentives has been legislation and quasi-legislation (by which is meant in this context, Statutory Instruments, Circulars, Guidance, Determinations, and the like). Equally, this could hardly be described as innovative practice. After all, the rise in legislation and quasi-legislation – increasing the power of the central executive – had been commented upon for some time (Harlow & Rawlings, 1997, Ch. 2 summarizes some of these arguments). What was different, however, was the purposive tone and specification within it. The pre-Thatcher legislative style was to give wide powers together with considerable discretion to local authorities in their operation (albeit with some blips, such as the 1972 Act). In this sense, law 'provided a structure within which the administrative understandings could evolve' (Loughlin, 1994, p. 268). This legislative pattern might be exemplified by the fact that there has never been any duty upon local authorities to have a stock of housing; this has simply been assumed (a fact of which, more recently, government has taken advantage: see Ch. 6). Legislation 'enabled' the central–local government relationship to evolve through administrative norm-setting. Until 1996, the waiting list for council housing had colloquial, but no legal, status. Equally, council housing proved, in the early part of this century, to be non-justiciable precisely because of this open-ended structure. In *Shelley* v. *London County Council* [1948] 2 All ER 898, the House of Lords had, for example, held that the council could pick and evict its tenants at will without judicial interference.

However, between 1979 and 1992, central government enacted 143 Bills relating to local government of which 58 were major (Wilson & Game, 1994, p. 95). Quasi-legislation has proliferated (as to which, see, for example, Ganz, 1991). Regulation to the minutiae has been the order of the day; much of the legislation has initially been presented to Parliament still requiring rewriting to make it workable. The style of the legislation is '*instrumental* . . . designed to establish the norms and to regulate the relationship' (Loughlin, 1997, p. 62; original emphasis). Increasing specification, however, left gaps which were exploited by local government and then tightened by regulation. Stewart characterizes the council housing finance regime, for example, as a 'cat and mouse game' (1996, p. 145). In this sense, legislation can equally be described as 'enabling', albeit this time enabling whichever Secretary of State to make extra-statutory regulations. Rather than describing the legal effect of sections in Statutes, commentators have been left describing the remarkable breadth of rule-making powers given by Statutes. Finally, this increasing specification has led to what has been termed a juridification of the central–local relationship, with councils increasingly challenging the powers, their interpretation, and their application before the courts (see, for example, Loughlin, 1994; 1996; *cf* Cooper, 1995, where the notion of juridification is examined).

Enabling is also a fairly consistent theme within the council housing regime, again with subtle shifts in meaning and emphasis (see Goodlad, 1993). So, for example, the post-war council housebuilding might accurately be described as having been 'enabled'. Councils borrowed money from private-sector lenders, they employed a private-sector workforce, and the land developed was owned privately (see, for example, Merrett, 1979, Ch. 2; Short, 1982). Indeed, as councils were often run by the municipal bourgeois, this self-serving behaviour was perhaps only natural.

When central government's housing White Paper in 1987 prescribed 'enabling' as the future role for local government, it was widely believed to foreshadow a very different programme for state housing:

'Local authorities should increasingly see themselves as enablers who ensure that everyone in the area is adequately housed; *but not necessarily by them.*' (DoE, 1987, para. 1.16; emphasis added)

'The future role of local authorities will essentially be a strategic one identifying housing needs and demands, encouraging innovative methods of provision by other bodies to meet such needs, maximising the use of private finance, and encouraging the new interest in the revival of the independent rented sector.' (para. 5.1)

This shift in emphasis, in other words, confirmed a radical reappraisal of the role of local government in the provision of accommodation. Thus, enabling was first the strategy used to bring council housing into being, and has been the strategy used to dismantle it.

The first section of this chapter analyses why council housing proved to be an easy target – a rabbit in front of a car's headlights. It also provides brief details of the mechanisms used by central government in their campaign which fell under the umbrella term of 'privatization'. It is important to appreciate that the fact that these mechanisms may actually have been ineffective in their original intention does not matter. What matters is their influence upon the climate of council housing. For example, a strategy which is ineffective can, nevertheless, have alternative consequences, perhaps unforeseen, which are not necessarily against the more general thrust of government policy.

The second section of this chapter details a key tool used by central government in their campaign. This tool influenced councils into a strategy of raising rents, competing against other councils for limited pots of money (which were, in any event, creamed off the total pot available to local government), implementing business strategies, as well as ridding themselves of their housing stock completely. This tool was money. Control over the finances of local government meant that central government could treat local government as a marionette (although occasionally the strings might become twisted, as in the 'militant' campaigns in Liverpool in the mid-1980s and the poll tax riots at the close of that decade) and, in the process, facilitate the broader programme of privatization. Housing finance is certainly not easy (deliberately) but crucial to an understanding of the nature of the beast. This section aims to provide the ball of string to guide readers through the maze.

The third section considers the way the new understanding of enabling has affected the terrain of housing management. Concentration is upon the various mechanisms used by central government to impose the overriding facets of its new public management ethos upon housing management. This ethos can be roughly summarized as providing 'value for money' and involved the 'three Es': economy, efficiency, effectiveness. As housing management had never adopted a professional core, it also proved an easy and willing target. In the 1990s, housing management has been subject to compulsory competitive tendering (DoE, 1992), contracting out (see, for example, Local Authorities (Contracting out of Allocation of Housing and Homelessness Functions) Order, SI 1996/3205), and (currently) 'best value' (DETR, 1997a). Each of these might be described as 'camouflaged centralism'.

5.1 The Privatization of State Housing

Privatization can take many forms, be partial or complete, and lead to vastly diverse regulatory structures. The privatization of housing has been encouraged and occurred through a variety of different direct and indirect mechanisms – from an individual council tenant's right to buy their home to the power of councils to sell their entire housing stock to a different organization. In this section, attention is first briefly given to the claims made by the Conservatives and New Right analysts that council housing was deeply problematic and it is suggested that this was a partial rewriting of history. A summary of the mechanisms used to deal with the supposed problems is provided and, then, consideration is given to the effects that this had on the housing service. Our consideration in this latter part essentially goes to the heart of the enabling process.

The Critique of State Housing

The first Thatcher government picked and chose those parts of New Right ideology in which she saw political advantage, and there was clearly such advantage in the policies developed out of the critique of state housing. The large-scale bureaucracy required to manage council housing had operated on a paternalistic basis – 'the oppressed, stigmatized and ignored consumer' (Cole & Furbey, 1994, p. 189) – as well as inefficiently and incompetently. Council housing itself was portrayed as being poorly designed, and charged out at rents which defied market principles. Finally, in tune with New Right ideology, it was argued that the state should adopt a minimal role (thereby also 'smashing the unions' to use the phrase of the Secretary of State for Environment in 1988, Nicholas Ridley MP). Thatcher argued this case not on the basis of ideology but because the state as a landlord had proved itself to be 'insensitive, incompetent and corrupt' (Thatcher, 1993, p. 599). Major's attack on council house design in 1995 was a further example of this trend to denigrate state provision (although see Meikle & Wintour, 1995). In short, for the Conservatives, the collective consumption of council housing represented a fundamentally flawed denial of the market (see Stewart & Burridge, 1989, p. 66); individual home owners were praised, council tenants attracted sympathy. One of the key successes of the Thatcher government was, then, their ability 'to consolidate the move from a crisis *of* council housing to a crisis *in* council housing' (Cole & Furbey, 1994, p. 212; original emphasis)

These critiques struck a chord because, in part, they were true. It was difficult to justify certain stultifying management practices (a sample of which can be found in Saunders, 1990, p. 88 *et seq*), particularly as council tenants themselves began to use home ownership as a comparator (Cairncross *et al.*, 1997, pp. 104–107). Allocation practices tended to favour the better-off working class who were regarded as the deserving, whilst the undeserving remained within the private rented sector. However, this part of the critique was based upon a lack of empirical appreciation, for management practices were, at worst, uneven in application. Some areas with strong commitments to the tenure often produced enlightened policies although the impact of Fabian mores ('the delivery of efficient public services through rational bureaucratic organisation': Cole & Furbey, 1994, p. 126) might have tended to undermine them. This paternalism was enhanced by the lack of enforceable rights given to council tenants (see, for example, *Liverpool City Council* v. *Irwin* [1976] 2 All ER 39) combined with the judicial approach of *laissez-faire* in respect of council house management (see generally, Loveland, 1992). It was no surprise that the rights agenda of the 1970s partly concentrated on housing.

Complaints about the design of the stock reflected the time at which the stock had been built. At different periods throughout the century, political pressure, the necessity for the housebuilding programme, central specifications, the need for economy (occasionally 'more for less'), all made the design of council housebuilding uneven. Some of it was very good, and some very poor (see, for example, Cole & Furbey, 1994, Ch. 4; Forrest & Murie, 1991, p. 36). The rise and fall of the tower block provides an example of the way housing was developed on the basis of powerful interest groups and the availability of funding, rather than a more comprehensive, rational schema:

> '[W]e can say that the state's switch to a high-density redevelopment strategy took the shape of high flats because of the formal hegemony in local authorities of architects who were zealots of the modern movement, and that simultaneously this sea change in the form of public sector housing was underpinned by the material interests of big capital in raising its degree of monopoly in the competition for contracts.' (Merrett, 1979, pp. 130–1)

Thus, the production of council housing was, in itself, a product of an alliance between different interest groups, the influence of which varied over time.

One of the crucial interest groups has been central government. The construction of council housing has been undertaken mainly by the private sector using private finance. Central government partly financed the servicing of these debts by providing fixed sums for certain periods (a system in practice until the 1972 Act). So, for example, central government provided subsidy under the Housing (Financial Provisions) Act 1924 at £9 per annum per house for 40 years (see Buck, 1991, p. 77). The figure varied, however, and it is this variable which is reflected in the quality of housing design. The quality of housing partly reflected the financial support when it was built. The remainder, including for example management and maintenance costs, was paid from other sources. One such source was council rents. The standard form of private lending involves heavy interest charges at the beginning of the loan when the amount of capital is highest. It follows that newer properties required higher rents than the older ones. After attempts at requiring council housing to adopt private-sector rent levels were abandoned (because the market itself was so variegated: Malpass, 1990, p. 67), the Housing Act 1935 instigated the process of rent pooling, although this was not explicitly central government policy until 1955 (see Malpass, 1990, Ch. 5). Rent-pooling enabled rents to be set across a council area and so offset the higher costs of new building against the lower costs of older developments on which the loans were running (or had run) their course.

This scheme of rent-pooling paid no heed to national policy, nor to local preferences nor the efficiency of local housing management and housebuilding. Rather, and this was the central argument levelled by the Conservatives against the system for some time, rent-setting depended upon when properties were built. The older the properties, the lower the rent; the newer the properties, the higher the rent. This factor was exacerbated by the accounting method adopted by local government, known as historic cost accounting, which valued properties on the basis of how much they cost to build as opposed to their current market value. The consequence of this was that authorities with similar stock would commonly have radically different rent structures and costs which neither reflected the market nor the efficiency of their management (see further Walker & Marsh, 1993).

The two points which come from this short discussion are, first, the important fact that council housing developed *locally*, on the basis of local initiative and was as influenced by local politics as by central subsidy. Locality – or the spatial dimension to council housing – also provides a focus for appreciating that general critiques are misjudged and unfounded in rigorous empirical data. Secondly, the quality of council housing also depended upon when it was built – the *temporal* dimension – for the nature and amount of subsidy differed over time as well as the central implementation of quality standards. Any general solutions to the 'problems' of council housing based upon a belief in a general malaise within the tenure are met with these two key points, which will be reflected when such solutions are implemented.

Solutions

Broadly, the *general* solutions developed after 1979 can be divided into three overlapping time periods. In retrospect, the first time period which occurred between 1979–1986 began with the privatization initiatives (and financial incentives) included in the Housing Act 1980. State provision was attacked in the following ways:

- Individual right of council tenants to buy the property they occupied at a discount (which increased over time).
- Individual right of council tenant to a mortgage from the local authority.
- Considerable enforcement powers vested in the Secretary of State
- A new financial agenda which effectively would require a considerable increase in rent levels as well as penalizing councils which developed housing. In this way, tenants would be encouraged to buy. Capital allocations from central government were directed at providing grants to home owners as opposed to financing further development.
- The grant of tenants' rights – known as the Tenants' Charter – in relation to their property, subsequently bolstered by the right to have defects repaired.

One of the rationales for this programme was that, by 1980, there was a crude surplus of property over numbers of households:

> 'I start off, and the Treasury knows that I start off, from a situation where we have the largest crude supply of houses over households that we have ever had in this country.' (House of Commons Environment Committee, 1981, para. 107, *per* Michael Heseltine MP, Secretary of State for the Environment; criticized by the Committee at para. 18; cited in Forrest *et al.*, 1984, p. 25).

What was required, then, was not more accommodation but a change in tenure structure to allow the 'normal' individual preference for home ownership to be expressed. Such preference was obviously affected by the sweeteners as well as the fact that the denigration of generic council housing did not allow for the fact that many council properties were highly desirable (see, further, Forrest & Murie, 1991; Ch. 12 below). The consequence was that councils' housebuilding declined, and the era of politicization and juridification was hastened into action. Councils' opposition to these changes was often bitter (Forrest & Murie, 1985) even though, for example, their implementation of the Tenants' Charter was uneven (Kay *et al.*, 1987). As we shall see in Chapter 12, though, any slight delay in implementing the right to buy was met with threats from the DoE. Thus, one might add that the government's priority was more concerned with dismantling the tenure than with the grant of tenancy rights to those remaining within it. Those tenancy rights had, in any event, been proposed by the previous Labour administration (although the 1980 Act was a watered down version: see Loveland, 1995, pp. 28–32)

The right to buy in this period played a critical role in bolstering the economy: 'Housing capital receipts between 1979–80 and 1985–6 totalled £9,527 million. Other privatization activities generated £7,732 million. In each year up to 1984–5 the housing programme yielded more capital receipts than all the other acts of privatization together' (Forrest & Murie, 1991, p. 93). Thus, the right to buy proved a powerful tool in the general tax cutting era which has often been assumed to have been part of the reason why Thatcher retained power for so long.

The strategy moved into a second phase in 1986 partly because it was recognized at this time that the policy to increase home ownership to its maximum level was being reached (*cf* DoE, 1995, where 1.5 million new home owners were predicted at p. 9). The Housing Act 1980 could plausibly be presented as an explicit attack on council housing for its incentives to individualism. The strategy unveiled in the 1987 White Paper was a more general attack on the continuing existence of the tenure itself. It was argued that:

'there are still too many estates where the quality of life is less than satisfactory. It is not what tenants want, and it is not what the original designers of the estates had in mind. Tenants live there not from choice, but because they have nowhere else to live. Many tenants feel that standards of maintenance are inadequate and that management is too remote.' (DoE, 1987, para. 5.3)

So the attack was on the environment created by council housing together with the, by now familiar, attack on council management. The solution was privatization on a grander scale than had hitherto been conceived and was put in place in the Housing Act 1988 and the Local Government and Housing Act 1989. Councils were to lose entire blocks of accommodation through a collective expression of dissatisfaction (a voting system which was rigged against council housing for it assumed that those who did not vote wished to leave the tenure):

- Large scale voluntary transfers (LSVTs) of the whole of the council's stock to RSLs:[1]
- The transfer of blocks of council housing to private landlords approved by the Housing Corporation – known as 'Tenants' Choice' or 'Pick a Landlord'.
- The transfer of the so-called worst council estates to Housing Action Trusts (HATs)
- A new, more stringent financial regime that effectively required councils to raise rents and almost completely stop development.

Subsequent legislation has merely tinkered with this regime, increasing tenants' rights as well as the attack on management practices (for example, through sponsoring innovative methods of buying individual council housing, such as shared ownership and rents-to-mortgages schemes).

The 1988 Act was based upon a particular ideological stance which was, unconvincingly, transposed onto tenants. The assumption made in that

Act as well as the White Paper was that council tenants were fed up with their housing management which should be conducted on a smaller scale. As Ginsburg suggests, 'The list of woes [presented in the White Paper] reveals the muddled and prejudiced thinking of the government and its advisors' (1989, p. 72). This list of woes was, however, based upon no empirical data considering the effectiveness of housing management. It was not until 1989 that any such research was published and, even then, it was noted that councils competed rather well with the alternatives (Centre for Housing Research, 1989). Thus, the 1987 White Paper was based upon ideologically prejudiced (as well as paternalistic) views of what council tenants actually wanted.

It may well, therefore, come as no surprise that the government's trumpeted policies in the 1987 White Paper proved rather more difficult to implement. Tenants' Choice was a failure – only two estates transferred to alternative management, both in Conservative-controlled areas such as Westminster – and has now been repealed. When repealing it, the then Housing Minister described it as 'silly, ineffective, adversarial, lengthy and costly' (HC Debs, Standing Committee G, Twenty Sixth Sitting, col 1041 (16 June 1996); see also National Audit Office, 1997, where the immense government support to Torbay tenants pursuing a failed attempt to exercise the Tenants' Choice provisions is laid bare). HATs also initially proved to be a costly failure as the first six estates chosen by the government to take part in the scheme failed, leaving the government's rationale and policies in a rather awkward vacuum.

In fact, the legislation appears to have caused, *inter alia*, three things: first, a re-establishment of tenants' protest groups (as to which, see, for example, Woodward, 1991; Ginsburg, 1989); and second rekindled the flame of the right to buy because of the uncertainty created by the new legislation. A third effect – a rethinking of housing management practices – was also driven by the new legislative landscape as councils recognized that their estates were under threat (see, for example, Cole & Furbey's discussion of the decentralization of housing management and other measures: pp. 217–231; Cole *et al.*, 1991). Thus, the paradox is that the result of the new policies might be regarded as a reaffirmation of the principles of collective consumption, as opposed to the government's 'muddled and prejudiced thinking', as well as fueling the success of earlier privatization initiatives.

The third phase began around 1991 and implicitly accepted that the centrepiece (Tenants' Choice and HATs) of the 1988 legislation had failed. The *Citizen's Charter* argued that housing management had 'seemed too remote, impersonal and out of touch with the day-to-day concerns of tenants' (Cabinet Office, 1991 p. 15). Consequently, it was proposed that, *inter alia*:

- Performance standards would be provided directly to tenants who could then 'identify the standards of service they [could] properly expect, and create pressure for improvement and action where performance is unacceptable' (p. 15).

- Compulsory competitive tendering (CCT) would be applied to housing management because 'Some councils still patronise their tenants, apparently believing that only the council itself can provide the required service' (p. 16).

- Tenants themselves would be given the 'right to manage' their estates (p. 16; this was an extension of rights granted in the Housing and Planning Act 1986).

This is not the place to provide a critique of the *Charter* (see Barron & Scott, 1992). However, these views of housing management plied old truths which, throughout the 1980s, had been radically altered. Decentralization had been one method already applied to housing management, since 1980 (Walsall MBC being the first council to decentralize its housing service), for precisely the reasons mentioned by the government in 1991. Thus, local government had already rejected the 'large is beautiful' ethic by the time that the *Charter* was published (Cole *et al.*, 1991, p. 149; more than a hundred councils had decentralized, with many more planning to do so: p. 153). Decentralization specifically employed localized, estate-based housing management techniques which required the housing service to be in touch with their tenants. The *Charter*, then, might be regarded in part as an ideologically driven attack on council management.

The Effects

Some of the effects of these policies have already been discussed, and will be discussed in later chapters. However, attention here will be focused on a more general analysis of the effect of these policies in practice. The two descriptions commonly associated with the effects of this legislation are *residualization* and *marginalization* (see Forrest & Murie, 1991, pp. 65–85; although these effects are true of all tenures: Murie, 1997b).

Before we proceed to analyse these terms, three preliminary matters require some thought. First, it is important to appreciate that these effects were 'in place and their impact was clear' even before the 1979 election (Murie, 1997a, p. 92). The various parts of the legislative agenda in relation to council housing after this time merely exacerbated these trends. Second, there is a spatial element to these trends. The uneven design and build quality of council housing, together with disparities in environmental quality, between areas and even within local authority catchment areas, renders a general analysis important but nevertheless slightly misleading (see further Dunn *et al.*, 1987). Third, these effects can also be spied occurring in other tenures and, whilst they are most closely associated with the trends in council housing, they reflect a broader restructuring of each tenure together with the creation of new 'zones of transition' (see Murie, 1997b, p. 447–8; Forrest & Murie, 1995; Rex & Moore, 1967).

Residualization

This refers to a direction of change in council housing, from one where it was to be a mass tenure for all, to one where it provides housing for marginal groups. Forrest and Murie's analysis drew attention to five particular aspects, although the term 'rarely refers to a *single* feature' (1991, p. 74–5; original emphasis): first, there has been a decline in the size of the public housing stock; second, there is the uneven quality of the stock; third, the changing characteristics of tenants; fourth, the nature of policy regarding council housing as residual; fifth, an increase in means testing (from general 'bricks and mortar' subsidy to means-tested allowances, such as Housing Benefit). So, residualization therefore relates to an examination of trends in housing.

Marginalization

This was the pivotal concept (Forrest & Murie, 1991, p. 82). It referred to the fact that the people remaining within the tenure were generally those with little political and economic muscle (p. 78). Increasingly, council housing provided accommodation for those in the lowest four income deciles, reflecting their unemployed or low-paid status (Murie, 1997a). This has occurred at a time of decline in the tenure share of the sector and so reflecting a greater concentration of such people in council housing than ever before. The better-off have generally left the tenure through the right to buy. This has incidentally creamed off the better quality properties from the council stock leaving within the sector (generally) flats and poor quality accommodation (see, for example, Forrest & Murie's analysis of the commodification of former council properties, 1995). Legislation giving priority to families and others within what are inadequately termed 'special needs' groups are commonly cited as reasons for the changing composition (see Part II of this book). The movement from 'bricks and mortar' subsidy to individual subsidy through Housing Benefit to pay increased rents is a further aspect of this, particularly as Housing Benefit contains strong disincentives through a tapering mechanism.[2]

Whether or not the principle of universalism had been applied to council housing, it now seems clear that council housing is a tenure for the most marginalized in society. This reflects a new role for council housing as a 'safety net', a role underlined by the DoE in 1994 when it clearly espoused the belief that council housing was 'for people whose overall needs were substantial and enduring' and that people should not 'expect the state to provide for them on demand' (paras 1.1 & 1.2 respectively). Council housing, ironically, has been more closely aligned with the dismantling of the welfare state than it was with the rise of the welfare state.

5.2 The Role of Finance in the Dismantling of Council Housing

In the Housing Finance Act 1972, the Conservative central government sought to control the level of rents charged by local authorities, together with a more widespread control over the housing revenue account through the payment of central subsidy. This policy was disastrous but it provided the preface to the first Thatcher government's consideration of housing finance. Finance can be regarded as the key to the whole housing programme implemented during the post-1979 period. That programme might be summarized simply as the promotion of home ownership. Deciding to become a home owner involves a complex decision-making process taking into account (say) the availability of mortgage finance (the council tenant's new right to a mortgage), the price (the right to buy included substantial discounts), as well as matters such as the comparative outlay between rent and mortgage together with the future of the tenure and effectiveness of management. The future of the tenure was uncertain, the effectiveness of council management was, as has been argued above, uneven.

The housing finance system introduced in the first and third Thatcher governments considerably altered the rent structure so effecting a huge increase in rent levels albeit (once again) unevenly distributed across the country initially. Furthermore, central housing revenue subsidy to local authorities and capital allocations were considerably reduced – squeezing the level of housing management in line with the new agenda, inspired by the 'three Es' and efficiency gains. In other words, council housing finance was *the most potent method of centrally regulating for the dismantling of the local housing sector and, ironically, requiring local authorities themselves to 'press the button'.* Essentially, central government took control of capital spending plans and revenue financing, whilst leaving rent-setting powers and management financing in the hands of the authorities. This was a brilliant and innovative schema.

The success of these reforms generally can be seen in considering two current problems. First, the success in making local authorities increase rents led to the assertion in the 1995 housing White Paper that rent levels were now placing too high a burden on Housing Benefit levels (the subsidy paid to individuals to assist with rent payments): '. . . we must strike a balance between helping all tenants through keeping their rents down, and helping individuals through Housing Benefit' (DoE, 1995, p. 26). Second, council housebuilding has effectively ended: in 1980, local authorities began building 37,394 new accommodation units; in 1995, this figure was 1,890 (Wilcox, 1997, Table 18). These two points are characteristic of a schema which has involved withdrawing general subsidy for housebuilding – bricks and mortar subsidy – to a reliance upon individual subsidy – Housing Benefit. The argument, throughout the past twenty-odd years, has been that *tenants should pay for what they are getting and subsidy should be a safety net,* not a generalized subsidy which cannot be targeted on those most in need.

The reform of council housing finance took place in two waves, occurring in 1980 and 1989. Critical to an appreciation of these regimes is the rather awkward split between two parts: capital and revenue. These are awkward because, at the margins, they overlap. For example, repairs generally fall on the revenue side, although they can be capitalized in standard accounting practice. One of the effects of the 1989 regime was a much clearer definition of what was revenue, but even this leaves room for doubt and discretion (see Sch. 4). The battleground of the 1980s and 1990s was *accountancy practice* with occasional judicial forays (see, for example, *R* v. *Secretary of State for the Environment ex parte Camden LBC* [1998] 1 All ER 937). The techniques of innovative and creative accounting have become widespread, ultimately leading councils to financial markets and Swap transactions declared *ultra vires* by the courts (see generally Loughlin, 1996, Ch. 6; also *Hazell* v. *Hammersmith and Fulham LBC* [1991] 2 WLR 372). Be that as it may, the following discussion splits capital and revenue financing because, essentially, they are governed by different legal structures.

Capital Finance

General
In November 1976, the Labour government announced a new system of capital allocations based upon a submission to the DoE from local authorities to be known as the Housing Investment Programme (HIP). The idea was that this programme would initiate 'a comprehensive assessment of the local housing situation' and capital allocations would be made on that basis over four-year periods (see DoE, 1977, para. 9.07). The 1977 White Paper stressed the flexibility of this new scheme, although central government was able to control the distribution of capital in a way in which it had not been able to hitherto. The first Thatcher government, however, (ab)used the HIP submission to control a reduced flow of capital into the system through political prioritizing as well as reducing the timescale of the programme to an annual allocation. So, for example, renovation grants (to home owners) were privileged by the system but new local authority building was denied:

> 'The local autonomy and planning objectives of the system have been almost fully subservient to central decisions on the distribution of resources, strong encouragement to follow national policy initiatives and a tightly controlled and uncertain financial climate.' (Leather, 1983, p. 223)

Thus, the HIP submission became more a matter of central government priorities and control than a local matter as had been the original intention (Cole & Goodchild, 1995, pp. 51–3 detail the local authority response to this; see also Loughlin, 1986, p. 111). Distribution also began to be based upon the General Needs Index, a supposedly objective assessment of the needs of each area (although political preference was consistently implied: see Leather & Murie, 1986, p. 49).

The main issue was what to do with the expected flow of receipts from the sale of council housing. The Local Government, Planning and Land Act 1980 solved this problem by allowing only 50 per cent of the total capital receipts gained in any one year to be included in the HIP allocation, enabling government to reduce further its capital outlay. This proportion was subsequently reduced to 40 per cent in 1984 and then 20 per cent in 1985.

The problem was that spending capital receipts from sales benefitted those areas with greater levels of receipts causing an imbalance in capital allocations: 'As those with the most capital receipts were not necessarily those with the biggest problems, capital spending was not directed towards the areas of greatest need' (Hills, 1990, p. 82). Even worse, from the government's perspective, it gradually became clear that the system allowed for a proportion of capital receipts not accounted for in one year to 'cascade' into subsequent years (which led to the reductions in proportions available in 1984/5). Finally, capital receipts could be used on renovations, which led to 'capitalized repairs' occurring, and interest generated on the receipts could be transferred to the housing revenue side.

All of this spelt change, which came in the Local Government and Housing Act 1989. The objectives in the housing finance White Paper were stated to be about providing effective government influence over expenditure and borrowing; a more equitable distribution of capital; *to promote asset sales and efficient asset management*; and to provide a sound basis for planning with confidence (DoE, 1988, p. 11; see also Malpass, 1992, pp. 20–1; emphasis added). The new system provides a method of calculating each local authority's capital borrowing allocation in respect of all its responsibilities. Housing borrowing only accounts for a percentage of the general amount.

The HIP submission remained in name only. It provided the basis for the government's assessment of the 'Basic Credit Approval' (BCA) – the capital borrowing allocation for each authority. From that amount was deducted 25 per cent of the value of council houses sold and 50 per cent of most other assets sold (known as receipts taken into account or RTIA). Finally, Supplementary Credit Approvals (SCA) would be added. In equation form, each authority's capital allocation equalled (BCA−RTIA) + SCA. This meant that, given a certain level of capital allocation to be distributed generally, the level of capital receipts would provide a counterbalance to the BCA. Areas with less capital receipts might therefore expect to get more (subject always to the BCA). However, decreasing right to buy sales in the 1990s have caused a significant downturn in capital receipts and RTIA.

The remaining proportion of capital generated through asset sales had to be used to pay off the council's debts. Significant incentives are given to those councils which have become debt free, thus providing an incentive to large scale voluntary transfer and other privatization mechanisms.

One example of an SCA is the capital allocation to some authorities that take part in the 'Cash Incentive Scheme' through which certain tenants are given financial incentives to purchase alternative accommodation, freeing up the unit of council housing for reallocation (*cf* the Tenant's Incentive Scheme for RSLs). SCAs have also been the mechanism chosen by the New Labour government when they introduced their Manifesto commitment to allow local authorities to phase in the capital receipts not already spent: Local Government Finance (Supplementary Credit Approvals) Act 1997. However, this only accounts for £147 million in its first year of operation. The government requires authorities to bid for portions of capital, taking account of the following selection of objectives: renovations and repairs to council stock, new building in partnership with RSLs, and renewal grants for home owners. The policy does not, therefore, involve a change in central government priorities, nor in central government control – indeed, precisely the reverse for the government will favour schemes linking to its other programmes such as the welfare to work scheme (see DETR, 1997b). SCAs are therefore a mechanism for further controlling the capital allocation of local authorities, specifically linked to central priorities.

Distribution Principles
Total credit allocations are set by the Treasury for all Departments of State. DETR distributes its allocation to ten regional offices on the basis of the General Needs Index. These local offices then distribute their largesse according to the 'efficiency and effectiveness of local authorities in meeting local housing need, taking into account both the authority's strategy and its performance' (DETR, 1997c, Appendix A, para. 28).[3] This is code. The HIP allocation is based upon how well councils aim to fulfill the 'enabling' role in their submissions. In 1989, DoE guidance on the presentation of HIP submissions drew attention to the importance of the private sector. Public spending could only be justified on projects required for those in need although: 'Need should be justified, . . ., by reference to the extent to which the private sector is able and willing to make provision for low-cost housing and the steps that the authority is taking both to maximise the private sector contribution, and to make the best use of its own stock' (cited in Cole & Goodchild, 1995, p. 54). Current HIP guidance is available on the internet and sets out very clearly the national policy priorities (Annex A: 'It is, of course, important that local authorities take account of national priorities') and reflects the fact that this is a *competition* for resources in that authorities submissions are judged against each other on the basis of a number of different factors (DETR, 1998a, paras 32–6).

In 1990, the DoE provided the 'clearest indication that local housing strategies which proposed new council houses would not be supported', whilst in 1991, effectiveness and efficiency were related to the development of the enabling role 'in co-operation with housing associations or other parts of the private sector' (see Malpass, 1997, p. 8). The centralization involved in the new HIP strategy is forcefully expressed in the following:

'The preparation of housing strategies is now, more than ever, governed by tactical considerations designed to please, or appease, the Department of the Environment and to demonstrate awareness of current political priorities at central government level. . . . One [survey] respondent noted the need "to follow government direction, or risk being penalised due to discretion." ' (Cole & Goodchild, 1995, pp. 54–5).

Councils now have their hands forced, first, because they lack control over the Housing Corporation's priorities (which are, in any event, set by central government); and second, because of the low level of capital available to finance other providers of new accommodation (see Warburton, 1996, pp. 119–121; Bramley, 1993). Thus, the enabling strategy has been about 'brokering deals' between different sectors.

Finally, the capital allocations have been 'topsliced', meaning that a proportion of the total capital allocation to housing has been sliced off the top to pay for particular projects or schemes which have taken place according to the priorities set by central government. A classic example of such a scheme was City Challenge, which has now been incorporated within the Single Regeneration Budget. Under this all-or-nothing scheme, councils bid for a proportion of a capital allocation as part of a broader regeneration programme. Failure meant wasted resources – success meant an increase in capital allocation which could be spent on deprived areas. However:

'The problem for some authorities was the nature of the strings attached to the funding, in the form of the competitive bidding procedure, requirements concerning the high profile involvement of private, voluntary and community partner organisations, and in particular the way that City Challenge was to be managed outside the direct control of elected local authorities . . . .' (Malpass, 1994, p. 307)

In other words, these projects invariably involved further centralized control and allocations according to central political preference.

This control has prompted the New Labour government to review the system of capital allocation as part of their programme to modernize local government and make it more accountable (DETR, 1997c). A principal part of the proposals relates to changes in the RTIA mechanism which is regarded as 'a tax on authorities' usable capital receipts (para. 6.2). Three problems are regarded as requiring solutions: first the gap between what is required and what is on offer; second, the short termism of the annual spending round; third, poor local management (para. 2.10; note the same concerns about management). Ironically, the HIP system of allocation is suggested as a solution to these more general problems (Ch. 3), as what is regarded as most appropriate is better targeting of resources (further code for no increase in resources). What can be argued, with some justification, is that this document is consequently about increasing central control, whilst retaining the illusion of localism.

In 1998, New Labour consulted on proposals to reform the capital allocations system by moving towards a 'single pot' for capital allocation. This reflected part of the DETR's responsibility, after having been granted an extra £3.6 billion following the Comprehensive Spending Review (other DETR responsibilities include the setting up of Best Value and a Housing Inspectorate – see below). The proposal also reflects an apparent willingness to accept that the DETR had been shaping council's spending priorities 'rather than enabling the council to respond to local needs' (DETR, 1998c, para. 2.10). Further, 'the prescriptive nature of the allocations can be seen to inhibit strategic planning, frustrate flexible policy implementation and prevent important local priorities being achieved' (para. 2.3). Clearly, these proposals need to be seen in the light of the more general movements in local authority finance, and through streamlining there are cuts to parts of the capital allocation (see Ch. 14).

Revenue

This era of increasing central control was repeated in the controls applied to revenue accounts. Since 1935 housing authorities had been required to hold 'housing revenue accounts' (HRA), although it has only been more recently that the HRA has been manipulated. Since 1919, central government has paid a subsidy to local government on the basis of what was required in order to achieve balance between revenue and expenditure (Malpass, 1991, p. 66). Other than in the 1972 Act, council rents have been charged on the basis of what is 'reasonable', with central subsidy making up the deficit. It was the flexible, non-justiciability of this reasonableness criterion which enabled the first Thatcher government to achieve its objective of reducing central government subsidy at the same time as rents massively increased. Between April 1980–1983 rents rose by 82 per cent (Malpass, 1990, p. 140). After this period rents generally rose in line with inflation until the new regime, under the 1989 Act, was implemented. The 1980–83 period suggests that the reasonableness concept was sufficiently malleable for the Conservatives to introduce their policies – the concept was a bland statement of general principle.

The 1980 Act

Central government was able to lever rents upwards between 1980–3 after it had altered significantly the housing revenue system in the Housing Act 1980. During the 1970s, cross-party consensus began to emerge on three broad principles: first, the historic cost accounting method required updating so that rents should thereafter be set on the basis of current property values; second, government subsidy should be calculated on a deficit basis to shore up any overdrawn balance at the end of the year;

third, means-tested rent rebates for those who could not afford the increased rents should be more generally applicable rather than available on a discretionary basis as had been the case previously (Malpass, 1991, p. 70). The regime brought into being in the 1980 Act borrowed substantially from that in the previous Labour administration's 1979 housing Bill.

The most important changes affected by the 1980 Act were, first, to remove the no profit rule from the HRA, so enabling authorities to make a surplus; second, to base government subsidy on *notional deficits*. Subsidy was, henceforward, to be based upon central government's assumptions about the appropriate levels of income and expenditure in individual local authorities. Consequently, assumptions of rent levels and expenditure on management and maintenance were set centrally, although councils were at liberty to depart from these levels (supposedly leaving councils' autonomy in place). The centrally set amounts were based on the levels spent in 1977–8 initially and the amount applicable to management and maintenance was raised on this basis in line with the rate of inflation. This 'impl[ied]' that the underlying "need to spend" on [it] was broadly constant' (Malpass *et al.*, 1993, p. 15) without allowing for the required expansion of the level of repairs and general maintenance (leading to capitalized repairs).

Central government's subsidy was only one element of the subsidy to the HRA. There were also contributions which could be made from the Rate[4] Fund as well as central subsidy in respect of the total rent rebate bill. Central government was given the power to reduce its own contribution to the Rate Fund – particularly that which related to housing expenditure – but this was too controversial for the first Thatcher government. Pressure from the Conservative-controlled Association of District Councils meant that the 'block grant mechanism' for raising rents was used only once in 1981–2 (see Malpass, 1990, pp. 142–4 generally).

From 1982–89, contributions from the Rate Fund to the HRA actually outstripped the amount of central government subsidy, although this was more prevalent in London and metropolitan areas than in rural areas (see Malpass, 1990, pp. 150–1). This meant that ratepayers in these areas were effectively subsidising the authorities' housing income. Conversely, interest on right-to-buy sales were more prevalent in *rural areas* thus subsidising the HRA in those authorities (*ibid*). In other words, the controls exerted by central government were undermined by their inability to reduce their subsidy levels (i.e. block grant through what was known as the E7 indicator), as well as a lack of controls on capital payments. It was this lack of control which, after about 1983, caused central government to lose its leverage over rents in many areas.

This lack of leverage became most apparent as local rent increases caused many councils to go 'out of subsidy' – that is, their HRA balanced or had entered surplus. By 1985–6, 258 councils did not require subsidy. Those still requiring subsidy were generally concentrated in the south (Malpass, 1990, pp. 147–8). The increase in rents was counterbalanced by an increase in targeted rent rebates (which became included in the Housing Benefit system in 1982) paid out of the Department of Health and Social Security (DHSS) budget. Not all council tenants required rebates, but it was generally the case that increasing rents also meant that there was a greater incentive to exercise the right to buy for those who could afford to do so.

For those councils with less interest to pay on historic debts, the system did not require rents to increase to such a great extent as others – the first to enter subsidy (and shake off central control) were those with less expenditure/debt. *Thus, central government lost control over the rents these councils were able to levy*[5] *whilst at the same time paying for increases in rent through rent rebate.* Furthermore, surpluses made on the HRA could be transferred to the Rate Fund. In such cases, the increased rents paid by council tenants and the treasury through rent rebate were subsidizing and reducing the amounts required from the ratepayers (who were also council tenants). Ginsburg puts it this way:

> 'Under the present system tenants are in effect swindled. Their rents often contribute to estate lighting, cleansing, rubbish collection, property development, playgrounds, etc, which are covered by the rates for owner occupiers and private tenants. In effect, council tenants often pay twice over both in their rates and their rents for council services.' (Ginsburg, 1989, p. 64)

As the system was based upon *notional deficits*, councils could also be in surplus but have a notional deficit. The actual surplus could be transferred to the Rate Fund but the government would cotinue to pay subsidy.

The Current System

The system was ripe for reform. The 1987 White Paper suggested that the provision and management of council housing 'needs to be carried out in a businesslike way, so that homes can be managed and maintained to a reasonable standard, and rents kept at an affordable level, without excessive and indiscriminate subsidies' (DoE, 1987, para. 5.7). The 1988 housing finance White Paper based its proposals on three principles: there was a need for a simpler system, giving consistent incentives; it needed to be fairer between tenants and local tax payers as well as between tenants in different areas; it should direct subsidy to areas which require it, providing incentives for good management 'rather than a cover for bad practice and inefficiency' (DoE, 1998, p. 6). In accordance with the second principle, rents were to be set by reference to what people could pay as well as what the property was worth on the basis of today's values. Here, then, 'reasonableness' of rent was related to market principles.

The Local Government and Housing Act 1989, Part VI, provided the principal mechanisms for the implementation of this policy. The system required councils to 'ring fence' their HRA so that it was no longer possible to make contributions from it to other accounts. Schedule 4 to the

Act set out what items might be regarded as credits and debits to the account and did not include interest on capital receipts. In common with most housing legislation, Schedule 4 provides a discretionary mechanism through which debits and credits can be massaged by the Secretary of State. The clearest example of this is item 8: 'Sums calculated for the year in accordance with such formulae as the Secretary of State may from time to time determine' which appears in both debit and credit sides. The 'Item 8 Credit and Item 8 Debit (General) Determination 1998–99' provides almost impenetrable formulae for the calculation of these items.

Central government's subsidy and the amount paid in respect of rent rebate became combined into one subsidy. Immediately, this simple adjustment put all councils' HRAs into deficit because rent rebate was now counted as expenditure (whereas before it had been an item of income, combined with rents). Councils therefore became reliant on central subsidy again, which returned the lever over rent levels to central government (see Malpass, 1991, p. 72). Central government believed that rents would eventually increase to levels which would reduce government subsidy, thus reducing government's exposure to rent rebate, so that (crudely) richer tenants would support poorer tenants.

Central government subsidy was to be calculated on a completely different basis reflecting the desire to individualize it for each council. This was supposed to be a 'fundamental' accounting basis, tailored to each authority's individual requirements. Central government would set a guideline rent increase, affecting income levels, as well as an allowance for management and maintenance, affecting expenditure. There was 'a desire to produce a pattern of rents which is more closely related to local and regional variations in the value of property in the private sector, and to encourage a pattern of [management and maintenance] spending which is related to differences in stock characteristics' (Malpass *et al.*, 1993, p. 21). However, councils could raise rents outside that guideline to the level they wished as well as increase the amount spent on management and maintenance. Thus, the basic tenet of the revolt against the 1972 Act – the loss of local autonomy in rent setting – had not been altered: councils could set their own rents outside the guideline if they so wished, but this power was heavily constrained by government influence through subsidy. Reductions in subsidy would require increases in rents.

Problems arose with the system from the beginning because it was implemented before 'certain key aspects . . . had been finalized' (Malpass & Warburton, 1993, p. 97). Thus management and maintenance allowances were based on *actual* spending levels between 1986–89 with a *three per cent* increase. However, during 1986–89, many councils had been capitalizing their repairs, and consequently the revenue basis of their repairs was generally less in that period. In the second year, however, management allowances were calculated on the basis of stock character-istics; management costs remained subject to a percentage uplift. Increasingly, however, it appears that levels of spending on repair and maintenance have been significantly cut in urban areas and much less so in more affluent areas: 'Intuitively, one would have to say that this pattern is the opposite of what one would expect on the basis of targeting resources on areas of greatest need' (Malpass *et al.*, 1993, p. 47). This has occurred because the level of management and maintenance required on the stock in urban areas is generally above that which tenants are able to pay outside the subsidy arrangements.

The New Labour Consultation

In December 1998, the New Labour government issued a Consulation Paper essentially considering the benefits of tinkering with the sorts of items included within the HRA, as well as moving towards resource accounting. The basis of these changes is to enable certain matters to be resourced through the HRA. In particular, stock valuations will be carried out and 6 per cent of the valuation will be used to gauge the Item 8 determination to make certain payments, such as to interest on outstanding loans. HRA subsidy will include either an element of depreciation or a major repairs allowance, which would enable the authority to catch up on historic repairs. Authorities will effectively bid for this in new Business Plans (DETR, 1998b, para. 3.2–3). Under the new scheme, rent rebates would be taken out of the HRA but this seems to be merely technical because 'the government would still need to 'capture' surplus rental income to offset the additional costs of funding rent rebates in full' (DETR, 1998b, para. 2.20).

Rent Setting

Rent levels have also been problematic:

> '[W]hen data were first run through the DoE computers in 1989 it quickly emerged that some form of damping mechanism would be needed in order to prevent very large increases in some London and south-eastern authorities, and large *reductions* in some northern authorities.' (Malpass, 1991, p. 73)

Rents were calculated on the basis of a percentage of right-to-buy valuations and local capital valuation plus five per cent real increase plus another five per cent for inflation. However, the government introduced a 'damping' mechanism so that the guideline rent increases set were between 95p and £4.50 per week for 1990–91; £1.38 and 2.50 for 1991–92; £1.20 and £4.50 for 1992–93. This damping remains, so for 1998–99 rent increases ranged from 72p to £1.22 (this reduction in increase is due to attempts to restrict the upward spiral of Housing Benefit). The new system, therefore, required north to subsidize south (because rents had to rise in the north, instead of being reduced, to offset the lower rent rises in the south).

Rent levels actually set by councils have generally overshot the guideline increases set centrally. Mainly, this was required to offset management and maintenance expenses greater than notionally allowed by central government under the new system. Rents rose fastest in London and the South, so that average rent levels in London in 1992 were 68 per cent higher than those in the north, as opposed to a 23 per cent differential five years earlier (Malpass *et al.*, 1993, p. 41). However, research also suggested differentiation on the basis of diverse factors, such as levels of voids (which are assumed to be at a certain percentage in the new scheme), and so geographical comparisons can only form general observations. When rent levels rise above a certain point in each individual authority, the amount of subsidy due from government is reduced. Subsidy is, as before, paid in deficit and related to notional amounts. Of the two elements of subsidy – the government element and the Housing Benefit element – by 1995/96, rent increases had eliminated government subsidy and were eating away at the Housing Benefit element.

Individually, then, the new system has created even greater incentives to opt out of the system through the right to buy and equivalent measures. Those tenants not in receipt of Housing Benefit, or who are required to contribute to their housing costs outside the benefit system, effectively subsidize the rents of those who do receive benefit because the greater the rises in rent the less subsidy (including Housing Benefit subsidy) is paid by the government:

'As rents rise relative to expenditure, so HRA subsidy will fall, and the better-off tenants will inevitably see themselves as paying for the rebates of their less well-off neighbours. . . . Tenants who buy will relieve themselves of the burden of subsidising their poorer neighbours, and will themselves become eligible for assistance through mortgage interest tax relief.' (Malpass, 1990, pp. 176–7)

Less subsidy paid to cover management and maintenance charges will also mean an increase in rents.

Rent rises, however, affect Housing Benefit; as they are linked to the Retail Price Index, they also affect inflation as well (see Warburton, 1996, p. 118). Affordability has now become the crucial issue reflecting the tense battle being fought between the DoE/DETR and the DSS over Housing Benefit levels (the latter being responsible for the rebate element of subsidy). The battle created 'all sorts of problems' between central government departments (Malpass *et al.*, 1993, p. 37) in the early stages. This was partly because rent rebates rise with actual rent rises (and not guideline increases set by the DoE). Localized rent setting therefore contains an element of chance. If actual rents bring about an overspend on the Treasury-set budget, the Treasury may require increases in subsequent years (*ibid*).

This battle became overt in the 1995 housing White Paper, by which point it was clear that the DSS had won. Guideline rent increases were to be reduced in each of the succeeding years because 'We are now approaching the limits of what can be achieved through higher rents. . . . To increase rents much further could increase the cost to the taxpayer, because of the increased benefits bill and damage to work incentives' (DoE, 1995, p. 27). Up to that point, most councils had been setting their rents on the basis of giving 'a specific number of points to particular characteristics of a dwelling' and without reference to private sector values (Walker & Marsh, 1997, p. 41). However, the 1989 Act did require councils, in setting 'reasonable rents' to

> 'have regard in particular to the principle that the rents of houses of any class or description should bear broadly the same proportion to private sector rents as the rents of houses of any other class or description.'
> (s. 24(3), Housing Act 1985, as amended by 1989 Act; known as the 'relative desirability' provision)

The 1995 White Paper promised to encourage councils to make greater use of this provision (so that tenants occupy properties best suited to their requirements: DoE, 1995, p. 27).

S. 24(3) does not require market-based rents to be set, simply that councils have regard to those rents in setting their rents. Guidance on rent-setting was subsequently amended so as to ensure that 'the social rented sector is used as efficiently as possible' (DoE, 1996, para. 8.4). A particular problem of implementing this provision in order to make most efficient use of properties is that tenants are often insulated from rent rises by Housing Benefit: '[Housing Benefit] entitlement is likely to blunt the impact of the new price signals, and in any event the ability of tenants to move in response to [the new signals] is severely limited by the lack of stock into which they can move' (Walker & Marsh, 1997, p. 44). For those not in receipt of benefit and living in better quality stock, higher rents are yet a further incentive to exercise the right to buy. Furthermore, it is unclear that there is any general rationale guiding private-sector rents and (of some interest given the general discussion as to their public/private status) RSLs are specifically included within the definition of private sector thereby further dimming any unifying, comparator (Walker & Marsh, 1998). Finally, rent setting itself is a 'lengthy, resource intensive exercise' which, in the context of changes in housing management through Compulsory Competitive Tendering (CCT) (Walker & Marsh, 1995, para. 3.31), suggests that legislative change will take time to seep into the system.

5.3   'In the Image of . . .': The New Housing Management

There has always been an uncertainty about the role of housing management. Does it extend further than simply collecting the rent and managing and maintaining properties? In other words, is there (or should there be) a public service ethos within council housing management, and, if so, how far should it extend? Decentralization had given rise to a welfare role within management – an acceptance that it was not only about providing housing but also maintaining tenants within it. Reducing management and maintenance elements of subsidy provided one message from central government against a backdrop of increasingly marginalized estates. In that context, it is not surprising that managers themselves view their role as 'one of contradiction, insecurity and even puzzlement' (Clapham & Franklin, 1997, p. 15). The impact of community care and children's legislation has sharpened the contrast. However, it is clear that no real answer was forthcoming, which made the area a perfect project for central government's crude tool of CCT.

The characterization of council housing management as 'inefficient, wasteful, and costly' has, since 1979, had an enduring appeal. In 1991, these criticisms re-emerged in the *Citizen's Charter* which prefaced a somewhat tortuous move towards putting housing management out to tender. This critique either was inaccurate, too general, or suggested that government policies since 1979 had failed to achieve efficient and effective management practice. In fact, the DoE's own research pointed to the 'business' culture' and 'customer awareness', which was traced back to 1980 'and the general philosophy of the 1980s' (Baker *et al.*, 1992, para. 4.16). The same study also suggested that there was a 'strong economic case' for (CCT) which could 'generate beneficial changes' for tenants (paras 7.2 & 7.24 respectively). It is difficult to appreciate quite how the research can have come to this conclusion, for alternative options had simply not been tested. Indeed, there was some doubt as to whether there could be effective competition as RSLs might not compete for fear of 'biting the hand that fed them'. Thus, the potential market was self-limiting.

Despite these concerns, the Consultation Paper (issued at the same time as the research itself was published) promised to introduce CCT 'on a tight timetable' whilst promising, in a potentially contradictory next sentence, that 'the prime consideration will be the welfare of the tenants' (DoE, 1992, para. 3.2). CCT was to be extended to housing management 'as a further stimulus to efficiency, as a means of ensuring that the councils examine their performance and seek maximum value for money' (para. 2.6). It was introduced in 1994 and phased in thereafter, depending upon size of council (see SI 1994/1671 which sets out the definition of housing management for these purposes, as well as SI 1994/2297).

CCT operates by requiring councils to place specified parts of the housing management out to tender so that their 'in-house' housing management is forced to compete with outside organizations (see Harden, 1992, pp. 17–22; *cf* 'contracting out' which does not necessarily involve competition). Its principal mechanism is a form of contract between the local authority (as 'client' or 'purchaser') and the organization which wins the contract (as 'provider') in an open tender. Where the outside organization wins the contract, that contract is enforceable in the usual way; where it is won internally, it is not so enforceable because the council cannot sue itself. Critically, though, the rhetoric of ensuring better service provision for tenants is undermined by the fact that tenants cannot enforce the contract on ordinary principles (third parties cannot enforce contracts to which they are not privy). Tenants must be consulted as to the contract specification but it was always proposed that they should have no right to veto a council's decision to tender particular estates (DoE, 1992, para. 4.7). Furthermore, 'it remains doubtful whether this combination of consumer voice, legal rights and compulsory competition does justice to the full range of the tenant interest in social housing' (Vincent-Jones & Harries, 1998, p. 51). Democratic empowerment of tenants through associations and other structures have, in one study, led to 'power struggles and factionalism' (*ibid*, p. 61).

CCT is a further example of the new "enabling" (reflected in the literature): 'In principle, this process should transform the state, locally and centrally, into *an 'enabling' organization*, responsible for ensuring that public services are delivered, rather than producing them directly itself' (Deakin & Walsh, 1996, p. 33; emphasis added). The more general claims of supporters of CCT and the contracting culture – of efficiency and cost-effectiveness – remain unproven, and there are doubts as to whether service quality has improved (see, for example, Parker, 1990; Cope, 1995; Deakin & Walsh, 1996). Shaw *et al.* argue that the Conservative government's agenda in relation to CCT was not so much concerned with improving service delivery as forming part of their 'attempted reorientation of the local welfare state towards a more business-led agenda' (1995, p. 70). They view CCT as a *political tool* designed to facilitate the changes required in public service. Five key aspects of this 'camouflaged centralism' are considered: first, CCT has concerned privatization and cost-cutting; second, it has undermined local initiatives such as equal opportunities; third, it has aided the 'depoliticisation of resource allocation decisions and helped to question the assumption that problems can be necessarily cured (or even ameliorated) by the allocation of increasing resources' and, in the process, aided the rise of managers as opposed to the welfare state professionals; fourth, CCT has considerably added to the power of officers at the expense of councillors and, in the process, removed decisions from democratic accountability processes; fifth, accountability has been shifted from elections to the market (pp. 70–71).

Of the eight areas chosen to pilot CCT for housing management, the private sector mainly secured the contracts (although without in-house bids: Blake & Fraser, 1995, p. 23). Outside those areas, it seems that RSLs have tended not to bid for the contracts on the basis that they cannot afford to have their links with the council threatened (as Housing Corporation funding is, to a certain extent, dependent upon these links: see Ch. 6 below). Thus, paradoxically, the centrally determined scheme in the development of housing has affected the competition for housing management. Other matters with which potential contractees might be concerned are, for example, the cost of bidding (Blake & Fraser estimate it at around £100,000) together with its complexity. The process has been summarized in the following way:

'The CCT process varies from council to council, but generally includes the completion of a questionnaire, a formal presentation to a council's selection or evaluation panel and the completion of a detailed submission. But in practice the selection process starts well before these formal stages.

Prospective tenderers will often sound out local authorities on their likely reaction to a bid. If a bid is perceived to be hostile by the council, it is unlikely to proceed. This is particularly true of [those RSLs] who have forged strong financial links by bidding on a hostile basis. . . .

But all of this activity has taken place against a background of limited information on the contract specifications and requirements. This changes dramatically at the tender stage. Then, bidders are over-whelmed with information. One recent bidder was told to collect their package by car and was given 19 bulky specification files to drive off with.' (Callan, 1996, p. 20–1)

A further factor was the specification in the regulations that contracts worth less than £500,000 would be exempted from CCT when these were precisely the type of contract for which RSLs and other organizations were most likely to bid (as smaller, more manageable contracts are most attractive to smaller organizations).

In the first round of CCT, it was perhaps unsurprising that around 95 per cent of councils' own housing management services won the contracts. It was alleged that councils had engaged in anti-competitive practices, as well as the then Housing Minister hinting at the Chartered Institute of Housing conference 'in his tetchy threat to delegates that he could force the transfer of the housing service into the private sector without any competition whatsoever if councils persisted with any rigging of the process' (Blake & Dwelly, 1996, pp23–4). The fall of the Conservative government meant that CCT had already reached its zenith. New Labour's manifesto promised to reform the system.

This promised reform has already begun with the setting back of the timetable for completion of the CCT programme, a Consultation Paper on a new system called Best Value, and pilot projects on the new system begun (see, for example, Owen, 1998). The Consultation Paper clearly highlights the failures of CCT (see DETR, 1997a, para. 1.5: 'In short, CCT has proved a poor deal for employees, employers and local people.'). The new approach is to be based upon the pragmatic principle of 'What matters is what works' (para. 1.6). However, it is clear that the 'three Es' are as important to Best Value as they were to CCT: 'Achieving Best Value is not just about economy and efficiency, but also about effectiveness and the quality of local services – the setting of targets and performance against these should therefore underpin the new regime' (DETR, 1997a,

Figure 1). Local authorities, furthermore, will be required to deliver the 'four Cs': challenge why and how services are being provided; compare with others in both public and private sectors; consult with tenants, residents and the 'wider community'; 'embrace fair competition' (DETR, 1999b, para. 4.5). Competition will remain a key to the process as will central government and auditors' control. Financial control is to be increased by the development of a Housing Inspectorate within the Audit Commission's Best Value team (DETR, 1999b, part 6).

Drawing upon the work of Teubner and others, Vincent-Jones has argued that the CCT regime inadequately attempted to enforce a particular approach of service provision through legal and other mechanisms: 'The case for the abolition of CCT is strengthened beyond economic and political arguments by the reflexive failures of the compulsory regime. There can be little justification for substantive legal regulation, monitoring and control of local authority choice in the making of arrangements for service provision' (1998, p. 374). Nevertheless, in certain circumstances CCT was made to work, for example, through developing pre-existing arrangements for participation. In general, 'local authorities were successful in neutralising the threat posed by CCT, mainly through the adoption of strategies of minimal compliance that appear to have left their 'core values' intact' (*ibid*, p. 373). Moving away from this overly rigid system may require the retention of some of the aspects of CCT but within a less restricting environment.

What is interesting about the new approach, though is the identification of the taxpayer as the consumer of services. Best Value is seen as a duty 'which reinforces rather than replaces the fiduciary duty which the courts have confirmed applies to local authorities' stewardship of their resources' (para. 2.2; see also *Bromley LBC* v. *GLC* [1983] 1 AC 768). Whilst the Consultation Paper hedges around the subject, it seems relatively clear that those who do not pay tax have no interest in Best Value. Cooper argues that the judicial technique of referring to the taxpayer is part of a justificatory matrix for judicial decision-making techniques:

> 'Taxpayers as a class are constructed in two ways. First, by what they are not. They are not public transport users, council employees or the elderly. . . .
> Second, the figure of the taxpayer is intended to symbolize the generic and universal, against the elderly, tenants and staff's particularistic interests. . . In this instance, the taxpayer is at least moderately affluent and male. He is not a socialist or feminist; nor does he want local government practising philanthropy. Limited benevolence may, however, be acceptable.' (1997, pp. 240–1)

From this angle, Best Value fits neatly into a contract culture which sidelines the interests of those who are not taxpayers.

Such a view may prove too cynical. In 1999, New Labour proposed the creation of Tenant Participation Compacts between the local authority and its tenants (DETR, 1999a – see Ch. 6 for discussion). The government has argued that 'local authorities should acively and meaningfully involve tenants and residents in the planning and delivery of their housing strategies and services' (DETR, 1999b, para. 3.7). There is much detail left to be worked out, however. For example, what should be the balance between the authority's tenant and other residents' views? Local arrangements are supposed to determine such questions.

Conclusion

It should not come as a surprise that, were the Conservatives to have won the 1997 general election, they would have pursued the final solution of withdrawing housing from local authority control completely. The piecemeal solutions operated between 1979–1997 had effectively created the environment for many authorities to have done so already. From the Housing Act 1980 to the Housing Act 1996, successive Conservative governments provided ever-greater incentives to individual council tenants to join the mass of home owners, through, for example, the right to buy; then, they concentrated on legislative provisions which gave powers to tenants and to central government to transfer whole or parts of council housing to different sectors; finally, they subjected housing management to contractual approaches, thus changing the nature of the public-sector ethos.

The backdrop to these measures has been a complex financial structure which was essentially put in place to provide the government with extra leverage over local authorities, as well as further incentives to tenants to exercise the right to buy. What could have been a greater incentive to leave the tenure than rents increasing by 80 per cent between 1980–3? Fairly consistently, central government exerted greater and greater pressure over local authorities' capital programmes and rents. Until around 1975, it might have been said that local government had pursued locally generated plans and had built up its housing tenure in a perhaps haphazard way, reflecting the authority's own appreciation of the level of housing need in the area together with the willingness of central government to provide development funds at any particular time. From 1979 onwards, the situation had changed to the extent that local government has become an arm of central government; something which has been controlled and subjugated by its greatest power.

Throughout the Thatcher/Major eras, the promotion of home owner-ship, and the dismantling of council provision of accommodation, have been the most significant (and related) themes. The key to these lies in the privatization initiatives. However, to appreciate fully the success of privatization policies, it is crucial to appreciate the manipulation of council finance which imposed rent increases (and made tenants subsidize the Housing Benefit of other tenants) whilst at the same time effectively reducing the subsidy available for management and maintenance. The deteriorating service consequently provided by housing management, combined with the uncertainty as to its core, consequently heralded further initiatives designed to privatize the service.

Further Reading

The reading on local authorities is voluminous. A small reasonably representative selection appears below.

On enabling (and housing): N. Rao (1990), *The Changing Role of Local Housing Authorities*, York: Joseph Rowntree; R. Goodlad (1994), 'Conceptualising 'enabling': the housing role of local authorities', vol 20, *Local Government Studies*, 570; R. Goodlad (1997), 'Local authorities and the new governance of social housing', in P. Malpass (ed.), *Ownership, Control and Accountability*, Coventry: Institute of Housing; Audit Commission (1992), *Developing Local Authority Housing Strategies*, London: HMSO.

On central-local relationships (generally): Various Consultation Papers from DETR; I. Loveland (1996), *Constitutional Law – A Critical Introduction*, London: Butterworths, Chs 10–11; G. Stoker (1995), 'Intergovernmental relations', vol 73, *Public Administration*, 101; G. Jones (1989), 'The relationship between central and local government', in C. Harlow (ed.), *Public Law and Politics*, London: Sweet & Maxwell.

On local government: (generally) J. Stewart & G. Stoker (eds), *Local Government in the 1990s*, London: Macmillan; S. Leach, J. Stewart & K. Walsh (1994), *The Changing Organisation and Management of Local Government*, London: Macmillan; (on accountability): M. Loughlin (1992), *Administrative Accountability in Local Government*, York: Joseph Rowntree; (on politics): D. Widdicombe, (1986), *The Conduct of Local Authority Business*, Cmnd 9797, London: HMSO; (on management): A. Cochrane (1994), 'Managing change in local government' in J. Clarke, A. Cochrane & E. McLaughlin (eds), *Managing Social Policy*, London: Sage; P. Hoggett (1991), 'A new management in the public sector?', vol 19, *Policy and Politics*, 243; W. Bines *et al.* (1993), *Managing Social Housing*, London: HMSO; Centre for Housing Research, University of Glasgow (1989), *The Nature and Effectiveness of Housing Management in England*, London: HMSO; A. Crook *et al.* (1996), *A New Lease of Life?*, Bristol: Policy Press; (on decentralization) V. Lowndes & G. Stoker (1992), 'An Evaluation of Neighbourhood Decentralisation', vol 20, *Policy and Politics*, 47 (Pt I), 143 (Pt 2); D. Burns *et al.* (1994), *The Politics of Decentralisation*, London: Macmillan; I. Cole (1993), 'The decentralisation of housing services', in P. Malpass & R Means (eds), *Implementing Housing Policy*, Buckingham: Open University Press; (on restructuring): C. Pycroft (1995), 'Restructuring local government: the Banham Commission's failed historic enterprise', vol 10, *Public Policy and Administration*, 49; R. Leach (1994), 'Restructuring local government', vol 20, *Local Government Studies*, 345.

On CCT: P. Vincent-Jones (1994), 'The limits of near-contractual governance: local authority internal trading under CCT', vol 21 *Journal of Law and Society*, 214; D. Chaundy & M. Uttley (1993), 'The economics of compulsory competitive tendering: issues, evidence and the case of municipal refuse collection', vol 8, *Public Policy and Administration*, 25; K. Walsh (1989), 'Competition and service in local government', in J. Stewart and G. Stoker (eds), *The Future of Local Government*, London: Macmillan; K. Walsh & H. Davis (1993), *Competition and Service: The Impact of the Local Government Act 1988*, London: HMSO.

Endnotes

1. LSVTs had begun prior to the 1987 White Paper – see Ch. 6 – under general powers contained in the 1985 Act. However, their existence was carefully nurtured by the DoE after 1987 and thus is included in this time period.
2. This mechanism reduces the amount of Housing Benefit payable disproportionately with the amount of income earned.
3. Until 1997, 40 per cent was allocated on the basis of the GNI, whilst 60 per cent was allocated on other more discretionary criteria.
4. The rates were a local tax – the forerunner of the Poll Tax and Council Tax. They were essentially based upon the value of property and were paid by home owners.
5. If the E7 indicator had still been available to be used, the government could have used the GRE to reduce the block grant and thus place greater pressure on council rents.

Bibliography

Baker, R., Challen, P., MacLennan, D., Reid, V. and Whitehead, C. (1992), *The Scope for Competitive Tendering of Housing Management*, London: HMSO

Barron, A. and Scott, C. (1992), 'The Citizen's Charter Programme', vol 55, *Modern Law Review*, 526

Blake, J. and Dwelly, T. (1996), 'Left in the starting blocks', September/October, *Roof*, 23

Blake, J. and Fraser, R. (1995), 'Sink or swim', March/April, *Roof*, 21

Bramley, G. (1993), 'The enabling role for local housing authorities: a preliminary evaluation', in P. Malpass and R. Means (eds), *Implementing Housing Policy*, Buckingham: Open University Press

Buck, T. (1991), 'Rents and income: a legal overview', in D. Hughes and S. Lowe (eds), *A New Century of Social Housing*, Leicester: Leicester University Press

Cabinet Office (1991), *The Citizen's Charter*, Cm 1599, London: HMSO

Cairncross, L., Clapham, D. and Goodlad, R. (1997), *Housing Management, Consumers and Citizens*, London: Routledge

Callen, P. (1996), 'Left out in the cold?', January/February, *Roof*, 20

Centre for Housing Research (1989), *The Nature and Effectiveness of Housing Management*, London: HMSD

Clapham, D. and Franklin, B. (1997), 'The social construction of housing management', vol 12, *Housing Studies*, 7

Clarke, A. (1993), 'Prejudice, ignorance and panic! Popular politics in a land fit for scroungers', in M. Loney, D. Boswell, and J. Clarke (eds), *Social Policy and Social Welfare*, Milton Keynes: Open University Press

Cole, I., Arnold, P. and Windle, K. (1991), 'Decentralised housing services – back to the future', in D. Donnison and D. Maclennan (eds), *The Housing Service of the Future*, Coventry: Institute of Housing

Cole, I. and Furbey, R. (1994), *The Eclipse of Council Housing*, London: Routledge

Cole, I. and Goodchild, B. (1995), 'Local housing strategies in England: an assessment of their changing role and content', vol 23, *Policy and Politics*, 49

Cooper, D. (1995), 'Local government legal consciousness in the shadow of juridification', vol 22, *Journal of Law and Society*, 506

Cooper, D. (1996), 'Institutional illegality and disobedience: local government narratives', vol 16, *Oxford Journal of Legal Studies*, 255

Cooper, D. (1997), 'Fiduciary government: decentring property and taxpayers' interests', vol 6, *Social and Legal Studies*, 235

Cope, S. (1995), 'Contracting-out in local government: cutting by privatising', vol 10, *Public Policy and Administration*, 29

Deakin, D. and Walsh, K. (1996), 'The enabling state: the role of markets and contracts', vol 74, *Public Administration*, 33

Department of the Environment (DoE) (1977), *Housing Policy – A Consultative Document*, London: HMSO

Department of the Environment (DoE) (1987), *Housing: The Government's Proposals*, Cm 214, London: HMSO

Department of the Environment (DoE) (1988), *New Financial Regime for Local Authority Housing in England and Wales: A Consultation Paper*, London: DoE

Department of the Environment (DoE) (1992), *Competing for Quality in Housing – Competition in the Provision of Housing Management: A Consultation Paper*, London: HMSO

Department of the Environment (DoE) (1994), *Access to Local Authority and Housing Association Tenancies*, London: HMSO

Department of the Environment (DoE) (1995), *Our Future Homes: Opportunity, Choice and Responsibility*, Cm 2901, London: HMSO

Department of the Environment (DoE) (1996), *Housing Revenue Manual*, London: HMSO

Department of the Environment, Transport and the Regions (DETR) (1997a), *Modernising Local Government: Improving Local Services through Best Value, A Consultation Paper*, London: DETR

Department of the Environment, Transport and the Regions (DETR) (1997b), *Capital Receipts Initiative: Guidance to Local Authorities*, London: DETR

Department of the Environment, Transport and the Regions (DETR) (1997c), *Modernising Local Government: Capital Finance*, London: DETR

Department of the Environment, Transport and the Regions (DETR) (1998a), *The Housing Investment Programme: 1998 Guidance Note for Local Authorities*, London: DETR

Department of the Environment, Transport and the Regions (DETR) (1998b), *A New Financial Framework for Local Authority Housing: Resource Accounting inthe Housing Revenue Account Consulation Paper*, London: DETR

Department of the Environment, Transport and the Regions (DETR) (1998c), *Proposed Single Allocation to Local Housing Authorities for Capital Investment in Housing*, London: DETR

Department of the Environment, Transport and the Regions (DETR) (1999a), *Tenant Participation Compacts Consultation Paper*, London: DETR

Department of the Environment, Transport and the Regions (DETR) (1999b), *Best Value in Housing Framework Consultation Paper*, London: DETR

Donnison, D. (1967), *The Government of Housing*, London: Harmondsworth

Dunn, R., Forrest, R. and Murie, A. (1987), 'The geography of council house sales in England 1979–1985', vol 24, *Urban Studies*, 47

Forrest, R., Lansley, S. and Murie, A. (1984), *A Foot on the Ladder? An Evaluation of Low Cost Home Ownership Initiatives*, Working Paper 41, Bristol: School for Advanced Urban Studies, University of Bristol

Forrest, R. and Murie, A. (1985), *An Unreasonable Act? Central-local Government Conflict and the Housing Act 1980*, Bristol: School for Advanced Urban Studies, University of Bristol

Forrest, R. and Murie, A. (1991), *Selling the Welfare State: The Privatisation of Public Housing*, London: Routledge

Forrest, R. and Murie, A. (1995), 'From privatization to commodification: tenure conversion and new zones of transition in the city', vol 19, *International Journal of Urban and Regional Research*, 407

Ganz, G. (1991), *Quasi-Legislation*, London: Sweet & Maxwell

Ginsburg, N. (1989), 'The Housing Act, 1988 and its policy context: a critical commentary', vol 25, *Critical Social Policy*, 56

Golding, P. and Middleton, S. (1982), *Images of Welfare*, Oxford: Basil Blackwell

Goodlad, R. (1993), *The Housing Authority as Enabler*, Coventry: Institute of Housing

Harden, I. (1992), *The Contracting State*, Buckingham: Open University Press

Harlow, C. and Rawlings, R. (1997), *Law and Administration*, London: Butterworths

Hills, J. (1990), *Unravelling Housing Finance*, Oxford: Oxford University Press

House of Commons Environment Committee (1981), *Third Report from the Environment Committee*, London: HMSO

Kay, A., Legg, C. and Foot, J. (1987), *The 1980 Tenants' Rights in Practice: A Study of the Implementation of the 1980 Housing Act Rights by Local Authorities 1980–83*, London: Blackrose

Leather, P. (1983), 'Housing (dis?)investment programmes', vol 11, *Policy and Politics*, 215

Leather, P. and Murie, A. (1986), 'The decline in public expenditure', in P. Malpass (ed.), *The Housing Crisis*, London: Croom Helm

Loughlin, M. (1986), *Local Government in the Modern State*, London: Sweet & Maxwell

Loughlin, M. (1994), 'The restructuring of central-local government relations', in J. Jowell and D. Oliver (eds), *The Changing Constitution*, Oxford: Oxford University Press

Loughlin, M. (1996), *Legality and Locality: The Role of Law in Central-Local Government*, Oxford: Oxford University Press

Loughlin, M. (1997), 'Understanding central-local government relations', vol 11, *Public Policy and Administration*, 48

Loveland, I. (1992), 'Square pegs, round holes: the 'right' to council housing in the post-war era', vol 19, *Journal of Law and Society*, 339

Loveland, I. (1995), *Housing Homeless Persons*, Oxford: Oxford University Press

Malpass, P. (1990), *Reshaping Housing Policy: Subsidies, Rents and Residualisation*, London: Routledge

Malpass, P. (1991), 'The financing of public housing', in D. Hughes and S. Lowe (eds), *A New Century of Social Housing*, Leicester: Leicester University Press

Malpass, P. (1992), 'Housing policy and the disabling of local authorities', in J. Birchall (ed.), *Housing Policy in the 1990s*, London: Routledge

Malpass, P. (1994), 'Policy making and local governance: how Bristol failed to secure City Challenge funding (twice)', vol 22, *Policy and Politics*, 301

Malpass, P. (1997), 'Introduction', in P. Malpass (ed.), *Ownership, Control and Accountability: The New Governance of Housing*, Coventry: Institute of Housing

Malpass, P. and Warburton, M. (1993), 'The new financial regime for local authority housing', in P. Malpass and R. Means (eds), *Implementing Housing Policy*, Buckingham: Open University Press

Malpass, P., Warburton, M., Bramley, G. and Smart, G. (1993), *Housing Policy in Action: The New Financial Regime for Council Housing*, Bristol: School for Advanced Urban Studies, University of Bristol

Meikle, J. and Wintour, P. (1995), 'The house that John built', *The Guardian*, 27 April

Merrett, S. (1979), *State Housing in Britain*, London: Routledge & Kegan Paul

Ministry of Housing and Local Government (1965), *The Housing Programme 1965–1970*, London: HMSO

Murie, A. (1997a), 'Beyond state housing', in P. Williams (ed.), *Directions in Housing Policy: Towards Sustainable Housing Policies for the UK*, London: Paul Chapman

Murie, A. (1997b), 'The social rented sector, housing and the welfare state', vol 12, *Housing Studies*, 437

National Audit Office (1997), *Housing Corporation: Tenants' Choice and the Torbay Tenants Housing Association*, London: HMSO

Owen, M. (1998), 'The best value yet?', March/April, *Roof*, 12

Parker, D. (1990), 'The 1988 Local Government Act and compulsory competitive tendering', vol 27, *Urban Studies*, 653

Rex, J. & Moore, R. (1967), *Race, Community and Conflict: A Study of Sparkbrook*, Oxford: Oxford University Press

Saunders, P. (1990), *A Nation of Home Owners*, London: Allen & Unwin

Shaw, K., Fenwick, J. and Foreman, A. (1995), 'Compulsory competition for local government services in the UK: a case of market rhetoric and camouflaged centralism', vol 10, *Public Policy and Administration*, 63

Short, J. (1982), *Housing in Britain: The Post-War Experience*, London: Methuen

Skinner, D. and Langdon, J. (1972), *The Story of Clay Cross*, Nottingham: Spokesman

Stewart, A. (1996), *Rethinking Housing Law*, London: Sweet & Maxwell

Stewart, A. and Burridge, R. (1989), 'Housing tales of law and space', vol 16, *Journal of Law and Society*, 65

Thatcher, M. (1993), *The Downing Street Years*, London: Harper Collins

Vincent-Jones, P. (1998), 'Responsive law and governance in public services provision: a future for the local contracting state', vol 61, *Modern Law Review*, 362

Vincent-Jones, P. and Harries, A. (1998), 'Tenant participation in contracting for housing management services: a case study', in D. Cowan (ed.), *Housing: Participation and Exclusion*, Aldershot: Dartmouth

Walker, B. and Marsh, A. (1993), 'Alternative rent setting regimes in the public sector: some implications', in D. Maclennan and K. Gibb (eds), *Housing Finance and Subsidies in Britain*, Aldershot: Avebury

Walker, B. and Marsh, A. (1995), *Rent Setting Policies in English Local Authorities*, London: HMSO

Walker, B. and Marsh, A. (1997), 'Rent setting in local government', vol 23, *Local Government Policy Making*, 39

Walker, B. and Marsh, A. (1998), 'Pricing public housing services: mirroring the market?', vol 13, *Housing Studies*, 549

Warburton, M. (1996), 'The changing role of local authorities in housing', in S. Leach, Howard David & Associates (eds), *Enabling or Disabling Local Government*, Buckingham: Open University Press

Wilcox, S. (1997), *Housing Finance Review 1997/98*, York: Joseph Rowntree Foundation

Wilson, D. and Game, C. (1994), *Local Government in the United Kingdom*, London: Macmillan

Woodward, R. (1991), 'Mobilising opposition: the campaign against housing action trusts in Tower Hamlets', vol 6, *Housing Studies*, 44

6   In Search of Voice – Putting the 'Social' Back into 'Social Housing'

It is unclear what criteria turn housing into *social* housing. If government subsidy is the essential element, then all housing would have to be regarded as social – indeed, government support for home ownership being what it was, that tenure would presumably have a greater right to call itself social than (say) council housing. Housing Benefit provides a buoy for a number of private landlords enabling them to charge market rents. If the essential element is low-cost (either to build or to occupy), then those RSLs which charge more than private landlords would surely be excluded; indeed, that portion of the private rented sector provided by companies for their employees would be included. If the essential element was that it was not to make a profit, then those councils that supplement (or have supplemented) accounts other than their Housing Revenue Account, and some RSLs which guard their surpluses gained from rents, and pay large salaries and bonuses to their respective executives, would be hard-pressed to justify inclusion in the category of social housing (*cf* Priemus, 1997, p. 555: 'This may be considered to be the crucial test: rented housing is defined as social rented housing when the landlord puts any surplus back into its property'). If the criterion was allocation according to need, the evidence suggests that 'need' is rarely as important as comparative bargaining power (see Clapham & Kintrea, 1991) or who is the most deserving (Cowan, 1997).

Yet these are the sorts of criteria suggested as being the essential elements of social housing. Other definitions consider vaguer criteria, such as including the notion of 'a socially responsible agency conforming to some form of tenants' charter or guarantee' (Bramley, 1993, p. 155). The introduction of dubious notions of social responsibility – hardly applicable to some RSLs or councils in the 'housing as business' era – or individualistic, often unenforceable, tenants' charters or guarantees hardly inspires confidence. Our attempts at defining the essential characteristics of 'social' housing fail partly because of the lack of coherence in definitions of the term 'social', partly because of the variety of organizations that might have a claim to fall within the category, and partly because the experience of the past twenty or so years has required the same organizations to (re-)join the housing market: 'What it comes down to is not a change in mission but a change in approach: the social rented sector has to become market-oriented' (Priemus, 1997, p. 557).

In this chapter, I will be arguing that whatever the term means, 'social' is at the very least about the people who live in the housing which the organization provides. 'Social' is about giving those people rights, in both the individual and collective sense. In the previous two chapters, our analysis of the regulation of RSLs and councils has concerned those organizations' relationships with the government and other organizations which hold regulatory power (such as private lenders). Here, our consideration turns to the missing regulators: the tenants.

We have already observed how housing management was dogged by its (probably deserved) reputation as being unresponsive and overbearing. This was mirrored in the lack of rights given to tenants. Until 1980, tenants could be evicted at the whim of the council (as they had no security of tenure); they rarely had contracts, but where they did these usually contained negative covenants (obligations) on the tenants with very little, if any, positive obligation on the landlord. Tenants were regarded as the 'passive recipients of landlord bounty' (Gilroy, 1998, p. 22), and were rendered powerless by their status.

One of the great benefits of the Thatcher/Major era was that tenants became 'empowered'. For example, the Housing Act 1980 gave them contractual rights as well as security of tenure. Subsequent legislation has improved upon this, although the emphasis through this period was in giving individual rights through market processes. Power, in this sense, was epitomized by the growing ability of tenants to participate in, and have an effect upon, management decisions affecting them. For rather different reasons, at the same time tenants groups have formed, enabling collective participation to occur. A key question underlying this chapter is how far power has been transferred to tenants, or whether this has given rise to more subtle methods through which the powerful have been able to control the protest of the powerless. Indeed, it is the very conception of power that makes its transference to social landlords' tenants of some difficulty. It is helpful to compare one definition of power-wielding with a description of tenants on a Newcastle housing estate:

'Being powerful involves possessing and mobilising resources, effecting and securing intended outcomes of decision-making, shaping and manipulating interests of other actors, controlling and filtering agendas of decision making and creating and maintaining structures of decision making.' (Atkinson & Cope, 1997, p. 208)

'But these [tenants] are people whose energies are often eaten up with the daily struggle of making ends meet and keeping their children out of crime. Housing managers in the north east talk of council estates which are full of unemployed people who have no sense of purpose; of places where the spirit is gone.' (Gilroy, 1998, p. 35)

Gilroy's point about the marginalization of many tenants, and particularly in certain areas, is an important one for all those interested in the participation agenda. Carr and Sefton-Green, in their work on the Tollington estate in North London (1999), have made a similar point in that the residents have no desire to participate in the management of their estate – their primary objective was to move (or transfer). This created a shifting, marginalized body of residents with no connection to the area. This marginalization is a challenge to those seeking to empower residents through participating in housing management.

The strategy adopted by the Conservatives involved inculcating market principles into social housing. So, for example, the past two chapters have discussed the changing financial structuring of council and RSL housing. At the same time, the influence of the private sector has been felt in the changing descriptions of tenants. However, occupiers' rights do not require, as their concomitant, a change in personality – from occupier or tenant, to client or consumer – as market-based ideologies often require. Whilst there may be a market (or quasi-market) amongst housing providers, tenants and their successors will most often be those who have no choice because of their exclusion from other tenures for one reason or another (Hambleton & Hoggett, 1987, p. 23). Furthermore, on no account can housing be equated with a consumer durable – you can take back a television which stops working but not a flat. These points did not stop successive Conservative governments from subjecting councils and RSLs to market-based ideologies so as to withdraw central financial support whilst, at the same time, increasing central control.

The mechanisms provided by those governments mainly involved giving tenants individual rights, which denied (indeed, broke up) the collective, monopolistic force. It was assumed that the downgraded council tenants would 'vote with their feet' and leave council tenure through exercising their right to buy. It was assumed that this was because they were fed up with the tenure, and wanted to pursue their individual rights as owner–occupiers, whilst less emphasis was given to the incentives constraining the choices of tenants. In this set of assumptions, the Conservatives were attempting to expose the 'voice' of tenants by providing them with a means of 'exit' from the tenure (Hirschman, 1970, p. 4). The larger numbers seeking to exit from the tenure, the greater emphasis given to voice. Mechanisms increasing the voice of tenants were almost always related to exiting from the tenure. Mechanisms which did not involve exit were often tokenistic. So, for example, the right of (council and RSL) tenants to information and consultation are extremely weak forms of 'giving tenants a say' in the management of their estates and, furthermore, do not include matters such as rent levels (which are, in any event, controlled by central government). Indeed, in the Local Government Act 1988, non-elected Councillor tenants specifically had their rights to vote on council (sub-)committees withdrawn.

It is also clear that the 1987–1992 Conservative government made a serious tactical error in misreading the support of council tenants for their landlords and for collective provision. The 1987 housing White Paper identified council housing management in cities as 'becoming distant and bureaucratic' (DoE, 1987, para. 1.9) and that 'there are still too many estates where the quality of life is less than satisfactory. It is not what tenants want, and it is not what the original designers of the estates had in mind. Tenants live there not from choice, but because they have nowhere else to live' (para. 5.3 – an argument against marketization of council housing). From this, it was argued that the necessary policy prescription was the ability of tenants to effect a change of landlord.

Tenants receiving 'a poor service from their council' were to be allowed to transfer to another landlord (Tenants' Choice; paras 5.9–5.11). For 'some of the inner urban areas, where social problems and housing disrepair are so serious', the government was going to introduce Housing Action Trusts (HATs) which would 'provide scope for tenants in these areas to have a diversity of landlord and ownership' (para. 6.3). These two policy options were premised on a slightly different version of the old individualized 'exit as voice' route. In the case of Tenants Choice, it was believed that tenants would vote to exit from council management *en masse*. In the case of HATs, the government themselves would choose the areas (the patrician Nicholas Ridley MP, then Secretary of State, argued that 'if you are trying to help somebody . . . you don't want them to vote against that being done': Ginsburg, 1989, p. 72). In the first section of this chapter, we consider these policies, and why they failed, together with the notable privatization successes gained through what has become known as the Large Scale Voluntary Transfer (LSVT). LSVTs were not even considered in the White Paper – they were then in their infancy – but have since outstripped the privatization initiatives included in it.

In the second section, our attention turns to those initiatives which have attempted to involve tenants in participating in housing management. Some of these have gone beyond the tokenistic and have involved the real devolution of *power* from councils to tenants. Whilst the form of Conservative legislation tended to marginalize tenants through giving individual rights and little role in management (until 1993), the substance of actual policy was markedly different. Tenant participation moved up the agenda because *all* political parties supported it, albeit for markedly different reasons (see, for example, Goodlad, 1991, pp. 118–9). The 'Priority Estates Project', sponsored by the DoE began the trend in the early 1980s, together with the move in some councils to decentralize their housing services (although 'we might conclude that managerial rather than political objectives were paramount' in such moves: Gilroy, 1998, p. 30). Bidding for certain capital allocations, such as Estate Action in the mid-1980s, was made conditional upon councils agreeing to institute some forms of tenant participation, although central government's perception was that local government was part of the problem (see also Ch. 4 –

discussion of City Challenge). It has been argued, however, that these capital allocations plans were already 'largely set before communities became involved' (Atkinson & Cope, 1997, pp. 219–20). Nevertheless, there have been substantial gains made by council tenants since the mid-1980s in a way in which earlier confrontational campaigns, such as rent strikes and the campaign against the Housing Finance Act 1972, perhaps were not as successful in achieving. Our spotlight also turns to a discussion of the formal powers of tenants to take over the management of their estates, contained in the Leasehold Reform, Housing and Urban Development Act 1993.

These collective rights have been matched by the emergence of individual rights to complain and the following section considers this development. These rights to complain constitute a critical part of the regulatory matrix of social housing. Whilst the development of such rights in the 1980s might have been described as 'jejeune' (Birkinshaw, 1995, p. 122), there has been encouragement in the 1990s for such systems coming particularly from the *Citizen's Charter* (Cabinet Office, 1991).

In the final section of this chapter, we will look at where these developments (as well as those considered in the previous two chapters) have taken us. The development of the Local Housing Company, often regarded as the saviour of 'social housing', has been slow and rather a long time in coming. Nevertheless, at the time of writing, at least four have been set up with more in the pipeline. We will consider their rationale, purpose, and capability for the task. At this stage, it is only necessary to point out that they represent a politically acceptable form of privatization of public housing.

6.1   Exit as Voice

The granting to tenants of a right to buy their property in 1980 (council tenants) and 1996 (RSL tenants) created a method of individualized exit from one tenure and entry into another. The large numbers who have exercised, and are expected to exercise, their rights are partly based on assumptions that tenants in the social sector wish to exercise control over their own lives and that social housing management cannot allow this to happen. These were also the assumptions underlying the policy prescriptions contained in the 1987 White Paper and subsequently included in the Housing Act 1988. Tenants' Choice and HATs were different methods of cracking the same nut. The former, it was believed, would broaden the base of social landlordism so as to include *commercial landlords* (DoE, 1987, para. 5.10). The latter concerned the setting up of a 'trust', albeit one appointed by central government, wresting control from the council: 'Tenants' interests will be deeply involved, for example in respect of refurbishment programmes and eventual disposal of property by the HAT' (para. 6.6). At this stage, tenants were not to be given the option to transfer. So, empowerment was given a rather different 'spin' depending upon which scheme was under consideration.

Tenants' Choice

Essentially, this programme empowered council tenants to change their landlord. The new landlord would have to be approved by the Housing Corporation and would have to agree to honour the tenant's guarantee (giving tenants rights over and above those in the Statute – these are now contained in the *Performance Standards:* Housing Corporation, 1997). This significantly undermined the potential for involvement of the commercial sector as the guarantee has always required rents to be set at below market levels. Thus, this part may well have been part of the political posturing, or simply thinking ahead. The most controversial part of the Tenants' Choice programme was the method used to implement it: a vote. The vote was rather bizarre, for any person who did not vote *was assumed to have voted in favour of transfer*. If the government had assumed that council tenants were desperate to leave their council landlord or were simply too apathetic to do so, they were mistaken. Only two estates transferred landlords, both to tenants' co-operatives and both in Westminster – tenants 'protect[ed] themselves from predators who are being actively courted by the Tory council' (Ginsburg, 1989, 67).

The programme backfired on the government in this sense, as well as being a principal cause of the (re-)generation of tenants federations apparently determined to remain in council tenure. As tenants had to organize against the threat of predator landlords, the response in some areas was the production of initially cohesive groups. On the other hand, if the government's central intention was privatization and/or improving council house management, one can argue it was hugely successful. Tenant's Choice is continually cited as a reason for decentralizing housing management as well as for LSVTs. Thus, it can be argued that superficially the programme was a failure but the reverberations in terms of housing practice more generally were massive:

'A typical comment of one officer, in a traditional authority, when asked the purpose of tenant consultation, was: 'Well the ultimate objective must be to make sure they [tenants] don't whizz off to somebody else.' (Cairncross *et al.*, 1997, p. 61)

Tenants' Choice caused each group to reassess their position. Whilst the *status quo* was preserved ('better the devil you know'), clearly the power differential between tenants and managers, as well as within each group, had been subtly altered by their experience and concerns for the future. Tenants' Choice was, in fact, repealed in the Housing Act 1996 (after £1.87 million had been paid to Torbay tenants attempting to transfer landlord. On a 93 per cent turnout, only seven per cent voted in favour: National Audit Office, 1997).

HATs

In 1987–88, 'Department of Environment officials and their private consultants were to be seen looking round estates for likely candidates' for the HAT programme (Ginsburg, p. 71). The first six estates were chosen and publicized on 11 July 1988, even before the 1988 Act had completed its course through Parliament. The six estates were not, as was originally argued, the most run down areas but a broad mix. The estates in Tower Hamlets were those where the problems identified in the White Paper 'had in fact been successfully tackled in recent years by initiatives such as Estates Action and the Priority Estates Project' as well as decentralization (in various forms) (see Woodward, 1991, p. 46 & 48). So, tenants had misgivings about the intentions behind HATs (as the Tower Hamlets areas, for example, were closely related to the Docklands site then under redevelopment and sale: *ibid*).

The basic idea behind HATs, it should be stressed, is one that most would sign up to – increasing diversity of tenure is commonly regarded as a panacea, for this will lead to diversity of income and 'it is the compounding impact of poverty that generates a significant element of the problem' (Lund, 1996, p. 132; *cf* Ginsburg, 1989, p. 72 where it is suggested that what was required was a more general renewal – 'Housing improvement may be just a cosmetic to hide social problems behind a prettier face.'). However, Parliamentary debate took place against a backdrop of political animosity, uncertainty about 'secret discussions', as well as the structure of the proposed legislation (see Karn, 1993). HATs were portrayed as an attack on *Labour* councils (all of the first six were Labour-controlled areas) and not as a positive measure to cure problems on estates. The legislation, in standard modern form, was 'enabling', leaving all of the detail and power to the less conspicuous method of quasi-legislation:

'The HAT legislation is framed in a way which sees little need to meet the anxieties of tenants, much less those of local authorities. Once the HAT is approved in principle there is no control over ministerial appointments to the board, no control over how the Trust exercises its functions and no right of return to local authorities with a guaranteed ability to repurchase properties.' (Gregory & Hainsworth, 1993, p. 114)

Initially, the fact that the legislation did not seek to assuage tenants' anxieties did not matter. They were not to have a choice anyway. This became the most highly contentious issue in the latter stages of Parliamentary debate and eventually the government conceded that tenants would be able to vote on the issue (either because this was conceded in a television interview, because of the effect of pressure groups, or because the Bill was running out of Parliamentary time: Karn, 1993, pp. 78–9, Ginsburg, 1989). By this time (the concession was made, at the earliest on 11 November 1988), the damage had been done, for the antagonism behind the legislation, as well as featuring in the language used within the legislation and the powers given to the government, could not be altered as well. Instead, a variety of non-statutory concessions were given, such as that estates could be transferred back to the local authority when the HAT had run its course; tenants and councillors could be represented on the board of the HAT.

By the time these concessions were made, however, anti-HAT campaigns were at full throttle. Public meetings of tenants to discuss the HAT proposals met with significant support (1000 people turned up to the first meeting in Tower Hamlets). In Tower Hamlets, 'tenant opposition was based on two principles – a fear for the consequences of a HAT for [the tenants'] security as tenants in low-rent housing, and an objection to the mechanisms by which a HAT would be established on their estates' (Woodward, 1991, p. 46). Four themes were apparent in the tenant mobilization: 'justifying council housing'; 'do we really need another Development Corporation?'; 'only tenant power can defeat the HATs'; 'HATs will not solve the housing crisis' (*ibid*, pp. 47–53). The dissatisfaction with the government's proposals, together with a dawning realization that their proposals might not be acceptable in the chosen areas, meant that only two areas proceeded to ballot. Both ballots were resoundingly anti-HAT. In one area, the ballot failed apparently because of concern about the enforceability of the government's extra-statutory concessions (Karn, 1993, p. 83). Indeed, the unifying factor about all the anti-HAT campaigns is that the government simply were not trusted by the communities involved after a considerable period of downgrading. Also, the attack on council management represented a 1970s view and 'municipal tenure may rarely have been as bad as caricatured' by the government (Gregory & Hainsworth, 1993, p. 115).

The failure of the first six HATs did not spell the end of the programme's existence. Indeed, just seven years after the 1988 Act, they have been touted as 'a role model' as well as being 'democratic and accountable' (Chumrow, 1995, p. 76). Such an amazing turnaround seems entirely due to the desperation of the government faced with the prospect of its primary policy objective failing. The balance of bargaining power had turned in favour of *local authorities* willing to implement the scheme. The first two, Hull and Waltham Forest, did not concern the worst estates, rather estates into which the councils were attempting to lever finance without success. Liverpool's HAT, on the other hand, was set up to deal with its tower blocks. All (there are now six) won significant concessions from the DoE as well as significant finance. In fact, the original budget for the HATs was £125 million but £170 million was allocated to Waltham Forest alone (subsequently increased to £227 million: House of Commons Public Accounts Committee, 1998, para. 10). Furthermore, the Leasehold Reform, Housing and Urban Development Act 1993 provided a statutory right for the tenants to return to the council, as well as government concessions that the necessary funding would be provided. Local authorities bargaining power has been used to the full, leading one commentator to suggest that the HAT scheme was completely unnecessary: 'some might argue that a good deal of time, negotiation and hard work could have been saved by giving the money straight to the council' (Owens, 1992, p. 19).

Karn suggests that 'it seems extraordinary that government thought that, even if HATs could have been imposed against the will of local authorities and tenants, they could have operated effectively in such a confrontational climate' (1993, p. 77). Yet, whilst the original proposals might be described as having ignored the voice of the tenant in favour of the exit option, apparently the DoE/DETR 'now seek to work more collaboratively with local authorities' (House of Commons Public Accounts Committee, 1998, para. 40). Furthermore, private finance has now been levered into the operation of each HAT suggesting that central government's initial objectives have been satisfied.

It might be argued that the HATs which were successfully set up were done so at the behest of the local authority and, in this way, the *status quo* was retained, for the council retained the power. Certainly in Hull, such a position might be justified by the fact that tenants were given four months before a vote on the HAT was taken and, by this stage, the proposals had all been sewn up between the council and the DoE: 'In North Hull there was no tenants association and the local authority campaigned hard for a yes vote, allowing only a very short preparatory period and limited opportunities for the tenants to take external advice' (Karn, 1993, p. 86). However, tenant participation has been observed throughout the HAT process because, quite simply, it could not succeed without their support. In addition to choices of fittings, tenants themselves have been able to extract concessions from the DoE. Waltham Forest tenants, for example, produced a tenants' expectations document which guided their negotiations with the DoE; the final version had a foreword from George Young, then Housing Minister (Chumrow, 1995, pp. 81–2). When appointing members to the HAT boards, it appears that the Minister has no role – tenant members are elected, councils propose their own members, and the chair proposes the other members (after consultation with the DoE/DETR): *ibid*, p. 85.

It might be argued that the crucial distinction between Waltham Forest, on the one hand, and Hull on the other lies in the *style* of authority, as opposed to the (op)position of tenants. Cairncross *et al.* draw distinctions between three types of authority: first, the traditional model that is built on notions of representative democracy; second, the consumerist model in which 'emphasis is placed on the individual household either to begin or continue to consume its product in preference to a competitor's' (p. 29); and third, the citizenship model, in which the emphasis is on the customer *and* citizen, in the collective sense, and '. . . a key element . . . is the existence of a dialogue between the producer, consumer and citizen . . .' (p. 32). Whilst they suggest that no one authority fits precisely into each particular model, it is possible from the above to suggest that Hull might be regarded as traditional and Waltham Forest the citizenship (although it may well be that after the HAT was negotiated, matters and models altered).

LSVTs

In December 1988, Chiltern District Council (a Conservative-controlled rural authority) sold off its entire stock to a RSL. This was the culmination of a series of discussions between the council and the DoE concerning the future of the housing stock. Disposal took place under powers conferred in s. 32, Housing Act 1985. This is a general provision – '. . . a local authority have [sic] power by this section, and not otherwise, to dispose of land held by them for the purposes of this part' – which contains a requirement that the Secretary of State consent to the transfer (s. 2). This was a *considerable, pioneering innovation* although, as will become clear, whether tenants were to benefit from the transfer is less apparent. Nevertheless, LSVT has become the most popular method amongst councils for privatizing their estates – by May 1995, 67 authorities had balloted their tenants, and 40 had transferred (Mullins *et al.*, 1995, p. 25); in March 1998, the New Labour government announced that a further 23 councils were to proceed to ballot their tenants on LSVT proposals (DETR, 1998). In each case bar one, transfer has been to an RSL (the exceptional case involved transfer to a housing association not registered with the Housing Corporation).

There is, in fact, considerable evidence that LSVTs were initiated by the officers within the councils. In 1987 and immediately thereafter, the climate of council housing must have been considerably depressed. Tenants' Choice, HATs, and the new financial regime that would cut back their capital allocation as well as change rent setting policy, meant that council housing as a tenure must have seemed moribund (it should be remembered that 'it was not until the 1988 Act had been in operation for a few years that the limited impact of Tenants' Choice became generally recognized, and fears of speculative or predatory activity were dispelled': Mullins *et al.*, 1993, p. 171). In that case, the officers own job security was pretty limited. On the other hand:

> 'Transfer brings the prospect of working for a growing, rather than a declining, organisation; of greater autonomy in being able to plan over the medium term, rather than on a strictly annual cycle; of less interference by elected politicians; and of improved working conditions, with higher status and enhanced career progression, as well as better salaries and fringe benefits. In general, officers may see greater opportunities in the more entrepreneurial and innovative atmosphere of a new organisation than in the bureaucratic, scrutinised approach of the local authority.' (Kleinman, 1993, p. 169)

> 'Usually the transfer process has been identified with and led by housing officers rather than by members and transfers have rarely been

specifically identified with 'privatisation' or related based political ideologies.' (Mullins *et al.*, 1995, p. 41)

For the councils involved, a transfer enables them to pay off their historic debts and thus regain control of their own finances. There are also considerable benefits in becoming debt-free (see Ch. 4 above). For the housing stock, the benefit comes from an injection of capital to make, for example, historic repairs. As the early transfers were in Conservative authorities, there was also political capital to be made out of the programme. The dominance of this option can be shown by the fact that 'none of the councils pushing transfer have taken seriously the option of a tenant-controlled co-operative, nor have they put forward a convincing case for remaining with the council' (Birchall, 1992, p. 182).

Much, however, has depended upon the valuation of the stock in the business plan. It should be remembered that, generally, LSVTs are financed *privately* and there is therefore the interests of the private lenders to be considered. Valuation in business plans was originally done on the basis of a Discounted Cash Flow Analysis – that is, income less expenditure: 'It is certainly not clear that the government is representing the taxpayer interest in these negotiations [as to price] as opposed to its more immediate concerns about implementing government housing policy' (Kleinman, 1993, p. 170). Key to this, however, were assumptions about levels of right-to-buy sales and spending on repairs. When right-to-buy sales fell, those new RSLs which had over-budgeted became more aware of the market risk of the transaction (Mullins *et al.*, 1995, Ch. 8 for comparison). For the lenders, an LSVT probably represents a good risk because their outlay has the security of being charged over the whole stock, as well as the tenants' rents being comparatively low (with, therefore, significant room to manoeuvre should it be required).

Tenants were given rent guarantees, often linked to the retail price index, for a period, usually around five years. One reason for this was that the DoE required tenants to be balloted in every case where an LSVT was proposed. These rent guarantees did *not* affect tenants allocated to the new RSL's property after transfer, thus 'illustrating the influence of existing tenants on the package' (Mullins *et al.*, 1993, p. 181). New tenants would therefore pay for the guarantees given to the old tenants and keep the RSL afloat – rent differentials were found to be 'substantial in the early years', with new tenants' rents being as much as twice those of the original tenants (Mullins *et al.*, 1995, p. 48). With the coming to an end of many of these rent guarantee periods, it appears that the original business plan assumptions have changed, so that the original tenants' rents are scheduled to rise substantially to make an 'earlier convergence' with new tenants' rents (Mullins *et al.*, 1995, p. 49). The difficulty for RSLs in this position, however, is the new *Performance Standards* which insists on the 'RPI + 1%' formula for LSVTs (unless the original rent valuations allowed for a greater increase) (Housing Corporation, 1997, pp. 30–1). RSLs, the Standard suggests, 'should charge rents which are appropriate to their financial and other commitments and circumstances, including the need to maintain their housing'.

The current uncertainty in many LSVTs over rents is indicative of the more general problem: tenants had to vote, by a majority of those attending, to transfer but could only do so on the basis of complicated assumptions. These assumptions related to *financial* matters, particularly the effect of the financial controls in the 1989 Act, *political* matters, for example the continuing benefits given to RSLs as opposed to councils, as well as the ability of the landlord to meet its new commitments. The difficulty of such assumptions is exacerbated when the council favours transfer and tenants are then kept in the dark:

'One finding of the research was the very limited involvement allowed to tenants in the transfer process. Tenants were consulted, but were not actively involved in the decision process about the future ownership of their homes. In only two of our early case studies was independent advice made available to tenants from a body other than the transferring council or new landlord. Many important decisions were taken in meetings from which the public were excluded.' (Mullins *et al.*, 1993, p. 180; suggesting a consumerist model)

The situation has slightly altered now, so that the DoE/DETR requires independent consultants to be appointed on behalf of the tenants (although early evidence suggested that this was little used: Mullins *et al.*, 1995, pp. 35–9). It is perhaps unsurprising then that votes are often marginally won or lost. Successful early ballots were often sold to tenants as the ' "least change option" under which they would retain the same housing staff, and enjoy a similar but better service for a reasonable rent' (Mullins *et al.*, 1993, p. 181). Nevertheless, it is clear that considerable change has resulted from LSVT, aptly summarized by the move from political to market risk (Kleinman, 1993). Market risk has a particular emphasis for tenants because, whilst their right to buy is preserved, their security of tenure is weakened by the change in landlord involving a concomitant change in tenancy regime from public to private. One may, therefore, characterize the LSVT process as disempowering tenants, although no doubt the original intention was to protect them

LSVT is commonly portrayed as being outside the government's interests. Whilst there was clearly privatization of public stock with commensurate reduction in public borrowing, the government lost control over their rent levels; the transfer commonly involved moving from one monopolistic provider to another (particularly true of the London Borough of Bromley); no private landlords entered the market; government cannot claw back any surplus on the rents (Kleinman, 1993, pp. 169–70). It can however be argued that LSVT fits naturally into a central–local government model in which local government submits and is subservient to central control. The DoE/DETR's role has involved them in behind-the-scenes negotiations throughout the process, beginning at an early stage. In these conversations, it is clear that the DoE/DETR has an important role, for ultimately it is up to them to approve the transfer: 'the Department's role is to provide advice and guidance throughout the process of transfer, to enable authorities to put forward applications which are *likely to be acceptable*' (DETR, 1998, p. 5). In other words, proposals will only go to ballot if they are already acceptable to the DETR. These regulatory conversations enable(d) the DoE/DETR to mould the formulation of the proposals and, thus, impose the stamp of central government on them. Indeed, some of the problems perceived to be against the DoE/DETR interest have since been resolved: the Conservatives imposed a limit on the number of properties to be transferred (5,000) and required councils to pay a levy to the Treasury of 20 per cent of the value of the transfer as an approximate amount to cover increased Housing Benefit payments as a result of the transfer.

If the LSVT programme were against government interest, it would be difficult to appreciate why the governments have let it continue for so long as a major policy innovation. Indeed, the 1995 White Paper said that the government 'would like to see *all* authorities consider transfer as one of the options for dealing with housing problems.' (DoE, 1995a, p. 29) A linked Consultation Paper also suggested ways of manipulating the costs so as to allow transfers where the 'price paid for the housing is less than the debt on it' (DoE, 1995b, para. 2.15). What is amazing is the cross-party support now apparent in favour of LSVT. The programme for 1998/9 'will involve over 85,000 dwellings . . ., generating capital receipts of over £482 million. . . . This reflects the government's commitment to a continuing programme of transfers as a means of generating private finance to repair and improve the condition of social housing' (DETR, 1998). Whereas, in 1995, no Liberal Democrat authority had transferred, and no Labour-controlled authority had voted on a transfer, it is apparent that this situation has now markedly changed. Whilst this benefits the government (as well as fulfilling their pre-election promise to engage in public–private partnerships) and the councils (most of which become debt-free),[1] it may well be to the detriment of the tenants whose voice may well have been marginalized in the early (and, possibly also, later) stages of the process.

6.2   Participation as Voice

Since 1980, tenants have had statutory security of tenure and other individual rights, such as the right to repair. Our concern here is with the implementation of rights given to tenants *collectively* to participate in housing management. It is important to appreciate that apocalyptic views of collective protest have, despite some blips (around, for example, the 1972 Housing Finance Act: Lowe, 1986), rarely come to pass. Whilst no general tendencies nor 'life cycles' of tenants' movements can be drawn

(Cairncross *et al.*, 1997, pp. 131–2; *cf* Lowe, 1986), there are also considerable obstacles to their development (see, generally, Cole & Furbey, 1994, pp. 150–161). Nevertheless, when they form they can be powerful, for example in their defeat of the HATs, although this is often the exception (only three councils attempted to avoid implementing the Housing Finance Act 1972). Furthermore, whilst agitational reasons may be given for their development, tenants' associations are equally likely to develop for 'social and welfare reasons' depending upon the level of council/RSL support (Cairncross *et al.*, 1997, p. 133).

Participation can take a variety of different forms which broadly correspond to, first, 'therapy' and 'manipulation' (for example, cynical consultation and poor information); second, 'degrees of tokenism' (information, consultation, and placation through which 'citizens may indeed hear and be heard. But under these conditions they lack the power to ensure that their views will be *heeded* by the powerful'); third, 'degrees of citizen power' (such as citizen control, delegated power, and partnership) (see Arnstein, 1969; Burns *et al.*, 1994, Ch. 6; Cowan, 1998). The Housing Act 1980 gave tenants the right to information and consultation, although this was not as significant a voice as had been proposed by the previous Labour government. These rights have been drafted in a way which makes the provisions servants of the council as opposed to the tenants (Kay *et al.*, 1987, p. 181). They have also been drafted in obscure fashion – tenants are entitled to be consulted when they 'are likely to be substantially affected by a matter of housing management' (s 105(1), 1985 Act). The authority need only 'consider any representations made to it' before making its decision. This consultation does not, however, apply to rent or charges for services levied by the authority (s 105(2)). The local authority must publish information relating to tenancies and its allocations policy.

These are generally individualist provisions, and/or have been interpreted in this way by the courts. So, for example, it has been argued that 'The whole point of publication is that applicants and their advisers should know the framework within which they should approach the council and in turn expect the council to deal with them' *R v Tower Hamlets LBC ex parte Khalique* (1994) 26 HLR 517. Furthermore, the limitations of the provisions have been exposed within the case law: see *Short v Tower Hamlets LBC* (1985) 18 HLR 171. Thus, it appears that these statutory duties do no more than provide 'degrees of tokenism'. It has been correctly suggested that the requirements 'can be met by engaging in very limited forms of contact between landlord and tenant' (Goodlad, 1991, p. 121). Furthermore, early research on the implementation of these rights suggested that the councils did little more than the minimum, as well as some which refused to implement them (Kay *et al.*, 1987, Ch. 7).

Nevertheless, the apparent development of an alliance on tenant participation between political parties in the late 1970s and early 1980s considerably aided the cause: 'Conservative MPs were more likely to want to expose public service professionals to customers' criticism and to break Labour's hold on big city local government; Labour MPs were increasingly concerned about the image of the welfare state and how to give it a human face' (Goodlad, 1991, p. 116). Since the mid-1980s at the latest, however, participation has been a watchword, although its shifting definition in practice reflects the dominance of different interests groups in different areas (for definitions, see Cairncross *et al.*, 1997, pp. 32–46; Furbey *et al.*, 1996, p. 251; Gilroy, 1998, pp. 22–3). Thus, the spatial distribution is important. For example, authorities in the 'consumerist model' are more likely to focus on individual rights, 'ensuring that the household can gain easy access to the product or service; providing information in a way which encourages take-up; promoting a positive image (advertising); and providing the consumer with a choice of product or service and giving them a means of redress if they have complaints' (Cairncross *et al.*, 1997, p. 29). Equally, such authorities are more likely expressly to *discourage* collective tenants groups.

There may well also be a further splintering of interest groups within authorities, between tenants themselves, between tenants and housing managers, and between tenants, housing managers and councillors (Cairncross *et al.*, 1997). The different interest groups often have different views as to the importance of tenant participation as well as why they participate in the first place. For example, tenants view managers' use of participation as a cynical exercise (p. 121), whereas managers view tenants as engaging in it for self-interest (p. 73). Neither perception was entirely accurate. The motivations of managers 'were a mixture of self-interest and altruism' (p. 65) but the same might also be said of tenants. Indeed, the alliance of interests might best be described as uneasy at any particular time. The same is true for RSLs, for whom this is the biggest issue arising out of the regulatory muscle of the Housing Corporation: 'they [21 RSLs surveyed] all argued that the blanket notion of participation is ill-thought through and ends up, therefore, as mere tokenism. Unless it is unpicked as a policy and the fuzzy parts are jettisoned, then many associations will agree to the policy on paper but implement it only symbolically' (Day *et al.*, 1993, pp. 23–4).

This uncertainty of the 1980s has since been transferred into a more proactive model in the 1990s, so that we are now in a position to discuss 'degrees of citizen power'. Development can generally be traced back to the cooperative movement (with which many Labour MPs in the 1970s were involved) (see generally Clapham & Kintrea, 1992). Estate Management Boards have developed as a partnership between the council and tenants: 'The Board negotiates a management agreement: this establishes the various tasks which the Board will undertake and allows for a budget to pay for these tasks' (Foley & Evans, 1994, p. 398). Housing cooperatives are another device used more recently (for example, it was the vehicle adopted by the Westminster tenants who opted to transfer landlord under the Tenants' Choice programme). Some Scottish estates have chosen to adopt a scheme known as 'community ownership'

(Clapham *et al.*, 1997). By 1992, at least 117 tenants groups were involved in managing their estates through one of these vehicles.

A further innovation is New Labour's attempts at standardizing tenant participation throughout local authorities, guaranteeing a minimum, and enforcing this through the Best Value approach. A Consultation Paper deals with the setting up and maintenance of 'Tenant Participation Compacts' which will be negotiated in each local authority area between tenants and councillors (DETR, 1999). A similar process is occurring with RSLs. Negotiations will have to include centrally imposed core standards, and the Compacts will have to be consistently monitored (in line with the 'four Cs' – challenge, compare, consult, and compete: para. 2.20). The Compacts 'should involve tenants in both strategic and local decisions on housing issues' (para. 1.5). The core standards go further then ever before, embracing (for example) rent-setting, budgets, finance, tenancy conditions, allocations and lettings, together with anti-social behaviour policies. The only limitation is that local authorities must operate within the current legislative framework (for example, they will therefore not be able to oust 'anti-social' tenants without a court order).

The most significant statutory development has been the provisions giving tenants the 'right to manage' their estates (Leasehold Reform, Housing and Urban Development Act 1993, ss. 129–134; these are skeleton provisions, and the main body of regulation can be found in the Housing (Right to Manage) Regulations 1994, SI 1994/627). The Tenant Participation Compact must give the tenants the opportunity to consider managing their own estates. Such organizations are known as Tenant Management Organizations (TMOs) but broadly correspond to both Estate Management Boards and tenant management cooperatives. They take over the management of the estates whilst leaving ownership with the council (or RSL under *Performance Standards*).

The programme has its own structural difficulties (although New Labour has no intention to abolish the programme: DETR, 1999, para. 2.18). First, the TMO must employ its own staff and not do so through the council. Secondly, the regulations create a complex pattern of notices, feasibility studies, ballots and agency reports to the extent that devolution of power to TMOs suffered as a result of the implementation of the legislation. Third, the regulations provide for a *confrontational* approach only, so that tenants have to serve a notice on the council before they have had the opportunity to consider all their options: 'Right to manage is seen as threatening to local authorities and as adversarial rather than partnership-building. The ending of the option whereby TMOs could use staff seconded from the local authority reinforces this view.' (Crossley, 1995). One reason for these obstructions might have been because all those estates which opted for a TMO were expressly excluded from the ambit of CCT. The greater complexity involved in setting up a TMO, the more organisations would be subject to CCT (although this was denied by Kensington & Chelsea RBC after tenants voted in favour of a TMO: McIntosh, 1994).

Furbey *et al.* argue that these contradictions – support and constraints – infused the Conservative approach to 'citizenship' (1996, pp. 254–258). On the one hand, there was the construction of the citizen as consumer – the individualist model emphasized by the positioning of the apostrophe in *Citizen's Charter* – and on the other hand there was the citizen as 'active' – a person who 'is able and willing to shoulder social obligation' (p. 256). The concern of Furbey *et al.*, however, lies in the broader issue of training and it is clear that 'to be effective, tenants need to develop a range of knowledge and skills' (Pearl with Spray, 1997, p. 94). Funding given to training organizations, as with other areas, was 'intended to increase the choices for the 'citizen-as-consumer' and to encourage the qualities of initiative, independence, autonomy and risk-taking characteristic of the 'enterprise culture' (Furbey *et al.*, 1996, p. 259). Whilst state sponsored training does not conform to Conservative policy:

> 'Nevertheless, it remains the case that government resourced TMO training embodies a diagnosis for the problems of council housing informed by notions of 'dependence' and 'enterprise' and finances the entry of consumer-citizens into a limited marketplace of options.' (p. 262)

The training therefore provides one rationale for the failure of estates and a Conservative-inspired solution. In other words, citizens were sponsored and encouraged to take power from their councils (and RSLs) but only on the ideological grounds propounded by central government. As with LSVTs, then, the TMO can be regarded as an example of the expansion of central control (particularly as TMOs fall directly under the regulatory shadow of central government).

6.3   Complaints as Voice

A central precept of consumerism is the right to complain when things go wrong. Until recently, local authority housing departments' methods of grievance redress were undeveloped. In one study, only 27 per cent of questionnaire respondents claimed to have a formal written policy which was publicized in various ways (Lewis *et al.*, 1987, para. 4A 2.2). Pursuing a complaint is a method of individual participation and, potentially, grievance redress. Over the years, there has been a diversity of persons/ organizations to whom tenants can complain: councillors, housing officers/managers, local MP, Commission for Local Administration (the local ombudsman), the courts, the local authority's own grievance redress machinery. Evidence suggests that tenants pursue more than one avenue in relation to the same complaint (Cairncross *et al.*, 1997, Table 5.3). Most complaints relate to repairs and management (which is not surprising bearing in mind that customer satisfaction surveys continually pinpoint this area as a grievance) (Karn *et al.*, 1997, Ch. 6). However, it also appears that tenants knowledge of complaints mechanisms is poor, particularly in the case of the local ombudsman, Independent Housing Ombudsman (for RSL tenants) and the Housing Corporation (Karn *et al.*, 1997, pp. 84–88). This lack of knowledge may well reflect tenants' more general feelings of powerlessness. So, for example, homelessness applicants who are rejected by councils have a right to have their case reviewed (Housing Act 1996, s 202). Questionnaire research has found that in the six months to January 1998, few aggrieved applicants (outside London) sought to exercise this right (Hunter & Cowan, 1998).

6.4 'Mix and Match': Local Housing Companies

Local Housing Companies are currently the panacea for the ills of housing generally. They were first suggested by the Duke of Edinburgh's *Inquiry into British Housing* in 1991 and further considered by Wilcox *et al.* (1993). It is, however, difficult to draw out precisely what is *different* about them. They are registered with the Housing Corporation, which has always registered not-for-profit companies limited by guarantee. Local Housing Companies take over part of a local authority's stock in a similar vein to RSLs, which take under an LSVT (of which they are one strand). Local Housing Companies have both tenant and councillor representation on their boards in the same way as many LSVTs and HATs (although LSVTs are subject to a strict 20 per cent councillor membership; HATs' board membership depends upon negotiation). They have to secure private finance (but this is a feature of the 'social' housing world anyway). The 1995 White Paper does not assist in differentiating these providers from others:

'[Local Housing Companies] would need to be clearly in the private sector: local authority nominees would need to be in the minority on the board and not able to exercise a dominant influence. Subject to that, local authorities have a key role to play.' (DoE, 1995a, p. 29)

The DoE, in fact, presented the idea as 'privatisation', summoning up the spirit of the anti-local authority campaign of 1987 (Dwelly, 1995; *cf* Raynsford, 1991)). However, a sanguine critique of the concept concludes that 'Given the limited independence of a housing association [from central control], it is doubtful whether the political balance of the governing body is of much significance' (Alder, 1997, p. 37). One reason why there is currently no difference is because it was proposed (until the last minute) to allow profit-making companies to become RSLs through the Local Housing Company route. Indeed, the whole (legislative) consultation process was based upon this assumption.

Amidst this confusing legal background, the first companies have been set up. They have been pigeonholed within the LSVT programme as well as attracting government funding through the Estates Renewal Challenge

Fund (which has taken over from City Challenge). Their acceptance by New Labour seems assured because of their ability to lever private finance into estates. However, they suffer from the same pitfalls as LSVT – rising rents, less security, market risk, central control through the Housing Corporation (*cf* Wheal, 1998, where it is suggested that the Local Housing Company in Poplar, Tower Hamlets, has been able to give firmer rent guarantees than the council).

Conclusion

This chapter began with the wish to 'put the social back into social housing' and identified the tenant interest as the crucial element of 'social housing'. This has provided the focus for an analysis of the changing power structures within local authority and RSL property. We have seen how the different methods of privatization have differentially affected the interest groups. It is notable that the main method of exit created by the Conservatives, which gave tenants the opportunity to exit council house management – Tenants' Choice – was deeply unsuccessful because the Conservatives had based their opposition upon outmoded perceptions of housing management. The other mechanisms provided in the late 1980s, HATs and LSVTs, were engineered by different interest groups so that the tenants' voice could often have been ignored. Yet the effects of change of landlord, of going from public to private, have been significant and could not have been constructed at the time (particularly because of the subsequent fluctuations in the housing market affecting the right to buy as well as the government's desire to cut back on its Housing Benefit budget leading to the 'RPI + 1%' restrictions on rent rises).

Our analysis turned to consider the role of tenants in restructuring the power relationship inherent in housing management. Collective tenant participation, however this is framed, has occurred despite the individualist approach taken in housing legislation until 1993. There have been significant steps forward here towards tenant control of housing management, although this progression has been characterized by spatial unevenness as well as political differentiation. A further element of social housing is an open and fair complaints mechanism enabling tenants voices to be heard (albeit individually). There has been a considerable improvement here in a short period of time, although the process is characterized by lack of knowledge and possibly also apathy.

Finally, we considered the innovation of Local Housing Companies. These vehicles have sought to borrow the best bits of each of the previously discussed mechanisms whilst, nevertheless, falling within the LSVT category. Whether these organizations will fulfill the hope vested in them is open to doubt, however, for the same pitfalls as exist with LSVTs are equally apparent with them.

Endnote

1. Subsequent practice suggests that difficulties arise after transfer in the relationship between the council and the RSL, particularly when the former attempts to interfere in the latter's operation (see Exford, 1994; Dwelly, 1995).

Bibliography

Alder, J. (1997), 'Social landlords and housing associations: a distinction without a difference', vol 1, *Journal of Housing Law*, 35

Arnstein, S. (1969), 'Ladder of citizen participation', July, *American Institute of Planners*, 216

Atkinson, R. and Cope, S. (1997), 'Community participation and urban regeneration in Britain', in P. Hoggett (ed.), *Contested Communities – Experiences, Struggles, Policies*, Bristol: The Policy Press

Birchall, J. (1992), 'Council tenants: sovereign consumers or pawns in the game?', in J. Birchall (ed.), *Housing Policy in the 1990s*, London: Routledge

Birkinshaw, P. (1995), *Grievances, Remedies and the State*, London: Sweet & Maxwell

Bramley, G. (1993), 'Quasi-markets and social housing', in J. Le Grand and W. Bartlett (eds), *Quasi-Markets and Social Policy*, London: Macmillan

Burns, D., Hambleton, R. and Hoggett, P. (1994), *The Politics of Decentralisation*, London: Macmillan

Cabinet Office (1991), *The Citizen's Charter*, London: HMSO

Cairncross, L., Clapham, D. and Goodlad, R. (1997), *Housing Management, Consumers and Citizens*, London: Routledge

Carr, H. and Sefton-Green, D. (1999), 'Tollington estate and the decline of contract: An examination of the failure of long-term contracting in the local authority housing regime', Paper delivered at the Social-legal Studies Association Annual Conference, Loughborough University, April 1999

Chumrow, J. (1995), 'Housing action trusts: a possible role model?', in F. Ridley and D. Wilson (eds), *The Quango Debate*, Oxford: Oxford University Press

Clapham, D. and Kintrea, K. (1991), 'Housing allocation and the role of the public sector', in D. Donnison and D. Maclennan (eds), *The Housing Service of the Future*, Coventry: Institute of Housing

Clapham, D. and Kintrea, K. (1992), *Housing Co-operatives in Britain*, London: Longman

Clapham, D., Kintrea, K. and Kay, H. (1997), 'Direct democracy in practice: the case of 'community ownership' housing associations', vol 20, *Policy and Politics*, 359

Cole, I. And Furbey, R. (1994), *The Eclipse of Council Housing*, London: Routledge

Cowan, D. (1997), *Homelessness: The (In-)Appropriate Applicant*, Aldershot: Dartmouth

Cowan, D. (1998), 'Introduction: Crossing Boundaries', in D. Cowan (ed.), *Housing: Participation and Exclusion*, Aldershot: Dartmouth

Crossley, R. (1995), 'Time to give tenants a hearing', May/June, *Roof*, 13

Day, P., Henderson, D. and Klein, R. (1993), *Home Rules: Regulation and Accountability in Social Housing*, York: Joseph Rowntree Foundation

Department of the Environment (DoE) (1987), *Housing: The Government's Proposals*, Cm 214, London: HMSO

Department of the Environment (DoE) (1995a), *Our Future Homes: Opportunity, Choice and Responsibility*, Cm 2901, London: HMSO

Department of the Environment (DoE) (1995b), *More Choice in the Social Rented Sector*, London: DoE

Department of Environment, Transport and the Regions (DETR) (1998), *Housing Transfer Guidelines*, London: DETR

Department of the Environment, Transport and the Regions (DETR) (1999), *Tenant Participation Compacts Consultation Paper*, London: DETR

Dwelly, T. (1995), 'So who buys it?', September/October, *Roof*, 26

Exford, K. (1994), 'West Kent row reverberates', November/December, *Roof*, 9

Foley, B. and Evans, K. (1994), 'Tenant control, housing cooperatives and government policy', vol 20, *Local Government Studies*, 392

Furbey, R., Wishart, B. and Grayson, J. (1996), 'Training for tenants: 'Citizens' and the enterprise culture', vol 11, *Housing Studies*, 251

Gilroy, R. (1998), 'Bringing tenants into decision making', in D. Cowan (ed.), *Housing: Participation and Exclusion*, Aldershot: Dartmouth

Ginsburg, N. (1989), 'The Housing Act, 1988 and its policy context: a critical commentary', vol 25, *Critical Social Policy*, 56

Goodlad, R. (1991), 'Tenant participation', in D. Donnison and D. Maclennan (eds), *The Housing Service of the Future*, Coventry: Institute of Housing

Gregory, P. and Hainsworth, M. (1993), 'Chameleons or Trojan horses? The strange case of housing action trusts', vol 8, *Housing Studies*, 109

Hambleton, R. and Hoggett, P. (1987), 'Beyond bureaucratic paternalism', in P. Hoggett and R. Hambleton (eds), *Decentralisation and Democracy*, Occasional Paper No 28, Bristol: School for Advanced Urban Studies, University of Bristol

Hirschman, A. (1970), *Exit, Voice and Loyalty: Responses to Decline in Firms*, Cambridge, Mass: Harvard University Press

House of Commons Public Accounts Committee (1998), *Waltham Forest Housing Action Trust: Progress in Regenerating Housing Estates*, HC 425, London: HMSO

Housing Corporation (1997), *Performance Standards*, London: Housing Corporation

Hunter, C. and Cowan, D. (1998), 'Internal reviews in homelessness cases', paper given at the European Network of Housing Research, University of Wales, Cardiff, September

Karn, V. (1993), 'Remodelling a HAT: the implementation of the Housing Action Trust legislation 1987–92', in P. Malpass and R. Means (eds), *Implementing Housing Policy*, Buckingham: Open University Press

Karn, V., Lickiss, R. and Hughes, D. (1997), *Tenants' Complaints and the Reform of Housing Management*, Aldershot: Dartmouth

Kay, A., Legg, C. and Foot, J. (1987), *The 1980 Tenants' Rights in Practice*, London: Housing Research Group, City University

Kleinman, M. (1993), 'Large-scale transfers of council housing to new landlords: is British social housing becoming more European?', vol 8, *Housing Studies*, 163

Lewis, N., Seneviratne, M. and Cracknell, S. (1987), *Complaints Procedures in Local Government*, Vol 1, Sheffield: Centre for Criminological and Socio-Legal Studies, University of Sheffield

Lowe, S. (1986), *Urban Social Movements: The City after Castells*, London: Macmillan

Lund, B. (1996), *Housing Problems and Housing Policy*, London: Longman

McIntosh, A. (1994), 'By-pass or no through road?', May/June, *Roof*, 10

Mullins, D., Niner, P. and Riseborough, M. (1993), 'Large scale voluntary transfers', in P. Malpass and R. Means (eds), *Implementing Housing Policy*, Buckingham: Open University Press

Mullins, D., Niner, P. and Riseborough, M. (1995), *Evaluating Large Scale Voluntary Transfers of Local Authority Housing*, London: HMSO

National Audit Office (1997), *Housing Corporation: Tenants' Choice and the Torbay Tenants Housing Association*, HC 170 1997/98, London: SO

Owens, R. (1992), 'If the HAT fits', January/February, *Roof*, 17

Pearl, M. with Spray, W. (1997), *Social Housing Management: A Critical Appraisal of Housing Practice*, London: Macmillan

Priemus, H. (1997), 'Growth and stagnation in social housing: what is 'social' in the social rented sector?', vol 12, *Housing Studies*, 549

Raynsford, N. (1991), 'Management at arm's length', vol 25, *Inside Communications*, 5

Wheal, C. (1998), 'A tonic for Eastenders', *The Guardian*, 25 March

Wilcox, S., Bramley, G., Ferguson, A., Perry, J. and Woods, C. (1993), *Local Housing Companies: New Opportunities for Council Housing*, York: Joseph Rowntree Foundation

Woodward, R. (1991), 'Mobilising opposition: the campaign against Housing Action Trusts in Tower Hamlets', vol 6, *Housing Studies*, 44

Part II

Access to Housing: Need, Affordability and Tenure Neutrality

'Shelter is one of the most basic human needs. Being without a home is a catastrophe. Not only are the roofless deprived of the means to improve their lot: an address holds the key to employment, credit, goods, support, and services. But a roof – any sort of roof – is often not enough. The quality of accommodation is important too, often a significant factor in an individual's health, security and well-being. The interconnection between unsatisfactory housing and social and personal ills such as high levels of crime, educational under-achievement, and ill-health is increasingly stressed . . . The Government's declared aim is a "decent home . . . within reach of every family" – to which one might add, in the words of one of the witnesses to this inquiry: "Access to decent housing implies that people should not be obliged to live in physically substandard accommodation because their incomes are too low to afford anything better." ' (House of Commons Environment Committee (1996), *Housing Need*, HC 1995/6 22-I, London: HMSO, para. 1)

Introduction to Part II

It is a common, some might even say cherished, assumption that social housing is allocated according to need whilst private sector housing is allocated according to affordability. Such assumptions underline much government thinking on allocations. So, for example, the DoE's 1995 White Paper is full of the notion of need, in terms of the allocation of social housing (DoE, 1995). Their 1994 Consultation Paper on homelessness and local authority allocations promised reforms to the relevant legislation because that legislation did not prioritize those in housing need.

It is the argument throughout Part II of this book that such concepts are far too blunt evaluative tools to explain and justify actual practice(s) as well as the legislation involved in many cases. Indeed, we do not need to draw up sophisticated analytical, jurisprudential, or any other theoretical interpretation of these concepts. Rather, although it might surprise the reader, we find that the law and policy combine to deny allocation according to need whereas the market (as well as government's influence in it) distorts the notion of allocation according to affordability. Some general strands become apparent as well. For example, throughout tenures, ethnic minorities face discrimination, women and young people often have difficulties gaining access to accommodation. It may well be that these difficulties are a reflection of societal values in the allocation process. However, more likely, this is a reflection of a much broader pattern of discrimination that becomes self-serving (for example, 'she is unemployed, so she cannot get a mortgage' hides various messages about the role and opportunities of women in society).

In fact, when we talk about need and affordability, we are employing a set of values which themselves flesh out the principles involved. These values are *political, historical, economic, class- and 'race'-based, geographical* and provide the basis upon which tenure choice is made. So, for example, it was not inevitable that home ownership should become the majority tenure. Indeed, as we have seen, this has only become true this century. Far more important, have been the political signals of favouritism (tax breaks and 'talking up'), the decline of other tenures for one reason or another, the incline of mortgage finance, together with the (at times) apparent economic benefits of home ownership compared to other tenures (capital gains). However, it is certainly the case that these benefits have changed over time and at any one time will be spatially differentiated. Furthermore, it is clear that these factors, broad as they are, contain only part of the matrix. All of this makes the task of providing a general account of allocations a daunting prospect. It is, therefore, crucial for the analyst to bear in mind that each of these factors will have a differential effect. We can draw certain themes from the available research but these must be interpreted with care.

It is in this context that the notion of 'affordability' must be interpreted. Accommodation becomes more affordable when government involves itself in providing individuals (effectively) with a subsidy to pay for it, and less affordable when government changes the rules so as to withdraw the benefit. Becoming a 'citizen' within the New Right agenda meant engaging in the market place as a 'legitimate' consumer (see Clarke *et al.*, 1992, p. 141). The principle of *laissez-faire* attached to the market place within true New Right ideology, but not within the Thatcherite (for a discussion of the meaning of Thatcherism in the welfare context see Hewitt, 1992, Ch. 4) and post-Thatcherite world. Ultimately, intervention in the market led to 100 per cent mortgage advances and the recipients of this largesse ended up with the most serious problems when the market bottomed out. Intervention in the private rented sector makes that market affordable for some. However, it may well be that government involvement creates a sub-market for those who need individual subsidy to access such accommodation. The trap attached to needing such individual subsidy is that it effectively operates in an exclusionary way. The fact that benefits can be lost disproportionately to increases in income means that receipt of benefits operates as an employment disincentive. Thus, access to housing for such people can often involve exclusion from other consumptive and labour rights. In other words, the market and its affordability are manipulated by government, as well as other forces, in ways that are not always obvious.

In our post-Thatcherite world, 'social' housing allocation takes place in an imperfect quasi-market. This quasi-market actually threatens our use of the terminology, for there is nothing particularly 'social' about social housing allocation. However, it becomes apparent that power is involved and exercised either individually or bureaucratically. An individual's power is based upon that individual's *knowledge* of the available options. So, for example, if you are unclear about the role of RSLs, you are less likely to pursue that avenue. Power is also exercised through the knowledge that bureaucratic processes will eventually mean that, if you can wait long enough, you may well be allocated a better property, although this depends upon the political context of the process. Thus, administrative processes place an interpretative layer upon the notion of need. This point is elegantly made in the following quotation:

'Housing consumption . . . is the arena in which systematic inequalities in the social structure are mapped on to systematic differences in the housing stock; and it is a medium through which qualitative variations in the housing stock themselves accentuate and sustain different forms of social differentiation. This occurs in a number of ways, relating to the rules and procedures routinely administered by public bureaucracies, to the market-related criteria invoked in the apportionment of housing finance, and to the broad shifts of power, resources and influence between different tenure sectors that are determined by central government, either directly through housing policy or indirectly through broader strategies for managing the economy.' (Clapham *et al.*, 1990, p. 65)

Need is also undermined in a simple way. If it is accepted that needs are relative – a contentious matter in itself (see the important Doyal and Gough, 1991) – that there are issues of resources involved in our underlying use of the word 'need' – another contentious matter (see the important *R* v. *Gloucestershire CC ex parte Barry* [1997] 2 All ER 1) – it is nevertheless clear that to exclude persons from consideration as to whether they have any need is a denial of that person's need. Simply to deny a person an assessment of their comparative housing need is to deny that person's need. Personally, I feel slightly insane in making the point for it seems so crystal clear. If you do not allow a person onto your housing waiting list or you do not allow a person to be assessed under the homelessness legislation, you are ignoring their real needs for accommodation. Indeed, for some, you are creating real needs for accommodation for they have no other avenues. In this sense, then, our use of the word 'need' might be regarded as Orwellian (or antithetical).

Often, what it comes down to is that social housing is allocated according to a set of centrally determined priorities that also enables morality – and, specifically, a person's deservingness – to pierce and influence the general principle of needs-based allocations. Certain priorities are set. The clearest example relates to persons with children who are prioritized throughout and within central social housing allocation systems. There is no reason why such people should be prioritized at the expense of, for example, single persons under 25, although Fitzpatrick and Stephens suggest that they 'fall into the somewhat nebulous category of greater "desert"' (1998). The principle guiding the Conservative's homelessness reforms undoubtedly related to their nebulous notion of 'Victorian values' or 'back to basics' (see Cowan, 1998). Thus, the distinction often made between the deserving and undeserving poor is as strong in certain influential quarters today as it was in (say) the nineteenth century. A further example is the notion of self-induced homelessness. Those who are assessed as falling into this category obtain limited, sometimes non-existent, duties owed to them – Loveland used the phrase 'sign here and sod off' (1992). This clause, introduced under a Labour government in 1977, probably saved the homelessness legislation from reform under Thatcher for it pursued the line of less eligibility.

However, a more plausible answer to why Thatcher's government never reformed that legislation links in Part I of this book with the themes in Part II. Loveland (once again) regards the homelessness legislation as 'an exercise in legislative deceit' (1995, p. 331). The Thatcher government were able to rest easy knowing that its existence meant that they could say that they had a commitment to housing the homeless when the opposite was the case because local authorities did not have sufficient units of accommodation to do so. On this basis, the reforms contained in the Housing Act 1996 can be portrayed plausibly as a response to the failing back to basics campaign as well as attempts to bolster Major's leadership credentials in the light of his failing control of his party. New Labour amendments have simply attempted to reimpose the previous situation and so, equally, qualify for Loveland's withering critique.

Finally, a consistent theme running through Part II is of *tenure neutrality* or at the very least *tenure reciprocity*. These terms require explanation. The latter, being the more obvious argument, can be dealt with first.

The succeeding chapters deal with issues of access in a broadly tenure based way, beginning with issues of access to council housing and ending with issues of access to home ownership. Our analysis begins with homelessness but this does not mean that homelessness issues do not infiltrate into other areas. For example, there is an intimate connection between housing solutions for homelessness and home ownership, as the DoE's 1994 Consultation Paper made clear:

'The Government is committed to fostering opportunities for the continued spread of home ownership, and has established a number of arrangements for assisting people on low incomes to become home owners. Such measures both reduce the pressure on subsidised rented housing, and free such housing for those who need it.' (para. 2.1)

In other words, one of the housing solutions to homelessness is to facilitate the transition into home ownership. This is an example of tenure reciprocity. So, Forrest and Murie found that 'many purchasers would have been categorized at earlier stages as 'problem' tenants with little prospect of purchasing' (1991, p. 132).

There are links in other ways too. Some public sector housing is prized because, whilst it leads to a council tenancy, it carries the further benefit of enabling tenants to purchase their accommodation at discounts which increase depending on length of residence. So, the process of bureaucratic, public-sector allocation feeds into, and influences, who purchases their council homes. This raises important questions about who is allocated which property, for there will always be those who are more inclined to buy as well as those properties which would fare well in the home-ownership market. The same point can now be made in relation to certain RSL property, after the implementation of the 1996 Act's 'right to acquire'.

This notion of tenure reciprocity actually raises questions for consideration as well. It seems clear from the above that tenure is fluid, not fixed. This is what I mean when using the term 'tenure neutrality'. I am not saying that there are no distinctions between the tenures – although I am placing a bookmark for the discussion in Part III – but that accessing the different tenures is not in itself tenure based. So, being accepted as homeless or at the top of the housing register does not automatically lead to being allocated local authority property. It can also lead to allocation in RSL property, in the private rented sector, or even home ownership (as we have seen). The underlying message, then, is that certain important parts of the allocations systems are not tenure based. However, and this is the point, how can we then justify having different methods, bureau-cracies, procedures, legislation (or anything else for that matter) of allocating housing which are tenure-based? If we are to have coherence in housing allocations, as seems entirely reasonable, we must accept this facet of post-Thatcherism and re-orientate the (broad) law of housing allocations.

Bibliography

Clapham, D., Kemp, P. and Smith, S. (1990), *Housing and Social Policy*, London: Macmillan

Clarke, J., Cochrane, A. and Smart, C. (1992), *Ideologies of Welfare*, London: Routledge

Cowan, D. (1998), 'Reforming the homelessness legislation', vol 55, *Critical Social Policy*, 275

Department of the Environment (DoE) (1994), *Access to Local Authority and Housing Association Tenancies*, London: HMSO

Department of the Environment (DoE) (1995), *Our Future Homes*, London: HMSO

Doyal, L. and Gough, I. (1991), *A Theory of Human Need*, London: Macmillan

Fitzpatrick, S. and Stephens, M. (1998), 'Homelessness, need and desert in the allocation of council housing', paper delivered at the Social-legal Studies Association Annual Conference, Manchester Metropolitan University

Forrest, R. and Murie, A. (1991), *Selling the Welfare State*, London: Routledge

Hewitt, M. (1992), *Welfare, Ideology and Need*, Hemel Hempstead: Harvester Wheatsheaf

Loveland, I. (1992), 'Administrative justice, administrative process and the housing of homeless persons: A view from the sharp end', vol 13, *Journal of Social Welfare and Family Law*, 4

Loveland, I. (1995), *Housing Homeless Persons*, Oxford: Oxford University Press

Readers might also consider some of the material cited on affordability in later chapters, together with more theoretical work, such as J Neale (1997), 'Homelessness and theory reconsidered', vol 12, *Housing Studies*, 47. For important work on the housing position of ethnic minorities, see Karn, V. (ed.) (1997), *Ethnicity in the 1991 Census, Volume 4*, London: HMSO, where various permutations of the 1991 census results are considered.

7 Homelessness

Nowhere is the Orwellian characteristic of 'access' laws exposed better than in the creation, formulation, and implementation of the homelessness legislation. The notion of access to housing can be and often is exposed as being as much (if not more) about exclusion from housing than in probably any other subject covered in this part of the book. One reason this is so derives from the history of the homelessness legislation (currently the Housing Act 1996, Part VII) which has more often been concerrned with punishing the (so-called) undeserving than with providing rehousing opportunities.

The Poor Laws, which provide the earliest indications of the existence of a welfare state, doled out welfare on the basis that its recipients were undeserving:

> 'The old Poor Law actually stigmatized the poor with moral delinquency in its statutory provisions. The leading example is the Act of 1697 (8 and 9 Will III, c30), which obliged all those receiving poor relief to wear the letter 'P' on the right shoulder of their uppermost garment (s. 2). Badging the poor was applied at the local level and seems to have continued in some areas even after the legislation was repealed in 1810.' (Cranston, 1985, p. 35)

Not only is this an indication of the moral precepts upon which that legislation is based, it also suggests that these moral precepts continued after the legislation was repealed. Indeed, this penalization is as evident today as in the past. When Michael Portillo was Chief Secretary to the Treasury, he argued that:

> 'Help from government has become widely available with scant regard to whether the recipients have behaved reasonably, or unreasonably, responsibly or irresponsibly. As a result the penalties for fecklessness have been diminished and the rewards for personal responsibility devalued.' (Wintour, 1994)

The quote from Cranston also suggests that such values do not depend upon the legislation for their existence, but upon the administrators.This was also true when the National Assistance Act 1948 abolished the previous version of the Poor Law: the implementation of the former did not differ markedly from the implementation of the latter. Unpealing the law revealed the same practice. This was shown most clearly in the BBC television play *Cathy Come Home* (in many ways, the pivotal moment in modern development of the homelessness legislation: Loveland, 1991a) in which administrators appeared to be more concerned with the moral and spiritual welfare of Cathy than about her housing.

It may be argued that the homelessness legislation since 1977 has enabled its administrators – local authority homeless persons units in the housing departments (hereafter HPUs) – to implement their policies using ideological values similar to those of their predecessors. This is done through the legislative obstacles (a word used by Watchman & Robson, 1981) that the homeless must cross in order to be defined as 'successful'. In contrast to popular belief, a person does not (and never did) gain access to permanent accommodation because they become pregnant. Rather, successful applicants must be (a) eligible, (b) homeless, (c) in priority need, and (d) not intentionally homeless.

These obstacles are not tightly defined but rather are *discretionary*. By their nature, discretionary criteria require an administrator to make a decision against broad criteria. In turn, even though there is centrally determined guidance (to which the authority is required to have regard: s. 182, Housing Act 1996) and other material (such as the authority's own departmental guidance), the administrator brings themselves and their own prejudices to the decision (individual diversity). There are often calls for greater conformity in decision-making from government (see, for example, DoE, 1989) and academics (see, for example, Niner, 1989) but the discretionary nature of the job of homelessness decision-making means that diversity is celebrated. When one adds to this equation the fact that the decisions can also be based upon the availability of accommodation in an area, and that availability differs from area to area, that diversity will be enhanced.

One example of this continuum is reflected in the types of accommodation used to house these apparently undeserving people. Even though the National Assistance Act abolished the old poor laws, the same accommodation was used to implement the 1948 Act as had been used before (see Rees, 1965; Bailey & Ruddock, 1972; Robson & Poustie, 1996, p. 38). Often, this was dormitory, single sex accommodation which required families to be split up and children taken away from their aberrant parents. After the implementation of the Housing (Homeless Persons) Act 1977 – on which the 1996 Act is based – families were generally kept together, but housed in similar style accommodation 'with standards and rules more appropriate to police stations and workhouses' ('bed and breakfast': see Carter, 1997; Watchman, 1988; Bonnerjea & Lawton, 1987, pp. 37–44; Robson & Poustie, 1996, pp. 49–51). The misery of living in such accommodation for considerable periods whilst awaiting the provision of other housing is difficult to imagine; but it was nevertheless an everyday experience of the law of access/exclusion to housing. Even then, the quality of final accommodation offered to successful homeless applicants was often the poorest accommodation in the authority's own stock.

The homelessness legislation is not an indicator of housing need. Rather, at any particular moment, the legislation can only tell us who the law regards as being the most deserving and therefore entitled to assistance. It is because of this that the concept of need – a valuable empirical research tool, particularly in housing and social security (see Doyal & Gough, 1991; Hewitt, 1993; Spicker, 1993; Darke & Darke, 1979; Cullingworth, 1979) – is, in fact, a red herring when discussing the homelessness legislation, for that legislation has already defined 'need'on its own terms:

> 'Legislation has always required us to oppress the homeless by making *moral judgments*, not about their housing need, but about *why* the homeless become homeless in the first place. Furthermore, the relationship between the criteria through which local authorities made (and make) these moral judgments have, since 1977, also explicitly been related to the *supply* of available units of accommodation.' (Cowan, 1997, p. 21)

In other words, 'need' is related to the cause of the person's homelessness as well as to the availability of replacement accommodation in their area. It follows that, if (say) there are two available units of accommodation in a particular area, only two people can have the requisite need and so the parameters of the moral judgments must be narrowed. At this stage, it seems that the law is more likely to become involved. For, in narrowing those parameters, it is often the case that legal questions arise on the margins of the legislation's construction.

The proper concern should be with the ways in which the legislators perceive and define the various concepts used in the homelessness legislation, as well as the ways in which administrators implement it. In fact, the legislators use need in a particular (and peculiar) way. In the debates leading to the 1996 Act, for example, David Curry, the Housing Minister, contrasted the short-term 'social' need of homelessness with long-term 'social and physical' needs (as if homelessness itself might not be a symbol of the reality of long-term need: Standing Committee G, 12 March 1996, cols 587–9). This distinction means that the response to homelessness contained in the 1996 Act controversially restricts successful homeless applicants to a minimum period of just two years' accommodation. Furthermore, the administrators personal conception of housing need is the basis for housing exclusion based on race, gender, sexual habits, and external factors, such as media publicity, etc..

The implementation of the homelessness legislation has been greatly researched from a variety of different perspectives and much is known about this process of decision-making. This is an appropriate place to begin our analysis, so as to appreciate the pressures of 'doing the job' as well as the influences on the final decision-making. The second section, the most substantial part of this chapter, analyses the legislative obstacles standing in the way of homeless applicants. Here, the consideration will centre upon (a) the formulation of each obstacle, (b) the legal construction of each obstacle, and (c) the practice of each obstacle. The third section considers the ways in which the accommodation duties are implemented.

7.1 Doing the Job

The Value of Law or Legal Values?

HPU officers engaged in implementing the homelessness legislation rarely have legal training. In Loveland's study of three such HPUs, only two officers had any legal qualifications and their attempts at inculcating colleagues in legal processes failed (Loveland, 1995, Ch. 5; Cowan, 1997; *cf* Halliday's study of an inner city authority in which 'legal competence . . . [was] regarded as a professional attribute': 1998, p. 200). Indeed, the perception of homelessness work is often that it is the first rung on the career ladder. Training for the job is limited, most commonly being 'on-the-job'. In this type of atmosphere, the experience of administering the 'law' is almost certainly going to be skewed by the advice of other colleagues (whose practice might involve a deviation from legislative obligations), the officer's own interpretation of the 1996 Act or the Code of Guidance (CoG) (which substantially fleshes out the Act with the views of the DoE), and the local authority's own internal guidance. The cost of external training is usually prohibitive and, often, of short-term benefit only; internal training sessions where officers discuss their cases and other matters would be more likely. A DoE questionnaire-based study of local authority practice found that only about 28 per cent of authorities set aside a regular training period (Mullins *et al.*, 1996, para. 4.11). More often than not, officers are therefore susceptible to being made in the image of their predecessors.

Comments from officers such as 'we go by the law here' usually refer to the fact that they follow the Code of Guidance. However, the Code is not meant to be a substitute for the Act; rather it is meant to be advisory. It is also intensely *political*. For example, the Code produced by the Conservative government after the 1996 Act made a number of unfortunate references to distinctions between married and unmarried households (DoE, 1996, para. 5.21). The current Code has been considerably amended by New Labour and, at the time of writing, a new version has been put out to Consultation (DETR, 1999). (*All references to the Code in this book are to that produced on 20 December 1996, together with subsequent revisions*). Sometimes, the courts hold it to be unlawful (see, for example, *R* v. *Secretary of State for the Environment ex parte Tower Hamlets LBC* [1993] 25 HLR 524). The Code does not provide answers to every question. Its approach is to provide the parameters of decision-making, what might be relevant considerations. It does not provide a concrete list of matters which must be considered in every case (which would be unrealistic).

In Cowan's fieldwork covering 15 HPUs, the use and value of internal written guidance was variable. Furthermore, whilst officers might have read the manual on their arrival, it was rarely referred to again. Indeed, internal policies are not always implemented for this reason as well as others: 'This was not "radicalism" but a conscious decision often taken by several or all of the members of the HPU after discussion as to the appropriate priority to be afforded to particular cases' (Cowan, 1997, p. 40). Loveland also draws attention to the 'subversive' employee who actively subverts council policy (1988) as well as the need for stability ('[officers] would prefer politically unpalatable policy as long as it was clear': 1994, p. 7). On the other hand, Halliday refers to internal guidance being strictly adhered to, for the following reasons:

'The manager explained that Timbergreens learned early on from its experience of judicial review that it needed to be able to *demonstrate* that it had considered the relevant facts in an applicant's case. Accordingly, as much information is obtained as possible so as not to be caught out in a subsequent legal challenge by the claim that it has not considered all the relevant factors. . . .
However, another reason lies behind information bingeing [which this approach required]. A general culture of suspicion exists in the Assessments Team in relation to the openness and truthfulness of homeless applicants. The widespread view is held that applicants 'change their stories' in order to circumvent the legal barriers which may prevent them from being eventually offered housing.' (Halliday, 1998, p. 217)

In other words, law can be relevant to, and decisive of, the administrative process (in this case because it suited the HPU officers' beliefs). There is a suggestion that the process of juridification has also had greater impact since (at the latest) 1989 (Loveland, 1995, Ch. 10). It can be argued that a central reason for this surgence is the limited availability of accommodation in some areas, which has constrained decision-making. Law is a valuable tool in the constraining process precisely because it enables officers to make the necessary decision. In other words, law can be perceived, not as a check on the administrative process, but as part of the legitimating process.

HPU officers are 'bullish' about their decisions, most often believing them to be legally defensible (Cowan, 1998). Thus, when applicants challenge them, sometimes after consultation with a solicitor or other advisory agency, resort might be made to the law (either the HPU's version of it or that of the authority's own legal service). The relevance of law to the administrative process rather depends upon the value that the authority places upon it. For example, if there is insufficient finance to seek legal advice, an HPU might well accede to such legal advances. Some authorities, on the other hand, are known to refuse to accede to such requests until they reach the door of the court, perhaps using this process as a means of weeding out those not desperate enough (Sunkin *et al.*,

1995). However, it is certainly true that academic lawyers are at an early stage in appreciating the impact of law on administrative practice.

The 1996 Act requires all HPUs to have a system of internal review of decisions in their authority (s. 202; The Allocation of Housing and Homelessness (Review Procedures and Amendment) Regulations 1996, SI 1996/3122; DoE, 1996, Ch. 17; Allocation of Housing and Homelessness (Review Procedures) Regulations 1999, SI 1999/71). The Regulations are fairly bland and unprescriptive. The only exception occurs where 'there is a deficiency or irregularity in the original decison, or in the manner in which it was made', but the authority is minded to make a decision against the applicant. in such circumstances, the applicant is entitled to make oral or written representations (SI 1999/71, para. 8(2)(b)).

It is likely that decision-making practice will be affected. This may depend upon a number of different factors such as the types of person conducting the review, the confidence of the officers in the review process achieving the 'correct' result, the procedures adopted by the review process (see Baldwin *et al.*, 1992; Cowan, 1998). Aggrieved applicants have the right to make a further appeal to the County Court on 'a point of law' (s. 204; as to the abstruse meaning of a 'point of law', see Arden & Hunter, 1996, paras 3.7–3.27).

There is some evidence that there is considerable variation in the use and success of the new internal review process (Cowan & Hunter, 1998).[1] Generally, there are more internal reviews than judicial reviews (although this does not account for those applicants who threatened judicial review, but did not for whatever reason, approach the court). However, most authorities hardly experienced any internal reviews in the six months before January 1998 (of our respondents, 68 per cent had fewer than five review applications, and only 8 per cent, mostly London authorities, had experienced more than 41 reviews).

The majority of the reviews take place in urban areas. This is not a surprising finding because urban areas tend to have the largest numbers of homelessness applicants. What is surprising, though, is the fact that this is not uniform and between apparently similar authorities wide variations are apparent. So, for example, in two northern metropolitan authorities (both with a housing stock of over 50,000 dwellings, both Labour controlled, and both having about the same number of homelessness applications), one had between 6–15 reviews and the other had considerably more than 66 reviews in the previous six months. What is most interesting about this is that the authority with fewer reviews is known to have considerably greater pressure on its housing stock, whereas the other authority is known to have a high turnover of stock. Similar striking variations were apparent amongst London respondents.

It appears that applicants are more likely to be successful if there are more reviews (perhaps suggesting that in some areas there is a learning process for all the 'players' which affects success rates). Amongst London authorities,[2] the average success rate was 20 per cent, but there were wide variations. So, for example, in one authority which had experienced 99 reviews, just four per cent had been successful; in another authority 41 per cent had been successful (this was the largest by some way, the next highest being 29 per cent).

Some brief preliminary observations may be appropriate, which highlight the critical need for further research in this important field. The first observation is that decision-making is now occurring in terms of a different adjudicative paradigm and much of the earlier research on decision-making requires reconsideration. How the internal review process (and, indeed, County Court appeals) impacts upon the original decision-making is an as yet unanswered question. Secondly, use of the internal review process may bear no relation to the factors which have been suggested to have influenced judicial review applications. It may, for example, be related to whether the local authority exercises its discretion to continue to provide accommodation pending the review. Third, the internal review process might be regarded as part of a delegalization of the homelessness legislation, in which the only relevance of law is to provide broad procedural guidelines as to how the review should be conducted. Fourth, the lack of use of the internal review process has no convincing explanation – all things are not equal between unsuccessful homelessness applicants.

Rationing: Gatekeeping Available Accommodation

The process of implementing the homelessness legislation is often a complex method of rationing access to a limited supply of accommodation. The question is not only about whether a person meets the criteria in the homelessness legislation but whether a person will also make the best use of the accommodation provided (*cf* the deserving–undeserving dichotomy). In fact, this process is one of rationing and operates in a number of ways (see, generally, Lidstone, 1994). For example, 'front of house' staff who are the public face of the authority can misdirect a person away from the HPU to a different part of the authority (*ibid*, p. 469; Anderson & Morgan, 1997). The HPU officers' interviewing techniques can be aggressive or make the applicant feel that they have no hope of accessing accommodation in this way (see Malos & Hague, 1993, p. 42). Decision letters might not be sent to applicants who are then expected to find out about decisions by osmosis or telephoning the authority (a daunting process in itself) (Cowan, 1998).

It also appears that there are practical concerns about 'opening the floodgates' – opening the gate so wide generally, or for a particular group. One example of this occurred in the early 1990s when HPUs were in the process of (re-)considering a housing response to persons who were HIV-positive. Some London HPUs, under most stress as regards the availability of accommodation, which accepted those who were HIV-positive provided they were homeless, were forced into changing this response because of fears that all their single person's accommodation near hospitals would be allocated to this client group. Partly, such a response was induced by the media panic about the numbers of persons who were forecast to become HIV-positive and, partly, it was a response to a diminishing stock of accommodation (Cowan, 1995a).

Gatekeeping is more generally associated with the notion of a resource-based rationing process. So, the HPU officer is said to have one eye on the availability of accommodation and one eye on the applicant. Carlen (1994) identifies bureaucratic or professional procedures which have the effect of deterring applicants (from calling themselves homeless), denying applicants (the legal status of homelessness), and disciplining applicants into withdrawing their status. However, there is an alternative meaning to 'resource-based' to the effect that decision-making depends upon the resources given by the authority to the HPU. The Audit Commission recommended 'a target of completing all enquiries within 30 days unless there are exceptional reasons why the case has to take longer' (1989, para. 66). However, it also noted that a result of increasing numbers of applicants was that in six out of seven authorities covered by their research 'interviewing staff had in recent periods carried excessive caseloads and the efficiency and effectiveness of their services had been adversely affected' (para. 72). A fifth of HPUs allocated more than 30 new cases per month to each interviewing officer (p. 26). Obviously the care taken in making enquiries, the quality of decision, and the impact of law will be experienced differently given this variable. It can be (and sometimes is) argued that making some decisions, such as concerning intentional homelessness (which is most heavily litigated – see below), is simply inefficient because they take too long. That the number of staff employed within HPUs has risen considerably since 1986 (Mullins *et al.*, 1996, para. 4.6) suggests that authorities may have taken the decision to employ more people rather than let more applicants through the gate.

Working Together

It would be wrong to suggest that the homelessness legislation considered here provides the only method of enabling the homeless to access accommodation. Both the Children Act 1989 (people under 21: ss 17, 20, 27; see Cowan, 1997, Ch. 4) and the NHS and Community Care Act 1990 (people over 18) contain rehousing provisions although one has to look quite hard in the latter case for their existence (LAC 10/94, reintroducing the repealed s. 21(1)(b), National Assistance Act 1948; see Cowan, 1995, where constitutional considerations are also considered). Rather than assisting in the cases where they apply, it is an unfortunate facet of this welfare-based legislation that they create a paradox:

'The paradox of social welfare bureaucracies is that although they might be ostensibly devoted to the wider public interest and to the interests of intended beneficiaries, frequently they appear to neglect these interests in what they do. . . . [Frequently] they act in a manner which seems deliberately to trample on the interests, rights and liberties of their clientele' (Cranston, 1985, p. 232)

In this case, the problem arises because the assessing and providing obligations have been given to the social services departments of local authorities. In non-unitary authorities, there is an awkward split (including, sometimes, of political control) between County Councils (social services authorities) and District/Borough Councils (housing authorities). It should not be assumed that the situation is much easier in unitary authorities as often social services and housing are physically separated in different offices in the same building.

The consistent findings of empirical research in this area support the view that inter-agency relationships, which are supposed to form 'joint assessments' (or similar) actually combine to do the opposite (for example, see Cowan, 1997, Chs 3–4; Means & Smith, 1996; McCluskey, 1994). Furthermore, this seriously affects the homelessness decision-making process when it is believed, rightly or wrongly, that 'aftercare' services and support are not provided because it is believed that this will affect the applicant's ability to retain their accommodation. If they are not able to retain their accommodation, then it is likely they will lose any entitlement that they originally had. Although there are other explanations, in the past I have argued that the overarching problem, which foreshadows all attempts at joint working, is the legislation itself (Cowan, 1997, Chs 2–5).

A Discriminating Process?

A recurrent concern in the implementation of the homelessness legislation is with discrimination by HPUs against certain persons on the basis of race, sex, age, criminal background, and mental capacity. Cowan and Fionda found that HPUs often made adverse findings against those coming out of prison because there might be a causal link between the offending behaviour and the loss of accommodation (1994a, especially pp. 453–454; see further, Paylor, 1995; Carlisle, 1996). Hawes found that older people are often given preferential treatment by local authorities (1997, p. 9) but other studies suggest that the same is not true amongst the young (Cowan, 1997, Ch. 4). Other studies suggest a patriarchal attitude operating within local authorities reinforcing male values. This is particularly evident in cases of 'domestic' violence against women (see, for example, Maguire, 1989; and below), perhaps based upon the male view of home as castle as opposed to female views (see Ch. 1).

There is considerable adverse criticism attaching to *institutional racism*[3] that has been found to occur in allocations policies, some of which will be considered in the next chapter. For now, it is simply necessary to say that 'the legacy of past antipathy still infuses a range of bureaucratic procedures regulating entry to the public sector' (Smith, 1989, p. 94).

However, it is apparent that structural processes considered in the previous chapters are all causes of homelessness amongst ethnic minorities. This is reflected in statistical analyses of homeless applicants. These reflect a consistently larger number of applications from ethnic minorities to HPUs than form part of the resident population: 70 per cent to 50 per cent in Brent (Bonnerjea & Lawton, 1987 – a study of homelessness amongst the Afro-Caribbean population). HPUs have been slow to monitor their applications on the basis of ethnic origin, although part of the cause was that Department of Environment statistics were not required on this issue.

Implementation of the homeless persons legislation led to early suggestions of bias. The London Borough of Hillingdon, close to Heathrow airport, apparently did the following:

'. . . the Chairman of the council's housing committee, Mr Terry Dicks, decided to have the Janmohammeds [a recently arrived family who had applied to the council for accommodation] taken by taxi to the Foreign Office and dumped on the pavement in a gesture, later described by Lord Justice Griffiths as in the worst possible taste and with inhuman disregard for the feelings of this unfortunate family. In contrast, Mr Turvey, an Englishman returning to England from Rhodesia, as it then was . . . was . . . secured accommodation by the housing authority.' (MacEwen, 1990, p. 515; see also MacEwen, 1991, ch. 7)

An attempt at making an investigation in this case by the Commission for Racial Equality (CRE) was subsequently stymied by the courts. However, a subsequent investigation in the case of Tower Hamlets' treatment of homeless Bangladeshis found that Tower Hamlets discriminated both directly and indirectly against them. This meant that the families were refused or not provided with permanent accommodation; waited longer for accommodation; were not accepted as homeless where part of their family was resident outside the UK; and disproportionately allocated housing on poor estates (CRE, 1988; see Ginsburg, 1992, pp. 121–122; Ginsburg & Watson, 1992; for a different scenario in the same authority, see *R* v. *Tower Hamlets LBC ex parte Khalique* (1994) 26 HLR 517; in respect of discrimination against travellers, see CLA 95/B/1009). A sophisticated study of institutional racism in Haringey and Lambeth found that 'despite all of the positive steps taken to reduce sources of subjective and institutional racism, black applicants were receiving inferior quality accommodation to comparable white applicants. . .' (Jeffers & Hoggett, 1995, p. 327). One suggested reason for this was based upon the fact that, as most black applicants entered the system through the homelessness route, they were keener than others to be rehoused quickly: 'when asked the question "where would you like to live?", [this was] reinterpreted in terms of "how long do you wish to wait for an offer?"'. They would therefore accept accommodation in the worse areas (*ibid*, p. 336).

7.2   Homelessness Law and Practice

The most appropriate way to conceptualize homelessness law is as a confusion of principle for that was the main characteristic of its formulation. This confusion relates to the *cause(s)* of homelessness. There appear to be four such principles, all of which are reflected in the 1996 Act. The first, as suggested above, is that homelessness is caused by personal inadequacy or fecklessness (*cf* Greve *et al.*, 1971; CHAC, 1968; Seebohm, 1969). There are at least three other less punitive rationales explaining why people become homeless. These relate, first, to the consequences of *structural* inequalities in housing; second, to the fact that inequalities in society act as *precipitating* causes; and, finally, to the view that any response to homelessness encourages people to make themselves homeless in order to *(ab-)use the legislation* (see, for example, the DoE's Consultation Paper, 1994, in which this was a dominant consideration – discussed in Cowan & Fionda, 1994b; Loveland, 1994; Carter & Ginsburg, 1994).

Each of these essentially contradictory principles is reflected both in the formulation and practice of the homelessness legislation. Broadly, the legislation requires applicants to jump over the following obstacles: (a) they must be eligible; (b) they must be homeless (c) they must be in priority need; and (d) they must not be intentionally homeless. Simply jumping one does not guarantee the provision of accommodation. The approach adopted in this section is to go through each, drawing attention to the following factors: first, their Parliamentary antecedents; second, their statutory definitions and some relevant comments from the Code of Guidance; third, some consideration of relevant case law is provided; and, finally, known actual practice is considered.

Eligibility

The Housing Act 1996, for the first time, makes certain homeless people ineligible for accommodation. These groups generally refer to asylum seekers and 'illegal' immigrants (see ss. 185–188 and The Homelessness Regulations 1996, SI 1996/2754, The Allocation of Housing and Homelessness (Amendment) (No. 2) Regulations 1997, 1997/2046; and CoG, Ch. 12 as amended 7/03/97). This is all considered in Chapter 10 below.

It is, however, also true that HPUs often adopt threshold-type criteria governing whether a person is able to make an application. For example, it is well-known that some HPUs require those subject to domestic violence to seek legal advice (and sometimes non-molestation or occupation orders under the Family Law Act 1996 and its predecessors: see Diduck & Kaganas, 1999) before accepting an application in those cases (Cowan, 1997, pp. 126–132; Thornton, 1989; Malos & Hague, 1993). Advice sometimes given is as follows:

'The applicant should be told they may be better off pursuing legal remedies rather than waiting a number of years in temporary accommodation for rehousing, with all the upheaval entailed in moving from one temporary accommodation address to another.'

Homelessness

The term 'homelessness' is susceptible to a multitude of different interpretations (see Robson & Poustie, 1996, pp. 10–16). The distinction that exercised the minds of Parliamentarians in 1977 was between the quality of accommodation and the level of occupation. It was believed that, if homelessness covered both, 'it would be expecting too much of human nature to think that no-one would do whatever he could to move out of poor accommodation into that other accommodation' (HC Debs, vol. 214, col. 955 *per* Hugh Rossi). So, homelessness occurs when a person has *'no accommodation available for his occupation'* (s. 175(1)). It did not cover the quality of accommodation available.

Despite that Parliamentary intention, it was apparent from an early stage, that the courts began considering the quality of accommodation suggesting that it was a relevant factor to be taken into account here. However, case law has centred around the meaning of the word 'accommodation', attempting to narrow its meaning quite considerably. In *R* v. *Hillingdon LBC ex parte Puhlhofer* [1986] AC 484, Lord Brightman suggested that

'Parliament plainly, and wisely, placed no qualifying adjective before the word accommodation [in s. 175] and none is to be implied. The word 'appropriate' or 'reasonable' is not to be imported. Nor is accommodation not accommodation because it might be unfit for human habitation . . . or might involve overcrowding.'

An immediate result of this judgment was that Parliament legislated to the effect that a person had no accommodation when there was no accommodation *'which it would be reasonable for him to continue to occupy'* (s. 175(3)). Parliament, in fact, accepted the observation that this amendment simply restored the position to what it had been before (and, indeed, made it potentially harsher: HC Debs, vol 103, col 740). Even though this ameliorating amendment was brought into force in 1996, the 'baleful influence' of *Puhlhofer* remains (Hoath, 1988, p. 43). In *R* v. *Brent LBC ex parte Awua* [1996] 1 AC 55, Lord Hoffmann argued that:

'A local authority could take the view that a family like the Puhlhofers, put into a single cramped and squalid bedroom, can be expected to make do for a limited period. On the other hand, there will come a time at which it is no longer reasonable to expect them to continue to occupy such accommodation.' (at p. 68)

'Reasonableness' is not capable of general exposition but must be considered in each individual case. Quasi-legislation makes the consideration of affordability a relevant consideration in each case (The Homelessness (Suitability of Accommodation) Order 1996, SI 1996/3204), which essentially applies a means test to the notion of 'reasonableness' and thus homelessness. The CoG suggests that the following other considerations are relevant: physical conditions of the property; overcrowding; type of accommodation; violence or threats of violence from persons *not* associated (see below) with the applicant; security of tenure (para. 13.8). Case law on the meaning of 'reasonableness' is often harsh. For example, the courts have suggested that just because accommodation is 'unfit for human habitation' does not automatically make it unreasonable to occupy it (see *R* v. *South Herefordshire DC ex parte Miles* [1983] 17 HLR 82); a similar result occurred in relation to the occupation of an HMO which was in breach of fire regulations (*R* v. *Kensington and Chelsea RBC ex parte Ben-el-Mabrouck* [1995] 27 HLR 564).

However, decisions about reasonableness, and homelessness generally, have to be made exceptionally quickly in practice. HPU officers do not visit the accommodation themselves and therefore have to make a judgment. Simple statistics provide an interesting, albeit incomplete, entry into the analysis. A 1993/4 DoE study illustrated the percentage of authorities which would consider an applicant homeless in the following circumstances: women's refuge, 86 per cent; accommodation statutorily unfit, 84 per cent; night shelter, 79 per cent; squat, 64 per cent; hostels, 58 per cent; accommodation statutorily overcrowded, 68 per cent; touring caravan, 57 per cent; bed and breakfast, 51 per cent; accommodation applicant cannot afford, 45 per cent (Mullins *et al.*, Table 5.1). The authors do not make the point that the law assumes in most of these cases that the person is statutorily homeless so that the percentage of authorities that do not make a homelessness finding in these cases is staggering. Loveland's qualitative research suggested that authorities have always adopted a restrictive practice (particularly in respect of certain applicants) (1995, pp. 171–175).

Three other parts of the statutory definition of homelessness also repay critical analysis. First, there is a requirement that the accommodation must be available for the applicant together with 'a member of his family' and/or 'any other person who might reasonably be expected to reside with him' (s. 176). If it is not so available, the applicant is homeless. This has been the premise of the homelessness legislation since 1977 – that families should not be split up. The splitting up of families, however, is commonplace, partly because of the discretion given to authorities in determining who is a member of the applicant's family and partly as a result of difficulties in proof (see Baker, 1996). For example, the Children Act 1989 allows for parents of a child to make an agreement as to a child's care and control without court interference. If a child spends two nights with its father, does this place the child in this category? The CoG, with commendable vagueness, suggests this is 'a matter of fact and degree' (para. 13.2).

Second, if the applicant has accommodation anywhere in the world, they will not be homeless in England or Wales. A front page article in the *Daily Mail* as the Housing Act 1996 proceeded through Parliament announced the judicial decision in *R* v. *Camden LBC ex parte Aranda* (1996) 28 HLR 672 under the headline 'Tenant's £20,000 worth of cheek' (Doran, 1996). Ms Aranda had been granted £20,000 to return to Columbia to buy a property with her husband (under a tenants' incentive scheme). The marriage had broken down and her personal circumstances had forced a return. On application to Camden, she was found to be intentionally homeless but this finding was (correctly) overturned by the court. The government evidently took the view that an applicant who has accommodation (wherever it may be) should not be found homeless in these circumstances. An amendment was made to the Act to this effect.

Third, in certain situations applicants are deemed homeless within the terms of the legislation, the most important of which was domestic violence (HC Debs, vol 926, col 902 (18 February 1977) *per* Stephen Ross). Until the 1996 Act, the legislation had drawn an ugly distinction between violence which took place within the home and that which took place outside the home (only the former being deemed automatically homeless; the latter on the basis of reasonableness: see Cowan, 1997, Ch. 6). The new Act draws the dividing line on the basis of whether the aggressor is 'associated with the applicant' (ss. 177–8) in line with the Family Law Act 1996. The homelessness legislation, however, has never provided a threshold of violence (other than widening it to include *threats of violence* as well, provided those threats are likely to be carried out). There is also the question of how to prove the violence. Much depends not upon legislative criteria or the CoG, but upon the way in which applicants are able to articulate their version of events. It also remains to be seen whether HPUs will adopt the associated person approach.

Other types of violence, including that which takes place from a non-associated person (such as, for example, racially motivated violence), is subject to the reasonableness criterion. There is some evidence (albeit limited) from Cowan's study that racial harassment is not accorded a high priority by HPUs despite governmental exhortations to adopt a victim-oriented approach (Home Office, 1989; 1991). This is mainly because cases of racial harassment within the council's own stock are dealt with as transfers (and therefore not under the homelessness legislation) and the only applications generally come from the private sector in which it is assumed that applicants are better able to access their legal remedies. Part of the problem is that the homelessness legislation encourages a climate of suspicion on the part of HPU officers, which is hardly conducive to a victim-oriented approach (Cowan, 1997, pp. 110–115).

Priority need

The priority need categories were taken directly from a 1974 Circular (LAC 18/74, para. 8). These categories do not really concern need generally. They determine which people are *most* needy according to one view. These categories are also not really about priority because, first, applicants within the categories must cross over the other obstacles as well as fit within a priority category. It is sometimes assumed that, if an applicant falls within a priority category, this automatically causes a rehousing obligation to arise. On its own, such an observation is incorrect even though academic research often assumes it to be true. Second, there are no gradations of priority – some are in, the rest are out. The priority need categories are as follows:

> 'a pregnant woman or a person with whom she resides or might reasonably be expected to reside;
> a person with whom dependent children reside or might reasonably be expected to reside;
> a person who is vulnerable as a result of old age, mental illness or handicap or physical disability or other special reason, or with whom such a person resides or might reasonably be expected to reside;
> a person who is homeless or threatened with homelessness as a result of an emergency such as flood, fire, or other disaster.' (s. 189(1))

A single person who is not pregnant and/or does not have a child can only fall within the final two paragraphs (the same is true of a married couple in that situation).

It is perhaps unsurprising that 'vulnerable' and 'emergency' have generally received restrictive definitions by the judiciary. The former occurs when a person is 'less able to fend for [themselves in finding and keeping accommodation] so that injury or detriment would result when a less vulnerable person will be able to cope without harmful effects' (*R* v. *Waveney DC ex parte Bowers* [1983] QB 238, 244; *R* v. *Bath CC ex parte Sangermano* (1984) 17 HLR 94). Far from applying a dictionary definition, the courts therefore impose a comparative test. 'Emergency' is not given a general meaning but must be related to the examples given, using the *eiusdem generis* method of construction. The immediate effect of such a construction was that a person unlawfully evicted from accommodation was not in priority need due to an emergency (*R* v. *Bristol CC ex parte Bradic* (1995) 27 HLR 584).

These categories are as important for the people who are not included as for those who are. Categories expressly excluded from vulnerability and emergency status are, for example, young people, those subjected to violence (who are deemed homeless), and those recipients of community care. They must be found 'vulnerable as a result of . . . some other special reason'. The CoG makes valuable reference to, and suggestions for, each group as well as referring authorities to alternative legislation (such as the Children Act 1989 and/or the NHS and Community Care Act 1990) but these exhortations appear to be forgotten in the process of implementing the Act. Table 7.1, taken from the 1993/4 DoE study, suggests that such positive exhortations often become lost (see also Cowan, 1997):

Intentional homelessness

This provision was introduced as a result of concerns that people would make themselves homeless to jump the housing queue and to take advantage of the beneficial effects of the Act (see HC Debs, vol. 926, col. 919, 929–30, 943–4, 957–8 (18 February 1977); HC Debs, vol. 934, cols 1608–75 (8 July 1977). This issue came to dominate the Parliamentary debates in 1977. Since that time, it has simply been assumed that the concept should remain. It was not questioned in the debates around the 1996 Act. Rather it was expanded to cover a further situation (see below). The fears were best expressed by William Rees-Davies MP, who used four examples to justify the argument favouring an expanded concept of intentional homelessness: first, there were rent-dodgers (who were 'people who are not meeting their rent obligations, many of them quite deliberately'). Second were those who 'come off the beach' during high season in a resort such as Margate (in his constituency) and required the local authority to help them; third, 'strangers to an area should [not] be treated in the same way as those who are resident in the area'; the fourth category was divided into two, 'what I call the in-laws and . . . the winter lettings case'. The 'in-laws' case encapsulated those who went to stay with their in-laws, caused friction, and were then 'kicked out. . . . They are then homeless and go to the local authority and try to crash the queue . . .' The 'winter lettings' case encapsulated those people who took on a winter letting and then approached the local authority when it came to its natural conclusion (see generally HC Debs, vol 926, cols 972–5).

This 'indictment' was framed in terms of moral blameworthiness. This was the key to each of the examples and was expressed in terms of the

Table 7.1 Priority need

Category	Sample	Yes	Depends	No
Leaving long-stay mental handicap or psychiatric hospital	344	92	2	6
Applicant with shared care of children	337	75	3	23
Women who have suffered violence at home, no dependent children	343	74	2	25
Children leaving care	339	66	3	31
Men who have suffered violence at home, no dependent children	336	64	2	34
Applicants aged under 18 (on basis of age alone)	344	17	2	81
Applicant leaving prison	338	5	2	93
Applicant with AIDS	174	98	–	2
Applicant HIV positive symptomatic (ill)	163	96	–	4
Applicant HIV positive asymptomatic (not ill)	145	53	–	47

Source: Mullins *et al.*, 1996, p. 53

reasons why the subject of each example had left their previous accommodation. It was not framed in terms of the deservingness or need of homeless persons as homeless persons. For example, earlier in the debate Rees-Davies and others had referred to homeless people, who potentially would use the legislation, as scroungers and scrimshankers, explicitly referring to the in-laws example (*ibid,* col 921).[4] The queue-jumping image is directly related to the availability or supply of accommodation. The Act was not allowing for more accommodation to be built – it was supposed to be cost neutral – rather it was concerned with re-ordering priorities and the administration. Thus the concern of Rees-Davies and others was that this re-ordering would mean that homeless people would infiltrate their (apparently beautiful) areas and take housing away from their residents.

There were, of course, opposing views but political reality meant that the Bill had to be palatable across the parties.[5] Applicants were therefore not entitled to indefinite accommodation under the Act if they were found to be intentionally homeless, whether or not they had a priority need. The intentional homelessness provision in the new Act, after several attempts at drafting it, read(s) as follows:

> . . . a person becomes homeless intentionally if he deliberately does or fails to do anything in consequence of which he ceases to occupy accommodation which is available for his occupation and which it would have been reasonable for him to continue to occupy. (s 191(1))

Described as 'gobbledegook', the provision has been subjected to microscopic examination by the judiciary, particularly in the late 1980s and 1990s. Case law suggests that four issues must be considered: the applicant must have deliberately done or failed to do something; this must have caused the loss of accommodation; that accommodation must have been available for the applicant; and it must have been reasonable for the applicant to continue to occupy it. At one time, it was believed that the relevant accommodation was the applicant's 'last settled accommodation' (*Din* v. *Wandsworth LBC* [1983] 15 HLR 73) and a considerable body of case law developed around that concept. That case law unhelpfully suggested that whether accommodation was settled or temporary was a 'question of fact and degree'. It has subsequently become apparent that leaving settled accommodation is not the only way in which a person might become intentionally homeless. Lord Hoffmann left open whether it was possible to find a person intentionally homeless after leaving other types of accommodation (*R* v. *Brent LBC ex parte Awua* [1996] 1 AC 55, 68; see, further, Arden & Hunter, 1996, Ch. 14; Hunter & Miles, 1997).

A few examples should suffice to illustrate the more general operation of the section:

- *Example* 1: The applicant left secure accommodation for a winter let which automatically terminated. It was held that the applicant's deliberate act of leaving the secure accommodation for insecure accommodation caused the homelessness.[6]
- *Example* 2: The applicants were incurring substantial arrears of rent on their accommodation. They were advised to await the result of possession proceedings by the local authority but they left before those proceedings had begun. The House of Lords upheld the local authority's finding of intentional homelessness because the voluntary decision to leave the accommodation was the cause of the homelessness (not the substantial arrears of rent).[7]
- *Example* 3: Deliberate failure to pay rent or mortgage payments which results in eviction is also likely to lead to a justifiable finding of intentional homelessness.[8]
- *Example* 4: Deliberately committing an offence (in this case, paedophilia), the result of which, if caught, would lead an ordinary reasonable person to expect that the applicant would be given a long prison sentence which would lead to the loss of the applicant's accommodation.[9]

It is tolerably clear that the judiciary have widened the ambit of the clause. For example, in *Dyson* v. *Kerrier DC* (Example 1 above), Brightman LJ was forced to change the tenses of the section in order to reach the 'desired' result. Indeed, the courts have accepted the proposition that the Act enables successful applicants to jump the queue (without referring to the fact that the intentional homelessness clause was designed to avoid this happening): see, for example, *R* v. *Eastleigh BC ex parte Betts* [1983] 2 AC 614.

Actual practice has been somewhat more difficult to investigate. It appears that the existence of the huge body of case law has deterred some HPUs from making these decisions (Cowan, 1995). However, bland statistical evidence unfortunately is no help whatsoever in assessing whether a particular decision is in line with this body of case law (see Mullins *et al.*, 1996, paras 5.43–5.52). Loveland (1993, p. 119) refers to a DoE-sponsored study of nine HPUs as 'tantalisingly inconclusive' on this point as well as 'legally misleading' (Niner, 1989) and a further DoE-sponsored study as unhelpful (Evans & Duncan, 1988)). There is, in fact, detailed qualitative evidence which suggests that HPU decision-making practices are characterized by unlawfulness (Loveland, 1993; 1995, Ch. 7; Widdowson, 1981; Birkinshaw, 1982).

For example, Thornton draws attention to a practice in some HPUs of finding applicants fleeing domestic violence to be intentionally homeless (1988; see also Binney *et al.*, 1981, pp. 78–85); a practice described by the House of Commons Home Affairs Committee as 'nonsense' (1992, para. 131). Other examples include housing debt, where research has suggested a divide being drawn between council rent arrears, private sector rent arrears, and mortgage arrears (Loveland, 1993). The complexity and exhaustiveness of the decision-making process is captured in the following instruction by a senior HPU officer to a junior officer:

> 'We need to satisfy ourselves that the applicants have made every effort to remain in their property. When they decided to sell, were they in arrears? Were there any other debts/court actions. Have they sought any advice about their finances? What did they think was going to happen to them after the sale? Have they made any plans other than coming to us? Why did the wife stop working?' (Loveland, 1993, p. 125)

Rees-Davies' 'in-laws' example returned in the DoE's Consultation Paper in 1994 in order 'to ensure that someone who is merely asked to leave by family or friends should no longer automatically qualify for assistance' (para. 8.2). This was explicitly linked with abuse of the legislation (i.e. families/friends making their children/friends homeless to take advantage of the Act). So, a further situation in which an applicant can be made intentionally homeless is now as follows:

> '[if]
> (a) he enters into an arrangement under which he is required to cease to occupy accommodation which it would have been reasonable for him to continue to occupy, and
> (b) the purpose of the arrangement is to enable him to become entitled to assistance under this part,
> and there is no other good reason why he is homeless' (s. 191(3); see the comment by David Curry, the then housing minister, in Cowan, 1997, p. 199)

When the homelessness legislation was first implemented, there were plenty of stories which surfaced about HPUs requiring parents/friends to obtain a court order evicting their children/friends in order to check the applicant's genuineness. The CoG issued in 1991 suggested that this requirement was undesirable but this provision might enable HPUs to test an applicants' genuineness in the same way.

7.3   Local Authority Duties

Until 1995 it was believed that the homelessness legislation required councils to provide *permanent* accommodation to applicants who successfully overcame each obstacle. However, in *Awua*, Lord Hoffmann argued that this was not necessarily the case; in fact the only general duty seemed to be to provide accommodation for more than 28 days (applicants with less than 28 days accommodation are 'threatened with homelessness' and thus the duty has not been discharged). Lord Hoffmann's reasoning was that, if a pregnant woman and her partner were in priority need (because of pregnancy) and were offered accommodation on this basis, but subsequently offered their child for adoption, the council should not continue to be under a duty to provide permanent accommodation (at p. 71). He found that the Act did not require permanent accommodation to be provided (see Cowan, 1997, pp. 282–284).

Policy, on the other hand, had already moved on by this stage. The argument was that single mothers 'got pregnant to get a council house', which neatly combined two different arguments: people abused the legislation; the legislation enabled successful applicants to 'jump the queue' for council housing (for a critique see Cowan, 1997, pp. 170–4). The DoE Consultation Paper argued that there was a 'perverse incentive' for people to apply as homeless (1994, para. 2.8) because people using the waiting list had to wait nearly twice as long as those accepted as homeless (para. 2.6; referring to Prescott-Clarke *et al.*, 1994). It was therefore suggested that only short-term accommodation should be provided and only if the applicant had tried to find alternative accommodation in the private sector (and so exercised personal responsibility and self-reliance: para. 6). Subsequently, the Housing Minister justified this also by arguing that the *Awua* decision had caused uncertainty (Curry, 1996).

Unsuccessful applicants are provided with advice and assistance (described by Loveland, 1991b, as sometimes being equivalent to 'sign here and sod off') and/or temporary accommodation (usually bed and breakfast or other hostel-type accommodation).

The following represent the stages of the decision-making process which lead to a successful applicant being provided with the short-term accommodation by the authority.

Local Connection

The applicant must have a local connection with the authority to which an application is made. If not,[10] and the applicant is successful, the applicant may be referred to another authority which will be obliged to perform the housing obligation. This provision was introduced into the 1977 Act because of fears that applicants would apply to certain authorities which might be regarded as the most desirable (*cf* the law of settlement under the old Poor Laws: Maude, 1922). The fear was expressed by Rees-Davies who wanted his own authority to be able to say to applicants from other areas the following explicit statement: 'No – a pox on you. Go back to where you come from. We will not be the local authority responsible for looking after you.' (HC Debs, vol 934, col 1659 (8 July 1977))

A local connection exists when the applicant (together with any person 'who might reasonably be expected to reside' with that person): 'is, or in the past was resident there, and that residence is or was of [the applicant's] choice'; has employment in that area; has family associations in that area; or has special circumstances (s 199(1)). Where an applicant has no local connection with the authority to which an application is made, that authority may refer the applicant to an authority where there is such a connection (assuming that there is one).[11] The only exception is where the applicant 'runs the risk of domestic violence, or threats of such violence, from a person with whom the applicant is associated (ss 198(2)(c), (3)). Whilst invocation of local connection in all other cases is permissive (and not a duty), most authorities do so.

In addition to the CoG, an inter-authority agreement also fleshes out the terms of the legislation (see The Homelessness (Decisions on Referrals) Order 1998, SI 1998/1578). So, for example, it is stated that 'a working definition of 'normal residence' should be that the household has been residing for at least 6 months in the area during the previous 12 months, or for not less than 3 years during the previous 5 year period' (Agreement on Procedures for Referrals of the Homeless, 6 June 1979, para. 2.5(i)). Judicial decisions have been rare[12] because, by virtue of quasi-legislation, where authorities disagree about a referral, a process of arbitration must be undertaken (Housing (Homeless Persons) Appropriate Arrangements Order 1978, SI 1978/69; Housing (Homeless Persons) Appropriate Arrangements Order 1978 (No 2), SI 1978/661). Nevertheless, Loveland is able to suggest that, by way of contrast with decisions on the key concepts, two of three study authorities adopted overtly unlawful decision-making processes. In one case, this was 'unwitting'; in another case, it was 'to simplify its decision making processes or to conserve its limited housing supply' (Loveland, 1995, p. 239). Decisions by arbitration rarely receive the attention they merit (see Thornton, 1995, where they are referred to as a 'jurisprudence worthy of analysis' and there is certainly evidence of inconsistent decision making by referees in these cases).

Suitable Alternative Accommodation

The most important amendment to the obligations in the 1977 Act made in the 1996 Act is this step, which applies 'where other suitable accommodation is available for occupation [by the applicant and family] in their district' (s 197(1)). If that is the case, then the only duty on the authority is to provide the requisite level of advice and assistance which enables the applicant to secure that accommodation (s. 197(2)). If the applicant fails to take 'reasonable steps to secure the accommodation', then the duty ceases (s 197(3)). However, what is reasonable (as well as the level of advice and assistance to be provided) depends upon the type of applicant as well as the state of the local housing market and type of accommodation available (s 197(4)). Quasi-legislation now specifies that any housing provided under this provision must be available for at least two years (although the applicant may be evicted before then, it seems) (The Homelessness (Suitability of Accommodation) (Amendment) Order 1997, SI 1997/1741).

These proposals were introduced because the assistance provided by the Act was to be 'a safety net' and not a route into permanent accommodation (DoE, 1994, para. 9.2). Furthermore, it was an attempt to ensure that applicants had the requisite level of 'self-reliance and personal responsibility' – the Major/Thatcher duologue – before any public housing would be provided. In other words, public housing was regarded to be a site of last resort. Actually, authorities have always been entitled to consider tenures other than their own accommodation, but DoE research suggested that only 2 per cent made use of private sector leasing (O'Callaghan & Dominian, 1996, para. 4.72 and Table 4.30; see also the HAMA arrangement considered in Ch. 2 above).

Whether the proposals will work out this way or not is another matter. Considerable concerns that lists of accommodation agencies operating in the area or lists of available accommodation could be handed to applicants in satisfaction of this duty were expressed about this provision during the passage of the Bill. At a late stage the government did amend the clause to ensure that the advice and assistance should not fall to this level (HL Debs, vol 574, col 94 (8 July 1996)) but, even so, such a response would fall within the letter of the Act.[13] There is a much greater concern that has emerged since publication of the White Paper: the ability and/or willingness of the private-sector rental market to house the homeless. This is considered in Chapter 11 below.

The whole point of the 1996 Act's accommodation provisions are to provide the legislative outline for what might be termed a 'mixed economy of housing' (adapting a phrase often used to describe the provision of care in the community: DoH, 1990). This means that the first port of call for the provision of housing the homeless does not need to be the local authority's own stock. Rather the authority should consider other private sector providers of accommodation. In other words, this is one method of partially *privatizing* the provision of accommodation. As with care in the community, the structure of the legislation is, in fact, weighted against the provision of public-sector accommodation for it should be noted that the duty to consider alternative providers must be considered before the authority's own duty to provide applies. As yet, it is unclear how strictly this section will be implemented by local authorities. It may be assumed that there will be a differential response, which might be based upon the political control of the authority.

The Main Housing Duty

The main housing duty is the duty owed to applicants who have successfully completed the obstacle course *and* for whom there is no other suitable accommodation available in the area. The duty is to provide 'suitable' accommodation for a period of two years (s 193(3)). At the end of that period, the authority may (i.e. a power) provide accommodation for a further period provided the applicant retains a priority need, there is not other suitable alternative accommodation in the area, and the applicant wishes the authority to continue providing the accommodation (s 194(2)).[14] The minimum period was initially to be one year but the

Conservative government accepted that two years would be more appropriate (particularly as the Prescott-Clarke *et al.* study found that the average time taken to be housed from a waiting list was 1.2 years). The basis for this significant amendment was that, under the old law (at least until *Awua*), homeless people were able to jump the queue for permanent accommodation. This important argument (actually, practically the only difference between the Labour and Conservative governments) is considered further in Chapter 8 below.

The requirement of 'suitability' was introduced as one of the amendments to the legislation required after *Puhlhofer*. There is a considerable jurisprudence as to its meaning. So, for example, in *Awua*, Lord Hoffmann suggested that it is 'primarily a matter of space and arrangement . . . I do not think that the courts should lay down requirements as to security of tenure' (at p. 71). Quasi-legislation makes affordability a critical criterion (as with reasonableness, see above). However, the quality of accommodation offered has been exposed, to a limited extent, by cases in the courts. For example, in *R* v. *Brent LBC ex parte Omar* [1991] 23 HLR 446, the authority provided accommodation which reminded the applicant of the place of captivity in which she was tortured to such an extent that she would rather commit suicide than continue to live in that accommodation. It was held that this was unsuitable.

However, the cases also expose the limitations of judicial review for in hardly any cases has the provision of accommodation by the authority been overturned. For example, in *R* v. *Camden LBC ex parte Jibril* [1997] 29 HLR 785, an applicant who was offered a five-bedroomed property with one toilet, but who had a family of 12, was met with the following judicial observation:

'I have considerable sympathy with the position of the applicant in relation to her concerns about the property that was offered, but it seems to me that I cannot properly conclude from the facts of this case that the decision which was reached by the council was one that was not reasonably open to it. I must have regard to the margin of appreciation, the room for the exercise of discretion, that is enjoyed by the council. . . and to the limited basis upon which the court is allowed to intervene in relation to a challenge of this kind.' (at p. 791)

This suggests that, when taken with the observation that most authorities do not allocate the best properties to homelessness applicants, judicial review is not a particularly useful adjudicatory tool.

Allocation of the worst properties occurs partly because these are the properties which are most often available and homeless people have most need for immediate re-housing (see Jeffers & Hoggett, 1995; Mullins *et al.*, 1996, paras 7.74–7.75). So, this obvious inequality might be regarded as situational, although it might be argued that such inequalities should be matched by policies to equalize the needs. However, such inequalities are further induced by, for example, the common policy of making just one offer of accommodation to a homeless applicant (if rejected, the applicant can be found intentionally homeless on reapplication); the limited choice available to applicants; certain systems which discriminate against applicants (for example, where Councillors take an active role in housing allocation). Loveland's research suggested that policies of offering homeless applicant's properties on 'dump estates' – euphemistically called 'difficult-to-let' housing – are caused by a complex of events (1995, pp. 261–265). It is nevertheless the case that, whilst the events may be different, the same result often occurs. Even at the end of the long, drawn out process, homeless applicants who last the course, are faced with a final obstacle impelling them into private sector accommodation.

Conclusion

In this chapter, it has been argued that various different factors affect the ability of homeless applicants to seek rehousing through the homelessness legislation. It has been argued that administrative practice (deterrence), the legislation, case law (denial), and a certain negativity all conspire against the homelessness legislation being regarded as a method of 'access' to accommodation. Rather, it might better be considered as a method of excluding applicants (privatization), a sort of giving accommodation with one hand but taking it away with the other. The very existence of the homelessness legislation is a fraud in that it suggests that our legislators have sought to ameliorate homelessness by providing rehousing opportunities. Those who apply as homeless subject themselves not only to complicated decision-making processes as well as complicated juridification, they also take part in a system which judges them against certain moral precepts. It is sometimes assumed that certain persons are able to access accommodation through the homelessness legislation in a rather simpler way than actually occurs ('getting pregnant to get a council house' is a phrase with a certain currency). What we have seen in this chapter is how a mixture of law and administrative precepts combine to *deny* a person's self-defined status as homeless and, in so doing, deny that person's 'right' to housing.

Further Reading

The so-called legal bible of the homelessness legislation is A. Arden & C. Hunter (1996), *Homelessness and Allocations*, London: Legal Action Group. Unfortunately, the illuminating (and more contextual) study by P. Robson & M. Poustie, *Homeless People and the Law*, London: Butterworths was published before the Housing Bill. It, therefore, was out of date for England and Wales almost immediately (even though much of the law remains relevant). D. Burnet's *Introduction to Housing Law*, London: Cavendish, 1996, Ch. 3, is an alternative to these more established texts (and up to date as well). See also L. Thompson (1988), *An Act of Compromise*, London: SHAC/Shelter. Equally useful, particularly as it gives examples of good practice, is L. Moroney & J. Goodwin, *Homelessness: A Good Practice Guide*, London: Shelter, and L. Moroney & K. Harris (1997), *Relationship Breakdown and Housing: A Practical Guide*, London: Shelter. Shelter, the pressure group for the homeless, has a constant stream of quality publications on the issue, some of which are referred to in the text.

Loveland's empirical study (*Housing Homeless Persons: Administrative Law and Process*, Oxford: Oxford University Press) remains important, despite now being unfortunately dated (fieldwork carried out in 1989–90), because of its appreciation of the impact of homelessness law in implementation processes. Other studies include P. Birkinshaw (1982), 'Homelessness and the law: the effects and responses to legislation', vol 5, *Urban Law and Policy*, 255; and, more specifically, D. Cowan & J. Fionda (1994), 'Meeting the need: the response of local housing authorities to the housing of ex-offenders', vol 34, *British Journal of Criminology*, 444; D. Cowan (1995), 'HIV and homelessness: intervention and backlash in local authority policy', in National AIDS Trust (ed.), *Socio-economic Implications of AIDS in Europe*, London: Cassells. Students might consider some of the research on 'impact', in particular G. Richardson & M. Sunkin (1996), 'Judicial Review: Questions of Impact', *Public Law*, pp. 79–103 and/or, in the homelessness context, S. Halliday (1998), 'Researching the 'impact' of judicial review on routine administrative decision-making', in D. Cowan (ed.), *Housing: Participation and Exclusion*, Aldershot: Dartmouth.

Critique of the DoE's 1994 Consultation Paper can be found as follows: D. Cowan & J. Fionda (1994), 'Back to basics', vol 57, *Modern Law Review*, 610; I. Loveland (1995), 'Cathy sod off! the end of the homelessness legislation', vol 16, *Journal of Social Welfare and Family Law*, 367; G. Pascall & R. Morley (1996), 'Women and homelessness: proposals from the Department of the Environment', vol 17, *Journal of Social Welfare and Family Law*, 189; S. Fitzpatrick & M. Stephens (1994), *Housing the Homeless: Policy and Legal Issues*, Glasgow: Centre for Housing Research and Urban Studies, University of Glasgow. Theoretical approaches are considered in J. Neale (1997), 'Homelessness and theory reconsidered', vol 12, *Housing Studies*, 47.

From a housing/social policy perspective, see the collection of essays from members and former members of the University of York's Centre for Housing Policy, edited by R. Burrows, N. Pleace, & D. Quilgars (1997), *Homelessness and Social Policy*, London: Routledge; P. Blachin (1996), *Housing Policy: An Introduction*, London: Routledge, Ch. 13; B. Lund (1996), *Housing Problems and Housing Policy*, London: Longman, Ch. 5; D. Clapham, P. Kemp, & S. Smith (1990), *Housing and Social Policy*, London: Macmillan, Ch. 5; P. Lidstone (1997), 'Women and homelessness', in C. Booth, J. Darke & S. Yeandle (eds), *Changing Places: Women's Lives in the City*, London: Paul Chapman. The feminist contribution to the debate is best put by S. Watson with H. Austerberry (1996), *Housing and Homelessness: A Feminist Perspective*, and also S. Watson (1985), 'Definitions of homelessness: a feminist perspective', vol 2, *Critical Social Policy*, 60; G. Pascall (1996), *Social Policy: A New Feminist Analysis*, London: Routledge, pp. 140–62.

Other useful contributions include G. Bramley (1991), 'Explaining the incidence of statutory homelessness in England', vol 8, *Housing Studies*, 128; on violence to women, the following might be consulted in addition to those materials cited in the text: N. Charles (1994), 'Domestic violence, homelessness and housing: the response of housing providers in Wales', vol 41, *Critical Social Policy*, 36; G. Hague

& E. Malos (1994), 'Domestic violence, social policy and housing', vol 42, *Critical Social Policy*, 112; S. Maguire (1988), 'Sorry love: violence against women in the home and the state response', vol 23, *Critical Social Policy*, 25; readers might also consider J. Bull (1993), *Housing Consequences of Relationship Breakdown*, London: HMSO, as well as (1995), *The Housing Consequences of Relationship Breakdown*, York: Centre for Housing Policy Discussion Paper 10, University of York.

The notions of 'denial' and 'deterrence' are expertly uncovered in the old law and administrative practice by P Carlen (1994), 'The governance of homelessness: legality, lore and lexicon in the agency-maintenance of youth homelessness', vol 41, *Critical Social Policy*, 18, and in (1996), *Jigsaw – A Political Criminology of Youth Homelessness*, Buckingham: Open University Press.

For a comparative, alegal perspective (despite its pretensions), see G. Daly (1996), *Homeless*, London: Routledge; M. Robertson & M. Greenblatt (1992), *Homelessness: A National Perspective*, New York: Plenum

Not considered in this chapter, but of considerable importance for those who are street homeless, is the Rough Sleepers Initiative, introduced by the government in the 1990s. Its review by the government in 1995 (as a Consultation Paper linked to the White Paper: DoE, 1995) is important as it sets out the stall (and spending plans) of the former government that still predominates: DoE, DoH, DSS, Home Office, DFEE (1995), *Rough Sleepers Initiative: Future Plans*, London: DoE.

Endnotes

1. In this paragraph, I am drawing upon questionnaire-based research conducted in January 1998 (Cowan & Hunter, 1998). Questionnaires were sent to all local authority HPU managers requesting information concerning: the details of the authority (such as housing stock and political control); types of procedures it had adopted; the numbers and outcomes of the reviews that had occurred in the previous six months; open-ended questions concerning the manager's perceptions. The response rate was 58 per cent. This research was funded by the Departments of Law at the Universities of Bristol and Nottingham.
2. 15 responses were received from London authorities.
3. Ginsburg (1992) defines this as 'Evidence of racial inequalities in housing linked to local institutional practices . . .'(p. 109).
4. Although it is no doubt true that Rees-Davies himself did believe that homeless people were as a group undeserving.
5. The Bill was introduced by Stephen Ross MP (a Liberal) at a time when the government (Labour) was in minority.
6. *Dyson* v. *Kerrier District Council* [1980] 1 WLR 1205.
7. *Din* v. *London Borough of Wandsworth* [1983] 1 AC 657; *cf R* v. *Wandsworth LBC ex parte Hawthorne* (1994) 27 HLR 59 (family unable to pay rent because of inadequacy of resources not intentionally homeless).
8. *Robinson* v. *Torbay Borough Council* [1982] 1 All ER 726, 1997.
9. *R* v. *Hounslow LBC ex parte R The Times*, QBD, 25 February 1997
10. There is evidence that applicants who do have a local connection with the area to which application is made are still referred to another authority: see Thornton, 1995, p. 22.

11. If no local connection exists with any authority, then the one to which application is made must adopt the obligation.
12. Although see *R* v *Newham LBC ex parte Tower Hamlets LBC* [1992] 2 All ER 767, where the referral procedure was heavily criticised; Cowan, 1993 for discussion.
13. The CoG is, in fact, much less confident than the Minister: 'Provision of minimal assistance – such as only providing copies of newspaper advertisements – is *not likely to* be sufficient to meet the duty' (DoE, 1996, para. 20.10; emphasis added)
14. It may be surmised that the final criterion is a reflection of the Conservative's belief that council housing is an undesirable tenure which would not be chosen by people.

Bibliography

Anderson, I. and Morgan, J. (1997), *Social Housing for Single People? A study of Local Policy and Practice*, Stirling: Housing Policy and Practice Unit, University of Stirling

Arden, A. and Hunter, C. (1996), *Homelessness and Allocations*, London: Legal Action Group

Audit Commission (1989), *Housing the Homeless: the Local Authority's Role*, London: Audit Commission

Bailey, R. and Ruddock, J. (1972), *The Grief Report*, London: Shelter

Baldwin, J., Wikeley, N. and Young, R. (1992), *Judging Social Security*, Oxford: Oxford University Press

Binney, V., Harkell, G. and Nixon, J. (1981), *Leaving Violent Men*, Women's Aid Federation England

Birkinshaw, P. (1982), 'Homelessness and the law – the effects and response to legislation', vol 5, *Urban Law and Policy*, 255

Bonnerjea, L. and Lawton, J. (1987), *Homelessness in Brent*, London: Policy Studies Institute

Carlen, P. (1994), 'The governance of homelessness: legality, lore and lexicon in the agency-maintenance of youth homelessness', vol 41, *Critical Social Policy*, 100

Carlisle, J. (1996), *The Housing Needs of Ex-Prisoners*, York: Centre for Housing Policy, University of York

Carter, M. (1997), *The Last Resort*, London: Shelter

Carter, M. and Ginsburg, N. (1994), 'New government housing policies', vol 41, *Critical Social Policy*, 100

Central Housing Advisory Committee (CHAC) (1968), *Council Housing: Purposes, Procedures and Priorities*, London: HMSO

Commission for Racial Equality (CRE) (1988), *Homelessness and Discrimination*, London: CRE

Cowan, D. (1995a), 'HIV and homelessness: lobbying, law, policy and practice', vol 17, *Journal of Social Welfare and Family Law*, 43

Cowan, D. (1995b), 'Accommodating community care', vol 22, *Journal of Law and Society*, 212

Cowan, D. (1997), *Homelessness: The (In-)Appropriate Applicant*, Aldershot: Dartmouth

Cowan, D. (1998), 'Homelessness internal appeals: serving the administrative process?', vol 27, *Anglo-American Law Review*, 66 (Pt I), 169 (Pt II)

Cowan, D. and Fionda, J. (1994a), 'Meeting the need', vol 34, *British Journal of Criminology*, 444

Cowan, D. and Fionda, J. (1994b), 'Back to basics: the government's homelessness proposals', vol 57, *Modern Law Review*, 610

Cowan, D. and Hunter, C. (1998), 'Homelessness internal reviews: a view from the sharp end', paper given at the European Network for Housing Research Conference, Cardiff, September 1998

Cranston, R. (1985), *Legal Foundations of the Welfare State*, London: Weidenfeld & Nicolson

Cullingworth, J. (1979), *Essays on Housing Policy*, London: Allen & Unwin

Curry, D. (1996), 'The government's response', *The Guardian*, 7 February

Darke, J. and Darke, R. (1979), *Who Needs Housing*, London: Allen & Unwin

Department of the Environment (DoE) (1989), *The Government's Review of the Homelessness Legislation*, London: HMSO

Department of the Environment (DoE) (1994), *Access to Local Authority and Housing Association Tenancies*, London: DETR

Department of the Environment (DoE) (1996), *Code of Guidance on Parts VI and VII of the Housing Act 1996*, London: DoE

Department of the Environment, Transport and the Regions (DETR) (1999), *Code of Guidance on the Allocation of Housing and Homelessness*, Consultation Paper, London: DETR

Department of Health (DoH) (1990), *Caring for People: Community Care in the Next Decade and Beyond*, London: HMSO

Diduck, A. and Kaganas, F. (1999), *Family Law, Gender and the State*, Oxford: Hart

Doran, A. (1996), 'Tenants' £20,000 worth of cheek', *Daily Mail*, 19 February

Doyal, L. and Gough, I. (1991), *A Theory of Human Need*, London: Macmillan

Evans, A. and Duncan, S. (1988), *Responding to homelessness: Local Authority Policy and Practice*, London: HMSO

Ginsburg, N. (1992), 'Racism and housing: concepts and reality', in P. Braham, A. Rattansi, and R. Skellington (eds), *Racism and Antiracism*, London: Sage

Ginsburg, N. and Watson, S. (1992), 'Issues of race and gender facing housing policy', in J. Birchall (ed.), *Housing Policy in the 1990s*, London: Routledge

Greve, J., Page, D. and Greve, S. (1971), *Homelessness in London*, Edinburgh: Academic Press

Halliday, S. (1998), 'Researching the 'impact' of judicial review on routine administrative decision-making', in D. Cowan (ed.), *Housing: Participation and Exclusion*, Aldershot: Dartmouth

Hawes, D. (1997), *Homelessness and Older People*, Bristol: Policy Press

Hewitt, M. (1993), *Welfare, Ideology and Need*, Hemel Hempstead: Harvester Wheatsheaf

Hoath, D. (1988), 'Homelessness law after the Housing and Planning Act 1986: the 'Puhlhofer' amendments', vol 10, *Journal of Social Welfare Law*, 39

Home Office (1989), *The Response to Racial Attacks and Harassment: Guidance for the Statutory Agencies*, London: Home Office

Home Office (1991), *The Response to Racial Attacks: Sustaining the Momentum*, London: Home Office

House of Commons Home Affairs Committee (1992), *Domestic Violence*, London: HMSO

Hunter, C. and Miles, J. (1997), 'The unsettling of settled law on 'settled accommodation': the House of Lords and the homelessness legislation old and new', vol 19, *Journal of Social Welfare and Law*, 267

Jeffers, S. and Hoggett, P. (1995), 'Like counting deckchairs on the Titanic: a study of institutional racism and housing allocations in Haringey and Lambeth', vol 10, *Housing Studies*, 325

Lewis, J. and Glennerster, H. (1996), *Implementing the New Community Care*, Buckingham:

Lidstone, P. (1994), 'Rationing housing to the homeless applicant', vol 9, *Housing Studies*, 459

Loveland, I. (1988), 'Housing Benefit: administrative law and administrative practice', vol 66, *Public Administration*, 57

Loveland, I. (1991a), 'Legal rights and political realities: governmental responses to homelessness in Britain', vol 18, *Law and Social Inquiry*, 249

Loveland, I. (1991b), 'Administrative law, administrative processes, and the housing of homeless persons – a view from the sharp end', vol 13, *Journal of Social Welfare and Family Law*, 4

Loveland, I. (1993), 'The politics, law and practice of 'intentional homelessness'', vol 15, *Journal of Social Welfare and Family Law*, 113

Loveland, I. (1994), 'Cathy Sod off! The end of the homelessness legislation', vol 16, *Journal of Social Welfare and Family Law*, 367

Loveland, I. (1995), *Housing Homeless Persons*, Oxford: Oxford University Press

MacEwen, M. (1990), 'Homelessness, race and law', vol 16, *New Community*, 505

MacEwen, M. (1991), *Housing, Race and the Law*, London: Routledge

Maguire, S. (1989), 'Sorry love: violence against women in the home and the state response', vol 23, *Critical Social Policy*, 35

Malos, E. and Hague, G. (1993), *Domestic Violence and Housing*, Bristol: School for Applied Social Sciences, University of Bristol

Maude, W. (1922), *Settlement and Removal*, London: Poor Law Publications

McCluskey, J. (1994), *Acting in Isolation*, London: CHAR

Means, R. and Smith, R. (1996), *Community Care, Housing and Homelessness: Issues, Obstacles, and Innovative Practice*, Bristol: Policy Press

Mullins, D., Niner, P. with Marsh, A. and Walker, B. (1996), *Evaluation of the 1991 Homelessness Code of Guidance*, London: HMSO

Niner, P. (1989), *Homelessness in Nine Local Authorities*, London: HMSO

Paylor, I. (1995), *Housing Needs of Ex-Prisoners*, London: Routledge

Prescott-Clarke, P., Clemens, S. and Park, A. (1994), *Routes into Local Authority Housing*, London: HMSO

Rees, B. (1965), *No Fixed Abode*, London: Stanmore

Robson, P. and Poustie, M. (1996), *Homeless People and the Law*, London: Butterworths

Seebohm, F. (1969), *Report of the Committee on Local Authority and Allied Social Services*, London: HMSO

Smith, S. (1989), *The Politics of 'Race' and Residence*, Cambridge: Polity

Spicker, P. (1993), *Poverty and Social Security: Concepts and Principles*, London: Routledge

Sunkin, M., Bridges, L. and Meszaros, G. (1995), *Judicial Review in Perspective*, London: Public Law Project

Thornton, R. (1989), 'Homelessness through relationship breakdown: the local authorities' response', vol 11, *Journal of Social Welfare Law*, 67

Thornton, R. (1995), 'Who houses? Homelessness, local connection and inter authority referrals under section 67 of the Housing Act 1985', vol 17, *Journal of Social Welfare and Family Law*, 133

Watchman, P. and Robson, P. (1981), 'The homeless persons obstacle race', *Journal of Social Welfare Law*, 1

Watchman, P. (1988), 'Heartbreak hotel', vol 10, *Journal of Social Welfare Law*, 147

Widdowson, B. (1981), *Intentional Homelessness*, London: Shelter

Wintour, P. (1994), 'Portillo lays into yobbos and feckless', *The Guardian*, 8 January

8   Housing Need: The Case of Local Authority Waiting Lists

In the post-war period, it has generally been accepted that council housing should be allocated according to need rather than ability to pay. Indeed, Conservative governments maintained their commitment to the principle of need to the end and the New Labour government has restated its commitment. So, for example, the Housing Act 1996, quasi-legislation and the CoG provide a list of persons 'to ensure that such housing goes to those with the greatest underlying needs' (DoE, 1996b, para. 1). Differences might reasonably exist as to what 'needs' might be regarded as the basis for a rational allocations policy in each area (*cf* Spicker, 1987), but allocation according to need is the general principle.

It should then come as something of a shock to learn that the way 'need' is identified in practice has led, in some areas, to institutional racial discrimination (GLC, 1976; CRE, 1984; Henderson & Karn, 1987); allocation of better[1] properties to those on higher incomes (Williams, *et al.*, 1986); 'problem' applicants being excluded from housing (for example, in Manchester, where the exclusion list is said to include around 10,000 people: Blake, 1997); transfer applicants allocated better properties than – for example – the homeless (Clapham & Kintrea, 1986); sexual discrimination (particularly against women after relationship breakdown: see, generally, Pascall, 1997; Bull, 1993). They have even stood accused of creating difficult-to-let or, to use the euphemism, 'dump', estates (see DoE, 1981; Power, 1987; *cf* the contextual approach adopted by Griffiths *et al.*, 1996). In other words, rather than redressing the imbalances created by 'allocation according to wealth' in the private sector, allocation according to need by local authorities paradoxically reflected wider institutional and/or societal discrimination.

Early studies concentrated on particular parts of the allocations process which showed how applicants were 'graded' according to preconceived notions of deservingness. Most clearly, this process often occurred when the 'housing visitor' came to discuss rehousing with the applicant(s). Malpass and Murie refer to this person as 'perhaps the most thoroughly discussed part of the implementation process in housing allocations' (1994, p. 284; for a sample, see Lambert *et al.*, 1978; CHAC, 1969). However, more recent research has suggested that it is important to consider the totality of the process, rather than actors in the chain. As Clapham & Kintrea suggest:

'[The] processes have been described as 'primary' rationing (who enters the sector) and 'secondary' rationing (who gets which house). . . . The outcome of housing allocation systems depends on three inter-related factors: the formally stated policy of the organisation; the way that policy is translated into practice; and the interaction between the household and the allocation process.' (1991, p. 55)

It should be noted that law does not appear in this triptych. This is partly because the law provided the equivalent of 'open planning'; that is, an open framework upon which the local authority imposed itself. Even when things went wrong, the courts refused to become involved. So, in *Shelley* v. *London County Council* [1948] 2 All ER 898, the House of Lords argued that the selection and allocation of properties was entirely within the Council's power and not subject to review by the courts. Judicial control has moved on from that particularly low point so that now, on one view, it would be reasonable to portray judicial controls as robust.

However, it will be argued that the legislation provides little control over allocation policies and practices, and does little to contain the inequality of bargaining between particular tenants. This remains the case notwithstanding the update in 1996 by a Conservative government which (on one view) has pursued a policy of juridification of local government. Furthermore, it will be argued that judicial controls are, in fact, negligible even with considerably increased judicial interest in allocations. This is despite the fact that the 1996 Act, as we saw in the previous chapter, has become the main battleground for those seeking permanent housing, for it was a central precept of that Act that, *subject to certain exceptions (such as transfers), allocations could only be made through the housing register (or waiting list)* (s. 161(1)). In other words, the scheme provides local authorities with so much discretion that it is unlikely that much will change.

Discretion, however, has been the central area for attack, the cause of institutional inadequacy (see Lewis, 1976; Lewis & Livock, 1979). Smith and Mallinson summarize the argument in the following way:

'. . . discretion was depicted as the bug in the system – a source of deviance which allowed short-term management goals to compromise the principle of social justice. It was the smokescreen behind which housing departments infused an agreed hierarchy of needs with a range of other, more dubious, allocative principles.' (1996, p. 341)

It can be argued that operationalizing allocations policies and legislation inevitably requires discretion, whether or not such policies are rule-based (for an important examination of this, see Sainsbury, 1992; Baldwin *et al.*, 1992; Smith & Mallinson, 1996). For example, how officers interview applicants, or the degree to which officers chase up material about applicants from external sources is, to a certain extent, up to the officers themselves. It is only once this is accepted that one can fully appreciate the diversity of allocations policies.

Before we discuss allocation schemes proper, an examination of exclusions from those schemes needs to take place. Hitherto, this has been an under-researched part of the process. However, in the context of a return to Victorian housing management policies, this has become a crucial area (Clapham, 1997). Furthermore, it can be argued that exclusions are one way of controlling demand, or keeping it to an acceptable level. The relationship between housing allocation and estate management is a crucial one, particularly as the roles often conflict. Allocators wish to ensure a quick take-up of void accommodation, whereas estate managers wish to keep problems on the estates to a minimum. We will explore these issues and use a case study (paedophiles and/or alleged paedophiles) to illustrate the process of exclusion.

Our consideration then takes us to the law and the relative importance of the Housing Act 1996. If discretion is an important key to unlock area variations, central government's attempts at providing a unifying strand to the exercise of the discretion must also be analysed. In particular, consideration will be given to the position adopted by the Conservative government, that single mothers became pregnant in order to jump the housing queue; as well as the belief, now reversed, that homeless people should not be preferred on waiting lists. In considering the law, we will also look at the way local authority allocation schemes operationalize the concept of 'need' in their policies and practices.

In the final section, we observe how authorities have weighted their policies so that they favour certain persons at the expense of others. Often it appears to be the case that allocation schemes tend to favour existing tenants at the expense of others on the waiting list. Furthermore, sometimes unwittingly, institutional practices and demands lead to racial discrimination.

Throughout this chapter it will be argued that need is rarely a consideration in housing allocations, despite plenty of rhetoric. Future New Labour proposals that will remove the obligation to provide accommodation according to need, in favour of the equally nebulous 'planned programme for creating mixed and stable communities' have already been mooted (speech by Housing Minister, Hilary Armstrong, to the Local Government Association: Winchester, 1999). These proposals have been mooted to halt local authorities 'unnecessary and wide-ranging' exclusions.

One final preliminary point needs to be made. Much of the research upon which this chapter is based draws upon data reflecting a mismatch between the demand for council housing and its supply. Allocation is therefore based upon a queuing system, subject to a number of criteria. However, the residualization of council housing has had important effects upon demand in certain areas. Certain types of unpopular housing, particularly tower blocks in some areas, have extremely limited demand (the production of such estates is considered in chapter 18). Councils have adopted innovative methods of wooing people into parts of their difficult-to-let housing. For example, one council has advertised its tower blocks in a glossy leaflet put through doors in the local bedsit community: 'Call in at the . . . Housing Office, meet our friendly staff and enjoy a free cup of coffee. You will be able to find out about the accommodation we have available and see around our show flat.' Some councils have set up shop fronts as letting agents for their property. Some people may continue to be excluded from this housing, particularly those with a history of rent arrears or anti-social behaviour, but such open access policies are symbols of a new era of housing selection and allocation.

8.1 W(h)ither Need? Part I – Exclusions and Exclusivity

In this section, I will argue that the ability of central and local government to *exclude* certain groups of people from even appearing on the housing register surely denies the belief that the housing register can be a register of need. Indeed, so many people can be excluded from the register that this lack of association can be exaggerated (depending upon the area). Central government, at an early stage, signalled its intention to exclude 'certain categories of persons from abroad [who are] excluded from entitlement to benefit' (DoE, 1996a, para. 12).[2] These provisions (s. 161(2) and various quasi-legislation) are considered in chapter 10. Here, it is important for us to consider exclusions usually considered by local government.

Local Exclusions

In the 1996 Act, local government, for the first time was given the power to 'decide what classes of persons are, or are not, qualifying persons' (s 161(4)) and therefore decide who is entitled to appear on the register (subject to statutory and quasi-statutory inclusions and exclusions). Authorities have always had their own exclusions – in 1993, 92 per cent had some form of exclusions (Bines *et al.*, 1993, para. 9.28). The 1996 Act provided statutory power to do so for the first time. Thus, for example, it was reported in 1993 that Warrington Borough Council sought to exclude drug dealers from their estates (Brimacombe, 1993). More recently, it has been reported that Manchester has almost 10,000 people on an 'rehousing exceptions list' (Blake, 1997). As Griffiths *et al.* point out, 'Clearly some of the restrictions on access to the waiting list . . . only make sense when there are more applicants than properties becoming available . . .' (1997, para. 4.19). The demand:supply ratio provides an important contextual factor governing exclusions/allocations systems. In low demand areas, the financial imperative to re-let properties means that authorities sometimes cannot afford to be too fussy (and it is this factor which is commonly blamed for the creation of 'dump' estates: see the analysis in Chapter 18)

The current CoG provides examples of the groups central government believe could be included:

'. . . people with a history of anti-social behaviour, people who have attacked housing department staff, or tenants with a record of rent arrears. Authorities could impose other qualifications, such as those related to residency in the authority's district or ownership of a property, although they may wish to consider the implications of excluding all members of such groups, e.g. elderly owner-occupiers.' (para. 4.27)

Quite what this says about housing need is hard to see. It also appears to be potentially unlawful advice. Case law has, fairly consistently, pursued the approach that local authorities may exclude but only if account can be taken of exceptional cases (see generally *British Oxygen Co Ltd* v. *Board of Trade* [1971] AC 610; and specifically *R* v. *Wolverhampton MBC ex parte Watters* (1997) 29 HLR 931, *R* v. *Lambeth LBC ex parte Ashley* (1997) 29 HLR 385; it may be possible that the existence of a right of review has a curative effect on general exclusions but this remains open to question: *Waters*).

It is well-known that many, if not most, authorities exclude certain applicants from their waiting list on the basis of a lack of connection with the area (90 per cent in 1993: Bines *et al.*, 1993, Table A9.7). Parliamentary debates around this issue *welcomed* this: 'Earlier in the Bill we all agreed and signed up to the proposition that . . . rural communities wish a certain amount of protection for their own community where there is a limited amount of housing' (HL Debs, vol 573, cols 345–346 (19 June 1996) *per* Lord Mackay). Nevertheless, most urban authorities impose residency as well as other qualifications. The recommendations of the CHAC report that residence qualifications should be unlawful – because they act as a barrier against an assessment of need (see CHAC, 1969, Ch. 4 for discussion; *cf* Niner, 1975, pp. 31–2) – have conveniently been forgotten in favour of political convenience.

Consider the following part of the policy of a hard-pressed London Borough:[3]

'2.   WHO CAN APPLY TO THE REGISTER

Anyone can apply for entry in the register so long as they are:
– over 18 years of age (younger, if supported by a rent guarantee) and
– resident in the borough
– placed in temporary accommodation by this council in another authority's area, under homelessness legislation,
or
– accepted under mobility or reciprocal arrangements

and **do not** fall within the following categories:
– owning or purchasing a property including shared ownership, which is reasonable to occupy

- suspended under Limitations of Offers policy
- placed by another authority who retain responsibility for their rehousing
- disqualified under Part VI of the Act by virtue of their residency status in the United Kingdom
- evicted in the previous twelve months on the following grounds:
  i) rent arrears
  ii) racial or sexual harassment, or
  iii) domestic violence
and were responsible for, or considered to have acquiesced in, the acts or breach of tenancy conditions which led to possession being granted. Such decisions would be based on the individual merits of the case.'

Many policies similarly have age exclusions despite the existence of accommodation duties to persons under 18 in the Children Act 1989 (ss. 17(10), 20(1), & 27). The Major government believed that this was reasonable on the basis that children apparently had no long-term need. However, most authorities pursue this exclusion because *legal* problems of granting tenancies to under 18s make it difficult to recover rent.[4] A further exclusion of this policy – owner–occupiers – is equally common as it is assumed that owner–occupiers will be able to provide for alternative accommodation. Its legality was called into question in *R* v. *Bristol CC ex parte Johns* (1992) 25 HLR 249 (where the policy was brought in specifically as a result of 'a large number of applications from those who had exercised their right to purchase their council homes': p. 254). The policy was held to be valid in that case because it made those 'in severe difficulties' an exception.

Rent arrears of former local authority tenants has recently been found to be the most common exclusion amongst local authorities (Butler, 1998, p. 12). Current thinking is to regard such people as 'problems' because of the management issues which they are said to create. Provided there are exceptional categories, such policies are lawful (although see below for cases where rent arrears cause loss of priority). As many of those excluded are also found intentionally homeless, it is also usual to find the intentionally homeless excluded.

A more recent concern has been to exclude those responsible for 'anti-social' behaviour. Anti-social behaviour – discussed in depth in Chapter 18 – is not susceptible to precise definition and, to a certain extent, use of this terminology legitimates the exclusion of people whom the authority regards as 'undesirable' for some reason. In Shelter's research, 24 local authorities apparently excluded persons whom the authority 'believed to have' a history of anti-social behaviour (Butler, 1998, p. 12). Two complaints to the Local Government Ombudsman exemplify this trend occurring in South Tyneside (97/C/3827; 97/C/2883). This authority had a policy of requiring councillor approval before some people were excluded. An agreement with the police under the Safer Estates Initiative enabled the council to request information about criminal convictions of their tenants, but only for the purpose of proving and commencing civil proceedings against them.

In the first complaint, a family sought accommodation after being subjected to continual harassment. Casual conversations between a housing officer, member of the police and a social worker suggested the male had convictions over a number of years and had assaulted a social worker. The case was referred to the Councillors' committee, containing 'extremely misleading' incorrect allegations about the family as a result of the casual conversations (including allegations of sex offences against children), and the family were excluded. A second report was equally flawed. In the second complaint, a single man applied for housing. The council found that he had been guilty of a number of offences including criminal damage and assault. Furthermore, the council also 'received information' that the man 'was associating with Ms Larch, a former tenant of the council who had been excluded from the waiting list because of a history of troublesome tenancies'. The man was excluded after yet another misleading report to the Councillors.

In both cases, the Ombudsman found maladministration causing injustice and recommended that the council urgently reviewed its practices. These complaints evidence the increasingly hysterical concerns about anti-social behaviour, fuelled in part by Councillors' beliefs that council accommodation has become a 'dumping ground' for society's undesirables. These concerns have come into sharp relief in the question over whether paedophiles should be allocated accommodation in the sector.

Policy in Action: The Case of Paedophiles

The current tendency appears to be towards social exclusion. One part of such exclusion involves exclusion from housing. Recent legislation has harshly responded to those convicted of sexual offences against children. Even on release from prison, such people are required to be supervised in ways which are more familiar to war-time conditions. For example, the Sex Offenders Act 1997 requires such people to provide to the police their name(s) and home address, as well as notifying the police of any changes (s. 2). This Act was a response to a period in which such people have been consistently vilified by the media. At the same time as the more general debate about the care and control of paedophiles was continuing, a quite separate issue arose in relation to their housing.

Local newspapers (such as the *Manchester Evening News* and *Bournemouth Evening Echo*) began to 'out' – that is, provide names and addresses of – local paedophiles. In November 1996, 'George Taylor fled his Birmingham flat under police escort after residents discovered he had been jailed for a child sex offence' (Millar, 1997a). Local vigilante attacks have been common, and there have been reports of evictions of paedophiles from council estates as a result of tenant protest (see Bowcott & Clouston, 1997). *The Times* reported one protestor in Scotland as making the following comment:

'Margaret Hanley, 54, a mother of eight leading the protest, welcomed Mr Christie's rapid departure but criticised the council for using Raploch as a "dumping ground for weirdos". Linking the case to that of Thomas Hamilton, the Dunblane murderer, she said: ". . . If we don't act, the council will wait until perhaps our children are raped and murdered and our schools shot up, and then they'll say 'Oh, we had a theory about him'. . . ." We will be making sure this doesn't happen again.' (English, 1997)

Lewisham council warned 8,000 residents that 'a 'very dangerous' convicted paedophile ha[d] moved into their area' (*The Guardian*, 27 March 1997). Sometimes even the wrong people are 'outed' with disastrous consequences.

All of this has had an effect on many councils' decision-making (as well as judicial: *R* v. *Hounslow LBC ex parte R*[5]). It may well be that, in the light of the political aspect of allocations through the waiting list together with the power of estate managers, this was almost inevitably reflected in some allocations policies and reported in national media. First, Middlesbrough Council was widely reported to be considering excluding 'child abusers . . . from getting a council house' (*Daily Mail*, 9 January 1997); one councillor was reported as saying ' "We can't afford to see the safety and security of our tenants jeopardised by accommodating paedophiles" ' (Ford, 9 January 1997). On the same day, a housing officer at Birmingham Council was suspended after informing local residents of the rehousing of a paedophile (after release from prison) (Murray, 1997). Two months later, the following appeared in *The Times* under the banner 'Council refuses to house sex offenders':

'Rhondda Cynon Taff council in South Wales is the first [sic] to demand that prospective tenants declare criminal records, especially those involving sex, children and drugs.

The council's housing committee acted after residents in the village of Hawthorn successfully fought to prevent David Simms, a convicted paedophile, being housed by the council when he left prison. Council officials visited Simms in jail and got him to agree not to live in the area.' (Tendler, 1997)

Housing exclusions and allocations now take place within a much broader context, in which the importance of crime control has surpassed the due process rights of individuals (see Part III). Local authority concerns about the type of person to whom they are allocating accommodation, and the effect this will have on their estates, masks a fundamental restrucuring of the whole process of housing allocation itself.

This restructuring, as yet in its infancy, is more concerned with *responsibility* than *need*, and has linked in with the shift amongst agencies of social control to the notion of 'risk' (Cowan & Gilroy, 1999; Ericsson & Haggerty, 1997; Giddens, 1999). The shift to risk has been apparent in housing allocation systems for some time. For example, in assessing any application for housing, authorities must consider the risk that rent will not be paid or that a person will commit anti-social behaviour. The South Tyneside scheme is the crudest example of this but, in a sense, local authorities have been making these assessments for some time (in relation to, say, those in receipt of community care services). More recently, it has become an overt consideration, such as in relation to sex offenders. The enormity of this shift is yet to be worked through. For example, the relationship between housing allocation and policing strategies involves a reworking of our understanding of both agencies, as well as questions relating to the desirability of panoptic surveillance (Cowan & Gilroy, 1999).

8.2   W(h)ither Need? Part II – Allocations, Law and Policy

Allocations from the waiting list – or housing register – are now the central method used for allocating social housing. The term 'social housing' reflects the increasing responsibility of local authorities to create 'common housing registers' through which local authorities filter out successful applicants and refer them to those social housing organizations (such as housing associations) with which the authority has agreements or nomination rights. This is a reflection and progression of the Conservative's housing policy of making local authorities 'enablers' (or facilitators) of social housing in their areas. In their Consultation Paper, the government warmly encouraged authorities to develop these (DoE, 1994, para. 22), which is the derivation of the strange (for lawyers anyway) legislative exhortation to keep such registers (see s. 162(3)).

Our purpose here is to examine the law, policy and types of allocations schemes. This, in many ways, is the denouement. Before we consider the types of schemes in operation, the first consideration is to approach the law through a consideration of which types or groups of persons should gain priority on housing registers. For some time, it has been a generally accepted proposition that some should have preference (indeed this was so before there was any legal duty on authorities to keep waiting lists). However, crucially, there have been differences of opinion as to who should gain this preference. We will see below that preference is often nominal and that, in practice, authorities' schemes favour others. The legal background provides the crux for the inventiveness of local policy-making, as it is totally dependent upon the exercise of discretionary decision-making by councillors (who set the policy) and officers (who implement it). It will be argued in this section that the judicial interpretation of the law further facilitates this decision-making, for it has lessened the preference given to these applicants. This will affect the legality of the waiting schemes in operation.

What is a 'Reasonable Preference'?

Since the Housing Act 1935, certain people have been given a 'reasonable preference' in the allocation of public housing. The 1935 Act gave preference to 'persons on occupying insanitary or overcrowded houses, persons having large families, persons living under unsatisfactory housing conditions'. There is some definition of overcrowding in sections 324–6, Housing Act 1985. However, the other terms have never been defined, leaving much to local discretion (see below). The Housing (Homeless Persons) Act 1977 added those homeless persons (and their families) accepted for the full housing duty by the local authority.

The Housing Act 1996 has radically altered these preference categories, so that they now (supposedly) cater for 'long-term housing need' which also includes 'social need'. Whilst this was Conservative legislation, the New Labour opposition substantively disagreed with only one point. In the Conservatives' formulation, the homeless were not given a reasonable preference whereas Labour would have done so as well as adding other categories of social need (see Standing Committee G, Seventeenth Sitting, cols 648–649). The Conservatives justified their exclusion on the grounds that, first, the priorities given to the homeless perversely encouraged people to become homeless;[6] and, second, that homeless people should not be able to jump the housing queue. In the period leading to the Consultation Paper in 1994, and for some time afterwards, the Conservatives propagated the belief that 'single mothers became pregnant to get council housing' (see Cowan, 1998), even though this argument was based more upon anecdote than hard data.[7] The Labour government has since overturned this exclusion.

At least since 1994, it has been assumed that the notion of a 'reasonable preference' was directly aligned with priority on the register (so, for example, the CoG appears to regard them as 'the priority categories': para. 5.3). This is, unfortunately, inaccurate as a matter of law. First, a number of cases have now held that 'reasonable preference' does not equate to anything like a priority. In *R* v. *Newham LBC ex parte Watkins*, it was suggested that:

> 'A reasonable preference to the named categories . . . must entail some preferred treatment. To inflate the preferred to a highly preferred status is entirely outwith the statutory function. To deflate the preferred might be "reasonable", so long as there was some degree of preferential treatment.' (1994) 26 HLR 431

From this, one gleans that whilst a 'reasonable preference' provides the applicant with some type of preference, the local authority also has the ability to downgrade such people at the same time. So, the phrase actually carries with it no priority at all, just 'some degree of preferential treatment'. One might surmise from this that the general policy of the courts is to disallow any person from gaining priority in the queue for housing, believing this to be inequitable.

Second, it is now absolutely crystal clear that authorities are entitled to exclude from their housing register those applicants to whom a reasonable preference is to be given (provided there is a right of appeal). In *R* v. *Wolverhampton MBC ex parte Watters*, Ms Watters and her five children had run up rent arrears of £2,300 on a council flat and been evicted. The family moved on to private-sector accommodation, and then applied to be put on the housing register. They were refused because of the outstanding arrears (even though their allotted Housing Benefit fell below their current rent by £10 per week). After an internal appeal, the council confirmed its refusal, which was upheld by the Court of Appeal. Judge LJ had this to say:

> 'The section is concerned with the process of selection of tenants by the housing authority and there is nothing to suggest that the suitability of the prospective tenants, or indeed any other relevant considerations, are to be ignored.
>
> The statutory obligations imposed . . . therefore require that positive favour should be shown to applications which satisfy any of the relevant criteria. To use colloquial language they should be given a reasonable head start. Thereafter all the remaining factors fall to be considered in the balancing exercise inevitably required when each individual application is under consideration.' (1997) 29 HLR 931, 938

In other words, 'the authority has a duty to have regard to the financial consequences of its actions and to balance its housing revenue account.' (*R* v. *Newham LBC ex parte Miah* (1996) 28 HLR 279). The CoG makes the same point, albeit more starkly: 'Authorities have a general duty to manage the resources at their disposal prudently. They may wish to take into account the characteristics of the people they select as tenants, both individually (as potentially good tenants) and collectively' (para. 5.6). So, even within preference groups, it is entirely reasonable for certain applicants to gain no priority, for applicants to be 'graded' differently, and for those who supposedly have long-term housing need (as they fit within the preference groups to be outlined below) to be ignored. Housing need is therefore subverted to the management role of the local authority.

Third, the authority is entitled to argue that it has no accommodation which it might allocate to a reasonable preference group. In *R* v. *Brent LBC ex parte Enekeme* (unreported, 10 June 1996) the applicants were seeking a transfer and were within a reasonable preference category (persons with large families – strangely absent from the current list). The council set the target for allocations of four bedroom properties at 15 for the homeless, 25 for decants (having recently approved a scheme to demolish a block of flats), and none for transfer cases.[8] The Court of Appeal upheld this scheme as being 'self-evidently correct'.

It follows from all of this that, rather than giving priority to certain persons, the statutory scheme actually enables local authorities to discriminate between different applicants. Indeed, the wording used by the legislation is exposed as being something of a sham, promising preference but granting nothing more than a 'reasonable head start'. On this basis, even if there were any credibility in the view that women deliberately get pregnant to jump the housing queue (Green & Hansbro, 1995; Ermisch, 1996), it would not lead to them gaining priority.

Categories to Whom 'Reasonable Preference' Attaches

On its face, the 1996 Act prescribes six categories who are entitled to 'reasonable preference'. They are:

'(a) people occupying insanitary or overcrowded housing or otherwise living in unsatisfactory housing conditions;
(b) people occupying accommodation which is temporary or occupied on insecure terms;
(c) families with dependent[9] children;
(d) households consisting of or including someone who is expecting a child;
(e) households consisting of or including someone with a particular need for settled accommodation on medical or welfare grounds;
(f) households whose social or economic circumstances are such that they have difficulty in securing settled accommodation' (s 167(2))

An applicant in one or more categories is entitled to cumulative preference. The only omission from the previous scheme (other than the homeless) is those with large families. Burnet explains this omission thus:

'This is probably not the thin end of the wedge of some eugenics policy, but explicable by the fact that adequate consideration can presumably be given to such families under one of the new categories, such as families with dependent children. However, against their exclusion it has been argued that they are disadvantaged in the public sector through lack of suitable housing stock, and bound to struggle in the private sector because of shortages and landlords' reluctance to let to families with many children.' (Burnet, 1996, p. 120)

This may be true, but the omission is no doubt precisely because authorities have no stock. It is surely an act of deceit to grant a reasonable preference to a person when there is no chance of fulfilling it. On the other hand, its omission means that such families are not entitled to the preference and, as the categories are cumulative, greater priority would have been given if this category had been retained.

The Conservatives' argument was that each of these categories reflected those in the greatest long-term housing need. However, this argument seems difficult to justify as, certainly for some of the categories, the provision of short-term housing simply removes that need in the same way as provision of housing alleviates homelessness. Furthermore, the categories are most certainly 'elastic linguistically', which suggests that long term housing need must be further refined in order to make this scheme workable. As has been remarked, 'No doubt an experienced housing officer can judge whether such conditions pertain, given a high degree of flexibility in applying general standards of sanitation, the size of family, and satisfactory living standards' (*R* v. *Newham LBC ex parte Watkins* (1994) 26 HLR 431). For those wishing to challenge a local authority's assessment, such a comment provides a stark warning that the courts will view housing officers as being best placed to make the decisions.

Some notion of the government's intent can be gleaned from a DoE Consultation Paper (1996b, paras 28–34) but this is limited. The CoG is hardly forthcoming either, although it does provide 'a number of possible indicators' of need in Annex A. The only other assistance provided by the CoG is that authorities may wish to give greater priority to a household which includes a woman who is pregnant and living in insanitary conditions as opposed to a household which includes a woman who is only pregnant (which is surely obvious):

> 'However, the fact that a household includes a woman who is both pregnant and has a dependent child . . . should not of itself give that household greater preference over a family which has two dependent children . . .' (para. 5.7)

The phrase 'settled accommodation' is a clear reference to the jurisprudence which developed under the homelessness legislation, which tended to use two criteria of temporal and physical conditions of the property (see Arden & Hunter, 1997, Ch. 14; Hunter & Miles, 1997). It certainly does not mean long-term accommodation and so the local authority can, quite justifiably, use this against applicants in the last two categories.

Securing Additional Preference

Sub-paragraph (e) of the 'reasonable preference' categories defined above has become the critical provision, as such people are given 'additional preference' in allocation schemes provided they 'cannot reasonably be expected to find settled accommodation for themselves in the future'.[10] Extrapolation of this sub-paragraph together with the proviso above is shrouded in obscurity. The CoG, once again, is unhelpful in providing standards although it does provide the following guidance which perhaps undermines the Conservatives' self-help ideology:

'[Welfare grounds] could include vulnerable people with care and support needs, who could be expected to find accommodation on their own initiative but have a need for a secure base; or vulnerable people who do not have care and support needs; but do have a need for a secure base' (para. 5.13)

'The provision is aimed at individuals who are particularly vulnerable, for example as a result of old age, physical or mental illness, and/or because of a learning or physical disability' (para. 5.10 – note the parallels with the single persons' priority need in the homelessness part: s. 189(1)(c)).

Community Care and Young Persons

The additional preference is designed to reflect the concomitant obligations upon local authorities to provide housing for certain people under the community care and children legislation. The Conservative government was heavily criticized for its introduction of the 'care by the community' policy (see DHSS, 1981) as well as deinstitutionalization by, *inter alia*, the *Daily Telegraph*. It has been convincingly argued that adequate ordinary housing is the foundation of community care, for without such housing requisite levels of care are more difficult to provide and assessments are difficult to make (see NFHA/Mind, 1989; Morris, 1993; Arnold & Page, 1992). Nevertheless, access to housing was forgotten in the creation of the NHS and Community Care Act 1990 (see generally, Griffiths, 1988; Cowan, 1995). Only in 1992 did central government accept its importance (DoH/DoE, 1992), although since then study after study has found significant turmoil surrounding its implementation (see Means & Smith, 1996).

On the other hand, the Children Act 1989 seemed to proceed on the basis that adequate housing was crucial for a child's well-being. Thus, there are a proliferation of access provisions in the 1989 Act, generally owed to 'children in need' (s. 17(10) & 20(1)). A succession of judicial pronouncements, though, have marginalized the role of the housing department in the provision of accommodation to this client group based upon the fact that housing departments only become involved when requested and can avoid involvement if that request is not 'compatible with their own statutory or other duties and obligations and does not unduly prejudice the discharge of any of their functions' (s. 27(2)). The House of Lords essentially marginalized the role of housing departments by saying that they could refuse the request after having considered the relevant facts and that the courts would not review the case ('Judicial review is not the way to obtain co-operation': *R* v. *Northavon DC ex parte Smith* (1994) 26 HLR 659; see Cowan & Fionda, 1993, 1994, 1995). In the event, the involvement of housing authorities could be as limited here as with community care.

A further problem created by these other parts of the welfare matrix is that primary responsibility for individual assessments rests with social services departments. The current position is that housing and social services should make 'joint assessments' in all such cases (DoH, 1990; it is unclear what is meant by 'joint'). This type of procedure is fraught with difficulty and antagonism (see Cowan, 1997, Chs 2–3) because the actors are working under different guidelines and their cultures represent different starting points. At heart, though, there is also the central problem of resources. If there are insufficient people to conduct the assessments or insufficient units of accommodation to meet the need, then problems will arise whatever the ideological and organizational under-pinnings.[11] Working together implicitly involves a threat to the professionalism of each agency for neither can be regarded as the 'sole possessor of necessary expertise' (Langan, 1993).

It may well be that, while the CoG advocates joint working at every opportunity, the 1996 Act will not facilitate it. First, there is no need for agencies to work together for there is nothing in this part of the Act requiring it. Second, the ability to exclude certain people, together with the additional pretence category, will be the cause of some antipathy, particularly if (as expected) this category is narrowly defined by local authorities. So, whilst a social work department might assess an applicant as 'in need' of accommodation, the housing department might not. Third, there are problems inherent in the term 'additional preference' as we shall now consider.

What is Additional Preference?
The CoG is absolutely clear on the meaning of additional preference which, in the morass of ambiguity, is refreshing: 'The provision does not require authorities to allocate the first available property of any sort in such cases, but it does assume that people meeting this description will have first call on suitable vacancies' (para. 5.10). Were this all, it would go a long way to meeting some of the issues that arise in practice. However, the government were caught between a rock and a hard place. They wished to give priority to people with an additional preference but at the same time were concerned at growing neighbourhood problems. So, in the Parliamentary debates, this concern appeared to be a key consideration:

> 'It could lead to many problems for a housing authority if it housed someone who perhaps had a history of mental illness which led him (or her) sometimes to be a difficult neighbour, should there not be a proper care package in place from social services in order to try to deal with the difficulty that the person had so that it would not spill over to the neighbours.' (HL Debs, vol 573, col 354 (19 June 1996) *per* Lord Mackay)

The CoG reflects this problem when it allows the local authority to take the following into account (presumably in its assessment): the availability of suitable accommodation, whether a package of care and support services is required in order to take up an offer of accommodation, as well as decisions by social services or health agencies about how the applicant's support, care or health needs should be met (para. 5.11). Yet Cowan found that many housing departments were already operating such policies in 1994, partly as a response to their perception of the failure of social services personnel to provide the requisite levels of care and support. So, it is perfectly possible for housing departments to refuse to house a person because of their perception of the failure of social services – indeed, the CoG justifies this. 'Allocation of accommodation . . . is to be guided by the effect of allocation and not by entitlement' (Cowan, 1997, p. 205). The additional preference can, therefore, be overridden fairly simply and, for some authorities, it appears to have been usual practice to do so. Equally, it should be noted that authorities tend to penalise those with mental problems but favour the disabled (Smith & Mallinson, 1996)

General Preference

The public debates about reforming housing priorities began at the Conservative party conference in 1993 when Sir George Young, then Housing Minister in the Major government, announced that he was reconsidering the allocations process. This was the infamous 'back-to-basics' conference at which minister after minister proclaimed the evils of teenage pregnancies. In his speech, Young asked, 'How do we explain to the young couple . . . who want to wait for a home before they start a family . . . that they cannot be rehoused ahead of the unmarried teenager expecting her first, probably unplanned child?' The DoE's Consultation Paper also seemed to argue that unmarried mothers had less need than married couples (1994). Indeed, the whole consultation process was infused with such moral indignation:

> 'Allocation schemes should reflect the underlying values of our society. They should balance specific housing needs against the need to support married life, so that tomorrow's generation grows up in a stable home environment.' (DoE, 1995, p. 36)

> 'Recognizing the importance of a stable home environment to children's development, the Government believes that local authorities should give priority to ensuring that families, particularly married couples, with dependent children or who are expecting a child have access to settled accommodation. Consideration should also be given to those who have delayed starting a family because of the inadequacies of their accommodation.' (DoE, 1996b, para. 29)[12]

The belief appears to have been both that single motherhood was a major contributor to the rise in demand for accommodation; and also that single motherhood itself was caused, not by circumstances such as divorce, but as a result of the fecklessness of teenagers who would seek to jump the housing queue by becoming pregnant. So, for example, it is a key criticism of the 'reasonable preference' categories that they do not include those, usually female, fleeing violence or harassment (Hague & Malos, 1998), even though many authorities often give people in such circumstances *priority*.

Nowhere on the face of the Act does this preference for marriage or the so-called nuclear family appear. However, as was observed earlier, even within the reasonable preference categories, it is open to local authorities to favour some individuals over others within the same category and authorities have plenty of discretion otherwise to decide upon priorities. The current CoG has sought to influence the exercise of this discretion by 'ensur[ing] that first priority should be the provision of housing for married couples with children, and for vulnerable individuals, who are living in unsuitable accommodation' (para. 5.21). The dubious status of this exhortation (for that is all it can be) nevertheless allows local authorities, if they so wish, to prejudice single parent families. In the context of providing housing supposedly based upon need, encouraging allocations based upon morality as opposed to real needs seems far from the original welfare ideology (although not from practice – see below).

The Labour Amendment

Within six weeks of taking office, the New Labour government consulted on changes to the 'reasonable preference' categories so that they included those who have successfully cleared the obstacles in the homelessness legislation (that is, those people who have been found homeless, in priority need, and not intentionally homeless). This has been implemented by way of quasi-legislation so that a reasonable preference category reflects this (The Allocation of Housing (Reasonable and Additional Preference) Regulations 1997, SI 1997/1902). Effectively, this restores the previously enjoyed preference. However, Loveland described that as 'an exercise in legislative deceit' (1995, p. 331) because, on the one hand, authorities were to give reasonable preference but, on the other hand, they had diminishing resources to fulfil that preference. Thus, the result was a bottleneck, with too many people pushing for too few units of accommodation, most of which was in any event of the worst quality (the better stock having been sold off).

Local Authority Practice

The complexity and ambiguity of the legislative scheme must be translated into actual practice by local authority housing departments. However, this practice must be within the realities of often hard-pressed, under-resourced housing departments (as we saw in the previous chapter); thus, 'the allocation of council housing is a form of rationing, in which housing officers seek to match supply and effective demand. The main determinant of allocations is the stock which the housing officers have to let' (Spicker, 1987, p. 25). A number of different types of schemes are used to ration accommodation, although most used are points and date order schemes. Often, these are different between waiting list and transfer applications (*ibid*). In the study by Prescott-Clarke *et al.*, 80 per cent of respondent housing departments operated the former and 26 per cent the latter, there being some crossover of scheme (1994, paras 3.7.3 – 3.7.4). Date order schemes have little to do with housing need but tend to favour those who are able to wait longest (see below):

> 'For example, in one of the case studies a two year residential requirement was combined with a strict date order allocation scheme. This meant that applicants had to wait another three years before an offer of accommodation would be made.' (Bines *et al.*, 1993, para. 9.30)

It is well known that some authorities operate 'merit' schemes where allocations are based upon merit, which, *prima facie*, suggests a degree of bias in the process. Nevertheless, Bines *et al.*'s benchmark study found 15 per cent of local authorities were still using some form of merit or 'discretionary' scheme (1993, Table 9.4).

Nevertheless, as the following section shows, whichever type of scheme is used the same results often appear, so that the process of rationing becomes a process of discrimination.

8.3 W[h]ither Need? Part III – The Effect of Discretion

Influencing Allocation

Housing management, which includes the allocation of council tenancies, has not really developed any form of professional ethic (Franklin & Clapham, 1997). It has been argued that this absence '. . . simply confirms the power of prevailing definitions of gender roles, 'deserving' and 'undeserving' working class households, and racial status to direct housing allocation' (Cole & Furbey, 1994, p. 143). In other words, housing management might be perceived as a microcosm of societal prejudices precisely because there is no professional ethic (see Henderson & Karn's observations on their case study data: 1987, p. 17). That being said, housing management has also been influenced by its historical antecedents, in particular the five per cent philanthropy of Octavia Hill,[13] although her role can be over-emphasised (Clapham, 1991). Nevertheless, for different reasons, current housing management appears to have adopted similar perspectives through exclusions and allocation of better properties to 'better' tenants, so that this now appears to mirror the style of Octavia Hill (Spicker, 1985).

The key to an appreciation of the rationale for this apparent denial of 'need', if only in terms of the *result* of allocations policy, lies in the relationship between demand and supply. The 'expressed demand' for council housing is 'the number of households seeking to enter or remain within the sector' which 'may be compared with the annual flow of units of social rented accommodation becoming available' (Bramley, 1989, p. 19; see also Bramley & Paice, 1987). When this is done, it was argued that there is an undersupply of units of social rented accommodation. The DoE's evidence to the Environment Committee made it clear that 'on current plans, social housing outputs will only reach the lower end of the Department's 60,000 to 100,000 unit range in the period 1996–97 to 1998–99' even though there were other factors which 'might lead to an increase in demand' (House of Commons Environment Committee, 1996, Vol. I, paras 99–100; for the DoE's evidence, see Vol. II). The effect of this is, therefore, that local authorities have to ration the resource of council housing.

This undersupply has been rendered considerably more important by the numbers of dwellings lost through government 'privatization' initiatives such as the right to buy (see Ch. 12 below). More than 1.5 million units of accommodation have been lost in this way, which must affect the throughput of allocations. However, it has also been the better quality dwellings which have been sold – so schemes which house the better-off families in better accommodation favour them twice-over. Leaving a rump of the worst regarded accommodation in the council housing sector has meant that there is greater pressure on the allocators when people refuse accommodation. This pressure has intensified in recent years as a result of performance indicators that depend, in part, on the amount of time taken to relet property and that are publicized in the national media (collated nationally by the Audit Commission of the numbers of void properties – see, for example, Audit Commission, 1993, pp. 18–20); financial incentives to provide 'best value' management or to keep management 'in-house' after CCT, as well as financial penalties affecting void dwellings, which mean that rental income must be maximized and thus properties relet as quickly as possible. This suggests that the process of rationing must have clearly defined goals of 'efficiency and effectiveness' – the Audit Commission's brief.

In addition to these pressures on housing allocation, there are pressures that derive from estate management objectives. Estate management is subject to similar financial pressures which ensure that, if they are given a say in allocation policies, estate managers want to house only those people who are not 'problems', which excludes those who have a history of neighbour harassment, rent arrears, or not fitting in. Management is assisted by 'homogeneity rather than diversity' (Pearl, 1997, p. 80). Furthermore, large scale privatization initiatives, such as Housing Action Trusts and the failed Tenant's Choice, might have encouraged councils to adopt policies favouring existing tenants 'to please and retain them' (Clapham & Kintrea, 1991, p. 60). So, the efficient and effective rationing process must also take account of the effect of the allocation on the local community as the following comment from an area office in Henderson and Karn's study in Birmingham, suggests:

'They've caused a lot of trouble, so they're not really suitable for the offer that has been placed on. . . . So we don't really want another problem family in there, causing any more trouble.' (p. 268)

The relationship between housing allocation and estate management is often a difficult one to negotiate, often engendering poor relations between them. Cole and Furbey make the following point, neatly encapsulating the various pressures referred to above:

'[H]ousing staff are more likely to secure career advancement through achieving rapid allocations, minimising empty properties, reducing rent arrears, containing disputes between neighbours, and reducing, through segregation, the risks of racial conflict, particularly given current enthusiasm for performance indicators. To adopt a less pragmatic, more progressive view of the social role of council housing, let alone a more forthright advocacy of social equality, is to court powerful opposition and reduced material prospects.' (p. 143)

This last comment brings home the *politics* of allocations, for Members of Parliament, Councillors and other political worthies often hear complaints about the allocation process in their surgeries. Depending upon the person, such people can be influential supporters of individual causes. Furthermore, it is Councillors who are responsible for setting the parameters of the scheme. Gray suggests that 'as the population on the waiting list changes, so local authorities may amend the rules of selection to maintain particular groups in a specific position'. He cites an illustration of Slough BC which 'increased the residential qualifications necessary so as to avoid rehousing a large number of Asians' (1976, p. 220). Councillors are often liable to favour their current constituency, which includes those already resident who are seeking a transfer (see Clapham & Kintrea, 1986; *ibid*, 1991), as well as exclude owner–occupiers. Finally, allocations are often made directly by Councillors (although such a scheme is [or should be] no longer possible). For those who believe this to be part of the history of this country, a reading of *R* v. *Tower Hamlets LBC ex parte Khalique* (1994) 26 HLR 517, where Councillors from the majority group set up a 'Homelessness Board' to direct allocations policy, might dissuade them.

Consumption

Thus, whilst council housing supposedly eschews market principles, surprisingly, a market of sorts exists as a result of the allocation processes. This market favours those applicants who can wait long enough for the best offers and are able to refuse offers with impunity. The 'reality is one of a complex bargaining process between the client and the bureaucrat':

'The result . . . is to establish a clear hierarchy wherein offers of good quality property are most often made to those most able to 'operate' the system whether by political influence, by possessing a bargaining counter, or by articulacy and social acceptability. Conversely property perceived by the Allocations staff as poor in quality will be offered to those least able to refuse, least articulate and least able to enlist effective support.' (Jones, 1988, p. 96; see also English, 1979)

Within these schemes, those able to wait the longest time generally are allocated the best properties. Those unable to wait because of personal circumstances are allocated the worst properties. This occurs because housing allocation is made as a result of 'matching', not of properties to people, but people to properties. This subtle distinction means that the management prerogative is to ensure that people on the waiting list accept the properties they are offered. It is accepted that the more desperate a person, the worse property they will be willing to accept. Henderson and Karn's study suggested that the work of the primary allocators:

'would be almost inconceivable without the ability of the controllers to develop an image of the social situation of the applicant . . ., and to use this image in conjunction with their (inevitably subjective) knowledge of particular streets and estates to effect potential offers of accommodation.' (p. 277)

Some applicants have even less bargaining power than others. For example, allocations to successful homeless people are often made on the basis of a 'one-offer policy', so that any unreasonable (in the authority's view) refusal implies a total discharge of duty. On the other hand, waiting list applicants in the same authority may be entitled to unlimited or (say) three refusals. Furthermore, transfer applicants are usually entitled to refuse accommodation. The longer an applicant can wait, the better property is offered because usually a percentage of points gained by the applicant is added to the applicant's total for each successive year the applicant is on the list; and the applicant's reasons for rejection are usually kept on record and reference is made to them on a subsequent offer (Clapham & Kintrea, 1986, p. 64).

This institutional bias is probably compounded by applicants' expressed preferences for accommodation types as well as areas. Policies will often inform applicants that they will have to wait a considerable period for properties in some areas, which might be reinforced by interviewing/ visiting officers (see, for example, Jeffers & Hoggett, 1995). Furthermore, if the better properties tend to be allocated to transfer applicants, who have the ability to wait, then it follows that their previous accommodation will become available for waiting list applicants. Thus, the market operates in circular fashion. Added to this circularity are those who are often known as 'decants' – those who have been decanted from estates which have been demolished. Most often these people receive the highest priority in allocations policies and therefore are allocated better properties.

Matching demand to supply also suggests difficulties for those applicants with large families where there is insufficient accommodation to match the size of family. In some areas, authorities may not even have any accommodation which has more than four bedrooms, and even then the larger accommodation may be in short supply and heavy demand. In acknowledging that there will always be a demand for such accommodation, Henderson and Karn made the following point:

> 'What emerges most forcefully from this study is that the management of public sector housing cannot be separated from its production. Only in the production of more suitable types of housing for families and for the elderly and single, and in the constant up grading of existing housing can many allocation problems be brought within manageable limits.' (p. 279)

Some results

Whatever type of allocations scheme is used (see below), whether discretion given by the Act is minimized by the organization's rules, the basic fact seems to be that allocations always end up discriminating against certain persons. So, Henderson and Karn's study of Birmingham found direct and indirect racial discrimination in the allocations process, due to the pressures and effects of consumption considered earlier. However, this was enforced by the 'dual allocations system' operated by Birmingham – allocations were made centrally but could be vetoed by area offices. In the 1980s, Glasgow operated allocations through a points system with override provisions in nine priority cases of exceptional needs. Applicants expressed preferences for the type of property and area on the basis of 36 different permutations. This system was 'very close to the type of allocation scheme which the Labour Party has argued should be 'carefully examined' by other local authorities' (Clapham & Kintrea, 1991, p. 59). Nevertheless, transfer applicants were favoured and subsequently Glasgow changed their scheme slightly to favour such applicants even further (*ibid*). Such a pattern appears to be replicated nationally for, despite the ever-declining numbers of local authority accommodation, residential mobility within the sector has increased (see Burrows, 1997, Ch. 2). Some schemes are so complex that academics as well as officers have trouble understanding their priorities.

Such institutional prejudices have obvious effects. Equally, however, individual prejudices affect the most positive allocations scheme as the following comments about the 'housing visitor' suggest:

> 'The role of the housing visitor was also unclear. When one did arrive eventually, many people became optimistic . . . Many believed that a lot depended on the visitor and that what he or she said counted;. . . .

No small wonder, then, that they sometimes became confused and a little anxious when they saw the visitor inspect bed-clothes and furniture. . . . Visitors would discuss an applicant's preferences and would sometimes warn them against naming only those areas where there were few council houses, or estates which were in high demand.' (Lambert *et al.*, 1978, p. 47)

'It is the way, then, in which the visitors culturally perceived the applicant and his/her family that had a crucial effect on the nature of the visit, and also on the visitors comments recorded on the application form . . .
In general the nature of the visit and the visitors comments recorded on the application form depended on the sympathy which the visitor had with the applicants situation' (Flett *et al.*, 1979; see also Murie, 1983, pp. 199–201; Sarre *et al.*, 1989, pp. 206–213 and Appendix 1)[14]

The vestiges of this system remain in some areas. Furthermore, the point is of more general application than simply relating to the role of the housing visitor, for it applies equally to the subjective perceptions of the allocators. Thus, in Smith and Mallinson's more recent study of allocations on the basis of medical priority, a clear distinction was drawn between physical difficulties (all right) and mental difficulties (not all right): 'Housing officers experience a general sense of unease when they are dealing with a problem which has no predictable physical manifestations' (at p. 348). Personal perceptions of applicants, reflecting societal considerations and prejudices, are always part of a scheme because, however computerized it is, the scheme always relies on humans. So, Niner comments that 'The personal interests of the officers making the decisions, their local knowledge, and other such informal factors appear as important in determining the outcome as any more formal policies' (1975, p. 26).

Conclusion

It is an unfortunate fact that a combination of different processes lead to housing allocations by local authorities which neither reflect need nor the legislation. Rather, they reflect the prejudices common in society together with the political prerogative of re-election. The literature suggests that one reason for this prejudice is that allocations decisions are made by people; people have prejudices, often in common with others; these prejudices, infiltrate the decisions which are made. However, our analysis suggests that prejudice can also begin at central level. Respected sociological (and socio-legal) studies are conducted into the use of law as a tool of social change (for example in the context of the Race Relations Act 1976: Lustgarten, 1986). In the housing allocations context, the law has been changed to reflect the dubious beliefs of central government as well as favour marriage and/or the nuclear family.

However, the overriding conclusion to be drawn from the legal material is that the increase in reasonable preference categories simply gives more people the opportunity of pressing their reasonable case for (re-)housing. All of this must, however, be reconsidered in light of the new supply/demand paradigm, in which some local authorities have an oversupply of properties which few people want. More recent, and expected, government pronouncements increasingly reflect this concern. Reform is on the agenda and this is expected to realign allocations with strategies to deal with anti-social behaviour and other issues of responsibility particularly considered in Ch.18 below.

Further Reading

The best legal text outlining types of allocations schemes can be found in D. Hoath (1989), *Public Housing Law*, London: Sweet & Maxwell; see also by the same author (1981), *Council Housing*, London: Sweet & Maxwell. However most such texts have been dated by the 1996 Act. This also applies to some of the non-legal texts, although others have a lasting resonance (such as Henderson & Karn's text).

Other work on race and housing allocations is summarized (brilliantly) by Ginsburg in (1992) 'Racism and housing: concepts and reality' in P. Braham, A. Rattansi and R. Skellington (eds), *Racism and Antiracism*, London: Sage; much can also be gleaned from the baseline study of M. MacEwen and H. Third (1998), 'Tenure choice and ethnic minorities in Scotland: recent research and some legal conundrums', in D. Cowan (ed.), *Housing: Participation and Exclusion*, Aldershot: Dartmouth; for a different, refreshing perspective, see R. Ward, 'Race and access to housing' in S. Smith & J. Mercer, *New Perspectives on Race and Housing in Britain*, Glasgow: Centre for Housing Research, University of Glasgow; see also S. Smith (1989), *The Politics of 'Race' and Residence*, Cambridge: Polity. Single persons' access to housing through the waiting list can be gleaned from I. Anderson and J. Morgan (1997), *Social Housing for Single People? A Study of Local Policy and Practice*, Stirling: Housing Policy and Practice Unit, University of Stirling.

On housing management, other than the standard materials (such as Malpass & Murie), see P. Kemp and P. Williams (1991), 'Housing management: an historical perspective' in S. Lowe and D. Hughes (eds), *A New Century of Social Housing*, Leicester: Leicester University Press; D. Clapham *et al.* (1990), *Housing and Social Policy*, London: Macmillan, provides useful and interesting perspectives; the Centre for Housing Research's 1989 report to the DoE, *The Nature and Effectiveness of Housing Management in England*, London: HMSO contains important data.

Empirical work on community care can be found (in numerous volumes) in DoH (1995), *Implementing Community Care*, London: DoH; see also J. Lewis & H. Glennester (1996), *Implementing the New Community Care* Buckingham: Open University Press. Legal aspects of community care are considered in L. Clements (1996), *Community Care and the Law*, London: Legal Action Group and B.Dimond, *Legal Aspects of Care in the Community*, London: Macmillan. Implementation of the Children Act 1989 is considered in J. McCluskey (1994), *Acting in Isolation*, London: CHAR. General problems of inter-agency working are considered in F. Kaganas, M. King and C. Piper (1995), *Legislating for Harmony*, London: Jessica Kingsley.

Endnotes

1. 'Better' here includes the following variables: satisfaction levels; area popularity; labour class; segregation (Williams *et al.*, 1986; Clapham & Kintrea, 1986).
2. Central government also has power to include and/or exclude any person or group by regulations: s 161(3), Housing Act 1996. So far, the use of this power has been to include (a) successful homelessness applicants over 18, (b) some refugees, some of those granted exceptional leave to enter the UK and some who have current leave to enter and remain; those excluded under this subsection are persons 'not habitually resident in the Common Travel Area' with some exceptions: see The Allocation of Housing Regulations 1996, SI 1996/ 2753; The Allocation of Housing and Homelessness (Amendment) (No 2) Regulations 1997, SI 1997/2046.
3. This has been anonymized.
4. 'Minors' are unable to take a grant of a tenancy at law. This creates difficulties as the only way to grant a tenancy to a minor (a person under 18) is to do so under a trust. This means that a person (often a social worker) is required to take the legal estate, with the child as beneficiary. This complex legal arrangement hides a further problem that children are not subject to contractual obligations, such as paying rent, unless they are 'necessities'. This term hides centuries of case law, although recent expositions suggest that accommodation is a necessity: see Goff & Jones, 1995.
5. The Acting Chief Executive at Hounslow made the following comment after the decision: 'When we made the original decision not to house R in October, 1995, paedophiles weren't so much in the national arena, and it was a decision based solely on housing issues' (as recorded in Millar, 1997).
6. As Charles Murray, the New Right sociologist, describes welfare legislation, 'the system [had been] designed to be exploited' (Murray, 1994, p. 22).
7. Of course, as we saw in the previous chapter, such a belief was wildly inaccurate. Pregnancy and/or having a child gives a 'priority need' but it does not enable the parent to jump over the other obstacles in the legislation.
8. Transfer cases do fall within the reasonable preference categories, even though they are now exempted from the 1996 Act's allocation scheme.
9. See *R* v. *Bexley LBC ex parte B* [1993] 2 All ER 65 for discussion of the meaning of this word; see also: *R* v. *Kensington and Chelsea RBC ex parte Amarfio* (1995) 27 HLR 543; *R* v. *Newham LBC ex parte Dada* (1995) 27 HLR 502.
10. As amended by SI 1997/1902, para. 3.
11. It has been suggested that there is a sharp distinction between 'people processing' agencies such as housing, and 'people changing' agencies, such as social services: (Hudson, 1987, p. 177).
12. As this was in the Consultation Paper which first contained the government's view of the new preference categories, it undoubtedly could have been drawn upon in judicial proceedings to cure any ambiguities in the legislation.
13. Octavia Hill was a Victorian estate manager who pursued evangelical Christian approaches to management, rewarding the 'deserving' by (for example) allocating better properties or repairing the properties they rented (see, for example, Clapham, 1991).
14. 'The allocation study endorsed the tendency for housing officers, particularly visitors, to reflect stereotypical perceptions of black (and white) allocations expectations based on implicit assumptions of suitability and appropriateness, . . .': p. 207.

Bibliography

Arden, A. and Hunter, C. (1997), *Homelessness and Allocations*, London: Legal Action Group

Arnold, P. and Page, D. (1992), *Housing and Community Care: Bricks and Mortar or Foundation for Action?*, Hull: Humberside Polytechnic

Audit Commission (1993), *Staying on Course*, London: HMSO

Baldwin, J., Wikeley, N. and Young, R. (1992), *Judging Social Security*, Oxford: Oxford University Press

Bines, W., Kemp, P., Pleace, N. and Radley, C. (1993), *Managing Social Housing*, London: HMSO

Blake, J. (1997), 'Exclusion units', Nov/Dec, *Roof*, 27

Bowcott, O. and Clouston, E. (1997), 'Nightmare on any street', *The Guardian*, 10 June

Bramley, G. (1989), 'The demand for social housing in England in the 1980s' vol 4, *Housing Studies*, 18

Bramley, G. and Paice, D. (1987), *Housing Needs in Non-Metropolitan Areas*, London: Association of District Councils

Brimacombe, M. (1993), 'Weed out the undesirables', Nov/Dec, *Roof*, 21

Bull, J. (1993), *Housing Consequences of Relationship Breakdown*, London: HMSO

Burnet, D. (1996), *An Introduction to Housing Law*, London: Cavendish

Burrows, R. (1997), *Contemporary Patterns of Residential Mobility in Relation to Social Housing in England*, York: Centre for Housing Policy, University of York

Butler, S. (1998), *Access Denies: The Exclusion of People in Need from Social Housing*, London: Shelter

Central Housing Advisory Committee (CHAC) (1969), *Council Housing: Purposes, Procedures and Priorities*, London: HMSO

Clapham, D. (1991), 'A woman of her time', in C. Grant (ed.), *Built to Last*, London: Roof

Clapham, D. (1997), 'The new Victorians', Nov/Dec, *Roof*, 26

Clapham, D. & Kintrea, K. (1986), 'Rationing, choice and constraint: the allocation of public housing in Glasgow', vol 15, *Journal of Social Policy*, 51

Clapham, D. and Kintrea, K. (1991), 'Housing allocation and the role of the public sector', in D. Donnison and D. Maclennan (eds), *The Housing Service of the Future*, Coventry: Institute of Housing

Cole, I. and Furbey, R. (1994), *The Eclipse of Council Housing*, London: Routledge

Commission for Racial Equality (CRE) (1984), *Race and Council Housing in Hackney*, London: CRE

Cowan, D. (1995), 'Accommodating community care', vol 24, *Journal of Law and Society*, 212

Cowan, D. (1997), *Homelessness: The (In-)Appropriate Applicant*, Aldershot: Dartmouth

Cowan, D. (1998), 'Reforming the homelessness legislation', vol 55, *Critical Social Policy*, 435

Cowan, D., & Fionda, J. (1993), 'New angles on homelessness', vol 15, *Journal of Social Welfare and Family Law*, 403

Cowan, D. and Fionda, J. [1994], 'Usurping the Housing Act', *Cambridge Law Journal*, 19

Cowan, D. and Fionda, J. (1995), 'Housing homeless families – an update', vol 7, *Child and Family Law Quarterly*, 66

Cowan, D. and Gilroy, R. (1999), 'The homelessness legislation as a vehicle for marginalization: making an example out of the paedophile', in T. Kennett and A. Marsh (eds), *Homelessness: Exploring the New Terrain*, Bristol: Policy Press

Daily Mail (1997), 'Child abusers may be barred from getting a council house', *Daily Mail*, 9 January

Department of the Environment (DoE) (1981), *An Investigation of Difficult to Let Housing* Vol 1: General Findings, London: HMSO

Department of the Environment (DoE) (1994), *Access to Local Authority and Housing Association Tenancies*, London: HMSO

Department of the Environment (DoE) (1995), *Our Future Homes: Choice, Opportunity and Responsibility*, London: HMSO

Department of the Environment (DoE) (1996a), *Allocation of Housing by Local Authorities: Consultation Paper Linked to the Housing Bill*, London: DoE

Department of the Environment (DoE) (1996b), *Allocation of Housing Accommodation and Homelessness*, London: DoE

Department of Health (DoH) (1990), *Caring for People in the Next Decade and Beyond: Policy Guidance*, London: HMSO

Department of Health(DoH)/Department of the Environment (DoE) (1992), 'Housing and Community Care', Circular 10/92, London: DoH

Department of Health and Social Security (DHSS) (1981), *Growing Older*, London: HMSO

English, J. (1979), 'Access and deprivation in local authority housing', in C. Jones (ed.), *Urban Deprivation and the Inner City*, London: Croom Helm

English, S. (1997), 'Jeering mothers drive paedophile off council estate', *The Times*, January 11

Ericson, R. and Haggerty, K. (1997), *Policing the Risk Society*, Oxford: Oxford University Press

Ermisch, J. (1996), *Household Formation and Housing Tenure Decisions of Young People*, Essex: University of Essex

Flett, H., Henderson, J. and Brown, B. (1979), 'The practice of racial dispersal in Birmingham, 1969–1975', vol 8, *Journal of Social Policy*, 289

Ford, R. (1997), 'Council considers ban on housing paedophiles', *The Times*, 9 January

Franklin, B. and Clapham, D. (1997), 'The social construction of housing management', vol 12, *Housing Studies*, 7

Giddens, A.(1999), 'Risk and responsibility', vol 62, *Modern Law Review*, 1

Goff, Lord Robert and Jones, G. (1995), *The Law of Restitution*, London: Sweet & Maxwell

Gray, F. (1976), 'Consumption: housing management', in S. Merrett (ed.), *State Housing in Britain*, London: Routledge

Greater London Council (GLC) (1976), *Colour and the Allocation of GLC Housing*, London: GLC

Green, H. and Hansbro, J. (1995), *Housing in England 1993/94*, London: HMSO

Griffiths, M., Parker, J., Smith, R. and Stirling, T. (1997), *Local Authority Housing Allocations: Systems, Policies and Procedures*, Rotherham: DETR

Griffiths, M., Parker, J., Smith, R., Stirling, T. and Trott, T. (1996), *Community Lettings: Local Allocations Policies in Practice*, York: Joseph Rowntree Foundation

Griffiths, R. (1988), *Community Care: Agenda for Action*, London: HMSO

The Guardian (1997), 'Council warns off paedophile', *The Guardian*, 27 March

Hague, G. and Malos, E. (1998), 'Facing both ways at once', in D. Cowan (ed.), *Housing: Participation and Exclusion*, Aldershot: Dartmouth

Henderson, J. and Karn, V. (1987), *Race, Class and State Housing: Inequality and the Allocation of Public Housing in Britain*, Aldershot: Gower

House of Commons Environment Committee (1996), *Housing Need*, vol I, London: HMSO

House of Commons Environment Committee (1996), *Housing Need*, vol II, London: HMSO

Hudson, B. (1987), 'Collaboration in social welfare: a framework for analysis', vol 15, *Policy and Politics*, 175

Hunter, C. and Miles, J. (1997), 'The unsettling of settled law on 'settled accommodation': the House of Lords and the homelessness legislation old and new', vol 19, *Journal of Social Welfare and Family Law*, 267

Jeffers, S. and Hoggett, P. (1995), 'Like counting deckchairs on the Titanic: a study of institutional racism and housing allocations in Haringey and Lambeth', vol 10, *Housing Studies*, 325

Jones, M. (1988), 'Utopia and reality: the utopia of public housing and its reality at Broadwater Farm', in N. Teymur, T. Markus and T. Woolley (eds), *Rehumanizing Housing*, London: Butterworths

Lambert, J., Paris, C. and Blackaby, B. (1978), *Housing Policy and the State: Allocation, Access and Control*, London: Macmillan

Langan, M. (1993), 'New directions in social work', in J. Clarke (ed.), *A Crisis in Care? Challenges to Social Work*, London: Sage

Lewis, N. (1976), 'Council housing allocation: problems of discretion and control', Vol 11, *Public Administration*, 147

Lewis, N. and Livock, R. (1979), 'Council house allocation procedures: some problems of discretion and control', Vol 2, *Urban Law and Policy*, 133

Loveland, I. (1995), *Housing Homeless Persons*, Oxford: Oxford University Press

Lustgarten, L. (1986), 'Racial inequality and the limits of law', vol 49, *Modern Law Review*, 68

Malpass, P. and Murie, A. (1994), *Housing Policy and Practice*, London: Macmillan

Means, R. and Smith, R. (1996), *Community Care, Housing and Homelessness: Issues, Obstacles and Innovative Practice*, Bristol: Policy Press

Millar, S. (1997a), 'Anger over paedophile list', *The Guardian*, 19 February

Millar, S. (1997b), 'Paedophile eviction 'right'', *The Guardian*, 20 February

Murie, A. (1983), *Housing Inequality and Deprivation*, London: Heinemann

Morris, J. (1993), *Community Care or Independent Living?*, York: Joseph Rowntree Foundation

Murray, C. (1994), *Underclass: The Crisis Deepens*, London: Institute for Economic Affairs

Murray, I. (1997), 'Tenants back official accused of tip-off about sex offender', *The Times*, 9 January

National Federation of Housing Associations (NFHA)/Mind (1989), *Housing: The Foundation of Community Care*, London: NFHA

Niner, P. (1975), *Local Authority Housing Policy and Practice*, Birmingham: University of Birmingham

Pascall, G. (1997), *Social Policy: A New Feminist Analysis*, London: Routledge

Pearl, M. (1997), *Social Housing Management*, London: Macmillan

Power, A. (1987), *Property before People*, London: Unwin Hyman

Prescott-Clarke, P., Clemens, S. and Park, A. (1994), *Routes into Local Authority Housing*, London: HMSO

Sainsbury, R. (1992), 'Administrative justice: discretion and procedure in social security decision-making', in K. Hawkins (ed.), *The Uses of Discretion*, Oxford: Clarendon

Sarre, P., Phillips, D. and Skellington, R. (1989), *Ethnic Minority Housing: Explanations and Policies*, Aldershot: Avebury

Smith, S. and Mallinson, S. (1996), 'The problem with social housing: discretion, accountability and the welfare ideal', vol 24, *Policy and Politics*, 339

Spicker, P. (1985), 'Legacy of Octavia Hill', *Housing*

Spicker, P. (1987), 'Concepts of need in housing allocation', vol 15, *Policy and Politics*, 17

Tendler, S. (1997), 'Council refuses to house sex offender', *The Times*, 6 March

Williams, N., Sewel, J. and Twine, F. (1986), 'Council house allocation and tenant incomes', vol 18, *Area*, 131

Winchester, R. (1999), 'Need loses top priority', *Inside Housing*, 5 February

9 Registered Social Landlords (RSLs) and Housing Need

RSLs now play a major role in allocating supposedly low-cost housing to low (and no) income households. In 1995/96, housing associations made approximately 114,000 lettings to new tenants and 26,000 lettings to the statutory homeless (compared with 62,000 and 9,000 respectively in 1990/91: Wilcox, 1997a, Table 94). This was just less than one-half of the allocations made by local authorities (250,000). So, in sheer numerical terms, RSL allocations play a critical part in the allocating process. Yet, the process of allocations also raises fundamental questions about the Housing Corporation and RSLs' purpose(s) as well as their independence.

Registration with the Housing Corporation obliges landlords to allocate properties in accordance with such Guidance as is produced by the Corporation. This Guidance has always made it clear that the general principle is that landlords should allocate property according to *need*. So, for example, the 1994 Tenant's Guarantee made it clear that:

'The essential purpose of registered housing associations is to provide accommodation to those who are inadequately housed or homeless, and for whom suitable housing is not available at prices within their means, or at all, elsewhere in the local market.' (para. A1)
'In determining their priorities for the provision of accommodation and the offer of tenancies, associations must take account of housing need and conditions in the areas in which they operate.' (Housing Corporation, 1994, para. A3; see now Housing Corporation, 1997b (*Performance Standards*), pp. 35–48)

Since performance standards were introduced, allocations policies and practices have formed part of the Housing Corporation's regulatory checks.[1]

Performance Standards, the Corporation's current regulatory guidance, has subtly shifted the pattern of allocation according to need. Questions must therefore be posed about the independence and purpose(s) of RSLs. The following is contained in *Standards*:

'RSLs selection and allocation policies and practices for new lettings should give reasonable preference to those in greatest housing need, except where this would lead to unsustainable tenancies or unstable communities. In letting homes providing accommodation on a long-term basis, this means giving priority to the categories of need set out in

s. 167 of the Housing Act 1996 (as amended).' (Housing Corporation, 1997b, para. F2.1)

Thus, the Corporation is requiring RSLs to use the same allocation principles as local authorities (as if the 1996 Act contains the final word on the meaning of 'housing need'), except where this 'would lead to unsustainable tenancies or unstable communities'. This latter point reflects the observation that allocation policies and practices have a marked effect on the 'balance' of estates. As RSLs have no direct responsibility to house those from the local authority's housing register, other than through any agreements between themselves and the authority, the Corporation's role as the agent of central government has infiltrated into allocations policies of individual RSLs.

Whilst research on local authority allocations has been fulsome (to say the least), qualitative research on housing association allocations is commensurably rare (for two exceptions, see CRE, 1983, Niner with Karn, 1985). Part of the problem may well be the sheer diversity of RSLs in each local authority area (47 in Bristol alone: Malpass, 1997a). However, this lack of research has not halted RSL allocations policies from being part of the reason for a 'spiral of decline' on RSL estates (Page, 1993). This is the derivation of the concept of 'unsustainable tenancies or unstable communities' in *Standards*. This spiral of decline, on one view, has been caused because RSLs have essentially been forced to house an increasing number of homeless (statutory and otherwise) as well as others prioritized on local authority housing registers (*cf* Griffiths *et al.*, 1996). This reflects an increasing level of external control on RSL allocations from a different source – local authorities. Local authorities have been able to exert control because the funding mechanisms for developing RSLs effectively require local authority support for such schemes; in return for their support, local authorities have learnt to negotiate greater nomination rights over RSL stock (that is, local authorities nominating particular applicant(s) for particular RSL properties). *Standards* requires RSLs 'to offer to make available at least 50% of their vacancies' to local authorities (p. 42) but authorities are often able to extract greater proportions (for example, where they have offered cheap land for RSL development).

Local authority use of nominations has particularly been evident since the housing White Paper in 1987 (DoE, 1987). That document made it clear that housing associations were to be the providers of low-cost social housing and that local authorities were to adopt an enabling role. Whilst the enabling role tends to mean different things in different places, one common theme has been an emerging realization by local authorities of the importance of RSLs (see Cole & Goodchild, 1995). So, for example, whilst authorities rarely used up their nomination rights in the 1980s, the most common concerns in the 1990s have been of excessive use of those nomination rights together with attempts by local authorities at gaining greater control over RSL allocations. In the 1980s, RSLs had greater power in bargaining with local authorities; but by the 1990s, this power has been subtly altered by a combination of need from local authorities and financial constraints imposed by central government upon authorities. These financial constraints have meant that Total Cost Indicators have favoured those RSLs bidding for funds with lower indicators as well as the (increasing) use of private finance. This has required RSLs and authorities to work in partnership (which is, in any event, a Housing Corporation criterion for the receipt of public funds).

The sheer diversity in size, geography, and type of RSL schemes, together with the lack of available qualitative research, makes comprehensive analysis of allocations processes practically impossible. Allocations processes and practices are fragmented within and between different RSLs. However, it is certainly possible to tease out some of the possible issues that arise in practice. Readers of earlier chapters will remember that local authority allocation policies are considerably affected by a number of conflicting matters: an applicant's ability to wait; the number of offers made by the authority to the applicant; perceptions of different estates and social problems; institutional bias, particularly against ethnic minorities; central government prejudices; and local authority eligibility criteria. All of these various pressures may well exist in RSL allocations, although the rationale for their existence is often different.

The first section of this chapter considers the external pressures affecting RSL allocations strategies. It will be argued that a combination of different external factors affect and infect the process of allocation according to (so-called) need. These include central government pressures, issues created by the involvement of private finance, public awareness of the existence and ethos of RSLs, together with Housing Corporation requirements. These pressures affect the primary rationing – who enters the sector – as well as the secondary rationing process – who is allocated which unit of accommodation (Clapham & Kintrea, 1991, p. 55).

The second section deals with the main sources through which RSLs gain potential occupiers. Generally (although not exclusively), this is done in two ways – through direct applications from households or indirectly from organizations referring (or nominating) households. The first method gives the RSL control over who is selected, whereas the second method might not. Our consideration in this section will revolve around the processes of selection and allocation and it will be argued that allocation according to need is as far away from actually occurring as with local authority allocations. As Niner has suggested, 'Successful registration requires luck, informal advice and/or persistence and ability to wait until the list is open' (1987, p. 231).

In the third section, we consider the moves towards what have become known as 'common housing registers' (CHRs) between local authorities and a number of RSLs operating in the authority's area. CHRs are widely regarded as good practice (Binns and Cannon, 1996) and RSLs have been exhorted to join CHRs operating in their area. At present, CHRs are in a minority but it is anticipated that they will become ascendant. This makes sense, on one view – the fragmentation of 'social housing' makes the selection of individual applicants a lottery based upon the applicant's knowledge of the operation of RSLs in any particular area. Despite this, though, there are a number of problems identified by the early research upon them.

In the fourth section, we face the problem of 'unsustainable tenancies or unstable communities' head on, considering the concerns of RSLs, together with the responses to them. In an era in which anti-social behaviour (a term without definition) and fear of crime are part of the *zeitgeist*, it is perhaps no surprise that RSLs are seeking to control their allocation processes more carefully. The 'local lettings' policy introduced by *Standards*, which effectively enables the RSL to avoid allocation according to need (however that is defined), provides an important counterbalance to notions of 'social' housing. Local, or 'community', lettings have been defined as follows:

> '[S]ocial housing allocations policies, which operate alongside or in place of a consideration of housing need and take account of the potential tenant's contribution to that community in which the vacancy has occurred.' (Griffiths *et al.*, 1996, p. 1)

The final section discusses RSLs role at the fulcrum of the tenure choice for, whilst the majority operate as housing organizations, many now manage properties in other tenures as well as build properties for sale (for example as part of the shared-ownership schemes). This neglected part of their role raises further questions about rigidly separating tenure and enables us to (re-)locate the role of RSLs in the breakdown of tenure.

9.1   Infecting and/or Influencing the Allocations Process

In this section, we analyse three external controls on RSL allocations: central government; the Housing Corporation; and financial controls. Each of these might be argued to form important influences upon the processes and practices of RSL selection and allocation; and, as a direct effect, in turn each in some way delimits the way housing need is and can be defined.

Central Government
The usual sources of central government law-making – legislation, quasi-legislation, and case law – are practically non-existent in this sphere. It is, after all, the Housing Corporation's responsibility to regulate RSLs (s 36, Housing Act 1996) and any attempt by central government to invade upon that process may be considered illegitimate (albeit lawful). Indeed, it is the concomitant of receipt of public money that RSLs give themselves up to regulation by the Housing Corporation. We have seen that the Corporation is 'close' to the government and is the body charged (and

appointed) by the government to fulfil this part of central government's housing policy (see Chapter 6 above).

It is this intertwined relationship between central government and the Housing Corporation which leads to concerns over the independence of the Corporation, and, in turn, the RSLs themselves. This intertwining of interest was most obvious in the 1990s (perhaps as central government became more aware of its bargaining power). We have already seen how the government, through the Housing Corporation, manipulated (or, at least tried to) the regulation of RSL's allocations policies in the 1994 Tenants' Guarantee (which superseded HC Circ 48/89, specifically covering allocations). The 'essential purpose' – providing accommodation for the inadequately housed and homeless as well as those who are unable to afford market rents – circumscribed in the Tenants' Guarantee chimed with the nature of many RSLs, which are 'there to offer housing to those in the greatest need' (Withers & Randolph, 1994, p. 11). Despite their diversity of origin, allocation according to need is commonly said to the a general principle to which RSLs sign up.

In a document 'linked' to the White Paper, the DoE described the cornerstone of what all RSLs bidding for grants would be expected to provide as the 'Social Housing Product' (DoE, 1995b).[2] One of the four key features of this 'product' was that '[RSLs] will be expected to deliver . . . tenancies allocated *in accordance with [g]overnment policy on access to social housing*' (para. 5.4; emphasis added). Furthermore, '*New tenants who are not local authority nominees should be selected in accordance with an allocation scheme approved by the [Housing] Corporation; this must reflect the Regulations and Guidance that the Secretary of State sets for local authority allocations policies.*' (para. 5.15; emphasis added)[3]

This is the derivation of *Standards'* requirement that RSLs give reasonable preference to 'the categories of need set out in s. 167 of the Housing Act 1996' (p. 38). Increasingly, then, RSLs have become tools of central government housing policy. The only diversity remaining to the RSLs is their ability to set their own objectives in their 'governing instrument' (for example, its memorandum of association). Even then, the parameters of this instrument must not exceed what the Corporation regards as acceptable in order to enable registration of the RSL with the Corporation.

Other examples of central government influence over the Corporation's allocations guidelines include the following. First, RSLs were told in December 1996 that where they provide temporary housing for a homeless person in 'long-term property', 'they should not do so for more than two years (continuously or in aggregate) in any period of three years' (HC Circ R3 – 49/96, para. 3.3). We will see in the next chapter how Corporation Guidance attempted to balance government policy on one hand – that various asylum seekers and immigrants should not have access to social housing – with the independence of RSLs – many of which 'have aims and objectives which include the provision of housing' to such client groups (HC Circ R3 – 04/97). The paternalistic Guidance indicated the following:

'RSLs are independent voluntary bodies. Before they make any decision to let accommodation direct to applicants from abroad who do not qualify for local authority housing, they should carefully consider whether their aims and objectives allow them to do so.' (para. 3.1)

'RSLs are also reminded that most of their housing has been provided for permanent homes. They should normally make lettings for such accommodation to applicants who have demonstrated that they are eligible for permanent housing.' (para. 3.3)

'RSLs should carefully consider the effect on their financial position if they house applicants who do not have the means to pay their rent and service charges.' (para. 3.5)

The message, whilst not exactly forcing RSLs to adopt central government's exclusions, nevertheless exhorts such adoption as it emphasizes the RSLs' aims and objectives, the obligation implied in the receipt of public funds, and their financial dependence on rents (and the assumed inability of this client group to pay).

Thus, the denial of certain groups' housing need can be implicit through Circulars whereas, for local authorities, such matters occur through (quasi-) legislation. The only distinction is that the regulation takes a different form. Indeed, Day *et al.*'s research into RSL regulation and accountability uncovered some concerns about the level of regulation exerted by the Housing Corporation, particularly the importance ascribed to 'open' waiting lists:

'The allocation problems of associations varied, with some objecting to 'foreigners' from outside their community and others complaining that they could not find any disadvantaged groups to put in their housing.
. . .
The regulators were really demanding active searches on allocations policy rather than passive open access and this was thought to be in excess of the regulators' brief.' (1993, p. 25)

So, central government's influence extends further than first appears (or certainly further than the available documentation).

Performance Standards[4]

For the first time, the Corporation has, in *Standards*, set out in great detail specific policies on allocations. Unsurprisingly, these are far more prescriptive than previous regulation which simply recited the old mantra that RSL's housing should be allocated according to need (without prescribing how RSLs should define 'need'). In *Standards*, the Corporation has had to balance the independence of individual RSLs, on the one hand, with the apparent need for more prescriptive regulation (as exemplified by central government's approach to the social housing product). RSLs have been concerned for some time over what they perceive as excessive regulation over their selection and locations policies (Day *et al.*, 1993).

In terms of allocation, *Standards* contains the prescriptive requirement that RSLs should base their judgment of need on the reasonable and additional preference categories in the 1996 Act (except where this would lead to unsustainable tenancies or unstable communities: p. 38). Selection should be 'consistent with their governing instrument' (p. 35). This explicit requirement for a conjunction of prioritization between local authorities and RSLs is to be welcomed because diversity causes fragmentation of opportunity. If local authorities and RSLs have different methods of selection, such fragmentation has adverse effects on individual households (quite apart from fragmenating the social sector). At present, RSLs are advised not to join "common allocation" systems (where all selections for local authority and RSL homes are prioritised in exactly the same way) unless the governing body has agreed that this would not threaten the RSL's aims and objectives and *independence*' (p. 35; emphasis added). Such an admonition suggests a practical contradiction and conflict. On the one hand, uniformity in selection is not required; on the other hand, most social housing organizations are supposed to be using similar selection principles.

Standards creates an *expectation* of uniformity, for each organization is, or should be, selecting tenants according to the same principles. However, local authority allocations schemes are dependent upon local practices, whereas RSLs working practices and operational criteria are different (particularly when the RSL operates on a national basis or for a specific client group). Expectations of uniformity may therefore be dashed, particularly when the Corporation requires RSLs to maintain their *independence* at the same time as requiring them to work according to the same principles as local authorities. It is this contradiction that may well prove difficult, and cause difficulties, in practice.

One immediate problem relates to 'local connection'. This generally tends to be a key concern in local authority selection schemes, but RSLs have always been required to ignore such a consideration (see, for example, the HC Circ 48/89). On this issue, *Standards* has an awkward compromise: 'An RSL may give some additional weighting to the priority of an applicant for having a connection with the local authority area in which the applicant would be rehoused. But . . ., any use of such additional weighting must not dominate the prioritising process at the expense of the priority categories' (p. 44). In other words, some priority can be given, but not such as to undermine the reasonable preference categories.

In general, other than as appears in their governing instrument, RSLs are not entitled to exclude applicants from their waiting lists. However, some limited exceptions to this do exist (p. 46). These exceptions are further examples of the difficult compromise that the Corporation has to make in its allocations standards between, on the one hand, the principle of allocation according to need, and, on the other, the principle of deservingness (or appropriateness). This balance is the same as appears in the local authority sector. As, by and large, allocation schemes tend to reflect societal prejudice at any given moment, this should not surprise us. Nor should it surprise us that RSLs, as we shall see in the next part of this chapter, have always excluded certain persons despite Corporation guidance. Nevertheless, the exclusions represent a significant shift in the Corporation's regulatory guidance away from need.

First, an applicant may be excluded 'if there is proven evidence that the applicant breached the terms of a tenancy for which there are statutory grounds for possession, or breached the terms of a mortgage, or committed acts of physical violence against staff or other residents . . .'. There are three provisos to this: the events must have taken place within two years of the application; there must be no blanket ban, 'but will only be considered alongside each applicant's relative housing need'; and the applicant can use an internal complaints procedure. The latter two provisos are similar to those operating in respect of local authority exclusions.

The second exclusion reflects what I term the 'community care problem' – these are the issues associated with the deinstitutionalization of persons with support needs that are not being met within the community setting. This has been a concern for some time (see Cowan, 1997 for discussion). Centrally, the issues relate to an applicant's ability to maintain a tenancy without support. If an applicant requires support, which is not (or may not be) forthcoming from the appropriate statutory agency, this is 'setting up that person to fail'. Furthermore, problems over rent arrears amongst this client group, together with the costs of eviction, cause income stream losses to the RSL. RSLs are entitled to exclude a person where there support needs are too high for the RSL or if 'the RSL has failed in its efforts to encourage another responsible body to provide that support'. If the latter, RSLs are required to be able to demonstrate that they have contacted the relevant statutory agency to secure the necessary additional support as well as showing that it is not contrary to the Disability Discrimination Act 1995.

The final permissible exclusion relates to particular types of schemes that have adapted facilities or are targeted at people with particular needs. In such cases, applicants may be excluded if they do not have the relevant needs or if the applicant 'needs support at such a level that the RSL could not meet them without seriously undermining its ability to provide for the current residents of the scheme', or is unable to afford to place the applicant in the scheme.

Before leaving *Standards*, one important additional point needs to be made. Whilst *Standards* appears mandatory, it is sufficiently flexible to be manipulated according to the individual RSL's desires. I would hazard a guess that few RSLs will be totally aware of the import of the standards relating to selection and allocation or, if they were, few would be willing to put them completely into effect. This reflects the weakness of the Corporation's monitoring of RSLs and its regulatory power (see Chapter 6 above)

Financial Influences

Allocations are also increasingly influenced by financial considerations. The link is explicitly drawn between financial influences and central government policies in HC Circ R3 – 04/97, in which RSLs are also reminded that Regulations effectively cut certain people's entitlement to Housing Benefit. After all, any threat to an RSLs income stream is also a threat to its solvency, particularly affecting those which have engaged with private finance.

This financial imperative is also refracted in terms of those households who wish, or are willing to be, housed in this sector. Rents have risen substantially since the advent of mixed funding; private sector tenancies now granted by RSLs (combined with the *Charters*) offer less security and fewer rights than local authority tenancies; the right to buy applies generally in local authority stock, but RSL tenants are only guaranteed it in relation to properties developed after the 1996 Act. In other words, the RSL tenure is, in some respects, not as desirable as local authority housing. RSL rents are generally higher than local authorities and are converging with the private rented sector (and in some areas have already converged: Wilcox, 1997b, Table 69).

Where RSL and private-sector rents are equalizing (or have equalized already), the selection of tenants becomes more difficult. The problems of high rents, and the risks involved in them, were considered in Chapter 6 above. They may well adversely affect housing selection and allocation. This might be because fewer tenants wish to live in those particular properties leading to the properties becoming 'hard to let' even though the design and construction standards might be higher in the RSL property. Rent maximization also requires a minimal time between a property becoming available and its being (re)let. Thus, the pressure to (re)let property is at least as great in RSL allocations as it is in local authorities. In Chapter 8, we noted that the need for speedy relets was a principal cause of inequality in allocation (the more desperate applicants being regarded by allocators as more willing to accept lower quality accommodation).

A final consequence of the financial strictures under which RSLs operate is the relationships that have to be generated with local authorities in order to have development schemes funded. Local authority support for development schemes is a prerequisite of public funding. Furthermore, the lower the costs of any scheme, the more likely it is that it will be funded. Authorities can, for example, provide low- or no-cost land for development (formerly known as 'HAG stretch'), affect the planning process, and even provide a percentage of the funding. In these ways, they influence which RSLs receive funding. They, therefore, have found that their bargaining power has considerably increased and they have become adept at using their bargaining position in this process to seek significant levels of nominations.

9.2 Selection and Allocation

RSLs select and allocate properties to tenants directly – under their own policies and procedures – as well as through nominations and/or referrals – from other agencies such as local authorities. Often RSLs will only accept nominations, and have no direct method of application (other than through transfers). Different considerations appear to apply depending upon the source and this section is divided accordingly.

Direct Applications

A significant proportion of RSL tenants received their tenancies after direct application to the RSL concerned. In the 1993 DoE baseline study of housing management, 35 per cent of total self-contained lettings were made to direct applicants (Bines *et al.*, 1993, Table A9.2) and 27 per cent in 1995/96 (Housing Corporation, 1997a, Table 12.1). A study of certain selected areas found 46 per cent of lettings being made to direct applicants (Parker *et al.*, 1992, Table 3.2). It appears that the available research points to the principle of 'allocation according to need' being undermined at three different phases of the process: application, selection and allocation.

By way of preliminary, two matters should be borne in mind. First, the nature, scale, variety, objectives, and philosophies are different between RSLs so that general statements often lack validity in relation to each RSL. Furthermore, even within one local authority area, there may be such a multiplicity of operating RSLs that 'certainly, to be familiar with all the associations operating . . . would be a considerable task' (Niner with Karn, 1985, p. 40). This is a point to which we will return below for, if even academics are unable to gain the requisite familiarity, how are applicants supposed to exercise their 'choice' (that watchword of privatization)?

Second, RSLs often have greater pressures on their selection and allocations than local authorities. This can be seen when one matches the level of direct applications against the number of lettings in any given year. Greatest stress is placed on smaller RSLs. Thus, with demand outstripping supply, there is a need for some form of *rationing*. This means that RSLs have to indulge in gatekeeping, although their methods of so doing might differ from local authorities.

Application
The principle factor affecting who applies to an RSL is the available knowledge and information about the existence and role of the RSL.

There is, apparently, a considerable degree of ignorance about RSLs amongst their client base. Whilst RSLs, like local authorities, are under duties to provide information about themselves and their allocation policies, it appears that they are chary of doing so in any great depth. This might be considered part of the gatekeeping undertaken by RSLs in order to lessen the number of applicants for 'by advertising their services [RSLs] were in danger of raising false expectations' (Parker *et al.*, 1992, para. 2.20).[5] The same study commented that 'most [RSLs] expressed the view that applicants got to know of them by word of mouth or because they were long established and had a local presence within a particular area of the local authority district' (para. 6.23). In the Prescott-Clarke *et al.* study, 40 per cent of those not interested in RSL accommodation were also unaware of some aspect of RSLs (1994, Table 5.28). Of 77 interviews of applicants in four study areas running common housing registers (see below), Mullins and Niner found that, when asked how much they knew about RSLs, 74 per cent of respondents knew 'only a little' or 'nothing at all' (1996, para. 7.46).[6]

A dated, but nevertheless relevant, qualitative study of two large RSLs suggested three more general factors influencing direct applications: geography/familiarity/image; channel of approach; and preliminary advice and guidance. As regards the first, the 'word of mouth' approach generally suggested that as one estate was predominantly white, such a policy 'favours white rather than black households' (Niner with Karn, 1985, p. 73). Furthermore, the location of the stock of one RSL 'in the more deprived inner and middle ring areas of Birmingham' meant that more applications from the deprived and vulnerable would be made (p. 72). Finally, there was a clear method of encouraging enquiry staff to act as gatekeepers: '. . . their instructions were to deter 'applicants' who would stand no chance of being housed, though to give out a form if the 'applicant' insisted' (p. 76).

Selection
Selection is not a matter of course. The individuality of RSLs is (as might be expected) reflected in who will be selected for (re)housing. Furthermore, as RSLs have no duties imposed upon them (other than through Housing Corporation Guidance and Performance Standards or what is agreed between themselves and any local authority), they can adopt any type of policy as regards selection. Selection is supposed to be based upon 'need'. We have seen how the Housing Corporation has defined need at different phases. However, a number of factors combine to deny need. First, as might be expected, RSLs restrict who may appear on their waiting list. Some restrictions might be obvious. For example, if an RSL provides sheltered accommodation for the elderly, it is likely to have lower age limits. However, more generally, it appears that RSLs operate restrictions which go beyond the obvious. The Bines *et al.* study found (Tables A9.7–8) that, from a base of 113 RSLs, 100 per cent of RSLs imposed restrictions on former tenants with arrears outstanding or with a

history of rent arrears (compared to 67 per cent of local authorities); 85 per cent restricted those deemed adequately housed (compared to 35 per cent of local authorities); 44 per cent restricted selection to those with a local connection (compared to 90 per cent of local authorities); 81 per cent of RSLs imposed restrictions on those aged 18 or under (compared with 92 per cent of local authorities: para. 9.31).

Whilst most RSLs operate waiting lists, it is apparent that they close these at particular times when the waiting list reaches unmanageable proportions (usually in terms of the expected annual number of lettings). Applicants who apply when the list is closed will, most likely, be rejected as a matter of course. The Parker *et al.* study found that RSLs said that open waiting lists were 'very time consuming' (1992, para. 2.27) and, in Bromley, of the (just) six RSLs which operated a waiting list:

'These associations indicated that they had to adopt some objective means of keeping the length of the list realistic. This had most commonly been achieved by closing the list to further applicants once there is little prospect of rehousing within a year to eighteen months. One association, for example, closed its lists once they exceeded 10 per cent of the number of units in a particular scheme' (para. 2.31)

No matter what sort of need is exhibited by applicants, it appears that they can be excluded during this period. RSLs are only able to do this because they are not obliged to keep waiting lists. There is also some evidence that applicants are 'discouraged from proceeding if they were likely to have to wait what was considered an unreasonably long time' (Centre for Housing Research, 1989, para. 4.7; Niner with Karn, 1985), although this is commonly found in studies of housing allocation (Cowan, 1997)

The method of selection is often ostensibly different between local authorities and RSLs. Most local authorities now give applicants points in order to work out their comparative housing need. RSLs, on the other hand, only use points schemes in 46 per cent of cases. Instead, 48 per cent use a 'merit discretionary' basis (compared to 15 per cent of local authorities: Bines *et al.*, Tables 9.4–9.5), under which applicants are prioritized on the basis of their individual merit (for comment see Chapter 8) A potential reason for the mismatch is that the Housing Corporation, hitherto, has tended to argue against using points schemes on the basis that they lack flexibility (*cf* Ch. 8, where it was suggested that such schemes provide as much flexibility as others). However, it may be thought that relying on overt discretion and a commensurate lack of checks suggests a more worrying balance has been drawn in RSL allocations.

The only research on selection decisions in two RSLs, both of which adopted discretionary decision-making with no formal rules, found that the key part of the decision-making was delegated to housing managers (Niner with Karn, 1985, pp. 82–90). In one RSL, decisions were made on the basis of 'fairly crude' information and the manager made a comparison on the basis of cases then under consideration (not on general principles). The researchers found that decisions seemed to involve the following: assessment of the degree of housing need ('the interpretation of need was flexible. . .'); urgency of housing need (the RSL could not deal with immediate housing need but 'a notice to quit or marriage date several months ahead was considered insufficiently 'urgent'); the manager's estimate of the ability of the RSL to provide rehousing within 12 months (pp. 82–3).

In the other RSL, personal contact was often supplemented with a home visit: 'The personal contact involved very rarely resulted in more personal comments being recorded, though examples were found of remarks both favourable and unfavourable' (p. 85). The Parker *et al.* study 'consumer' survey found the following:

> 'Respondents also had negative views of the home visit/interview process, where many felt they were being 'checked-up' on and 'judged'. Some lines of questioning were seen as intrusive whilst others saw the interview either as falsely raising expectations of being rehoused or dashing hopes. Overall, the interviewer was seen as being in control of the process with the applicant as subordinate, which discourages applicants from asking questions.' (para. 6.36)

Cases would be forwarded on to a committee comprised of all management, the Director, and a social worker. The decision hinged upon: the degree of housing need; urgency of need (as this RSL could respond quickly); availability of suitable property; availability of alternative accommodation (through income levels and position on other waiting lists). The paradox, however, was that despite the degree to which 'housing need and the needs of families' were taken into account, the process did not favour these groups. This occurred because they lost contact with a number of applicants; their housing stock and availability meant that those requiring three or more bedrooms could not be helped; and finally, those in greatest need tended to be prioritized on the council's waiting list anyway. The study, in fact, concerned racially fair allocations practices and, on this point, concluded that this policy 'may have disproportionately affected West Indian applicants' (p. 88).

The lack of openness associated with RSL allocations tends to generate suspicion of their motives as well as their objectives and fairness. The lack of research only enhances these.

Allocation

It is impossible to separate allocations from the selection process, for the availability and type of accommodation are reflected in who is selected. This clearly comes across in the second RSL studied by Niner with Karn (above). Thus, despite ever increasing demands emanating from central bodies that RSLs should house the statutorily homeless, often these people are not selected, perhaps because they are most likely to require larger accommodation than is available. Despite recent programmes to increase the numbers of larger properties in the sector, the majority of properties tend to be smaller, with one or two bedrooms; only three per cent of RSLs have 'large family dwellings with four or more bedrooms' (Housing Corporation, 1997a, para. 2.5).

At this stage, the links between local authorities and RSLs become more apparent. For example, the level of the applicant's bargaining power – expressed in terms of ability to wait – seems crucial, particularly as RSLs tend to allow more offers without penalty (Niner with Karn, p. 90; Bines *et al.*, Table A9.10); RSLs are faced with similar pressure to relet their properties as quickly as possible and so this must surely affect the process (the person suiting the property rather than the property suiting the person: Niner with Karn, p. 96–97); the number of transfer applicants and the importance attached by RSLs to 'keeping them happy' by allowing transfers might be expected to affect the new lettings process. All of the factors which contributed to institutional bias in local authorities are, in other words, present in many RSL schemes. Furthermore, as Niner with Karn observed in sixteen cases considered by one RSL, morality enters into the process in, for example, some of the factors considered: 'favourable view of someone enterprising enough to find work'; 'possible friction with neighbours in future'; 'tenant "deserts" and quality of property (where a transfer was being made following neighbour complaints)'. Clearly, then, in that RSL (at least), the estate management perspective was also considered.

Indirect Applications

The majority of indirect applications to RSLs come from nomination agreements with the relevant local authority. These arrangements usually allow local authorities to nominate a proportion of first and subsequent lettings. The Housing Corporation requires that this proportion should be 50 per cent or greater as part of the RSL obligations to assist local authorities 'to such extent as is reasonable' (s. 170, 1996 Act; Housing Corporation, 1997b, p. 42). There is no rule that RSLs need to offer nominations to local authorities, although it seems to have been assumed that this will be done. Once again a Housing Corporation Circular 'expected' RSLs to enter into such agreements (HC Circ 48/89). In London, the various representative bodies agreed slightly higher percentages so that RSLs offer 75 per cent of available lettings of family-sized housing and 50 per cent of one-bed 'true voids' (NFHA, 1989).

One commentator has suggested, 'nominations have become the Stonehenge of housing allocations: everybody knows that they're there, but nobody is quite sure why or what they are' (Jones, 1997, p. 20). However, RSLs are under certain statutory duties (both new and old). Under the homelessness legislation, they are obliged to comply with a request for assistance from local authorities 'as is reasonable in the circumstances' (s. 213(1) Housing Act 1996); where the authority requests assistance, 'a [RSL] shall cooperate to such extent as is reasonable in the circumstances in offering accommodation to people with priority on the authority's housing register' (s. 170 Housing Act 1996). These specific duties are weak and probably unenforceable (*cf* s. 27(2), Children Act 1989; *R* v. *Northavon DC ex parte Smith* (1993) 25 HLR 656). It would appear that these nomination arrangements are part of the Housing Corporation's attempts to enforce compliance with these statutory obligations. Furthermore, nominations are 'often conditions of Housing Corporation finance' (Alder & Handy, 1996, p. 336) or conditions of local authority support for RSL development.

Increasing concern is now being generated by RSLs as to the numbers and types of persons nominated by local authorities. This has not always been the case. The Parker *et al.* study found that nomination rights were not being taken up, although this was less common with larger properties: 'associations tend to use nominations for family-sized accommodation but use other sources to find tenants for their traditional client groups of single people and older people' (para. 4.28). A survey of London Boroughs in 1992 indicated that 'a sizeable proportion of nominations are rejected by [RSLs]' but that despite an inability to use their own stock for statutory homeless households, no London authority used up all its nomination rights (Association of London Authorities *et al.*, 1992, pp. 4–5). In 1992/3, information provided by 137 RSLs found that 39 per cent of non-take up of nomination rights were of one-bedroom properties together with 21 per cent of family housing. It has only been more recently that local authorities have seen the value of exploiting their nominations both through 'HAG stretch' as well as because:

'. . . the changing power relationship between local authorities and housing associations has led to a degree of competition amongst housing associations to gain the favoured "development partner" status with local authorities [which carries greater funding opportunities]. This has contributed to the growing willingness of housing associations to agree higher nomination levels and to improve their nomination relationships. The effect has been to drive up agreed nomination quotas, not only for new schemes, but also for existing developments.' (Withers & Randolph, 1994, p. 45)

Nevertheless, the variation in types of nominations arrangements, together with the variation in take-up of nominations, are considerable. Furthermore, nominations are only as good as the individual local authority's housing register. For example, if that is operated in a discriminatory way, this will in all likelihood, be reflected in who is nominated.

Jones divides nominations arrangements into three types: *pool*; *individual*; and *assumed* (1997, pp. 42–4). Pool nominations occur when local authorities nominate a pool of applicants for no specific vacancy. RSL interviewees seemed to regard these as least satisfactory as ' "A mess

. . . chaos". This was thought to be because "A [local authority] letting officer is just getting an application off their backs" '. Pool systems are generally not favoured in practice (see also Parker *et al.*, 1992, paras 4.42–4.45). Individual nominations occur when one or more nominations are made for a direct vacancy. Here, the RSL 'is dependent on the efficiency (or otherwise)' of the local authority's allocation schemes. Assumed nominations occur when the RSL allocates accommodation to a council tenant so that their property is freed up for others on the council's waiting list. These are contentious because they do not come from the local authority and 'It's just playing a game really, making the figures look alright at the end of the day' (p. 44). The important factor in assumed nominations is that the RSL *retains control* over whom it accepts, as well as affecting the statistics.

Control can also be retained even in the first two systems (as well as others) by the RSL reinterviewing nominees as well as rejecting some applicants. This is particularly the case where RSLs are given a choice of three or more people for a particular property in the 'individual' approach, and RSLs are known to favour such schemes. In 1991/92, Withers and Randolph found that, from a survey of 113 RSLs, 2753 out of 5852 nominations were unsuccessful. Of these, only 28 per cent were untraceable; of the rest, 20 per cent were rejected by the RSL, 8 per cent not selected, 12 per cent withdrew, and 25 per cent refused an offer (Table 6.25). Parker *et al.* made the following observation about this process:

'When associations were asked how the choice was made, it was said to be on the basis of need in accordance with the association's own criteria. It was not clear how this was done when nominations were of very different types (e.g. a transfer because of harassment, a transfer to reduce under-occupation, or a homeless family) – a dilemma which can be expected quite often if the local authority is strictly following its own priority system.' (para. 4.56)

Of the RSLs in two areas we interviewed about their allocations policies (after the publication of *Standards*), it was the *norm* to re-interview applicants nominated to the RSLs. This reflected the concern held by all RSLs that the quality of nominations was commonly poor, in that information was out of date or the nominees were not considered sufficiently appropriate for the particular property on offer (Cowan *et al.*, 1999).

It seems to be the case that the system entitles the 'social landlords' to play a game of double jeopardy. Applicants must be successful through the local authority route and then must be successful through the RSL's allocations scheme. Common reasons for rejecting applicants seem to relate to nominees lacking eligibility for the RSL and different occupation standards between local authorities and RSLs (Withers & Randolph, 1994, pp. 84–5), together with high RSL rents, and oversupply in some areas (Jones, 1997, pp. 64 *et seq*; see also Cole *et al.*, 1996, p. 31 for RSL tenants' perspectives). It may well be that RSLs use particular [poorer] parts of their stock for local authority nominations, as they have allocated them on an ad hoc basis in the past (Parker *et al.*, 1992, para. 4.35–4.40). Thus, local authorities have tended to believe that RSLs were 'not considered as attractive a proposition as formerly and some applicants would no longer consider one' (Parker *et al.*, para. 4.47).

Whilst RSLs are accused of 'cherry picking' by local authorities (that is, only accepting the nominees likely to cause no management problems), RSLs tend to accuse authorities of giving poor quality nominations or 'dumping' those the authority does not want to house upon RSLs. Part of the problem lies with the quality of the initial information gathering exercise – Niner with Karn argue that, in Birmingham's case, 'Not only was the city likely to be nominating people who had no interest in an association tenancy, but also it was failing to inform applicants that they had been nominated' (p. 115). *Standards* reflects the concern that 'nomination agreements should not remove RSLs' independence in the letting of their homes' (p. 42); it also states that, as RSLs and local authorities have similar prioritization regulations, 'local authority nominees can normally be assumed to be in sufficient need or appropriate to be rehoused' (*ibid*). Such statements (again) expose a policy conflict and also make it reasonably clear where the power lies in allocation. If the local authority nominates, then the RSL should normally accept that household.

9.3   Common Housing Registers – Managing Governance

CHRs are in vogue. Central government welcomed their development in the 1995 White Paper (DoE, 1995, p. 36); the Chartered Institute of Housing has produced a Good Practice Guide (Binns & Cannon, 1996); *Standards* encourages RSLs to join CHRs (p. 35); the Housing Corporation has completed an evaluation of those CHRs in action (Mullins & Niner, 1996),[7] and there is much to be said for them in the era of social housing fragmentation. In most areas where there are large numbers of RSLs operating, access to social housing can hardly be said to be equitable. Rather, it is based upon a household's knowledge of available options and its desperation. The greater knowledge a household has of the different operating RSLs in the area, the more options it will have in seeking access to housing; the more desperate a household is, the more likely it will be to settle for poorer quality stock.

The use of a CHR generally requires most RSLs and local authorities to have a single application form and database of applicants. Other than this, there are large variations amongst those operating. Some, for example, operate common allocations policies that give one organization the responsibility to prioritize applicants, who are then rehoused by each member according to their position on the register. Such schemes are frowned upon by the Corporation because of concerns about loss of independence by RSLs (*Standards*, p. 35; *cf* Mullins & Niner, 1998, p. 189 where it is suggested that within such schemes RSLs are commonly entitled to set 'matters such as occupancy standards, bedroom category assessments and estate child densities'). At the other end of the spectrum, they may provide a formalized method for local authority nominations through a single application form. The benefit of this is that it tends to short-circuit allegations about 'cherry picking' by RSLs and 'dumping' by local authorities because providers take on those at the top of a single list (although RSLs may well re-interview).

Whichever system is used, the great benefit of the CHR is that it reduces the distortions caused by differentiated, fragmented knowledge and desperation. For applicants, though, Mullins and Niner argue that it *reduces* choice and increases competition between households:

> 'From the customers' point of view, the ability to choose to go to different providers is lost, and competition from other customers increased by the pooling of information on potential customers by providers. . . .
> If there are policies to limit the number of offers made to applicants, the introduction of a CHR almost always reduces the degree of choice available to the determined applicant who would previously have shopped around. One offer only might mean a total of six or seven offers for an individual applicant where each housing association in an area maintains their own waiting list, but only one offer under a CHR.' (1996, paras 2.38–9)

Such a finding suggests a weakness in the CHR but should be contrasted with the degree of ignorance amongst applicants (however determined) that the same study found about RSLs (paras 7.46–50). Fragmentation means that those with greater knowledge are able to benefit over those without that level of knowledge. Thus, if the CHR reduces choice to those with greater knowledge, it restores equity between applicants (which is surely the way access to social housing should be).

Mullins and Niner found very little evidence to support the view that common housing registers have radically affected lettings, other than possibly reducing the number of transfers and increasing the number of moves between tenures (paras 7.55–7.63). Other than Information Technology difficulties (i.e. systems compatibility), the retention of independence from the authority remains an important consideration. For larger RSLs, 'decisions to participate tended to reflect local factors such as current housing stock in an area, expectations of future development funding, the rate of generation of vacancies and nomination rights, and potential costs savings on waiting list administration' (para. 8.48). Where, for example, social housing is in surplus, the fragmentation of providers means that they are all in competition with each other to fill their voids. In these areas, providers see themselves 'as competitors for customers rather than "partners in meeting housing need" (Mullins & Niner, 1998, p. 191).

The development of CHRs is commensurate with the mechanisms required to manage the new 'governance' of social housing. Governance 'recognises the interdependence of organisations. The essence of governance is the interactive relationship between and within govern-mental and non-governmental forces' (Stoker, 1995; cited in Malpass, 1997b, p. 3). The management of CHRs reflects the increasing professionalization in the management of governance, because officers are usually the driving force behind these innovations. For Mullins and Niner, this raises issues of accountability (1998, p. 192), although political influence in individual allocations is commonly frowned upon.

The jury is still out on CHRs. Their merit is clear, but perhaps less clear are some of the difficult issues that they raise for RSLs about independence, competition, nominations and transfers. Whatever, they are set to become a key method of overcoming the problems of fragmentation and differentiation amongst social housing providers.

9.4   'Creating Communities or Welfare Housing?'[8]

The massive expansion of RSLs, the increase in their role as social housing providers, together with greater responsibilities towards local authorities, rising rents and reliance on benefits have all led to questions being raised about the role of RSLs. Are they supposed to be 'creating communities'[9] or providing welfare for the marginalized? The argument is that: '. . . the challenge now is to maximise the numbers and minimise the price. Although the scale is different, the 'numbers game' which led directly to the housing disasters of the sixties, is being played again, this time by [RSLs] instead of councils' (Page, 1993, p. 4). Page argues that one of the problems is that too many low-income families are now being housed by RSLs, 'problem families' are being dumped on RSLs through nomination rights: 'A new way of thinking is required which meets housing need but pays attention to the social fabric of the community on a new estate.' These concerns are not new – criminologists have drawn a link between 'problem estates' and allocations policies for some time (see Bottoms & Wiles, 1997, and Ch. 18 for discussion). It has never been argued that the one is the consequence of the other but, rather, that the creation of 'problem estates' is a dynamic process depending upon a number of different factors (see Damer, 1974, for example).

Many of Page's assumptions have been challenged by subsequent research. For example, Page recited an argument about high 'child densities' on estates causing problems. Cole *et al.* found, by contrast, that residents felt that 'a high proportion of children could often enhance a sense of belonging and increase social interaction, rather than threaten a sense of community'. The notion of 'tenure mix' – that housing estates should reflect all tenures – is also open to challenge 'although images of the divide between owners and tenants persisted' (*ibid*, p. 39). Indeed, tenure hierarchies can operate to negate 'community' (Griffiths *et al*., 1996, p. 22). Page's 'assumption that a needs-based system of allocations will not produce sufficiently balanced and settled neighbourhoods' has equally been challenged. A better correlation might be between the degree of choice applicants have in moving to the estate ('volunteers not conscripts': Griffiths *et al*., p. 6) and their sense of commitment to the estate (Cole *et al*., pp. 30–34).

It may well be that the notion of community lettings comes down to two factors which can be interrelated: (a) RSLs wish to recapture control over their allocations partly because they believe that (b) they are being forced to house troublemakers (with a concomitant effect on their management roles). Thus, some community lettings policies make the questionable assumption that 'the problem of anti-social behaviour is best dealt with by excluding or removing anti-social elements' (Griffiths *et al*., p. 21). In turn, this brings various stereotypes to the surface and so community lettings policies can become policies which exclude certain types of person – for example homeless people and/or 'anti-social applicants' – from certain areas.

In all this debate, the principal complaint has been of insensitivity in local authority nominations, together with an increasing requirement to house homeless applicants. Thus, *Standards* requires RSLs to allocate housing according to need (as defined by the 1996 Act) 'except where this would lead to unsustainable tenancies or unstable communities', although this can only occur in exceptional cases (p. 38). Furthermore, allocations do not have to be made to those in the greatest need in difficult-to-let stock or 'if steps are needed to prevent or reverse social conditions in an area threatening the housing rights of most residents or the value of the stock' (p. 45). RSLs transfer policies are regarded as 'one means of stabilising communities, since [the policies] can reduce concentrations of deprivation or needs' (p. 40). Whilst the available research clearly shows that allocations policies, on their own, cannot turn around estates, the local lettings policies suggested by the Corporation appear to suggest that they can do so. The unidimensional solution proposed is, therefore, not only discriminatory and based on principles designed to undermine the notion of allocation according to need, but also is unlikely to have the desired effect.

9.5   RSLs as the 'pivot'

RSLs operate as the pivot between different tenures. In addition to managing their own property for rent, more than 40 RSLs have taken a significant proportion of local authority accommodation after a large-scale voluntary transfer, many build accommodation for low-cost home ownership, some have won contracts to manage particular parts of local authority estates (see, for example, Miller, 1996) and some take part in schemes under which they manage private-sector property (see Chs 4 & 6).

As regards the former, 88 per cent of transferring authorities have retained the assessment of housing need and the rest have retained it in part. All transferring authorities have retained some part of the homelessness decision-making role. On the other hand, the obligation to maintain the housing register has been transferred to the RSL in 68 per cent of all cases (statistics drawn from Aldbourne Associates, 1997, Table 3.1.1). Whilst judicial authority conflicted on the matter, it now seems that it is perfectly possible for authorities to transfer all their homelessness decision-making obligations to RSLs and many of their housing register functions (The Local Authorities (Contracting Out of Allocation of Housing and Homelessness Functions) Order 1996, SI 1996/3205). Very little is known about allocations in transfer areas, although it is assumed that taking over local authority property will involve the local authority requiring the new RSL landlord to accept 100 per cent nominations.

As regards the management of private rented accommodation (HAMA or housing associations as managing agents: see Ch. 2), these have generally been set up to provide short-term housing for statutory homeless households instead of the staged accommodation prior to an offer of permanent accommodation (under the Housing Act 1985, Part III). The scheme was originally meant to ensure that such households do not live in bed and breakfast accommodation. It was also designed to stimulate the private rented sector (London Research Centre, 1995, pp. 5–6), although the objectives of schemes have shifted in different directions since their commencement (see London Research Centre's evaluation for detail).

Accommodation built for low-cost home ownership is often targeted on those already occupying 'social housing' so as to free up that unit of accommodation for other households. The key criterion for allocation is the ability of applicants to be in priority need as well as obtain a mortgage, whilst not able to afford private rented accommodation nor mainstream home ownership (Housing Corporation, 1997b, p. 39; for further discussion, see Ch. 5). Demand from existing social housing occupiers appears to be low (less than the Housing Corporation requirement of 60 per cent: see Bramley *et al.*, 1995 for an evaluation).

Conclusion

Once again, the conclusion must be that the pinnacle of 'allocation according to need' has not been met and will not be met. Such a conclusion must be tentative, for the lack of research that has permeated the above discussion cannot merit a firm conclusion. Furthermore, the diversity of RSLs must mean that there will equally be a diversity of responses to the notion of 'allocation according to need'. However, a number of general messages can be gleaned. First, there is a confusion as to roles and obligations. Centrally prescribed allocations requirements have wrested some control away from RSLs as to the types of households they might have expected to accommodate less than two years ago. The confusion is also exhibited in the gradual retreat of central government from financing the RSL movement which partially causes higher rents (and higher costs to Housing Benefit). The management imperative for cost effectiveness and risk avoidance both affect allocations and selection in the same way as they imperatives do for local authorities (although for different reasons). Allocations themselves have exposed the true dimension of the debate to be the confusion in the role of RSLs. This question can be expected to dominate discussions in the coming years.

Further Reading

The National Housing Federation (formerly the National Federation of Housing Associations) publishes regular updates on lettings by RSLs in *Housing Today* together with research reports which sometimes deal with allocations. Publications based on the Housing Corporation's 'CORE' (Continuous Recording of data on new lettings by RSLs) provide valuable information. Additional material from the Housing Corporation can be found in research reports; see, for example, M. Harrison, A. Karmani, I. Law, D. Phillips, and A. Ravetz (1996), *Black and Minority Ethnic Housing Associations*, Research Source 16, London: Housing Corporation.

As regards legal materials, Alder & Handy seems unfortunately out of date, particularly as it does not take account of the Social Housing Standards. Thus, reliance must be placed on the Housing Corporation Circulars directly, which are the crucial source of quasi-legal data. H. Cope (1990), *Housing Associations: Policy and Practice*, London: Macmillan provides a useful and interesting source of information but it too is dated (although its blend of materials means that it retains its appeal). Additionally, slightly dated but relevant material might be gleaned from J. Hales and S. Shah (1990), *New Lettings by Housing Associations*.

The Commission for Racial Equality's 1983 report: *Collingwood Housing Association Ltd: Report of a Formal Investigation* remains a useful source of information but this is mainly background reading. Accountability studies tend not to discuss allocations which seems strange considering the fact that the accountability of the allocators is such a key issue (*cf* local authority allocations).

A subject which has not been dealt with in any depth above is the role of tenant participation in the allocations process. It might be argued that tenants have a right to be involved in allocations to a degree as allocations might affect the estate (see Griffiths *et al.*). Certainly Tenant Management Organisations have much to offer in the process. However, this is undeveloped as yet and there are fairly obvious dangers of such involvement (see generally Chartered Institute of Housing Tenant Participation Advisory Service (1994), *Tenant Participation in Housing Manage-ment*, Coventry: CIH; M. Pearl with W. Spratt (1997), 'The role of tenants in managing housing', in M. Pearl (1997), *Managing Social Housing*, London: Macmillan).

Endnotes

1. Note the important qualification about performance standards that 'they [are] designed to concentrate on the outcome of associations' performance rather than on the process of achieving it.' (HC, 1996, p. 3) This suggests that Housing Corporation data will not provide qualitative data about the operation of allocations by social landlords.
2. Commercial terminology appears to be used because 'Taken together this package of 'outputs' defines the social housing 'product' which government is 'buying' . . .' (para. 5.5).
3. At this time, the DoE still planned to regulate allocations schemes through regulation and guidance (DoE, 1996).
4. Local Lettings are not discussed in this section.
5. 'This was particularly so in Bromley where most associations had leaflets or handouts which could be given to applicants once they had found their way into the system and which explained their allocation policies and practices – but produced nothing specifically designed to attract applicants' (*ibid*, para. 2.20).
6. 22 per cent were unsure whether RSL rents were higher or lower than local authorities; 26 per cent believed they were about the same.
7. Once again, central government policy appears to have been driven by supposed 'good practice' from local authorities: see Miller, 1992 where the first common housing register (in Wrekin) is discussed albeit briefly.
8. With apologies to Cole *et al.*, 1996.
9. For consideration of the notion of 'community', an overused and underdefined concept, see Cole *et al.*, 1996, pp. 10–12 and the collection edited by Hoggett, 1997.

Bibliography

Aldbourne Associates (1997), *Vision into Reality: The Role of Transfer Authorities as Housing Enablers*, Aldbourne: Aldbourne Associates

Alder, J. and Handy, C. (1996), *Housing Associations: the Law of Social Landlords*, London: Sweet & Maxwell

Association of London Authorities, London Boroughs Association and National Federation of Housing Associations (1992), *Nominations and Statutory Homeless Households*, London: NFHA

Bines, W., Kemp, P., Pleace, N. and Radley, C. (1993), *Managing Social Housing*, London: HMSO

Binns, J. and Cannon, L. (1996), *Common Housing Registers: A Good Practice Guide*, Coventry: CIH

Bottoms, A. and Wiles, P. (1997), 'Environmental criminology', in R. Morgan & R. Reiner (eds), *The Oxford Handbook of Criminology*, Oxford: Oxford University Press

Bramley, G., Dunmore, K., Durrant, C. and Smart, G. (1995), *Do-It-Yourself Shared Ownership: An Evaluation*, London: Housing Corporation

Centre for Housing Research, University of Glasgow (1989), *The Nature and Effectiveness of Housing Management in England*, London: HMSO

Clapham, D. and Kintrea, K. (1991), 'Housing allocation and the role of the public sector', in D. Donnison and D. Maclennan (eds), *The Housing Service of the Future*, Coventry: Institute of Housing

Cole, I. and Goodchild, B. (1995), 'Local housing strategies in England: an assessment of their changing role and content', vol 23, *Policy and Politics*, 49

Cole, I., Gidley, G., Ritchies, C., Simpson, D. and Wishart, B. (1996), *Creating Communities or Welfare Housing? A Study of New Housing Association Developments in Yorkshire/Humberside*, York: Joseph Rowntree Foundation

Commission for Racial Equality (CRE) (1983), *Collingwood Housing Association Ltd. Report of a Formal Investigation*, London: CRE

Cowan, D. (1997), *Homelessness: The (In-)Appropriate Applicant*, Aldershot: Dartmouth

Cowan, D., Gilroy, R., Pantazis, C. and Bevan, M. (1999), *Allocating Social Housing to Sex Offenders*, York: Joseph Rowntree Foundation

Damer, S. (1974), 'Wine alley: the sociology of a dreadful enclosure', vol 22, *Sociological Review*, 221

Day, P., Henderson, D. and Klein, R. (1993), *Home Rules: Regulation and Accountability in Social Housing*, York: Joseph Rowntree Foundation

Department of the Environment (DoE) (1995a), *Our Future Homes: Opportunity, Choice and Responsibility*, London: HMSO

Department of the Environment (DoE) (1995b), *More Choice in the Social Rented Sector* Consultation Paper Linked to the Housing White Paper *Our Future Homes*, London: DoE

Department of the Environment (DoE) (1996), *Allocation of Housing by Local Authorities: Consultation Paper Linked to the Housing Bill*, London: DoE

Griffiths, M., Parker, J., Smith, R., Stirling, T. and Trott, T. (1996), *Community Lettings: Local Allocations Policies and Practices*, York: Joseph Rowntree Foundation

Hales, J. and Shah, S. (1990), *New Lettings by Housing Associations*, London: HMSO

Hoggett, P. (ed.) (1997a), *Contested Communities: Experiences, Struggles, Policies*, Bristol: Policy Press

Housing Corporation (1997a), *Registered Social Landlords in 1996: General Report*, London: Housing Corporation

Housing Corporation (1997b), *Performance Standards: Performance Standards and Regulatory Guidance for Registered Social Landlords*, London: Housing Corporation

Jones, A. (1997), *Can't Nominate or Won't Nominate?*, London: Anchor Trust

London Research Centre (1995), *The Use of the Private Rented Sector to Meet Housing Need: The First Year of the HAMA Initiative*, London: Housing Corporation

Malpass, P. (1997a), 'Introduction', in P. Malpass (ed), *Ownership, Control and Accountability: The New Governance of Housing*, Coventry: CIH

Malpass, P. (1997b), 'The local governance of housing', in P. Malpass (ed), *Ownership, Control and Accountability: The New Governance of Housing*, Coventry: CIH

Miller, K. (1992), 'Pointless waiting?', March/April, *Roof*, 34

Miller, K. (1996), 'They called it mission impossible', Sept/Oct, *Roof*, 32

Mullins, D., Niner, P. and Riseborough, M. (1995), *Evaluating Large Scale Voluntary Transfers of Local Authority Housing*, London: HMSO

Mullins, D. and Niner P. (1996), *Common Housing Registers: An Evaluation and Analysis of Current Practice*, London: The Housing Corporation

Mullins, D. and Niner, P. (1998), 'A prize of citizenship? Changing access to social housing', in A. Marsh and D. Mullins (eds), *Housing and Public Policy: Citizenship, Choice and Control*, Buckingham: Open University Press

National Federation of Housing Associations (NFHA) (1989), *Partners in Meeting Housing Need*, London: NFHA

Niner, P. (1987), 'Housing associations and ethnic minorities', in S. Smith and J. Mercer (eds), *New Perspectives on Race and Housing in Britain*, Glasgow: Centre for Housing Research, University of Glasgow

Niner, P. with Karn, V. (1985), *Housing Association Allocations: Achieving Racial Equality – A West Midlands Case Study*, London: The Runnymede Trust

Noble, D. (1981), 'From rules to discretion: the Housing Corporation', in M. Adler & S. Asquith (eds), *Discretion and Welfare*, London: Heinemann

Page, D. (1993), *Building for Communities: A Study of New Housing Association Estates*, York: Joseph Rowntree Foundation

Parker, J., Smith, R. and Williams, P. (1992), *Access, Allocations and Nominations: The Role of Housing Associations*, London: HMSO

Prescott-Clarke, P., Clemens, S. and Park, A. (1994), *Routes into Local Authority Housing*, London: HMSO

Wilcox, S. (1997a), *Housing Finance Review 1997/98*, York: Joseph Rowntree Foundation

Wilcox, S. (1997b), 'Incoherent rents', in S. Wilcox (ed.), *Housing Finance Review 1997/98*, York: Joseph Rowntree Foundation

Withers, P. and Randolph, B. (1994), *Access, Homelessness and Housing Associations*, NFHA Research Report 21, London: National Federation of Housing Associations

10 Importing Housing Need? Asylum-seekers and Other 'Persons from Abroad'

'What kind of country do we live in when frail old ladies are turned out of their home to make way for fit young asylum seekers?' (Woodward, 1998)

In 1986, 4,300 applications for asylum were made, of which 350 were accepted and 2,100 were granted 'exceptional leave to remain'.[1] In 1995, the number of applications for asylum had risen tenfold, although only 1,300 grants of asylum were made together with 4,400 grants of exceptional leave to remain. Generally, it seems that only about one in ten of the applications for asylum are now accepted. Nevertheless, about 57,000 applications for asylum were left outstanding for decision at the end of 1996. The numbers of non-asylum-seekers who seek to abuse the immigration system are generally unknown, although much political and media capital is made out of headline figures. Indeed, the social and legal construction of this category of abuse or bogus claimant is, in itself, unclear (which no doubt suits those employing this terminology).

Indeed, throughout the twentieth century (at least), the backdrop to any discussion of asylum and immigration has involved the extrapolation of a dichotomy between those who are perceived to be genuine and those who are bogus (for analysis, see Phillips & Hardy, 1997; Kennedy, 1999). Michael Howard, then Home Secretary, drew upon this distinction when, opening debate on his 1995 Asylum and Immigration Bill, he argued that Britain should be a 'haven' and not a 'honeypot' (Howard, 1995). In the 1990s, this dichotomy has been developed by legislators and the media, so that two major pieces of legislation have been passed through Parliament (Asylum and Immigration Appeals Act 1993; Asylum and Immigration Act 1996) and, at the time of writing, a further Asylum and Immigration Bill has been published with 138 clauses and 14 Schedules. Asylum and immigration legislation has become as frequent as criminal justice legislation. As with criminal justice, legislation in this area has restricted severely the liberty of those seeking asylum and immigration. Not only has this manifested itself in greater use of detention, but also severely restricted entitlements to the so-called safety net of welfare.

The words 'abuse' and 'bogus', when used in this context, actually refer to a much broader category of people than might initially be thought the case. The social construction of such terms has been inspired by concerns over employment, crime, and welfare. These have been willingly reported (and embellished) by the media. Often asylum-seekers and others are regarded as economic migrants – that is, those people who come to Britain to gain access to the supposedly generous welfare benefits (see, for example, Levy & Pukas, 1995; Rose & Austin, 1995). Sometimes they are individualized – for example in the report that Svetlana Stalin was living in Britain on benefits (Jones, 1996); and sometimes collectivized suggesting much greater abuse of the system (Burt & Purnell, 1997). Sometimes there is a suggestion that the system itself poses much greater threats to the nation's wealth because of other countries inflicting trade barriers when Britain 'gives houseroom' to these people (see Torode, 1996a, 1996b).

The pejorative language used in the debates has been part of a stigmatization process which has legitimized central government's attempts to subject many of these people to absolute penury. In earlier work, I have referred to this process as the social construction of a sub-category of persons who are inappropriate – or so morally blameworthy that the issue of resources becomes irrelevant – and this justifies penalizing legislation which affects the broader category of persons (Cowan, 1997, Ch. 7; 1998). Describing the effect of such policies, Rutherford uses the term 'eliminative ideal' – 'Put bluntly, the eliminative ideal strives to solve present and emerging problems by getting rid of troublesome and disagreeable people with methods which are lawful and widely supported' (1997, p. 117). Each piece of asylum and immigration legislation in the 1990s has included cutbacks on the welfare entitlements of those affected (although this might be regarded as the crescendo: see Dummett & Nicol, 1990). Crude distinctions have been adopted to manufacture categories of appropriate and inappropriate. We can see this most clearly in Conservative party conference speeches. For example, Peter Lilley, then Secretary of State for Social Security, made these comments at the Conservative Party Conference in 1993 (the 'back-to-basics' conference):

'We have all too many home grown scroungers, but it is beyond the pale when foreigners come here expecting handouts. . . .
'It's not so much a cook's tour but a crooks' tour. . . . Just imagine the advice you might find in a European phrasebook for Benefit Tourists.
'Wo is das Hotel?' – where is the housing department? 'Ou est le bureau de change?' – where do I cash my benefit cheque? 'Mio bambina e in Italia' – send child benefits to my family in Italy. 'Je suis un citoyen de l'Europe' – give me benefits or I'll take you to the European Court'.[2]

The link between access to housing, on the one hand, and asylum and immigration, on the other, has formed part of the debates for some time. Smith, for example, suggests that concerns over settlement patterns in the post-war period – 'residential segregation' – were used as justification for immigration controls (1993; see also Cowan, forthcoming):

'Political imagery associated with the organisation of residential space has, through its role in initiating and legitimizing policy change, contributed to the racial categorization of groups and individuals according to who they are or where they come from, where they live, and how they act or what they are presumed to think.' (Smith, 1993, p. 129)

In the 1990s, legislation turned to the restriction of asylum seekers' and others' rights of access to social housing. This was, in part, justified by, and predicated upon, the inability of a proportion of such people to pay for the accommodation (an irony, as the government had already removed their ability to pay by withdrawing entitlement to Housing Benefit). The combined effect of this legislation has left many living and begging on the streets (which, in turn, has linked in to the moral panic about begging: Bamber, 1999).

At first, the Conservative government's approach was compounded by the judiciary, which in fact extended the reach of the 'crackdown'. Subsequently, however, the judiciary have been portrayed by the media as countering the government's every move. The judiciary have been regarded as 'liberals' countermanding the instructions of their government masters (see Lightfoot & Prescott, 1995; Cohen, 1995). It is, however, apparent that the judiciary have only courted controversy when rights of appeal have been threatened (and, thus, the absolute penury of the asylum seekers has only been a subsidiary issue) – their concerns have been the traditionally legalistic ones about the withdrawal of due process rights, as opposed to the withdrawal of welfare rights.

The first part of this chapter outlines the effect of this welter of restricting legislation. So far, our approach has been to consider how the process of housing management discriminates in the implementation of housing policy. The apparent distinction between earlier chapters and this is that here the government itself has given authorities the ability to discriminate between particular types of applicant. The important point being made is that the principle of social housing being allocated according to housing need has been completely ignored because these people are regarded as *inappropriate*.

The second part of this chapter considers the effect this has had, or potentially will have, on the role and operation of housing management. More specifically, we will be discussing the inevitable requirement of housing managers to act as a further crutch to the immigration system. Local housing authorities and, to a certain extent, RSLs have become 'responsibilized' (Garland, 1996) within the state immigration machinery (see also Ginsburg, 1992, pp. 160–1). It is argued that this has affected *all* welfare claimants because all such people now have to show that they are *not* asylum-seekers *nor* 'persons from abroad' *nor* 'illegal' immigrants.

In the third part, we will consider judicial pronouncements that have uncovered and extrapolated a statutory means to provide support for those affected by the restrictive legislation. These did seem to undermine the Conservative government's legislative ambition, but the cases show a deep-rooted dissatisfaction amongst the judiciary, together with retrenchment, which has caused much uncertainty within the system.

It is this uncertainty which the New Labour government has sought to eradicate in its current Parliamentary Bill. In the final part of this chapter, we will analyse the new housing provisions and the way the Home Office intends them to operate. In this part, we will also consider the media's construction of the need for further legislation. This is an important – indeed, crucial – part of the examination of the Parliamentary process because the media has controlled the discourse of asylum and immigration, or as Mathieson has put it, the media 'directs and controls or disciplines our *consciousness*' (1997, p. 231). Needless to say, the media's concentration has been upon the *inappropriate* and has thus provided further justification for the New Labour programme of restrictions.

10.1   Need *v.* Abuse

In 1992, asylum-seekers were entitled to an exceptional grant payment of 90 per cent Income Support that also enabled them to claim Housing Benefit. They were entitled to claim housing through local authorities' waiting lists as well as through the homelessness legislation. If successful, they were (in those pre-*Awua* days), or should have been, provided with long-term accommodation. If their asylum application was unsuccessful, they would be deported and thus lose their right to accommodation.

In 1992, those non-asylum seekers coming to England and Wales from countries which were members of the European Community were entitled to apply for housing as homeless persons, as well as to apply for benefits and housing through the waiting list. In 1992, other non-asylum-seekers who entered the country from abroad, usually on the basis that they were not entitled to public funds, were nevertheless entitled to apply for public housing as a homeless person (although not through the waiting list).

Since 1992, these rules have altered radically to the extent that all welfare entitlements have been withdrawn from a substantial proportion of these people. The shift towards housing exclusion has been swift and extreme, but there has also been a welter of legislation, quasi-legislation, and case law which has propelled it. This shift has been parallelled by a Circular from the Housing Corporation reminding RSLs that they 'should carefully consider' whether they should accommodate persons from abroad who are ineligible for Housing Benefit.

Table 10.1 overleaf provides a chronology of the most significant of these events. The table shows, in basic form, the lengths to which successive governments have gone to withdraw assistance from these people. The result of this chronology, in terms of the structure of access to social housing, is that we can no longer openly argue that social housing is allocated according to housing need (even if that position was

Table 10.1   Chronology of events impacting upon the housing rights of asylum-seekers and other persons from abroad

Date	Event	Effect
1992	Asylum and Immigration Bill	Potentially restricting rights to housing of asylum-seekers and dependents. Lack of Parliamentary time forced withdrawal prior to election
7 April 1993	*R* v. *Secretary of State for the Environment ex parte Tower Hamlets LBC* [1993] 25 HLR 524	Local authorities under a duty to inquire into immigration status of applicants. No duties owed to 'illegal immigrants'
	Asylum and Immigration Act 1993	Restricts rights under homelessness legislation of asylum-seekers and dependents.
6–8 October 1993	Conservative Party Conference	'Clampdown' on benefit tourism promised
1 August 1994	The Income-related Benefits Schemes (Miscellaneous Amendments) (No 3) Regulations 1994, SI 1994/ 1807	'Habitual residence' test introduced, together with 'persons from abroad' test, into Housing Benefit eligibility
5 February 1996	Social Security (Persons from Abroad) Miscellaneous Amendment Regulations 1996, SI 1996/30	Asylum seekers ineligible for all social security benefits unless they applied for asylum at port of entry
21 June 1996	*R* v. *Secretary of State for Social Security ex parte B* (1997) 29 HLR 129	SI 1996/30 *ultra vires* the Secretary of State
	Asylum and Immigration Act 1996	'person[s] subject to immigration control' not entitled to local authority accommodation through waiting list, ineligible through homelessness legislation, unless of a class specified by the Secretary of State; unable to work; enabling power to disentitle such persons from claiming benefit
19 August 1996	The Housing Accommodation and Homelessness (Persons subject to Immigration Control) Order 1996, SI 1996/ 1982	Specifies 'persons from abroad' who are eligible together with others who are ineligible

Table 10.1 (cont.)

Date	Event	Effect
19 August 1996	Housing Act 1996	'persons from abroad' not eligible to appear on waiting list nor for assistance as homeless; other persons subject to immigration control ineligible
January 1997	Housing Corporation Circular, R3–04/97, 'Lettings to Certain Persons from Abroad'	RSLs advised that they 'should carefully consider' whether they should accommodate persons from abroad who are ineligible
20 January 1997	Allocation of Housing Regulations 1996, SI 1996, 2753; Homelessness Regulations 1996, SI 1996/ 2754	Specify eligibility and ineligibility under Housing Act 1996
17 February 1997	*R* v. *Hammersmith and Fulham LBC ex parte M* (1998) 30 HLR 10	Asylum-seekers entitled to 'care and attention' under s 21(1)(a), National Assistance Act 1948, including food and accommodation
5 March 1997	Special Grant (no 24)	'Asylum Seekers Accommodation Special Grant' to be paid to local authorities incurring expense as a result of *ex parte M*
28 March–1 April 1997	Allocation of Housing and Homelessness (Amendment) Regulations 1997	Amends SI 1996/2753, 2754
27 August 1997	Allocation of Housing and Homelessness (Amendment) (No2) Regulations 1997, SI 1997/2046	Amendment in favour of certain persons from Montserrat who became eligible
4 February 1998	The Housing Accommodation and Homelessness (Persons Subject to Immigration Control) (Amendment) Order 1998, SI 1998/139	Specifies others to whom the local authority is entitled to grant a tenancy or licence of their own property; including asylum-seekers owed a duty under National Assistance Act 1948 and those owed a duty under Housing Act 1996.
27 July 1998	Publication of New Labour's White Paper, *Fairer, Faster, Firmer*	Voucher system proposed for accommodation, food and other living essentials
9 February 1999	Publication of Asylum and Immigration Bill	Implements the White Paper

sustainable). Here, it is most apparent that social housing access has been denied on the basis of (lack of) resources.

Asylum-seekers and their Dependents

The current position is that asylum-seekers are ineligible to appear on the local authority's housing register, as well as ineligible for assistance under the homelessness part of the Housing Act 1996, unless they are in a class specified in regulations (in which case they are eligible). The only asylum-seekers able to appear on a housing register are essentially those whose claims have already been determined in their favour either completely, or because they have been given exceptional leave to enter, or those who have leave to enter, and remain (reg 4, SI 1996/2753).

The same persons are also entitled to make a homelessness application with one major exception. Those who apply for asylum at the 'port of entry' are also eligible (those who apply 'in country' are ineligible). The homelessness legislation was made to tally with Housing Benefit regulations in this respect and, thus, those eligible under that legislation are also entitled to benefits, and vice versa. Eligibility ceases when a negative decision is made by the Immigration and Nationality Department (IND); so, if the asylum-seeker wishes to appeal against the decision, they have no entitlement to accommodation nor welfare benefits.

However, even those asylum-seekers who are eligible under the homelessness legislation have restrictions attached to their entitlement. If the asylum-seeker has 'any accommodation in the United Kingdom, however temporary, available for his occupation', that person is ineligible. Although there was some doubt, it is now accepted that those eligible without any accommodation in the United Kingdom are entitled to be rehoused as with other applicants (see *R* v. *Kensington & Chelsea RBC ex parte Korneva* (1997) 29 HLR 709).

The rationale for the homelessness eligibility criterion was, as suggested already, to bring this legislation into line with entitlement to Housing Benefit (see, for example, Standing Committees G, 19 March 1996, col 742, *per* David Curry MP). There was an attempt to introduce the exclusion of 'in-country' asylum applicants through regulations in early 1996. This was prefaced by a report by the Social Security Advisory Committee (SSAC, 1996) together with a report by the House of Commons Social Security Committee (1996). These, supplemented by a House of Commons debate on the regulations, provide ample evidence of the government's case (HC Debs, Vol 269, cols 331–345, 11 January 1996).[3]

The government's case was as follows: about 90 per cent of applications for asylum were unsuccessful; the vast majority were economic migrants; 'the current benefit arrangements encourage abuses of the asylum system . . . [which] are detrimental to both the taxpayer (who foots the bill) and to genuine refugees (who suffer from delays created by unfounded applications and appeals)' (SSAC, para. 11); those who undertake to enter the UK on the understanding that they should have no recourse to public funds 'should be held to that undertaking whether they make an asylum claim or not' (*ibid*). Benefit was cut off after the first decision, because:

> 'under the [former] rules, asylum-seekers are allowed to retain benefit during an appeal. Not surprisingly, the vast majority of asylum-seekers appeal against rejection. Yet 96 per cent of their appeals turn out to be unfounded.' (HC Debs, col 332, *per* Peter Lilley MP)

This would also bring asylum-seekers into line with British citizens when their benefit claims were rejected. The benefit budget was to save £200 million 'in the long term' (col. 335).

The Social Security Committee and Social Security Advisory Committee were heavily critical, for, they argued, these proposals, whilst aimed at the fraudulent, were also admitted to affect the genuine: 'It would be difficult to overstate the degree of alarm expressed by our respondents, and disbelief that the Government would willingly countenance leaving such people with no income to buy food or the means to house themselves' (SSAC, 1996, para. 24). Furthermore, it was noted that the government's belief that they would be able to save £200 million was unlikely, bearing in mind the greater administrative requirements of the regulations (para. 90)

The Court of Appeal found the regulations to be *ultra vires* on the basis that, effectively, they meant that asylum-seekers would be unable to exercise their due process rights if they were denied entitlement to benefit:

> 'Parliament cannot have intended a significant number of genuine asylum seekers to be impaled on the horns of so intolerable a dilemma: the need either to abandon their claims to refugee status or alternatively to maintain them as best they can but in a state of utter destitution. Primary legislation alone could in my judgment achieve that sorry state of affairs.' *R* v. *Secretary of State for Social Security ex parte B* (1997) 29 HLR 129)

The Asylum and Immigration Act 1996 and Housing Act 1996 were, in consequence, widened to achieve that sorry state of affairs.[4] The decision to allow benefits only to those who made an asylum application at 'port of entry', and disallow benefits to those who apply 'in country', is a crude tool to weed out the bogus from the genuine based upon no empirical evidence of where the supposed, so-called abuse occurred. It was simply assumed by the government that those who applied for asylum at the port of entry were most likely to be genuine. The facts of *R* v. *Hammersmith & Fulham LBC ex parte M* (1998) 30 HLR 10 provide an illustration of just how crude this distinction is. Each of the applicants had applied for asylum either the same day as they arrived in England, or the following day. As none of the applicants had applied at their entry point, they were denied benefits irrespective of the genuineness of their claims. One slept rough under Waterloo Bridge and another 'had not eaten for some time, he was friendless, penniless and completely destitute'.

Other 'Persons from Abroad'

Peter Lilley's speech to the Conservative party conference in 1993 concerned what has become known as benefit tourism – that is, persons coming to Britain to take advantage of the supposedly generous welfare benefits. Some months earlier, in fact, the Court of Appeal had made the first dent on this subject in the homelessness legislation.

In *Tower Hamlets LBC* v. *Secretary of State for the Environment* (1993) 25 HLR 524, legal counsel agreed between themselves that illegal entrants (that is, those who enter the country clandestinely; those who obtain leave to enter as a result of false and deceitful statements as to the availability of accommodation) were owed no duty under the homelessness legislation. It was also conceded that it is the duty of the local authority to make enquiries as to the immigration status of an individual, which might include enquiries of the Home Office. Furthermore, it was conceded that the local authority were under a duty to report to the Home Office that a person might be an illegal entrant. In fact, the only point of argument in the case was whose responsibility it was to make a decision as to the immigration status of the applicant. The Court of Appeal decided that it was for the local housing authority (who should then report their decision to the Home Office). This was despite the fact that 'immigration decisions are, plainly, decisions for the immigration authorities' (at p. 531, *per* Lord Donaldson MR). Stuart-Smith LJ felt that this was the most commendable solution because 'it is the housing authority . . . who will most probably discover that there has been deception by the immigrant in relation to availability of accommodation' (at p. 530). From what were these points of law drawn? No process of construction justified them, as Donaldson admitted; rather:

> 'It can only, I think, be the inference, derived from common sense and fortified by the Immigration Rules and *R* v. *Hillingdon LBC ex parte Streeting* [1980] 1 WLR 1425, that Parliament cannot have intended to require housing authorities to house those who enter the country unlawfully.' (at p. 532)

The government retained these exclusions in the 1996 Act. A Home Office press release talked about an 'efficiency scrutiny' which would cause £100 million of savings, including a procedure for staff to notify the IND about 'suspected illegal immigrants' on the following rationale: 'Resources must be spent upon those who have a right to live here and who contribute to our society'.

Other 'persons from abroad' who are not entitled to assistance from the housing authority through the register or the homelessness legislation are those not 'habitually resident' in the Common Travel Area[5] and those European Economic Area nationals who are required to leave the UK by the Secretary of State (the latter is a narrow category and not pursued below for this reason: see *Chief Adjudication Officer* v. *Wolke* [1998] 1 All ER 129). Similar regulations have been in place for Housing Benefit since August 1994 (see Adler, 1995; Bolderson & Roberts, 1995 for discussion). The DSS justified the Housing Benefit regulations as 'part of a process of narrowing access to benefit for people the taxpayer should not be asked to support' but they admitted that they did not have 'reliable estimates' of those who would be affected (about 5,000 EEA nationals, it was thought, might be affected: Explanatory Memorandum from the DSS, SSAC, 1994, paras 3 & 12 respectively). The Social Security Advisory Committee commented that:

'The basic difficulty with an habitual residence test was summed up by our correspondents very succinctly – it allows for the construction of a case for or against the claimant in almost every circumstance. . . . [W]e take the view that such a complex and subjective test would inevitably lead to cases of doubtful adjudication, refusal of benefit and consequent hardship.' (SSAC, 1994, para. 34)

The evidence suggests that the SSAC may well have been correct (see NACAB, 1996; CPAG, 1995). The test certainly appears to have caught a significant number of British citizens (up to 31 March 1996, 14,032 EEA nationals and 9,738 British citizens had failed the test). Nevertheless, the DSS refused to change the test because EEA nationals, particularly (apparently) Spaniards were claiming benefit: 'The news had got around in Europe, and more and more were coming. Unless and until something was done, the problem would not have diminished or remained static, but would have grown' (HC Debs, Vol 276, col 881 (29 April 1996), *per* Roger Evans MP).

The habitual residence test is subject to a number of exceptions (to make it accord with European Law as far as possible). Nowhere is the test defined, however. This startling fact is compounded by the current CoG which blandly states that it 'is intended to convey a degree of permanence in the person's residence in the Common Travel Area' (para. 4.16). Income Support Commissioners have generally refused to give minimum periods of time after which a person's residence is sufficiently permanent for it to become 'habitual' (although a UK citizen might do so after three to six months settled residence in the UK: CIS/1067/1995 (Howell)). It has been suggested that the residence must have been viable without resort to benefits (*ibid*), although subsequent decisions have disagreed with this (CIS/2326/1995 (Mesher)).

In *Nessa* v. *Chief Adjudication Officer*, *The Times*, 11 February 1998, the Court of Appeal, with Thorpe LJ dissenting, argued that presence for some appreciable period of time was necessary before a person could be habitually resident. Morritt LJ argued that:

'It does not seem to me that physical presence in the United Kingdom together with a settled intention to remain but without the lapse of any appreciable period of time since arrival is best calculated to introduce the restriction intended. The additional requirement for the lapse of an appreciable period of time since arrival adds to the fact of physical presence a further fact more easily ascertainable than and confirmatory of a settled intention to remain.'

So, this notion of habitual residence, in fact, operates to exclude any person willy-nilly on the basis of lack of residence in a particular area. It operates quite irrespective of that person's housing need – indeed, assessments of housing need become irrelevant in such cases.

10.2 Issues of Implementation

Asylum and immigration law is complex (something of an under-statement). HPU, Housing Benefit, and housing register officers are now required to apply it. Few officers are qualified to do so; some may have been on training courses, although the value of such courses (often for a day or an afternoon) might be limited. Waddington also argues that the authority is required to ask unanswerable questions for, in order to prove their status, applicants will have to prove a negative (1998, p. 223). The body to whom the authority must turn for assistance in individual cases is the Immigration Status Enquiries Unit, which is also the body responsible for deporting individuals. Thus, complexity, confusion, and these unanswerable questions effectively mean that between the authorities and the Home Office there will be 'organizational interdependence'. Neither body can function effectively without the other (*ibid*, pp. 221–2).

This panoptic surveillance of housing and welfare applicants ensures that social housing forms part of the web of social control. In the *Tower Hamlets* case, Stuart-Smith LJ justified this extension of state control by arguing that: 'It is the housing authority rather than the immigration authority who will most probably discover that there has been a deception by the immigrant . . .' (at p. 530). This is the fear – the actual or perceived failure of the immigration service to control and uncover abuse or bogus applicants then requires other agencies to assist them in their responsibility (see Garland, 1996 for similar argument in the context of criminal justice). These processes actually create an excluding community of welfare authorities (an irony in itself), which operate to *deny* entitlement and *deter* any application (see Carlen, 1994, where these terms are employed in the context of youth homelessness).

However, this excluding community operates on a much broader level for these events affect *all* welfare applicants, in tune with, for example, generated concerns about Housing Benefit fraud. This arises because local authorities (and the Housing Corporation) have been given a major role to play in promoting 'equality of opportunity, and good relations, between persons of different racial groups' (s. 71, Race Relations Act 1976). It is difficult to see how this might be done in the current state, particularly when passports and documentation have to be checked but not in all cases. The answer seems to be that all welfare applicants should be required to provide proof of identity *and* nationality – to adopt Hillyard's evocative phrase, all welfare applicants have become part of the 'suspect community' (1993). If they are unable to do so, they will be denied entitlement. Good practice guidance suggests that applicants be given the opportunity to withdraw their applications if their status needs to be checked with the Home Office (Shelter & CRE, 1997). If authorities accept that guidance then many may be deterred from making an application as good practice.

Housing Benefit entitlement is a key element in the welfare restrictions discussed in the previous part. It is also a significant method through which central government is able to control the decision-making of local authorities and RSLs in this area. Local authorities and RSLs (not to mention private-sector landlords) who provide accommodation to those in these groups will simply find themselves out of pocket when accommodation is allocated but Housing Benefit is unavailable. Local authorities and RSLs can hardly afford this in this era of financial controls and performance indicators. Thus, they are forced (if need be) to cooperate with central government. Indeed, rumours abounded that as soon as the 1996 welfare controls were implemented, asylum-seekers were immediately evicted (see, for example, Meikle, 1997a). Fears have also been expressed that the benefit cuts together with cuts to housing rights were brought in with inadequate support systems which are now at breaking point (Meikle, 1997b).

The element of control is further exacerbated by the inability of local authorities to make any decision without confirmation from the IND. One might assume that the IND would respond suitably quickly to requests made by local authorities. That appears not to be the case. Limited analysis of the 1991 CoG found that, in two case study areas, only two out of 50 replies had been received in one area over a period of a year and 30 cases were outstanding in the other (Mullins *et al.*, 1996, para. 4.47). The facts in *R* v. *Brent LBC ex parte Miyanger* (1997) 29 HLR 628 provide further evidence of extreme delays which caused the court to issue mandamus against the council, partly because 'there is no information as to when the Secretary of State's response is likely to be available' (at p. 632). Local authorities are unable to make a decision (and not even able to start their enquiries) until they have the Home Office response; if it does not come within a reasonable period the authority will be subject to mandamus. The authority itself is truly caught between a rock and a hard place.

10.3 Legal Innovations

Other than the mainstream Housing Acts, advisers have a considerable amount of other legislation which can assist applicants requiring accommodation. It has never been disputed that the Children Act 1989 – under which those children in need (s. 17(X)) are entitled to be provided with accommodation by local authorities (s. 20) – will assist those under 18. That Act also effectively provides for families to be housed together. Such a lacuna seems to have passed the Conservative administration by in their attempts to exclude housing entitlements from asylum-seekers and other persons from abroad. What use of the 1989 Act does, though, is change the sphere of decision-making and the *locus* of the obligation. Under the Children Act, duties are incumbent upon the social services department to perform (and presumably cannot be referred to the housing department under s. 27, as that department is expressly under no obligation).

In *R* v. *Hammersmith and Fulham LBC ex parte M* (1998) 30 HLR 10, the Court of Appeal held that the National Assistance Act 1948, s 21(1)(a) was applicable in some asylum-seeker cases. That section reads as follows:

> '[local authorities are under a duty to provide] (a) residential accommodation for persons aged 18 or over who by reason of age, illness, disability or any other circumstances are in need of care and attention which is not available to them. . . .'

Circulars provide that local authorities come under a duty 'to provide temporary accommodation for persons who are in urgent need thereof in circumstances where the need for that accommodation could not reasonably have been foreseen' (LAC 93(10), para. 2(2); this is discussed in Cowan, 1995). This Circular was a direct result of the lack of accommodation provisions in the community care legislation and, in fact, repeats the homelessness legislation as existed between 1948–77.[6]

The Court of Appeal held that 'any other circumstances' in the 1948 Act included some asylum-seekers because of the 'problems under which they are labouring':

> 'In addition to the lack of food and accommodation is to be added their inability to speak the language, their ignorance of this country and the fact they have been subject to the stress of coming to this country in circumstances which at least involve their contending to be refugees. Inevitably the combined effect of these factors with the passage of time will produce one or more of the conditions specifically referred to in section 21(1)(a).' (at p. 20)

The repercussions of this decision are still being worked out in the courts. Some backtracking has taken place perhaps because, as Carnwath J put it, 'I feel instinctively that the provisions of the 1948 Act were probably not designed to cover the situation which has now arisen': *R* v. *Newham LBC ex parte Gorenkin* (1998) 30 HLR 278. It has been successfully argued that, if an asylum seeker has accommodation, food and other services cannot be provided under the Act (it must all be provided as a composite service:

R v. *Newham LBC ex parte Gorenkin* (1998) 30 HLR 278. On the other hand, if accommodation is provided under the Act, no food or other services need to be provided as well: *R* v. *Newham LBC ex parte Medical Foundation for the Care of Victims of Torture* (1998) HLR 955. It has also been successfully argued that authorities are not entitled to provide cash payments to asylum-seekers in order to buy food; rather, the authority can issue vouchers or provide supermarket food free: *R* v. *Secretary of State for Health ex parte Hammersmith and Fulham LBC, The Times*, CA, 9 September 1998. Illegal entrants are not entitled to the benefits of this relief (*R* v. *Brent LBC ex parte D* (1998) 1 CCLR 234), although a person who lawfully overstays their permission to remain in the UK may be (*R* v. *Lambeth LBC ex parte Sarhangi, The Times*, 9 December 1998). In one case, the courts abrogated their jurisdiction to the relevant Minister because the Secretary of State provided the necessary funds and partly because the question concerned the construction of the Secretary of State's own guidance (two reasons which surely make an impartial judgment most important): *Ex parte P, The Times*, QBD, 31 March 1998. Despite the universalism inherent in the concept of need, local authorities are entitled to refuse to provide accommodation where the applicant 'had brought the problem on his own head' by being evicted from bed and breakfast accommodation (*R* v. *Kensington and Chelsea RBC ex parte Kujtim, The Times*, 2 April 1999).

Court action was also threatened over the quality of food provided by the authorities ('A nutritionist had examined the food and concluded it provided only 60 per cent of a man's daily needs and 80 per cent of a woman's': Donegan, 1997; see also Brogan, 1997b). The government, 'bought off' challenges by the local authorities (Brogan, 1997a) by providing a special grant covering expenditure under s. 21 from August 1996 to March 1997 (which was then extended).

As the majority of asylum-seekers apparently settle in London, and are concentrated in a few boroughs, the majority of the burden has fallen on those borough authorities. Equally, the type of accommodation required to be provided (bed and breakfast accommodation 'on a considerable scale': *ex parte Hammersmith and Fulham LBC*) in those boroughs is expensive. Only in April 1998 did the government sanction the use of local authority property as accommodation which might be used to house such people under these duties (see The Housing Accommodation and Homelessness (Persons Subject to Immigration Control) (Amendment) Order 1998, SI 1998/139). Accessing this accommodation requires the social services departments to negotiate such access with their housing department. Also, some such accommodation, in which persons are provided a package of services, apparently is hard to find ('We have run out of accommodation. We have 444 asylum seekers in 40 locations inside and outside [Westminster]. We are often forced to put them three to a room': Travis, 1997). Authorities have therefore sought to 'export' asylum-seekers to other areas where such accommodation is also cheaper. Eastbourne Council's leader apparently argued, in a fit of nimbyism, that,

'If you get a large number of people coming into Eastbourne it could cause us problems, for instance in housing our own people' (*Evening Argus*, 1997).

10.4   The Asylum and Immigration Bill 1999

Justification and Proposals[7]

'Piecemeal and ill-considered changes over the last 20 years have left our immigration control struggling to meet [ ] expectations. . . . [T]he system has become too complex and too slow, and huge backlogs have developed. Perversely, it is often the genuine applicants who have suffered, while abusive claimants and racketeers have profited.'

The current arrangements for supporting asylum seekers are a shambles. New arrangements are needed to ensure that genuine asylum seekers are not left destitute, but which minimise the attractions of the UK to economic migrants.' (Home Office, 1998 – preface by Home Secretary, Jack Straw)

There is no doubt that the current system of supporting asylum-seekers and other persons from abroad are 'a shambles', caused mainly by judicial whim that 'produced an unplanned and unwelcome new burden on local authorities and local taxpayers' (para. 3.11). However, the White Paper issued in July 1998 was also predicated on the familiar belief that 'the asylum system is being abused by those seeking to migrate for purely economic reasons. Many claims are simply a tissue of lies' (para. 1.14). Yet, remarkably, the document also accepted that abusive applications 'are difficult to assess accurately'. Instead, it concentrates on the numbers of applicants rejected and deported (paras 1.15–1.21), as if rejection automatically implies systemic abuse. Specific examples of abuse provided in the White Paper, such as human 'trafficking', clandestine entry and forged documentation, can each be differently constructed as examples of desperation, ignorance, and need on the part of the asylum seeker. The White Paper offers such casual empiricism for its assertion, in the form of short case studies, which only serves to highlight further the absence of rigorous analysis.

The White Paper proposed that the underlying basis for support of asylum seekers should be a safety net in cases of genuine hardship, 'in a way which minimises the incentive for abuse by those who do not really need the support or who would make an unfounded asylum application in order to obtain the provision' (para. 8.19). A voucher-based system was regarded as better than cash-based because it 'is less attractive and provides less of a financial inducement' (para. 8.20). Accommodation would be provided but on a 'no choice basis' (para. 8.21; they 'would be expected to take what was available, and would not be able to pick and choose what was available': para. 8.22). To oversee this new system, the

White Paper proposed a new national body which would contract with 'a range of providers'.

Controlling Discourse

The White Paper's assertion of systemic abuse of the system by economic migrants and others mirrors the media's discourse, which has controlled debates about asylum and immigration throughout the 1990s. Tuitt refers to this concern in her discussion of the debates leading to the Asylum and Immigration Appeals Act 1993: 'More worrying still [than the lack of empirical evidence] was the demonstrably poor understanding of the political and economic conditions which affect most asylum seekers, which might lead to their unfairly being characterised as fraudulent' (1996, p. 147). Similar considerations permeated the debates about the Asylum and Immigration Act 1996 (see Cowan, 1997, pp. 154–160).

In this section, I will draw upon newspaper reports[8] in the period 23 November 1998 to 10 January 1999. This period begins with the Queen's Speech, which announced government's intention to bring forward a Bill in this area, and ends with the publication of the Bill itself. In this period, I argue, the media has reconstructed the asylum seeker and other persons from abroad as *inappropriate*, or so morally blameworthy as to justify the removal of the obligation to provide welfare assistance. Thus, the principle of need is subverted to our whipped-up concerns about assistance going to the inappropriate. Even further, I argue that in the same periods in 1993 and 1996, exactly the same observations could have been made. It may well be argued that the Home Office has carefully orchestrated public debate through a series of press releases which subsequently form the basis for media reporting. The casual empiricism of the White Paper is therefore bolstered and regarded as unarguable – indeed, the only way to argue the opposite is to embrace the discourse of inappropriateness itself.

In what follows, I want to refer to four particular strands of this media reporting. This is a division made for convenience sake, and the strands do overlap. Not all of the reports relate to asylum and immigration, however these have been the major stories (judging by column inches and headlines):

- The first strand of reports relate to concerns about the influx of asylum seekers, particularly after the Archbishop of Canterbury used his New Year address to appeal for greater understanding of the problems they face (see Williams, 1998a; Williams, 1999b; Bamber & Baldwin, 1999). In some reports, the rising numbers are specifically related to concerns about costs to the taxpayer: 'The cost of supporting the colossal system which processes asylum applications could reach £3 billion this year, the equivalent of 1.5p on income tax, official figures disclose' (Williams, 1999a); 'Asylum seekers £300 million handout' (Williams & Purnell, 8 December 1998); 'Refugee rise brings 7pc increase in homeless'

(Hetherington, 1998). The 'soaring numbers of asylum seekers' are specifically blamed for the major housing crisis in London (Salman, 1999).

In a special report about the 12,000 Somalis living in Ealing, West London, concerns are expressed by the *Daily Mail* about drug taking and female circumcision, but mostly about the cost to the taxpayer, expressed in economic terms: 'There are 12,000 Somalis living in Ealing, each costing taxpayers enough to keep 80 children alive in Africa. So are our well-meaning attempts to help third world victims of oppression doing them, as well as us, more harm than good?' (Goodwin, 1999). The *Evening Standard* linked the costs of housing asylum-seekers with 'massive' cuts in grant aid given to the arts (Blamires, 1999).

- A strand relates to the relationship between crime and asylum-seekers. One set refers to the concerns exposed by the White Paper, for example about sham marriages (Taylor, 1999), fake asylum certificates (Bamber, 1998), and fake passports (Davenport, 1999). A further set seeks directly to link criminal activity with asylum seekers and thus justify further controls and limits on the immigration system – 'Brutal crimes of the asylum seekers' was a *Daily Mail* front page headline designed for maximum impact (Williams, 1998b); and 'Asylum drug den' (Craven, 1998). Then there is Simon Heffer, the *Daily Mail* columnist, who argues that most beggars seen during his Christmas shopping were 'East European vagrants who have moved on to London after years of picking pockets on the Paris Metro' (1998).

- Third, there are a number of reports concerning housing. Despite the ineligibility of most asylum seekers from appearing on the housing register, the *Daily Mail* reported that Hammersmith and Fulham LBC had rearranged its priorities and awarded asylum seekers an extra 75 points: 'Asylum seekers took my place on council house list' (Clark, 1998). This meant that a 'working mother won't get her new home for Christmas'. Fuelling this inaccurate report, Sir Norman Fowler, Shadow Home Secretary, is reported as saying that

> 'This issue raises serious questions as many of those seeking asylum in this country are pursuing bogus claims. It cannot be right that they should go straight to the top of a housing list.'

Some reports relate to the problems caused by the 1948 Act, and particularly the decanting of asylum seekers to seaside areas. So, for example, 'there is an increasing resentment in Dover, which considers itself a reluctant host to the new arrivals and regards their descriptions of harrowing events in their former homelands with some scepticism' (Millward, 1998; also Johnston, 1998). The *Daily Mail* drew attention to a 'holiday camp for refugees', linked with local people's complaints about a 'spate of vandalism and petty crime recently in the area'

(Woodward, 1999); additionally, that organ referred to 'frail old ladies [being] turned out of their home to make way for fit young asylum seekers' (Woodward, 1998) and widows being 'ordered out' so that asylum seekers could move in (Sawyer & Maguire, 1998) – apparently, some landlords decided that it was more profitable to provide accommodation for asylum seekers under the 1948 Act.

Most fury was, however, vented when an NHS hospital opened two wards which were then used to provide accommodation for 60 Romanian female refugees and their children (their male partners having been placed in a detention centre). The wards had been used in 1903 as a smallpox isolation unit (Carroll, 1998), but the tenor of the reporting suggested that hospital wards which could have been used for NHS patients were being used instead for Romanian gipsies: 'They couldn't find my dying granny a bed but they open the wards for gipsies' (Davies & Judd, 1998); 'Hospital houses asylum seekers' (Rowinski, 1998); 'Hospital wards open for illegal refugees' (Waddell & Laville, 1998); 'Protest as empty ward used to house Romanian refugees' (Carroll, 1998). Later in the same month, the *Daily Telegraph* recorded the desire by some of the 'Romanian stowaways' to be sent home. The local Labour MP, Howard Stoate, is recorded as arguing that 'If these people are prepared to return voluntarily to their country of origin, it would seem to suggest that they are not asylum seekers fleeing persecution' (although being forcibly separated from one's partner and then locked in a detention centre, as well as being the subjects of media antipathy, may well have been regarded by these people as worse than persecution at home) (Piening, 1998).

• The fourth strand is the tenor of the reports about the new Bill itself. Just nine of the 138 clauses and 14 Schedules to the Bill relate to housing. Yet, this was the focus of most newspaper reporting of the Bill (although extra reporting referred to other parts of the Bill: Johnston, 1999a; Travis, 1999b), reflecting a Home Office press release issued the day the Bill was published (048/99, 9 February 1999: 'New asylum arrangements will discourage abuse'). Indeed, the same day, *The Guardian* included the results of an opinion poll which recorded a majority backing the withdrawal of welfare benefits to asylum seekers (Travis, 1999a).

Voluntary arrangements between councils are to be set up to enable best use to be made of vacant council accommodation. However, the Home Secretary does take power to force councils to provide accommodation (clause 81) and this was the focus of commentary in the examined newspapers (respectively Johnston, 1999b; Ford, 1999; Travis, 1999c; Clark, 1999). In a 'leader' in *The Times*, it was argued that: 'Most council taxpayers in those areas [which formerly provided accommodation to asylum seekers] will support Mr Straw's proposal to deny migrants a choice of accommodation'. Those asylum-seekers who do not continue to occupy the accommodation will automatically have their benefits withdrawn. A subsequent report in *The Times* referred to the creation of a new currency termed the 'Asylo' – the belief that the vouchers provided to asylum seekers would be sold ('the fraud in tokens could reach £20 million a year': Kennedy, 1999).

Some of the newspaper reports are wildly inaccurate; some take partial views of more complex structures (like the reporting of the Bill); some, like the *Daily Mail*, have a particular opinion about asylum generally and their reports follow a familiar pattern. The singular feature of the vast proportion of these reports throughout the examined newspapers, however, is their *negativity*. Asylum-seekers are constructed as 'fraudulent' and/or 'bogus', the system is constructed as designed to be abused. The assumption is that economic migration is rife and that we (the taxpayers and local taxpayers) should not pay for it. All of this legitimizes the government's penalizing response. Whilst all media harrowingly reported the civil wars in Europe, the former USSR and Africa, where the refugees are produced, that same media has constructed those same refugees as a drain on our resources. Against this barrage of negativity, the assumption of social housing being allocated according to need has simply been ignored.

Conclusion

The result of the Conservative administration's attempts to save money by restricting (and, in some cases removing) the rights to housing and benefit of asylum-seekers and others were, to a certain extent, thwarted by the courts. Rumours currently surfacing are that costs to authorities of providing accommodation and services under the National Assistance Act 1948 have reached somewhere in the region of £125 million per annum. This does not account for the increased administrative costs involved in the surveillance of applications from those affected, together with the increased time it will take to assess applications. Even before the impact of the 1948 Act was known, the savings from these restrictions were not thought to be that much in excess of what is currently being paid out. When it is appreciated that the total benefit budget is around £80–90 billion, the savings seem hardly worthwhile, particularly when authorities are required to fight fraud and abuse of the system. On this basis, it can be argued that asylum-seekers and others affected have been sacrificed at the altar of good copy and xenophobia. Much the same is true of the New Labour proposals, both in terms of their production by a government willing to adopt the unproven assumption of wide-scale bogus and fraudulent use of the immigration system, and its consumption by a willing media.

It has been argued that bogus asylum-seekers and other persons from abroad form a category of persons who are socially constructed to be so inappropriate as to cause the issue of supply and resources to be irrelevant.

What becomes relevant in these cases is the need for a clampdown or war to be waged against these people. This clampdown/war affects *all* asylum seekers and other persons from abroad, whether or not they are bogus or fraudulent (terms which are left undefined for convenience sake).

What does all this tell us about housing need? Housing need has been a neat but meaningless concept. This fact has enabled successive governments to pay lip service to a welfarist principle whilst at the same time providing them with the necessary degree of lattitude to ignore need whenever they deem necessary. For this reason, our adherence to the concept of allocation according to need has been damaging. The case of asylum and immigration provides a paradigm of this.

Further Reading

The legal restrictions are covered in C. Hunter (1998), 'Asylum seekers' rights to housing: new recipients of old Poor Law', in F. Nicholson & P. Twomey, *Current Issues of UK Asylum Law and Policy*, Aldershot: Ashgate. In the context of a rising media panic about homelessness, see D. Cowan (1997), *Homelessness: The (In-)Appropriate Applicant*, Aldershot: Dartmouth, pp. 154–160).

Waddington notes the paucity of texts in this area from a housing law and policy perspective, mainly (it might be suspected) because of its novelty. The background is expertly covered in S. Dummett and A. Nicol (1991), *Subjects, Citizens, Aliens and Others*, London: Weidenfeld & Nicolson; see also S. Juss (1993), *Immigration, Nationality and Citizenship*, London: Mansell. The validity of the habitual residence test is, at the time of writing, being considered by the European Court of Justice. Other useful studies are R. Cohen (1994), *Frontiers of Identity – The British and the Others*, London: Longman; P. Tuitt (1996), *False Images – The Law's Construction of the Refugee*, London: Pluto; S. Cohen (1985), 'Anti-semitism, immigration controls and the welfare state', vol 13, *Critical Social Policy* (it can also be found in D. Taylor (ed.), *Critical Social Policy*, London: Sage).

Endnotes

1. 'Exceptional leave to remain' is granted to those whose asylum application is rejected but whom, nevertheless, are given leave to remain in the UK (for example, as a result of illness).
2. Apparently this was the first the DSS had heard of any 'clampdown'.
3. Peter Lilley wrote to all asylum-seekers claiming benefit on 8 January 1996 saying that their benefit would be cut off.
4. The decision was subsequently blamed for being the cause of a sudden increase in asylum applications: Doughty, 1996.
5. That is, Great Britain, Republic of Ireland, the Channel Islands and the Isle of Man
6. Interestingly, 'residential accommodation' has been interpreted in the line of authority under discussion as 'no more than accommodation where a person lives': *ex parte Medical Foundation*. This is so, even though the context of that legislation suggests that it should mean 'institutionalized' accommodation.

7. This part only refers to those proposals affecting the support of asylum-seekers and other persons from abroad.
8. From the following: *Daily Telegraph, The Times, The Guardian, Daily Mail,* and *London Evening Standard.* Each has a significant readership and is at the more salubrious end of the market.

Bibliography

Adler, M. (1995), 'The habitual residence test: a critical analysis', vol 2, *Journal of Social Security Law,* 179

Bamber, D. (1998), 'DIY certificate offered to 'refugees'', *Sunday Telegraph,* 13 December

Bamber, D. (1999), 'Beggars who exploit children targeted', *Sunday Telegraph,* 3 January

Bamber, D. and Baldwin, D. (1999), 'Labour blamed for asylum 'chaos'', *Sunday Telegraph,* 7 February

Blamires, D. (1999), 'Refugees blamed for massive arts cuts', *Evening Standard,* 3 February

Bolderson, H. and Roberts, S. (1995), 'New restrictions on benefits for migrants: xenophobia or trivial pursuits?', January, *Benefits,* 11

Brogan, B. (1997), 'Battle over food bill for asylum seekers', *Daily Mail,* 11 February

Brogan, B. (1997), 'It's hard to stomach', *Daily Mail,* 14 February

Burt, J. and Purnell, S. (1997), 'Scandal of the immigrant benefit industry', *Daily Mail,* 30 June

Carlen, P. (1994), 'The governance of homelessness: legality, lore and lexicon in the agency-maintenance of youth homelessness', vol 41, *Critical Social Policy,* 18

Carroll, R. (1998), 'Protest as empty wards used to house Romanian refugees', *The Guardian,* 8 December

Child Poverty Action Group (CPAG) (1995), 'The habitual residence test one year on', June, *Welfare Rights Bulletin,* 7

Clark, J. (1998), 'Asylum seekers took my place on council house list', *Daily Mail,* 11 December

Clark, J. (1999), 'Asylum seekers to get empty council homes', *Daily Mail,* 10 February

Cohen, N. (1995), 'The long arm of the law', *The Independent on Sunday,* 5 November

Cowan, D. (1995), 'Accommodating community care', vol 22, *Journal of Law and Society,* 212

Cowan, D. (1997), *Homelessness: The (In-)Appropriate Applicant,* Aldershot: Dartmouth

Cowan, D. (1998), 'Reforming the homelessness legislation', vol 57, *Critical Social Policy,* 433

Cowan, D. (forthcoming), 'State support for ethnic minority households: spatial segregation and ghettoisation', in J. Murphy (ed), *Ethnic Minorities and Family Law,* Oxford: Hart

Craven, N. (1998), 'Asylum drugs den', *Daily Mail,* 12 December

Davenport, J. (1999), 'Refugee jailed for passport racket', *Evening Standard,* 10 February

Davies, B. and Judd, T. (1998), 'They couldn't find my dying granny a bed but they open the wards for gipsies', *Daily Mail*, 8 December

Donegan, L. (1997), 'Refugees allege diet inadequate', *The Guardian*, 14 February

Doughty, S. (1996), 'How asylum judges opened the floodgates', *Daily Mail*, 16 August

Dummett, A. and Nicol, A. (1990), *Subjects, Citizens, Aliens and Others*, London: Weidenfeld & Nicolson

Evening Argus (1997), 'London is to send homeless to Sussex', *Evening Argus*, 28–29 June

Ford, R. (1999), 'Councils will be forced to house refugees', *The Times*, 10 February

Garland, D. (1996), 'The limits of the sovereign state', vol 36, *British Journal of Criminology*, 445

Ginsburg, N. (1992), *Divisions of Welfare*, London: Sage

Goodwin, J. (1999), 'Suburbia's little Somalia', *Daily Mail*, 12 January

Heffer, S. (1998), 'How to stem this flood of fake refugees', *Daily Mail*, 12 December

Hetherington, P. (1998), 'Refugee rise brings 7pc increase in homeless', *The Guardian*, 11 December

Hillyard, P. (1993), *Suspect Community*, London: Pluto

Home Office (1998), *Fairer, Faster and Firmer – A Modern Approach to Immigration and Asylum*, Cm 4018, London: SO

House of Commons Social Security Committee (1996), *Benefits for Asylum Seekers*, HC 1995/96 Cm 81, London: HMSO

Howard, M. (1995), 'Why Britain should be a haven and not a honeypot', *Daily Mail*, 12 December

Johnston, P. (1998), 'Struggle to house 104 lorry refugees', *Daily Telegraph*, 5 December

Johnston, P. (1999a), 'Still a long way to go before the floodgates can be closed', *Daily Telegraph*, 10 February

Johnston, P. (1999b), 'Councils will be forced to take refugees', *Daily Telegraph*, 10 February

Jones, D. (1996), 'Her father was one of this century's most evil dictators, so why on earth is Svetlana Stalin living on state benefit in Britain', *Daily Mail*, 15 February

Kennedy, D. (1999), '"Asylo": a singular new currency', *The Times*, 11 February

Kennedy, D. (1999), 'History repeats itself', *The Times*, 19 February

Levy, A. and Pukas, A. (1995), 'Scandal of benefit millionaires', *The Sunday Times*, 17 December

Lightfoot, L. and Prescott, M. (1995), 'Too big for their wigs?', *The Sunday Times*, 5 November

Mathieson, T. 'The viewer society', vol 1, *Theoretical Criminology*, 215

Meikle, J. (1997a), 'Asylum seekers 'face living in tents'', *The Guardian*, 20 March

Meikle, J. (1997b), 'Asylum seekers' support system near collapse', *The Guardian*, 14 June

Millward, D. (1998), 'Seeking sanctuary in the guest houses of Dover', *Daily Telegraph*, 23 November

Mullins, D. and Niner, P. with Marsh, A. and Walker, B. (1996), *Evaluation of the 1991 Homelessness Code of Guidance*, London: HMSO

National Association of Citizen's Advice Bureaux (NACAB) (1996), *Failing the Test*, London: NACAB

Phillips, N. and Hardy, C. (1997), 'Managing multiple identities: discourse, legitimacy and resources in the UK refugee system', vol 4, *Organization*, 159

Piening, J. (1998), 'Romanian stowaways ask to be sent home', *Daily Telegraph*, 23 December

Rose, P. and Austin, H. (1995), 'The bomber on benefit', *Daily Mail*, 6 November

Rowinski, P. (1998), 'Hospital houses asylum seekers', *The Times*, 7 December

Rutherford, A. (1997), 'Criminal policy and the eliminative ideal', vol 31, *Social Policy and Administration*, 116

Salman, S. (1999), "London needs 100,000 homes", *Evening Standard*, 27 January

Sawyer, N. and Maguire, C. (1998), 'Widows ordered out, then asylum seekers move in', *Daily Mail*, 7 December

Shelter and Commission for Racial Equality (CRE) (1997), *Housing Act 1996 and Asylum and Immigration Act 1996: Shelter and CRE Guidance on Eligible and Qualifying Persons*, London: Shelter & CRE

Smith, S. (1993), 'Residential Segregation and the Politics of Racialization', in M. Cross & M. Kieth (eds), *Racism, the City and the State*, London: Routledge

Social Security Advisory Committee (SSAC) (1994), *The Income-related Benefits Schemes (Miscellaneous Amendments) (No 3) Regulations 1994*, Cm 2609, London: HMSO

Social Security Advisory Committee (SSAC) (1996), *The Social Security (Persons from Abroad) Miscellaneous Regulations 1996*, Cm 3062, London: HMSO

Taylor, D. (1999), 'War on sham marriages', *The Express*, 1 February

Torode, J. (1996a), 'Why do we give this bigot houseroom', *Daily Mail*, 19 April

Torode, J. (1996b), 'The madness of letting this racist remain in Britain', *Daily Mail*, 18 June

Travis, A. (1997), 'Westminster to cut costs by sending asylum seekers to Liverpool hostel', *The Guardian*, 16 May

Travis, A. (1999a), 'Majority backs ending asylum seekers benefit', *The Guardian*, 9 February

Travis, A. (1999b), 'Straw's welcome for asylum seekers', *The Guardian*, 10 February

Travis, A. (1999c), 'Refugees to lose benefits', *The Guardian*, 10 February

Tuitt, P. (1996), *False Images: The Law's Construction of the Refugee*, London: Pluto

Waddell, D. and Laville, S. (1998), 'Hospital wards open for illegal refugees', *Daily Telegraph*, 7 December

Waddington, M. (1998), 'Too poor to stay here: 'illegal immigrants' and housing officers', in D. Cowan (ed.), *Housing: Participation and Exclusion*, Aldershot: Dartmouth

Williams, D. (1998a), 'And still they flood in', *Daily Mail*, 28 November

Williams, D. (1998b) 'Brutal crimes of the asylum seekers', *Daily Mail*, 30 November

Williams, D. (1999a), 'Refugee tide rising', *Daily Mail*, 11 January

Williams, D. (1999b), 'Last year another 63,000 people claimed asylum in Britain. That is the true scale of the immigration crisis we face, Mr Straw', *Daily Mail*, 23 January

Williams, D. and Purnell, B. (1998), 'Asylum Seekers £300 million handout', *Daily Mail*, 8 December

Woodward, T. (1998), 'What kind of country do we live in when frail old ladies are turned out of their home to make way for fit young asylum seekers?', *Daily Mail*, 3 December

Woodward, T. (1999), 'Holiday camp for refugees', *Daily Mail*, 11 February

11 Access to the Private Rented Sector: Controlling Deregulation

The private housing sector is supposedly characterized by ease of access. The Housing Act 1988, through a process of deregulation and decontrol of the private rented sector (PRS), supposedly injected market principles into the sector (see Ch. 2). It was 'a result of statutory restrictions' that the private rented market was unable to flourish (DoE, 1987, para. 3.1; *cf* Ch. 2). This affected landlords' willingness to use their property for letting as well as potential tenants' ability to find quality accommodation because of a lack of supply (para. 3.2). The opening out of the market has supposedly been the 'key element' in the rebirth of this sector (DoE, 1995a, p. 20–1). One might add that opening the market to competition might, on one view, enhance the quality of accommodation offered for private renting (as people would be prepared to pay more for better quality accommodation) as well as removing all barriers (other than affordability of parts of the sector) to accessing this accommodation.

On the other hand, it can be argued that this market is imperfect for at least two important reasons affecting access to this sector. First, in some areas there is excessive demand for a limited (and possibly decreasing) supply of accommodation. Excessive demand suggests that landlords will be able to use poor quality accommodation as well as charge rents that might have been higher than expected. It appears that the supply of accommodation predominantly contains three or more rooms (assumed to be two or more bedrooms) – 77 per cent of the total flow of accommodation through the sector in 1994 (Rhodes & Bevan, 1997, pp. 26–29) – whereas the sector's primary client base in recent years has been the provision of temporary accommodation to the young and/or mobile who have difficulties accessing accommodation in the 'social' sector (see, for example, Kleinman *et al.*, 1996, pp. 15–16). Essentially, those unable to gain access to social housing (predominantly childless persons) as well as those unable or unwilling to enter the owner-occupier market generally form the client base of the PRS.

Government policies in the 1990s have sought to effect a considerable change to this client base and will, in the future, potentially alter the demand:supply structure. Principally, this position reflected the Conservative policies of using the PRS as staging-point accommodation for the (statutory) homeless. The Housing Act 1996 fits neatly into this stream of disjointed tenure structure – that is, the neat, vertical tenure structure of the early 1980s has given way to a more tenure neutral structure in the 1990s:

> 'Essentially what is happening is that it is becoming more possible, and more acceptable, to separate the component parts of a rental sector – finance, ownership and management. In the past all these were typically provided by the same organisation or individual, and hence there were distinct sub-sectors defined by ownership: local authority, housing association, private landlord. Increasingly, rented housing will involve different combinations of agents in this chain of provision.' (Kleinman *et al.*, 1996, p. 11)

We have already considered one (non-statutory) mechanism of this neutrality in the schemes operated by RSLs in the HAMA scheme, whereby RSLs manage property in the private sector which is then commonly used to house the homeless (Ch. 2). Thus, there has been a link between the private sector and the discharge of local authority responsibilities to the homeless. A more direct involvement was through the 'private-sector leasing' scheme, earlier known as the 'North Wiltshire' scheme (see Cowan, 1992), where landlords leased accommodation to local authorities who then used it to discharge part of their statutory obligations (for an example of its use see Cowan, 1997, p. 93). At the same time as this was being used, some (Conservative) local authorities, such as Wandsworth, began schemes through which the PRS was used to discharge all local authority obligations (see *R* v. *Wandsworth LBC ex parte Crooks* (1995) 27 HLR 660). Other authorities and voluntary agencies used 'access schemes' (Rugg, 1996) to assist predominantly non-statutory homeless people in their search for PRS accommodation. The first section of this chapter considers the implications of this shift towards tenure neutrality in the sector from the perspective of access to the sector.

The second way in which the PRS is an imperfect market is, somewhat bizarrely, because this deregulated and decontrolled market has a sub-sector which *is controlled by the State*. It will be remembered that under the Rent Acts 1977 and 1965, landlords were restricted to claiming a fair rent (which could be registered with the rent officer). Partial deregulation and decontrol in the Housing Act 1980 did not have much effect but the ability to claim a market rent on assured and assured shorthold tenancies after the introduction of the Housing Act 1988 considerably altered the legislative landscape. The 1987 White Paper provided the government's thinking, which appeared to be skewed in the direction of giving landlords the ability 'to secure a reasonable rate of return on their investment' as well as giving 'reasonable security' to tenants (para. 3.16). Quite apart from the latter objective (and we shall consider later whether this security is sufficient), it was appreciated even then that Housing Benefit would be a critical source of achieving the objective:

'The Housing Benefit system will continue to provide help to those who need it. However once rents are deregulated it will be necessary to ensure that landlords cannot increase the rents of benefit recipients to unreasonable levels at the expense of the taxpayer.' (para. 3.18)

Thus, the government realized that some form of rent regulation was bound to occur through Housing Benefit. Even though Housing Benefit was administered by local authorities, a complex network of influencing factors nevertheless leads back to central control over administration and level of payment.

The then government was seeking to provide state benefits directly to its natural constituency (landlords) as an incentive to that constituency to increase their share of the market (and thus increase its profits). Housing Benefit, in this sense, was not a benefit to the occupier but a direct subsidy to the landlord on top of the capital gain caused by a sale of the property. Indeed, the claimant can have their benefit paid direct to their landlord (subject to certain considerations: Housing Benefit (General) Regulations 1987, SI 1987/1971, reg 93, as amended by SI 1997/2434). Further, for those tenants on Income Support, Housing Benefit initially was supposed to cover all of the rent, provided that the rent was not unreasonably high nor the property too large for the claimant's needs. Even where there was 'unreasonableness', the local authority had discretion to pay the extra amount through Housing Benefit. Nevertheless, this concept of 'unreasonableness' seemed inconsistent with the notion of a market value and, in any event, where the market was governed by access to Housing Benefit (and, thus, the amount of the benefit payable in any case), one might expect this correlation to influence the contractually payable value.

In the mid-1990s, the concern has turned not to the values payable in this so-called market but to the fecklessness of the so-called recipients of the benefit – the occupiers. Thus, Thatcher's government used the notion of 'benefit hotels' and the 'Costa del Dole', together with the belief that the 'fabric of society' was breaking up, to link this with benefit dependency amongst the young. Rather than considering whether to redress the balance caused by the benefit 'taper' for those in work, under which such persons lose more benefit than they earn, they chose to reduce the allowable benefits for the under 25s. Thatcher believed that the under 25s should stay at home with their parents (unless they were in work) and thus benefits were reduced (1993, p. 604). The Major government further reduced the Housing Benefit available for this particular group in 1995 (see Kemp & Rugg, 1998).

Subsequently, the Major government, in a desperate search to reduce the benefit bill, found potential sources within the Housing Benefit criteria. In May 1996, approximately 1,153,000 households received Housing Benefit, with an average payout of £53.15 per week (Wilcox, 1997, Table 111a). Average rents have doubled from £30 per week in 1988 to £60 per week in 1993. In 1987/88, before the introduction of the 1988 Act, the total Housing Benefit bill was £3.9 billion; in 1995/96, the total was £11.9 billion. This spiralling increase in the welfare bill attributable to Housing Benefit seems to have turned the Major government against the 'fat cat' landlords who, it was occasionally argued, were partly responsible for this significant increase (an interesting volte-face). New controls were needed, not to stem the ability of landlords to charge market rents, but because there was no incentive on Housing Benefit recipients (that is, the occupiers) to shop around for the best rent and negotiate with their landlords. In other words, benefit cuts were proposed and executed in order to facilitate the better operation of the market that was the primary cause for the upward spiral of Housing Benefit in the first place. It is only more recently that concerns have been expressed at central government level over the affordability of rents in both the private and social sectors (see Wilson, 1998).

In this chapter, we consider two fundamental controls over the 'free' PRS market. The first concerns the type of accommodation available, as well as the client groups for whom this sector is thought to provide. Both constrain choice because the type of accommodation available is often of poor quality (would you live there?) and is thought to provide mostly for marginalized individuals (which then determines the sort of accommodation provided as well as the level of security considered appropriate). In the second section, we consider the Housing Benefit rules and their effect – it is argued that the Housing Benefit scheme provides an important limit on the PRS market and this has become more particularly so in the recent past as its availability has been further reined in.

The PRS raises a fundamental dilemma within housing policy for governments. Most landlords will only enter the market if they can obtain a reasonable rate of return/profit. In order to obtain that level of profit, market rents (and above) need to be charged. For those who can afford such rents, home ownership often represents a better deal. For those unable to afford such rents, as we are now finding, the state is unable to finance market rents. Reduction in levels of individual state subsidy presumably implies a reduction in profit levels, which also presumably implies that landlords in this sub-sector of the PRS will either withdraw from the PRS itself or withdraw from the Housing Benefit sub-sector.

11.1   Access to What and for Whom?

Supply: Demand

The share of the housing market attributable to the PRS has diminished during this century in line with the rise in owner–occupation, so that the market share of the PRS remains at or below about 10 per cent (see Ch. 2 above, where the reasons for this decline are considered). This decline in market share is partly reflected in the changing client group of the PRS. In the early part of this century, the demand of households using the PRS was for long-term, unfurnished accommodation. Tied accommodation (that is, rented accommodation linked to employment) was a further important part of the market. Increasingly, however, as current tenure preferences spread through the market, the PRS is required to provide ready-access, short-term, furnished accommodation for the mobile and young. There are also what might be termed 'sub-sectors' of the PRS in which properties are earmarked for certain types of person, for example, students. Thus, a study in York 'found that many landlords preferred to let to students and were unlikely to let outside that niche market' (Rugg, 1997, p. 174).

The DoE has suggested that:

'A healthy private rented sector can:
- provide an essential first stage for young people leaving home, including students and those saving a deposit to buy their own home;
- contribute to a healthy economy by assisting labour mobility;
- provide a home for people facing a change in their personal or domestic circumstances;
- accommodate anyone who prefers to rent rather than own.' (1995, p. 20; for similar sentiments see DoE, 1987, para. 3.3)[1]

The weight of this type of belief about the role of the PRS has favoured the provision of short-term accommodation. Thus, the little regulation available reflects the supply of accommodation for the supposed needs of these potential client groups (perhaps more by chance than deliberate policy).

The 1988 Act attempted to stimulate the market by creating two new types of tenancy – the assured tenancy and the assured shorthold tenancy. Both provide limited security, although the latter is essentially geared towards the short-term market. That type of tenancy has to last for a minimum of six months and, other than in particular types of PRS market (such as students), this is usually the maximum period. At the end of that period, the landlord is entitled to evict the tenant after two months notice has been given. It is unsurprising that this is the most commonly used form of arrangement in the PRS. Indeed, so few tenancies are now made on an assured basis that the 1996 Act made the assured shorthold the 'default tenancy'. This limited security makes the PRS an unreliable source of long-term housing (even though the longer a tenant stays the greater security is given to the landlord in terms of the rental flow), as well as making the owner-occupied market appear to offer greater security.

If the PRS is supposed to cater for groups of persons such as the young, mobile, those who have suffered relationship breakdown (of some form or other), the type and nature of accommodation must be relevant for that client group. These types of groups are generally characterized as non-family, or at least having young families, as well as (most often) single persons who are not accepted as homeless by the local authority (as the priority need categories exclude most single people: Ch. 7), and therefore the type of accommodation required will generally be smaller. It is also the case that those who are rejected from the social rented sector for one reason or another end up in the PRS (where else could they go?). Whilst there are geographical distortions in the data, the pattern is that most accommodation has two or more bedrooms – only 16–28 per cent of available accommodation had one bedroom in 1994 (Rhodes & Bevan, 1997, p. 28). Thus, it appears that the area where there was the greatest supply deficiency is precisely the area where accommodation was most in demand.[2] The relatively small size of the sector also has consequences for the demand-led market:

> 'One of the problems is that [the PRS] is an area where good news seems to turn into bad. A case in point is the behaviour of young people. Any reduction or delay in younger people entering home ownership is likely to result in an increase in private renting. But this is not unalloyed good news because: 'the effect of an influx of people who could afford to buy but choose to rent . . . would squeeze out people whose ability to rent in the private rented sector would depend on Housing Benefit.' (House of Commons Environment Committee, 1996, para. 91)

In other words, if the market is based upon ability to pay, then it is likely that those able to afford higher rents will steadily push those unable to out of the sector (it is presumed into the social rented sector, although the capacity and willingness of that sector is unclear in this regard).

Standards

A further issue relates to the standard of accommodation offered. It was suggested above that a perfect market might lead to increased standards in the sector. However, it is clear that the greatest number of rented dwellings which are 'unfit for human habitation' (s 604, Housing Act 1985, as amended) are in the PRS (24.6 per cent in the PRS; 19.6 per cent in local authority tenure; 3 per cent in RSL: DoE, 1993). Furthermore, unlike any other sector, a majority of its properties were built before 1919 and thus to different standards than currently apply (see Leather & Morrison, 1997, pp. 29–36). HMOs form a significant part of the PRS including the number of converted flats (see Ch. 2) and standards of accommodation in most HMOs are poor and safety is often under prioritized (Thomas & Hedges, 1986; Everton, 1997; Smith, 1998, pp. 167–8). The surprising result of the government's 1995 review of HMOs was that they believed extra regulation would 'lead to excessive cost and bureaucracy' in this sub-sector (DoE, 1995, para. 2.1) although reform is currently on the agenda.

Discrimination

Demand for and standards of accommodation in the PRS form a significant inter-connecting barrier to accessing accommodation in this tenure. However, there are other barriers which belie the current image of the PRS as 'easy access'. What was true in 1976 appears to be the case today: '[A]ppearances can be deceptive and, *in practice*, simple economic factors and the realisation of individual preferences and opportunities do not entirely account for the pattern of occupancy that can be observed' (Murie *et al.*, 1976, p. 198). It may well be important, for example, to distinguish between the practices of letting agencies (including estate agents), on the one hand, and direct lettings on the other (see, for example, Harloe *et al.*, 1974). The former are, perhaps, most likely to have formal letting policies which may exclude certain people. A classic example of exclusion of certain people from this tenure is to request a deposit and a month's rent in advance, or even some sort of payment in advance (such as 'key money' or a 'premium'). Those on benefits are unlikely to be able to comply, as Housing Benefit does not include payment of a deposit and is now paid in arrears. Discretionary payments are available from the Social Fund, but rank low in priority. Other methods of exclusion include, for example, checks on financial credit, requirements for a bank reference, and/or considering any criminal convictions. The lack of willingness by some landlords to let to those on Housing Benefit is considered below, but is clearly relevant here as well.

There is considerable evidence of racial discrimination in relation to accessing PRS (for a relatively early study, see Burney, 1967; more recent evidence can be found in Bevan *et al.*, 1995, p. 53). Smith suggests that 'in the absence of explicit sets of allocation rules, there is maximum potential for direct racial discrimination by landlords' (1989, p. 82). In 1986, a survey conducted by the Greater London Council found that, on average, black households paid more for worse conditions and less security (1986). Settlement patterns of ethnic minorities, most commonly in the PRS, have often tended to reflect community ties of one sort or another. However, this should not be considered to be choice:

> '[I]f we accept that Asian people prefer to live in close-knit communities, this does not explain why they have 'chosen' to live in overcrowded conditions, in houses that are generally in a poor state of repair, in the declining areas of Britain's inner cities with all of the accompanying disadvantages.' (Morris & Winn, 1990, p. 88)

Patterns of settlement, in fact, tend to reflect discrimination and disadvantage within all sectors but particularly within the PRS. Anti-discrimination legislation may well have simply forced such discrimination underground. Instead, the problem of discrimination has been rectified through ethnic minorities avoiding landlords who discriminate, in favour of a smaller group of landlords. Letting agents have also been found to discriminate unlawfully against ethnic minority applicants (see CRE, 1980, discussed in MacEwen, 1991, pp. 291–294). It is, then, no surprise that black people are disproportionately represented amongst the homeless population, many of whom were rehoused in squalid bed and breakfast accommodation in the PRS anyway (Bonnerjea & Lawton, 1987).

The Homeless

This cycle of disadvantage is perhaps the most appropriate way to consider the Conservative government's response to homelessness. Local authority duties to successful homeless applicants are prefaced by the requirement that, where there is 'other suitable available accommodation' for the applicant in the authority's area, the authority is simply under a duty to provide to the applicant 'such advice and assistance as the authority consider is reasonably required to enable him to secure such accommodation' (s 197, 1996 Act). This limited obligation (see Ch. 7) actually raises serious questions about the appropriateness and viability of the PRS to accommodate a significant proportion of the homeless population. Even using the DoE's homelessness statistics, it has been shown that in certain areas the PRS would be swallowed up entirely by the homeless (Rhodes & Bevan, 1997). At the same time, the usual sources of demand for PRS accommodation, such as the non-statutory homeless, may simply be frozen out.

This reliance on the PRS potentially will have a considerable impact on the sector. Landlords are being exhorted to take over the role of social housing – or, on another view, the homeless are being privatized (Cowan, 1997). The PRS was also being encouraged to join in with local authority and RSL in the creation and operation of the common housing registers (s 162(3)). That encouragement being so, there remain considerable doubts as to the willingness of the PRS to engage in this relationship. A study of PRS landlords' attitudes found that:

'A number of landlords had negative perceptions of people who were homeless. Some landlords felt that it would not be fair on other tenants or neighbours to accept homeless households. One landlord went so far as to suggest that a separate building would have to be provided which was specially sound-proofed. . . . [M]any landlords prefer not to let to families with children. Some landlords tended to be dismissive of the idea of providing accommodation for homeless households in general, because they felt that the accommodation they were providing was not suitable for families. . . . A number of landlords considered that they would only let to homeless households as a last resort, if they could not find 'preferred' tenants.' (Bevan *et al.* 1995 p. 58)

Thus, there is suspicion that some parts of the PRS will be unwilling to assist and this, when combined with the fact that many also do not wish to let to those in receipt of benefits, suggests that the PRS will be a marginal player in the provision of social housing.

11.2   The Importance of Housing Benefit

In May 1995, approximately 1,039,000 households received Housing Benefit in England at an average payment of £55.40 per week (Wilcox, 1997, Table 113). This was just short of 50 per cent of the total number of dwelling in the PRS. In Wales, the proportion was just above 50 per cent. This suggests that a considerable part of the demand for PRS accommodation comes from low-income households. Housing Benefit pays up to and including 100 per cent of the rent. This willingness to pay the full rent has led to various accusations being levelled at both landlords and tenants – for example, it has been suggested that claimants are able to move 'up-market' or do not need to negotiate with landlords for lower rent (*cf* Bevan *et al.*, 1995; Kemp & McLaverty, 1996). As Hills explains:

> 'The up-marketing potential in this is a problem both for those who want to increase market influences in housing decisions (which are almost entirely removed by it) and for those concerned at the distributional consequences of the restrictions imposed to try to limit its effects . . .' (1991, pp. 173–4).

In this part, the Housing Benefit scheme will be explained together with a consideration of its effects upon the PRS. The scheme itself is tremendously complex but repays careful examination. As the Social Security Advisory Committee concluded:

> 'The increasing cost of the scheme is a measure of its importance in protecting low paid and unemployed people from the effects of high rents. Radical changes or drastic cuts would be likely to increase poverty, force people into unsatisfactory housing or homelessness and reduce the supply of rented accommodation (SSAC, 1995, para. 7.1)

It might be said that the housing cycle of the deprived is linked up by the availability and level of Housing Benefit. Only if rents are more affordable to those on low incomes will the system deliver.

In no way can the following provide an adequate summary of Housing Benefit law (for which see Zebedee & Ward, 1997; Arden & Partington, 1994, as updated). However, the major parts of the scheme are summarized in the opening section. The second section draws attention to the method used by central government to control the outflow of Housing Benefit. The final section considers the relationship between Housing Benefit and access to the PRS. It will be argued that the ever-increasing constraints on the Housing Benefit budget have caused a considerable crisis of confidence in the PRS and raise questions about the continuing involvement of the PRS in housing those on low enough incomes to claim Housing Benefit.

Hitherto, central government's concerns about Housing Benefit have manifested themselves in two ways: first, through reductions in benefit to specific groups, such as asylum-seekers and other persons from abroad and the under 25s; and second, through a continuing 'crackdown' on Housing Benefit fraud (the widely advertised benefit fraud 'hotline' to 'shop a cheat' and unscientifically calculated headline figures of levels of fraud of up to £8 billion). The first phase of the New Labour government, as concerned with Housing Benefit levels as the previous government, has continued both strands (see, for example, DSS, 1998). What these obfuscate, though, is the lack of a strategy for the PRS.

The law

Housing Benefit law is largely found in two amended Statutory Instruments: Housing Benefit (General) Regulations 1987, SI 1987/1971 and the Rent Officers (Housing Benefit Functions) Order 1997, SI 1997/1984 (under the Social Security Contributions and Benefits Act 1992 and the Housing Act 1996). Local authorities are charged with the implementation of these regulations. The former has been heavily amended, but provides instructions (often down to the minutiae) regarding the calculation of an individual's Housing Benefit. Essentially, a person's entitlement depends upon (a) their eligible housing costs, (b) not having greater income and capital than prescribed, and (c) the maximum Housing Benefit payable.

Eligible Housing Costs
Eligible housing costs are generally those costs incurred by a claimant in respect of the *occupation of a home* and which are *eligible*. Ineligible housing costs are, for example, that portion of costs which relate to service charges (Sch. 1, 1987; for discussion of the problems which have arisen in respect of this, see Oldman & Wilcox, 1997; *R* v. *Housing Benefit Review Board for Swansea ex parte Littler*, Unreported, Court of Appeal, 15 July 1998). Certain arrangements are deemed to give rise to no eligible liability because, *inter alia*, they have arisen either from living with a close relative or partner or as a result of a non-commercial arrangement between them; or where the arrangement has 'been created to take advantage of the Housing Benefit scheme' (Reg. 7 (a) & (b)).

   Other than the exemptions, Housing Benefit will pay the eligible rent *except where it is greater than the maximum rent*. The maximum rent depends upon the decision of the rent officer. The authority must refer the claim to the rent officer for a determination. This process is meant to provide a check on the amount of benefit payable. The 1997 regulations prescribe the types of determinations which can be made by the rent officer. Each determination is shrouded with discretion.

Rent Officers. The following determinations, together with their definitions, can be made by rent officers: that the rent 'is *significantly higher* than the rent which the landlord might reasonably have been expected to obtain under the tenancy at that time' (Sch. 1, para. 1); the dwelling is too large, or in the words of the regulation 'exceeds the *size criteria*' (Sch. 1, para. 2; the criteria are specified in Sch. 2); the rent payable is '*exceptionally high*' (Sch. 1, para. 3); a *local reference rent* which is the mean of the highest rent a landlord 'might reasonably have been expected to obtain for an assured tenancy' and 'is not an exceptionally high rent' and the lowest rent on the same principles (Sch. 1, para. 4 – the supposed dwelling must be in the same locality, in a reasonable state of repair and have the same number of bedrooms (provided this accords with the size criteria)); a *single room rent* divined on the same principles as the local reference rent except that the exclusive use of one bedroom only together with a shared toilet and kitchen facilities are assumed (Sch. 1, para. 5); finally, the rent officer must determine whether any of the rent 'is fairly attributable to the provision of services which are ineligible (Sch. 1, para. 6).

If the rent officer makes a determination that the rent falls within any of the first three, the rent officer must also determine the highest rent which 'might reasonably have been expected to obtain at the relevant time', having regard to rent levels in the 'locality' and on the assumption that the potential occupier is not entitled to Housing Benefit. The notion of locality and the disregard of Housing Benefit entitlement are also part of the consideration in the local reference rent and the single room rent.

It might fairly be said that these determinations are characterized by their discretionary nature. It has been suggested that their introduction (in fact, in 1995), required 'increased cognitive' skills on the part of the rent officer (Gibb, 1995, p. 14). The nature of 'locality' for example is unclear from the regulations:

> 'Although the DSS paper asserts that this is a familiar concept to rent officers, with some legal recognition, it would appear to be essentially subjective and is difficult to reconcile with any rigorous definition capable of being applied statistically. . . . Basically, the broader the area used, the larger will be the discrepancies between the local reference rents and the actual market rents, and the more certain it will be that households will lose benefit.' (Bramley, 1995, p. 24)

The Social Security Advisory Committee has drawn attention to an example where the single room rent of £39 was set for the whole of Greater Manchester without apparent recognition of geographical variations for smaller towns such as Bury within that area (SSAC, 1997, para. 14).

Five other points need to be made. First, legal challenges through judicial review on *Wednesbury* principles (that is, that the rent officer's decision is so unreasonable that no reasonable person would have come to the same decision) would surely be improbable for the breadth of the discretion available would mean that the margin of appreciation would be too wide. Put another way, quite simply there are too many 'reasonables' involved.

Second, the breadth of the discretion, in many ways startling, probably means that no two rent officers will come to the same decision on any particular case. This suggests that rent officers even in the same area will probably come to different decisions leading to allegations of arbitrary decision-making on their part (see Bramley, 1995, p. 14). The available evidence suggests that there is considerable inconsistency in decision-making (see Kemp & McLaverty, 1994, p 113). So, for example, if a redetermination is requested, it is likely to be different (particularly as the rent officer must consult and have regard to the advice of 'one or two' colleagues: Sch. 3, para. 2).

Third, rent determinations are clearly not an 'exact science' (Kemp & McLaverty, 1993, p. 98) and rent officers do not have reference to some hidden, carefully constructed formula(e). Rather, it appears that rent officers look at local newspapers, shop window advertisements, contact with letting agencies and agents: 'we use whatever source we can get hold of' 1993. So, there is a further level of vagueness in the methodology apparently used by them. Many rent officers conduct physical inspections of the property, particularly if they are considering reducing maximum levels (p. 103)

Fourth, there is an air of unreality about some of the assumptions which the rent officer has to make. For example, the regulations presuppose the existence of a market for the type of accommodation as well as that this market is not dependent upon Housing Benefit. How does one estimate a market value for bedsits on the basis of a non-Housing Benefit market when that market does not exist? As Kemp and McLaverty argue 'The concept of "reasonable market rents" can only have meaning if they can be estimated from similar accommodation which is let in a market transaction between landlords and tenants who are paying out of their own income' (p. 99; for similar comments and some thoughts on the matter, albeit under earlier regulations, see *R* v. *Waltham Forest LBC ex parte Holder* (1997) 29 HLR 71, esp. 79–81).

Finally, the regulations require a distinction to be drawn between 'exceptionally high' rents and those rents which are 'significantly higher' for these are different possible determinations. Surely this is close to being a distinction without a difference. In fact, as might be expected, rent officers interpret the 'significantly higher' phrase in very different ways, one rent officer describing such determinations as 'a bit of a sham really' (*ibid*, p. 100).

Calculating the maximum rent. The relevance of the rent officer's determination(s) are that they will determine the maximum rent for Housing Benefit purposes. Whereas in the pre-1995 days of the scheme, the rent officers' determinations could be exceeded in the amount of the actual payment, the current regulations give enormous power to the rent officer. So, the maximum rent depends upon the determinations which the rent officer may take into account. The following are the possible permutations which are contained in regulation 11 of the 1987 SI:

- If the rent officer has fixed a 'reasonable' rent, but not a local reference rent, that will be the maximum rent.
- If the rent officer has fixed a local reference rent, but not a 'reasonable' rent, then the maximum rent cannot exceed twice the local reference rent. Somewhere in between appears to be all right.
- If the rent officer has determined a single room rent for a person under 25, then that will be the maximum, subject to certain exceptions.
- If the rent officer has determined both a local reference rent and a 'reasonable rent', and the latter is higher than the former, then the maximum rent is the local reference rent. If the local reference rent is higher than the 'reasonable' rent, then the maximum rent is the 'reasonable' rent.

Local reference rents and single room rents. Local reference rents were introduced in May 1995 (SI 1995/1644) and the single room rent was introduced in October 1996 (SI 1996/965). Both are attempts at reducing the maximum available rent on which Housing Benefit is payable. Thus, the background is a money saving exercise together with, as the euphemism goes, better targeting of benefits. The detailed rationales are slightly different for each scheme. Local reference rents were introduced partly as an incentive to tenants to negotiate rent with their landlords (or choose cheaper accommodation) as well as to put a stop to a separate market developing for those in receipt of Housing Benefit. Single room rents for under 25s were introduced so that the state would not be required to pay for rents which would be more than they could afford to pay from their own resources (if they actually had any). The Conservative government attempted to apply the single room rent to all claimants under 60 years old (SI 1997/852),[3] although the Labour government has since repealed that requirement (SI 1997/1975).

It will become apparent below that these determinations may have significantly altered the ability of recipients of Housing Benefit to access accommodation in the PRS. They also raise considerable issues for providers of social housing (particularly RSLs, to whom the changes do not apply unless a reference to the rent officer is made, which, in turn, is within the local authority's discretion: Reg. 11(3D)(a)).

Income and Capital Thresholds

A person with income and capital above the threshold limits is subject to a deduction in the amount payable strictly in line with regulations. This deduction, known as a 'taper', is steep so that benefit is lost quickly if the limits are exceeded (65 per cent of benefit is lost for every extra pound of income above allowable Income Support levels). The impact of the taper is simple. If benefit is lost quicker than income is gained through employment, there is a disincentive to seek employment on those in receipt of benefit. This is exacerbated by higher rents: 'Rents of £70 per week extend the poverty trap for couples with two children up to almost £280 gross earnings per week' (SSAC, 1995, para. 5.4).

Maximum Housing Benefit
The maximum Housing Benefit is generally the maximum rent reduced according to the taper (as necessary). A further deduction is made where there is a 'non-dependent' of the claimant who resides with the claimant (see Witherspoon *et al.*, 1996). The local authority is entitled to pay more than the maximum rent, to the level of the actual rent payable by the claimant, where the 'claimant's circumstances are exceptional' (1987 SI, reg 61(2)(a)) or the claimant would 'suffer exceptional hardship' (Reg. 61(3)(c)). These payments are rarely made.

Central Government Control

There is now a considerable body of evidence to suggest that central government effectively controls the Housing Benefit bill. Central government pays to local authorities, by way of a subsidy, only a proportion of the benefit actually paid out to claimants. This level of subsidy is set annually by central government. Currently, local authorities receive 95 per cent of their expenditure (SI 1997/1004, reg 4(1); this is paid into the authority's general account and which, therefore, includes the authority's administration costs). However, the amount of subsidy is restricted where the authority pay backdated benefit, higher rents, more than a rent officer determines, errors by the authority resulting in an overpayment (see regs 5–11; from 50 per cent to 25 per cent). Furthermore:

> 'The government's contribution to discretionary payments will be £2.5 million in England each year, a figure which approximates to an average of about £6,000 for each local authority per annum. . . . (Based on the average Housing Benefit reduction of £910 per annum, . . ., £6,000 will on average allow each local authority to provide discretionary payments up to the full rent level for less than seven households per year).'
> (Rhodes & Bevan, 1997, p. 55)

Not only do rent officers restrict the amount of benefit available to the claimant, they also have a concomitant effect on the amount of benefit subsidy payable to the authority. It is not surprising, therefore, that a number of studies have found that the rent officers' determinations not so much guide as determine the amount of benefit given to claimants (see Kemp & McLaverty, 1994; Audit Commission, 1993). The generosity of local authorities has had to be curbed, or as one Housing Benefit head apparently commented, '[b]ecause the subsidy rules are so tight, [our] policy is to follow the letter of the law' (Kemp & McLaverty, 1994, p. 119).

Increasingly, local authorities have begun to employ the technical 'letter of the law' to reduce benefit levels. For example, the law requires that no benefit is payable where arrangements are made which attempt to take advantage of the Housing Benefit system (SI 1987/1971, reg 7). Local authorities have, it seems, attempted to exploit this rule to avoid obligations to pay out Housing Benefit where there is a gap between the rent officer's determination and the actual rent. This exploitation has probably particularly occurred in relation to residential accommodation *R* v. *Manchester CC ex parte Baragrove Properties Ltd* (1991) 23 HLR 337) and, more recently, in respect of family arrangements (see, in particular, *R* v. *South Gloucestershire Housing Benefit Review Board ex parte Dadds* (1997) 29 HLR 700). It has been assumed that these cases have been brought because they involve attempts by local authorities to avoid being exposed to loss of subsidy (see Rahilly, 1995; 1997; Partington, 1998).[4]

Access to the PRS and Housing Benefit

Often, the availability of benefit is portrayed as a key to the profit of many landlords. However, the relationship between landlords and Housing Benefit is more complex. A variety of studies have shown how recipients, rather than willingly be manipulated by landlords into paying greater rent than is available, have sought to be discerning when moving (see Kemp & McLaverty, 1995). Reliance on Housing Benefit was seen as a constraint for the following reasons:

- delays in processing benefits claims;
- landlords not taking claimants on Housing Benefit;
- the difficulties of paying deposits and rents in advance whilst living on benefit income and the sparsity of places that required neither;
- the uncertainty about whether all the rent would be met through Housing Benefit or not; and
- the perceived attitudes of Housing Benefit and benefits agency staff (Kemp *et al.*, 1994, p. 31).

Each of these is now considered in turn. Local authorities are required to process benefit claims within 14 days. Whilst it appears that most do so, many cases are not processed within the time limit for whatever reason (such as, for example, claimants not providing relevant information or delays in rent officer determinations). Such delays lead to arrears of rent. Authorities are, in certain circumstances, required to pay an interim Housing Benefit but many avoid such obligations either out of ignorance or because such payments are penalized (Kemp, 1992). Problems of delays are further exacerbated by the current requirement that Housing Benefit is paid four weeks in arrears (and not in advance as most tenancy contracts require). The introduction of payment in arrears was caused by the government's desire to avoid overpayment of Housing Benefit (and seems to have ignored the practical reality of contractual rent in advance). Some local authorities have operated 'fast-track' procedures to certain landlords and access schemes ((Bevan *et al.*, 1995, pp. 62–3; Rugg, 1996).

Rugg found that 'the introduction of payment in arrears was a final blow to [access schemes] attempts to persuade good-quality landlords to let to people on Housing Benefit' (1997, p. 36). In practice, the unwillingness of landlords to let to people on Housing Benefit can usually be checked in local newspapers which feature the usual signs 'No DSS', 'Professionals only', 'Students acceptable'. Empirical evidence supports the finding that the choice of claimants is narrowed by landlords' ability to discriminate against claimants. A 'good' tenant appears to be a person in work, who dresses well and is polite and responsible; some landlords, apparently, draw a distinction between Housing Benefit recipients and others in this regard (Bevan *et al.*, 1995, pp. 51–54). Young persons, particularly those under 25, are avoided (Kemp & Rugg, 1998). The result is that some landlords are unwilling to let to people on Housing Benefit, particularly because the prospective tenant's entitlement may be nil or reduced after moving in. Most studies have found about two in five landlords who do not wish to let to people on Housing Benefit (see Bevan *et al.*, 1995; Kemp & McLaverty, 1995). This must partly be a response to the uncertainty created within the system but also to the publicity given to government's attempts to rein in the system (Kemp & Rugg, 1998).

A further factor that narrows down the accommodation on offer to benefit recipients (who, by the very receipt of benefit, have low and/or no income), is the need of landlords to charge a deposit and rent in advance. From the landlord's perspective, the deposit is security against damage and/or non-payment of rent in the future; payment of a month's rent in advance is also common (in Kemp & McLaverty's study, about 77 per cent of tenants paid rent in advance: Table 3.11). It is possible to receive a discretionary payment from the Social Fund to pay a deposit but the benefits agency rarely prioritize such payments. Access schemes had been particularly important in breaking down the barriers constructed by advance payments through, for example, offering rent guarantees (Rugg, 1996), although much of this work has now been threatened by the changes to the availability of benefits (Rugg, 1997).

There are at least two strands to the problem of uncertainty about the correlation between rent and Housing Benefit. First, since 1995, prospective tenants have been entitled to a 'pre-tenancy determination' which requires the rent officer to determine the availability and amount of Housing Benefit against the contractual rent. Only a prospective tenant can request this and it is supposed to be completed within a short timescale. However, even some delay can affect the ability of prospective tenants in high demand areas and/or for cheaper accommodation for there will always be those who are willing to take on the accommodation despite uncertainty. The taper (if any) is not worked out at this stage and, therefore, the benefit actually payable may be different from the determination. Also, knowledge of the Housing Benefit system amongst claimants is diverse and if nothing or little is known then the availability of this determination may not matter because its existence is not known (see Kemp *et al.*, 1994, pp. 44–5; Kemp & Rugg, 1998 suggest that ignorance is particularly common amongst the young).

Second, there are the restrictions on entitlement to the reference rent level or lower. The rent officers' discretion has meant that certain areas will feel this disproportionately, particularly as rent officers now effectively determine the amount of Housing Benefit. So, it is no surprise that Rugg's research has found (albeit amongst a sample of access schemes) that some areas are experiencing local reference rents at lower than the current market rents: 'In at least one area where the reference rents were low, however, *"landlords have gone into a panic"* ' (1997, p. 25; original emphasis). Landlords who rely on Housing Benefit 'could do little but bear the loss and take what they could get' whereas smaller landlords were withdrawing their properties from access schemes (p. 26). Thus, in some areas there is more likely to be a shortfall.

Finally, the attitudes of benefits staff are bound to influence people's decisions particularly when those decisions are being made often without appropriate information as to the Housing Benefit scheme. The advice and assistance given by benefits staff will also affect the expectations of potential claimants. Lengthy, invasive application forms (sometimes more than 26 pages long), now required as part of the 'crackdown' on Housing Benefit fraud make all *applicants suspect* which may well be reflected in the scheme's administration.

Reflections on the Housing Benefit Scheme

A restricted PRS market is restricted even further for those in receipt of Housing Benefit. A decontrolled rent is controlled, in certain circumstances, by the receipt of Housing Benefit because of the centrally imposed benefit controls. About 40 per cent of landlords do not want to rent to a person in receipt of Housing Benefit, whereas about 50 per cent of private-sector tenants need it. Increasingly government is relying on the PRS to take over the responsibility of social housing. The government's controls in the mid-1990s have been premised partly on the belief that tenants should negotiate with their landlords (although most only know of the restriction once they have signed their agreements and, thus, the scope for negotiation is limited anyway). How far this is possible in an expanded demand and limited supply market is unclear. What is clear, though, is that Housing Benefit claimants have taken the brunt of the government's desire to cut the Housing Benefit budget when the government appeared to blame landlords for taking advantage of the scheme. The cycle of homelessness creation amongst the low and/or no income groups becomes complete with the decline of benefit. In this light, it is ironic that the 1996 Act sought to encourage local authorities to place successful homeless applicants in the PRS.

Conclusion

Increasingly, the PRS is becoming the 'choice' of the marginalized and excluded. That choice is restricted and constrained by the unwillingness of the social rented sector to provide accommodation for certain persons, together with the great demand for social rented accommodation as against its supply. The marginalized and excluded are rarely afforded the opportunity to finance the purchase of their own accommodation precisely because they are marginalized and excluded, and this usually (if not always) extends to the labour market. Yet it remains unclear whether the PRS has the requisite capacity and willingness to provide accommodation for these groups. Profit for landlords in the PRS needs to be consistent (although most often it does not reach the levels which landlords might obtain on other investments). Reliance on the section of market demand that itself relies on Housing Benefit will, it is suggested, lead to a gradual withdrawal from this market, for Housing Benefit cannot be relied upon into the next millennium. Rather, it is likely that the PRS will become even more fragmented after the potential withdrawal of business landlords (although the Housing Investment Trusts scheme might curb this withdrawal but, in all likelihood, for those who can afford to pay).

Paying 100 per cent of rent through Housing Benefit implies central government control over rents in a supposedly decontrolled market. It is a fallacy to believe that this market is decontrolled in any sense. However, the declining availability and amounts of benefit payable will – there is no doubt of this in my mind – lead to a dual market for those in receipt of benefit (who will only be able to afford the worse type of accommodation) and for those who can afford to pay 'market' rents without reliance on benefit (who will be able to 'cherry pick' the better quality accommodation). This dichotomy is already particularly the case in respect of the under 25s, who are only entitled to a 'single room rent' with shared facilities payable through Housing Benefit.

The Housing Benefit scheme was conceived in the 1987 White Paper as a means of enabling landlords to raise their rents to a 'market' level. In this sense, the Conservatives were providing a subsidy not to the needy but to landlords. What was formerly achieved through rent control is now being achieved through cuts to the Housing Benefit budget as landlords have sought to raise the lid on the market. Those who suffer are those who are searching for decent quality accommodation at a price they can afford.

Further Reading

Housing Benefit law is constantly being updated and readers are advised to look at one of the encyclopaedias (which, themselves, are constantly updated). A. Arden & M. Partington's (1994), *Housing Law*, London: Sweet & Maxwell, provides a commentary on the rules and is recommended for this purpose.

Studies on Housing Benefit and its impact are (at the time of writing) constantly emanating from the Centre for Housing Policy, University of York, some of which can be found in R Burrows, N. Please & D. Quilgars (eds), *Homelessness and Social Policy*, London: Routledge. The Centre's web site will provide updating details. A useful, thoughtful analysis of the situation in 1995 can be found in SSAC, *The Review of Social Security*, Paper 3: Housing Benefit, Leeds: Benefits Agency; see also I. Gibbs and P. Kemp (1993), 'Housing Benefit and income redistribution', vol 30, *Urban Studies*, 63–72. Other more historical considerations include: P. Kemp (1987), 'The reform of Housing Benefit', vol 21, *Social Policy and Administration*, 171–186 and by the same author (1991), 'The administration of Housing Benefit', in D. Donnison and D. Maclennan (eds), *The Housing Service of the Future*, Coventry: Institute of Housing; I. Loveland's interesting analysis of three authorities' implementation of the pre-1987 scheme can be found at (1988), 'Housing Benefit: administrative law and administrative practice', vol 66, *Public Administration*, 57–75.

For consideration of the reform of Housing Benefit, see P. Kemp (ed), *The Future of Housing Benefits*, Glasgow: Centre for Housing Research, University of Glasgow; K. Gibb (1995), *Housing Benefit: The Future*, London: National Federation of Housing Associations; J. Hills (1991), *Unravelling Housing Finance*, Oxford: Oxford University Press, Part IV provides an economic analysis. An economic analysis of the HAMA scheme (considered in Ch. 2 above) can be found in C. Giles, P. Johnson and J. McCrae (1996), *Financing Temporary Accommodation in the Private Rented Sector*, London: Stationery Office (this research was conducted before the impact of the 1996 changes).

Endnotes

1. 'Private renting has significance, too, as far as the government's concept of 'sustainable home ownership' is concerned. [This] implies that alternative tenures are available to people prior to, and when departing from, home ownership either voluntarily or not.' (House of Commons Environment Committee, 1996, para. 87).
2. As we shall see, Housing Benefit is reduced if a property is underoccupied. However, if there is no available accommodation with less than two bedrooms as may be the case in some areas at some times, it may well be that underoccupation will occur causing problems for Housing Benefit payment.
3. The Social Security Advisory Committee had this to say about the draft SI: 'We find it ironic that the Government, having introduced a lower rate for under 25s on the grounds that such young single people should have lower accommodation expectations, should now argue for an equally reduced rate for over 25s, by applying a principle of equality of treatment for everyone under 60.' (SSAC, 1997, para. 28).
4. It should be added that, under the scheme pertaining in 1995, local authorities had more discretion in deciding whether to pay out greater than a 'reasonable' rent. At that time, the local reference rent and single room rent determinations did not exist.

Bibliography

Arden, A. and Partington, M. (1994), *Housing Law*, London: Sweet & Maxwell
Audit Commission (1993), *Remote Control*, London: HMSO
Bevan, M., Kemp, P. and Rhodes, D. (1995), *Private Landlords and Housing Benefit*, York: Centre for Housing Policy, University of York
Bonnerjea, L. and Lawton, J. (1987), *Homelessness in Brent*, London: Policy Studies Institute

Bramley, G. (1995), *Too High a Price: Homeless Households, Housing Benefit and the Private Rented Sector*, London: Shelter

Burney, E. (1967), *Housing on Trial*, Oxford: Oxford University Press

Commission for Racial Equality (CRE) (1980), *Report of Formal Investigation into Allan's Accommodation Bureaux*, London: CRE

Cowan, D. (1992), 'Policy and the 'North Wiltshire' Scheme', *Local Government Review*, 587

Cowan, D. (1997), *Homelessness: The (In-)Appropriate Applicant*, Aldershot: Dartmouth

Department of the Environment (DoE) (1987), *Housing: The Government's Proposals*, London: HMSO

Department of the Environment (DoE) (1993), *English House Condition Survey 1991*, London: HMSO

Department of the Environment (DoE) (1995a), *Our Future Homes: Opportunity, Choice and Responsibility*, London: HMSO

Department of the Environment (DoE) (1995b), *Improving Standards in Houses in Multiple Occupation*, Consultation Paper Linked to the Housing White Paper 'Our Future Homes', London: DoE

Department of Social Security (DSS) (1998), *Beating Fraud is Everyone's Business*, London: DSS

DTZ Pieda Consulting (1998) *Rents in Local Authority and Registered Social Landlords Sectors*, London: National Housing Federation

Everton, A. (1997), 'Fire precautions – legal controls in houses in multiple occupation: safe havens . . . or . . . any port in a storm?', vol 19, *Journal of Social Welfare and Family Law*, 61

Gibb, K. (1995), *Housing Reforms to Social Security*, Glasgow: Centre for Housing Research and Urban Studies, University of Glasgow

Greater London Council (GLC) (1986), *Private Tenants in London: Counting the Cost*, London: GLC

Harloe, M., Isaacharoff, R. and Minns, R. (1974), *The Organization of Housing: Public and Private Enterprise in London*, London: Heinemann

Hencke, D. (1997), 'Watchdog counts £122,000–per-family cost of homes facelift for tenants', *The Guardian*, 29 January

Hills, J. (1991), *Unravelling Housing Finance*, Oxford: Oxford University Press

House of Commons Environment Committee (1996), *Housing Need*, HC 1995/96 22–I, London: HMSO

Kemp, P. (1992), *Housing Benefit: An Appraisal*, London: HMSO

Kemp, P. and McLaverty, P. (1993), 'Determining eligible rent for rent allowances: a case study of public policy implementation', in P. Malpass and A. Baines (eds), *Housing and Welfare: Housing Studies Association Conference Proceedings Spring 1993*, Bristol: School for Advanced Urban Studies, University of Bristol

Kemp, P. and McLaverty, P. (1994), 'The determination of eligible rents for Housing Benefit: the implementation by local authorities of central government policy', vol 12, *Environment and Planning C*, 109

Kemp, P. and McLaverty, P. (1996), *Private Tenants and Restrictions in Rent for Housing Benefit*, York: Centre for Housing Policy, University of York

Kemp, P., Oldman, C., Rugg, J. and Williams, T. (1994), *The Effects of Benefit on Housing Decisions*, London: HMSO

Kemp, P. and Rugg, J. (1998), *The Single Room Rent: Its Impact on Young People*, York: Centre for Housing Policy, University of York

Kleinman, M., Whitehead, C. and Scanlon, K. (1996), *The Private Rented Sector*, London: National Housing Federation

Leather, P. and Morrison, T. (1997), *The State of UK Housing*, Bristol: Policy Press

MacEwen, M. (1991), *Housing, Race and Law*, London: Routledge

Morris, J. and Winn, M. (1990), *Housing and Social Inequality*, London: Hilary Shipman

Murie, A., Niner, P. and Watson, C. (1976), *Housing Policy and the Housing System*, London: Allen & Unwin

Oldman, C. and Wilcox, S. (1997), *Rents and Service Charges: Definitions and Debates*, London: The Housing Corporation

Partington, M. (1998), 'The reintroduction of rent control' vol 1, *Journal of Housing Law*, 8

Rahilly, S. (1995), 'Housing Benefit: the impact of subsidies on decision-making', vol 2, *Journal of Social Security Law*, 196

Rahilly, S. (1997), Case note, vol 4, *Journal of Social Security Law*, 177

Rhodes, D. and Bevan, M. (1997), *Can the Private Rented Sector House the Homeless?*, York: Centre for Housing Policy, University of York

Rugg, J. (1996), *Opening Doors: Helping People on Low Income Secure Private Rented Accommodation*, York: Centre for Housing Policy, University of York

Rugg, J. (1997), *Closing Doors? Access Schemes and the Recent Housing Changes*, York: Centre for Housing Policy, University of York

Smith, N. (1998), 'Bureaucracy or death: safeguarding lives in houses in multiple occupation', in D. Cowan (ed.), *Housing: Participation and Exclusion*, Aldershot: Dartmouth

Smith, S. (1989), *The Politics of 'Race' and Residence*, Cambridge: Polity

Social Security Advisory Committee (1995), *The Review of Social Security, Paper 3: Housing Benefit*, Leeds: BA Publications

Social Security Advisory Committee (1997), *The Housing Benefit and Council Tax Benefit (General) Amendment Regulations 1997*, CM 3598, London: Stationery Officer

Thatcher, M. (1993), *The Downing Street Years*, London: HarperCollins

Thomas, A. and Hedges, A. (1986), *The 1985 Physical and Social Survey of Houses in Multiple Occupation in England and Wales*, London: HMSO

Wilcox, S. (1997), *Housing Finance Review 1997/98*, York: Joseph Rowntree Foundation

Wilson, W. (1998), *Rent Levels, Affordability and Housing Benefit*, House of Commons Research Paper 98/69, London: House of Commons Library

Witherspoon, S., Whyley, C. and Kempson, E. (1996), *Paying for Rented Housing: Non-Dependent Deductions from Housing Benefit*, London: HMSO

Zebedee, J. and Ward, M. (1997) *Guide to Housing Benefit and Council Tax Benefit*, London: Shelter

12 'This is Mine! This is Private! This is where I belong!':[1] Access to Home Ownership

'Even the use of the English language is affected in government statements. "Despite the continuing growth of *home* ownership, there are still over 8 million rented *dwellings*." Owner occupiers have homes, tenants have dwellings. Council tenants have homes when they are being urged to buy them. The use of the emotive word in the one context rather than the other reflects the attitudes of those making the statements.' Murie *et al.*, 1976, p. 171

Homeowners pay no income tax on the imputed rental value of their property. They pay no capital gains tax on the sale of the property (provided it has been their principal private residence). They are often able to command high proportions of the purchase price in mortgage advance (up to 100 per cent). Alternative tenures are talked down (council housing), limited (RSLs), difficult to come by and offer limited security of tenure (private renting). Access to other tenures is rationed. Furthermore, all government literature 'talks up' the value and role of ownership, arguing on the basis of surveys (conducted by MORI on behalf of the Building Societies Association) that it is what most people want (in 1996, 77 per cent).[2] There is no party political bias in this, for all have jockeyed for position in the post-war period to be regarded as the party of the homeowner. So, it might be argued that Blair's repositioning of New Labour as the 'party of the homeowner' was a crucial step in the party's transformation. Even after the worst post-war recession, the Conservative government's 1995 housing White Paper argued:

'A high level of home ownership, alongside a healthy rented market, is good for the country and good for the individual. 80% of people favour home ownership over other forms of tenure. They value independence and control over their own home. Buying a home is often cheaper than renting. Home owners know that in later life, when the mortgage has been paid off, they will have the security of an asset which will help maintain their living standards.' (DoE, 1995, p. 12)

The promotion of home ownership is seen as satisfying the male's 'deep and natural desire . . . to have independent control of the home that shelters him and his family' (DoE, 1971; see also Gilroy's critique: 1994, p. 35). Whilst the 1995 White Paper also talked about a 'sustainable' level of home ownership, the message was clear: the government wanted to help as many as possible into this tenure.

Sustained academic analysis has followed suit arguing that home ownership represents a 'search for ontological security' (Saunders, 1990, p. 293). This term:

'refers to the confidence that human beings have in the continuity of their self-identity and in the constancy of the surrounding social and material environments of actions. A sense of the reliability of persons and things . . . is basic to feelings of ontological security . . . but it is an emotional, rather than a cognitive, phenomenon, and it is rooted in the unconscious.' (Giddens, 1990, p. 92)

Saunders argues that 'a home of one's own offers both a physical (hence spatially rooted) and permanent (hence temporally rooted) location in the world'. Despite accepting that the concept is 'difficult to operationalize empirically', he suggests a number of indicators which, he argues, lend support to his thesis that ontological security is 'enhanced' by accessing home ownership. This viewpoint has been subjected to critiques, based upon substantial empirical evidence (see generally Forrest *et al.*, 1990). The first part of this chapter reviews the available evidence. We might observe at this stage that ascribing a certain set of values and principles to those who fall within the *generic* term 'home ownership' should generate a certain amount of scepticism.

A further perspective is the massive development since the 1980s of *low-cost* home ownership (see Forrest *et al.*, 1984, Ch. 4). Commonly, this has implied the creation of home ownership through discounts and/or incentives. For example, rather than continue to allow sales of accommodation to council tenants on a discretionary basis, the Housing Act 1980 created the 'right' of such a tenant to buy their own accommodation at a progressive discount depending upon the duration of their tenancy. Between 1979–1991, the sale of council housing to sitting tenants accounted for 46 per cent of the rise in home ownership nationally (from 55 to 68 per cent) (Forrest & Murie, 1995, p. 408). The 1995 White Paper heralded the expansion of the accumulative process to RSL tenants (p. 15), subsequently brought into effect in the Housing Act 1996 as the 'right to acquire'. Shared-ownership schemes, for example through the local authority, RSL, or building societies, have been further, less heralded methods of enhancing low-cost home ownership. However, these forms of ownership further erode the notion of generic home ownership as part of the continuing need for innovation to progress the ideological goal of reducing welfare through increasing property ownership. A number of legal and policy issues present themselves here for discussion.[3] Central to the discussion, though, is the way the implementation of the preference for home ownership, as opposed to council housing, impacts upon a local authority's obligations to the homeless. Local authorities (and RSLs) are required to provide accommodation to certain parts of the homelessness population without adequate resources, as these have been privatized. Inescapably, this takes us to the Westminster City Council alleged gerrymandering scandal of the 1990s.

Before commencing the analysis, two introductory points are necessary. These are, to a certain extent, dependent upon each other. First, the backdrop to this chapter is one of considerable change in the terrain of home ownership. In the mid to late 1980s, there was an overflow of market success as home owners were faced with rising prices. Many jumped on the bandwagon, possibly afraid of not being able to afford to buy at a later stage. This boom was enhanced and influenced by policy-makers, and exchange professionals such as mortgage 'advisers' and the legal profession. For example, mortgage relief at source (MIRAS) was available to two persons taking out a mortgage on the same property. This was abandoned in 1988, so that only one person became entitled to the benefits of MIRAS. However, three months' notice of this abandonment was given, causing a greater flow of properties (and panic) as buyers rushed to meet the deadline. The 'bust' which closely followed the 'boom' in the early 1990s led to the introduction of a new phrase into legal language and everyday use: negative equity. This affected those people whose mortgages were greater than the value of their property and was combined with a separate phenomenon of increasing (re-)possessions of property by mortgagees. At the time of writing, the 'bust' cycle has probably ended. Thus, if one was writing between 1992–4, the focus might have been on how negative equity was created and the repossession 'crisis' (see, for example, Forrest & Murie, 1994; Gentle *et al.*, 1994; Dorling & Cornford,1995); in 1998, the current focus is on '*sustainability*' of those accessing home ownership (see, for example, Dwelly, 1997) together with '*coping strategies*' of those whose property has suffered from negative equity (Forrest and Kennett, 1996; see also Munro and Madigan, 1998). (This time frame is, of course, a caricature, in that it suggests neat patterns when there are, in fact, overlaps and concentrations throughout). The optimism of the 1980s boom era (reflected in Saunders 1990) has given way to more sanguine analyses (Forrest *et al.*, 1990).

Second, the housing market does not respond uniformly to house price booms and busts. There are significant spatial variations, often within the same area (*cf* the five TCI bands which do not respect such diversity: see Ch. 9). Generally, it appears that there is an epicentre (London) which then ripples out to the surrounding areas (Bramley, 1994). Thus, the bust cycle particularly affects, and did affect, those in London and the South East/West. This also meant that negative equity was largely a phenomenon of Southern England, with the North relatively unaffected, in part due to lower entry prices. Other aspects of the 'bust' period involved the types of person affected by negative equity. This was dependent upon the mortgage advance (the higher the proportion of advance, the greater the possibility of negative equity), the date of purchase, the income of the home owner(s), age of home owner, occupation of homeowner, as well as the value of property (see Dorling

& Cornford, 1995). Thus, we need to make the important point that the boom-bust cycle, which affects access points, has temporal, spatial and life cycle foci (see Forrest & Murie, 1994).

12.1 The Value(s) of Home Ownership

Despite the recession, the impact of negative equity does not appear to have overly dulled the desire, shown by surveys, for home ownership (although it may well be that the 'under 25s' have been so affected: Pannell, 1997, p. 10). It seems that, whatever the market throws at people, the desire for home ownership remains constant. The British Social Attitudes survey consistently find high proportions extolling the virtues of home ownership.[4] Governments of whatever hue have for most of the post-war period argued that there is a 'deep and natural' desire for home ownership. Saunders has put flesh on these bland assertions by suggesting that the advantages of home ownership are so significant that, if not genetic, people *desire* to become home owners. Using survey evidence from three towns (Burnley, Slough, and Derby), he suggests that:

'Two principal motives are mentioned time and time again when people are asked why they prefer to own rather than rent their homes. One is financial – buying is seen as cheaper in the long run, or rent is seen as a waste of money, or rising prices are seen as a means of saving for the future or accumulating capital. The other has to do with the sense of independence and autonomy which ownership confers – the freedom from control and surveillance by a landlord and the ability to personalize the property according to one's tastes.' (1990, p. 84)

Saunders goes on to argue that home owners, as a class, have an intersection of interests in, for example, rising prices. Drawing on the work of Dunleavy, he argues that housing tenure forms part of a realignment of society through the creation of a 'sectoral cleavage' (pp. 332 *et seq*). This sectoral cleavage has a 'material basis as well as a political and ideological expression' (p. 333). Such a cleavage arises 'wherever the state is involved in providing goods or services to one group while another is able to provide or buy them for itself in the private sector' (p. 334). This cleavage, opened by the expansion of home ownership, leads to emphasized societal divisions between the haves and the have nots. The cleavage operates when one consumes any item – thus the term 'consumption sector cleavage' – in the private sector ('the exercise of consumer power') or the public sector ('the experience of consumer powerlessness'). The underclass, increasingly, is that class which is dependent upon state welfare.

The notion that home ownership provides financial advantages was certainly true, as implied in the opening paragraph of this chapter (income tax and capital gains exemptions). The statistical extent of negative equity, and mortgage repossession, can also be exaggerated (although, perhaps, not in one's consciousness). As Forrest and Murie suggest, 'tenure preferences are not formed in a vacuum but are heavily influenced by the pattern of subsidy, general housing policies and the individual judgements regarding financial expectations and changes in family circumstances' (1991, p. 123).

On the other hand, government did its best to maintain the notion that home ownership was 'a basic and natural desire' (DoE, 1977, p. 50). This was achieved through tax incentives:

> 'In this kind of thinking the encouragement of owner-occupation takes on a duty of satisfying innate desires. There is a neat logical trick here: people desire owner–occupation as it is more financially attractive because state policies have made it so; this desire is seen as natural; it is thus up to the government to meet this natural desire. What could be more natural?' (Short, 1982, p. 119)

In other words, governments acted, through tax incentives and advantages, to make home ownership more desirable than other forms of tenure. Kemeny argues that the explosion in numbers of home owners could not have been inevitable but was due to subtle shifts in incentives and subsidies, actively implicating the state in this process (1981, 1992). A principal incentive was mortgage interest tax relief, which became deducted at source in 1982 (hence MIRAS). This tax relief was 'regressive' in the economic sense, for the greater the income tax a person paid the greater the tax relief on their mortgage payments (see, for example, Karn *et al.*, 1986, pp. 125–127). Whilst the limit of MIRAS was pegged to £30,000, on the assumption of interest rates at 15 per cent, a higher rate taxpayer (at 40 per cent) would receive an extra £675 per annum, increasing their total tax relief on their mortgage payment (Hills, 1990, p. 196). Furthermore, Hills extrapolates that mortgage interest relief actually led to a greater subsidy being given to home owners than to tenants (pp. 27–8). Indeed, Forrest and Murie refer to a 'paradox that, as owner occupation has expanded, it has become progressively what it is not supposed to be. It has become dependent in its present form on large-scale public support' (1990, p. 164).

Thus the income incentives to buy were significant even though the hidden costs of home ownership, such as maintenance and repairs, may well make it more expensive in the long run (see Kemeny, 1981, Ch. 3). Furthermore, as mortgages have become pegged to variable interest rates, the cost of buying with a mortgage is directly linked to the national (and thus the global) economy. When interest rates go up, so do mortgage costs (a fact not missed by popular media which concentrates on interest rate rises – see Gurney, 1990, pp. 8–10). Those with large mortgages are disproportionately affected as their housing costs dramatically increase with interest rate rises. Generally, those who have borrowed the largest amounts proportionate with the value of their properties have been most at risk, although the risk of unemployment is ubiquitous. The spatial aspect must also be considered, for in some areas it remains much cheaper to rent than to own (see Forrest & Murie, 1990, p. 48).

The present situation also provides a crucial contrast with past experience. Mortgage interest tax relief is reduced with reduced rates of taxation and lower interest rates. However, other changes have altered the regressive nature of this relief so that over a period of time it has become associated with lower marginal taxation rates. Currently, this tax relief can extend to no more than 15 per cent and is likely to be phased out over time. In 1990/91, £7.7 billion was spent in mortgage tax relief compared with £2.4 billion in 1997/98 (Wilcox, 1997, Table 100), at a time when the market share due to home ownership was increasing. It is suggested that 'The reductions in owner-occupier tax relief have the appearance of being almost purely fiscal with the objective of raising more revenue from income taxation without raising the basic rate of tax' (Holmans & Whitehead, 1997, p. 41). The economic incentives which skewed preferences in favour of home ownership are in the process of considerable flux. It is unlikely that these incentives will ever return. The paradox of central regulation has altered its trajectory so that, instead of subsidy, regulation impacts through manipulation of interest rates which themselves are heavily dependent upon the global economy and the risks inherent in that:

'And it is through the manipulation of interest rates, the monetarist vehicle for achieving its goals, that home owners have become locked into the circuit of fiscal regulation. As the potential for risk, insecurity and instability has increased within the global arena, at the level of the nation-state universal support for home owners has been eroded.' (Forrest & Kennett, 1996, p. 374)

As regards capital accumulation – that is, the rising values of owner–occupied property – it now seems clear that this is considerably stratified in the general sense that those who started off with more make greater profits than those who begin with less: 'Home ownership may be a game all can play, but the chances of winning are skewed heavily in certain directions' (Forrest & Murie, 1990, p. 90). Thus, home ownership should be construed as a 'continuum' with a low income end which is indistinct from renting (*ibid*, p. 198; see also Doling & Stafford, 1989, p. 150). Evidence from a study conducted by Karn *et al.* (in the late 1970s) of areas of low income home ownership in Birmingham and Liverpool – considered further below – suggested that home ownership was 'a squalid trap':

'Unlike many owners who might expect capital gains on their property and the possibility of movement to a different strata of the market, these owners may suffer real capital losses and far from being able to move they will be forced to stay in a deteriorating asset which will be in a deteriorating condition.' (1985, p. 106)

So, even before negative equity became associated with home ownership, the diversity of experience was mirrored by differential returns, with some people receiving negative returns. The employment consequences resulting from the lack of mobility are by-products and are reflected in settlement patterns. The 1990s' housing collapse also had a differential effect but this time in the Conservative heartlands of the South East:

'The collapse has occurred in the heartland of British home ownership – in areas where in some cases 90 per cent of households are in that tenure. It is in these areas where the professional and managerial classes are concentrated, where the new service class of Thatcher's Britain invested heavily in a booming housing market and where large numbers of households extended their mortgage credit to the limit to enter an owner occupied market which in the late 1980s was pulling further away in price terms from other regions' (Forrest & Murie, 1994, p. 60)

Here Saunders' notion of consistent and constant capital gain, with upward mobility from starter home, looks a product of its time.

The notion of 'independence' is closely bound up with that of 'ontological security', that essential element of control and security missing in other more public aspects of our lives. Drawing on questionnaire-based evidence in three towns, he uses three indicators which, he suggests, go some way to showing that access to home ownership enhances individuals' ontological security: the meaning of home; the strength of attachment to homes; the personalization of dwellings. Owners tended to associate 'home' with relaxation and personal possession, whilst renters defined it in terms of family or neighbourhood – 'One possible explanation for these variations is that tenants are less able than owners to express a sense of self and belonging through their houses' (p. 294). The differences were most marked for council house purchasers. Tenants were 'much less inclined to develop attachments to their houses than owners' (*ibid*). Because of local authority control through the tenancy agreement, tenants were less likely to have personalized their homes (particularly because they had little or no choice over the property allocated to them).

However, it can be argued that, in fact, these findings are only true of particular segments of home owners. So, for example, the home may also be regarded as the location for gender distinctions: 'The organisation of power and responsibility within the 'home-as-haven' may result in misery, repression, violence and frustration' (Gurney, 1990, p. 25; see also the material in Ch. 1). We are becoming used to reports of violence occurring within the home, by one family member against another – in many ways, our growing knowledge of the extent of this, together with other issues such as paedophilia, reflects the greater willingness to pierce the ownership veil. It is the distinction drawn between home, household and dwelling which Kemeny criticizes:

'The home cannot be understood except as a product of the social organisation of the household in relation to the dwelling as a spatial reflection of that organisation and the limitations that this places on, and the possibilities that it opens up for, household members' activities and relationships. Therefore the neglect of that relationship must necessarily impoverish any understanding of the home.' (Kemeny, 1992, p. 158)

In their critique of Saunders' thesis, Forrest *et al.* (1990) argue that Saunders' data also admit of other explanations, more in line with the findings from other studies. For example, council tenants who purchased their property (under the pre-1980 power of local authorities to sell the property) 'were more likely to identify rent levels and rent rises as the most important gain associated with buying rather than consideration of investment, security or freedoms and independence associated with home ownership' (p. 171). Furthermore, home owners form a considerable proportion of those on the housing register (29 per cent in 1991: Prescott-Clarke *et al.*, 1994, p. 78). They argue that the data also suit a 'less preoccupied explanation':

'This would shift from trying to demonstrate that tenure produces certain attitudes and would regard it as an achieved status reflecting housing histories, strategies, choices, opportunities and constraints. It is the output of processes. . . . Indeed, there is a great danger that by presenting home ownership as a superior, exclusive tenure it is implied that anyone not in it has not made rational choices. *All housing choices operate within constraints.*' (p. 178; emphasis added)

This latter point is discussed in the next section. However, we should also observe, as do Forrest *et al.*, that the proprietary rights of home ownership are temporally based. So, for example, the status of private renting was, at one time, regarded (by lawyers) as a 'status of irremovability' with proprietary rights attached to it (see Hand, 1980). Furthermore, the reality of home ownership for many is of *in*security, exacerbated by legal rules favouring mortgage lenders.

12.2 Choice *v.* Constraint

Greater levels of home ownership are encouraged by the poverty of alternative options. So, if there simply is no private rental market in an area, or the area is already dominated by owner–occupation, it makes sense that ownership will flourish. As we have seen in previous chapters in this part, access to public sector accommodation is resource-led and heavily dependent upon availability of accommodation together with moral/political overtones. Earlier chapters have suggested that govern-ment has successfully manipulated subsidy to the public sector with the effect of increasing rents. Accessing RSL accommodation is commonly hidebound by similar issues as well as higher rents. Thus, governments fuelled the expansion of home ownership by creating the circumstances best equipped to enable it to expand (Kemeny, 1981). As Forrest and Murie suggest:

> 'Certainly ineligibility for council housing among certain groups, long waiting lists, the prospect of being allocated an unpopular flat or maisonette, the lack of private rented accommodation, rising rents and a general decline in investment in public housing are all factors which can fuel preferences for home ownership.' (1991, p. 123; see also Karn *et al.*, 1985, pp. 51–57)

Thus, the desire for home ownership can arise because of constraints inherent in accessing other tenures. Sometimes, people buy because they have no other option available to them (and precisely the same is true as Forrest & Murie's study of Hyndburn shows: 1991, pp. 183–188). This is termed the 'coerced exchange', to which we return later in this chapter.

Affordability of housing to buy in certain areas also creates a differentiated market with certain segments of low-income home owner-ship. These areas are linked with both issues of 'race' and gender. Commentators have drawn attention to the high proportions of Indian and Caribbean and the low proportions of Bangladeshi households in owner–occupation (see generally, Karn, 1997). The reasons for this are complex and draw on the above as well as the analysis in earlier chapters which has suggested patterns of discrimination. For example, even when they managed to access council housing, Afro-Caribbean households most commonly occupied accommodation a class of property lower than white households (Peach & Byron, 1994, p. 366; a point to which we return below).

It is perhaps unsurprising in the light of this evidence that Karn *et al.*'s research in inner city areas in Birmingham and Liverpool uncovered a high density of ethnic minorities in this accommodation: 'Disadvantaged in the labour market, in the bureaucratically managed public housing system and in the private rental market, many of these households 'opted' to buy cheap inner city dwellings' (1985, p. 2). This segregation has, in many cases, not dissipated amongst white dominated dwellings, partly because discrimination exists in the institutions which govern access to home ownership. When account is taken of socio-economic differentials thrown up by the census, as well as geographical differences between ethnic groupings, interesting patterns remain. Pakistani households are 19.9 per cent more likely to become owner-occupiers, and 18 per cent less likely to be found in council housing, than expected; Black-African households are 17.6 per cent less likely to be owner occupiers and 9.5 per cent more likely to be in council housing than expected. As Dorling puts it: 'Most of the tenure patterns of ethnic minorities cannot be explained by the jobs they do, their household structure or by where they live. *"All else" is not equal in housing in Britain in 1991.*' (Dorling, 1997, pp. 155–6; original emphasis)

This completes the circle of discrimination against ethnic groups in accessing accommodation in whatever sector. In answering the suggestion that this might be part of the exercise of choice, Smith makes the following point:

> 'Even if black people prefer segregation, it is hard to understand why they should pursue this in the more run-down segments of the housing stock, rather than in areas where they could secure the symbolic and economic benefits associated with suburban life.' (1989, p. 37)

Early examples of discrimination involved building societies 'redlining' certain areas,[5] stereotyping area preferences, or even stereotyping credit ratings on ethnic lines. All of this suggests that 'building society activity (and inactivity) has probably been most decisive (directly or indirectly) in sustaining the 'racial' dimension of residential segregation at a local level in the private sector' (Smith, 1989, p. 89). Other examples of 'exchange professionals' mediating discrimination include estate agents re-enforcing segregation (CRE, 1990).

It is unclear how far this pattern exists today, particularly as the profit-motive dominates mortgage lending and dictates the searching out of new markets. A snapshot of two new-build estates in Bristol and Luton found an under-representation of ethnic group households (Forrest *et al.*, 1997, p. 16) but no general conclusions can be drawn from this. More than anything, the effect of differential labour market access and reward provides a neat excuse to building society managers:

> 'Institutional racism in the owner-occupied sector . . . is the result of a blend of common-sense subjective racism and structural factors. The exclusion of certain areas, properties or people with low or insecure incomes has a common-sense financial and administrative legitimation, to the extent that a building society manager can claim that lending on such properties or to such people is too risky' (Ginsburg, 1992, p. 119)

Drawing on 'structuration theory' – which posits relationships between structures and individual agency taking account of factors such as individuals' knowledge, capability over a period of time – Sarre *et al.* have drawn attention to a more complex social reality than one based upon a binary choice:constraint division (1989). Thus, for example, one needs to consider broader structural factors, such as the *political* meanings ascribed to phrases such as 'racial segregation' (see Smith, 1993).

A similar pattern affects women's access to home ownership. The available data from the 1991 census (which may be tarnished: Gilroy, 1994, p. 31) and other sources, suggest a fairly consistent picture of access to owner-occupation being dependent upon men: 'Women's home ownership, then, is generally one of ownership and not purchase and that ownership has been arrived at through their relationship with a man' (Gilroy, 1994, p. 36; see also Pascall, 1997, p. 136). This reflects women's weaker economic position in the labour market and impacts upon women's opportunities in the housing market (the evidence is reviewed by Gilroy, 1994, pp. 45–49). Thus, women's movements on relationship breakdown reflect a tenure change from owner-occupation to local authority (see Bull, 1995),[6] although such a tenure change is often hampered by the gatekeepers within the authority (see Ch. 7). Single parents, typecast in the media, are likely to be similarly typecast by mortgage lenders although the latter are able to legitimate this by reference to lower wages.

12.3   Regulation and Choice: Entering the Mortgage Contract

In this part, we put mortgage lenders under the spotlight. So far in this chapter, we have paid only scant attention to the contract of mortgage. However, it was the most powerful tool in the hands of the Conservative Party (short of local government) of expanding the tenure of home ownership. What I wish to show is that the mortgage contract, despite the rhetoric of consumerism, is largely unregulated (except at the margins). Consumerism is perhaps better explored through the notion of choice. In this context, the final part of this section considers the response of mortgage companies to the recession – sustainability apparently now equals flexibility.

A Narrow Legal Jurisdiction

Most people require a mortgage when they buy property. In Chapter 3, we saw how the mortgage market was revolutionized in the 1980s in order to facilitate the rise in home ownership. Mortgage lenders and mortgage borrowers are clearly in an unequal position. A series of judicial decisions at the turn of the century balanced the desire to retain the sanctity of the contractual bargain inherent in the mortgage transaction against the evident possibility of exploitation. The result is an extremely narrow jurisdiction: the courts will only become involved in mortgage transactions where the agreement is '(1) unfair and unconscionable, or (2) in the nature of a penalty clogging the equity of redemption, or (3) inconsistent with or repugnant to the contractual and equitable right to redeem' (*Kreglinger* v. *New Patagonia Meat Company Ltd* [1914] AC 25, *per* Lord Parker). Unfairness and unconscionability, in this triumvirate, do not bear their ordinary meaning. Rather they seem to have a specific, narrow construction, as Browne-Wilkinson J suggested:

  '. . . it is not enough to show that, in the eyes of the court, [the mortgage bargain] was unreasonable. In my judgment a bargain cannot be unfair and unconscionable unless one of the parties to it has *imposed the objectionable terms in a morally reprehensible manner*, that is to say, in a way which affects his conscience.' *Multiservice Bookbinding Ltd* v. *Marden* [1979] Ch 84 (emphasis added)

Thus, judicial intervention in a mortgage bargain on these principles is rare. This is particularly so as few standard mortgages these days affect the right of redemption (that is, the right to pay back the mortgage lender in full). The Consumer Credit Act 1974 explicitly excludes building societies from its terms (s 16) although it does affect banks and finance companies. A credit bargain can be found to be 'extortionate' (s 137) but the definition of this word once again narrows the jurisdiction: 'grossly exorbitant' or 'otherwise grossly contravenes ordinary principles of fair dealing' (s 138). Thus, its effect seems to be marginal (see Bentley & Howells, 1989).

Regulation 'By the Back Door'

Standard term contracts – that is, those contracts which are presented by one party for signing by the other without being negotiated – are now subject to a much more rigorous, but little known, regime. These contracts are 'complex transactions [which] can be made with a minimum of negotiation and by relatively unskilled personnel, and that supplier's risks are reduced and standardised. . . . Even if a customer is aware of what is in the standard form and protests, it is likely to be met with a take-it-or-leave-it attitude' (Beale, 1994, pp. 231–2). Protection against 'unfair terms' in consumer contracts has hitherto not extended to property transactions, including mortgage lending.

By virtue of an EC Council Directive (93/13/EEC, 5 April 1993), member states were required to implement regulations relating to unfair terms in standard term contracts which *do* now affect property transactions. This potentially important regulation (brought into effect as the Unfair Terms in Consumer Contracts Regulations 1994, SI 1994/3159) is limited where it is most needed, however, for it provides that 'no assessment shall be made of the fairness of any term which . . . concerns the adequacy of the price or remuneration, as against the goods or services sold or supplied' (Reg 3(2)(b)). This means that assessments of the fairness of such matters as interest rates on the transaction do not fall within the ambit of the regulations (although if the term is not expressed in 'plain, intelligible language' it will be given the 'interpretation most favourable to the consumer': Reg 6).

Self-regulation

The narrowness of the jurisdiction is matched by the narrowness of the legislation affecting the mortgage contract. The political strength of the building society and mortgage lending lobby is also considerable, with a concomitant impact on the breadth and acceptability of legislation affecting lending. Direct regulation is, therefore, minimal in a supposedly deregulated market. In this context, together with the increased competition of the 1980s, many mortgage lenders sought to maximize their markets by reducing their credit tests and increasing the amount they were willing to grant (up to 100 per cent of the value of the property in many cases[7]). This increased availability of credit fuelled the house price rises of the 1980s and has been posited as a major cause of the boom-bust scenario.

One effect of the 1990s bust part of the cycle has been the move to *self*-regulation, rather than risk the increasing reliance on credit. Self-regulation also reflects the ethos of corporate regulation in the 1990s, in which home buying is regarded by governments as an example of the exercise of consumer choice: 'The reliance placed on mortgage finance, as the means of gaining access to the social entitlement of decent housing, is indicative of the new conception of an individual in society as 'consumer-citizen" (Whitehouse, 1998b, p. 189). The presumption has always been that the consumer-citizen will exercise rational choice in the market place. Rational choice assumes knowledge of the terms of different mortgage contracts. However, first, it appears that borrowers rarely consider the 'small print' of the contract, but concentrate on the price to be paid (Whitehouse, 1998b); second, until recently this small print was dominated by 'legalese' – or deliberate complexity. The first batch of self-regulation in 1992 required lenders to put terms into plain English, although as Whitehouse notes:

'Terms incorporated into these standard contracts include, for example, making the mortgagor liable for much of the cost involved in the mortgage transaction. The fact that these terms are put into 'plain English' merely ensures that the mortgagor is absolutely clear about what the rights of the mortgagee are.' (1998a, p. 136)

One example of such a term is the common requirement in mortgages of more than 75 per cent of the purchase price that the borrower pay the lender an extra premium to create extra security against negative equity (the lender most often uses this to buy mortgage indemnity insurance). The lender, in this way, is protected against negative equity through insurance as well as the borrower's contract to repay the full amount of the loan whatever the value of the security.

The Labour Party's manifesto for the 1997 general election included the threat that 'Mortgage buyers also require stronger consumer protection, for example, by extension of the Financial Services Act, against the sale of disadvantageous mortgage packages'. However, the Council of Mortgage Lenders – the body representing 98 per cent of lenders – issued its own voluntary, self-regulatory document in March 1997. This document – *The Code of Mortgage Lending Practice* (CML, 1997) – is essentially about the level of service a consumer might expect from the lender. It is an anodyne document, putting into 'plain English' the current practice of mortgage lenders. The only concession appears to be that the mortgage lender should provide a greater level of information to the borrower (Ch. 3). The result of this, then, is that entry into the mortgage contract is largely unregulated by the law. Given that most people require mortgages to buy property, the imbalance in the relationship between lender and borrower can only be explained by the symbiotic relationship between government's desire to increase home ownership and the lenders' evident desire to increase their market share.

Sustainability and Flexibility

Rational choice requires a market in which the consumer can exercise that choice. The Conservative government provided that market with the deregulation of the financial services industry. Increased competition led to different lenders offering different products. In the climate of instability during and after the recession, it became clear that borrowers required greater flexibility in types of mortgage as well as mortgage payments. A significant portion of those most affected by negative equity were the younger home owners. These people are particularly affected by the mortgage contract because most mortgage payments are 'frontloaded' – that is, payments at the beginning of the mortgage are greater than at the end because the amount outstanding is greater. This problem, together with the problems of intermittent unemployment within the casualized labour market, has meant that lenders have had to offer different products. In this case, then, it may reasonably be characterized as the dog (the labour market) wagging the tail (the mortgage market).

The 1995 White Paper talked about 'sustainable' home ownership and suggested that government would encourage lenders to create 'flexible mortgage products suitable for the growing number of self-employed and people on fixed term contracts' (DoE, 1995a, p. 13). Added emphasis was provided by the New Labour Party manifesto which suggested that a New Labour government 'would work with mortgage providers to encourage greater provision of more flexible mortgages to protect families in a world of increased job insecurity'. The message from governments has therefore been clear: they will work with lenders to establish new types of mortgage in order for the lenders to establish greater market control and so further fuel the inexorable rise of home ownership, undimmed by the downside(s) of home ownership.

Lenders have, however, stolen a march on the prospect of government intervention. For some time, they have considered, and some offered, 'flexible' mortgage packages. Indeed, *Which?* Magazine provided examples drawn from 18 different lenders (cited in Williams, 1997, p. 45). The most flexible package was offered by the Bank of Scotland Mortgages Direct. This package enabled customers to borrow up to 95 per cent of the value of the property; interest was calculated monthly and borrowers had to make at least ten payments per annum. Borrowers were entitled to increase their payments, pay lump sums (subject to conditions), make lower payments, take payment 'holidays', and to loan draw-downs.[8] All of this is useful but low take-up rates suggest that they are not popular. One reason for low take-up is provided by Williams:

> 'Due recognition has to be given to the costs of servicing such loans which by their very nature are more complex and staff intensive. This is then reflected in pricing and charges and this in turn will impact upon consumer demand' (*ibid*, p. 46)

In other words, consumer choice and flexibility (and, thus, sustainability) is possible, but at a price. In *Roof*, the Director-general of the CML suggested that governments wanted flexible mortgages but the 'jury is out' on whether consumers actually wanted them (Birch, 1997, p. 24). Cynically, it might be argued that the proletarianization of lenders' workforce, combined with the standardization of documentation, meets certain market circumstances and is beneficial to lenders; it is not, however, beneficial to borrowers.

12.4   Low-cost Home Ownership

The Conservative governments between 1979–1997 will forever be associated with the facilitation of low-cost home ownership. The essence of New Right philosophy – reduce welfare by increasing personal responsibility and self-reliance – was perceived to coordinate with electoral advantage. The best-known example of the pursuance of this philosophy was the privatization of individual units of council housing through giving council tenants the 'right to buy' their council houses. Previously, local authorities had a discretion to sell their stock (see Murie *et al.*, 1976, for analysis). In the juridified 1980s, policies were put in place in the Housing Act 1980 to force councils to sell their accommodation. The sales have tended to benefit the better-off tenants who were able to purchase the better quality accommodation. This must be seen in the broader context of councils' allocations policies: the better quality accommodation is always going to be the most desirable but it is allocated most often to those who have the greatest bargaining power.

It is right to concentrate on the right-to-buy council housing, for it has been the means through which the Conservatives engineered a massive withdrawal from local authority tenure. About two million council sector units of accommodation have been sold off since 1980. However, the phrase 'low-cost home ownership' refers to a much broader, lengthier programme than council house sales. Most recently, for example, slightly different issues have been raised in relation to the right to acquire RSL accommodation.

Apparently, in June 1980, Michael Heseltine, then Secretary of State for the Environment, announced that the drive to expand home ownership would take into account a programme of seven elements (which built on earlier innovations):

'1. Selling council houses to sitting tenants.
 2. Selling local authority-owned land to private builders with planning permission for starter home schemes.
 3. Building starter homes for sale on local authority land in partnership with private builders.
 4. Improving homes for sale.
 5. Selling unimproved homes for improvement by the purchasers.
 6. Offering shared ownership as an alternative to outright sales wherever possible.
 7. Using the new local authority mortgage guarantee power to facilitate down market lending by building societies.' (See Forrest *et al.*, 1984, p. 37)

In this section, I want to discuss three elements from this programme: shared ownership; right to buy; right to acquire. This is because the former, whilst being marginal in the 1980s, is now gathering impetus as a potentially expandable tenure; also because it does not fit neatly into the conventional notions of home ownership. It therefore provides a neat method of exhibiting the diversity within the tenure. The right to buy is obviously a crucial part of this section and needs no further explanation. The new right of RSL tenants to acquire their properties should be contrasted with the right to buy. The right to acquire has been framed differently, which leaves awkward questions about different rights within the 'social' sector. The impact of the right to buy has been substantial, not only on central and local governments, but also upon tenure structures. Thus, Forrest and Murie argue:

'But again, to borrow from Rex and Moore (1967), [British cities where most of the sales have been concentrated] are areas where principal forms of access to housing are being transformed, where the rules of competition for housing are changing and where legitimation "in terms of the values of the welfare state" is giving way to legitimation in terms of the ideal of 'a property-owning democracy' (*ibid.*: 274–5).'(1995, p. 409)

Shared ownership

Shared ownership has recently been discussed as one of the 'flexible' 'sustainable' responses to recession (DoE, 1995a, p. 14). Essentially, shared-ownership schemes rest upon the basis of some form of equity sharing. A purchaser buys part of the equity in the property (usually up to 75 per cent) with the rest being paid for by somebody else, such as a housing association, building society,[9] or local authority. The purchaser can buy larger shares at a later time – known as 'staircasing' – but until the property is 100 per cent owned the buyer usually pays rent as a proportion of the outstanding amount. The legal construction of these agreements is most commonly that the purchaser takes the property on a long lease, granted at a premium to reflect the proportionate share, with the equity sharer retaining the larger interest (in simple transactions, this will be the freehold) and taking a second charge on the lease (the purchaser's mortgagee taking the first charge). Commonly also in the social sector, if the purchaser subsequently decides to sell the property on, the equity sharer will have a right of pre-emption (that is, a right of first refusal).

From one perspective, 'shared ownership' is nothing more than the grant of a long lease at a premium – there is certainly nothing innovative about that. Leaseholds are all part of the feudalism inherent in property law. However, this hides something rather different. Leaseholds may be feudalistic but here they are being used as an *innovation*. The real differences lie in the fact that the lease represents a share in the property for the 'tenant' and the 'landlord' also retains a real stake in the property (the remaining proportion). The use value of the property is granted to the tenant, as is usual with a lease, but the exchange value is rather different as it reflects the proportion owned by the tenant and not the value of the lease itself. Anachronistic legal concepts legitimate the device but the nomenclature adopted – 'shared ownership' – reflects neither the bargain nor its legal construction.

In the public sector, early attempts to provide shared ownership in the Housing Act 1980, together with a *right* to shared ownership subsequently granted in the Housing and Building Control Act 1984, were largely perceived as failures. There was a low take-up and the arrangements were overly complicated. In the Leasehold Reform, Housing and Urban Development Act 1993, a new scheme was brought into force, known as the 'rents-to-mortgages scheme'. This has also met with minimum take-up (in single figures) partly because of its complexity (see Hughes & Lowe, 1995, pp. 75–82, where the law is outlined in the full regalia of legal complexity) and partly because it is unavailable to those who are entitled to Housing Benefit. As a significant proportion of council tenants are entitled to Housing Benefit, and those not entitled are probably able to obtain a competitive mortgage to finance the purchase of their property at considerable discount, the scheme was perhaps more symbolic than real. It was a further way in which central government flexed its control over local government.

In the RSL sector, shared ownership has a rather longer history, although, once again, it has recently been revived. Funding comes direct from the Housing Corporation which subsidizes the RSL's share. It is a significant part of the 'social housing' programme, accounting for about 13,500 units of accommodation, which itself represents about 28.5 per cent in 1996–97 (Bramley & Dunmore, 1996, p. 110). One of the perceived benefits is a tie-in with the concerns about tenure diversity on RSL estates, for shared ownership is nothing if not an encouragement to diversity (Page, 1993). The predominant motive has, however, been widening access to home ownership (Bramley & Dunmore, p. 107). Shared ownership is available to all RSL tenants. However, the variant Do-it-Yourself Shared Ownership (DIYSO) is also open to others. DIYSO is a significant part of the overall programme and differs from mainstream shared ownership only in the sense that prospective purchasers find their own property anywhere (up to a maximum value and maximum number of bedrooms, depending on their financial status).

Allocations into shared ownership are regulated by the Housing Corporation (1997, p. 39), which requires that applicants be in priority need, an existing local authority or RSL tenant; *and* should not be able to afford other private provision; *and* should be able to obtain their own mortgage together with having ability to meet the other costs of purchase (such as solicitor's costs); *and* would release rented accommodation if part of the Tenants' Incentive Scheme; *and*, if the scheme is for the elderly, the applicant should be over 55. These criteria limit the applicability of the scheme, but it is further restricted by the Corporation's own interpretation of these criteria:

'The Corporation will expect RSLs to give reasonable preference to:
a applicants in greater housing need, taking into account their ability to meet that need in the local housing market
b their ability to meet the outgoings without hardship
c existing social housing tenants or tenants that have been nominated by the local authority for home ownership or have some priority under the RSL's policy for letting rented accommodation but would prefer to become home owners.' (*ibid*)

The Housing Corporation insists that DIYSO must include at least 60 per cent of current RSL or council tenants because this frees up the units of accommodation they leave behind for others. The 60 per cent level gives rise to tensions within the movement because it is difficult to find enough 'social' tenants to fill the allocation (particularly as this sector has become such a residual one), leading to a certain creativity in interpretation (Bramley *et al.*, 1995, paras 6.18 *et seq*).

The advantages of shared ownership are considerable for some, although this is a relatively small category of people who cannot afford (or do not want) full home ownership, are nevertheless able to obtain a mortgage, and want to own rather than rent in other tenures. It is noticeable that those opting for DIYSO generally take high proportion mortgages: 27 per cent took 100 per cent mortgages (Bramley & Dunmore, 1996, p. 119). Furthermore, the scheme takes a long time, is bureaucratic (see Bramley *et al.*, 1995, Table 3.1, now modified by HC Circ F2 – 07/97, para. 3), which increases the costs of the exchange professionals. It is, thus, not unusual for buyers to seek mortgages of greater than 100 per cent.

It is not yet clear what current and future demand there is for shared ownership, particularly since the introduction of the right to acquire and the discounts applicable to that scheme (see Bramley & Dunmore, 1996,

p. 119–20 for pre-right to acquire consideration). Nor is it clear whether shared ownership is cost effective and has other advantages for providers. For applicants, there is considerable difficulty in obtaining a mortgage for shared ownership although, no doubt, this is because its complexity makes lending more expensive; and the ability to staircase 'injects an additional element of uncertainty regarding the repayment profile of loans' as well as an irrational response to innovation (*ibid*, p. 128).[10] Whilst a shared-ownership buyer would be entitled to Housing Benefit to cover the rent part of the outgoings, Bramley and Dunmore provide the following example (based on 1995 entitlement) of the relevance of Housing Benefit:

> 'In a typical example (50 per cent share of £60,000 house for a couple with two children), gross income would need to fall from the initial affordability threshold of £14,000 by 35 per cent to £9,600 before [Housing Benefit] started. However, at that level of income the net rent:income ratio would be a decidedly unaffordable 47 per cent and the residual income the household would have to live on would be £1200 *less than* the Income Support poverty line.' (p. 121)

Thus, shared ownership actually involves considerable risk (although other risks, such as negative equity, are marginalized). Whilst there is staircasing upwards to greater proportionate shares, what is currently missing is the flexibility to staircase *down* (Bramley *et al.*, 1995).

'Coerced exchange' I: The Right to Buy

'Coercion'
In Chapter 4, we saw how the Conservative governments in the 1980s and 1990s gradually withdrew subsidy from local authorities, which led to a concomitant increase in rents payable by tenants. It is certainly true that local government's approach to housing management could border on, or could simply be, paternalistic (examples can be found in Saunders, 1990, pp. 95–6). Such factors form the backdrop to the successive legislation in 1980, 1984, 1986, and 1993 that first introduced the right for council tenants to buy their homes with a discount, then extended the range of the legislation, and then extended the discounts and the methods used. Put together, this considerable body of legislation provides the most astounding ingredients of sweeteners and incentives for individual privatization. Capturing this mix of central pressures on local authorities, together with sweeteners for tenants, Cole and Furbey suggest that:

> '. . . it is not clear that this exodus [of council tenants to home owners] is to be viewed as an historical inevitability produced by ineluctable deficiencies in public housing. Faced with an exceptional deal, the relatively affluent households which form the majority exerting the Right to Buy have certainly voted with their feet, but their votes have been cast against an already strongly residualised, increasingly

centralised, unmodernised tenure which was not resourced or managed to meet their changing aspirations.' (1994, p. 172)

If local authorities did not want to take part, they were forced to do so by sweeping powers granted to the Secretary of State for the Environment in the 1980 Act. Few other statutory provisions better represented the changed relationship between central and local government than s. 23 of the 1980 Act. This empowered the Secretary of State to intervene and take the powers of the local authority, including the powers to complete individual sales, where 'it appears to the Secretary of State that tenants . . . have or may have difficulty in exercising the right to buy effectively and expeditiously'. In other words, implicit coercion on tenants to buy their property was matched by coercion on local authorities to engage in the process of selling them. Even Lord Denning regarded s. 23 as 'a most coercive power' (see *Norwich CC* v. *Secretary of State for the Environment* [1982] 1 All ER 737 and Forrest & Murie, 1991, Ch. 9). Unlike practically all other statutory duties on local authorities, the DoE put authorities' response to the new duties under rigorous surveillance: 'Impressions of progress or delay were also obtained from letters of complaint from or on behalf of tenants, from press reports and from informal discussion between the Department and local authorities' (Forrest & Murie, 1991, p. 208). Any sign of delays would be met with formal approaches. The Norwich saga is instructive, for their refusal to sell was neither absolute nor based on inefficiency. Rather the council was concerned at being able to balance their obligations to those in housing need against those who wished to purchase their accommodation (*ibid*, p. 212). These motivations will be returned to below.

Enforcing the right to buy

The basic position (at the time of writing) is that any secure council tenant, who has been such for two or more years, is entitled to exercise the right to buy their accommodation (be it house or flat) at a discount. The exact level of coercion in the process of exercising the right to buy can be shown in flow diagram format (Fig 12.1)

The process is simple and effective. At every stage, either the tenant or the landlord can force the other's hand. As such, it was a brilliant scheme, designed to reduce local discretion and power, and in the process dismantle the notion of council housing.

Who Buys What, Where?

The short answer to this question is that the better quality properties have been sold to the more affluent council tenants, who themselves are generally middle-aged two-parent families with children of (or older than) school age (see Forrest & Murie, 1991; Dunn *et al.*, 1987; Williams *et al.*, 1986). This suggests spatial, class, and life-cycle dimensions in answering the question. (As interesting is who did not buy their property, despite the significant inducements to do so.) It might be deduced from the

Figure 12.1   The right-to-buy process

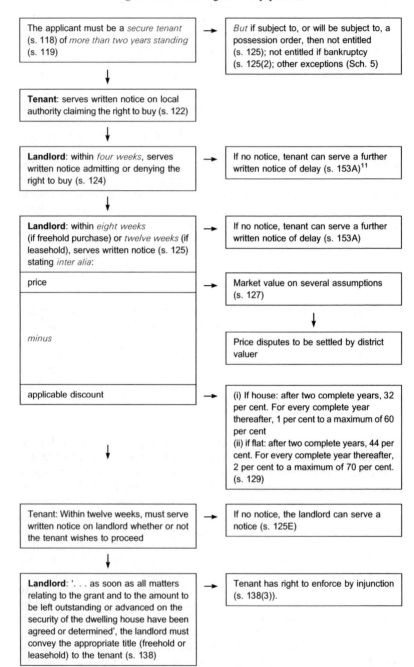

differential discounts applicable between houses and flats, higher discounts applying to the latter, that flats were harder to sell. Dunn *et al.* posit five potential factors explaining the spatial differentiation of the right to buy: pre-existing tenure patterns (pent-up demand in areas where low rates of home ownership exist); characteristics of tenants (life-cycle factors together with employment, income and class); characteristics of the council stock (the spectrum of quality); housing cost factors and local economic circumstances; political and administrative factors (areas which had not sold under discretionary policies might lead to pent-up demand): (1987, pp. 52–54).

Forrest and Murie's study contrasted the various factors operating in favour of, and against, purchase in four areas in which significant tenure differences might have affected the dimensions of the right to buy: the New Forest (predominant high-cost home ownership); Hyndburn (predominant low-cost, poor quality home ownership); Derwentside (predominantly good quality, cheap council housing); and Hackney (predominantly council housing of different quality and price). Not surprisingly, the right to buy had an uneven impact in each area, depending upon various factors such as the cost of the rent against the cost of buying (1991, Ch. 8). Despite the high level of differentiation, the authors argue that:

'In the strict sense every locality is unique. There are nevertheless a number of general processes at work which can be abstracted from the detailed case studies. Moreover, . . ., local housing market factors such as the relative sizes of the tenures, the level of differentiation within the council stock, and the buying/renting cost gap can interact with broader socio-economic processes to produce quite different outcomes. Equally, apparently similar outcomes can be the product of a different combination of factors.' (p. 195)

Belying its image, council housing has been of a high enough standard to persuade people to buy and others to lend money to facilitate the purchase. Certainly, the available evidence on former council homes now being re-sold in the market place is that they have been absorbed into the market and are bought by people who are moving within the owner-occupied sector, although there are spatial divisions (Forrest & Murie, 1995; Forrest *et al.*, 1996). Thus, the movement from sitting tenant purchase (privatization) to market place (commodification) suggests that the quality of the initial dwellings sold compares favourably with the private sector.

If one considers that the best properties were originally allocated to those either who could afford to wait for them or who were favoured by some part of the allocation process – for example, by discretionary transfers – then the right completes the web or circle of preference for those who had already been preferentially treated. The ability to buy at considerable discount simply maintained the web or circle of affluence for those people. Nevertheless, the characteristics of the tenant purchasers' housing histories also suggest that 'many purchasers would have been characterised at earlier stages as 'problem' tenants with little prospect of purchasing' (Forrest & Murie, 1984, p. 37). Those treated unfavourably at allocation stage are thus treated unfavourably at purchasing stage. For example, it is clear that far fewer flats than houses have been sold under the right-to-buy provisions (partly because of the quality of these flats and partly because those allocated to them are generally the worse off who have less bargaining power). Within this part of the web or circle, we might expect to find a particular concentration of ethnic minorities because of discrimination in allocation. Whilst noting a high proportion of sales amongst Afro-Caribbean tenants in Wandsworth compared to Birmingham, it was suggested that:

> 'Tower blocks contain a disproportionate amount of the Caribbean population and very few sales. However, the tower blocks contain an even more disproportionate amount of single Caribbean women with dependent children. This marginalised group would appear to lack access to more appropriate housing types and the purchase option. Tower blocks are becoming, oxymoronically, vertical sinks.' (Peach & Byron, 1994, pp. 379–80)

What is becoming clear, then, is that council house allocations and council house sales are involved in a self-fulfilling prophecy – privilege leads to greater privilege; exclusion leads to further exclusion.

Unabashed Capitalism – Drug Dealers and Racial Harassment

The right to buy has always been premised upon the belief that a significant proportion of tenants would want to exercise it and a suspicion that local authorities would do their utmost to wriggle out of the legislative straitjacket. Central government adopted the approach that would provide maximum control over recalcitrant local authorities under the guise of protecting the choice of tenants:

> 'Tenants wishing to become owners will expect the House to ensure that they have a right to buy which cannot be circumvented or ignored. If Parliament enacts this legislation it is right to expect all councils and landlords falling within the provisions of the Bill to carry out their duties responsibly and speedily.' (HC Debs, Vol 976, col 1447, *per* Michael Heseltine; cited in Forrest & Murie, 1991, p. 205)

In taking this policy option, central government clearly opted for individual rights (the tenant purchaser) against collective provision (local authority and its other tenants). It was anti-socialism in the broadest sense, but what was to happen about anti-social tenants who sought to exercise their right to buy?

Figure 12.1 shows that if there is a possession order made against the secure tenant, then the tenant is not entitled to exercise the right to buy. Case law has made clear that this exclusion applies if, at any time prior to the *exercise* of the right to buy, a possession order has been made against the tenant (*Enfield LBC* v. *McKeown* [1986] 1 WLR 1007). In other words, at any stage before completion of the purchase, if a possession order is granted, the right to buy ceases to be operable. Equally, if (for some reason) the tenant loses their secure status, they also lose their right to buy (*Muir Group Housing Association* v. *Thornley* (1992) 25 HLR 89).

Such protection against (allegedly) anti-social tenants has proved inadequate in certain cases so far. In *Taylor* v. *Newham LBC* [1993] 25 HLR 290, the applicant had reached the stage where she was entitled to apply for an injunction to enforce the right to buy. Before she had done so, however, Newham issued proceedings to recover possession of the property on the basis of 'acts of an aggressive, violent, insulting and offensive nature, and being, as it was alleged, the product of hostility born of racial enmity [against the local Asian community].' It was on this basis that the council sought to defend Ms Taylor's subsequent application for an injunction. This defence was unsuccessful for, as it was held, the injunction can only be set aside on narrow grounds. Sir Thomas Bingham MR made it clear that the intention of Parliament overrode all other considerations:

> '[The history of the right to buy is that] it was introduced for the first time in 1980 at a time when a number of local authorities strongly resisted parting with the ownership of publicly owned accommodation to those who then lived in it, and it seems to me that we should be doing great violence to the obvious intention of Parliament if we did not recognise that it was Parliament's intention to block to the maximum the opportunities open to reluctant landlords to obstruct the acquisition of title by their tenants.' (at p. 298)

It followed that Ms Taylor's rights overrode the obvious social problems caused by enabling an alleged racist to buy her property in the area where the alleged acts had taken place.

In *Bristol City Council* v. *Lovell* (1997) 29 HLR 528, a similar issue arose for the Court of Appeal in the following way. Lovell, an alleged drug dealer, had 'suitably adapted [his property] to the trade, with steel grilles over doors and windows, kennels for Rottweiler dogs, surveillance cameras to check visitors, a radio scanner tuned to police frequency and equipment for locating covert listening devices' (*per* Lord Hoffmann). He had accepted the terms of the Council's proposed conveyance. He sought to defend the Council's possession proceedings by counterclaiming for an injunction to complete the transaction under s. 138(3). Before the possession proceedings had been heard, an interlocutory application for the injunction was brought and decided in Mr Lovell's favour. Sir Thomas Bingham MR, in a somewhat tortuous judgment, ultimately came to the conclusion that, whilst 'it would be wholly inconsistent with what I would have thought would be the intention of Parliament' (at p. 537) if the allegations proved founded, Mr Lovell was entitled to the injunction. No possession order had been made and it followed that an injunction should be granted. Hobhouse LJ put the matter in this way:

> '. . . the "moral" argument of the landlord Council is based upon the concern it has to protect the interests of its remaining tenants on the estate. It is clearly in the public interest as well as the interests of others living in the neighbourhood of this property that antisocial illegal activities should come to an end. . . .' (at p. 541)

> 'The broader considerations which have understandably motivated the City Council's opposition to the grant of an injunction to this tenant under s. 138 are considerations which have been expressly excluded from the policy of Part V of the 1985 Act.' (at p. 543)

From these cases, one might extrapolate that the drive to increase home ownership, exhibited in the Housing Act 1980 and its successors, was potentially at the expense of social considerations. From government's inaction in shoring up this obvious gap (and the opportunity was there in the Housing Act 1996), one can only assume that this is what was intended.

Rather than focussing on such broader considerations, the House of Lords decision in *Lovell* reflected a narrower approach. The majority overturned the Court of Appeal's decision on two grounds, one essentially practical, the other substantive. The practical ground was that the court is entitled, in the exercise of its discretion as to case management, to hear cases in whatever order it wishes on the basis of what appears 'just and convenient' (Lord Lloyd dissented on this ground). This is difficult to accept in the light of the other accepted assertion that this discretion cannot be used to overrule the policy of the statute nor the rights which it gives to tenants (*per* Lord Hoffmann). The policy of the Act, as we have seen, was to give rights to the tenant at the expense of the landlord. It was only in defeating the purpose of the enforcement provisions of the Act – to force recalcitrant landlords to convey the property – that this discretion might be exercised. Thus, in order to do what was undoubtedly (on the alleged facts) just and convenient, the House of Lords had to remould the policy of the legislation. *Taylor* could be distinguished because, in that case, there was no question as to the judge's discretion on this point, only as to whether the injunction was discretionary or not.

The substantive ground related to a concession made by counsel for Lovell that the council would have been able to continue with their possession action *after* the grant of the injunction on the basis that Lovell remained a tenant until the actual conveyance. Lord Lloyd found that concession surprising ('To my mind Parliament cannot have intended that the Council should be able, in effect, to reverse a mandatory injunction by obtaining a subsequent order for possession') but nevertheless accepted it. Other members of the House of Lords believed the concession proper. Indeed, Lord Clyde based the majority of his reasoning upon this point. The difficulty with it, though, is precisely that raised by Lord Lloyd. The effect of a grant of possession after the grant of the injunction does violence to the nature and rationale of the injunction: to force the council to make the grant. Of course, as Lord Clyde points out, other matters require checking (in the ordinary way of the conveyancing process) but this does not answer the point that the council can avoid the effect of the injunction by subsequently seeking possession of the property.

In this case, then, we might say that the policy of the Act was superseded by the factual matrix of the case.

Unabashed Capitalism – 'Building Stable Communities'[12]
In the *Norwich CC* case, the Court observed that the council was 'stalling' in its performance of its obligations in order to consider how the right to buy fit in with its other obligations, such as its duty to the homeless and others in housing need. That this balancing act between individualism (home ownership) and collectivism (housing those in need) came down on the side of individualism has since become apparent in the infamous occurrences in Westminster. On 8 July 1987, Westminster City Council decided to extend its statutory obligations by using discretionary powers to sell 500 vacant properties every year (under s. 32(1), 1985 Act, and General Consents granted by the Secretary of State by letter dated 2 June 1981). Furthermore, the Council decided to extend a programme of cash grants to pay tenants to purchase accommodation within Westminster or outside (for operation of these, see Boggan & Blackhurst, 1994; Boggan, 1994). These decisions were termed 'Building Stable Communities' in council documentation. In seeking to expand the scope of home ownership in the borough they became the subject of a dispute, part of which concerned the relationship between sales' programmes and duties to those in housing need.

Ironically, in the week before the Conservative government introduced its proposals to curb obligations to the homeless, the District Auditor for Westminster produced an interim report containing provisional findings and views as to the legality of these decisions. Broadly, it was argued that Westminster, a Conservative 'flagship' council, had engaged in gerrymandering and that in so doing it had acted improperly as well as in defiance of its obligations to the homeless. Subsequent newspaper coverage referred to a confidential internal report which alleged that over 100 homeless families and their children were placed 'in tower blocks which it knew were riddled with asbestos, some of it in a most dangerous and virulent form – "It was only when the council workmen came in dressed like spacemen that we found out about the asbestos."' (Hencke, 1995)

At the local elections in 1986, the Conservatives secured Westminster but with a reduced majority on the council. The leading Conservative councillors formed a cabal to attempt to determine methods of keeping the borough in Conservative hands. In March 1988, Councillor Lady Porter explained the policy to her colleagues: 'Conservative members of the council have identified *eight key battlezone wards*. The result of the 1990 local elections will depend on how people vote in these wards.' (Magill, 1996, para. 504). At a seminar conducted on 6 September 1986 for the Conservative members of the council, Porter outlined what was meant by 'gentrification': 'In short it is ensuring that the right people live in the right areas. The areas are relatively easy to define: target wards identified on the basis of electoral trends and results.' (*ibid*, para. 536). Targets for increasing Conservative party support in each of the eight wards were subsequently set out (*ibid*, para. 659). Other papers referred to 'our long term aim must be to move as many homeless as possible out of Westminster' (*ibid*, para. 660). Even on 25 June 1987, Chief Officers 'were reminded of the *paramount* importance of the Building Stable Communities strategy in the development of *all* council policy' (*ibid*, para. 670; emphasis added).

Our concern here is not with the 'gerrymandering' aspect – however crucial that is to the nature of local government obligations, as well as the implicit belief that home owners are Conservative voters (see, for discussion, Saunders, 1990, Ch 4; Forrest *et al.*, 1990, pp. 166–170; Williams *et al.*, 1987). Our focus is on the relationship between the council's sales policies and its other statutory obligations (broadly Magill, 1996, Volume 2, Part (F)(1)-(6)). The simple problem was that the loss of an extra 500 units of accommodation in 1987/88 would mean, *inter alia*: (a) 'if the council maintained its policy to house certain other homeless households (which it did), the number of homeless households to whom it owed a statutory duty but for whom it would not secure suitable permanent accommodation in that year would be 236 (or over 26%)' (Magill, 1996, para. 238); (b) a net reduction of almost 75 per cent of vacant dwellings available for letting within the councils own stock (*ibid*, para. 241); (c) obligations to house people from the waiting list would be restricted. It was argued that target groups would, nevertheless, accord with those within the General Consent. However:

> 'The effect of large scale designation of dwellings leased at a premium is that, even if such individuals are given a reasonable preference by the authority when it decides to whom it may grant a lease of a designated dwelling, such individuals will in practice only receive such a preference if they can also afford to pay whatever premium is highlighted.' (*ibid*, para. 275)

In other words, it seems that a crucial aspect of the problems associated with designated, discretionary sales was the failure to take account of the obligations to households in housing need (a potential issue in Wandsworth, another Conservative 'flagship' authority: Bates, 1994). If that is the case on this rather small scale, then a combination of such policies together with sitting tenant sales under the right to buy might largely be responsible for many of the current low-cost housing problems. The notion of creating 'stable communities', paraded by the Conservative government as an important objective of the right to buy and a feature of current discussions amongst social landlords, remains tinged with doubt.

None of these questions seem to have been subjected to adverse comment by subsequent court proceedings, in which the findings of the District Auditor were impugned. In the Divisional Court, certain persons found guilty by the Auditor of wilful misconduct were found innocent because they did not believe they were doing anything unlawful. In fact, only Porter and Weeks (the Deputy Leader of the council) were held to be liable: 'Their purpose throughout was to achieve unlawful electoral advantage' *Porter* v. *Magill* (1998) 30 HLR 997, 1022. The Chairman of the council's housing committee was guilty of misconduct, but, because he had a proper purpose and did not appreciate the unlawfulness of his conduct, he was found not guilty of 'wilful misconduct' (p. 1033). Before the Court of Appeal (*The Times*, 6 May 1999), Porter and Weeks escaped liability on the ground that, as the Divisional Court had absolved the other accused from liability, Porter and Weeks must likewise be absolved. The reasoning appears to have been that the council's housing committee voted for the discretionary sales policy on a proper basis and no improper pressure had been placed upon the other members of that committee; Porter and Weeks had taken eminent legal advice, which had accepted the legitimacy of the policy, on which they were entitled to rely; and it followed that 'wilful misconduct' had not been proved. The case is apparently being appealed to the House of Lords.

Retrenchment – New Labour Proposals

The implementation of two New Labour proposals suggest a degree of retrenchment from the unabashed capitalism of the Thatcher era. First, the level of discounts has been pegged back to a maximum of '70 per cent of the average value of local authority houses and flats in each government region, and 65 per cent in London where pressure on social housing is currently greatest' (DETR, 1998a, para. 19): The Housing (Right to Buy) (Limits on Discounts) Order 1998, SI 1998/2997. The slightly lower level for London is because 'the pressure on social housing resources is considerably greater in this region' (para. 23) meaning that buyers should pay a slightly higher proportion of the market value.

Second, for some purchasers, the right-to-buy scheme has been something of a disaster. Specifically, these households bought flats through the medium of long leaseholds. Long leaseholds retain the relationship of landlord and tenant, albeit in modified form. The tenant is responsible for paying any rent and service charges (the latter were pegged back for the first five years in the legislative scheme). Service charges have, however, been enormous in some cases and purchasers of long leaseholds have been particularly affected. Furthermore, commodification has, for some, not brought the expected benefits:

'But for some people, the cost and strain of home ownership is too much and they want to become a tenant again. Others want to move and buy elsewhere (for employment, health, family or other reasons) but cannot find a buyer, or the prospective buyer cannot find a lender willing to give a mortgage.' (DETR, 1998b, para. 10)

DETR has implemented a scheme that enables the local authority to purchase its former stock using a proportion of capital receipts from the sale of its stock (The Local Authorities (Capital Finance) (Amendment No 3) Regulations 1998, SI 1998/1937). Local authorities are entitled to set up and maintain their schemes giving preference to whichever owners they wish (para. 17). This renationalization programme is quite remarkable, albeit small, because it appears to be totally out of step with the rest of housing policy which encourages home ownership and privatization of stock. However, it can be explained by reference to the notion of 'sustainability', for some purchasers have been locked into unsustainable relationships with either landlords or lenders, and the perceived need for mobility. More cynically, it might be argued that the policy represented a method of silencing the protests of disaffected purchasers, which gained much local and national publicity and which might have affected the privatization programme.

'Coerced Exchange' II: The Right to Acquire

A curious and relatively ignored facet of the debate about the right to buy is that many RSL tenants were never given the right to buy the property allocated to them until the 1996 Act. For some time, the Tenants Incentive Scheme has provided grants to RSL tenants to purchase accommodation outside the control of the RSL (to free up the unit for others in housing need). Perversely, then, it may well have been that this has made RSL accommodation less attractive than council accommodation. RSLs are able to sell properties on a voluntary basis with the consent of the Housing Corporation but this was rarely done. The introduction of common methods of allocation between local authorities and RSLs, together with local authority rights commonly to nominate a proportion of RSL tenants, have made the absence of such a right seem anachronistic.

For many RSL tenants, purchase of their accommodation would make financial sense for similar reasons to those of council tenants with the added bonus of the fact that, as RSLs have been building significant numbers of accommodation units recently (certainly compared to local authorities), much accommodation is 'first hand'. We have already seen that RSL rents are rapidly reaching the levels of private-sector rents and, whilst the Housing Corporation has attempted to stem these rises, purchase may compare favourably depending on the location and level of discounts.

Two schemes are now in place which potentially provide RSL tenants with the capability to purchase, although both schemes have crucial limitations (limitations have already been placed on the Tenants Incentive Scheme so that it does not apply to tenants who are in receipt of Housing Benefit or who have been so 12 months prior to their application: HC Circ F2 – 07/97, para. 2(ii)).

The first new scheme is the Voluntary Purchase Grant scheme (see DoE, 1995b for background). This is a cash-limited scheme and RSLs must bid for an allocation from the Housing Corporation. Essentially, the conditions are precisely the same as those applicable to the right to buy (although assured tenants are also eligible). The only exception is that tenants are ineligible if the RSL 'is seeking to take possession of the dwelling' (Voluntary Purchase Grant General Determination, para. 11(g)) suggesting that the Housing Corporation has heeded the lessons of the right to buy as exposed in *Taylor*. RSLs are expected to prioritize 'according to date order of application and, within that, length of tenancy with the association' (HC Circ F2 – 06/96, para. 3.3; see Ch. 8 for consideration of date order schemes). RSLs have discretion over which properties they include in the scheme ('RSLs may also decide to target properties for sale where there is low demand or because they wish to introduce tenure mix on an estate': HC Circ F2 – 31/97). Unlike the right to buy, however, discounts are based neither on percentages nor on length of stay. Rather, discounts are based upon the five Total Cost Indicator areas. Discounts ran from £9,000 to £16,000 depending on area (para. 6). These are crude indicators, for within each of these five areas it will surely be more of an incentive to purchase in some rather than other areas (for example, because of differences in house prices within each TCI area). Discounts on this basis are also part of the general incentives to purchase under the other major scheme introduced in the Housing Act 1996 – the right to acquire (The Housing (Right to Acquire)(Discount) Order 1997, SI 1997/626). These are blunt tools: discounts of £16,000 are given to those in certain areas (Schedule 1) which include Lambeth and Merton. These adjoining parts of London conceal vastly different types of property as well as prices – from the highest to the lowest – and benefits will reflect priorities granted in allocations schemes.

For some time, this right will be in abeyance, for it only applies to properties built or improved using grant from the Housing Corporation under the 1996 Act. Essentially, the right to acquire operates in exactly the same way as the right to buy (Figure 12.1 above, subject to the difference as regards discounts) although the exceptions are slightly different. For example, the Schedule 5 exceptions have been increased to reflect the source of the finance used to build the property and other associated matters (see The Housing (Right to Acquire) Regulations 1997, SI 1997/ 619, Sch 1, para. 40). The government has also been forced to designate certain areas which do not form part of the scheme (SI 1997/620–SI 1997/ 624).

There are now similar schemes governing council and RSL tenants' rights to buy or acquire their property (an interesting contrast of expression), although there are differences in their application. RSL tenants' rights are greatly limited both by the cash-limited nature of the Voluntary Purchase Grant scheme (apparently covering only about 2,000 properties in its first year of operation) and the limitations in the availability of the right to acquire. However, the crucial difference lies in the scale of the discount for council and RSL tenants. The proportionate discount regime, surely better equipped for a differentiated market, has found no place in the less property-specific cash-related regime. This is a factor which will, no doubt, reduce demand.

A further factor, related to this, is that RSL tenants who have no right to a mortgage will have considerable difficulties in gaining access to mortgage finance as many mortgagees will not lend to those in receipt of Housing Benefit – so the right to acquire will only benefit the better-off. It is likely that this reflects the limited scope for government invention in the sector because of its reliance on private finance. Overtly interfering with this relationship, and offering discounts which affected the involvement of private finance, would have been disastrous to the politically weakened Conservative Party in 1995–6. The root cause of the weakness of many of the changes in the 1996 Act, as well as many of the concessions made by the Major government, reflected the political reality at that time which was not the case in 1980 at the time of the right to buy legislation. Housing law, in other words, is as affected by temporal and political vicissitudes as all aspects of government policy.

Conclusion

Access to home ownership has played a pivotal role in post-war housing policy, the prominence of which has been enhanced by successive Conservative governments from 1979 onwards. At the level of politics, it has been argued that home ownership is the most natural tenure, which the population generally desires, although this is at best debatable. Rather, it reflects the fact that alternative tenures have declined leaving little else other than properties for sale into home ownership in some areas. The movement into home ownership has also been facilitated (and engineered) by the largely unregulated credit movement. The ease with which money became available in the 1980s, as well as sporadically throughout the twentieth century, has enabled the mortgage contract to become so important. That such a contract remains unregulated, and lenders so powerful, has been discussed.

The ideological supremacy ascribed to home ownership by all major parties provides the most important context for any discussion of the tenure. This has found expression in the various aspects of government policy that have made it the most attractive tenure. In addition, it provides the context for the discussion of the expansion in low-cost home ownership and the many sweeteners used by government to influence people into the tenure. The influence of these sweeteners suggests that, often, it is the tail which wags the dog and not vice versa. This is because the deal offered to tenants is so good and credit so available that swapping tenures to home ownership often makes sound financial sense. The drive towards ever-increasing numbers of home owners in the 'low-cost' sector has consequences which should have been foreseen. These include the vital consideration, which seems to have been forgotten, that a balance needs to be drawn between home ownership and a constant source of accommodation to house those in need.

Further Reading

There is a wealth of literature covering the issues raised by Saunders. Saunders's other work is also relevant (although much is encapsulated in the 1990 text): see, for example, (1986), *Social Theory and the Urban Question*, London: Hutchison. Other than the material used in the text, readers may wish to refer to F. Gray's chapter on 'Owner-occupation and social relations' in S. Merrett (1982), *Owner Occupation in Britain*, London: Routledge, which is a brilliant, if early, analysis of different approaches to home ownership; additional material might include the contextual approach adopted by A. Dupuis and D. Thorns (1998), 'Home, home ownership and the search for ontological security', *Sociological Review*, 24; A. Franklin (1986), *Owner Occupation, Privatism, and Ontological Security: A Critical Formulation*, Working Paper 62, Bristol: School for Advanced Urban Studies, University of Bristol; P. Somerville (1989), 'Home sweet home: a critical comment on Saunders and Williams', vol 4, *Housing Studies*, 113; N. Yip and P. McLaverty (1993), *Tenure Preferences*, Discussion Paper 4, York: Centre for Housing Policy, University of York. Saunders' claims extend to housing *inheritance*, although research completed after 1990 suggests that, contrary to Saunders' claims, the 'incidence of housing inheritance is strongly class and tenure related': C. Hamnett (1992), 'A nation of inheritors? Housing inheritance, wealth and inequality in Britain', vol 20, *Journal of Social Policy*, 509. Research also considers the notion of consumption sector cleavages in relation to older people: see, for example, M. Evandrou and C. Victor (1988), *Differentiation in Later Life: Social Class and Housing tenure Cleavages*, London: International Centre for Economics and Related Disciplines, London School of Economics.

On gender and home ownership, see S. Watson (1988), *Accommodating Inequality*, Sydney: Allen & Unwin, Chs 3 & 5; relationship breakdown is considered also in P. McCarthy & B. Simpson (1991), *Issues in Post-Divorce Housing*, Aldershot: Avebury. Useful data and analyses on racial issues can be found in P. Sarre, D. Phillips & R. Skellington (1989), *Ethnic Minority Housing: Explanations and Policies*, Aldershot: Avebury, esp. Chs 2 & 7; P. Burton (1997), 'Urban policy and the myth of progress', vol 25, *Policy and Politics*, 421; see also, M. MacEwen (1991), *Housing, Race and the Law*, London: Routledge.

Material on sustainability can also be found in relation to home ownership in different chapters in P. Williams (ed.), *Directions in Housing Policy*, London: Paul Chapman. On 'flexibility', see R. Terry (1996), *Changing Housing Markets: The Case for Flexible Tenure and Flexible Mortgages*, London: National Housing Federation.

Standard textbooks on land law contain a great deal of case law on the mortgage contract, much of it though is rather antiquated (see, for example, K. Green (1995), *Land Law*, London: Macmillan). On self-regulation, see C. Harlow & R. Rawlings

(1997), *Law and Administration*, London: Butterworths, Ch. 10 and R. Baldwin & C. McCrudden (1990), *Regulation and Public Law*, London: Weidenfeld & Nicolson.

Endnotes

1. Saunders, 1990, p. 304.
2. *Cf* Forrest & Murie, 1991, where it is argued that 'Expressed preference for home ownership conflates a preference for a collection of housing attributes, such as space, quality, a house with a garden, the desire for a particular location as well as reflecting specific tax and subsidy advantages.' (p. 124).
3. As the right to buy involves the transfer from one housing tenure – council – to another – ownership – it is usually regarded as a method of 'exit' (using Hirsch's terminology). Repositioning some of the issues here reflects a personal belief that such an approach is unidimensional and does not reflect on the constantly evolving nature of an individual's housing history.
4. Kemeny admonishes that 'questions concerning tenure 'preferences', and 'attitudes' towards tenure are largely irrelevant as far as understanding the relationship between tenure and broader values and ideologies is concerned': 1981, p. 63.
5. 'Redlining' is/was a process, first uncovered in America but which was also found to exist in British building societies. It involved literally drawing a red line through a town and refusing to loan money on mortgage to those on the wrong side of the line. For examples of this process, see Karn *et al.*, 1985, Ch. 5.
6. Bull's warning that relationship breakdown is better seen 'as a process rather than an event' (p. 4) largely concerns the role of often complex legal proceedings which are brought out in the fuller study (Bull, 1993, p. 17).
7. This was a particular feature of the context of home ownership in 1980s but it should be remembered that lenders had been granting 100 per cent mortgages for some time, reaching an earlier peak in 1965: Forrest *et al.*, 1984, p. 11, referring to DoE Housing Statistics in 1971. What was different in the 1980s was the *scale* on which such mortgages were made.
8. The latter essentially requires the lender to operate as a bank (in ordinary terms) by enabling the borrower 'to withdraw overpayment, or have an automatic extra borrowing facility'.
9. Little is known about building society's involvement in shared-ownership schemes (other than through providing finance for other shared ownership schemes). However, Williams draws attention to the 'shared appreciation mortgage': 'Here the choices are between making an interest payment or not and sharing with the lender a variable amount of any price appreciation in the dwelling.' (1997, p. 44; see also pp. 49–50)
10. This last reason seems least plausible as shared ownership schemes have such a long history.
11. The effect of the s. 153A notice is that, if the landlord does not serve a counter notice, the tenant may serve an 'operative notice of delay'. After this point, any further payments made by the tenant as rent are also regarded as being made on account of the purchase price (s. 153B).
12. I am grateful to Professor Martin Loughlin for his assistance with the account provided in this section.

Bibliography

Bates, S. (1994), 'Second Tory council accused on housing', *The Guardian*, 17 January

Beale, H. (1994), 'Legislative control of fairness: the Directive on unfair terms in consumer contracts', in J. Beatson and D. Friedmann (eds), *Good Faith and Fault in Contract Law*, Oxford: Oxford University Press

Bentley, L. and Howells, G. (1989), 'The judicial treatment of Extortionate Credit Bargains', vol 53, *Conveyancer*, 164 (Pt I), 234 (Pt II)

Birch, J. (1997), 'Flexible friend', Nov/Dec, *Roof*, 23

Boggan, S. (1994), 'Tenants given cash to buy abroad', *The Independent*, 21 January

Boggan, S. and Blackhurst, C. (1994), 'Council used grants in second votes deal', *The Independent*, 19 January

Bramley, G. (1988), *Access to Owner Occupation*, Bristol: School for Advanced Urban Studies, University of Bristol

Bramley, G. (1994), 'An affordability crisis in British housing: dimensions, causes and policy impact', vol 9, *Housing Studies*, 103

Bramley, G. and Dunmore, K. (1996), 'Shared ownership: short-term expedient or long-term major tenure?', vol 11, *Housing Studies*, 105

Bramley, G., Dunmore, K., Durrant, C. and Smart, G. (1995), *Do-it-yourself Shared Ownership: An Evaluation*, London: Housing Corporation

Bull, J. (1993), *Housing Consequences of Relationship Breakdown*, London: HMSO

Bull, J. (1995), *Housing Consequences of Relationship Breakdown*, York: Centre for Housing Policy, University of York

Cole, I. and Furbey, R. (1994), *The Eclipse of Council Housing*, London: Routledge

Commission for Racial Equality (CRE) (1990), *Racial Discrimination in an Oldham Estate Agency*, London: CRE

Council for Mortgage Lenders (CML) (1997), *The Code of Mortgage Lending Practice*, London: CML

Department of the Environment (DoE) (1971), *Fair Deal for Housing*, Cmnd 4728, London: HMSO

Department of the Environment (DoE) (1995a), *Our Future Homes – Opportunity, Choice, Responsibility*, London: HMSO

Department of the Environment (DoE) (1995b), *Proposals for a Purchase Grant Scheme for Housing Association Tenants*, Consultation Paper Linked to the Housing White Paper 'Our Future Homes', London: DoE

Department of the Environment, Transport and the Regions (DETR) (1998a), *Secure Tenants' Right to Buy: Proposals to Change the Maximum Discount Cash Limit on Right to Buy and other Home Ownership Incentive Schemes in England – A Consultation Paper*, London: DETR

Department of the Environment, Transport and the Regions (DETR) (1998b), *A Financial Incentive for Local Authorities to Buy Back Homes from Leaseholders or others in Difficulty – A Consultation Paper*, London: DETR

Doling, J. and Stafford, B. (1989), *Home Ownership: The Diversity of Experience*, Aldershot: Gower

Dorling, D. (1997), 'Regional and local differences in the housing tenure of ethnic minorities', in V. Karn (ed.), *Ethnicity in the 1991 Census*, vol 4, London: HMSO

Dorling, D. and Cornford, J. (1995), 'Who has negative equity: How house price falls in Britain have hit different groups of home buyers', vol 10, *Housing Studies*, 151

Dunn, R., Forrest, R. and Murie, A. (1987), 'The geography of council house sales in England: 1979–85', vol 24, *Urban Studies*, 47

Dwelly, T. (1997), *Sustainable Home Ownership: The Debate*, York: Joseph Rowntree Foundation

Forrest, R., Gordon, D. and Murie, A. (1996), 'The position of former council homes in the housing market', vol 33, *Urban Studies*, 125

Forrest, R. and Kennett, T. (1996), 'Coping strategies, housing careers and households with negative equity', vol 25, *Journal of Social Policy*, 369

Forrest, R., Kennett, T. and Leather, P. (1997), *Home Owners on New Estates in the 1990s*, Bristol: Policy Press

Forrest, R., Lansley, S. and Murie, A. (1984), *A Foot on the Ladder? An Evaluation of Low Cost Home Ownership Initiatives*, Working Paper 41, Bristol: School for Advanced Urban Studies, University of Bristol

Forrest, R. and Murie, A. (1984), *Right to Buy? Issues of Need, Equity and Polarisation in the Sale of Council Houses*, Working Paper 39, Bristol: School for Advanced Urban Studies, University of Bristol

Forrest, R. and Murie, A. (1990), *Moving the Housing Market*, Aldershot: Avebury

Forrest, R. and Murie, A. (1991), *Selling the Welfare State – The Privatization of State Housing*, London: Routledge

Forrest, R. and Murie, A. (1994), 'Home ownership in recession', vol 9, *Housing Studies*, 55

Forrest, R. and Murie, A. (1995), 'From privatization to commodification: tenure conversion and new zones of transition in the city', vol 19, *International Journal of Urban and Regional Research*, 407

Forrest, R., Murie, A. and Williams, P. (1990), *Home Ownership: Differentiation and Fragmentation*, London: Allen & Unwin

Gentle, C., Dorling, D. and Cornford, J. (1994), 'Negative equity and British housing in the 1990s: cause and effect', vol 31, *Urban Studies*, 181

Giddens, A. (1990), *The Consequences of Modernity*, Cambridge: Polity

Gilroy, R. (1994), 'Women and owner occupation in Britain: first the prince, then the palace?', in R. Gilroy and R. Woods (eds), *Housing Women*, London: Routledge

Ginsburg, N. (1992), 'Racism and housing: concepts and reality', in P. Braham, A. Rattansi and R. Skellington (eds), *Racism and Antiracism: Inequalities, Opportunities and Policies*, London: Routledge

Gurney, C. (1990), *The Meaning of Home in the Decade of Owner Occupation: towards and Experiential Research Agenda*, Working Paper 88, Bristol: School for Advanced Urban Studies, University of Bristol

Hand, C. (1980), 'The statutory tenancy: an unrecognised proprietary interest', *Conveyancer*, 351

Hencke, D. (1995), 'Homeless 'put at risk' in asbestos-ridden tower blocks', *The Guardian*, 30 November

Hills, J. (1990), *Unravelling Housing Finance*, Oxford: Oxford University Press

Holmans, A. and Whitehead, C. (1997), 'Trends in housing assistance for owner-occupiers and local authority tenants', no 35, *Housing Finance*, 38

Housing Corporation (1997), *Performance Standards – Performance Standards and Regulatory Guidance for Registered Social Landlords*, London: Housing Corporation

Hughes, D. and Lowe, S. (1995), *Social Housing Law and Policy*, London: Butterworths

Karn, V. (ed.) (1997), *Ethnicity in the 1991 Census, Volume 4*, London: HMSO

Karn, V., Doling, J. and Stafford, B. (1986), 'Growing crisis and contradiction in home ownership', in P. Malpass (ed.), *The Housing Crisis*, London: Routledge

Karn, V., Kemeny, J. and Williams, P. (1985), *Home Ownership in the Inner City: Salvation or Despair?*, Aldershot: Gower

Kemeny, J. (1981), *The Myth of Home Ownership*, London: Routledge

Kemeny, J. (1992), *Housing and Social Theory*, London: Routledge

Magill, J. (1996), *Westminster City Council Audit of Accounts 1987/88 to 1994/95: Designated Sales*, Vol 2: Introduction, Decisions and Statement of Reasons on the Section 19 Objection, London: Westminster City Council

Munro, M. and Madigan, R. (1998), 'Housing strategies in an uncertain market', *Sociological Review*, 714

Murie, A., Niner, P. and Watson, C. (1976), *Housing Policy and the Housing System*, London: Allen & Unwin

Page, D. (1993), *Building for Communities*, York: Joseph Rowntree Foundation

Pannell, B. (1997), 'Tenure choice and mortgage decisions: 1996 market research findings', no 33, *Housing Finance*, 9

Pascall, G. (1997), *Social Policy: A New Feminist Analysis*, London: Routledge

Peach, C. and Byron, M. (1994), 'Council house sales, residualisation and Afro-Caribbean tenants', vol 23, *Journal of Social Policy*, 363

Prescott-Clarke, P., Clemens, S. and Park, A. (1994), *Routes into Local Authority Housing*, London: HMSO

Sarre, P., Phillips, D. and Skellington, R. (1989), *Ethnic Minority Housing: Explanations and Policies*, Aldershot: Avebury

Saunders, P. (1990), *A Nation of Home Owners*, London: Allen & Unwin

Short, J. (1982), *Housing in Britain: The Post-War Experience*, London; Methuen

Smith, S. (1989), *The Politics of 'Race' and Residence*, Cambridge: Polity Press

Smith, S. (1993), 'Residential segregation and the politics of racialization', in M. Cross & M. Kieth (eds), *Racism, the City and the State*, London: Routledge

Stewart, A. (1981), *Home Ownership in an Industrial Suburb*, London: Academic Press

Whitehouse, L. (1998a), 'The impact of consumerism on the home owner', in D. Cowan (ed.), *Housing: Participation and Exclusion*, Aldershot: Dartmouth

Whitehouse, L. (1998b), 'The home owner: citizen or consumer?', in S. Bright and J. Dewar (eds), *Land Law: Themes and Perspectives*, Oxford: Oxford University Press

Wilcox, S. (1997), *Housing Finance Review 1997/98*, York: Joseph Rowntree Foundation

Williams, N., Sewel, J. and Twine, F. (1986), 'Council house sales and residualisation', vol 15, *Journal of Social Policy*, 273

Williams, N., Sewel, J. and Twine, F. (1987), 'Council house sales and the electorate: voting behaviour and ideological implications', vol 4, *Housing Studies*, 274

Williams, P. (1997), 'A more flexible system of finance for home ownership', in T. Dwelly (ed.), *Sustainable Home Ownership: The Debate*, York: Joseph Rowntree Foundation

Part III

Rights and Responsibilities: From Due Process to Crime Control

'I remember also hearing at about this time a parable which Saul Alinsky, the radical American community organiser, used to tell. It went something like this. A man is walking by the riverside when he notices a body floating down stream. A fisherman leaps into the river, pulls the body ashore, gives mouth to mouth resuscitation, saving the man's life. A few minutes later the same thing happens, then again and again. Eventually yet another body floats by. This time the fisherman completely ignores the drowning man and starts running upstream along the bank. The observer asks the fisherman what on earth is he doing? Why is he not trying to rescue this drowning body? "This time," replies the fisherman, "I'm going upstream to find out who the hell is pushing these poor folks into the water"' (Cohen, 1985, p. 236). Part III is concerned with the social and legal construction of individual rights in housing. As in earlier chapters, we are concerned to flesh out and explain the disparities, actual and theoretical, between law, policy and practice. After discussing the (legal) security experienced by occupants of housing as well as the state and condition of property, we move on to discuss the lawful and unlawful methods through which occupants can be excluded from housing. The framework which guides this discussion explicitly recognizes that the current focus no longer reflects the grants of rights to occupants.

Introduction to Part III

The shift in focus is significant for it is also a shift in the way we think about housing and the home. Our concern is not with security but with adapting the way we think about housing and the home towards the furtherance of criminal justice ideals. Rutherford refers to criminal justice as having shifted towards the adoption of the 'eliminative ideal': 'Put bluntly, the eliminative ideal strives to solve present and emerging problems by getting rid of troublesome and disagreeable people with methods which are lawful and widely supported' (1997, p. 117). Such a statement could have been written about recent developments and thinking in housing.

Drawing upon models of criminal justice developed by Packer (1969), it can be argued that housing discourse has moved away from a 'due process' model, in which our principal concern lies with the protection of rights: 'The aim of this process is at least as much to protect the factually innocent as it is to convict the factually guilty' (p. 165). Instead, we are moving towards a 'crime control' model in which 'the repression of criminal conduct [is] viewed as by far the most important function to be performed by the criminal process' (Sanders & Young, 1994). It is because of this that 'the law-abiding citizen then become the victim of all sorts of unjustifiable invasions of his interests' (Packer, 1969, p. 158).

Garland has argued that the criminal justice system has, out of necessity, extended its reach into other domains (1996). This is because the failure of the state to control the upward spiral of crime has represented a challenge to the state's capacity to protect the public. The concentration now is upon the '*criminologies of everyday life*' (p. 450; original emphasis) – the acceptance that crime affects us all – and this has influenced moves towards, amongst other things, joint (or inter-agency) working: 'Its primary concern is to devolve responsibility for crime prevention on to agencies, organizations and individuals which are quite outside the state and to persuade them to act appropriately' (p. 452). However, at the same time as these strategies have been developed, 'the political arm of the state has frequently engaged in a form of denial which appears increasingly hysterical in the clinical sense of that term' (p. 459). This has led to a 'show of punitive force' that attempts to re-establish the sovereign authority of the state: 'punishment is an act of sovereign might, a performative action which exemplifies what absolute power is all about' (p. 461). Such statements could have been written about recent developments and thinking in housing.

All of this reflects a marked shift from the 1960s and 1970s when the central concern of housing lawyers lay in the protection of individual rights ('due process'). Our concern now lies with individual responsibility. Responsibility relates to the moral obligation upon individuals to behave in a particular way, usually in accord with the management principles. This is conceived much more broadly than ever before – we are not just concerned with the individual responsibility to keep up rent or mortgage payments and the effects of not doing so. A less clear example of a similar trend occurs in relation to housing renewal grants. Reforms in the late 1980s were explicitly based upon the premise that housing renewal was the responsibility of the householder, and not the state.

Housing has now become a key tool in the criminal justice process – in the monitoring and control of the occupation of, and exclusion from, property ('crime control'). So, for example, in Chapter 16, it is argued that the development of pro-arrest policies in cases of domestic violence have employed the criminal justice process to provide a temporary housing solution. This shift is further reflected, for example, in the adoption of the Introductory Tenancy regime, sometimes referred to colloquially as 'probationary' tenancies, in the 'war' against anti-social behaviour; in the increasing use of closed-circuit television (CCTV) surveillance on housing estates and High Streets; or in zero tolerance housing management strategies.

Despite this move towards crime-control models of housing management, there are still some pockets of housing rights which have remained unaffected. One example of this has been the consistently low levels of prosecution in cases of illegal eviction. This is an area untouched by pro-arrest policies or zero tolerance. Despite our fears about rachmanism and the apparent desire to stamp out any semblance of bad practice by private landlords, fines are low and prison sentences rare. Of course, this contrasts strongly with our approach to 'deviant' tenants against whom the full force of the law is mounted. In Chapter 15, we consider why this issue remains under-prosecuted and why there appears to be a class bias in those prosecutions which are brought. The simple answer is that landlords, as a class, tend to be favoured within the legislative schema. However, such an answer proves too simplistic. The explanation lies in the role of the local authority, which is usually responsible for bringing prosecutions in this area (termed 'non-police prosecutions'). Drawing upon analysis of non-police prosecutions more generally, we find that the under-prosecution of illegal eviction fits neatly within this genre. In similar vein, we draw upon this literature in Chapter 14 to explain local authorities' differential action in respect of properties found by them to be unfit for human habitation.

A second theme of Part III follows on from the shift towards crime control. Housing law is now more geared than ever before towards *exclusion* with a battery of different methods and procedures. The introduction of notions of social responsibility into housing rights has meant that those who are irresponsible will be excluded from their housing. The implementation of these new rights has, in itself, been the subject of differentiation as different local authorities, RSLs, and private landlords consider their appropriateness. So, for example, the recent rise in social housing evictions has had a spatial dimension. One commentator has suggested that areas with heavy demand are more willing to evict and exclude because they are then able to fill the vacancy quickly (Birch, 1999). The Social Landlords Crime and Nuisance Group has developed to press central government for change. In part, one can put these developments down to the particular construction given to the notion of 'citizenship' by the various governments. It links in with the growing awareness by some landlords that no sphere of housing should be used as a 'dumping ground' for society's undesirables. But there is an unpalatable remaining question: what happens to the excluded? Once excluded from social housing, it is unlikely that they will be able to access it again because access laws enable them to be excluded. Home ownership and mortgages are often out of the question. Consequently, there is a developing realization that the excluded commonly end up in the poorest end of the private rented sector.

The shift towards crime control has generally been *tenured*. This is the third principal theme of Part III – that, *despite attempts to argue that tenure does not matter, tenure is a crucial aspect of the debate*. Hilary Armstrong, the Housing Minister, has argued that 'Housing policy is too often regarded tenure-by-tenure. I want to see a more comprehensive and integrated approach applied at both the national and the local level' (1998, para. 4). It has been argued in earlier chapters that such approaches have been in operation for some time, albeit within a housing system dominated by home ownership. We have discussed, for example, the creation and use of cross-tenurial interests – 'what matters is what works' (*ibid*, para. 5); the fact that applying to a local authority for housing does not necessarily mean that one will be provided with local authority housing; nor that the local authority will continue even to provide housing.

What is argued here is that tenure *is* important. In fact, the only way one can regard housing rights is through tenure because it is the tenure that *defines* the rights that individuals obtain. Significantly, this is the starting point for Part III when we analyse security of tenure. Private-sector tenants get private-sector tenancies; public-sector tenants get public-sector tenancies; RSL tenants get an awkward mixture between the two (reflecting the awkward public:private distinction inherent in the RSL operation). Thus, one can only regard housing rights by tenure and this causes, I argue, manifest absurdity because of the cross-tenurial developments considered in previous chapters of this book. The rights that a person has in their housing depend upon their point of access (and, to a certain extent, exit). The rights gained through home ownership, paradoxically, are fewer than those in other sectors because of the legal construction of the mortgage relationship between lender and borrower. That relationship, in theory anyway, requires the borrower to give up their possessory rights to the property.

Tenure explains the repairing strategies employed by occupiers and landlords (although this is shown to be dependent upon the methods used to regulate each tenure). Legal conceptions of tenure are primarily responsible, also, for the concentration of the law upon repairing obligations in leasehold (particularly short-term), as opposed to freehold.

Tenure is also a key tool in examining the repossession process. Currently, different processes are employed when excluding any particular occupier from property. First, the decision to exclude is governed by different principles in different tenures. Second, the perception of housing debt seems to be tenurially based which, to a certain extent, determines arrears strategies and eviction processes. Third, tenure has been used as a powerful motif in the redefinition of the boundaries of the criminal justice system and the concomitant delimitation of rights. It is argued in Chapter 18 that there has been a move towards a 'crime control' model of housing management prefaced by an apparent belief that social sector tenants, particularly local authority tenants, are responsible for committing 'anti-social behaviour' (whatever that may be). Single tenure responses ('unitenurialism') were particularly prevalent under the last Conservative administration which brought in Introductory, or Probationary, Tenancies into the *local authority* sector.

The main blip in this argument is in Chapter 16, which is concerned with domestic violence. Domestic violence provides an important counterbalance to this argument, for recent legislation in this area has provided a cross-tenurial response to the issue (although not in relation to *access* to accommodation after leaving a violent relationship). Here, the law regulates the occupation of property as between cohabitants as well as broadening rights to injunctions. As regards the regulation of occupation rights, it is argued that, even though tenure is irrelevant, the new law is still problematically based upon the relationship of the parties and their respective property rights. Outside this legislation, however, tenure *remains* important because of the use of certain parts of housing law to regulate the occupation of the home.

Bibliography

Armstrong, H. (1998), *Principles for a New Housing Policy*, London: DETR

Birch, J. (1999), 'Eviction epidemic', January/February, *Roof*, 23

Cohen, S. (1985), *Visions of Social Control*, Cambridge: Polity

Garland, D. (1996), 'The limits of the sovereign state', vol 36, *British Journal of Criminology*, 445

Packer, H. (1969), *The Limits of the Criminal Sanction*, California: Stanford University Press

Rutherford, A. (1997), 'Criminal policy and the pursuit of the eliminative ideal', vol 31, *Social Policy and Administration*, 116

Sanders, A. and Young, R. (1994), *Criminal Justice*, London: Butterworths

13 Conflicts and Manifest Absurdities: Security of Tenure

Few people own their homes outright. A considerable number of people occupy their homes under a lease (or a tenancy). It might be said that a person with a lease for more than 21 years is a 'home owner', partly because lawyers regard such a time frame as 'long', although this is not free from doubt. The landlord can evict the tenant for breaching the terms of the lease/tenancy, but eviction can only be through a court order and only on narrow grounds. Where a mortgage lender lends money to the tenant to buy their home, the lender is entitled to take possession of the home 'as soon as the ink is dry' on the mortgage document. This right of the mortgage lender is heavily constrained by legislation and common, self-regulatory practice, leading to the leaseholder having 'security'. This means that the occupier can only be evicted from their accommodation on certain grounds and, even then, only with a court order.

The relationship that exists in a long lease is exactly the same where a person occupies property under a periodic lease in the private rented, RSL or local authority sectors. There is a landlord and tenant and, commonly, there is some form of agreement between the parties as to the rent payable and other terms. In strict law, on the expiry of a fixed term, the lease ends and the landlord is entitled to occupation. A periodic tenancy (by which is meant a tenancy for a period, such as a week or a month, which is repeated) ends when one or other party gives notice that it will end. The security provided by such arrangements is limited in time. By virtue of statute, however, the general rule is now that a landlord can only retake possession under a court order and, in many cases, such a court order can only be given on the basis that the landlord can show certain grounds. Thus, there is greater security, although that security depends upon the regime under which the tenant occupies.

'Security', then, has a technical meaning which refers to the fact that the rights of 'owners' to possession of the property are constrained by statute to certain grounds and also require a court order to be effective. It is the purpose of this chapter to analyse the statutory interventions broadly, within a framework which allows us to compare the differences between tenures. This is important because, as we saw in Part II of this book, often the type of tenure accessed is not related to the point of entry. This chapter seeks to expose the conflicts of, and manifest absurdities in, the *different* security of tenure regimes affecting *different* sectors and *different* occupiers. It is argued that the current position is quite simply unjustifiable (see also Miller, 1997). Some examples should provide ample illustrations of the inequity.

If a person successfully approaches a local authority for rehousing, they might be allocated accommodation in the authority's own stock. They might also be nominated to an RSL for rehousing. Equally (and likely in some areas), they might be allocated accommodation in the private rented sector. In 1994, the Conservative government were convinced that home ownership might also be suitable for some people seeking rehousing (DoE, 1994), but, in any event, it may be possible for some to move into shared ownership. On the other hand, if a person seeks private rented accommodation, that is usually what they will get (where they are able to find a suitable property within their, or Housing Benefit's, means). The level and type of security that people obtain from these sets of circumstances is different; the means of, and reasons for, evicting persons from their new accommodation are different – indeed, the enforceability of some of the supposedly granted 'rights' is unclear; the ability to obtain cheap or free legal advice is spatially orientated and of uneven quality – but lawyers are needed because of the complexity of the statutory framework as well as the individual or collective contracts.

All of this seems manifestly wrong – it is your *point of access* and the *local circumstance* which commonly will determine the type of rights you get.

There is worse though – for the rights that you may get, as well as the level of payments you might have to make, will be directly related to *when* you accessed your accommodation. If you accessed private rented accommodation prior to 1989, it is likely that you will now enjoy what lawyers termed the 'status of irremoveability' – a 'statutory tenancy' under the Rent Act 1977 – although this will depend on whether or not your landlord successfully managed to evade the protection granted by that legislation. After 1989, provided your landlord has complied with the appropriate formalities, you are likely to have been granted an assured shorthold tenancy, which might be regarded as a 'status of moveability'. The point is that rights granted to persons, in whatever tenure, change over time through the media of legislation, case law, agreements between housing providers, and individual knowledge of individual rights.

A perhaps unusual example of all of this is provided by using, and embellishing, the facts of *R v Brent LBC ex parte Jerke* (Unreported, QBD, 8 May 1998). In 1994, Brent transferred some of its estates to a Housing Action Trust (HAT). For the tenants, this did not involve a change in tenancy rights, just a change in landlord (from the authority to the Trust) because both landlords must normally grant secure tenancies to their residents. If the council had, like many authorities, transferred their stock to an RSL, this would have involved a change in the type of rights of the occupants because an RSL can (no longer) grant a secure tenancy – currently, RSLs generally have to grant assured tenancies, supplemented by a Tenants' Charter.

Be that as it may, this was a transfer to a HAT. The local authority had an agreement with the HAT that, so long as the HAT accepted nominations from the council for its tenancies, the authority would reciprocate by allowing all the former Brent tenants to apply for transfers to the authority, should the tenants so wish. Jerke, a former Brent tenant now with the HAT, sought a transfer.

If Jerke had successfully reached the top of the transfer list, the council might have used accommodation from its own stock; it might have nominated Jerke to an RSL using its nominations route; it might have nominated Jerke for a shared-ownership scheme (commonly run through RSLs). Alternatively, Jerke might have got fed up of waiting and applied directly to an RSL, another authority, or sought private rented accommodation or a mortgage.

What actually happened was that the arrangement between the HAT and the authority broke down because the HAT refused to accept any more nominations from the council (for practical reasons). The local authority deleted Jerke from its transfer list, and informed all potential transferees that they could instead put themselves on their housing register in the usual way (but without granting extra points for the length of time they had been on the transfer list). The authority's actions were upheld – we are not here concerned with the correctness of that decision, even though it seems unfair – but the point is that any number of permutations might have arisen from that one circumstance of seeking a transfer. *Each of those permutations would have involved a change to Jerke's level of security and rights.*

This example illustrates what might be termed the *fragmentation of tenure*. And, rephrasing the problem addressed in this chapter, quite simply the law has not kept pace with this fragmentation. Housing rights are tenure bound – they do not allow for the diversification within methods of access, and their temporal nature makes them uncertain. The question we face in this chapter is whether this is an adequate response of the law in the late modern world. In order to do this, we need to be appraised of the different levels of security in each tenure and such a discussion forms the main bulk of this chapter.

This argument is, at the time of writing, being rehearsed in the realms of central government and policy makers (including the Local Government Association and the Chartered Institute of Housing). At this stage, it appears that discussion is centring around the creation of a single Social Housing Tenancy – enabling local authorities and RSLs to grant the same rights to their tenants. Such a move would be eminently sensible – the current regime has grown up according to the exigencies of the Public Sector Borrowing Requirement (and the need for RSLs to obtain greater levels of private finance). Why stop with 'social' housing, though? As we have seen, fragmentation has affected the other tenures as well. The fear is, though, that any further regulation of the private rented sector will adversely affect the level of its supply – at present, any root and branch reform of the security regime is not politically palatable. This does not make the current system 'right' – clearly it is awkward and its effects are unfortunate. It is the purpose of this chapter to show just how awkward and unfortunate this situation is.

Somewhat unusually in the context of a discussion about security, I will also be discussing the levels of security enjoyed by home owners. This is partly because the security provided by home ownership should be compared with the security provided in other tenures as part of the consideration as to whether it is a *preferable* tenure; and partly because fragmentation has equally affected home ownership. Take, for example, a lease for 99 years – we say that the purchaser of such a lease becomes a home owner and that terminology extends throughout the currency of the lease. What happens, or should happen, when there is less than (say) four years left on the lease? What level of security does this provide to the owner?

In the final section, we will consider how far the human rights angle affects security by considering one particular aspect of the security of tenure legislation. We will look at the rights granted to all protected tenants to succession. This means that, on the death of the initial tenant, a further person is entitled to take the benefit of the protection of the tenancy. The successor generally must be in a relationship of husband and wife or be blood-related to the initial tenant. These rights do *not* apply to gay couples. We therefore consider their validity in this context. Human rights provide a critical context for our examination because of the incorporation of the European Convention of Human Rights, to which the UK is a signatory, into English law by virtue of the Human Rights Act 1998.

In the first section, though, we need to raise once again the awful spectre of the distinction between the lease and the licence. This was discussed in Chapter 1, where the lease was used as a vehicle to distinguish housing law from other subjects within the law curriculum. We need to discuss it again for two reasons. First, there is the simple rationale that much of the security provisions rely on the distinction and, consequently, we need to appreciate it. Second, it will be argued that this dichotomy provides an inadequate basis for drawing the line between security and insecurity – what is needed is an appreciation of the *purpose* of the landlord, not an abstruse discussion of legal technicality drawing upon anachronistic principles of land law.

Before commencing this analysis, the reader's attention should be drawn to a distinguishing characteristic between this book and other books on housing law. In this book, security provides an example of tenure-differentials, in what has become a cross-tenurial housing situation. We are, therefore, not concerned with all the technicalities nor are we interested in fleshing out all the relevant legal principles. Housing law texts tend to go into great detail on both the technicalities and the principles (although those texts do not then mark the subject out from landlord and tenant law), and many do not deal with home ownership. Subsequent chapters in this volume consider certain aspects of security: 'domestic' violence; unlawful/illegal eviction and harassment; crime and anti-social behaviour; and housing debt. What distinguishes all of these, though, is that they are generally tenure neutral. People experience housing debt in similar ways and for similar reasons. Why, then, do we have different methods of repossessing property depending upon tenure? Anti-social behaviour presumably occurs in all tenures. Why then have specific provisions been drawn up to affect council tenants? Put simply, Part III of this book is concerned with drawing out problems within our understanding of tenure. One, but only one, aspect of that relates to the differential levels of security.

13.1 Leases, Licences and Purposes

The lease plays a critical part in the arrangements provided by legislation by which an individual occupier is granted security. Most legislation only 'bites' when a lease has been granted. The lease is an important concept in land law because it is 'durable' – in other words, third parties are generally bound by the rights it creates (subject to the technicalities of land law). It is a concept of housing law because, without the right, the occupier can generally be ejected with a court order which is relatively easily granted. On the other hand, where the legislative protection bites on a lease, then the occupier can only be evicted where certain grounds have been proved and, in some cases, it would be reasonable to evict the occupier.

Licences are not durable – they are personal rights – and neither are they recognized, in the most part, by the security of tenure legislation in housing law. The main exception to this rule that statutory protection only bites on a lease relates to certain licences granted by local authorities and HATs. Under the Housing Act 1985, most tenants of local authorities and HATs are granted security. This level of security also applies where such landlords grant a licence: 'The provisions of this Part [relating to security of tenure] apply in relation to a licence to occupy a dwelling-house (whether or not granted for a consideration) as they apply in relation to a tenancy' (s 79(3), 1985 Act). At first sight, all licences are protected. However, in *Westminster CC* v. *Clarke* [1992] 1 All ER 695, the House of Lords held that the legislative history of this particular provision meant that only those licences under which the occupier is granted *exclusive possession* are protected by the Act.

The distinction between a lease and a licence, whilst critical to housing law, is one which is (unfortunately) left to land law. In *Street* v. *Mountford* [1985] 1 AC 809, the House of Lords made clear that the intention of the parties to the agreement was irrelevant. The only relevant intention was whether the agreement granted the occupier *exclusive possession, for a term, at a rent*. The 'term' must be a certain period at the outset. So, for example a weekly tenancy has a certain period of one week (even though it runs on until it is determined by either party). It is uncertain whether a rent is necessary. Strictly, it is not (see the analysis in *Ashburn Anstalt* v. *Arnold* [1988] 2 All ER 147), but in *Street* it was included as an indicia of a tenancy.

Exclusive possession was not an issue in the *Street* case at all. We know that it means that the occupier must have the right to exclude allcomers (including the landlord) from entering the property. In *Clarke*, Westminster reserved the right to move Clarke to an alternative place or to place other people in Clarke's bedsit with him. This reservation, which was never exercised, showed that Clarke did not have exclusive possession. Other clauses in agreements which show that an occupier does not have exclusive possession are, for example, where the grantor provides services such as room cleaning, linen changes, or requires the accommodation for part of the day. Sometimes such clauses are a 'pretence' and courts will ignore them (see *Antoniades* v. *Villiers* [1988] 3 WLR 1205; see Lee, 1996).

Exclusive possession is the hallmark of a tenancy but some licence agreements also grant exclusive possession to the occupier (as the analysis of s. 79(3) tells us). A licence where the occupier has exclusive possession commonly occurs where, for example, the grantor is unable for some reason to grant a lease, or the grantor does not intend to enter into legal relationships (such a category embraces a situation where personal rights of occupation are granted out of friendship: *Errington* v. *Errington* [1952] 1 KB 290). It seems also that those RSLs which are almshouses are unable to grant leases because they can only grant rights under a trust (which cannot include a landlord–tenant relationship) – for an excellent example, see *Gray* v. *Taylor* [1998] 4 All ER 17.

In this summary, I have expressly discounted the status of the landlord for, as a matter of law, the same principles should apply between tenures. Furthermore, the type of accommodation should be irrelevant if the only question is whether the occupier has exclusive possession. However, as Lord Templeman tells us in *Clarke*, the nature of the landlord's obligations and the accommodation are important:

'In reaching this conclusion [that Clarke did not have exclusive possession] I take into account the object of the council, namely the provision of temporary accommodation for vulnerable homeless persons, the necessity for the council to retain possession of all the rooms in order to make and administer arrangements for the suitable accommodation of all the occupiers and the need for the council to retain possession of every room not only in the interests of the council as owners of the hostel but also for the purpose of providing for the occupier supervision and assistance.' (at p. 703).

In this breathless sentence, Templeman undermines the position taken by land law. He begins to appreciate that the land law position shrouds a much more complex reality. The purpose of the organization, and the type of accommodation, generate at least an assumption of the type of right granted to the occupier. Take, for example, an RSL set up to provide short-term accommodation to single homeless persons in a hostel setting – it would be absurd, and against the organizational purpose, to say that this RSL has granted a tenancy and consequential rights of security to the occupier. But that is the position to which the land law approach should take us. It is only Templeman's taking account of the position of Westminster and the type of accommodation that enables us to take into account organizational purpose. This, however, is applied inconsistently by the courts (Carr, 1998).

One can also spy tenure distinctions being drawn by judges – these are irrelevant if all we are supposed to do is to draw conclusions from documentation. Templeman in *Clarke* clearly argued that this was a 'very special case', in part because of '. . . the totality, immediacy and objectives of the powers exercisable by the council . . .' (p. 703). In *Camden LBC* v. *Shortlife Community Housing* (1992) 25 HLR 331, Millett J made a great deal out of the relationship between the organizations – Camden licensed accommodation to Shortlife to provide accommodation for non-priority homeless persons (at p. 345–6) – but also the nature of the accommodation:

> 'The flats were at the end of their useful life; they were taken gradually out of use for letting to tenants; and they became part of the rolling stock of short-life property to be dealt with quite differently. It was of the very essence of the arrangements that properties should be made available and handed back on a rotating basis and at short notice. Such a system sits uneasily with the concept of the grant of a [tenancy].' (at p. 347).

Similar points are raised in *Gray* v. *Taylor*, but this time the Court was most concerned with the *type of person* whom should occupy accommodation owned by an almshouse. An example was raised of almshouse residents who win the lottery and decide to remain in the accommodation:

> 'Lottery winners often announce that they do not intend that their good fortune should be allowed to change their pattern of life. The almshouse would then become something like a rich persons' club. It cannot seriously be suggested that the change from being a poor to being a rich person would be a ground falling within [the security of tenure legislation] on which the court could make an order for possession.' [1998] 4 All ER 17, 22, *per* Sir John Vinelott

These are just some of the comments which suggest that arcane legalism has given way to a recognition that organizational purpose has become an essential facet of the dichotomy.

13.2   Security of Tenure

The security of tenure provisions differ between tenures. This reflects the regulation of each tenure. So, for example, in the long history of council housing, council tenants only gained rights against their landlords in 1980, as the era of 'patronage' came to an end and the era of consumerism was beginning. Security given to RSL tenants has varied according to the directions from which the RSL has gleaned development funds. The current position of mixing public and private funds means that RSL tenants' security commonly falls between the public and private regimes. The need to encourage the private rental market has affected the level of security given to tenants in that sector. No matter how and by whom the accommodation is accessed, the regulation of each sector predetermines the level of security given to occupiers in each sector.

This focus on regulation, as opposed to access, is perhaps not unnatural because of the concentration on regulation and finance at central government level. The Conservative governments were keen to deregulate and decontrol as far as possible because it was believed that excessive regulation and control of the private-sector was constraining that sector's development. Regulation of private-sector landlord or lender interests was regarded almost as expropriation, a removal of those people's rights over their property or security (see also Honore, 1980). Such views are often replicated within the judiciary, where a concentration on strict contractual rights conflicts with statutory security. This principle is an underlying feature of much of the case law, which means that the legislation is often narrowly construed (i.e. construed against the interests of the occupier). Hand makes this point when she argues that:

'[T]he courts made no secret of their dislike for the whole idea of a statutory tenant since he did not fit easily into the accepted categories of proprietary interests. They therefore moved towards the position that he had a purely personal right. Parliament had not made its intentions sufficiently clear. To give the statutory tenant property rights was to remove them from the landlord and this the courts were unwilling to do.' (1980, p. 358)

Partington comments, however, that no study has been conducted on judicial views of security of tenure and thus any 'casual empiricism' should be treated with some caution (1980, p. 30). Robson and Watchman are more vituperative and methodologically sound in making comments about Lord Denning's role in the restriction of legislative intention as expressed in security of tenure legislation:

'Since the first of these Acts was introduced in 1915, . . ., the judiciary have indulged in a particularly pernicious form of judicial sabotage. At times stopping just short of squeezing the life from the policy.' (1981, p. 187)

'Under the mask of providing a more flexible approach to distinguishing between leases and licences, Lord Denning has slowly eroded the statutory rights of tenants until they are virtually deprived of the protection which Parliament introduced to prevent exploitation of shortages of supply in the housing market.' (p. 208)

Whilst Templeman sought to refocus on the agreement, and was explicit in his rejection of the relevance of the security of tenure legislation in this process, it is arguable that the deregulating legislation in the Housing Act 1988 had more effect than *Street* v. *Mountford* in that process. The Conservative government effectively removed the private rental occupier's status of irremoveability, and thus the judicial concern has been removed. In the 1990s, one might argue that the courts have, to a certain extent, been reconstructed and have been prepared to protect occupier's security (particularly owner-occupiers: *Palk* v. *Mortgage Services Funding* [1993] Ch. 330) but this has only occurred now after the occupier's rights have effectively been statutorily delimited.

In this section, we will consider each tenure separately (and in no particular order) and consider (a) qualifying conditions, (b) excluded agreements, (c) any rights granted to the occupier by statute, (d) the level of security (i.e. the ways in which, and reasons why, an occupier might be evicted).

Local Authorities and HATs I: The 'Secure Tenancy' Regime

Tenants of council housing have, for most of this century, not been regarded as requiring protection against their landlords. Indeed, until 1980, such tenants had few enforceable rights against their landlords. In part, this was because council tenants were not deemed worthy of protection; in part, this was because council housing had been provided at the expense of other ratepayers. Tenants were objects of local munificence. Loveland argues that a further important context was the relationship between central and local government: 'Tightly drafted statutes or interventionist case law would have overridden the traditional expectation that councils should govern their local areas, rather than simply administer centrally defined services on an agency basis' (1992, p. 344). The move to tightly drafted statutes and interventionist case law occurred when this relationship began to break down in the mid 1970s. Whilst it has been argued that tenants were granted rights *in order to* grant them the right to buy (Smith & George, 1997), it seems clear that the rights granted in the Housing Act 1980 were the culmination of a lengthy campaign. The Labour government's 1979 Housing Bill contained a set of individual rights which mostly found themselves put into the Conservative's 1980 Act, signalling the importance of consumerism within the Thatcherite ideologue.

Qualifying conditions
The security of tenure provisions, now contained in the consolidating Housing Act 1985, bite *at any time* when the occupier meets the 'tenant condition' and the landlord meets the 'landlord condition' (ss. 81 and 80

respectively). The property must also have been let[1] 'as a separate dwelling' (s. 79(1)), which has been taken to mean that living rooms (such as kitchens) must not be shared with other people (*Central YMCA* v. *Saunders* (1990) 23 HLR 212). Unlike the security provisions governing the private rented sector, the phrase 'at any time' means that the occupier can 'move in and out of secure status' (Morgan, 1998, p. 132).

The landlord condition is simply that the landlord is, amongst others, a local authority or a HAT. This means that HATs fit within the security regime affecting council housing and not the private sector regime.

The tenant condition is that the tenant must be 'an individual' (that is, not a company), and occupies the dwelling-house as 'his only or principal home'. The tenancy can be granted to two or more persons jointly, in which case only one of them must occupy the property as their only or principal home. The latter phrase implies that continued residence is not necessary. In *Brown* v. *Brash* [1948] 2 KB 247, it was held that the tenant must have both an 'inward intention to return' as well as some 'formal, outward, and visible sign of [possession]' (at p. 254). This case actually concerned the meaning of the word 'residence' but it has been applied in full force to cases under the 1985 Act (see, for example, *Crawley BC* v. *Sawyer* (1988) 20 HLR 98).

Excluded Agreements

There are a number of excluded agreements, which include long leases, certain short-term agreements (commonly referred to as the North Wiltshire scheme, whereby a landlord leases or licences accommodation to an authority with vacant possession for a specified period), and certain employment-related exclusions. Accommodation granted to homeless persons in satisfaction of the two-year duty to successful applicants is not secure unless the landlord gives notice to the contrary.

Statutory Rights

Prior to the 1980 Act, tenancy agreements commonly placed many obligations on the tenant without giving tenants any rights. The 1980 Act included what was termed the 'Tenants' Charter'. It has since been amended but the following are a selection of the rights granted. For example, tenants were given the right to assign their tenancies in certain circumstances, take in lodgers, make improvements to the property and be compensated for them, and to repair and recover the costs of the repairs. As important have been the rights to information and consultation that were discussed in Chapter 6. Each of these rights is delimited in some way or other so as to reduce their potency. For example, the right to be consulted does not go so far as to cover the level of rents, 'one of the most important collective concerns for tenants' (Gilroy, 1998, p. 26); and 'the economic disadvantage of most tenants limits their right to undertake improvements (Stewart, 1996, p. 153). Indeed, authorities took some time to implement the Charter, partly because of the political context and partly because of the implementation of the right to buy (see Kay *et al.*,

1987, Ch. 2). Furthermore, 'While the right to buy was advertised several times on television and in national newspapers, the DoE confined promotion of the rest of the Tenants' Charter to a slim official pamphlet' (Loveland, 1992, p. 352). Thus, the national structures meant that little information was given to individual tenants, who were then unable to exercise their rights for which, in any event, the authorities themselves were not ready.

Security of Tenure
In order to terminate a secure tenancy, the local authority or HAT must serve a 'notice of seeking possession' on the tenant(s), containing specified information. In the notice, the landlord must write which ground for possession they are relying upon. In the 1996 Act, new provision was made to dispense with notice where a court considers it 'just and equitable' to do so (s. 147, 1996 Act). This new provision was meant to salve the apparent concern of local authorities that possession proceedings took too long (although the 'just and equitable' process could take just as long in practice). There are 16 such grounds and the landlord must show not only that the ground is made out *but also* that it is reasonable for possession to be granted. For some of the grounds, the local authority must also show that suitable alternative accommodation is available to the occupier. Proceedings take place in the County Court before a District Judge. The criterion of 'reasonableness' means that the judge must take into account all relevant circumstances and 'he must do so in what I venture to call a broad, common-sense way as a man of the world, and come to his conclusion giving such weight as he thinks right to the various factors in the situation . . . but it is quite wrong for him to exclude from his consideration matters which he ought to take into account' (*Cumming* v. *Danson* [1942] 2 All ER 652, *per* Lord Greene MR). In recent cases, by contrast to this broad approach, the courts have been concerned to narrow down the available discretion. In *Shrewsbury & Atcham BC* v. *Evans* (1998) 30 HLR 123, possession was sought by the authority on the basis that the applicant had lied to gain accommodation (Ground 5). Beldam LJ argued as follows:

'Those who are on the housing list who have an equal or greater claim to public housing would, in my view, be justly indignant to find that the court did not think it reasonable in circumstances where someone has obtained accommodation by a deliberate and flagrant lie, to make an order for possession merely because the effect of the order would result in the occupant having to be considered by the local authority as homeless or intentionally homeless.' (1998) 30 HLR 123, 132

Thus, in some cases, reasonableness is a rather easy hurdle to overcome. Some factors are accorded rather less weight, if any, in some situations (particularly where, as here, Evans had apparently received her tenancy on the basis of a 'deliberate and flagrant lie').

Of the grounds for possession, subsequent chapters of this book concern themselves with claims for possession on the following grounds (none of which require the provision of suitables alternative accommodation): where rent lawfully due has not been paid or another obligation of the tenancy has been broken or not performed (Ground 1); where the tenant has committed a nuisance or anti-social behaviour (Ground 2); and where the remaining occupant has committed domestic violence (Ground 2A). Bearing in mind how easy it is to prove Ground 1, most notices specify this ground and most possession orders are made on this basis. Most orders that are made are suspended to enable the occupier to remedy their breach (and repay money owed in instalments). However, if the terms of a suspended order are broken, the occupier can be evicted without further court order. Until the eviction, the tenant can apply to the court to vary the order and revive the secure tenancy (*Burrows* v. *Brent LBC* (1997) 29 HLR 167).

Local Authorities and HATs II: The 'Introductory Tenancy' Regime

The introductory tenancy regime was set up as part of the 'fight against nuisance neighbours' in the Housing Act 1996, Part V. This regime was specifically requested by a number of authorities which were concerned about the rise of anti-social behaviour on their estates. It only applies to local authorities and HATs and only if those landlords decide, after consultation, to exercise their discretion to introduce the regime. After deciding to enter the scheme, every subsequent grant of a tenancy and exclusive possession licence (ss 124 (2) and 126(1)) is an *introductory* tenancy and not secure. So far, 40 landlords have begun a scheme, and more than 24,500 introductory tenancies have been created (although the information base is inadequate) (Social Landlords Crime and Nuisance Group (SLCNG), 1998). The largest landlord to have implemented the scheme is Manchester, with a housing stock of 82,000 and 6,200 introductory tenancies.

Qualifying Conditions
Every periodic tenancy or exclusive possession licence granted after the landlord decides to enter the regime is an introductory tenancy.

Excluded Agreements
Where the new occupier has been a secure tenant before, or an assured tenant of an RSL, they are excluded from the regime.

Statutory Rights
Introductory tenants have broadly similar rights as secure tenants. These have been granted by Statutory Instrument and do not appear on the face of the Act itself.

Security of Tenure
The central difference between a secure and introductory tenant lies in the ability of the landlord to seek possession of the property. The introductory tenancy only lasts a year (after which it automatically becomes secure). It was rightly termed a 'probationary' tenancy because, during that period, the introductory tenant can be evicted much more speedily. The procedure is simple: the landlord serves a notice of proceedings on the tenant and that must contain certain information (s. 128, 1996 Act). The tenant is entitled to seek an internal review of the decision to seek possession of the property (along similar lines to that which operates under the home-lessness legislation). Once the review, if any, has been conducted and the landlord decides to continue to seek possession, application is made to the County Court. That court must grant an order for possession, unless the landlord has not complied with the detail (*Manchester CC* v. *Cochrane*, Unreported, CA, 21 December 1998). Thus, the landlord can proceed from notice to eviction in a short period of time. Manchester, for example, has commented that the court proceedings itself is much shorter: 'the court hearing now only takes 10 minutes which removes the delay incurred by the Court administration process of having to book two or more days for a trial' (SLCNG, 1998). It is for this reason that many have expressed concern about the operation of the introductory tenancy regime. Other concerns reflect the possibility that a person might be evicted simply for not 'fitting in' and that communities might seek to use the legislation as a means of forcing new tenants out. This might particularly affect, for example, those with mental health problems, or black people placed on predominantly white estates. It is too early to tell whether these concerns are prescient. Some landlords clearly see their use as beneficial and those who already have tenancies may well approve of the scheme. Nevertheless, research on their impact is desperately required as more and more areas enter the schemes without any data to back up their effectiveness.

One might well wonder about the effectiveness of the one-year term to the tenancy. Anti-social behaviour and nuisance can arise at any time, not just in the first year of a tenancy. Indeed, it is perhaps more likely for the new tenant to experience the effects of nuisance and anti-social behaviour in the first year of a new tenancy as they are the new 'face'. In Chapter 18, we also question why the new regime only applies to council and HAT housing.

Private Renting I: The Rent Act Tenancy

The Rent Act 1977 was a consolidation of earlier legislation (Rent Act 1965 and Rent Act 1974). Under the protection of this Act, the tenant has been described as having a 'status of irremoveability' during the currency of protection. This term was used to denote the limits on the landlord's rights to evict the tenant, as well as the right (until 1989) of *two* successions given to the tenant. On the death of the tenant, their successor would be entitled to take the tenant's interest; and, on the death of the successor, a further succession was permitted. Rights of succession are considered below.

The Act's provisions bite on the initial term – which is called a 'protected tenancy' – and makes specific provision for occupation at the end of that term – the 'statutory tenancy'. In Chapter 2, we examined the argument of the Conservative government that the grant of such rights to tenants effectively makes landlords less willing to rent their properties out. We noted that landlords sought to avoid giving the protection offered by the Acts, usually successfully, to tenants either through licence agreements or other mechanisms. To a certain extent *Street* v. *Mountford* stymied such attempts, although by this time it was 'rapidly neutralized' by the effect of the Housing Act 1988 to be discussed below (see Vincent-Jones, 1987; Chapter 1 above).

Qualifying Conditions

The protected tenancy arises when a dwelling-house is let as a separate dwelling. There is no requirement for the property to form the tenant's only or principal home, nor must the tenant be an individual. Where there was a resident landlord, the qualifying conditions were not met and the tenant would have what the 1977 Act termed a 'restricted contract'. Such contracts cannot now be created and, instead, are currently not protected. The 'fair rent' system attaches to protected tenants.

On the termination of the protected tenancy, a statutory tenancy would result 'if and so long as [the tenant] occupies the dwelling-house as his residence' (s. 2). The statutory tenant is entitled to retain possession until the security has been exhausted. A company cannot be in 'residence' and, thus, the benefits of the statutory tenancy do not accrue to companies. The *Brown* v. *Brash* test applies to the word 'residence', and it is perfectly possible for a person to have two residences both of which qualify as statutory tenancies (in other words, residence does not have to be permanent).

Whilst the secure tenancy arises at any time that the conditions are fulfilled, the Rent Act tenancies must fulfill the conditions at all times otherwise the tenancy is not protected.

Excluded Agreements

Tenancies of properties at a high rent (or above a high rateable value) together with those granted for a low rent are excluded. These categories actually caught few properties as Partington explained: '. . . although Rent Act protection was initially designed to concentrate on housing occupied by the poorest tenant only, there has been a gradual, if haphazard, extension to more and more types of property. Today, very few properties are excluded on the rateable value ground though they may be excluded for other reasons' (1980, p. 156). One might regard this aspect of the legislation as an example of creeping regulation. Other examples of excluded agreements were those where there was 'board or attendance' provided (hence the move of many to the provision of bed and breakfast), lettings to students by educational institutions (covering halls of residence), and holiday lettings (leading to people taking holidays in unlikely places).

Statutory Rights
One of the most significant rights of protected tenants was the right to a fair rent (and all that went with that right). The statutory tenancy is generally incapable of assignment (although there is a potential exception in Sch. 1, para. 13: see Hand, 1980, pp. 354–5).

Security of Tenure
As usual, a court order is required to determine the possession of the tenant. This court order can be made if either the landlord has provided suitable alternative accommodation (and it would be reasonable to make an order for possession), or on the basis of 10 discretionary cases for possession (where the judge can only grant possession if it would also be reasonable to do so) and 10 mandatory cases for possession (where the judge must grant possession to the landlord where the ground has been proved). Reasonableness is decided on the basis of the principles adduced in *Cumming* v. *Danson* that all matters should be taken into account and weighed accordingly.

Some of the cases are similar to the grounds applicable to secure tenants under the 1985 Act. For example, Case 1 relates to unpaid rent and breach of other obligations. Case 2 relates to nuisance or annoyance to neighbours – this was the same as Ground 2 in the 1985 Act, but in the 1996 Act Ground 2 was amended, whilst Case 2 was (surprisingly) not. Nor did the 1996 Act update the 1977 Act so as to enable a Rent Act tenant to be evicted on the basis of domestic violence. Other cases specifically relate to the private sector, so as to include (for example) discretionary grounds for eviction where the landlord wishes for themselves or a member of their family to go into occupation of the property (Case 9) and the property is required for an employee of the landlord (Case 8). The mandatory grounds tend to be narrower in scope and generally also require the proof of other factors (contained in Part V, Sch. 2).

Private Renting II: The 'Assured Tenancy'

In the Housing Act 1988, the Conservative government sought to revive the private rented sector by deregulating the levels of security available to tenants under the 1977 Act, as well as enabling landlords to charge a market rent. This much is well-known. However, the 1988 Act contained *two* new statutory regimes for the private sector. No more Rent Act tenancies could be created (and amendments were made to the right of succession of Rent Act tenants – see below). The first, known as the assured tenancy, in fact closely resembles the 1977 Act regime, particularly as regards the level of security of tenure (albeit more simplified). There are, however, significant alterations to the grounds on which courts may grant possession orders.

Initially, all tenancies granted after the 1988 Act came into force were assured tenancies *unless* the landlord served a notice on the tenant that the tenancy was to be an *assured shorthold tenancy*. In the 1996 Act, however, the notice requirement was swapped around so that, at the time of writing, the landlord must serve a notice on the tenant that the tenancy is to be an assured tenancy. Where no notice is served the tenancy is an assured shorthold. The government's case for change was that many landlords were being caught out by the notice requirement and granting assured tenancies rather than assured shortholds (see DoE, 1995). However, it can be argued that the new system reverses the burden of this so that it is tenants who will be caught out by the notice requirement.

Qualifying Conditions
The main difference between the Rent Act protected tenancy and the assured tenancy is that for the latter, the tenant must occupy the property as their 'only or principal home'. A further difference is that the tenant must be an individual (and, therefore, companies are completely excluded from the ambit of the Act). Under the 1988 Act, assured tenancies cannot arise where there is a resident landlord and such agreements are unprotected.

Excluded Agreements
The assured tenancy regime only applies to tenancies created after the Act came into force. Similar exclusions exists as under the Rent Act 1977 (except that the rateable value exclusion now refers solely to high rent).

Statutory Rights
Assured tenants are entitled to assign or sublet their interests but only with the consent of the landlord.

Security of Tenure
The landlord must serve a notice of proceedings (although the court may dispense with it where it is 'just and equitable' to do so) which sets out all of the relevant information, including the grounds relied upon. There are eight mandatory and ten discretionary grounds for possession. By contrast to the 1977 Act, there are *three* grounds for possession based upon arrears of rent, one of which is *mandatory*. For monthly tenancies, the mandatory ground was shown where more than three months rent was in arrears (Ground 8). In the 1996 Act, this period was reduced to two months (and eight weeks for weekly tenancies): s. 101. The government's reason for this change was that for a private landlord 'having a tenant who does not pay the rent can be financially very difficult' (DoE, 1995, para. 2.14). Yet, where the tenant is reliant on Housing Benefit (which is now paid four weeks in arrears, whereas rent is practically always claimed in advance),

concerns have been expressed that this reduction could prove problematic. The Conservative government's answer was that, after service of the notice, it still takes a few months to obtain a court order and, provided the rent is paid off by that time, the ground can no longer be shown.

The discretionary grounds concerned with rent enable a landlord to gain possession where some rent lawfully due remains unpaid when possession proceedings are begun and at the date of service of the notice; and where the tenant is persistently late in paying rent.

The 1996 Act also included a ninth discretionary ground for possession by enabling landlords to gain possession where the tenancy has been granted after a false statement (as in the secure tenancy regime). It is difficult to see how the comments made in the *Shrewsbury* case on the question of reasonableness would apply in the private sector. The court specifically concerned itself with the question of local authorities and the inequity to others on the housing register. In the case of the private rented sector, the discretion may well be fulsome (although one might suspect the judiciary would strain for a converse solution).

As with the secure tenancy regime, the 1996 Act also included provisions enabling landlords to regain possession of properties after domestic violence (Ground 14A) and extended the ground of nuisance and annoyance to neighbours (Ground 14).

Private Renting III: The 'Assured Shorthold Tenancy'

The principal difference between the assured and assured shorthold tenancy regimes lie in the level of security of tenure (otherwise the regime are broadly similar). Essentially, the assured shorthold tenancy can be brought to an end at any time after the tenancy has been in existence for six months. The procedure for retaking possession is simplicity itself: the landlord serves a notice on the tenant in writing, giving the tenant not less than two months to leave, and the landlord must obtain a court order unless the tenant leaves earlier (which is mandatory). The other grounds of possession available in respect of assured tenancies equally apply (but are not entirely necessary because of the two month rule).

Thus, the central advantage of the assured shorthold is that the landlord can retake possession with minimal requirements and the tenant's security is consequently minimal. It is hardly surprising, then, that the assured shorthold has become the tenancy most commonly granted by landlords because they are able to obtain possession so quickly and neatly. Even if this is not what the landlord wants – many landlords want a secure let so that the income generated by the property is secure – the assured shorthold provides the landlord with the means to terminate the tenancy at their own whim.

Thus, we are far removed from the position where private sector tenants had a 'status of irremoveability' – perhaps a 'status of moveability' would be more appropriate.

RSLs: A Magic Mixture

We have noted in earlier chapters how RSLs have, at different times, been regarded as being private sector, public sector, or quasi-public sector. This is reflected in the types of tenancy that they are able to give. Importantly, though, this is now directly related to the source of funds. As we saw in Chapter 5, RSLs have been required to generate funds for development from private lenders (and this has often affected their management styles). It has always been assumed that private lenders would only be willing to make loans to RSLs if the security of tenure available to tenants was the same as in the private sector and (importantly) rents were subject to market principles: 'This [use of assured and assured shorthold regimes] should give [RSLs] the essential freedom and flexibility in setting their rents to enable them to meet the requirements of private sector finance instead of relying on funding from public sources' (DoE, 1987, para. 4.6). A further reason for this tmove to private-sector regimes was so that RSLs themselves would fall out of the public-sector regime and, thus, not be counted as part of the Public Sector Borrowing Requirement. Indeed, amongst the Conservative government, this was the main rationale for the desire to see RSLs develop.

Such analysis provides an appropriate introduction to the area, but the situation is rather more complex. First, at different times, RSL tenancies have been subject to different tenancy regimes as Table 13.1 shows.

Table 13.1   RSLs and security of tenure: 1977 to the present

Period	Type of Security	Type of Rent Regulation
1977–1980	nil	Fair rents – 1977 Act
1980–1989	Secure – 1980/1985 Acts	Fair rents – 1977 Act
1989–1998	Assured/Assured shorthold + Tenants' Guarantee	Market rents – 1988 Act
1998–	Assured/Assured shorthold + Tenants' Charter(s)	Market rents – 1988 Act

In the period 1977–80, RSL tenants had no security of tenure ('presumably because the landlords were non-profit making bodies and considered socially responsible': Stewart, 1996, p. 199). Between 1980–1988, RSL tenants were put within the secure tenancy regime, principally (it seems) because the Conservative government was keen to widen the definition of the public sector in order to widen the scope of the right to buy. However, the right to buy, by amendment in the House of Lords accepted by the Conservative government, did not apply to charitable RSLs. The 1980 Act regime applied to all tenancies granted by

RSLs prior to its introduction. Between 1989–1998, RSLs have only been able to grant private-sector tenancies because of the move to private finance. The regime introduced in the 1988 Act (which came into force in 1989) only applies to tenancies granted after its introduction. However, the Housing Corporation required RSLs to comply with the Tenants' Guarantee (reissued in 1994). The Guarantee made it clear that RSLs were to grant 'the most secure form of tenure possible', which meant that other than in 'exceptional circumstances' RSLs were to grant assured periodic tenancies (para. C3). The move in 1998 to a 'Tenants' Charter' system is, in part, a recognition that different RSLs grant different rights. The following are a selection of Charters: leaseholders who are shared owners; licencees living in supported housing; secure tenants; assured tenants; members of fully mutual housing cooperatives; shorthold tenants. These show clearly which rights the occupier has as a matter of law and which rights the Corporation requires the RSL to give to occupiers. The Charters basically tell the occupier what the regulatory document, *Performance Standards* (Housing Corporation, 1997), tell RSLs.

Standards contains similar comments to the Guarantee about the level of security of tenure ('the most secure form of tenancy possible compatible with the purpose of the housing means issuing all new tenants with assured periodic tenancies': para. G1.1). However, there are exceptions to this rule (other than fully mutual cooperatives which are unable to grant tenancies). In two particular circumstances, *Standards* enables an RSL to grant assured shorthold tenancies: under a 'local lettings' scheme or under an 'introductory tenancies' scheme. The Corporation is particularly concerned that RSLs 'take reasonable steps to know where social conditions put at risk residents or the value or lettability of their housing, and should liaise with other agencies on these problems' (Standard H2.2). The Corporation also suggests that 'RSLs should consider the use of starter tenancies [i.e. assured shortholds] as part of a strategy for dealing with community breakdown which includes a range of other measures to respond to local conditions and involves other local agencies' (Housing Corporation, 1998, para. 14).

All of this follows closely upon the research of David Page discussed in earlier and later chapters. Both local lettings and introductory tenancies can be granted for the same reasons, generally relating to what the Corporation terms the 'stability of communities' (section 2, p. 44). The main circumstances where assured shortholds can be used relate to where 'better use' needs to be made of the stock (for example, under occupation); 'if the stock concerned is difficult to let to those in priority need, and flexibility would significantly reduce the number of empty homes'; 'if steps are needed to prevent or reverse social conditions in an area threatening the housing rights of most residents or the value of the stock' (p. 45). The types of persons who may be restricted from obtaining accommodation under a local lettings policy relate to reducing child density levels, where applicants have a history of anti-social behaviour, and giving priority to applicants with family or work in the area (Housing Corporation, 1998, para. 7). One can divine two strands (at least) from these provisions. First, the Corporation has taken a view that the needs of the tenants sometimes outweigh the needs of those next on the list. Second, the RSL needs to preserve the value of the stock because otherwise the security for (public and private) loans is at stake. RSLs must have the support of the local authority before they can enter the local lettings scheme (because this affects the nominations, if any, of the authority), although the lack of consent of the authority can be overridden by the Corporation itself.

A further way in which the structure of security of tenure of RSL residents is more complex than types of security relates to the fact that RSLs do not simply grant periodic tenancies. Many are involved in different types of schemes, so that their residents will have different rights. For example, an RSL may have a local lettings policy affecting part of their stock, shared-ownership schemes in other areas, and the same RSL might also build property for other low-cost home ownership schemes. In other words, different tenure structures, and different security structures will apply in each scheme. Our concentration here is on periodic tenancies – we will consider shared ownership below, at the same time as home ownership. Finally, certain types of RSL cannot grant tenancies (and thus tenants fall outside the statutory regime) – such RSLs include cooperatives and almshouses.

In terms of the structure of this part of this chapter, the qualifying conditions (a) and excluded agreements (b) are the same as for private sector tenants. What is different are the types of rights given to occupiers and the level of security.

Statutory Rights

RSL tenants are granted all the rights of tenants in the regime in which their tenancies fit. However, *Standards* grants RSL residents many rights additional to those which 1988 Act tenants are granted. The desire is to equalize RSL tenants with council tenants. So RSL tenants are given additional rights to consultation on certain issues, to information, to participate in housing management, to repair, to take in lodgers, to assign tenancies, to exchange properties, as well as to alternative complaints mechanisms (using the Independent Housing Ombudsman scheme). These rights are not incorporated into the tenancy agreement and questions arise as to whether they are legally enforceable. The view commonly adopted is that the Guarantee and Charter create a 'legitimate expectation' that the RSL will respect those rights (see Stewart, 1996, p. 223; Alder & Handy, 1996, p. 108). Such an expectation may be misjudged on the basis that RSLs commonly seek exemptions from the *Standards*, have to balance the occasional conflicts created by private-finance systems and lenders (Day & Klein, 1993), as well as our knowledge that many RSLs disagree with some of the Standards (*ibid*). Furthermore, it is likely that many RSLs simply are not aware of the *Standards* document or have forgotten about it (therefore, how can they give those rights?). Finally, there are concerns about the extent of the doctrine of 'legitimate expectations' and whether it will provide a ground for claiming against an RSL landlord outside the tenancy contract.

Whilst there are questions about the *legal* enforceability of *Standards*, it seems relatively clear that the statutory ombudsman scheme, to which RSL tenants may apply for determination of any claim, will apply it. The ombudsman can filter cases into mediation or arbitration schemes (on the cost-effectiveness of mediation, see Dignan *et al.*, 1997). The ombudsman considers whether the RSL has been guilty of 'maladministration', a term wide enough to enable the ombudsman to take into account and enforce the requirements of *Standards*. The ombudsman's findings are unenforceable, but *Standards* makes clear that RSLs 'are expected to co-operate fully with the independent ombudsman and comply with any findings or recommendations he makes' (p. 57). The success of the ombudsman scheme is, however, open to question. First, residents are only entitled to complain to the ombudsman after exhausting the RSL's own internal complaints scheme; second, there are doubts as to the effectiveness of the ombudsman, as many complaints are filtered to other jurisdictions and few complaints are upheld (of course, RSLs may be perfect organizations but one must be sceptical). So, in 1996–7, the ombudsman received and scrutinized 1115 complaints; 226 were outside the jurisdiction and 734 were referred back to the RSL's internal complaints schemes. Of the 225 complaints actively considered, 139 were resolved as a result of the ombudsman's intervention: 12 informally settled; 54 settled by mediation; 2 by arbitration; maladministration was found in 30 other cases and maladministration was not found in 41 other cases.

Security of Tenure
Standards also makes important comments on when RSLs should bring proceedings for possession and thus constrains the RSLs' rights as landlord. Standard G1.3 makes clear that '[RSLs] should only seek possession once all other reasonable steps have been taken'. How far this statement is taken into account must be considered in terms of the empirical evidence as well as whether RSLs make full use of the powers available to them. For example, under the 1988 Act regime, RSLs are entitled to use the mandatory ground of eviction due to rent arrears. In a Scottish study (under similar legislation), Scottish Homes found that about three out of ten would use this provision (although 75 per cent had included the Ground in their contracts with residents) (1997, pp. 43–4). Not surprisingly, the study found that associations' practices vary widely, although generally the research found that RSLs 'spend more time and effort on the pre-litigation stages of arrears recovery than public sector landlords' (p. 48). Chapter 17 considers the comparative housing debt approaches of different landlords.

Home Ownership: 'So This Isn't Mine . . .'

In this section, I will be dealing with two separate problems of home ownership. The first concerns the extra statutory rights given to long leaseholders where the leases are running out. The second concerns the level of security given to home owners where there is a mortgage.

Statutory Rights
'Home ownership' is legally fragmented into, on the one hand, freehold tenure and, on the other, leasehold tenure. Leaseholds equally fit into the category of private renting (see Stewart, 1996, pp. 110–116) because the leaseholder pays rent, albeit commonly much lower, to a landlord. The landlord is the 'home owner', although it is unlikely that they will have ever occupied the property. Most leaseholders, however, would regard themselves as home owners – they pay a premium for their interest, which usually will require them to take a mortgage, and their rights are commonly long-term (more than 21 years and, in some cases, 999 years). This fragmentation has important consequences.

The long lease for 99 years was particularly in vogue in the nineteenth century, when landowners would let property on a building lease to a developer; after accommodation was built, the property would be let on short term bases. The rise of home ownership meant that many of these long leases were bought by occupiers. Problems arose in the 1950s as the long leases began to run their course. A further problem arises because, under English law, it is not possible for flat owners to buy freeholds (because obligations would not be mutually enforceable). Thus, they can only take leaseholds.

When long leases in areas begin to run out, the area itself also changes. For example, repairing the property is not worthwhile. Lenders tend to avoid properties with less than 40 years remaining on their lease, making potential purchasers seek alternative forms of finance (Stewart, 1981, p. 22). Perec Rachman, the notorious slum landlord, made enormous profits out of buying short ends of long leases very cheaply and using the properties for short-term letting. The properties were particularly affected by the diminishing premiums attached to them, making them suitable for low-cost home ownership (see Chapter 12). The developing problems of these areas began to be recognized more and more in government policy.

These problems mask an important conflict in the property relations of this segment of home ownership. On the one hand, the occupiers of these properties 'began to claim recognition of their investment in the property' (Stewart, 1996, p. 112). The desire of all political parties to expand home ownership means that these problems need solutions. On the other hand, the freeholders regard the grant of additional rights to long leaseholders as an expropriation. A few people own a considerable amount of valuable property. When, in the 1992 election campaign, the Conservative Party made it clear that it would introduce greater rights for long leaseholders, the Duke of Westminster resigned his membership of the party. The history of the development of the legislation suggests that much of its complexity is caused by the power reflex of different interest groups.

In 1967, the Leasehold Reform Act gave long leaseholders of houses with low rents the right to enfranchise (that is, purchase the freehold) or a further leasehold term. The Act proved complex and difficult to use, because it was so poorly drafted (it was subsequently regularly amended). As it turned out, landlords were able to stymy attempts to sell freeholds or leaseholds when they wanted to and, as Stewart shows in a study of Saltley in Birmingham, it was only the changing dynamics of the broader property market in the mid-1970s (during a down part of the cycle) which persuaded corporate landlords to part with their interests as part of a commercial restructuring of their interests:

> 'The position with L.C. & W. [a property company] was slightly different. By 1976 they needed financial assistance. Lonrho bought in shares during 1976 and finally took them over for £13 million later in the year. We judged that Lonrho would not be interested in freeholds in Saltley and that they too would sell off this part of the L.C. & W. portfolio. We proved to be correct.' (1981, p. 177)

In other words, the restructuring of tenure in the area occurred partly because of corporate restructuring due to changes in the property market cycle.

The 1967 Act has now been supplemented with legislation giving flat owners similar rights, as well as the right of leaseholders in a block to group together and purchase the freehold (Leasehold Reform, Housing and Urban Development Act 1993, Part I). The 1996 Act has amended the 'low rent' test, which excluded many from its provisions, so that any leaseholder granted a lease for more than 35 years is entitled to the benefit of the provisions. Basically, though we are left with a set of legislation which is regarded as being 'too restrictive, too complex, and too expensive' (Clarke, 1998, p. 400). The Acts can be avoided by freeholders and the need for reform remains (as has been recognized by DETR, 1998).

Security of Tenure
It is commonly said that home ownership offers the greatest security of all tenures. For those fortunate enough to own their homes outright, this is mostly true.[2] For the considerably larger proportion of home owners requiring a mortgage, the level of security is rather different and, perhaps unexpectedly, theoretically less than granted in other tenures. As Harman J. said in *Four-Maids* v. *Dudley Marshall Ltd* [1957] Ch. 317 the mortgage lender is entitled to go into possession of the property 'before the ink is dry on the mortgage' unless this right is excluded in some way or other. This reflects the history of the mortgage which involved the home owner basically conveying (or selling) their property in full to the lender for the duration of the loan. On repayment of the loan, the lender would be required to reconvey the property back to the home owner. All the home

owner generally has left is the right to repay the lender (*City of London BS* v. *Flegg* [1988] AC 54). Most lenders do now restrict this right in the mortgage contract by saying they will only seek possession if the borrower defaults on the mortgage (Whitehouse, 1998a, p. 191).

The lenders' right to repossession of the property for default on the mortgage is, however, circumscribed by the Administration of Justice Act 1970, s. 36 (as amended). This enables a court to make arrangements for repayment of the arrears on the mortgage. Nevertheless, bizarrely, this only applies *if* the lender seeks possession through application to the court. If the lender repossessed the property without making an application to the court, then no such protection applies. In Chapter 17, we consider the practical operation of this relief for home owners.

We take it for granted that lenders always seek possession through court order because, for them, it is a commercial imperative to be seen to act 'honourably'. We also take it for granted that what lenders want is payment and not possession, which should mean that they will only bring possession proceedings at the last resort. Nevertheless, as Whitehouse's research clearly shows, lenders begin actions for possession at different times, charge different amounts for telephone calls and the like, and approach the matter rather differently (1998b). Once a lender begins on the process of chasing up arrears, the costs start mounting and they are all *added* to the mortgage liability of the borrower.

13.3   Human Rights and Succession

On their death, the home owners' property is generally distributed according to their will. An exception to this rule is where the property is owned jointly with others. In that case, the property will go to the survivor(s) according to established rules of the law of property (known as the right of survivorship). When the legislation giving private renters security of tenure was being framed, it was considered essential to give private renters a similar right. Thus, security of tenure extends even after the death of the initial tenant, although this right has always been carefully delimited. First, at the moment, whatever the tenure only one succession is allowed (although tenancies protected under the Rent Act 1977 were given two successions until the 1988 Act changed this to one). The wider the group to which rights of succession are granted, the narrower the rights left with the landlord. As a balancing act, therefore, secondly, the rights of succession are granted to particular groups of persons, although as might be expected (given the deplorable state of the legislation) these are different between tenures.

In secure tenancies under the 1985 Act, the right of succession is given either to the 'tenant's spouse' *or* to another member of the tenant's 'family' who lived in the property for 12 months prior to the tenant's death (s. 87). The 1985 Act defines 'family' as specifically including a person living with the tenant 'as husband and wife' (s. 113).

Under the Rent Act 1977, the right of succession is given to the surviving spouse if and so long as that person occupies the dwelling house as their residence. 'Spouse' includes 'a person who was living with the original tenant as his or her wife or husband' (Sch. 1, para. 2(2)).[3] Under the Housing Act 1988, rights of succession are granted in similar circumstances (s. 17).

The question arises as to whether gay and lesbian couples enjoy, or should enjoy, these rights (see Dearden, 1998). Before considering this question, reference should be made to Articles 8 and 14 of the European Convention on Human Rights, now incorporated into English law by the Human Rights Act 1998:

'1. Everyone has the right to respect for his private and family life, his home and the correspondence

'2. There shall be no interference by a public authority with the exercise of this right except such as is in accordance with the law and is necessary in a democratic society in the interests of national security, public safety or the economic well-being of the country, for the prevention of disorder or crime, for the protection of health or morals, or for the protection of the rights and freedoms of others.' (Article 8)

'The enjoyment of the rights and freedoms set forth in this Convention shall be secured without discrimination on any ground such as sex, race, colour, language, religion, political or other opinion, national or social origin, association with a national minority, property, birth or other status.' (Article 14)

It is likely that the European Court of Human Rights will find that gay men and lesbians should enjoy the same age of consent as heterosexuals in conformity with both these articles (after the decision of the European Commission of Human Rights in *Sutherland* v. *UK* Application No 25186/94). In *Sutherland*, the European Commission of Human Rights made the following comment: 'in matters concerning alleged discrimination on grounds of sex, very weighty reasons would have to be put forward before the Convention organs could regard a difference of treatment based exclusively on the ground of sex as compatible with the Convention' (cited in Dearden, 1998, p. 54). The 'weighty reasons' advanced by the Conservative government against an amendment giving gay and lesbian couples succession rights were that they would give Guidance to local authorities on the use of joint tenancies in such cases (Standing Committee G, Thirteenth Sitting, cols 513–522, David Clappison MP). On the point of principle, no comment was made. The government lost that vote after David Ashby MP voted with the opposition (and was subsequently ousted by his local Conservative constituency party), although in the full House of Commons they were able to remove the amendment. Thus, only Guidance to local authorities (which, clearly, does not affect the private sector nor is it legally enforceable) advises them to grant joint tenancies in order to take advantage of the right of survivorship.

The issue has arisen twice before the courts. In *Harrogate BC* v. *Simpson* (1984) 17 HLR 205, the claim concerned a lesbian couple. The Court of Appeal found that the phrase 'living as husband and wife' did not include a lesbian couple: 'By some very antiquated view of lesbianism, partly encouraged by counsel for the appellant, Watkins LJ even managed to consider the two as acting, one the husband, the other the wife, making reference to [the deceased partner] as masculine and wearing men's clothing and the appellant as her female counterpart' (Dearden, 1998, p. 54).

In *Fitzpatrick* v. *Sterling HA* (1998) 30 HLR 576, the Court of Appeal were concerned with the rights of succession of a gay couple. The case is, quite frankly, one of the most remarkable judgments of modern times both for its stridency as well as for the dissenting judgment of Ward LJ. The actual result was that heterosexual succession was permissible (as the words of the statutes suggest) but that the bar on gay and lesbian succession remained, even though as Waite LJ recognized this was 'offensive to social justice and tolerance because it excludes lesbians and gays. It is out of tune with modern acceptance of the need to avoid any discrimination on the ground of sexual orientation' (at p. 588). It would be for Parliament to make the necessary changes, however, because of the consequential questions that arise, such as whether carers should be entitled to succeed to tenancies. For Waite LJ, there was, however a further policy consideration which had to be balanced against 'social justice and tolerance':

'These questions have to be judged in the light of a further policy consideration – fairness to home owners. Every enlargement of the class of potential successors to rent controlled tenancies involves a deeper invasion of rights of house-owners to possession of their own property.' (at pp. 588–9)

Thus, this case fits neatly into the line of authority which is most concerned with the expropriation of the landlord's interest.

Ward LJ's dissenting judgment was, on any measure, unusually strident and undoubtedly will find itself in the mainstream shortly ('If I am to be criticised – and of course I will be – then I prefer to be criticised, on an issue like this, for being ahead of the times, rather than behind the times': p. 607). He considered other legislation which uses the phrase 'as husband and wife' and concluded that there was nothing 'clear-cut' ('The truth may be the Parliamentary draftsman, omniscient though he is, sometimes simply did not think about these matters at all, but it is heresy to say that': p. 599). In an erudite discussion of the construction of the legislation, in which he considered teleological interpretations – 'those who occupy the property as their home should wherever it is possible . . . be given protection against eviction' (p. 604) – and concluded this section on construction as follows:

> 'To exclude same-sex couples from the protection the Rent Act proclaims the inevitable message that society judges their relationship to be less worthy of respect, concern and consideration than the relationship between members of the opposite sex. The fundamental human dignity of the homosexual couple is severely and palpably affected by the impugned distinction. The distinction is drawn on grounds relating to their personal characteristics, their sexual orientation. If the law is as my Lords state it to be, then it discriminates against a not insignificant proportion of the population who will justly complain that they have been denied their constitutional right to equal treatment under the law.' (p. 605).

Having therefore found the statute to be ambiguous on the word 'family', Ward LJ found that word catered for gay couples. The only distinction between heterosexual, gay and lesbian couples was sexual activity and that 'is a matter of form not function' (p. 605). Drawing upon the Guidance given to local authorities on joint tenancies, he argued that his position was more likely to reflect current Parliamentary intention. He might have added that *Standards* makes clear that gay and lesbian succession is acceptable

The case is, at the time of writing, on appeal to the House of Lords.

Conclusion

In this chapter, we began by recapping on cross-tenurial methods of accessing accommodation as well as briefly examining the effect that a change of landlord has upon the residents' status under the multifarious security of tenure legislation. The manifest absurdity of tenure security differentials, particularly when stripped to their practical application, makes the case for a single structure for security of tenure. Our subsequent discussion into the legal meanderings of the current different security regimes affecting all the sectors, as well as the quaintly ridiculous lease:licence distinction, makes the same point, albeit from a more technical standpoint. Different types of agreements are protected, different qualifying and exclusions exist, different rights are given, and different levels of security of tenure are provided. When the security of tenure provisions were updated in the 1996 Act, nobody appears to have thought that the 1977 Act should be affected!

Of course, most ridiculous of all are the differences between local authorities (secure) and RSLs (generally assured plus rights granted through the regulator). If RSLs form part of the private sector, then what is the point in the Charter and the rights guaranteed in *Standards*? If they are not different from local authorities, then why should they not grant secure tenancies? The real problem lies with the PSBR which generated the need to grant 1988 Act tenancies, but the form of the tenancy granted by the RSL is practically the same as that granted by the local authority. Furthermore, the current regime relies on its own ombudsman to give it the shroud of legality. The truth is that this distinction tells us as much about the Conservative government's intentions and needs as anything else – security of tenure was sacrificed at the alter of tax cuts. The move to a social housing tenancy cannot happen soon enough.

The home ownership regime has its own absurdities. One of the beliefs is that home owners have the greatest level of security. However, the right of the lender to take possession immediately is reflected in the ameliorating legislation that provides that, on default, the lender may take possession *unless* the borrower is able to pay the arrears. In other words, from the beginning, the legal position is stacked against the borrower. The owner's security lies in making the monthly mortgage payments.

Finally, the rights of succession to property provide the epitome of hetero-centric society's obsession with denying gay and lesbian rights. However, this may be just incidental to the main judicial project that has underlined their approaches to the legislation – that the grant of rights of any sort to tenants outside those given by the 'freely made' contract should be delimited because they involve some form of expropriation of the landlord's property. Such an explicitly class-based analysis no doubt does an injustice to the many different appreciations of judicial whim. Textual analysis will, no doubt, find different tensions appearing, and *Fitzpatrick* provides an example of clashing ideologies. Nevertheless, one is left with the unappealing proposition that often the judges have done their utmost to constrict the ambit of the legislation as best they can.

Further Reading

There are many texts which cover the security of tenure legislation. Those that pursue arguments, rather than simply outline the legislation are more interesting: see S. Bright & G. Gilbert (1994), *Landlord and Tenant Law: The Nature of Tenancies*, Oxford: Oxford University Press; P. Beirne (1977), *Fair Rent and Legal Fiction*, London: Macmillan; A. Murie, R. Forrest, M. Partington & P. Leather (1988), *The Consumer Implications of the Housing Act 1988*, SAUS Working Paper 77, Bristol: School for Advanced Urban Studies, University of Bristol; M. Partington (1980), *Landlord and Tenant*, London: Weidenfeld & Nicolson. For a useful text covering all the legislation and the main case law, see J. Morgan (1998), *Textbook on Housing Law*, London: Blackstones and J. Martin (1994), *Residential Security*, London: Sweet & Maxwell. On leaseholders' right to enfranchise or take a new lease, see D. Clarke (1993), *Leasehold Enfranchisement – The New Law*, Bristol: Jordans; D. Clarke (1996), 'Leasehold reform', in D. Cowan (ed.), *The Housing Act 1996: A Practical Guide*, Bristol: Jordans.

Endnotes

1. This includes licences where exclusive possession has been granted to the licensor.
2. The most significant exception to this lies in long leaseholds where there are a series of covenants affecting the 'owner's' user of the property. Other exceptions, for example, would arise if the local authority were to exercise their powers of compulsory purchase or there are other restrictions on the owner's use of the property (such as those covenants imposed on purchasers under the right to buy).
3. After the introduction of the 1988 Act, complicated rules exist as to the type of tenancy taken by the successor who is not a spouse: see Arden & Hunter, 1996, para. 5.15.

Bibliography

Alder, J. and Handy, C. (1996), *Housing Associations: The Law of Social Landlords*, London: Sweet & Maxwell

Arden, A. and Hunter, C. (1996), *Manual of Housing Law*, London: Sweet & Maxwell

Carr, H. (1998), 'The sorting of the forks from the spades: an unnecessary distraction in housing law?', in D. Cowan (ed.), *Housing: Participation and Exclusion*, Aldershot: Dartmouth

Clarke, D. (1998), 'Occupying 'cheek by jowl': property issues arising from communal living', in S. Bright and J. Dewar (eds), *Land Law: Themes and Perspectives*, Oxford: Oxford University Press

Day, P. and Klein, R. (1993), *Home Rules: Regulation and Accountability in Social Housing*, York: Joseph Rowntree Foundation

Dearden, N. (1998), 'Same sex succession: a family matter?' vol 1, *Journal of Housing Law*, 51

Department of the Environment (DoE) (1987), *Housing: The Government's Proposals*, Cm 214, London: HMSO

Department of the Environment (DoE) (1995), *The Legislative Framework for Private Renting*, Consultation Paper linked to the Housing White Paper 'Our Future Homes', London: DoE

Department of the Environment (DoE) (1994), *Access to Local Authority and Housing Association Tenancies*, London: HMSO

Department of the Environment, Transport and the Regions (DETR) (1998), *Residential Leasehold Reform in England and Wales – A Consultation Paper*, London: DETR

Dignan, J., Sorsby, A. and Hibbert, J. (1997), *Neighbour Disputes: Comparing the Cost-Effectiveness of Mediation and Alternative Approaches*, Sheffield: University of Sheffield

Gilroy, R. (1998), 'Bringing tenants into decision making', in D. Cowan (ed), *Housing: Participation and Exclusion*, Aldershot: Dartmouth

Hand, C. (1980), 'The statutory tenancy: an unrecognised proprietary interest?', *Conveyancer and Property Lawyer*, 351

Honore, T. (1980), *The Quest for Security: Employees, Tenants, Wives*, London: Stevens

Housing Corporation (1997), *Performance Standards*, London: Housing Corporation

Housing Corporation (1998), *Briefing Supplement to the Performance Standards: Managing Anti-social Behaviour by RSL Residents*, London: Housing Corporation

Kay, A., Legg, C. and Foot, J. (1987), *The 1980 Tenants' Rights in Practice: A Study of the Implementation of the 1980 Housing Act Rights by Local Authorities 1980–83*, London: Blackrose

Lee, N. (1996), 'The concept of sham: a fiction or reality?', vol 47, *Northern Ireland Legal Quarterly*, 377

Loveland, I. (1992), 'Square pegs, round holes: the 'right' to council housing in the post-war era', vol 19, *Journal of Law and Society*, 339

Miller, J. (1997), 'Time to end the two-tier tenancies', September/October, *Roof*, 12

Morgan, J. (1998), *Textbook on Housing Law*, London: Blackstone

Partington, M. (1980), *Landlord and Tenant*, London: Weidenfeld & Nicolson

Robson, P. and Watchman, P. (1981), 'Sabotaging the Rent Acts', in P. Robson and P. Watchman (eds), *Justice and Lord Denning*, London: Butterworths

Scottish Homes (1997), *Tenancy Rights and Repossession Rates: In Theory and Practice*, Research Report 55, Edinburgh: Scottish Homes

Smith, N. and George, G. (1997), 'Introductory tenancies: a nuisance too far?', vol 19, *Journal of Social Welfare and Family Law*, 307

Social Landlords Crime and Nuisance Group (SLCNG) (1998), *Introductory Tenancies: Report on Survey of Local Authorities Practice as at 1 May 1998*, Coventry: SLCNG

Stewart, A. (1981), *Housing Action in an Industrial Suburb*, Edinburgh: Academic Press

Stewart, A. (1996), *Rethinking Housing Law*, London: Sweet & Maxwell

Vincent-Jones, P. (1987), 'Exclusive possession and exclusive control of private rented housing: a socio-legal critique of the lease-licence distinction', vol 14, *Journal of Law and Society*, 445

Whitehouse, L. (1998a), 'The home owner: citizen or consumer?', in S. Bright and J. Dewar (eds), *Land Law: Themes and Perspectives*, Oxford: Oxford University Press

Whitehouse, L. (1998b), 'The impact of consumerism on the home owner', in D. Cowan (ed.), *Housing: Participation and Exclusion*, Aldershot: Dartmouth

14 Repairs and Unfitness: in Search of Reform

About 1,522,000 dwellings in England were unfit in 1996, representing 7.5 per cent of the total stock (DETR, 1998a, Ch. 6). This was almost exactly the same proportion of unfitness in the stock which was found to exist in 1991. Whilst most unfit properties are in home ownership (about 829,000), proportionately most properties in the private rented sector are unfit. Indeed, the proportions are *considerably* skewed: 6 per cent of owner-occupied properties are unfit, 7.3 per cent local authority, 5.2 per cent RSL, and *19.3 per cent* of private rented (representing about 25.8 per cent of all unfit properties). The highest levels of disrepair are found in the private rented sector for properties built before 1964 (for post-1964 buildings, local authority stock is in the worst state of repair). Even so, there are less unfit properties and lower levels of disrepair in the private rented sector than in 1991 (reflecting the different types of property being rented during property market recession).

What is most remarkable about the general levels of unfitness are that they have remained fairly constant – although the method of determining unfitness has changed (and is differentially interpreted in different areas), there is some evidence that levels of unfitness have not changed appreciably since 1971 (Leather & Morrison, 1997, p. 19). This is remarkable because considerable public expenditure has been channelled into housing renovation in all sectors over this period. Since 1969, when policy began to concentrate on the rehabilitation of properties, grants have been available to home owners and private landlords, through the agency of local authorities, to renovate their properties (although the terms and types of grant have changed over time). Never fewer than 50,000 grants were awarded between 1969 and 1995, and in 1983–4 more than 400,000 grants were awarded to carry out works. Between 1981 and 1992, grant aid accounted for about £8.3 billion (Leather & Mackintosh, 1997, p. 139). Furthermore, it is estimated that £28 billion was spent by individual owners on the upkeep of their properties in 1991. Despite greater numbers of local authority stock being renovated than private sector, there is a 'consensus' that between £20–30 billion is required to put local authority stock into repair (McNaughton, 1994). In total, it has been estimated that a minimum of £54 billion is required to deal with the 'current backlog of disrepair in the UK housing stock . . ., of which 83% relates to owner occupied and privately rented housing' (Leather & Mackintosh, 1997, p. 144).

For local authorities and RSLs, the finance to do repairs, a backlog of which have often built up over a long period, is often not available because of the public sector spending constraints that we discussed in Part I of this book. One reason for the backlog of repairs in the private sector is that it is not economically efficient to do them (hence the increasing role of DIY: Davidson *et al.*, 1997). The law places no obligations on home owners to make repairs, unless the local authority, through its Environmental Health Officers (EHOs) or similar, takes action in respect of properties which are unfit. More commonly, however, EHOs will seek to negotiate with the owner to make the necessary repairs without the need for enforcement procedures to commence. In the private rented sector, there are considerable disincentives for both landlords and tenants from conducting repairs – for the landlord, repairs reduce profitability; for the tenant, requesting that the landlord do repairs can lead to the early demise of a tenancy, particularly an assured shorthold, the tenant having been pigeon-holed as a 'complainer' (even though the landlord's responsibilities only begin when given notice of a defect in the property: *O'Brien* v. *Robinson* [1973] 1 All ER 583). In fact, repairing obligations placed upon landlords give them an incentive to let the property in such poor condition as to make it uneconomic to repair (Reynolds, 1974, pp. 384–5).

The move to concentrate on the rehabilitation of existing stock only really began in earnest in 1969. Prior to this, it was the usual policy to engage in site/slum clearance. That involved the compulsory purchase of properties (at site value only) and the rehousing of occupants in disparate council stock. A central reason for the redeployment of, and reduction in, resources was a realization after the first house condition survey that unfit properties were not congregated in certain areas but in disparate locations. Even so, the change in direction from clearance to rehabilitation may well have been inevitable (Balchin, 1995, p. 59) because the decision was made at a time of crisis in public spending in 1967, when sterling was devalued (Leather & Mackintosh, 1992, p. 110).

It also came at a crucial time in terms of the role of the state in housing production. Clearance involved local authorities pulling down private properties and replacing them with public stock, whereas rehabilitation retained the stock in the private sector: 'The shift from [clearance] to rehabilitation was therefore part of a shift away from the social democratic model of provision and towards the market alternative' (Clapham *et al.*, 1990, p. 36). 'Perhaps the innovation was promoted in the civil service and the cabinet, not because a spatially bounded programme was seen to be genuinely more cost-effective but because bureaucrats and politicians understood that the policy redirection required, for ideological purposes, tangible symbols of the new humanism of environmental policy' (Merrett, 1982, p. 203).

Clearance was also opposed by those households who supposedly were to benefit from it, and it was also clear that many of the houses designated for clearance were not unfit (Thomas, 1986, p. 70). The incrementally greater number of home owners affected (having purchased at a discount as sitting tenants) opposed it also because of the 'inconvenience and disruption' as well as low compensation (Leather & Mackintosh, 1992,

p. 111). Merrett summarized some of the rationales for the policy change in the following way:

'The origins . . . include the widespread belief that clearance smashed up long-established community networks of personal relationships which it would take years or even decades to renew; the personal distress and the loss of housing accommodation during the long gestation period from the initiation of clearance to the site's re-inhabitation; the popular discontent with the built form that redevelopment took; and the massive reduction in state expenditure promised by the replacement of public redevelopment by private rehabilitation. . . .' (1982, p. 203)

Subsequent legislation has generally provided a series of grants that can be claimed by home owners and private landlords, with a concentration in certain areas ('the 'halo' impact of area selectivity': Lund, 1996, p. 107). As we shall see, one by-product of concentrating grant activity in certain areas, such as inner London, was the development of 'gentrification', 'resulting in the displacement of existing, mainly low-income residents, and the conversion of private rented accommodation into owner-occupied properties or luxury flats' (Balchin, 1995, p. 67).

In this chapter, we begin our analysis with a consideration of the rationales of disrepair. In many respects, this involves cross-referencing with Parts I and II of the book. Regulation and access are principal reasons for disrepair. Our analysis is tenurially based, partly because the research has developed along these lines, and partly also because of the tenurial emphasis of regulation as conceived in Part I. However, it is important to remember that, for many, tenurial distinctions are accidental because access is accidental. If your point of access leads you to private renting, then you are proportionately more likely to be occupying unfit property or property requiring repair. If you are excluded from the public sector and find it difficult to obtain private rented accommodation, you are likely to occupy the worst sort of properties in home ownership because these are the cheapest to purchase.

In the second section, we analyse the development of the law in relation to repairs in the social and private rented sector. This has been the traditional interest of the law, which only recently has become concerned with the home ownership sector. In many ways, the development of the law relating to repairs mirrors the development of the rise of the state's involvement in the processes of housing production and consumption, for repair laws were borne out of worry about sanitary conditions and the living conditions of the poor ('the accumulating evidence of social malaise': Reynolds, 1974, p. 378). These worries have now resurfaced, in part because of the inadequacy of these laws, in suggestions for law reform made by the Law Commission. Whilst these proposals will, no doubt, be overlooked by government, they raise important considerations about the role/value of law in the process of improvement of properties.

In the third section, our attention turns to consider the operation of the public system of controlling unfit property in the private sector and providing for the repair of such property. Here, we also consider the operation of the grant system. Despite considerable funding, as we have seen, there has been no great improvement in the stock. In our analysis of the different grant regimes, we seek some potential answers to this question. The grant regime was brought into the mainstream of practice in part because of the expense of clearance. However, since it became mainstream, it is clear that successive governments have also tried to restrict levels of grant. This has had an effect on the numbers and types of properties deemed unfit by local authorities (because grant became related to unfitness). Furthermore, we consider the operation of the fitness legislation as an example of 'compliance' or 'accommodation' strategies that, rather than rely on enforcement mechanisms, seek to upgrade the stock through negotiation. We see this again in Chapter 15, but we explore some of the context-related factors leading to such approaches. It is argued that the legislation and funding mechanisms encourage such negotiating approaches to enforcement.

In terms of the structure of Part III of the book, this chapter neatly fits in a number of ways. First, in terms of grants, there has been a move away from general entitlement towards an attachement to the notion that the state and condition of property is part of the *responsibility* of the owner, and not the responsibility of the state. This fixation of responsibility on the owner has reconstructed the problem of unfitness as the fault of the owner. Second, as is shown in the next section, disrepair is a product of the regulation of, and access to each individual tenure, and, as such, requires tenured responses. Third, legislation relating to repairs and unfitness is mostly defined according to the duration of the lease, and only part of it affects local authority housing. Tenure is, therefore, shown to be a more complex device than is conceived by the adherents to tenure neutrality.

14.1   Explaining Disrepair

Before we consider methods used to exhort or require public and private owners to repair their property, it is necessary to analyse the explanations for disrepair. Only when these explanations are acknowledged can we then appreciate the scale of the problem. Different explanations exist in relation to each tenure, although (to anticipate slightly) it is of interest that access to accommodation is a critical factor. For example, those excluded from public sector accommodation will commonly find accommodation in HMOs, which are known to have poor conditions, or even in what is euphemistically termed 'low-cost' home ownership,[1] made up of unimproved properties. It is also unsurprising that most properties needing repair are in the home ownership sector because this is the largest sector of the housing market. Furthermore, prior to 1979, a considerable proportion of the sector was bought either by sitting tenants or had been privately rented. As much of this stock was constructed pre-1919, it may well be that a considerable proportion of it is in need of repairs (Leather & Mackintosh, 1992, p. 109). It is also important to appreciate that sectoral interests are not always equal – individual repairing strategies differ between sectors. Most clearly this is true of private landlords, who rent properties for different reasons and purposes.

Home Ownership

Concerns have been expressed that much of the building work in the private sector has been of decorative value but has done 'little to improve the structure', particularly in the worst quality housing. Primarily, this appears to be caused by the income of the occupants because they are simply unable to afford improvements to their property but are able to enhance 'the use-value and appearance of their property relatively cheaply' (Karn *et al.*, 1985, p. 122). After all, were sums of money expended upon the improvement of the property, such sums would probably not be recovered on a sale of the property or would considerably reduce any capital gain (known as the 'valuation gap', the value of the improved property may not be more than the value of the unimproved property: Thomas, 1986, p. 38–9). Lack of investment also arises because the capital gain on an improved property would not be significant unless surrounding owners improved their properties at the same time (known as the 'prisoner's dilemma': see Balchin, 1995, p. 72):

'Investment returns to individuals would be reasonable where all maintained their homes: but because of the narrow divergence between improved and unimproved prices, individuals would be better off not maintaining their property while others did. In this fundamental market contradiction, it is the dislocation between condition and value which is at the root of the valuation gap . . . [I]t is usually cheaper to buy a better house than carry out major repairs . . .' (Thomas, 1986, p. 40; Karn *et al.*, 1985, pp. 122–3).

Even with grant aid from local authorities, owners themselves were commonly required to contribute a proportion of the costs, which, in itself, acted as a disincentive to low income owners. More recent research has, however, doubted the importance of broader areal investment strategies, suggesting that 'investment criteria are not systematically used to influence repair and improvement investment decisions' (Leather *et al.*, 1998, 24). Three reasons were given for this finding: first, there was no evidence that people consider their neighbourhoods, except in extreme circumstances; second, the language of 'investment' commonly hides the fact that works are done for 'comfort or status'; third, even when properties requiring substantial investment are bought, purchasers had seldom costed out the work (*id*).

Together with income levels, other factors affecting home owners' improvement include life-cycle stages (younger households are more likely to do work than older ones) and stage of occupancy within the house (the earlier the occupancy, the more work is done): *ibid*, pp. 27–30; problems associated in the popular imagination (if not existing in fact) with 'cowboy' builders (see Merrett, 1982, pp. 199–200; DETR, 1998b); as flat-ownership involves complex interlocking legal and financial obligations, improvements require negotiation, which may mean that work is postponed (commonly among people at different life-cycle stages) (Littlewood & Munro, 1996, p. 505); or negative equity (Leather & Mackintosh, 1997, p. 147).

One final factor here is that it has been suggested that home owners do not make repairs because they are 'ignorant' of the true state of their properties. Findings from the 1991 English House Condition Survey suggested this (as did other similar surveys), particularly when compared with professional surveyors' opinions (DETR, 1998c). Such findings are, however, controversial. Heywood has pointed out that 'the fact that people say they are 'satisfied' with their housing does not prove that they are objectively unaware of its physical condition', suggesting that a number of external factors influence owners' responses to questions about repairs (1997, pp. 42–3):

'There has in the past been an idea, almost colonial in its assumptions, of the poor ignorant slum dwellers living in darkness and needing missionary efforts to make them aware of their condition or to rescue them from it. . . . There is a crucial distinction to be made between lack of knowledge and reluctance to acknowledge, . . . Perhaps it is distrust not ignorance, that has been the problem. People will not talk about the problems if they fear the consequences.' (*ibid*, p. 44)[2]

We consider the grant system in more depth in the third section of this chapter.

Private Rented

We have already seen that proportionately the greatest fitness and repair problems exist in the private rented sector, although this has improved between 1991 and 1996. Earlier chapters have shown that landlords have different reasons for letting property out, that different rent control/regulation and security provisions have applied at different times (of which landlords may well be unaware), and during periods of regulation (as opposed to deregulation) landlords have sought to circumvent the relevant schema. Repairing strategies might be expected to depend upon income and potential capital gain. However, it is important to remember that landlords' reasons for renting out property will also be reflected in repairing strategies – the nature of the landlord, and not the property, determines the level of repair (Crook *et al.*, 1998). Those for whom renting was their business, and other corporate and employment-related landlords were more likely to do repairs than those for whom rented property was an 'investment' or who had a single property rented out (*ibid*).

The problem, as we identified in Chapter 2, is that private renting is not as profitable as other investments. Those who rent out properties for non-investment purposes, such as to employees, tend to be more willing to invest in repairs despite lower profits. However, for other landlords, profit-making can only be maintained without increasing rents if repairs are not done. Such processes are particularly prevalent during periods of rent control or significant regulation because profit-making is curtailed and landlords are unable to recoup the costs of repairs through increased rents. When landlords are able somehow, in the words of the judges, to 'drive a coach and horses through the Rent Acts', repairs may not be done because of the lack of profit-making. As a general rule, then, it seems that rent control/regulation acts as a disincentive to repairing property. On the other hand, the state and condition of the property has always been relevant in determining a fair rent under the Rent Acts from the mid-1960s. This, together with the current rapidly rising 'fair' rents in the post-1988 era, suggest that the disincentive may be less important than the general problem of profitability (even with market rents).

Local Authorities

One result of the individual council tenant's right to buy their property was that the quality of stock left in local authority control diminished as a proportion of total stock because generally the better quality stock was sold off leaving a residual sector. We have also seen that the way council housing was and is financed has involved a continuing reduction in the revenue available to management and maintenance that has a knock-on impact upon the repairs service offered by authorities, although this is expected to change in the future as a result of the proposed changes to the HRA. Many of the collective privatization initiatives have been entered into, and sold to tenants, on the basis that they will enable the new landlord to access funds for repairs – the development of HATs and LSVTs are clearly linked to this. Involvement in 'undercover' privatization operations, such as City Challenge, now the Single Regeneration Budget, were also methods of levering money into the sector's repairs. Even though a considerable level of funding was provided to local authorities, it was never enough (which provided further incentives to tenants to exit).

On the other hand, it is commonly stated that one of the considerable advantages of being a public sector tenant is 'getting repairs done'; a poor repairs service commonly leads to a poor rating for housing management (Cairncross *et al.*, 1997, pp. 109–11). Satisfaction ratings are strongly correlated with speed of the repairs service (Bines *et al.*, 1993, para. 11.36). Indeed, repairs are the subject of most tenants' complaints (Karn *et al.*, 1997). Tenants are entitled to do their own repairs and be reimbursed by the council, but just nine per cent of tenants had taken advantage of this scheme (Bines *et al.*, 1993, para. 11.41).

Research based upon the Scottish House Condition Survey has found that poorer and more disadvantaged local authority tenants are less likely than other tenants to have repairs done to their properties. Such a finding is 'counter-intuitive' because we know that the more disadvantaged tend to accept the worse quality stock (because they tend to be more desperate for accommodation). Two reasons are suggested by the research: first 'those with a medium or high benefit dependency level, those with the lowest incomes and households headed by older people or women are *less likely to have requested the works* that had been done to their properties than male-headed, younger and less financially constrained households' (Littlewood & Munro, 1995, p. 7; emphasis added). Second, 'the current housing condition of less well-off households, older households and female headed households is *not* significantly worse than other household groups. In fact, in many cases their household condition is significantly superior to those who are better-off' (*ibid*).

RSLs

In 1974, RSLs' potential was regarded as being most useful in terms of the rehabilitation of stock. They were heavily funded for this purpose. Such funding continued, although not at the same levels, during the 1980s. However, the move to 'centre stage' after the White Papers' review (DoE 1987a, 1987b) also implied a change in focus. Whilst previously HAG had been paid on the costs of development, the move to frontloaded HAG, under which RSLs were required to keep to particular costs, have militated against rehabilitation of property because such work is expensive and its costs unpredictable. Frontloading HAG meant that development costs needed to be clear at the outset (otherwise the RSL would be liable for the overrun) but rehabilitation costs are least susceptible to precise calculation in advance (see Randolph, 1992; Langstaff, 1992). Furthermore, government funding was no longer available to cover the costs of repairs, which therefore required rents to be raised to account for repairs (as well as to generate surpluses to provide for future repairs).

14.2   Repairs and Unfitness

The law's concentration on the repairing obligations entailed in the leasehold agreement, as opposed to freehold ownership, reflects the fragmentation of ownership rights in property. Freehold ownership essentially is the closest one can come, in the English legal system, to land ownership; leasehold, on the other hand, implies both a contractual relationship with a 'superior' owner (often, the freeholder or a previous leaseholder) as well as a property relationship, as the leaseholder's rights to possession of the property are usually protected against all others. Because the freeholder only has a relationship with the land, and is the most absolute form of land ownership, the law did not require the owner to conduct repairs (other than as a result of public health matters). If the freeholder wished to let their property fall into disrepair, this was entirely up to them and the law would not interfere.

Legal obligations to repair were therefore a matter of contractual agreement between tenant and landlord. The law generally only intervened when those obligations were unclear or incomplete, entirely within the *laissez-faire* spirit of the nineteenth century when many of these cases were litigated. The development of extra-contractual obligations in the mid to late nineteenth century were, in fact, hotly contested, leading to quite illogical distinctions being drawn. In the famous case of *Smith* v. *Marrable*, Sir Thomas Marrable took a weekly tenancy of a furnished house in Brighton. On taking up occupation, the property was found to be infested with 'bugs' (the report does not go into detail) and, whatever was tried, the bugs could not be exterminated. Marrable surrendered the tenancy, and the landlord (Smith) sued for the rent. Parke B found in favour of Marrable in the following way:

'. . . [I]f the demised premises are incumbered with a nuisance of so serious a nature that no person can reasonably be expected to live in them, the tenant is at liberty to throw them up. This is not the case of a contract on the part of the landlord that the premises were free from this nuisance; *it rather rests in an implied condition of the law, that he undertakes to let them in a habitable state.*' (1844), 11 M & W 6 (my emphasis)

If the law had developed in this way, placing implied conditions on landlords that the property they were letting was habitable, it is arguable that the property developed during the late nineteenth century would have been of rather better quality than it actually was. However, just a year later, Parke B recanted and held that *Smith* should be kept to its own facts: '[*Smith*] was the case of a demise of a ready-furnished house for a temporary place at a watering-place. It was not a lease of real estate merely' (*Hart* v. *Windsor* (1945) 12 M & W 68, 87). The *Smith* principle was thereafter found to apply only in the exceptional case of the short-term let of *furnished* property. Most property at this time was unfurnished leasehold and so the common law did not touch upon the ordinary living conditions of the majority. The reason for moving away from the implied condition partly reflected a fixation upon the agricultural leases but, as Reynolds points out,

'the social reality was that the Industrial Revolution of the previous decades had seen the very structure of English society change from one dependent upon an agrarian economy to one based upon industry. . . .

It was at this crucial time of urbanisation and slum formation that the judges looked to the agrarian lease as providing a justification for their decisions' (1974, p. 378)

The failures of the common law to provide appropriate remedies for unfitness and disrepair gave way to statutory reform that attempted to ameliorate health issues in insanitary housing.

Unfitness[3]

Section 15 of the Housing of the Working Classes Act 1885 included an implied condition that the letting of property for habitation should, at its commencement, be 'in all respects reasonably fit for human habitation'. The Marquess of Salisbury said that 'I look to this clause more than to any other to diminish the death-rate that is caused by insanitary dwellings' (cited in Law Commission, 1996, para. 4.8). Subsequently, legislation made it clear that landlords and tenants were not able to contract out of its protection. In the common law world, the fitness provision was startlingly bold for the period and at least 80 years ahead of its time. It was not until 1970 that the US Court of Appeal in the District of Columbia held that similar provisions should apply to rented accommodation (*Javins* v. *First National Realty Corporation* (1970) 428 F.2d 1071).

Yet by this time, the English provision, which has never been repealed, had fallen into disuse (it is now s 8, Landlord and Tenant Act 1985). Attached to the provision were rent limits which, whilst they were low, covered 'with the exception of London, nearly all of the working classes of the Kingdom' (John Burns MP, cited in Law Commission, 1996, para. 4.9). The rent limits were increased in the early part of the twentieth century, and the provision upgraded after certain judicial assaults upon its impact (see Reynolds, 1974 for a consideration of these unfortunate judicial attempts to undermine the statute). Rent limits were finally increased in the Housing Act 1957. The rent limits then put in place, which remain today, are £52 generally and £80 for inner London – these are *per annum* figures, not weekly. The Law Commission suggest a number of reasons why the rent limits were not updated, whilst accepting that it is not 'easy to account' for this: 'the extension of local authority housing, the decline in private sector lettings engendered by the Rent Acts [sic], and the rise in owner occupation' (1996, para. 4.13). Additionally, they suggest that the development of the implied covenants to repair (see below) and made provision anachronistic (paras 4.14–7).

Indeed, the Law Commission made it clear that they wished to see the duty revived, and applied to all landlords in whichever sector letting property for less than seven years (Ch 8; *cf* Smith, 1994). Three objections were considered (paras 8.17 *et seq*): the proposals would lead to increased costs which would have to be borne by landlords or tenants; the applicability to local authority lettings; and the effect on renovation grants (the latter to be considered in the next section). The (perhaps surprising) stridency of the Law Commission's rejection of these criticisms ('we consider that the cost is justified by the injustice we seek to remedy' para. 8.18; 'we can see no case for a blanket exclusion of local authority lettings . . .' para. 8.25) have a slightly unreal air.

If government's central concerns were to entice more property onto the private rented market through deregulation and diminishing obligations upon landlords, attempting to make renting more profitable, then they would hardly be keen to implement the suggested reforms. Furthermore, if government is worried about rising rents (because of the Housing Benefit bill), then broadening the implied condition is hardly going to be flavour of the month because it is likely to lead to higher rents. These are the conundra of the implied condition of fitness. When one also considers the broader interest in the rehabilitation and renovation of the stock, the conundra are multiplied. There is an uncomfortable reality that, whilst meant to benefit a class of people who occupy the worst sort of property in the sector, such laws actually work to their detriment because cheap accommodation becomes scarce(r), and upgraded accommodation becomes more expensive (see Hirsch, 1981; Meyers, 1975).

The evidence that the impact of common law fitness rules had this effect in the United States is unclear, because it took place at a time when there were more general moves to improve the housing stock: 'During the seventies all income classes of tenants enjoyed more spacious accommodations with better facilities and lower rents, after adjusting for inflation and differences in quality' (Rabin, 1984, p. 561; see also pp. 561–578). In other words, legal developments on their own rarely have the revolutionary effect claimed – partly this relates to the method of enforcement and partly this relates to external factors (such as demand and supply). As far as the former is concerned, individual enforcement through the courts is costly, lengthy, and in the current private-sector climate of assured shorthold tenancies, largely a waste of time because by the time the tenant makes it to the court, the tenancy will have long since been determined. In many ways, this is the trap of the assured shorthold, and the dilemma for those seeking to increase standards in the sector.

Much more difficulty, however, occurs in applying similar arguments to the public sector stock because tenants are more likely to have a long-term interest in their property. However, to impose such a condition on local authorities and RSLs would practically place those landlords as well as the government in an awkward position. After all, if the property needs to be put into a fit standard, somebody has to pay or the stock will simply have to be taken out of commission (and we are talking about at least 300,000 dwellings that are occupied and unfit). Of course, it is known that obligations are placed upon local authorities that they cannot be expected to meet (Loveland's description of the homelessness legislation as 'an exercise in legislative deceit': 1995, p. 331; and see below); however, this is more like cutting off one's nose to spite one's face.

Repairs

'. . . it is a phenomenon, certainly known at common law, that there may be situations in which there is no repairing obligation imposed either expressly or impliedly on anyone in relation to a lease' (*Demetriou* v. *Poolaction Ltd* (1991) 1 EGLR 100)

Since 1961, in all leases for less than seven years, there have been obligations upon landlords to repair the structure and exterior of the dwelling-house. This also includes common parts, where the dwelling forms part of a larger building (after a restrictive interpretation applied to the section in *Camden Hill Towers* v. *Gardner* [1977] QB 823). Additionally, the landlord must keep in repair all installations, such as gas, water, sanitation, and electricity (now s. 11, Landlord and Tenant Act 1985). The landlord may not contract out of these provisions but they can hardly be regarded as extensive – the standard is explicitly related to the age, character, expected life and locality (*Newham LBC* v. *Patel* (1978) 13 HLR 77). A run-down property in a run-down area would, no doubt, conform with the statutory obligations.

Bright and Gilbert question 'whether it is part of landlord and tenant law to impose such a system of indirect welfare' upon tenants because the effect of the statute is the 'redistribut[ion of] wealth from the richer landlords to the poorer tenants' (1994, p. 350). However, a better view is Stewart's that 'the legislation constructs the landlord as potentially harmful to the tenants interests and in need of policing' (1996, p. 98). The obligations first came into effect in 1961, just prior to the phenomenon of rachmanism becoming strewn across the media but at a time when the effects of the decontrolling 1957 Act were beginning to be appreciated. Landlords were socially constructed as a class from whom tenants needed protection.

As usual, the court's construction of these statutory obligations has been to narrow them at almost every opportunity (see Reynolds, 1974). In *Quick* v. *Taff-Ely BC* [1986] QB 809, for example, the Court of Appeal found that the covenant did not protect the tenant against loss of amenity, although the covenant might require the remedying of an inherent defect. The property itself had an inherent defect which caused condensation at such a rate that all the tenants' fittings became mouldy and ruined. Amazingly, the Court held that this property was not in disrepair as the covenant only applied to the physical exterior of the property and not to its 'lack of amenity or inefficiency'. Dillon LJ argued

'[T]he liability of the local authority was to keep the structure and exterior of the house in repair, not the decorations. Though there is ample evidence of damage to the decorations and to bedding, clothing and other fabrics, evidence of damage to the subject-matter of the covenant, the structure and exterior of the house, is far to seek.

. . .[T]here is no evidence at all of physical damage to the walls, as opposed to the decorations, or the windows.'

Part of the problem in the case relates to a willingness to restrict the meaning of 'repair' (see also *Newham LBC* v. *Patel* (1978) 13 HLR 77; *Wycombe AHA* v. *Barnett* (1982) 5 HLR 84). Earlier cases had found that repairs could include the remedying of inherent defects in the property but Dillon LJ was concerned that this should be restricted to circumstances when it was 'the only practicable way of making good the damage'.

Even despite these limitations, the Law Commission have noted that 'actions to enforce [the implied covenant] are a commonplace and appear routinely in the daily lists of some county courts' (1996, para. 5.12). It should be noted that for local authority and RSL tenancies which commenced after October 1980, the statutory covenants do not apply (as these tenants have the right to repair granted in the Housing Act 1980). Also, whilst there is no empirical evidence proving or disproving this proposition, the implied covenant has (to my knowledge) never been stated to be a reason for the demise of the private rented sector. Given its limitations, however, this can hardly be surprising.

In *Southwark LBC* v. *Mills* [1999] 2 WLR 409, the question for the Court of Appeal was whether the council were under an obligation to soundproof a jerry-built dwelling (built at the end of the first world war) as a result of the covenant for quiet enjoyment. Such a covenant can be express or implied (in this case, it was express). The occupants 'hear pretty well everything (and I mean everything) that is said or done by their neighbours' (p. 411). The court held by a majority that, as the building lacked proper insulation at the time of each letting, the lack of sound insulation did not fall within the covenant. Showing a distinct lack of appreciation of the relationship between local authority landlord and tenant, the court found that the tenants could have bargained for soundproofing before taking the tenancy: 'if [the tenant] wants more [the tenant] should bargain for it and be prepared to pay the extra rent' (p. 419, *per* Mantell L.J.).

Environmental Protection Act 1990
A separate remedy is available for 'statutory nuisances', defined by section 79(1), Environmental Protection Act 1990 as 'any premises in such a state as to be prejudicial to health or a nuisance'. The phrase 'prejudicial to health' is defined as 'injurious, or likely to cause injury, to health' (s 79(7)). There are certain matters which are explicitly regarded as being prejudicial, such as smoke, fumes or gases. Where a nuisance occurs, is likely to occur or recur, the local authority must serve an 'abatement notice' (s 80), requiring the person responsible to abate the nuisance to the property and/or requiring certain works to be done to the property. In *R* v. *Bristol City Council ex parte Everett* [1999] 2 All ER 193, the Court of Appeal held that the phrase 'prejudicial to health or nuisance' did not

include physical accidents (or their likelihood): 'It is very unnatural to describe a physical accident as causing injury to health' (p. 203, *per* Buxton L.J.). The court based its judgement also on the history of the legislation – its foundations lie in the mid-1840s which, it was said, related to disease as opposed to physical injury. The import of this Act has therefore been significantly reduced.

14.3   Unfit Housing and the State

Other than the contract between landlord and tenant, the state has a legitimate role in pursuing the quality of its housing stock. This role began in the mid nineteenth century when interest began to be expressed in the poor sanitation of accommodation, together with its poor quality. As we saw in the previous section, the state believed this to be such an issue that, even during a period when sanctity of contract was at its most significant, it interfered in the contract between landlord and tenant. Local authorities were, even before this, given powers to curb and deal with unfit properties, including demolition of properties. In the early part of this century, indeed until beyond 1969, clearance schemes played a significant role in the control of such properties (see Hughes & Lowe, 1995, pp. 289–95; Leather & Mackintosh, 1994, p. 5).

In this section, our concern is with two inter-related aspects of such state intervention: the 'fitness for human habitation' regime under the Housing Act 1985, s. 604 (as amended); and the development of public sector grants to private owners and landlords to renovate their properties. Both are infused with socio-legal phenomena including differential 'policing' of and amongst private owners, as well as a willingness to engage in cooperative strategies (that we come across again in Chapter 15); the better-off doing better than the worse-off; and legislative deceit through which people are given rights which are impossible to fulfil (and appropriate responses by local government).

The Fitness Regime

Since 1989, the definition of 'fitness for human habitation', and the response to unfit properties, have been related to private-sector grants. Between 1989 and 1996, when grants for unfit properties were mandatory, authorities tended to avoid proactively identifying unfit properties and 'it [was] clear that some local authorities [were] only identifying as unfit those properties which resources permit them to tackle' (Leather *et al.*, 1994, p. 44). The relationship between fitness standards and the private sector is clear, particularly because the standards do not apply to local authority housing.[4] Considerable discretion, in fact, exists in relation to the standard of, and responses to, fitness. A dwelling-house is fit for human habitation, unless it fails to meet one or more 'standards' and 'by reason of that failure, is not reasonably suitable for occupation' (Housing Act 1985, s. 604(1) as amended). The standards are

'(a)   it is structurally stable;
(b)   it is free from serious disrepair;
(c)   it is free from dampness prejudicial to the health of the occupants (if any);
(d)   it has adequate provision for lighting, heating and ventilation;
(e)   it has an adequate piped supply of wholesome water;
(f)   there are satisfactory facilities in the dwelling-house for the preparation and cooking of food, including a sink with a satisfactory supply of hot and cold water;
(g)   it has a suitably located water-closet for the exclusive use of the occupants (if any);
(h)   it has, for the exclusive use of occupants (if any), a suitably located fixed bath or shower and wash-hand basin each of which is provided with a satisfactory supply of hot and cold water; and
(i)   it has an effective system for the draining of foul, waste and surface water.'

Where the property is a flat or an HMO, other factors need to be considered as well in relation to the common parts (s. 604(2) & (4)).

The 'primary concern should lie in safeguarding the health and safety of occupants' but the standard is related to the condition of the property. The standard is, to a certain extent, contradictory for, on the one hand, it is said that it does not relate to any particular types of occupants; but, on the other hand, the property must 'be reasonably suitable for all household sizes and types of potential occupant', particularly considering that 'the elderly and young children tend to spend the greatest time in and around the home' (DoE, 1996, pp. 58–9). There is a Code of Guidance which amplifies each of the criteria, but even so local authroities have considerable discretion in its interpretation. The current guidance is also 'largely silent' on when a property is not reasonably suitable for occupation. This causes concern for central government for the lack of unifomity of application potentially implied by this (particularly when related to the resources of the authority).

Where a property is unfit, an authority has a number of options. The first stage is that it must issue a 'minded to take action' notice upon the owner or landlord (Housing Grants Act 1996, s. 86). This notice is primarily designed 'to help local authorities reach sensible decisions with owners and landlords by giving them the right to make representations; and to help reduce the burden that can arise from having to take formal enforcement action' (DoE, 1996, p. 84). After this, the authority can decide to take formal action through serving one of five orders upon the owner or landlord: a repair notice specifying certain repairs which are required to make the property fit; a deferred action notice, specifying the repairs needed to be done to make the property fit but also that the authority will not take any further action for a specified period; closing order; demolition order; or declare a clearance area.

Decisions about appropriate enforcement action have been found to be related to a number of different factors. However, the general strategy appears to be one of accommodation, or cooperation, relating to securing compliance with the standard as opposed to direct enforcement action. The process itself, particularly with the 'minded to' notice, is geared towards accommodation strategies. Indeed, authorities and owners or landlords are forced together by the 'minded to' notice at an early stage. The legislation has always been 'fundamentally ambivalent' about enforcement in part because of its origins in the nineteenth century (Hutter, 1988, pp. 24–30; for historical antecedents, see Law Commission, 1996, paras 4.31–2). The current guidance clearly reflects the need for bargaining between the authority and the owner or landlord. For example, in deciding whether to serve a repair notice, the guidance suggests that the authority 'consider the circumstances and wishes of the owner and occupants, including the extent to which they are willing and able to carry out the repair; and the advice and assistance that might be available, or made available, locally to help with that' (DoE, 1996, p. 88). Compliance is a long-term strategy, secured through informal methods that have been typified as being either 'persuasive' or 'insistent' (Hutter, 1988). Links to particular local authorities mean that locality determines the interpretation of the officers' role.

A further consideration relates to funding generally and particularly for grants. Certain enforcement action, such as repair notices, required local authorities to provide mandatory grant aid to owners or landlords, but, as we shall see, authorities were underfunded. Consequently, repairs notices declined to 4,721 served in the final year of the mandatory grant regime. However, when grants and their level became discretionary, 17,048 notices were served suggesting that funding determined types of enforcement action (CIEH, 1998). It is also 'known that, in practice, there is a reluctance to enforce against owner-occupiers, particularly if they are elderly. Nor is it necessarily accepted that the state should intervene in an individual's choice to live in an unfit dwelling' (Legal Research Institute, 1998, para. 3.46). The situation, however, is different 'where a property is let for financial return' (*ibid*, para. 3.47). Indeed, reforms have been suggested to place greater duties upon landlords because 'it is justifiable on consumer protection grounds and in the interests of health policy' (*ibid*, para. 3.56).

The fitness standard and methods of enforcement are the subject of a Consultation Paper issued by the DETR (DETR, 1998). This suggests a move away from the fitness standard to a 'fitness rating' which would enable 'all the important health and safety issues [to be identified], and also to rank them according to the severity of risks' (para. 5.10). Only when a property fell below a particular rating on a scale would it be deemed unfit. This would enable authorities to focus upon those properties 'genuinely', as opposed to 'technically', unfit and would be more flexible (para. 5.11). It is also considered whether the current duty to take appropriate enforcement action should become a *power* or whether there should be a power in relation to owner-occupied property but a duty in relation to the private rented sector ('landlords are letting the property for commercial gain and tenants have a right to expect the property to be fit': para. 5.23). The movement from duty to power implies a continuing ambivalence regarding the regulatory status of fitness legislation and would cause further uncertainty over the role of environmental health in local government (see Hutter, 1988, pp. 48–9). Differentiating between tenures is part of an ever-diminishing targeting process which implies cost saving (lower enforcement action concomitantly implies lower levels of central expenditure) and also suggests that the commitment to cross-tenurialism is skin-deep.

The Grant Regime

Pre-1989 Criticisms
The grant regime was reformed in the Local Government and Housing Act 1989 and subsequently by the Housing Grants, Construction and Regeneration Act 1996. Before we consider these schemes, we should briefly outline what the 1989 Act was trying to remedy. Local authorities provided grants to home owners and private landlords but there were two essential problems.

First, 'the durability of work which was carried out with grant aid was open to question' (Leather & Mackintosh, 1993, p. 327). Work was supposed to last for thirty years, although it rarely did (*ibid*, 1992). Local authorities simply doled out money without responsibility for checking on the quality of the work. Furthermore, grants were related to the provision of amenities and not disrepair. Between 1981 and 1986, just 14 per cent of grants went to properties which were unfit or in disrepair (Leather & Mackintosh, 1994, p. 14; 1992, p. 115, referring to an unpublished DoE study).

Second, grants were ineffectively targeted. This was because, first, the actual application required a certain degree of technical knowledge which favoured certain persons over others; second, grants were meant to lever in private investment (i.e. the owner's own money), but this assumed that the owner was willing and/or able to spend their own capital on works (see above, particularly the 'valuation gap' and 'prisoner's dilemma'). Indeed, the situation was exacerbated by the fact that allowable amounts for payment were rarely updated, thus leaving a greater contribution for the homeowner. The result was that 'not only were grants going to the relatively better housed, rather than being focussed on the worst stock; but they were going to help the more affluent groups' (Thomas, 1986, p. 69). There were also concerns that people were defrauding the system through gaining grants and then selling off the property. This loophole was effectively closed in 1974 when reforms to the scheme restricted grantholders' sale of the property for a specific period (which was subsequently reduced in the Housing Act 1980).

Pre-1989 policies had also involved the designation of certain areas as 'General Improvement Areas' (GIA) (the Housing Act 1969) or 'Housing Action Areas' (HAA) (Housing Act 1974). Both were intended to have major impact upon substandard stock located in certain areas and where improvement grants were concentrated (and greater proportions of grant available), although the HAAs were supposed to be more targeted on housing stress areas. Both largely failed partly because the level of grant take-up was low and investment was rarely concentrated in these areas. Few HAA areas were designated because of local authority concerns about central government's financial commitment to HAAs, although those designated were successful (see Thomas, 1986, p. 92). Other than this, the designation of a GIA meant that 'the local authority may just as well have been putting a flag on the developer's office wall map to show where he might operate with the best return on investment' (Babbage, 1973). There were plenty of stories about winkling out and general movement of households from the area (Thomas, 1986, p. 76):

> 'Improvement grants intended to benefit the residents of areas of substandard housing were manifestly not benefiting the residents. They were adding to the profits of developers, increasing the capital value of the properties of often non-resident landlords and helping to provide new homes for former commuters. Simultaneously communities were being destroyed as quickly as if major clearance schemes had been undertaken . . .' (Balchin, 1995, p. 67)

In general, the failure of the schemes meant that grant aid was 'pepper-potted' in most areas amongst disparate properties (Leather & Mackintosh, 1994, p. 15). Furthermore, the HIP funding allocation method 'had never directed resources to the authorities with the greatest concentrations of poor condition housing' (Leather & Mackintosh, 1992, p. 116). Indeed, variations in the levels of central government funding (at times increased, for example, to boost employment in the building industry: Leather & Mackintosh, 1994, p. 19) meant that long-term strategies have never occurred.

Post-1989 Scheme and Criticisms

The 1987 White Paper heralded a change in approach from previous schemes. First, a clear statement that 'ownership carries with it responsibility to keep the home in good repair' (DoE, 1987b, para. 2.14), suggesting that government assistance would not be provided to home owners generally. Second, the government accepted that certain people 'are unable to afford the full costs of essential repair and improvement work' (para. 2.17). Finally, the government accepted that mandatory grants covering the full costs of works should be given to bring properties up to a new standard of fitness (as discussed previously).

Essentially, the new scheme promised up to 100 per cent grants to applicants to do essential works, provided their means fell below a certain pre-determined means-tested level.

In practice, though, the scheme produced a crisis. The demand for mandatory renovation grants (together with the new Disabled Facilities Grant: Leather & Mackintosh, 1997, p. 144) was not backed up by a supply of capital to meet the obligations. The new scheme took effect at the same time as the new funding regime for local authorities came into effect. Grants were paid to local government as specified capital grants, which were reduced from 1992. Thus, quite simply there was a funding deficit. Not surprisingly, the numbers of renovation grants provided by local government slowed down in the early to mid-1990s. Bearing in mind these were mandatory grants, though, the methods used by local authorities to reduce their obligations were important in explaining a rational response to a funding deficit:

'In most areas, there is little or no publicity for what is, in effect, a statutory welfare benefit. In some cases, local authorities are attempting to limit demand by placing enquirers on waiting lists for surveys or the [means test]. Other authorities have developed systems to prioritise mandatory grant applications, including policies to restrict entitlement to particular areas. All of these measures are open to challenge as they restrict the right of those living in unfit housing to a grant.' (Leather *et al.*, 1994, p. 43)

In other words, local authorities sought rational methods of restricting and prioritizing demand for the grants. Even so, the complexity of the means test required local authorities to invest in new staff and computer software to make the necessary calculations (Leather & Mackintosh, 1992, p. 120). The test was, in any event, flawed as it did not initially include any allowance for mortgage interest payments.

The 1989 Act also introduced Housing Renewal Areas, as opposed to GIAs and HAAs. This was to 'focus attention on the use of a broader area strategy which may include environmental and socio-economic regeneration' (DoE, 1990, p. 5). By July 1992, just 45 renewal areas had been designated. One reason for the slow start was the need to carry out socio-environmental surveys, called a Neighbourhood Renewal Assessment, before designating areas. Local authorities had insufficient staff and financial resources to carry out such surveys (see Couch & Gill, 1992, Ch. 1).

The 1996 Act and Beyond
'The fact that yet more rationing mechanisms are now required demonstrates that a policy of selectivity and targeting does not mean more resources for the poor; it simply leaves them exposed to further cuts because they lack the economic and social power to protect their interests.' (Lund, 1996, p. 114)

In the 1995 White Paper, the government argued that 'the case for help to private owners needs to be considered alongside other local housing priorities' (DoE, 1995a, p. 17) and that in order to make 'best use of resources' through the development of a more 'strategic approach', the system was to be reformed. More honest was the linked document which argued that 'both cost and logistics preclude the immediate repair of all unfit houses' (DoE, 1995b, para. 2.2). The mandatory grants became discretionary in the Housing Grants Act 1996. It was also suggested that landlords should be excluded from grants because 'maintenance costs are a normal overhead of the business of letting property' (para. 3.2). This provision was subsequently dropped.

The Act is accompanied by a considerable Code of Guidance (276 pages long, and updated) (DoE, 1996; DETR, 1998e). Resources are allocated through the HIP allocation process (on the basis of a separate calculation), half on the basis of need and half on the basis of 'a judgment of the quality of each authority's strategy and performance' (DETR, 1998e, Annex J1, para. 2). Central government subsidy accounts for 60 per cent of the total grants, and the authority must find 40 per cent themselves (*ibid*, para. 5). The Guidance shows how far the provision of grants has come since the heyday periods: 'The Secretary of State would consider that a local authority was failing in its duty as a housing enabler and in its responsibility to consider the condition of the local private sector stock if it did not have *some* provision for grant assistance' (DoE, 1996, para. 5.2.1; emphasis added). Judgments need to be based upon a distinction between immediate needs, on the one hand, and 'bringing a property up to a standard which will require little further work for a number of decades' (para. 5.2.3). Thus, the focus has changed from works to see the property through in the long term to short-termism.

This separate capital grant will, if New Labour's proposals are implemented, shortly be phased out and local authorities will be expected to meet the costs of such grants from other areas (such as Single Regeneration Budget funding or usable capital receipts) (DETR, 1998f, part 4). In future, any grant will be included within each authority's Annual Capital Grant. This means that capital receipts taken into account in the allocations process will reduce the amount of private sector grant allocated. However, in general, the DETR will not provide any allocation for private sector renewal. It is not difficult to imagine how this will affect the 'policing' of unfit properties.

Conclusion

This chapter has considered a wide sweep of law, policy and practice in relation to the repairs and fitness levels of property. It is apparent that we have been left with a variety of nineteenth century principles which are insufficient to match the current needs in terms of property renovation. We began with statistics relating to fitness and disrepair and ended with an examination of the legislation and determination of fitness together with the available grants. All of these have a bearing on the types, locations and variations of properties determined to be unfit. Reform of the fitness standard will, no doubt, also reduce the numbers of properties deemed to be unfit or in disrepair. Of major significance in this process has been an appreciation of contracting levels of public expenditure available for property rehabilitation (at a time when concerns have been expressed about over-development on 'greenfield' sites).

This lack of funding is matched by an apparent unwillingness within the tenures to renovate property. Even the RSL sector, the 1970s' roots of which were firmly embedded in rehabilitation, have moved away from it (because the funding system no longer provides an incentive in this direction). Home owners do a considerable amount of DIY and spend considerable amounts on property renovation but this does not seem to affect the statistics of disrepair and unfitness. A number of reasons were suggested for this, which reflect economically rational behaviour on the part of some owners. As for private renting, a sector which has the worst record of disrepair and unfitness, its lack of profitability and the lack of recoupment of outlay militate against repairs being completed. The law of landlord and tenant hardly provides landlords with an incentive to conduct repairs. As we have seen, duties outside of those expressed in the contract, have been restrictively interpreted and marginalized by ridiculously low rent levels. The area is ripe for reform but this has been true for some time, as the Law Commission has pointed out practically throughout its lifespan.

Further Reading

This chapter has not covered all the various ambulations of the law of repair, improvement, nor of the impact of environmental legislation. For detailed examination of these, see A. Arden and M. Partington (1994), *Housing Law*, London: Sweet & Maxwell; D. Hughes and S. Lowe (1995), *Social Housing Law and Policy*, London: Butterworths; A. Arden and C. Hunter (1997), *Manual of Housing Law*, London: Sweet & Maxwell. The Law Commission's proposals had their genesis in (1992), *Landlord and Tenant: Responsibility for State and Condition of Property*, Law Com 123, London: HMSO; for other Law Commission Reports in this area, see (1975), *Obligations of Landlords and Tenants*, Law Com No 67, London: HMSO. The following is a sample of relevant work not cited in this chapter: DoE (1993), *Monitoring the New Housing Fitness Standard*, London: HMSO; P. Leather & S. Mackintosh (1992), *Maintaining Home Ownership: The Agency Approach*, London: Longman; P. Leather & S. Mackintosh (eds) (1994), *The Future of Housing Renewal Policy*, Bristol: School for Advanced Urban Studies, University of Bristol; P. Leather & S. Mackintosh (eds) (1992), *Home Improvement under the New Regime*, Occasional Paper No 38, Bristol: School for Advanced Urban Studies, University of Bristol; P. Leather and M. Reid (1989), *Investing in Older Housing*, Occasional Paper 34, Bristol: School for Advanced Urban Studies, University of Bristol; V. Karn and L. Sheridan (1994), *New Homes in the 1990s*, York: Joseph

Rowntree Foundation; C. Paris and B. Blackaby (1979), *Not Much Improvement*, London: Heinemann; P. Niner and R. Forrest (1982), *Housing Action Area Policy and Progress: The Residents' Perspective*, Birmingham, Centre for Urban and Regional Studies, University of Birmingham.

Endnotes

1. For this purpose, we are not concerned with those low-cost home ownership initiatives induced by the Conservative governments of the 1980s and 1990s. In general, it was, as we have seen, the better quality properties, including those which had been renovated by the local authorities, which were purchased.
2. One consequence, for example, was the local authority's Environmental Health Officers taking more interest in the property for clearance or declaration of unfitness (and thus requiring money to be spent on the property).
3. It should be noted that the Act provides its own definition of unfitness (s. 9, Landlord and Tenant Act 1985) which is now anomalously *not* related to the current definition of fitness in s 604, Housing Act 1985.
4. This was a product of a rather dubious legal decision, *R* v. *Cardiff CC ex parte Cross* (1982) 6 HLR 1.

Bibliography

Balchin, P. (1995), *Housing Policy: An Introduction*, London: Routledge
Bines, W., Kemp, P., Pleace, N. and Radley, C. (1993), *Managing Social Housing*, London: HMSO
Bright, S. and Gilbert, G. (1994), *Landlord and Tenant: The Nature of Tenancies*, Oxford: Oxford University Press
Cairncross, L., Clapham, D. and Goodall, R. (1997), *Housing Management, Consumers and Citizens*, London: Routledge
Chartered Institute of Environmental Health (CIEH) (1998), *Environmental Health Report 1996–1997*, London: CIEH
Clapham, D., Kemp, P. and Smith, S. (1990), *Housing and Social Policy*, London: Macmillan
Couch, C. and Gill, N. (1992), *Renewal Areas: A Review of Progress*, Working Paper 119, Bristol: School for Advanced Urban Studies, University of Bristol
Crook, A., Henneberry, J. and Hughes, J. (1998), *Repairs and Improvements to Private Rented Dwellings in the 1990s*, London: DETR
Davidson, M., Redshaw, J. and Mooney, A. (1997), *The Role of DIY in Maintaining Owner Occupied Stock*, Bristol: Policy Press
Department of the Environment (DoE) (1987a), *Home Improvement Policy: The Government's Proposals*, London: DoE
Department of the Environment (DoE) (1987b), *Housing: The Government's Proposals*, Cm 214, London: HMSO
Department of the Environment (DoE) (1990), *Area Renewal, Unfitness, Slum Clearance and Enforcement Action*, LAC Circ 6/90, London: HMSO
Department of the Environment (DoE) (1995a), *Our Future Homes: Opportunity, Choice, Responsibility*, Cm 2901, London: HMSO

Department of the Environment (DoE) (1995b), *The Future of Private Housing Renewal Programmes*, Explanatory Paper Linked to the Housing White Paper 'Our Future Homes', London: DoE

Department of the Environment (DoE) (1996), *Private Sector Renewal: A Strategic Approach*, LAC 17/96, London: HMSO

Department of the Environment, Transport and the Regions (DETR) (1998a), *English House Condition Survey1996*, London: DETR

Department of the Environment, Transport and the Regions (DETR) (1998b), *Combatting Cowboy Builders: A Consultation Paper*, London: DETR

Department of the Environment, Transport and the Regions (DETR) (1998c), *Encouraging Home Owners to Repair and Maintain their Homes: A Review of Initiatives*, London: SO

Department of the Environment, Transport and the Regions (DETR) (1998d), *Housing Fitness Standard: A Consultation Paper*, London: DETR

Department of the Environment, Transport and the Regions (DETR) (1998e), *Housing Grants, Construction and Regeneration Act 1996, Part I*, LAC 4/98, London: SO

Department of the Environment, Transport and the Regions (DETR) (1998f), *Proposed Single Allocation to Local Authorities for Capital Investment in Housing*, London: DETR

Heywood, F. (1997), 'Poverty and disrepair: challenging the myth of ignorance in private sector housing', vol 12, *Housing Studies*, 27

Hirsch, W. (1981), 'Landlord-tenant relations law', in P. Burrows and C. Veljanovski (eds), *Economic Approach to Law*, London: Butterworths

Hughes, D. and Lowe, S. (1995), *Social Housing Law and Policy*, London: Butterworths

Hutter, B. (1988), *The Reasonable Arm of the Law*, Oxford: Oxford University Press

Karn, V., Kemeny, J. and Williams, P. (1985), *Home Ownership in the Inner City: Salvation or Despair?*, Studies in Urban and Regional Policy, 3, Aldershot: Gower

Karn, V., Lickiss, R. and Hughes, D. (1997), *Tenants' Complaints and the Reform of Housing Management*, Aldershot: Dartmouth

Langstaff, M. (1992), 'Housing associations: a move to centre stage', in J. Birchall (ed), *Housing Policy in the 1990s*, London: Routledge

Law Commission (1996), *Landlord and Tenant: Responsibility for State and Condition of Property*, Law Com No 238, London: HMSO

Leather, P., Littlewood, A. and Munro, M. with Lancaster, S., Maginn, P., Rolfe, S. and Smith, J. (1998), *Make do and Mend? Explaining Homeowners' Approaches to Repair and Maintenance*, Bristol: Policy Press

Leather, P. and Mackintosh, S. (1992), 'Housing renewal in an era of mass home ownership', in P. Malpass and R. Means (eds), *Implementing Housing Policy*, Buckingham: Open University Press

Leather, P. and Mackintosh, S. (1993), 'Towards a sustainable housing renewal policy', in R. Smith and J. Raistrick (eds), *Policy and Change*, Bristol: School for Advanced Urban Studies, University of Bristol

Leather, P. and Mackintosh, S. (1994), *The Future of Housing Renewal Policy*, Bristol: Policy Press

Leather, P. and Mackintosh, S. (1997), 'Towards sustainable policies for housing renewal in the private sector', in P. Williams (ed), *Directions in Housing Policy*, London: Paul Chapman

Leather, P., Mackintosh, S. and Rolfe, S. (1994), *Papering over the Cracks: Housing Conditions and the Nation's Health*, London: National Housing Forum

Leather, P. and Morrison, T. (1997), *The State of UK Housing – A Factfile on Dwelling Conditions*, Bristol: Policy Press

Legal Research Institute (1998), *Controlling Minimum Standards in Existing Housing*, Warwick: Legal Research Institute, University of Warwick

Littlewood, A. and Munro, M. (1995), *Investing in Housing: A Comparison of Landlord and Home Owner Repair Behaviour*, Glasgow: Centre for Housing Research and Urban Studies, University of Glasgow

Littlewood, A. and Munro, M. (1996), 'Explaining disrepair: examining owner occupiers' repair and maintenance behaviour', vol 11, *Housing Studies*, 503

Loveland, I. (1995), *Housing Homeless Persons*, Oxford: Oxford University Press

Lund, B. (1996), *Housing Problems and Housing Policy*, London: Longman

McNaughton, R. (1994), 'Repairs and maintenance in the public sector', in D. Donnison and D. Maclennan (eds), *The Housing Service of the Future*, London: Longman

Merrett, S. (1982), *Owner Occupation in Britain*, London: Routledge

Meyers, C. (1975), 'The covenant of habitability and the American Law Institute', vol 27, *Stanford Law Review*, 879

Rabin, E. (1984), 'The revolution in landlord-tenant law: causes and consequences', vol 69, *Cornell Law Review*, 517

Randolph, B. (1992), 'The re-privatization of housing associations', in P. Malpass and R. Means (eds), *Implementing Housing Policy*, Buckingham: Open University Press

Reynolds, J. (1974), 'Statutory covenants of fitness and repair: social legislation and the judges', vol 37, *Modern Law Review*, 377

Smith, P. (1994), 'Repairing obligations: a case against radical reform', *Conveyancer and Property Lawyer*, 186

Stewart, A. (1996), *Rethinking Housing Law*, London: Sweet & Maxwell

Thomas, A. (1986), *Housing and Urban Renewal*, London: Allen & Unwin

15 Unlawful Eviction and Harassment

In 1990, nine per cent of a sample of those renting privately said that they had suffered from harassment by their landlord (Rauta & Pickering, 1992). Extrapolating this to the full size of the private rented sector would suggest 144,180 households who had been, or were being, harassed by their landlords (Jew, 1994). At the same time, however, just 104 people were prosecuted for unlawful eviction, and 77 for harassment (in a residential setting). Even allowing for the fact that the earlier survey effectively required the tenants to self-define harassment, there seems to be a massive under-prosecution rate in these cases (although this is true of most crimes). When one considers that the current principle underlying the criminal justice system in the UK is *punitive*, insisting that people are brought to book (in the most efficient and effective way, of course) for their crimes, then this begins to look even more suspicious. Just three people were given custodial sentences for unlawful eviction and harassment in 1990 (lest one thinks 1990 was a blip, just four were given custodial sentences in 1996). At a time when one Home Secretary after another (since 1991) has praised the penal motive under some sobriquet or other ('prison works!'), it is time to reconsider why the penalties for unlawful eviction and harassment are so low.

Approaching the issue from the perspective of civil law, one might suspect that the civil law would adopt a particularly robust view of unlawful eviction and harassment. After all, as landlords generally require court orders to evict tenants, unlawful eviction and harassment is therefore effectively a challenge to the power and value of the civil law system because (almost by definition) such civil wrongs occur when landlords avoid court procedures. The general principle should be that the landlord is obliged to disgorge the profit made through the unlawful eviction and harassment, as well as compensate the former occupier for any physical or mental injury. In other words, the landlord should not be entitled to take advantage of their *deliberate exploitation of wrongdoing* (Birks, 1989, p. 326).

It was not until 1988 that unlawful eviction and harassment became a tort – or, a civil wrong – and then only by force of statute (ss. 27 & 28, Housing Act 1988). Of course, the civil law did penalize landlords before then but this was on more general grounds of, for example, breach of the implied or express covenant of *quiet enjoyment*. The principle employed in the statute was that the landlord should disgorge their profit, which was defined as the market value of the property with the occupier less the value without that person. In one case, more than £30,000 damages were awarded to a tenant (*Tagro* v. *Cafane* (1991) 23 HLR 250). However, more recently, the courts have adopted the position that the market value with the tenant should reflect the speed with which that person may be (lawfully) evicted. As an assured shorthold tenant may be evicted relatively speedily, the value of damages will be tiny in such situations (on the statutory basis).

One might argue that, in these post-Housing Act 1988 days of assured shorthold tenancies with their limited security and the broader context of a move towards the 'casualization' of housing (Morgan, 1996), incidences of unlawful eviction and harassment will become fewer in number as more and more tenancies can be terminated relatively simply. Around 50 per cent of tenants have an assured shorthold, a resident landlord, or no security, and can therefore be evicted extremely quickly and for relatively small cost. On the other hand, there are a large number of remaining tenancies protected under the Rent Act 1977. The ability to deregulate tenancies by getting rid of such tenants and replacing them with 1988 Act tenants will be greater (the well-known effect of 'creeping decontrol'). Research for Shelter also suggests that causes include landlords wishing to sell their properties; Housing Benefit-related problems (such as late payment); tenants' complaints about repairs; and more personal forms of harassment concerning the occupier's race, sex and sexuality, age and HIV status (Burrows & Hunter, 1990, Ch. 2). These are largely neutral as regards the type of occupation rights. Jew also found that the majority of complaints related to Housing Benefit problems (1994, pp. 33–41), which can only have been exacerbated by the reductions in allowable benefit (see Ch. 11).

Furthermore, all the evidence suggests that it is precisely these short-term types of occupation right in which unlawful eviction and harassment actually occur. The official committee which drew attention to the problem, as well as being partly responsible for drawing up the criminal law provisions, referred to this as 'the most startling fact to emerge' (Milner Holland, 1965, p. 259); this finding was also reflected in the report of the committee set up to investigate the implementation of the Rent Acts (Francis, 1971, p. 105). Thus, contrary to expectation, it is the areas where the occupier has less security in which a considerable proportion of the incidents of unlawful eviction and harassment occur. One factor which may be expected to emerge from the move towards casualization is, by contrast, an increase in *under-reporting* of harassment and unlawful eviction because there is little point in reporting such acts if the landlord can simply give you two months notice.

It may well be that such a fact is contrary to expectation because our image of the landlord on the margins of the legal process is sensitized by the affairs of Rachman in the 1950s and 1960s. Rachman and his pursuits provide the common reference point (even though the first Protection from Eviction Act was passed in 1924). Rachman's methods were threefold (at least): he would offer secure tenants a sum of money to give up their occupation (a practice known as 'winkling'); he would introduce tenants into the properties whom, he or his agents believed, would make life difficult for the secure tenants living in the property, making the latter gradually leave the property; third, he charged exorbitant rents for slum property. Yet, such actions would not breach the criminal law, nor would they constitute a civil wrong. Winkling was, and still is, regarded as a *legitimate commercial practice* and not harassing action; there would be considerable difficulty in finding a landlord responsible for the acts of others;[1] and the third was not an offence *per se* – rather the law simply required the landlord to repay any overcharging to the tenant.

It was the main finding of Nelken's classic study of unlawful eviction and harassment that the legislation had been successful because 'the response to Rachmanism reflected and reinforced established boundaries of propriety and impropriety in the use and abuse of property rights' (1983, p. 27). Offering a secure tenant money to leave a property might have been regarded as a harassing act, but the law did not make it so because this was regarded as legitimate. Thus, the law tends not to treat commercial practices by commercial landlords as unlawful. The law tends to catch small landlords who are not renting for the income generated (this applies to most small landlords: Bevan *et al.*, 1995).

The introduction of Rachman into our narrative underlines the fact that politics has been intimately involved with the development of this branch of the law. The 1964 general election, it is commonly said, was lost by the Conservatives partly because of the influence of Rachman. Rachman was implicated in the Profumo affair (the war minister, Profumo, sleeping with prostitutes who were involved with Russian agents) which led to the downfall of the Macmillan government. It was the abuses of the 'creeping decontrol' Rent Act 1957 – under which protected tenancies would become decontrolled once the protected tenant left the property – that also turned people off the Conservative government. Rachman was regarded as responsible for these abuses but he was also regarded as the worst example of a broader brand of exploitation. Publicity given to his practices led to an emergency debate in the House of Commons, as well as the setting up of the Milner Holland committee. One of the first acts of the incoming Labour government in 1964 was to pass 'emergency' legislation protecting people from eviction. It is perhaps ironic that, whilst so much political blood has been spilt over the issue, only limited use has been made of the legislation.

Indeed, since that time the 'ghost of Rachman' has been said to haunt the Conservative Party's dealings with the security of tenure issue (Kemp, 1992). Against the nature of the New Right, which, if it had any core ideology, concerned itself with deregulation, it was not until the third Thatcher government that the private rented sector was reformed and deregulated. Even then, that government was particularly careful to protect itself from being damaged by landlord abuses by creating the statutory tort and making prosecutions for unlawful harassment easier by changing the required *mens rea* (i.e. the mental state which a landlord must have to be convicted of the offence). These changes were regarded as 'an important additional deterrent to harassment' (DoE, 1987, para. 3.17). However, as the sector had largely deregulated itself prior to the 1988 Act as well as market rents commonly being charged, there was no great incentive for landlords to harass or unlawfully evict their tenants: 'In this sense, Rachmanism has not returned, because it never really went away' (Kemp, 1992, p. 119).

Discussions of the civil and criminal wrongs in housing law have tended to proceed upon narrow, insular lines. We discuss the law, making brief reference to how few prosecutions are begun, or how small are the damages awarded. But we rarely place this discussion within the broader perspective (for a classic exception, see Nelken, 1983). What will be attempted in this chapter is a broader analysis, taking advantage of some classic socio-legal studies into the effectiveness of non-police prosecutions. We will argue that the enforcement of the criminal legislation itself reinforces the distinctions between public (a place for regulation) and private (a place for self-regulation), as well as between 'real' crime (*mala in se*) and those acts which are not 'wrongs in themselves, but merely things that society requires to be better regulated' (*mala prohibita*) (Sanders & Young, 1994, p. 244).

The regulatory approach adopted appears to be one of securing *compliance* through negotiation or conciliation, and not prosecution. Those who are prosecuted are those with whom negotiation proves impossible for some reason (Nelken, 1983). Often, when one reads the case law concerning prosecutions, judges make comments similar to the following: 'It should be said at the outset that this is not a serious instance of the kind of case for which the legislation was designed. Mr Nelson was clearly a difficult lodger, and there is much to be said in favour of the defendant' (*R* v. *Yuthiwattana* (1984) 16 HLR 49, *per* Kerr LJ). The point is that most often the types of landlords who are prosecuted are those who have a personal 'issue' with the occupier because such landlords are the ones who are most unlikely to negotiate.

We then turn to consider the civil law. It will be argued that the relevance of the civil law has been downgraded in part by its own ineffectiveness and in part by judicial whim. There are a panoply of potential civil law actions and remedies open to occupiers who are subjected to unlawful eviction and harassment. An immediate remedy which can be gained by the occupier is an injunction (an order requiring the landlord not to do something or to take positive action). However, injunctions have been shown in other contexts to be rather ineffectual. Further, the statutory tort introduced in the 1988 Act has been interpreted so as to provide minimal damages in situations in which it would have been most valuable. Judicial interpretations have *not* accorded with Parliamentary intention. However, that intention was so poorly expressed in the legislation in the first place as to defeat most valuers who provide assessments of damages (although this may also reflect the difficulty that the law has in directing other 'systems').

15.1   Criminal Law

Establishing the Boundaries

Background
Before we discuss the uneven ways in which the criminal sanctions are applied in cases of unlawful eviction and harassment, it is appropriate to establish the boundaries of the offences. In fact, there is a neat correlation between the *complexity* of the law, and the fact of non-prosecution, as well as the non-involvement of the police in these disputes. Complexity is partly used to justify non-prosecution and police inaction. A conspiracy theorist might suggest that making the legislation so complex was one particular objective of lawmakers. However, such a perspective generally ignores the fact that the criminal sanction was the product of a bizarre conjunction of interests.

First, the Conservative Party had been badly stung by its involvement in landlord and tenant law in the 1957 Rent Act and wished to portray itself as being against criminal behaviour by any landlord: 'Thus Conservative speakers criticized the police for failing to enforce the 1964, temporary, Protection from Eviction Act, and stressed the need for stiff deterrent penalties to be imposed when the Bill became law' (Nelken, 1983, p. 38). Second, the large commercial landlords generally wanted criminal legislation so that they could 'divert the stigma that was being attached to all landlords' as part of the negative publicity induced by the Rachman affair (Nelken, 1983, p. 30). However, landlords cannot be regarded as an homogeneous group, all of whom wanted the same things. We saw in Chapter 2 that there are many different types of landlord who become landlords for a variety of reasons not all of which are related to profit-making. It can be assumed that the interests of commercial landlords were well-served by Parliament, but such assumptions must be tempered by the lack of political weight accorded to landlords in the immediate post-Rachman era.

Thirdly, the Labour government's election manifesto had promised such legislation. They offered a compromise position and, in doing so, were much assisted by the Milner Holland committee and its report. This report approached the issue of unlawful eviction and harassment by first discarding the term 'rachmanism' because 'it has no precise meaning and is used by different persons to mean different things' (Milner Holland, 1965, p. 162). They classified 'abuses' into the following 12 headings:

'(1)   Tenants unlawfully turned out of or excluded from their homes.
With the object of securing vacant possession, tenants subjected to:
(2)   Assault
(3)   Interference with their accommodation or its services
(4)   Interference with personal possessions
(5)   Deliberate introduction of unwelcome or undesirable tenants into other accommodation in the building

(6)   Any other deliberate or persistent annoyance
(7)   Threat of any items (1)–(6)
(8)   Tenants tricked or misled into leaving controlled accommodation
(9)   Rents in excess of controlled rents obtained for controlled property by threats of other improper means
(10)   Exorbitant rents demanded as the alternative to eviction
(11)   Deliberate withholding of rent books or the information which should be shown in them
(12)   Any other form of abuse, persecution, ill-treatment or unfair practices to which tenants have been subject' (pp. 163–4).

They characterized headings 1–8 as landlords trying to get rid of tenants 'by unlawful or reprehensible means'; 9–10 were 'unlawful and oppressive' means of gaining higher rents; 11 was already covered by earlier legislation (and not dealt with in this book); and 12 a catch-all category. Noticeably absent from these headings was winkling or other 'commercial' practices. The committee were directly responsible for the shape of the subsequent legislation as part of the 'kitchen cabinet' of the housing minister, Richard Crossman. Thus, only headings 1–8 fell to be dealt with under unlawful eviction and harassment legislation. Practices 9–10 were dealt with by allowing the tenant the means to have reimbursement of any excess.

Protection from Eviction Act 1977

The direct result of these various forces was the introduction of criminal offences relating to both unlawful eviction and unlawful harassment in the Rent Act 1965. These offences are now contained in the Protection from Eviction Act 1977. They can be committed by any person – not just the landlord – and against a 'residential occupier'. The phrase 'residential occupier' is given a specific meaning in the Act (s. 1(1)). This requires two things to be shown: first, that the person is 'occupying the premises as a residence', which suggests that the *Brown* v. *Brash* test applies (which requires evidence of occupation together with an intention to return to the premises if the applicant is elsewhere – see Ch. 13). Second, the occupation must be 'under a contract or by virtue of any enactment or rule of law giving [the person] the right to remain in occupation or restricting the right of any other person to recover possession of the premises'. This broad criterion seems to include all persons who are entitled to occupy the premises until the expiry of a court order for possession, or otherwise up to the termination of their right of occupation (where there is no statutory requirement for possession proceedings). For example, assured and assured shorthold tenants are residential occupiers. They remain so until the landlord has successfully brought possession proceedings and the court order has expired. After the possession order has expired, the person is no longer a residential occupier. Other than cases where there is a resident owner (either landlord or licensor), the Act makes it unlawful to recover possession without a court order (s. 3(1)). In these cases, the person remains a residential occupier until the court order has run its course.

There is a difference of opinion as to whether a trespasser (or squatter) can be a residential occupier (compare the 4th and 5th editions of *Quiet Enjoyment* on this point: Hunter & McGrath, 1994, p. 76; Carter & Dymond, 1998, p. 113). The better view is that a trespasser cannot be a residential occupier because it is not unlawful for an owner to recover possession without a court order, although the owner might be ill-advised to do so. There is judicial support for the view that a trespasser would not be protected (*R* v. *Phekoo* [1981] 1 WLR 1117). However, the alternative view relies on the restrictions upon owners' rights to recover possession of property contained in the Criminal Law Act 1977, s. 6. This makes it a criminal offence to recover possession by intentionally or recklessly using violence to secure entry to premises when a person occupying the premises objects to such entry.

Unlawful Eviction   The offence of unlawful eviction is committed in one of two circumstances. First, it occurs where 'any person unlawfully deprives the residential occupier of any premises of [that person's] occupation of the premises or any part thereof'; second, it occurs where any person 'attempts' to do the same (s. 1(2)). Whilst the word 'eviction' is not explicitly used, it is said that the act must have the character of an eviction. Locking up part of the premises, or obstructing the occupier's use of part of the premises would count for this purpose because the offence can occur in relation to part of the premises. An eviction is unlawful when the owner does not use the correct procedure for terminating a person's occupation. The Act does not prescribe a particular mental state (*mens rea*) which is required before the offence is proved. This either means that no particular mental state is required, or (and more likely) the general principle of criminal law that guilt is shown only if the defendant intended the act, or was reckless (see below), applies.

In *R* v. *Yuthiwattana* (1984) 16 HLR 49, the Court of Appeal found that the offence of unlawful eviction would not be committed in cases which they described as 'locking out' or not admitting the occupier on one or even more isolated occasions, so that in effect he continues to be allowed to occupy the premises but is then unable to enter, . . .' – such matters were better regarded as falling within criminal harassment provision (see below). Whilst the deprivation did not have to be permanent, the offence was committed when the occupier 'effectively has to leave the premises and find other accommodation' (at p. 63). However, in *Costelloe* v. *Camden LBC* (1986) Crim LR 250, the Court of Appeal made the apparently contradictory point that the temporal quantity of the exclusion was immaterial. The critical question was said to be 'what was the nature of the exclusion; was it designed to evict the occupier? If so the conduct fell within s. 1(2).'

Harassment 1   There are two offences of harassment of a residential occupier. The first (original) offence must be split between the required *mens rea* and the acts which the defendant must do (*actus reus*) in order to fit within the offence.

The mental element is as follows: when any person *intends* to cause the residential occupier to give up occupation of the premises or any part thereof, *or* to refrain from exercising any right or pursuing any remedy in respect of the premises or any part thereof. Whilst the prosecution do not need to prove that the defendant has breached the civil law (*R* v. *Burke* [1991] 1 AC 135), the requisite level of intention is nevertheless difficult to prove. The defendant must specifically intend either that the occupier give up the premises or that the occupier will not exercise any rights in relation to the premises: 'This means that the court is not entitled automatically to draw the conclusion that the defendant had the necessary intent just because the harassing conduct caused the victim to give up occupation, etc.' (Carter & Dymond, 1998, p. 126). If the defendant is *reckless* as to the result, this may also found a criminal prosecution (Ashworth, 1978, p. 78). In this context, recklessness would probably be decided according to a subjective test (liability would exist if the person knows or suspects or is aware of the risk that the occupier would give up the premises or that the occupier would not exercise any rights in relation to the premises).

In *Schon* v. *Camden LBC* (1986) 18 HLR 341, the landlord wanted to build a bathroom in a room directly above the tenant's flat. The landlord requested the tenant leave for two weeks offering a hotel room (which was rejected by the tenant). The works went ahead and the tenant's ceiling caved in. The Court of Appeal held that these actions did not show an intention to cause the tenant to give up the occupation of the premises. Rather, it disclosed an intention only to require the tenant to leave the accommodation for a limited period of time.

The *actus reus* are that the act(s) complained of must be likely to interfere with the peace or comfort of the residential occupier or members of the household, or that the services reasonably required for the occupation of the premises as a residence are persistently withdrawn or withheld. The first limb (acts likely to interfere with the peace and comfort) must relate to a positive act, and not an omission to act (although one act is sufficient: *R* v. *Polycarpou* (1978) 9 HLR 129). The second limb (persistently withdrawing or withholding services) does not apply to those services which are provided voluntarily by the landlords (although this is controversial: *cf* Carter & Dymond, 1998, p. 123); equally, the requirement of persistence means that there need be only one act but there must be deliberate continuity (for example, leaving gas or electricity cut off for a period of time).

Harassment 2   The second offence was introduced in the Housing Act 1988 by way of amendment to the Protection from Eviction Act 1977, s. 1(3A). This was in response to the claims that the requirement to prove a specific intent made convictions rather difficult. The new offence differs from the old one in the following ways: the offence can only be committed by the landlord or the landlord's agent (such as a letting agent) and not by any other person; the *mens rea* required is that the landlord or agent must *know, or have reasonable cause to believe*, that the acts are likely to cause the residential occupier to give up occupation of the premises or any part thereof, *or* to refrain from exercising any right or pursuing any remedy in respect of the premises or any part thereof. Otherwise the offence is the same as harassment 1.

Defence Where the landlord believes, or has reasonable cause to believe, that the residential occupier had ceased to reside in the premises, there is a good defence. In *R v Phekoo*, a landlord honestly believed that the occupiers were squatters (they were sub-tenants). It was suggested that such a belief was sufficient, provided it was honestly and reasonably held. However, in *West Wiltshire DC* v. *Snelgrove*, an *obiter* distinction was drawn between mistake of fact and mistake of law, the former being a defence and the latter going to mitigation: 'No doubt a mistaken belief as to whether or not they were contravening the statute would have been highly relevant by way of mitigation and thus on the issue of penalty. In my judgment, however, it could not have provided them with a defence . . .' (1998) 30 HLR 57,63. This dictum has been qualified by the Court of Appeal to the extent that certain civil law mistakes can act as a defence (see *Osei-Bonsu* v. *Wandsworth LBC* [1999] 1 All ER 265).

Protection from Harassment Act 1997
Somewhat dislocated from the argument hitherto because it has its roots in issues arising outside the subject matter, the Protection from Harassment Act 1997 nevertheless has the potential to be dramatically important. It can be surmised from our discussion of the 1977 Act that its complexity potentially makes successful prosecutions rather difficult. The 1997 Act, by way of contrast, seems to enable prosecutions to be brought on much simpler grounds. The 1997 Act was a product of a different set of events and political pressures. Before the 1997 general election, a debate arose about the proper protection of people from 'stalkers', as well as more general concerns regarding the limits to a person's privacy. These debates are ongoing. However, the Conservative government were able to resuscitate their proposed protection for people in these circumstances amidst what might be described as a law and order auction, in which the main bidders (Michael Howard MP, the then Home Secretary, and Jack Straw MP, his opposition shadow) espoused more and more punitive ideals in order to outbid each other. Thus, the Protection from Harassment Act 1997 was rushed through Parliament at this time without proper debate or questioning as to its ambit.

The Act creates three offences which are relevant for our purposes:

- A person is guilty of an offence if they pursue a 'course of conduct' which amounts to harassment of another *and* which that person knows or ought to know amounts to harassment of the other (s. 1; there are certain exceptions in ss (3)). The phrase 'Ought to know' is judged against what a 'reasonable person in possession of the same information would think'. An offence is committed in these circumstances (s. 2).

- In the same circumstances, the person against whom the harassment has occurred may claim damages and an injunction. Breach of that injunction entitles that person to apply for a warrant of arrest (s. 3).

- A person whose course of conduct causes another to fear, on at least two occasions, that violence will be used against him is guilty of an offence if he knows or ought to know that his course of conduct will cause the other to fear on each of those occasions (s. 4; there are certain exceptions in ss (3)). Once again, the phrase 'Ought to know' is judged against what a 'reasonable person in possession of the same information would think'.

The definition of these offences suggests that they are broad enough to cover a significant proportion of unlawful eviction and harassment cases. Their introduction makes it clear that the pre-existing complexity of the law cannot be used as an excuse for non-prosecution now.

15.2   (Non-)Enforcement

It is a common finding of studies of prosecution policies that there is often a class and race bias in the types of persons prosecuted. This is also reflected in the types of landlords who are prosecuted for unlawful eviction and harassment. It was well known at the time of the 1965 legislation that the offences were committed in urban stress areas, and generally by resident landlords (who, at that time, only needed to serve four weeks written notice on the tenant). Nelken's study of a sample of those landlords who were prosecuted found that these people tended to lack 'financial resources and legal competence' (1983, p. 91) and most commonly prosecutions occurred in the 'twilight areas' described by Rex and Moore against ethnic minority landlords (1967). In this section, I will seek to explain why these biases exist by considering the prosecution policies of the police and local authorities.

I do not wish to suggest in this section that prosecution is always the best or most appropriate course of action. In many cases, conciliation and negotiation, sometimes backed up with the threat of prosecution, are the best ways of dealing with 'low level' crimes. Sometimes, landlords simply need to be informed of the proper legal procedure or the relevant law (although landlords should know what they are getting themselves into before they enter into a contract for the rental of property). The point that is pursued below, though, is an explanation of the low level of prosecutions and why local authorities, as prosecutors, have tended to adopt compliance-based strategies.

The Police

Until the mid-1980s, the police commonly refused to become involved in domestic violence cases. Their response was to regard such crimes as 'domestics' and adopted a 'no-criming' approach (i.e. taking no action and not recording such crimes). They have adopted a similar approach to cases of unlawful eviction and harassment. Whilst they have gradually adopted more positive prosecution policies in relation to domestic violence (Morley & Mullender, 1992), the analogy ends there because they have not pursued the same approach to unlawful eviction and harassment. It appears that they have continued to no-crime these disputes, although a report is often sent to the local authority, which is given power to prosecute under the Protection from Eviction Act (and Criminal Law Act 1977). Local authorities' role in relation to the Protection from Harassment Act 1997 is more limited because they have no power to prosecute (unless it can be said to fall within their general duty under the Crime and Disorder Act 1998 – see below).

The assumption seems to be that these disputes are 'more suitable for civil proceedings' (Carter & Dymond, 1998, p. 147), although the police are likely to take action where the dispute involves something that can be pigeonholed as an offence (for example, actual bodily harm or other violence). The Francis report in 1971 drew attention to the following difficulties faced by the police in these cases: a police constable on the spot is in no position to work out whether the occupier is a 'residential occupier'; in the case of allegations of harassment, these take some time to investigate, and constables are in no position to take immediate action (although this does not include the subsequently created harassment action); the police have no power of arrest in these circumstances (Francis, 1971, p. 106). Nelken adds that the police probably see their role as limited because 'in all cases of domestic types of dispute the normal police response is to try and sort out the matter and maintain order rather than strive to bring any prosecution' (1983, p. 104) – to which one might add, unless there is strong public support for a more active role on their part.

Much of the Francis report's reasoning is concerning, but particularly so in relation to their comments about police involvement in harassment and unlawful eviction. There is, in fact, plently of anecdotal evidence that the police themselves take part in unlawful evictions. Simple training for police on the 1977 Act might be a start to avoiding such situations. After all, it is only at the margins that the concept of 'residential occupier' is confusing. Tenants are residential occupiers and so are licensees. Such agreements count for most residential occupation. A constable 'on the spot' should be able to work this out. Harassment may take some time to investigate (an efficiency argument), but then a number of other crimes do as well and this has never been used to deny police responsibility. After all, harassment and unlawful eviction are *property crimes*; their nearest relation is theft, because essentially the landlord is intentionally depriving the tenant of the tenant's property (the definition of theft); the law is supposed to abhor property crimes, particularly theft. Thus, the lack of police involvement cannot be explained other than as a symptom of broader structural issues about the sector.

Local Authority Prosecutions

There is now a considerable body of socio-legal research that considers the exercise of prosecutorial discretion amongst non-police agencies (see generally, Sanders & Young, 1994, pp. 240–6 for a summary). One aspect of that literature discusses the process of regulatory capture (under which the regulator takes on the perspective of the regulated) (see, in the context of the Housing Corporation, Ch. 5). In these studies, two regulatory strategies are commonly found to operate. First, 'compliance' strategies seek to remedy existing problems and prevent others arising through the regulator using cooperative and conciliatory approaches. Second, 'deterrence' strategies involve the regulator giving prosecution a pivotal role for any number of reasons (from retribution to utilitarian) (Hawkins, 1984). Hutter has found evidence of 'persuasive' and 'insistent' strategies within the 'compliance' category and has drawn attention to the probability that different areas may have different policies and practices *and* these may also vary within one area (1989). The type of strategy adopted tends to reflect the agency's background philosophy.

Our starting point is to consider briefly the background factors, which include central government guidance, official reports, and other external pressures to adopt compliance strategies. Next, using Cotterell's summary of the broader literature on why organizations adopt compliance strategies (1992), it will be argued that each reason is as appropriate to explain the local authorities' role. Finally, I will draw attention to the findings of the use of local authority discretion in these cases (referring to Nelken, 1983; Jew, 1994), drawing comparisons and contrasts with the approach of authorities in the associated area of racial harassment (see Bridges & Forbes, 1990; Cowan, 1997).

Towards 'Compliance'
Under the Protection from Eviction Act 1977 and the Criminal Law Act 1977, local authorities are entitled, but not obliged, to prosecute those persons who indulge in unlawful eviction and harassment. This power to prosecute is bolstered by the various duties imposed by the Crime and Disorder Act 1998:

> 'Without prejudice to any other obligation imposed on it, it shall be the duty of each authority . . . to exercise its function *with due regard to the likely effect of the exercise of those functions on, and the need to do all that it reasonably can to prevent, crime and disorder in its area*' (s. 17(1); emphasis added)

The predecessor to this section entitled local authorities to prosecute where they considered 'it expedient for the promotion or protection of the inhabitants in their area' (s. 222, Local Government Act 1972). The stronger provision in the 1998 Act suggests that greater legislative pressure is brought on local authorities to consider their role in unlawful eviction and harassment cases (although the impact of the provision is supposed to affect its policing of neighbour nuisance on its own estates – see Ch. 18). Nevertheless, the history of local authorities' role in these cases does not suggest that they will accept an increased prosecutorial role. Furthermore, it can be argued that conflicting pressures may enhance the need for conciliation as opposed to prosecution.

Before we place the local authorities' role in a more general context of non-police prosecutions, we should consider the immediate factors which have influenced the development of the conciliation strategy. Perhaps the most apparent demonstration of this sentiment has been the switch from the relevant officers in authorities being known as 'harassment officers' to 'tenancy relations officers' – a semantic shift which suggests that the officers' role is more concerned with relations between landlord and tenant than with prosecutions for harassment. This shift was probably induced by the impact of various official reports and government Circulars. Officially, many of the problems between owner and occupier are simply not 'criminal':

> '[T]he bulk of [complaints] reflect *not criminal action but mutual ill-feeling* of landlords and tenants – often people of different cultural backgrounds – which is frequently aggravated if not indeed caused by constrained proximity. When cases of sheer ill-will and mutual provocation are disregarded, there remain a number where an offence is being committed or contemplated, *many of them in ignorance that they are offences and terminable with a warning.*' (Francis, 1971, p. 105; emphasis added)

Thus, the view of the Francis committee was that most acts were not criminal and that most of them occurred because of ignorance of the law (although, as law students are regularly told *ignorantia iuris non excusat* – ignorance of the law is no excuse). The solution proffered by that committee follows naturally from this belief:

> 'We feel sure that the best way of tackling this problem is for local authorities in the stress areas, and elsewhere if considered necessary, to appoint a 'Harassment Officer' or 'Tenancy Relations Officer' charged with the duty of investigating complaints, *do what he can by way of conciliation in appropriate cases*, and where necessary collect evidence to support a prosecution by the local authority.' (*ibid*, p. 111)

These sentiments are echoed in central government's Circular issued after the introduction of the Housing Act 1988 (DoE, 1989). In one paragraph, the Circular suggests that 'It is important that local authorities should know and use their powers under the [Protection from Eviction] Act' (para. 7). However, subsequent paragraphs inform local authorities of *other* non-penal powers that can be used in circumstances amounting to harassment (paras 10–16). The Circular does not advise local authorities that they should appoint an Harassment/Tenancy Relations Officer unless the workload is sufficient (even though it is probably difficult to gauge the workload without having such a person in post). The Circular also makes the following point: '*The possibility of securing agreement between landlord and tenant (or licensor and licensee) and preventing harassment or an unlawful eviction should always be considered*' (para. 22). Thus, central government's exhortation is towards compliance policies (although taking no action at all will usually lead to a finding of maladministration by the Commission for Local Administration: Complaint No 94/A/3711, Wealden DC; 90/A/1356, Barnet LBC; 89/A/1581, Lewisham LBC).

Compliance policies are surely reinforced by the requirement that local authorities work together with private landlords (considered in previous chapters). This movement is evidenced, for example, by the Housing Act 1996, which requires authorities to find suitable accommodation in the private rented sector for successful homeless applicants where possible (s. 196); and local authorities were specifically given power to 'make arrangements with a private landlord to provide accommodation' (s. 209). At least since 1991, the Code of Guidance has also suggested that authorities should 'build up contacts with reputable private landlords, and might consider contracts with private landlords to provide a readily accessible service' (DoE, 1996, para. 21.24; see also DoE, 1991, para. 12.8). Schemes such as HAMA are practical examples of the development of these relationships. In other words, there are positive obligations on local authorities to negotiate with private landlords for the mutual benefit of both.

Finally, a complainant can also pursue their civil remedies, which will 'punish' the landlord with the award of damages and/or an injunction (see below). The award of damages is supposed to compensate complainants for what they have gone through. Thus, it may seem reasonable to require such people to adopt civil law strategies. Local authorities are also required by the 1996 Act to set up free housing advice services, which might assist those people in pursuing their complaints in the civil system. From this perspective, local authority personnel are able to act as gatekeepers between the civil and criminal systems, diverting the complainants between them according to their perception of the dispute(s).

Rationalizing Compliance
Drawing on the considerable amount of research into non-police prosecutions, most of which discuss the paucity of such prosecutions by regulatory agencies, Cotterell suggests that six factors at least seem of 'major significance' in understanding why agencies adopt compliance

strategies (1992, pp. 267–9). Each of these has a resonance for the study of the actions of local authorities in unlawful eviction and harassment cases.

First, there is the problem of the 'general inadequacy of agency resources to confront the problem of business regulation'. This is particularly evident when these agencies deal with large commercial operations (see, for example, Cranston, 1979). Most prosecutions for unlawful eviction and harassment take place against small, often resident landlords far from the image of the Rachmanite who transfers properties between companies in attempts to avoid enforcement proceedings. Large commercial landlords are most often able to organize their affairs so that they coincide with what is regarded as 'lawful' because this does not affect their operation. Furthermore, the process leading to prosecution is expensive and for local authorities that are already cash-strapped, particularly as regards their housing budget, prosecution is not an attractive option when it will be vigorously defended by companies with sufficient resources to frustrate the operation.

Resources also affect the organization of the authority's personnel. The DoE Circular did not exhort local authorities to employ a Harassment/ Tenancy Relations Officer. Subsequent research on behalf of the Campaign for Bedsit Rights (Jew, 1994) found that 72 per cent of authorities (in a sample of 61) had either a Tenancy Relations Officer or Housing Adviser, although many officers identifying themselves as such also had other duties within the authority (for example, Hackney Carriage Licensing); at best, this meant one full-time officer covering 2,686 private rentals and, at worst, one per 21,096. Training was non-existent in over 50 per cent of 'main departments' responsible for the issue. Twenty-seven authorities either had neither a 24-hour service nor an answer phone which referred the caller to the police (although many of those that did have an answerphone simply left the police's telephone number). Few authorities recorded complaints in a comprehensive manner. Finally, 62 per cent of authorities had no written procedures (Jew, 1994, pp. 50 *et seq*; see also Burrows & Hunter, 1990, p. 12). In this light, it is perhaps not surprising that so few prosecutions are brought.

Second, it is commonly said that available sanctions against law breaking are highly inadequate: 'Fines may often be sufficiently low to constitute mere licence fees for unlawful conduct' (Cotterell, p. 268). Available fines for unlawful eviction and harassment in Magistrates' courts are up to £5,000 and/or up to six months' imprisonment; in the Crown Court, an unlimited fine and/or up to two years' imprisonment. Despite the government writing to Magistrates' associations in 1988 warning them that 'making it easier to secure convictions may be of little avail if the penalties imposed by the criminal courts do not reflect the adequacy of the offence' (Letter from DoE, dated 13 October 1988, reprinted in Burrows & Hunter, 1990, pp. 78–80), it appears that fines awarded are extremely low and imprisonment a rare punishment.

Nelken's evidence suggests that calls to increase the level of fines belied the experience of Harassment/Tenancy Relations Officers, since the cases in which prosecutions were sought 'were rarely ones in which the landlord was deliberately seeking to evict for financial gain' (1983, p. 108). This also suggests a possible reason why fines are so low. Magistrates 'appear to treat harassment as an offence which is sometimes a serious matter but more often has something of the nature of a domestic or neighbour dispute . . . the level of fining increases in accordance with the evidence of genuine instrumentality in the offence' (Nelken, 1983, pp. 179–80).

Third, the often insecure basis of agency authority tends to encourage the adoption of compliance strategies. Regulatory agencies often need the support of those subject to their regulation in order to give the agency kudos. In the local authority context, in which the cost-effectiveness of services is continually considered against benchmarked standards, one might regard this as important. By contrast, however, one might point to the fact that councillors themselves are often keen to adopt pro-prosecution policies and the basis for the agency in these authorities is commonly secure. Nevertheless, there is a culture which suggests that the 'vast majority of landlords are good landlords' (see the DoE's Circular for confirmation of this view) and when they make a mistake it is because they don't know the law (*cf* Burrows & Hunter, 1990, p. 13: 'the line between ignorance and defiance is often a fine one').

This culture is highlighted – indeed, put in neon – by the fact that local authorities only have a power to prosecute. This means that they only need to consider whether to use their powers. They are under no duty to prosecute or to organize themselves so that greater account might be taken of these crimes. The fact that this is a power presumably deprioritizes this area of expertise in many authorities, particularly when there are a myriad of other enforceable obligations owed by authorities.

Fourth, agency personnel often complain of a low level of support and understanding from the courts. It is generally believed that Magistrates' courts operate in favour of landlords and that the crime is not taken seriously by Magistrates (*cf* Nelken). Authorities might point to their regular complaints about the level of fines or sentences imposed, which can hardly be said to make prosecution worthwhile on their own.

Fifth, 'lack of clear, unequivocal public support for regulatory agencies' work encourages caution and a compliance approach'. This factor tends to cover the whole sphere of 'white collar crime' and might be supposed to be encountered in respect of actions to recover the landlords' 'own' property. The distinction is summarized in the Latin phrases *mala in se* ('real' crimes) and *mala prohibita* (not crimes in themselves but those matters which society requires to be better regulated) (Sanders & Young, 1994, p. 244). On the other hand, as Sanders points out, 'perhaps it is the lack of enforcement which creates the non-criminogenic image' (1996, p. xvii). This is an important, essentially circular argument. Unlawful eviction and harassment might not be regarded as a 'real crime' precisely because it is rarely prosecuted. Were it prosecuted more, then our views might be different.

Unlawful eviction and harassment is a crime because of a conjunction of events largely based upon the response to Rachman. By way of contrast, one might point to the Conservative government's desire to deregulate business as being a dominant ideological position, an extrapolation of New Right ideology. As Snider argues,

'The popularity of [compliance] models does not surprise those who have studied the social diffusion and transmission of ideas. At particular ideological junctures, ideas are seized upon, disseminated, popularized, and thereby transformed into instruments that increase the power of the dominant class.' (1990, p. 382)

In this context, we should not be surprised that those prosecuted have tended to reflect a class bias because this reflects the dominant ideological position that 'respectable business people do not commit crimes intentionally' (*ibid*).

Furthermore, this position asserts that over-regulation is a detriment to business practices that will cause businesses to seek out other areas of profit-making. From this perspective, a compliance strategy enables profits to be made whilst retaining the strength of the industry.

Sixth, compliance polices are often pursued because of the complexity of the circumstances in which the alleged offences occur. The complexity of the law on unlawful eviction and harassment (other than the 1997 Act) is mirrored by the complexity of the disputes between owner and occupier. Nelken found that most complaints which led to prosecution (66 per cent) fell into what he described as personal harassment, in which the landlord either had a moral claim or personal dispute with the tenant (p. 72). Almost inevitably, such disputes are complex, particularly because the prosecutions in Nelken's sample generally involved resident landlords who had fallen out with their tenant for some reason (thus, the oft-heard judicial refrain, 'this is not the type of case for which the legislation was designed').

Locating Discretion[2]

The actual prosecution is the final stage of the process in which discretion is exercised by all parties. It will be argued that in each stage of the process, cases are filtered out so that only certain ones remain and these tend to reflect a class and race bias.

First, adopting Felstiner *et al.*'s approach for considering when a grievance becomes a complaint (1981), the occupier must 'name' the actions taken by the landlord as an offence, and 'blame' the landlord for such acts, as well as 'claim' against the landlord by *approaching the local authority*. At each filtering-out stage, it appears that middle-class occupiers tend not to seek the assistance of the local authority. This may be because they do not occupy properties in the so-called urban stress areas or because they are able to adopt alternative enforcement strategies (for example, through the civil system). There is a suggestion also that tenants may well complain partly because they are trying to improve their housing situation (even though the Harassment/Tenancy Relations Officer is often not a Rehousing Officer).

Second, the Harassment/Tenancy Relations Officer has discretion on how to pursue the case, if at all. So, for example, some cases might be regarded as irrelevant or as social problems. The officers themselves have been observed as having varying commitments to prosecution. However, it appears that, crucially, the types of cases put forward for prosecution are those in which the landlord refuses to accept conciliation or mediation by the officer: 'But it is clear that such judgments as 'no option' or 'refusal to have a dialogue' are intensely subjective ones, both in principle and in the context in which they are made' (Nelken, 1983, p. 120). Such judgments often reflect the personal prejudices of officers involved. Cases involving non-prosecution tend to fall into categories such as 'prosecution not practical' or 'not felt to be right' (for example, because the tenant is not a 'deserving' victim, or because the officer has sympathy with the landlord, or because the case is not sufficiently serious to put to the Magistrates). Table 15.1 summarizes the statistics kept in two study authorities.

Table 15.1 provides an excellent example of the different ways in which discretion can be employed in different areas. Although different definitions might be employed by each authority as to the action taken, the fact that Authority Two's use of mediation is so considerable, and that Authority one makes greater use of the warning letter as well as the rehousing of certain applicants, raise points of contrast at this stage.

Table 15.1   Results of enquiries in two local authorities

Percentage of total complaints	Result	
	Authority 1	Authority 2
Complaint not pursued: tenant's decision	14.9	28.9
Complaint not pursued: officer's decision	18.6	16.8
Resolved by mediation	19.6	51.5
Warning letter sent to landlord	83.7	67.1
Landlord prosecuted	2	1
Tenant referred to solicitor	17.1	9.4
Tenant referred to other agency	3.7	1.6
Civil action taken by tenant	3.5	2.2
Referred to homeless person's section	29.5	n/a
Injunction granted to tenant	5.7	n/a
Rehoused by local authority	22.5	n/a
Complaint not pursued	n/a	4.5
Tenant did not keep in contact	n/a	11.6

n/a = not available
Source: Jew, 1994, p. 62

Third, local authority legal advisors' discretion to prosecute is often made on the basis of councillors' policies. They exercise limited discretion because they 'do so little actual investigation of the cases'. In the context of the failure of local authorities to use their powers in cases of racial harassment, it has been suggested that local authority lawyers are not organized appropriately and that this influences non-prosecution: the legal department was often overworked; cases were assigned on an *ad hoc* basis (and therefore to non-specialists); entrenched attitudes amongst lawyers lead them to avoid seeing the witnesses; investigation and interviewing was expected to be done by the housing department (who received no training in investigation and legal skills; see Jew, 1994, for discussion in the eviction/harassment context). Thus:

'the general picture that emerges is one of legal departments maintaining a degree of professional distance from housing field-workers and of the initiative resting with the latter in seeking legal action on particular racial harassment cases, despite their limited training in the requirements of legal action. This, in turn, can create resentment, and in some cases equally entrenched attitudes among housing workers towards what they see as the 'negative' role of lawyers.' (Bridges & Forbes, 1990, p. 3).

One might, therefore, reasonably conclude that legal departments' organization must be improved if more prosecutions are to be brought.

15.3 Civil Law

Conservative concerns that they might be implicated in a further Rachman scandal after they deregulated the rented sector in the 1988 Act led them to strengthen the civil law proceedings under which a tenant could claim. Until that point, there had been no tort of unlawful eviction and harassment. Tenants had to rely on rather arcane principles such as the breach of the implied (or express) contractual term of 'quiet enjoyment' or a species of trespass and conversion (two tortious wrongs). It might be assumed, therefore, that the statutory tort introduced in sections 27 and 28, Housing Act 1988 would have made civil law solutions somewhat easier as well as adequately compensate the occupier appropriately (after all, these are criminal acts). Early cases brought under these provisions suggested that this would be so (see, for example, *Tagro* v. *Cafane* (1991) 23 HLR 250). However, subsequent cases have considerably reduced the level of damages awarded.

The tort can be committed by the landlord or any person acting on the landlord's behalf – although damages are only payable by the landlord[3] – and is in similar terms to the offence of attempted unlawful eviction *and* harassment 2. Damages are assessed as the difference between:

'(a) the value of the interest of the landlord . . . determined on the assumption that the residential occupier continues to have the same right to occupy the premises as before that time; and
(b) the value of the interest determined on the assumption that the residential occupier has ceased to have that right.' (s. 28(1))

The general principle is that the damages compensate the residential occupier for the landlord's profit from the eviction. However, the level of compensation can be mitigated by the conduct of the occupier where this is reasonable. In Parliamentary debates it was suggested that 'The conduct of a tenant will have to be very bad indeed for a court to decide that it is reasonable to mitigate damages that are clearly designed as a penalty for committing an unlawful act' (HC Debs, col 392 (9 November 1988)). In *Regalgrand Ltd* v. *Dickerson* (1997) 29 HLR 620, the landlords changed the locks on the door whilst the tenants were moving out. They claimed £707 arrears of rent and the tenants counterclaimed for unlawful eviction. Statutory damages assessed at £12,000 were reduced by £10,500 by the judge, and upheld on appeal, because the tenants were in arrears of rent. This could hardly be described as 'very bad' conduct, or certainly not such as to reduce the level of damages so significantly. It now appears that conduct does not have to be related to the landlord-tenant relationship. In *Osei-Bonsu* v. *Wandsworth LBS* [1999] 1 All ER 265, the Court of Appeal held that the plantiff's violence to his wife, which eventually led to an unlawful eviction by the council, was conduct which could reduce the level of damages.

The purpose of the new procedure was that it was designed as 'an important additional deterrent to harassment' (DoE, 1987, para. 3.17). Considerable problems have, however, arisen over the valuation for the purpose of assessing the level of damages. For example, in *Jones* v. *Miah* (1993) 26 HLR 60, four different sets of valuers were instructed and each interpreted the formula incorrectly (according to the Court of Appeal). In the beginning, this meant that the level of damages awarded was often rather high. However, more recently, two Court of Appeal decisions have removed the deterrent effect of this statutory remedy in most situations in which unlawful eviction and harassment occur (according to the Milner Holland report – i.e. multiple occupation and where the level of security is low).

In *Melville* v. *Burton* (1997) 29 HLR 319, M was a tenant of premises that also contained two other tenants. M was unlawfully evicted and, at first instance, was awarded £15,000. In the valuation, no account was taken of the presence of other occupiers. In the Court of Appeal, it was held that the proper basis for valuation was a 'factual' as opposed to a 'notional' basis ('otherwise that which the landlord is ordered to pay to the tenant is not the value of the profit occasioned by his wrong but a fine which may be far greater'). This meant that the damages reflected the market value of the property with *all the occupiers* less the market value without the complainant. In multiply occupied property, the difference in value will be minimal.

This was expanded upon in *King* v. *Jackson* (1998) 30 HLR 539. K was let a flat on an assured shorthold tenancy and was unlawfully evicted six days before her interest came to an end. At first instance, K was granted £11,000 damages. The Court of Appeal found that such an amount for being deprived of six days occupation was 'manifestly wrong' and the amount was in fact 'extremely small'. K was granted £1500 damages, but for breach of the covenant of quiet enjoyment. It also seems that as an assured shorthold can be terminated after two months notice, the level of damages would be minimal in *all* cases outside the original term of the tenancy.

The reasoning in *Melville* (which can, on this point, all be found at p. 325) provides an important counterbalance to the original legislative purpose of providing an important deterrent against such actions. It was argued by counsel for the plaintiff that where a property has ten tenants, it would make nonsense of the law if each of the first nine tenants were to receive nominal damages but the tenth 'would scoop the pool'. All that could be offered against that argument was the belief that it would be as 'incongruous' if each of the ten tenants was to claim full damages. However, one can surely posit that this was precisely the intention of Parliament, for how else could the section provide an effective deterrent?

It was then argued that the background to the sections was that it was enacted at the 'height of the property boom' to counteract the incentive that landlords had to 'winkle out inconvenient tenants whose presence was preventing their making large profits'. Whilst this was found to be 'persuasive' by the Court, the next step in the argument did not find favour. That step required the Court to 'ensure that the legislation continues to provide real protection to tenants, real deterrence to landlords'.

The Court found that three opposing arguments counterbalanced the position. First, Courts should not make assumptions about meanings because of some such 'extraneous and supervening reason'. Parliamentary intention, then, is irrelevant here (even though it might be observed that such intention is relevant where it suits the Court). The second reason is more bizarre, for the Court, totally oblivious to the evidence, makes the following startling anti-empirical proposition: 'in the much changed conditions that now obtain, the incentive to landlords to evict tenants is much reduced indeed, it is difficult to see why in the ordinary case a landlord should wish to evict a tenant at a rack rent who is paying his rent.' Surely, also, the reason why a landlord commits the civil wrong is irrelevant on the damages issue – it is the fact of unlawful eviction and/or harassment which creates the right to damages. The third reason was that there was no reason to think that the Act was meant to provide all tenants with substantial damages – 'had that been the intention some means of calculation not dependent on changing values would have been adopted'.

Such a statement rather begs the question as to the relevant method of assessing the damages (include all the other occupiers or not?). Finally:

> 'It is legitimate to reflect that, whereas during the property boom [the other civil law] rights were perceived to provide an inadequate deterrent to wrongful eviction, the position may well be different in the current climate. It should also be remembered that harassment and wrongful eviction are criminal offences.'

One might respond by asking why, if they are criminal offences, the level of damages is so paltry? (Melville was awarded £500 – not the £15,000 awarded in the County Court).

There is an important practical consequence of the decision to restrict the level of damages in this way. In *Tinker* v. *Potts* Unreported, Court of Appeal, 30 July 1996, the sole question for the Court was whether the damages likely to be awarded exceeded £5,000. If it was less, then the case would be referred to the small claims procedure in the County Court at which point the award of legal aid would stop. The small claims procedure essentially involves arbitration between the parties which, in many of these cases that involve personal disputes, does not appear satisfactory (although it has been promised to reduce the £5,000 limit, this has not yet occurred). Thus, in many cases where this award has been supposed to provide an effective deterrent to landlords, it appears perversely to *give landlords a licence to commit the tortious wrong itself.*

Conclusion

In this chapter, I have sought to provide a contextual analysis of the criminal and the statutory civil laws affecting unlawful eviction and harassment. I have shown how, despite these acts being crimes, they are not effectively punished; nor is the occupier effectively compensated through the statutory tort. It appears that the wheels of the criminal system are induced to start in few cases and these are mostly cases in which the landlord is pursuing a moral claim against the occupier as opposed to seeking to profit from their actions (as Rachman did). Those prosecuted tend to 'lack financial resources and legal competence', reflecting a class bias which can be found more broadly in non-police prosecutions. The reasons for this can be found by considering the advice given to local authorities, as well as more broadly in the literature concerning non-police prosecutions. It may well be that there is a systemic belief that landlords are seeking to recover *their* property, assuming that ownership is matched by the desire to protect the rights that flow out of it. Whichever motive is dominant, the result is that the criminal system is hardly ever employed. The civil courts have seen to it that the statutory remedy for unlawful eviction and harassment is hardly compensatory.

Further Reading

On the law, the major text is D. Carter & A. Dymond (1998), *Quiet Enjoyment*, London: LAG; otherwise all the major texts and Encyclopaediae cover the relevant provisions; additionally, J. Hill (1986), 'Section 1 of the Protection from Eviction Act 1977: the meaning of "occupation"', *Conveyancer and Property Lawyer* 265, provides a useful analysis. On non-police prosecutions, other than the texts referred to here, readers might consider the following: B. Hutter (1988), *The Reasonable Arm of the Law?*, Oxford: Clarendon; G. Richardson (1983), *Policing Pollution*, Oxford: Clarendon; W. Carson (1970), 'White-collar crime and the enforcement of factory legislation', vol 10, *British Journal of Criminology*, 383; F. Pearce & S. Tombs, 'Ideology, hegemony and empiricism: compliance theories of regulation', vol 30, *British Journal of Criminology*, 423, and Hawkins' response at p. 444. For a useful theoretical discussion of the role of prosecutors, see J. Fionda (1995), *Public Prosecutors and Discretion*, Oxford: Clarendon.

Endnotes

1. Rachman tended to introduce prostitutes and black people, taking advantage of the wider societal prejudice against both.
2. What follows is a summary of Nelken's findings: 1983, Ch. 4.
3. This has caused problems in cases where the landlord is not in the country: see, for example, *Sampson* v. *Wilson* (1997) 29 HLR 18.

Bibliography

Ashworth, A. (1978), 'Protecting the home through criminal law', *Journal of Social Welfare Law*, 76–85

Bevan, M., Kemp, P. and Rhodes, D. (1995), *Private Landlords and Housing Benefit*, York: Centre for Housing Policy, University of York

Birks, P. (1989), *An Introduction to the Law of Restitution*, Oxford: Oxford University Press

Bridges, L. and Forbes, D. (1990), *Making the Law Work against Racial Harassment*, London: LAG

Burrows, L. and Hunter, N. (1990), *Forced Out! Harassment and Illegal Eviction*, London: Shelter

Carter, D. and Dymond, A. (1998), *Quiet Enjoyment*, London: Legal Action Group

Cotterell, R. (1992), *The Sociology of Law*, London: Butterworths

Cowan, D. (1997), *Homelessness: The (In-)Appropriate Applicant*, Aldershot: Dartmouth

Cranston, R. (1979), *Regulating Business: Law and Consumer Agencies*, London: Macmillan

Department of the Environment (DoE) (1987), *Housing: the Government's Proposals*, Cm 214, London; HMSO

Department of the Environment (DoE) (1989), 'Housing Act 1988: Protection of Residential Occupiers', Circular 3/89, London: DoE

Department of the Environment (DoE) (1991), *Homelessness Code of Practice for Local Authorities*, London: HMSO

Department of the Environment (DoE) (1996), *Code of Guidance on Parts VI and VII of the Housing Act 1996*, London: DoE

Felstiner, W., Abel, R. and Saret, A. (1981), 'The emergence and transformation of disputes', vol 15, *Law and Society Review*, 631

Francis, H. (1971), *Report of the Committee on the Rent Acts*, Cmnd 4609, London: HMSO

Hawkins, K. (1984), *Environment and Enforcement*, Oxford: Oxford University Press

Hunter, C. and McGrath, S. (1994), *Quiet Enjoyment*, London: Legal Action Group

Hutter, B. (1989), 'Variations in regulatory enforcement styles', vol 11(2), *Law and Policy*, 153–174

Jew, P. (1994), *Law and Order in Private Rented Housing: Tackling Harassment and Illegal Eviction*, London: Campaign for Bedsit Rights

Kemp, P. (1992), 'The ghost of Rachman', in C. Grant (ed.), *Built to Last?*, London: Roof

Milner Holland (1965), *Report of the Committee on Housing in Greater London*, Cmnd 2605, London: HMSO

Morgan, J. (1996), 'The casualization of housing', vol 18, *Journal of Social Welfare and Family Law*, 445

Morley, R. and Mullender, A. (1992), 'Hype or hope? The importance of pro-arrest policies and batterers' programmes from North America to Britain as key measures for preventing violence against women in the home', vol 6, *International Journal of Law and the Family*, 265

Nelken, D. (1983), *The Limits of the Legal Process – A Study of Landlords, Law and Crime*, London: Academic Press

Rauta, S. and Pickering, R. (1992), *Private Renting in England 1990*, London: HMSO

Rex, J. and Moore, R. (1967), *Race, Community and Conflict*, Oxford: Oxford University Press

Sanders, A. (1996), 'Prosecution in common law jurisdictions', in A. Sanders (ed.), *Prosecution in Common Law Jurisdictions*, Aldershot: Dartmouth

Sanders, A. and Young, R. (1994), *Criminal Justice*, London: Butterworths

Snider, L. (1990), 'Co-operative models and corporate crime: panacea or cop-out?', vol 36, *Crime & Delinquency*, 373

16 Domestic Violence and the Regulation of Occupation Rights

There were an estimated 835,000 incidents of 'domestic' violence in 1997 (Home Office, 1998a), and it is also known that this type of crime is considerably under-reported. Further, there are different interpretations of the sorts of actions which fit within the compass of domestic violence. The Law Commission has suggested that violence is employed in two different ways: first, it is used to describe the use or threat of physical force; second, there is a broader meaning which extends to 'any form of physical, sexual, or psychological molestation or harassment which has a serious detrimental effect upon the health and well-being of the victim' (1992, para. 2.3). In many cases, domestic violence occurs as part of 'controlling behaviours' by the perpetrator, 'an ongoing strategy of intimidation, isolation, and control that extends to all areas of a woman's life' (Stark, 1995; cited in Kaganas & Piper, 1999, p. 188).

The government's response to the welter of cases of domestic violence has exposed a contradiction in its family policy 'in terms of [government's] commitment to push through policies bolstering the traditional family versus its desire to be seen to be strongly opposed to violence and abuse, and protective of women not only in the traditional conservative way, but also in a more up-to-date fashion (and fashion it may well be)' (Hague & Malos, 1994, p. 112). Spiralling concern about domestic violence impacts upon the promotion of the family as the ideal household. So, when the Home Secretary Jack Straw issued a White Paper entitled *Supporting Families* in 1998, he began it with the argument that: 'Family life is the foundation on which our communities, our society and our country are built. Families are central to the Government's vision of a modern and decent society' (Home Office, 1998b, p. 2). This conflicts with what appears to be regarded as the proper role of government – or rather, it is clearly believed that government's should not be 'interfering in family life' (*ibid*, p. 3).

This contradiction was exposed when the Conservative government first put their version of the Law Commission's draft Family Homes and Domestic Violence Bill before Parliament in 1995. The Bill was presumed uncontroversial. The previous civil remedies against domestic violence were a mish-mash of different statutory provisions and common law additions, which differentially applied depending upon the parties' previous relationship as well as the type of court to which an application was made. The 1995 Bill was to provide a single, coherent body of law applying to all persons in some kind of family relationship. Under the banner 'How could MPs fail to spot this blow to marriage', William Oddie argued in the *Daily Mail* (1995) that the Bill was biased in favour of cohabitees because they would gain new rights to a share of their partner's property, as well as remedies for domestic violence. Even though Oddie's appreciation of the Bill was inadequate, his article swayed a number of Conservative MPs who, bearing in mind the then small Conservative majority, had considerable power in determining what was and was not acceptable legislation.

A slightly amended version of that Bill became enacted in the Family Law Act 1996. The new Act enables a person to gain a 'non-molestation' order against an 'associated person' (usually with a power of arrest where the order is breached), or to gain an occupation order which affects the occupation of a particular property. Occupation orders are generally based upon the applicant's interest in the property concerned. Thus, this particular branch of the civil remedies for domestic violence depend not upon the violation of the woman but upon the type of rights which the woman has in the property as identified through the normal principles of property and family law. After all, as the Law Commission put it, 'the grant of an occupation order can severely restrict the enjoyment of property rights' (1992, para. 4.7).

Redefining occupation rights is, perhaps, an unusual arena for housing law; one into which it has been forced by popular opinion, as well as an appreciation of the housing consequences of domestic violence. It is an unusual arena for housing law because only in isolated instances does it seek to regulate the occupation rights of households between themselves (a further example is the regulation of succession to statutory tenancies). In this part of the book, housing law is generally regarded as affecting the rights and obligations of households in their external relationships with the state, landlord and mortgage lender. The role of housing law here is partly as regulator of the occupants' relationship *inter se* or between themselves, partly as a mechanism through which affected persons can be rehoused temporarily and permanently (through the homelessness legislation and housing register particularly), and also as one crucial part of a multi-agency approach to tackling domestic violence. It is true that the usual enforcement role of housing law also plays a part – for example, the perpetrator might be evicted by their landlord (ss. 145 & 149, Housing Act 1996) and found *intentionally homeless* in any subsequent application to a local authority; or where the couple were joint tenants (as opposed to tenants in common),[1] one of the joint tenants is entitled to terminate the tenancy (*Hammersmith and Fulham LBC* v. *Monk* [1992] 1 AC 478; see also *Newlon Housing Trust* v. *Alsulamein* (1998) 30 HLR 1132).

The provision of temporary and permanent housing itself has been regarded as a crucial tool in enabling a person to cope with the effects of domestic violence. The beginning of the social movement dealing with violence against women was linked with the provision of refuge accommodation – temporary accommodation providing a haven for women away from the violence (Dobash & Dobash, 1992, p. 12). Safe, secure accommodation in the long run is a critical requirement of those seeking to escape the violence (*ibid*; Hague & Malos, 1993) and 'its absence a chief obstacle to escaping violence', 'it ranks as one of the crucial factors affecting women's ability to find viable alternatives to a violence relationship' (Dobash & Dobash, 1992, pp. 66 & 93).

Yet, as we saw in Part II of this book, women commonly have considerably more problems than men in finding accommodation. This partly reflects women's economic dependence upon men (in Gilroy's phrase, 'first the prince, then the palace': 1994) and partly this also occurs because women's histories are not believed: 'Women's accounts of violence are frequently not believed or taken seriously, their own behaviour is often pathologised, and loopholes are often found by which to exclude or defer their claims (e.g. for rehousing)' (Hooper, 1996, p. 151). These twin modern facets also provide the justification for housing law's involvement in regulating the occupation of the parties. If women are more marginalized in their labour/housing relations than men, it follows that women should have greater entitlement to occupy the home. Logically also, the interest which the parties have in their property should also be irrelevant, as should the format of the parties' relationship (married or cohabiting). That the law is not this neutral says more about our lawmakers than about providing a rational, coherent response to domestic violence.

In this chapter, we will consider the role and value of the legal process(es) in seeking to regulate housing rights in these circumstances. We will also consider the tenure movements of women after they leave violent relationships. In particular, the role of the homelessness legislation in facilitating this process will be considered.

The fragmentation of this chapter into three parts (criminal, civil, rehousing) should not be mistaken for a fragmentation in the practical consequences of domestic violence. Often, all three occur together – indeed, rehousing might not occur without criminal and civil sanctions being pursued. Furthermore, legal and other practitioners within these areas have commonly begun to work together through the development of inter-agency initiatives (protocols, joint working and the like) with varying degrees of success (Hague *et al.*, 1996; Women's Unit, 1998, paras 2.1–2.19). The Home Office encouraged police forces to develop such networks in a 1990 Circular (60/1990) and a follow-up Circular was specifically designed to encourage such networks (Home Office, 1995). Inter-agency working, part of the current policy *zeitgeist*, forms a crucial part of the attempts by the state to control domestic violence.

16.1 Criminal Law

Violence is a crime. That the violence involved here is 'domestic' (whatever that may mean) does not, or should not, affect the approach of criminal law. Nevertheless, it is tolerably clear that, until recently, the police tended to treat domestic violence less seriously than other crimes because of its domestic attachment. The fact of the criminal law was commonly less than the reality. As a Home Office Circular put it, 'The Home Secretary regards a violent assault or brutal and threatening behaviour over a period of time by a person to whom the victim is married, or with whom the victim lives or has lived, as seriously as a violent assault by a stranger' (Circular 60/1990, p. 1). The Home Secretary had been forced into outlining these comparators because of the ways in which the police dealt with cases of domestic violence. The police commonly 'no-crimed' cases of domestic violence. That is, domestic violence was treated as a matter between partners and not one in which the police should intrude. Thus, no action would be taken in these cases and the crime would not be recorded (see Sanders, 1988).

The same Circular exhorted the police to adopt a more proactive approach, making the point that:

> 'Experience in other countries suggests that the arrest of an alleged assailant *may act as a powerful deterrent against his reoffending – at least for some time – and it is an important means of showing the victim that she is entitled to, and will receive, society's protection and support.*' (para. 16; emphasis added)

The importation of pro-arrest policies from the USA, under which police officers are required to arrest the perpetrator, whether or not the victim is reluctant to take such a step, have radically changed the way in which the police deal with cases of domestic violence (for discussion, see Morley & Mullender, 1992). These policies have, however, proved controversial. Leading commentators have denounced them as being based upon a 'naive belief in the individual deterrent effect of arrests' and they assume 'that victims have little agency and that the police and policy makers know what is best for them' (Hoyle & Sanders, 1999). Indeed, Hoyle & Sanders' research data suggest that the police are called not because of a desire to see the perpetrator prosecuted but because:

> 'most women who call the police wish to be separated, albeit sometimes temporarily, from the offender. Arrest is sought by many of these women only if it is necessary to achieve their goal of temporary or permanent separation.'

The police response has been variable. In Nottinghamshire, for example, it was estimated that 2,567 domestic violence reports were called in to police stations over a two-year period, but only 302 calls were recorded as involving domestic violence. It seems that decisions to charge a perpetrator were most closely related to the severity of the violence, the presence of a 'mitigating factor', and the nature of the relationship between the two parties (Wright, 1998, pp. 404–5).

Pro-arrest policies are not successful on their own. Hoyle and Sanders argue in favour of a 'victim empowerment' model in which the victim is put in a position in which they are able, as far as possible, to take an objective view about what is best for themselves. Such a model is based upon our understanding that domestic violence often occurs after, or as part of, *controlling behaviours* by the male partner (Dobash *et al.*, 1996; Hoyle & Sanders, 1999). These controlling behaviours often involve isolating the victim from their networks and threatening retaliation if arrested/prosecuted. Hoyle and Sanders argue that arresting the perpetrator should be only part of the equation, and that the victim also needs to have a new support network on which to draw (such as a domestic violence unit, which many police forces have).

Hague and Malos argue that the government's pro-arrest 'solution' was inspired more by cost-saving than other motivations, because the more comprehensive services required (such as funding temporary and permanent accommodation) have been subject to chronic underfunding (1994, p. 117). It is cheaper to arrest somebody than to fund further temporary accommodation. The funding balance has been tipped in favour of police action (including through the domestic violence unit) and against the funding of civil legal aid or refuge bedspaces. In 1975, it was estimated by the Select Committee on Violence in Marriage that one refuge bedspace would be needed for every 10,000 of the population; by 1995, less than one-third of the required bedspaces had been created (see Hague *et al.*, 1995, p. 1; House of Commons Home Affairs Committee, 1992, para. 129). Thus, the criminal law has been used, as a matter of expediency, to provide temporary respite – a *housing* 'solution'. Developing this approach will, in itself, involve a manipulation of occupation rights as the violent partner becomes excluded from the home by virtue of their involvement in criminal processes.

16.2   Civil Law

The civil law was reworked in the Family Law Act 1996 so as to provide a comprehensive range of remedies within a single statute. It provides for two remedies: a non-molestation order (s. 42), which operates in a similar vein to an injunction and prohibits the molestation of one person by another; an occupation order, which regulates the occupation of a property. The new law was first suggested by the Law Commission (1992), and was partially reformulated after the abortive attempt to introduce it in 1995. This new law provides an alternative to the use of the criminal law, which many women are unhappy using:

'From the point of view of the woman experiencing the abuse, it may seem preferable to apply for protection in the civil courts rather than to give evidence in a criminal prosecution of her partner. Firstly, the process seems to be more under her control: she instructs the solicitor, who will represent her in court, or will instruct a barrister on her behalf. Secondly, in most cases the hearing will be in a closed court or the Judge's chambers, and there will be no publicity. Thirdly, her partner will not acquire a criminal record, which could hamper his employment prospects and hence indirectly affect the economic situation of the woman and her children.' (Barron & Harwin, 1992, para. 8.3)

The civil law thus compliments the woman's need, and often is more in tune with them than is the criminal law. However, it may well be that the provision of legal aid to those entitled may not be forthcoming whilst criminal proceedings are ongoing. The benefit of the civil law in such cases may only be hypothetical when the woman is unable to afford such action.

In this section, our concern is not only to extrapolate upon and provide a critique of the law, but also to consider the systemic failings of the legal system in providing adequate protection to women in these circumstances. Whilst the remedies are newly incorporated into legislation, much of the previous empirical research findings remain relevant. As the Law Commission itself accepted, 'legal remedies can be undermined by the gap which exists between the letter and spirit of the law and the law in practice' (1992, para. 2.8). So, for example, Barron (1990) found that law officers, including solicitors and barristers, can adopt unsympathetic attitudes to women seeking protection from violence, or may not know the law, all of which operate to *deter* women from pursuing civil law remedies. Under the previous law, it was, for example, common for the woman to be advised to accept an undertaking from a violent partner that no further violence would occur, and the woman would be asked to give a cross-undertaking (thus penalizing the woman for the acts of her partner). Furthermore, no power of arrest can be attached to an undertaking, which meant they commonly went unenforced. On one view, the use of undertakings should not be so common after the new Act (Murphy, 1996);[2] on another view, undertakings were regarded as the norm prior to the 1996 Act and there is no evidence that this will change (Bird, 1995). Whatever the picture, such an example shows the way law officers would (unconsciously) act against the interests of the woman – rather than pursuing civil law actions, many were left with an unsuitable and unenforced 'undertaking'.

Non-molestation Orders

A non-molestation order is to be granted to prohibit the perpetrator from 'molesting [a woman] who is associated with the [perpetrator]' or any 'relevant child'[3] (s. 42). In deciding whether to grant the order, the court must consider 'all the circumstances including the need to secure the health, safety and well-being' of the applicant or relevant child (s. 46(5)). An 'associated' person refers to 'spouses, cohabitants and a curious list' of other persons (Hayes, 1996) including those who have lived in the same household, relatives, and fiances (s. 62(3)). Cohabitants refers only to a man and woman living together and does *not* apply to same sex couples (who are nevertheless able to apply if they live, or have lived, in the same household). A non-molestation order may be granted in an emergency without the perpetrator being given notice of the proceedings (*ex parte*): s. 45.

Research considering the effect of the types of orders granted under the previous regime showed that they were breached at least once in more than 50 per cent of cases (Barron, 1990). Commonly, there would be little enforcement of the orders by the police and courts so that the orders were 'not worth the paper they were written on' (*ibid*). The 1996 Act attempts to surmount this obstacle by effectively presuming that a power of arrest will be attached to non-molestation orders where the perpetrator 'has used or threatened violence' against the applicant or relevant child.

However, there remains some residual concern as to whether the power of arrest will, in fact, be attached to most orders. Some problems include, for example, the belief that powers of arrest should be confined to 'serious cases' (Law Commission, 1992, para. 5.15); the provision only applies where there has been some actual or threatened violence; the presumption does not apply in relation to *ex parte* applications; also, the power of arrest will not be attached where the applicant will be adequately protected without such a power (Diduck & Kaganas, forthcoming). Even when a power of arrest is attached, an order does not guarantee that the perpetrator will comply with it. Thus, many of the concerns about enforcement remain in place (together with the more general concerns such as solicitors' knowledge, willingness to accept undertakings, legal aid funding).

Occupation Orders

An occupation order can be granted to serve 'two broad functions' in relation to a property occupied by the woman and a person 'associated':

> 'First, they can be obtained to secure for the applicant . . . the right to enter and occupy a dwelling house, or part of a dwelling house, which is, or has been, her home. Alternatively they can be used to exclude or restrict the rights of the [perpetrator] to occupy or come near the home in relation to which the order is made.' (Murphy, 1996, pp. 846–7)

These orders are granted on different criteria depending upon two variables: the nature of the applicant's property interest, if any, and the nature of the relationship between the applicant and the perpetrator. *Neither of these variables depends upon the way the victim experiences the violence nor the effects of the violence.* Rather, they reflect the concerns of property lawyers (that ownership rights should not be expropriated) and moralists (that marriage means that the parties are more committed to each other).

The legal concern was to balance the rights of the victim with the rights of the perpetrator: 'The grant of an occupation order can severely restrict the enjoyment of property rights, . . . Such consequences may be acceptable when both parties are entitled to occupy, but they are more difficult to justify when the applicant has no such right' (Law Commission, 1992, para. 4.7). Such a concentration on legal rights is difficult to justify. If one begins with the proposition that the ability to obtain (re-)housing depends upon factors such as disposable income (or entitlement to Housing Benefit), then it would seem more rational to begin with the proposition that the person with most difficulty in securing rehousing should be entitled to go into occupation. Instead, the Act makes resources for rehousing just one of the criteria that a court is required to consider in deciding whether to make an order (unless, as regards certain orders, the applicant or relevant child is 'likely to suffer significant harm attributable to the conduct of the [perpetrator]': ss. 33(7), 35(8), 37(4)). The other specific criteria involve an examination of the financial resources of each of the parties; the likely effect of any order 'on the health, safety or well-being of the parties'; and the conduct of the parties in relation to each other and otherwise (giving plenty of scope for the 'she asked for it' school of jurisprudence): s. 33(6)(a)–(d).

Unless the applicant has some type of property interest, the Act distinguishes between the relationship of the parties. Different criteria apply in relation to different types of relationship. *Same sex couples are completely excluded unless they have some kind of property interest* – an exclusion that can only be explained as the prejudice of MPs. Spouses are entitled as if they have a property interest (because they are entitled to occupation under the Matrimonial Homes Act 1983). This differential protection is unlikely to survive the implementation of the Human Rights Act 1998 for long.

Former spouses are entitled even if they have no property interest but they must first gain entry to the property through court order and then the court must decide to exclude or restrict the perpetrator's occupation. In order to gain access to the property, the court must consider all relevant factors a well as take into account the factors relevant where the applicant has a property interest, *as well as* the length of time that has elapsed since the parties lived together, the length of time since the marriage was legally terminated, and the existence of other matrimonial or property-related proceedings (s. 35(6)(e)–(g)). Once access has been ordered, the court must then *reconsider* the factors relevant where the applicant has a property interest as well as the length of time since they ceased to live together.

Cohabitants and former cohabitants (provided they are male and female) are entitled to an order where they have no property interest, but on different grounds from former spouses. The process, however, is the same in that the applicant must first gain access and then exclude or restrict the perpetrator's occupation rights. The court must consider all relevant factors but specifically take into account the same four factors as where the applicant has an interest *as well as* the nature of the parties' relationship, the length of time they lived together, the existence of any children, the length of time since they ceased to live together, the existence of some other proceedings. Once access has been ordered, the court must then *reconsider* the same four factors as well as whether any relevant child is likely to suffer significant harm attributable to the respondent, and whether the harm 'likely to be suffered' by the perpetrator (in making the order) is 'as great as or greater than' the harm suffered by the applicant (caused by the violence). The final comparative exercise requires a hypothetical future to be compared against past acts, a not entirely simple exercise.

In particular with cohabitants and former cohabitants, the court is required to consider the 'nature of the parties' relationship' where one cohabitant is solely entitled to the property (s. 36(6)(e)). When considering that factor, the court is required to 'have regard to the fact that they have not given each other the commitment involved in marriage' (s. 41(2)). Quite how that affects the matter is unclear. Indeed, most commentators suggest that s. 41(2) will have limited impact. On the other hand, its presence in the Act clearly delimits Parliamentary intention to provide orders depending upon the differential 'quality' of relationships.

The existence of property interests and the nature of the parties' relationship are also relevant in relation to the length of the orders. Where the applicant has a property interest (or is married to the perpetrator), the order can last for as long as the court directs (s. 33(10)). Where the parties *were* married, the order can only last for six months but may be extended for successive six month periods (s. 35(10)). Where the parties were cohabiting, the order will last for six months but can only be extended for one further six month term (s. 36(10)). Thus, in terms of the criteria before an order is granted as well as in the duration of the order, the scope of the Act clearly favours those who marry.

Whatever the nature of the relationship or property interests of the parties, it has proved extremely difficult for an applicant to gain an occupation order (in its previous incarnations) (see, for example, Bull, 1995, p. 14). Even so, an application for an occupation order may not even be made as a result of the controlling behaviours of the perpetrator. Drawing upon data partly derived from women fleeing domestic violence, Bull found:

'. . . most of those fleeing violence did not stay and did not return home at a later time. Although they often expressed reluctance to leave what had been their home, they rarely had aspirations to return because of fear of reprisals from their ex-partner. The degree of fear felt by some respondents was so great that they had felt it necessary to move out of the area they had lived in with their partner, even if this meant isolation from family support networks.' (Bull, 1993, para. 2.36)

Bull notes that 'there was a striking lack of confidence' in the legal system amongst her respondents (para. 2.38). Such a lack of confidence may well be compounded by local authority housing departments requiring women to seek legal remedies before offering alternative housing and refusing to provide housing where the applicant is successful; where the woman does not wish to pursue civil legal remedies, or is unsuccessful, the housing department may, in a dreadful Catch-22, regard the woman as not homeless or as intentionally so.

16.3   Housing/Home Law

Regulating Occupation

Housing law provides mechanisms regulating the occupation of property after acts of violence. There are differences between home ownership and renting (in whatever tenure) – a point of some contention within the theme of this part of the book – although the main point of distinction is derived from the different ways in which the sectors are financed. The practical application may well differ, also depending upon the type of landlord involved.

The clearest method occurs where two or more persons hold a joint tenancy under a rental agreement. In such circumstances, it has been held since 1982 that one of the joint tenants is entitled to terminate the tenancy, provided that a notice is correctly served (*Greenwich LBC* v. *McGrady* (1982) 6 HLR 36; *Hammersmith & Fulham LBC* v. *Monk* [1992] 1 AC 478). In order to justify such a result, the House of Lords in *Monk* sought to rely on the *contractual* effect of the tenancy (which rather went against the grain of previous judgments in which the property law element of the tenancy had been placed uppermost).

The *McGrady* principle is well known and is practised by social landlords. Many local authorities and RSLs require their tenants (and others seeking rehousing) to take advantage of the principle in order to qualify for rehousing (see, for example, Cowan, 1997, pp. 130–1). This does not appear to be a universal demand but, if the opportunity is not taken, the woman conceivably could be saddled with two obligations to pay housing costs, in respect of her former and current home (as joint tenancies imply an obligation on either or both parties for the whole rent).

Alternatively, a public or private landlord might employ the new ground for eviction added to the relevant legislation by the Housing Act 1996 (ss. 145 & 149). Originally, this ground was designed to avoid the situation where the remaining partner *underoccupied* the property, the ground now enables the landlord to evict the remaining partner (once again, this does not apply to same sex couples) where the other partner has left 'because of violence or threats of violence' and the court is satisfied that the other partner is unlikely to return. The use of such a provision is currently unknown, although private landlords are most unlikely to use it if the rent remains paid; other landlords are unlikely to use it where other grounds are also available (particularly as all landlords must show that possession is also reasonable).

For women fleeing a property which is subject to a mortgage, the position is rather different. The only obligations on lenders are to serve a notice on the woman prior to seeking possession (although this only applies to former spouses and not to cohabitants or same sex couples): s. 56. Payments to lenders by one spouse, who has no legal relationship with the lender,[4] in respect of a matrimonial home are regarded as the payments of the borrower spouse (s. 30(3); once again this does not apply to cohabitants or same sex couples). The only payments to lenders by unmarried cohabitants that the lender is bound to accept occur during the period of an occupation order under the Family Law Act 1996 (s 36(13)). Apparently, *no* mortgage lender has a policy or practice in respect of domestic violence. Lenders are known to refuse to accept payments from women who have fled. The Halifax Building Society is reputed to send all correspondence, including notice of increases in interest rates, to the person whose name appears first on the mortgage document (which is usually the man within the Halifax's policy) (see Taylor, 1998).

Rehousing

Whilst women may seek rehousing in the private rented sector, it appears that the most common subsequent accommodation of women fleeing violence is in the 'social' sector. Of those moving out of women's refuges in Wales during 1990–1, just 3.4 per cent moved on to accommodation in the private sector (Charles, 1994, p. 41). Other research shows that women are more likely to move out of the private sector on relationship breakdown (Bull, 1995). This tallies with knowledge of mortgage lending patterns and landlord perceptions of tenants. Accessing the 'social' sector after violence commonly involves the applicant proving their genuineness to the local authority or RSL. Cowan's research found that local authority homeless persons units commonly put 'threshold tests' in the way of applicants:

> 'The proportion of female applicants claiming violence, the perception that such claims were sometimes not genuine and the system was being abused, (in some cases) the belief that successful applicants sometimes return to their violent partners, all militated in favour of placing further obstacles (or gatekeeping techniques) in the way of applicants. This was not always the case, but even in authorities with relatively "generous" policies, where it was believed that an applicant was abusing the system these obstacles would arise in an ad hoc way.' (Cowan, 1997, p. 126)

More subtle techniques are commonly employed by some homeless persons units, which require applicants claiming violence to be told that they are entitled to seek civil remedies and that this might be their best option (because the authority will be unable to match the quality of their previous accommodation and/or it will take some time before the accommodation is to be provided). The 'gut feeling' of officers about applicants' truthfulness is commonly found to be a key element in decision-making practices, particularly in respect of domestic violence (see Loveland, 1995; Thornton, 1989; Malos & Hague, 1993).

The homelessness legislation was updated, in line with the Family Law Act 1996, so that a person is *automatically* homeless if it is probable that their continued occupation of accommodation will lead to domestic violence from an associated person (ss 177–8, Housing Act 1996). Despite this change, single women are still required to 'fit within' either an emergency category or, rather more debilitating, to be regarded as 'vulnerable' in order to gain priority need. Even then, although rare these days, it is not unheard of for a woman to be found intentionally homeless after fleeing domestic violence (particularly if she is entitled to gain an occupation order): see, for example, Binney *et al.*, 1981.

Conclusion

The domestic violence laws and practice(s) reflect society's prejudice. Pro-arrest policies adopted by the police are regarded as being imposed upon women, without an appreciation of what individuals may require ('It seems presumptuous that policy makers or the feminist advocates who have influenced them can easily determine what is best for, or in the interests of, a diverse group of battered women': Hoyle & Sanders, 1999). The civil law has been drafted on the basis that supremacy is given to the format of the parties' relationship as well as the different interests which the parties have in the property. The nature and degree of violence, unless likely to cause significant harm, is not relevant; and the relative resources of the parties only one factor to be taken into account. Housing law has methods at its disposal to regulate occupation rights, but this depends upon the policies/practices or whim of the landlord, and not upon the individual circumstances. Rehousing in the local authority and RSL sectors is fraught with hidden catches. It is nevertheless correct to argue that the law in this area is better than it was, but how much better remains an open question.

Further Reading

Family law textbooks detail the relevant laws on domestic violence; see S. Cretney (1997), *Family Law*, London: Sweet & Maxwell; B. Hoggett, D. Pearl and P. Bates (1996), *The Family, Law and Society: Cases and Materials*, London: Butterworths; S. Lowe (1998), *Bromley's Family Law*, London: Butterworths. On the provisions of the 1995 Bill, see A. Kewley (1996), 'Pragmatism before principle: the limitations of civil law remedies for the victims of domestic violence', vol 18, *Journal of Social Welfare and Family Law*, 1. There are many other academic articles and other texts in this field. Readers may care to consult some or all of the following: N. Charles (1995), 'Feminist politics, domestic violence and the state', *Sociological Review*, 617; N. Charles (1994), 'The housing needs of women and children escaping domestic violence', vol 23, *Journal of Social Policy* 465; S. Grace (1995), *Policing Domestic Violence in the 1990s*, Home Office Research Study 139, London: HMSO; S. Maguire (1989), '"Sorry love" – violence against women in the home and the state response', vol 23, *Critical Social Policy*, 34; J. Pahl (ed) (1985), *Private Violence and Public Policy*, London: Routledge; S. Edwards (1996), *Sex and Gender in the Legal Process*, London: Blackstone; C. Smart (1989), *Feminism and the Power of Law*, London: Routledge.

Housing law texts in this area generally discuss relationship breakdown more generally – see L. Moroney & K. Harris (1997), *Relationship Breakdown and Housing: A Practical Guide*, London: Shelter; D. Hughes & S. Lowe (1995), *Social Housing Law and Policy*, London: Butterworths; there are texts discussing the *McGrady* line of authority, of which see, for example, A. Arden (1997), 'From Greenwich to Harrow: a trip down memory lane', vol 1, *Journal of Housing Law*, 3; on the potential effects of the government's 1994 Consultation Paper on home-lessness, see R. Morley & G. Pascall (1995), 'Women and homelessness: proposals from the Department of the Environment', vol 18, *Journal of Social Welfare and Family Law*, 327; G. Hague & E. Malos (1998), 'Facing both ways at once', in D. Cowan (ed), *Housing: Participation and Exclusion*, Aldershot: Dartmouth.

There is a developing literature considering the role of inter-agency initiatives: see, for example, C. Lyon (1995), in Feminist Legal Research Unit (ed), *Law and Body Politics*, Aldershot: Dartmouth; A. Kewley (1994), *The Inter-agency Response to Domestic Violence in Hull*, Hull: Humbercare.

Endnotes

1. A joint tenancy occurs where there are unity of time, title, possession and interest between two or more persons interested in property. Classically, a joint tenancy would arise where two persons signed the same tenancy agreement, guaranteeing the total rent obligation, to last for the same period for each person.
2. An undertaking will now only be accepted when no power of arrest would be added (s. 46(3)). However, there is a presumption that a power of arrest will be attached in all cases in which the perpetrator has used or threatened violence against the woman (unless the woman will be adequately protected without such a power, which is unlikely given the belief that the police rarely enforce without such a power): s. 47(2).
3. A 'relevant' child is defined by s. 62(2).
4. Where the partners were joint borrowers, the mortgage lender must accept payments from either or both parties because the obligation of the borrowers is joint and several (where the mortgage is joint as is most likely, as opposed to being 'in common').

Bibliography

Barron, J. (1990), *Not Worth the Paper . . .?*, Women's Aid Federation, England

Barron, J. and Harwin, N. (1992), *Written Evidence to the House of Commons Home Affairs Committee Inquiry into Domestic Violence*, Women's Aid Federation, England

Binney, V., Harkell, G. and Nixon, J. (1981), *Leaving Violent Men*, Women's Aid Federation, England

Bird, R. (1995), *Domestic Violence: The New Law*, Bristol: Jordans

Bull, J. (1993), *Housing Consequences of Relationship Breakdown*, London: HMSO

Bull, J. (1995), *Relationship Breakdown*, York: Centre for Housing Policy, University of York

Charles, N. (1994), 'Domestic violence, homelessness and housing: the response of housing providers in Wales', vol 41, *Critical Social Policy*, 36

Cowan, D. (1997), *Homelessness: The (In-)Appropriate Applicant*, Aldershot: Dartmouth

Diduck, A. and Kaganas, F. (1999), *Family Law, Gender and the State*, Oxford: Hart

Dobash, R. and Dobash, R. (1992), *Women, Violence and Social Change*, London: Routledge

Dobash, R., Dobash, R., Cavanagh, K. and Lewis, R. (1996), *Research Evaluation of Programmes for Violent Men*, Edinburgh: Scottish Office

Gilroy, R. (1994), 'Women and owner-occupation in Britain: first the prince, then the palace?', in R. Gilroy and R. Woods (eds), *Housing Women*, London: Routledge

Hague, G. and Malos, E. (1993), *Domestic Violence – Action for Change*, London: New Clarion

Hague, G. and Malos, E. (1994), 'Domestic violence, social policy and housing', vol 42, *Critical Social Policy*, 112

Hague, G., Malos, E. and Dear, W. (1995), *Against Domestic Violence: Inter-agency Initiatives*, SAUS Working Paper 127, Bristol: School for Advanced Urban Studies, University of Bristol

Hague, G., Malos, E. and Dear, W. (1996), *Multi-agency Work and Domestic Violence*, Bristol: Policy Press

Hayes, M. (1996), 'Non-molestation protection: only associated persons need apply', *Family Law*, 368

Home Office (1995), *Inter-agency Circular: Inter-agency Co-ordination to Tackle Domestic Violence*, London: Home Office

Home Office (1998a), *British Crime Survey*, London: Home Office

Home Office (1998b) *Supporting Families*, London: Home Office

Hooper, C-A (1996), 'Men's violence and relationship breakdown: can violence be dealt with as an exception to the rule?', in C. Hallett (ed.), *Women and Social Policy*, Hemel Hempstead: Harvester Wheatsheaf

House of Commons Home Affairs Committee (1992), *Domestic Violence*, London: HMSO

Hoyle, C. and Sanders, A. (1999), 'Police response to domestic violence: from victim choice to victim empowerment?', *British Journal of Criminology*, forthcoming

Kaganas, F. and Piper, C. (1999), 'Divorce and domestic violence', in S. Day and C. Piper (eds), *Undercurrents of Divorce*, Aldershot: Dartmouth

Law Commission (1992), *Family Law: Domestic Violence and Occupation of the Family Home*, Report No 207, London: HMSO

Loveland, I. (1995), *Housing Homeless Persons*, Oxford: Oxford University Press

Malos, E. and Hague, G. (1993), *Domestic Violence and Housing: Local Authority Responses to Women and Children Escaping Violence in the Home*, Bristol: School of Applied Social Studies, University of Bristol

Morely, R. and Mullender, A. (1992), 'Hype or hope? The importance of pro-arrest policies and batterers' programmes from North America to Britain as key measures for preventing violence against women in the home', vol 6, *International Journal of Law and the Family*, 265

Murphy, J. (1996), 'Domestic violence: the new law', vol 59, *Modern Law Review*, 845

Oddie, W. (1995), 'How could MPs fail to spot this blow to marriage', *Daily Mail*, 5 March

Sanders, A. (1998), 'Personal violence and public order: the prosecution of 'domestic' violence in England and Wales', vol 16, *International Journal of the Sociology of Law*, 359

Stark, E. (1995), 'Re-presenting women battering: from battered women syndrome to coercive control', vol 8, *Albany Law Review*, 973

Taylor, D. (1998), 'Black, blue and in the red', *The Guardian*, 23 November

Thornton, R. (1989), 'Homelessness through relationship breakdown', vol 10, *Journal of Social Welfare Law*, 67

Women's Unit (1998), *Tackling Violence against Women – Local Authority Response on Examples of Good Practice*, London: Women's Unit

Wright, S. (1998), 'Policing domestic violence: a Nottingham case study', vol 20, *Journal of Social Welfare and Family Law*, 397

17 Recovery of Arrears: Cross-tenurial Comparisons

In 1997, 67,073 mortgage possession[1] actions were begun in the courts; 107,861 possession actions bought by 'social landlords' (local authorities and RSLs); 22,302 possession actions brought by private landlords (Lord Chancellor's Department, 1998). The number of households in arrears on mortgage repayments increased in the first half of 1998 for the first time since 1991, when repossessions by lenders peaked (Hunter, 1998). The vast majority of tenancy possession actions are brought on the basis of rent arrears (around 98 per cent according to most studies), although it is commonly suggested that landlords use this ground for possession because of difficulties in proving alternative grounds (Bridges & Forbes, 1990). By way of contrast with previous parts of this book, it is (again) important to note that the law effectively prescribes different grounds for possession between tenures. The move to cross-tenurialism has not particularly affected the possession process. Indeed, even within the different tenures, we will see that different landlords/lenders operate different policies and practices on the issue of possession.

Perhaps the most vivid example of this tenured approach to possession occurred outside the judicial process, but as part of the political discourse of home ownership. In December 1991, it was reported that the Conservative government gave mortgage lenders 48 hours to come up with appropriate rescue schemes to halt the increasing numbers of possession actions brought as a consequence of the widening recession. Afterwards, John Major announced on Desert Island Discs that the repossessions crisis was over (although, by 1993, when repossessions peaked, such a view seemed overly complacent). No similar schemes were forced upon landlords, social or otherwise, to cope with the effects of recession and, in 1998, social landlords' possessions have apparently risen to a record high (Birch, 1998).

One reason for this distinction between home ownership and other tenures may well derive from the discourse about housing debt between tenures. In a study of the content of reports about housing debt in the London *Evening Standard* in 1989, Hunter and Nixon were able to show how that newspaper differentially portrayed housing debt:

'The articles on owner-occupiers clearly acknowledge that the causes of debt must be understood in relation to economic and social structural factors. . . . All the[] images are of a group of people without fault, who are doing their best to manage in circumstances beyond their control.'

'. . . [T]he articles relating to rental debt at no point acknowledge the fact that rent arrears can be caused by the same underlying factors of unemployment, matrimonial breakdown and sudden illnesses.' (1997)

Such tenured discourse was also reflected in the ways District Judges related to different housing debtors. Borrowers were often sympathetically treated, whereas tenants 'were either victims . . . who needed protecting or as households incapable of financial management who needed to be "taught a lesson". This discourse of housing debt should be related to the discussion in Chapter 12 about the desire for home ownership, for it is in this political discourse that the artificial tenured distinctions are first drawn – the political requirement for households to seek a private solution to their housing needs is clearly reflected in the discourse and practice of possession. Equally, during the Thatcher era and beyond, the success of lenders (particularly in financing the right to buy) was reflected in their political muscle, to the extent that lenders and the government 'principally structured' the debate about possession actions (Ford, 1994, p. 238). In other words, lenders have been able to delimit the debate's confines, for example by setting out the key definitions and collating the statistics themselves: 'The way in which rent arrears are measured has the effect of maximizing their apparent levels, whereas the way in which mortgage arrears are measured minimizes their apparent levels' (Doling & Wainwright, 1989, p. 82).

By contrast to home ownership, the stigma attached to tenants in other tenures has been enhanced by the limited public debate about rent arrears. What debate there has been has emphasized the view that many tenants have sought to 'milk' the system as part of widespread Housing Benefit fraud (see, for example, DSS, 1998), or as part of the broader attack on local authorities' effectiveness as landlords (leading to financial penalties for having rent arrears above a certain level). Yet, there are real causes for concern both in the level of possession actions brought (about double that of home ownership), as well as in the procedures operated. The tenant's 'day in court' is often transmuted to the tenants' depersonalized 'two minutes in court'. The procedure, different from that which pertains to mortgage arrears, has been characterized as 'administrative' as opposed to adjudicative (Nixon & Hunter, 1998, p. 102). Carlton has argued that, despite the various legislative protections given to tenants in the 1980s, judicial proceedings have tended to apply the same principles as prior to the 1980s (1998).

The point is that the negative image of tenants' housing debt is reflected in the possession process. There is, thus, a real and considerable cause for concern that the judicial process is a simple rubber-stamping exercise, with some humiliation thrown in for good measure (see Nixon & Hunter, 1996). The mortgage possession process throws up some similar issues but the characteristics of the hearings are rather different: tenancy possession hearings are heard in open court and are often dealt with en masse; mortgage possession hearings are heard in chambers, in private, and individually. These characteristics are undoubtedly partly responsible for the differential results between tenures (although other factors, such as the nature of the lender/landlord, skew the process as well)

What is surprising about these distinctions is that the reasons borrowers and tenants get into debt often correlate – people get into housing debt for similar reasons. Why, then, should they be treated differently within the judicial process on the basis of the way they hold the property? What we are most commonly dealing with are people who are in danger of losing their home – or, in academicspeak the 'use value' – and this is *the* cross-tenurial problem. This chapter's analysis begins by taking a step back from the court procedures which characterize the formal possession process. We look at the reasons why people get into debt and consider the responses of those in power, for it is at this more informal stage that tenurial differences actually become apparent. The whole process is conducted on a tenure basis because each party has different bargaining tools, reflecting their power/bargaining position (and lack of it).

Throughout, the lender/landlord is in a strong position but in each tenure the lender/landlord's right to possession on the ground of financial arrears is inhibited in some way or other:

- So, for example, there is political pressure on lenders not to take possession of homes and to arrive at some sort of accommodation between themselves and the borrower, even though their essentially commercial operation will be affected. A commercial decision whether or not to take possession would be made on the basis of the relationship between mortgage and current market value, whether or not there is a sufficient mortgage indemnity guarantee,[2] and the impact of large-scale possession on the mortgage market. Additionally, the needs of the borrower would have to be matched with the needs of shareholders or depositors. The alternative position is reinforced by the Mortgage Code produced by the Council of Mortgage Lenders, as well as the broad political position of the lender (1998). The impact of the 1991 compact between lenders and the government provides a gauge of the importance ascribed to the issue by political parties. The New Labour manifesto promised more flexible mortgage provision in 'a world of increased job insecurity' and so the pressure remains on lenders to operate less commercial arrears strategies. The conflict between commercialism and these other factors is reflected in actual arrears management practice.
- RSLs, as we have seen (Ch. 13), now provide private-sector tenancies. Yet, their ability to take possession after rent arrears is curtailed by Regulatory Guidance from the Housing Corporation (1997; 1998), although they are faced with the competing interests of those private lenders who have financed new developments. The need to retain and enhance surpluses is an important contraindication, signalling a move towards more commercially orientated arrears programmes.
- Local authorities grant so-called secure tenancies but the current financial package that they receive from the government by way of

subsidy relies on them having less than a set percentage of rent arrears throughout their stock. Various performance indicators, which are relied on as a gauge of levels of performance, relate to rent arrears levels and these are used as part of the assessment of level of central capital grant. The importance ascribed to rent arrears by local authorities is shown by the fact that the vast majority of exclusions from the waiting list relate to rent arrears (Shelter, 1998).

- Private landlords, by way of contrast, might be expected to react to housing debt in diverse ways, reflecting landlords' different reasons for engaging in renting in the first place. The availability of Housing Benefit will often be a key determinant, as will willingness to put up with delays in processing the claim (see, for example, Bevan *et al.*, 1995; Kemp & McLaverty, 1995). The type of tenancy – assured, assured shorthold, or protected – or other occupation right may well influence any decision. Nevertheless, in general terms, one might suspect that private landlords will be more willing to begin actions for possession on the ground(s) of rent arrears than other tenurial landlords because they are not 'social landlords' and are not subject to the ethic of 'social housing'. This is an empirical question yet to be answered. The suspicion may prove unfounded because of the more commercial ethic of post-Thatcherite social housing as well as the fact that a considerable proportion of landlords are not seeking to engage in commercial letting.

These conflicting pressures are reflected in the methods used to manage levels and types of arrears. We will consider some of the more prominent methods in the opening section of this chapter.

Better arrears management was one comparatively minor part of the mortgage rescue package worked out between the government and the lenders in the 1991 compact. Three other initiatives were set up: the payment of Income Support for mortgage interest direct to lenders (as opposed to being paid to borrowers who then passed it on to the lender); mortgage rescue schemes under which home owners would sell part of the property to RSLs and/or the lender under shared-ownership schemes; possessed properties being used by RSLs to house statutory homeless households; conversion from owning to renting (see Ford & Wilcox, 1992, p. 7). In the second section, we concentrate on evaluating these initiatives, more particularly in the light of the 1995 reductions in Income Support for mortgage interest payments. These reductions were, in part, designed to stimulate a private insurance market covering risks to mortgage payments, such as unemployment and illness. It will be argued that research has shown that there are causes for concern – those most at risk of falling into arrears are most often those who have most difficulty in obtaining insurance, as well as being those most unlikely to take up the insurance.

In the third section, we move on to consider the formal, legal possession process. The different approaches to possession, based upon tenure, will be analysed. Drawing upon research conducted on the possession process, it will be argued that despite these differences the process is still skewed in favour of the landlord/lender who, once they have begun the formal legal process, can thereafter only gain through its use (together with having their costs paid by the borrower/tenant). This can be shown through a consideration of the formal law governing the process; tenant/borrower participation in the process; the perceptions of tenants/borrowers about the process; the rationales for, and readiness of, landlords/lenders in using the process; the views of District Judges, who are primarily responsible for the process; and the actual results of the legal process.

17.1   Risk of Arrears: Reasons, Levels and Management Strategies

Reasons

It is or was commonly believed that housing debt is caused by the borrower/tenant's fecklessness – that housing debt is a product of current societal *mores*:

> 'The defaulter is seen as "feckless", someone who "won't pay" rather than "can't pay". The arrears represent a "wilful" refusal by the mortgagor to meet his or her legal obligations. A more sophisticated version of the social pathology explanation would stress that defaulters lack the initiative, education and social skills (especially budgeting) to remedy their situation. In short, their value system and life style engender mortgage default.' (Doling & Stafford, 1989, p. 71; see also Duncan & Kirby, 1983, pp. 50–1).

Such views perpetuate the success of capital in its ability to reproduce itself, for prejudice against default(ers) means that most will try to avoid it. Thus, there are apocryphal stories of households virtually starving themselves so that they are able to pay the rent/mortgage (see, for example, Nixon *et al.*, 1996, p. 6).

Most studies of housing debt have found that, rather than fecklessness being the principal cause, changes in various structures have had key influences (Ford & Seavers, 1998). Most significantly, changes in the labour market have provided the stimulus for housing debt. This goes beyond redundancy and into the restructuring of the labour market. Amongst those in serious rent arrears in the local authority and RSL sectors, only around 30 per cent were actually in full-time employment at the time of the DoE study in 1994 (Table 7.10), and the median gross pay was £6,552 and £8320 respectively. The move towards higher rates of unemployment, low pay, and the casualization of labour – that is, a move towards part-time or short-term contract work – has affected *all* sections of the labour market, from manual to managerial (Ford and Wilcox, 1998). In the late 1980s and 1990s, this was linked to strong recessionary pressures that also affected small businesses (Ford *et al.*, 1995, pp. 23–30; Ford, 1997). The recession, together with government management of the economy, also combined to create rises in interest rates (which had a knock-on effect on mortgage interest rates). This was particularly the case after the failed attempt by the UK government to join the European Exchange Rate Mechanism in 1990. Interest rates rose from 9.5 per cent in May 1988 to 15.4 per cent in February 1990, with a commensurate rise in mortgage payments.

A key structural change has also occurred within the consumer credit market. This not only affects mortgage lending but also credit for consumer items. Without doubt, the increased competition in the market place has been a significant cause of housing debt. Housing debt is usually found in conjunction with other debts: 'Financial management for many tenants and borrowers was impossible because of lack of sufficient income to maintain all regular payments of all bills and expenses' (Nixon *et al.*, 1996, p. 8). So the DoE study of local authority and RSL rent arrears found that 33 and 29 per cent respectively of households had other bills/ commitments/expenses which had to be paid before the rent (DoE, 1994, Table 8.1). The most apparent correlation between housing debt and the deregulation of consumer credit has been in mortgage lending. In Chapter 3, we analysed the deregulation of mortgage lending.

Increased competition for lending encouraged lenders to break the shackles of their previous lending policies. Most lenders increased the ratio of amount of loan to value of the property, as well as amount of loan to income(s) of borrowers. These increases meant that borrowers had larger loans which were more difficult to sustain in the subsequent employment climate and at a time of rising interest rates. It was also the principal cause of the negative equity crisis in the early 1990s (occurring when the value of the loan outstanding is *more than* the market value of the property) (Gentle *et al.*, 1994). The effects of deregulation were also reflected in the fact that, of those in arrears, a considerable proportion had taken out loans on the basis of multiples of *joint* incomes (Ford and Wilcox, 1998) so that when one of the borrowers lost their job or had their jobs restricted in some way, arrears mounted. There is also evidence that the changed environment particularly affected lending to younger people on their first house purchase, and in the early stages of family formation: 'This was not surprising since they were the ones with the highest loan to value mortgages, who were paying the largest proportion of their incomes in mortgage repayments, and who were most susceptible to strains on their finances as they had children and frequently lost the wife's earnings' (Ford *et al.*, 1995, p. 32; Ford, 1994, p. 231). Furthermore, those lenders that developed innovative mortgage types, such as 'low-start mortgages', where the interest rate rose considerably after a short period, were at risk of default as payments increased in an uncertain financial and labour market. Arrears also affected those who took out a mortgage *after* their purchase – commonly a second mortgage – and those who purchased council houses under the right to buy (Ford *et al.*, 1995, pp. 35–8).

A third factor affecting housing debt is relationship breakdown. This would clearly be the case in the event of mortgages based on multiples of joint incomes, but 'people with mortgage arrears were four times more likely to have split up from a partner than borrowers who had kept up on their mortgages' (although less actually blamed their arrears on this factor: Ford *et al.*, 1995, p. 30). Changes in personal/domestic circumstances were also responsible for levels of rent arrears in 35 and 23 per cent of cases in local authority and RSLs respectively (DoE, 1994, Table 8.1).

The final cause of housing debt to which reference must be made is the so-called 'safety net'. A considerable proportion of tenants and borrowers blame social security failings for their arrears. Tenants and landlords, in whichever tenure, particularly blame delays in processing Housing Benefit claims (Bevan *et al.*, 1995; Kemp & McLaverty, 1995, p. 57; DoE, 1994, pp. 82–6; Ford & Seavers, 1998). Other problems arise from overpayment of benefit, followed by a subsequent clawing back of that overpayment leaving the tenant in arrears. This probably occurs in a minority of cases but leads to substantial levels of housing debt (DoE, 1994, para. 8.27). The restrictions in Housing Benefit levels are undoubtedly also a cause for arrears, particularly when claims are reassessed and paid in arrears (Birch, 1999). Home owners are entitled to Income Support, which covers part or all of their mortgage interest payments, as opposed to Housing Benefit for tenants. We will look more closely at this in the next section of this chapter, but here it is necessary to point out that around one in five people mentioned problems with it in the interviews conducted by Ford *et al.* of those in mortgage arrears (1995, p. 38).

Levels

Having drawn comparisons between the reasons for housing debt between tenures, there are clear differences in proportions of debt. So, for example, in the DoE study of rent arrears in local authority and RSL accommodation, it was found that 43 and 49 per cent of tenants were in arrears of any amount (1994, para. 6.2), although this contrasted strongly with tenants' perceptions in which around 20 per cent acknowledged they were in arrears (para. 6.12). About 1.5 million local authority tenants and 400,000 RSL tenants were found to be in arrears. On the other hand, around one in 16 borrowers are in arrears on their mortgages, which is a grossed up figure of about 629,000 households (Ford *et al.*, 1995, p. 13). Certain lenders were found to be more likely to have borrowers in arrears (*ibid*, p. 17), perhaps reflecting weaker controls on lending policies.

Management Strategies

Whilst organizations representing, or regulating, borrowers and landlords have set out guidance or regulations encouraging their individual members to avoid possession proceedings whenever possible, it is clear that management strategies to deal with rent arrears depend upon the individual agency. Few general principles can be gleaned from the available research. In this section, the divide that will be drawn is between the 'social' sector, that is local authority and RSLs, and the mortgage sector.[3] This divide is partly because the available research is based upon this distinction, and partly also because approaches to arrears provides us with a further tool to analyse how 'social' social housing really is (or is able to be).

'Social' Housing

As might be expected there are comparisons and contrasts between local authorities and RSLs in their rent arrears strategies. Many local authorities and RSLs are known to have tightened their arrears strategies in the late 1990s, as a response to a number of different factors, such as constricted financial regimes. This is particularly true of RSLs, which are now more willing to begin court proceedings, threaten and implement evictions (Ford & Seavers, 1998). There are also 'huge variations around the country' depending upon a number of different factors, such as whether any vacancy can easily be filled (Birch, 1999). Here we will discuss the development of these strategies under the headings of Guidance and Management Strategies.

Guidance   There are tensions in the approaches adopted by the regulators in respect of the recovery of rent arrears in social housing. For example, the Housing Corporation *Standards* states that '[RSLs] should only seek possession once all other reasonable steps have been taken' (1997, Standard G1.3), which is reflected in the Residents' Charters; at the same time, though, RSLs are required to 'maximise the collection of rent due' (Standard H.1) which requires them to collect at least 97 per cent of the rent receivable and no more than 5 per cent outstanding arrears. A further criterion is the importance of rental income in meeting interest payments on private loans for post-1988 development, and private finance will have been based upon a particular percentage of rental income being collected (see Ch. 5). Although not strictly Guidance, the Independent Housing Ombudsman, to which all RSLs subscribe, has made it clear that she may 'regard it as unfair if associations start to threaten tenants with or issue notices seeking possession on the ground of rent arrears where they have, or should have, appropriate information about the [housing] benefit issue and the extent of any underpayments by the local authority' (Independent Housing Ombudsman, 1997, para. 2.6.4).

One of the more public criticisms of local authorities during the 1980s was their inefficiency in collecting rent arrears. Consequently, various agencies published potential strategies for efficient and effective rent collection (see, for example, Audit Commission, 1984; 1989). Ministerial Guidance has followed this pattern so that, rather than being concerned with the welfare of tenants, local authorities were encouraged to consider the effects of rent arrears on their other tenants as well as on those in arrears themselves 'who have to manage a burden of debt' (DoE, 1987, para. 2). Authorities were also warned that 'This inefficiency in the use of resources also damages the case for the allocation of resources to local authorities for housing' (*ibid*). Furthermore, to the acknowledged differences between authorities on the collection of rents, 'Ministers agree with the Audit Commission that the only consistent factor explaining differences in levels of arrears between otherwise comparable authorities is *the quality of their housing management*' (para. 3, emphasis added; see also Ch. 6). The post-1989 financial settlement assumed that authorities collected 100 per cent of the rent due and arrears were accounted for in the year after they were due, which detrimentally affected those authorities with high levels of rent arrears (Malpass *et al.*, 1993, p. 88).

Management Strategies   Early research suggested that there was a correlation between methods of rent collection and levels of arrears. Low levels of arrears were associated with door-to-door collection practices, although it was accepted that this method of rent collection was becoming obsolescent due to safety and cost considerations (Duncan & Kirby, 1983). Few RSLs have ever adopted this practice (Centre for Housing Research, 1989, para. 5.2; Bines *et al.*, 1993, para. 8.13). The 1994 DoE study, by contrast, found that this correlation did not exist, although certain methods of rent collection were associated with higher levels of arrears: payment through the post office and direct to the landlord through Housing Benefit (para.s 10.5–10.10). Low rent arrears are associated with weekly rent payments, as opposed to longer time scales, as these enable landlords to take earlier action to recover less money.

For local authorities, but not RSLs, arrears are also related to stock size; the larger the stock size, the larger the arrears (Bines *et al.*, 1993, para. 8.44). The DoE study of rent arrears also found that the location of the landlord's stock was the critical factor, noting that there was an urban/rural difference (DoE, 1994, para. 14.8). That same study found that those landlords who had decentralized, either to districts or to neighbourhoods, were as likely to be associated with high rent arrears as any other; those local authorities and RSLs with officers responsible for rent collection in smaller numbers of properties were as likely to have higher levels of arrears as others. It is commonly assumed that early contact with those in arrears can help reduce the possibility that the arrears will rise, although this is not necessarily the case. Central to this is the development of effective debt counselling and benefits advice. However, before the Housing Act 1996, such services were spatially distributed, of uneven quality, and different agencies had different focuses (see Nixon *et al.*, 1996). RSLs with low levels of arrears were 'most likely to always or usually refer people in arrears to a debt counseling service' (Bines *et al.*, 1993, para. 8.55). After the 1996 Act, local authorities are required to have advisory services and matters may change (although research on the level and quality of the services provided is required).

It now seems that early use of the formal legal process for recovery is less closely related to performance levels than was the case. Local authorities, on average, serve the Notice of Seeking Possession (NSP) – the first stage in the formal recovery process – earlier than RSLs (Bines *et al.*, 1993). Contrary to the views of housing officers, a substantial majority of tenants believed that the notice could lead to eviction, although 'for the most part the NSP did not significantly reduce arrears' (para.s 19.49–51). However, policies were radically different from *actual practice* and, in fact, RSLs and local authorities usually sent out NSPs at around the same times. The reason for this is that policies tend to account for 'normal' cases of rent arrears but such normal cases (the tenant who pays little or no rent over a period) rarely exist: 'In such cases landlords did not follow the process mechanistically but tended to return to reminder and then warning letters. It might be that a tenant had been in arrears for a considerable number of weeks before an NSP was served because attempts had been made on the part of the tenant to reduce the debt' (DoE, 1994, para. 19.43). Sensitivity to the tenant's circumstances, together with giving every opportunity to pay and gradually reduce the arrears was given priority over formal written policies (Cameron & Gilroy, 1997, p. 41; *cf* Birch, 1999, where it is suggested that current practice may be less sensitive because of central financial controls *inter alia*).

Strategies designed to reduce rent arrears are often a *response* to a particular level of arrears, as opposed to being the *cause* of those levels. A particularly good example of this is the 'emergency approach' to very high levels of arrears adopted by some urban authorities. Associated with this approach are, first, a specialist centralized arrears team of officers, and second, the use of more 'drastic forms of legal action' such as eviction or distress (Cameron & Gilroy 1997, p. 42). Distress is a self-help remedy available to landlords, under which they are able to enter the property, seize certain items, and sell them in lieu of rent. Use of formal legal process as a management strategy is part of control of arrears: 'in attempting to challenge a perceived culture of non-payment the routine use of eviction may become part of a deliberate policy to impress on tenants a determination by the landlord to reduce arrears' (p. 43). In this sense, 'positive' eviction policies are designed to 'send a message' to tenants.

Lenders

Before deregulation and the recession, lenders' arrears strategies were generally *jejeune*. Lenders would enter into 'forbearance' agreements, under which they would agree not to take possession action provided the borrower kept to a repayment schedule. Out of ten possible types of repayment schedule, the majority appeared to require the borrower to make the usual repayments plus arrears (Ford, 1989, p. 44). Forbearance arrangements were usually imposed, and in a sample of 40 cases, only one appeared to have been set with reference to the borrower's actual income and expenditure (*ibid*, p. 45). The level of information available to lenders about borrowers, allied to the relatively inflexible arrangements and common refusal to accept payments of social security alone, meant that arrears strategies were worse than useless. It was only as a response to the changing housing market post-1989 (in which both a sale and price were 'increasingly uncertain': Doling & Ford, 1991, p. 113) that building societies and other lenders began to implement better arrears management policies (through 'improved data collection and analysis procedures', 'in-house telephone helplines and debt counseling').

Additionally, the Council of Mortgage Lenders (CML), perhaps predicting the oncoming rise in arrears and repossessions as well as their political unacceptability, drew up an arrears policy. This attempt at self-regulation was largely designed to forestall any more formal attempts to regulate the industry and so retain the privileges of deregulation. So far, this approach has been successful, with the New Labour government agreeing to abide by the self-regulatory Code unless intervention becomes necessary at some stage in the future. Helen Liddell, then Treasury Minister, said that 'We have no plans at present to extend the scope of regulation into these areas but standards of conduct in these markets and the risks faced by consumers will be kept under review' (7 April 1998). The Code made clear that lenders would seek to develop forbearance agreements more in line with ability to pay as well as being 'consistent with both our interests and yours'. The lenders' interests will reflect the balance of the equity available in the property, the interests of the depositors and/or shareholders, and the cost of managing arrears levels.

Nevertheless, a study of arrears management strategies in one building society after the CML's guidelines were published found that the lenders were 'initially remote and impersonal', and a majority of borrowers agreed to make the usual monthly mortgage repayment plus a proportion of arrears (on the basis of a preconceived concern to recover arrears over a period of around 2 years): 'This reliance on a strategy that required borrowers to repay more than they were paying previously may well be counter-productive' (Ford & Wilcox, 1992, p. 18). A further study found that a large number of lenders had instituted procedural changes in their debt recovery policies, relying upon early intervention and in-depth assessment: 'The aim was to provide a structured regulated approach within which individual, workable agreements could be identified, implemented, monitored and assessed. The changes reflected a stronger recognition amongst lenders that default was associated with an inability to pay as opposed to wilful disregard of their commitment' (Ford *et al.*, 1995, p. 44).

However, despite such policies, actual practices showed that lenders relied principally on three strategies: reduced payments (17 per cent of agreements); current monthly payment only (12 per cent); current monthly payment plus arrears (27 per cent): *ibid*, p. 51. In other words, actual practices have shifted, but only marginally. Furthermore, 'Roughly equal proportions of borrowers with concessionary agreements and borrowers with agreements to pay the normal monthly payment plus arrears had broken the arrangement, 29 and 34 per cent respectively. The failure to sustain concessionary agreements is further evidence of a fundamental problem with regard to affordability.' (Ford *et al.*, 1995, p. 53). It is this context which suggests that forbearance agreements need to be more flexible than they currently are.

17.2 Mortgage Rescue

In December 1991, the government and the mortgage lending industry came to an 'understanding' which involved the government legislating to enable Income Support payments to be made direct to lenders; in return, lenders would not take possession action against those borrowers. That understanding was interpreted differently by lenders (Ford *et al.*, 1995, p. 56). Additionally, other initiatives were announced to stem the anticipated increase of possession actions: rescue schemes enabling borrowers to convert to shared ownership or to swap tenures to private renting; RSLs were supposed to rent repossessed properties to home-lessness applicants on short-term leases. Norman Lamont, then Chancellor, announced that these measures would reduce the expected repossessions by 40,000 (see Ford & Wilcox, 1992, p. 7). We have already seen that the assurance given to tighten-up arrears management practices has been less successful than it perhaps might have been because of the restricted types of agreements lenders are willing to make with their borrowers. In this section, we will briefly evaluate these schemes, and also consider the government's subsequent reduction of Income Support for mortgage interest payments (on the basis that individuals should take out private insurance).

Income Support for Mortgage Interest

Income Support is available to pay certain proportions of mortgage interest for those out of work. Criteria for receipt are, however, tight – those in work, whether full or part time, are not eligible, nor are those where another member of the household is in work or where the household's capital is greater than £8,000. Consequently, a majority of borrowers are excluded from the largesse (Ford *et al.*, 1995, p. 57). From 1987, Income Support was limited to 50 per cent during the first 16 weeks of the claim in order to 'preserve work incentives and equity between those on benefit and those on similarly low incomes in work' (Wikeley, 1995, p. 168). After the 16-week period, mortgage interest was paid in full. Until 1992, it was not possible for the Benefits Agency to pay the money direct to the lender. Lenders argued that 50 per cent of all borrowers failed to transfer the money to the lender, although 'the basis for this estimate is . . . unclear' (Ford & Wilcox, 1992, p. 15). Ford and Wilcox estimated that 80 per cent of those receiving assistance were not in arrears, but 44 per cent of the others were, in fact, passing on their Income Support in full.

Estimates of the effect of the 'understanding' reached between lenders and the government were governed by the lack of clarity as to that understanding. Some lenders believed it covered any payments of Income Support, others that it covered only those where the full mortgage payments were being met. Early estimates suggested that it would assist between 8,500–10,500 borrowers. However, the growing outlay of Income Support, and the commensurate need to reduce its scope further, meant that cuts to the scheme were proposed and effected during 1995. The basis for these cuts was that, on the one hand, the Income Support scheme only partially covered those who needed support, 'discourages a return to work, it bails out poor lending and it discourages the further growth of private finance' (see Pryce, 1998, where this latter claim is rejected). It was this development of private finance that the government wished to see through the development of private insurance covering arrears caused by unemployment. Consequently, for the first nine months of any claim for Income Support, borrowers are to receive no help with their Income Support (Social Security (Income Support and Claims and Payments) Amendment Regulations 1995, SI 1995/1613, para. 8(1)). In this gap, it was believed that private insurance would/should cover those in need of assistance.

The move from a publicly funded safety net to a privately funded insurance scheme has been fraught with difficulty. This can hardly have been surprising. In 1995, fewer than 12 or 13 per cent of borrowers had private insurance and there were concerns that the products on offer would not cater for those most at risk. Premiums are also expensive, in part because the insurers seem to have great difficulty in assessing the risk and, in part, because the risk of unemployment is particularly prevalent during certain periods of the economic cycle (Burchardt & Hills, 1997a; 1997b). Thus, there is a risk that a considerable number of policy holders will become unemployed at a particular time, which would make the policies unsustainable. Furthermore, in order to limit the possibility of 'adverse selection' (a disproportionate number of high-risk clients), insurers placed eligibility restrictions on the basis of age, length of time in employment, excluding self-employed persons, as well as only offering policies to those taking out mortgages with the same company (Burchardt & Hills, 1997a, p. 25). More recently, it appears that cover has been extended to certain groups, but *subject to certain special conditions* (Ford & Kempson, 1997, pp. 28–30). Take-up and marketing of the policies has been variable – the policies are commonly offered after the mortgage interview and 'Having just arranged a loan they were reluctant to start putting doubt in borrowers' minds about whether they would always be able to keep up payments. In part, this was a matter of ethics, but it was also driven by commercial considerations' (*ibid*, p. 43). Of those who would potentially be entitled to Income Support on losing employment, *three out of four have no private insurance* (*ibid*, p. 48). There are, consequently, serious doubts as to whether the Conservative government's attempt to make the nascent private insurance market universal have been successful.

Other Rescue Schemes

After initial optimism, it is apparent that these schemes failed. By the end of 1993, apparently only 700 borrowers had taken advantage of the schemes and only seven per cent of lenders were involved in them. Three reasons have surfaced (Ford *et al.*, 1995, pp. 65–6). First, borrowers wanted more time, and not to swap to a (perceived) less attractive tenure. The government having created the desire for home ownership, swapping to renting was not regarded as desirable (Ford & Wilcox, 1992, p. 24). Second, regulatory bodies, such as the Building Societies Commission and the Housing Corporation made regulations that both cut down the purview of the schemes as well as reducing their desirability. As one lender commented '. . . demanding mortgage lenders and institutions to rectify (the crisis) overnight . . . coming out with some half-cocked scheme which everyone says "Well, how legal is this?" . . . even the Commission running around because "can't do this"' (Ford *et al.*, 1995, p. 66). Third, those involved in the crisis talks seemed to assume that borrowers' debts were relatively simple (perhaps reflecting the beliefs about borrowers' 'fecklessness'). However, 'the parties to the mortgage rescue had to make decisions as to how complexities such as first and second charge holders, and unsecured loans and arrears would be handled' (*ibid*).

In *Cheltenham & Gloucester Building Society* v. *Krausz* (1997) 29 HLR 597, a rescue scheme came unstuck because the scheme offended the right of the mortgagee to take possession of the property unless the mortgage arrears could be met within a reasonable period. In this case, the scheme involved an RSL purchasing the property and letting it to the borrower. The RSL valued the property at £65,000, the building society at £90,000. As the society was taking active steps to take possession of the property, they were entitled to possession and so the sale to the RSL fell through. The case is discussed further below but the point here is that the scheme failed because, as the housing market had picked up, the society was able to cover the borrower's debts entirely through a sale by itself. The aim of keeping the borrower in the property was secondary.

Negative Equity: A Judicial Scheme

Krausz has been responsible for delimiting a line of judicial authority which has sought to equalize the relationship between borrower and lender when matters go awry. The particular issue arose over who was able to sell a property when there was negative equity, and when it was to be sold. As those most likely to have negative equity were also those most likely to be in mortgage arrears (young, first-time buyers), schemes developed for dealing with negative equity also have a resonance in respect of arrears. A strong case can be put for arguing that the decision over sale should be the borrower's. First, where there is negative equity, the lender is also usually protected by a Mortgage Indemnity Guarantee policy. These policies were developed to cover situations in which borrowers sought to obtain loans covering more than a certain proportion of the purchase price. Lenders required borrowers to pay the insurance premium, which then protected the lender. In other words, the debt is usually satisfied either through the sale price or through insurance. Second, it is generally accepted that repossessed properties command less in the marketplace. Third, where there is any outstanding debt, the lender is entitled to pursue the borrower even after the sale of the property. This is because the original mortgage contract still exists even after the sale of the property unless the loan is repaid (or redeemed) in full.

In law, however, the existence of the mortgage contract was the critical device which enabled the lender to protect their interests, at the expense of the borrower. Unless excluded, the mortgage contract entitles the lender to go into possession 'as soon as the ink is dry'. This is a powerful element which, whilst rarely exercised (although for confirmation, see *Ropaigea-lach* v. *Barclays Bank*, Unreported, Court of Appeal, 18 December 1998), nevertheless significantly influences the way lawyers think about the mortgage relationship. A borrower signs over their rights in the property to the lender and, by way of return, the borrower is entitled to redeem the mortgage. The cases to be discussed here show that lenders are most concerned to recover their security, rather than with 'rescue' or flexibly dealing with problems in individual cases.

In *Palk* v. *Mortgage Services Funding Ltd* [1993] Ch. 330, the Court of Appeal was faced with a disagreement over the sale of a property in negative equity. The borrower wanted to sell the property as soon as was possible, even though there would be a considerable debt outstanding. The lender wished to rent the property out until the property market increased again, although it was uncertain when this would be. Even with the property rented, there would still be a shortfall of £15,000. The jurisdiction of the court was wide – under s. 91(2), Law of Property Act 1925, the court is entitled to make an order 'on such terms as it thinks fit' in relation to the sale. In *Palk*, the Court ordered that the mortgagor should be entitled to sell the property. What seemed to influence the court was that the lender was effectively gambling on the state of the housing market and using the Palk's property as stake money. As Nicholls V-C suggested, if they wished to do this, the lenders could purchase the property themselves.

Palk and subsequent decisions have based themselves upon the assumed characteristics of the parties before them. *Palk*, for example, took place during the recession and the increasing numbers of repossessions. This fact particularly affected the court which, it may be argued, was swayed by their views of the lender. In *Barrett* v. *Halifax Building Society* (1995) 28 HLR 634, the lenders central argument was that allowing a borrower in this situation to sell the property would break their established policy not to allow borrowers to sell the property without making arrangements for paying any excess. In *Polonski* v. *Lloyds Bank* [1998] 1 FLR 896, the court ordered a sale in similar circumstances to *Palk*. Jacobs J was influenced by two factors: first, he argued that the bank would only be disadvantaged by the sale because the 'mortgage payments are currently being met by the state'. Second, the borrower was regarded as wanting to do the right thing (move from a relatively poor neighbourhood where she feared for her child's future to a more affluent neighbourhood):

> 'What [Polonski] wants to do seems to me a perfectly legitimate exercise of her undoubted right to live where she wants. . . . She has behaved – and it is not suggested otherwise – thoroughly responsibly financially over the years as far as she can and I cannot see that it can be just in effect to require her to stay where she is. Actually she probably cannot be required to stay where she is. She could just walk out next week, take up a tenancy in Salisbury and give the bank the keys.'

By contrast to *Polonski*, the Court of Appeal previously had attempted to circumscribe the jurisdiction in *Krausz*. In *Krausz*, the court was influenced by the judges' 'past experience of hopeless applications for leave to appeal against possession orders . . . There will be a danger, if the mortgagee does not obtain possession, that the mortgagor will delay the realisation of the property by seeking too high a price or deliberately procrastinating on completion [of the sale].' (at p. 603). Two other reasons provided were that the court would enter into an 'area of difficult factual enquiry' as to the common benefit of the lender and borrower; and there would be difficulties in lenders 'monitoring the negotiations of [borrowers] who are permitted time to market their properties' (*ibid*). Consequently, it was held that the jurisdiction opened up by the decision in *Palk* only applied where the lender was not actively seeking possession (and, in the process, casting doubt over the decision in *Barrett* and by implication also *Polonski*). Cynically, one might observe that the jurisdiction was opened to deal with what the courts perceived to be an emergency – the repossessions 'crisis' – and was just as quickly closed when that 'crisis' was perceived to have finished. The interests of the lender have now regained their prominence (although, it might be observed that those interests were never undermined even by the decision in *Palk* because the lender's interest was equally taken into account and served by the decision).

17.3 Possession Proceedings

Formal possession proceedings are the successors of the informal methods of arrears management. They are almost a natural step where the informal methods have failed for some reason. Given the similarity in circumstances in which arrears arise, irrespective of tenure, it is perhaps surprising that there are differences in the results of possession actions between tenures. It is more surprising to find that borrowers are considerably more likely to find themselves facing outright possession orders and their enforcement than tenants (21 per cent against 4 per cent), and suspended possession orders are used in a greater proportion of tenancy cases than mortgages

(54 per cent against 33 per cent) (Nixon *et al.*, 1996, pp. 36–7). This is explained by the following factors; the law; the procedures involved including the participation of the borrower/tenant; the types of orders that landlords/lenders request and their reasons for starting the proceedings in the first place; the level of arrears at the time of the hearing; together with the factors which judges take into account in the exercise of their discretion. We now consider each of these in turn.

Law

Actions for recovery depend upon the rights initially given to the debtor. These rights commonly are based upon the debtors' tenure but this is not completely the case. As we saw in Chapter 13, RSLs have been able to grant different tenancy levels at different times and this will affect their rights to gain possession of the property for rent arrears. The following discussion is split along the lines of tenure because, as will be argued, tenure is critical to the process and the law is effectively divided along those lines (even if not in fact).

Mortgage Possession
Strictly, a lender can go into possession as soon as the mortgage is granted (unless this right is excluded). Indeed, there is no need to bring a possession action at all. The fact that most lenders bring possession actions is because of a curious blend of antipathy towards self-help remedies (both in law and commercial practice), the right to take possession is delimited by certain potential criminal law offences (Criminal Law Act 1977, ss. 6 & 7), and the existence of a statutory right enabling the borrower to resist possession on certain grounds (a somewhat bizarre right given that there is no duty to bring proceedings in the first place). The protracted legislative history of the latter protection of the borrower is indicative of its complexity. However, by virtue of the Administration of Justice Act 1970, s. 36, as amended by s. 8 of the Administration of Justice Act 1973, courts are empowered to delay the grant of possession to the lender '*if it appears to the court that in the event of it exercising the power [of delay] the mortgagor is likely to be able within a reasonable period to pay any sums due under the mortgage . . .*'.[4]

This is a negative proposition in that, whilst accepting the lender's right to possession, it simply enables that right to be suspended where the borrower can pay all sums due (which includes the arrears and future payments of interest). In other words, the court has discretion to broker a forbearance agreement provided the borrower is likely to be able to repay the sums owing within a reasonable period. On this basis, the lender will be successful if a possession order is made, but they will also be successful if the judge exercises the discretion to delay the grant of possession in order to make an order as to payment (because the lender will potentially recoup their losses) (see Whitehouse, 1997, p. 172). Furthermore, the lenders' costs of bringing the actions in the first place are added to the amount owed by the borrower (see *First National Bank* v. *Syed* [1991] 2 All ER 250). The existence of this legislation does not, however, make it necessary for lenders to take possession proceedings against borrowers ('a curious anomaly': *Ropaigealach* v. *Barclays Bank*, Unreported, Court of Appeal, 18 December 1998).

The sole discretion in most actions open to the judge is as to the length of the reasonable period. The lengthier the term used, the smaller the amount to be paid by the borrower. In the 1980s, the standard period was two years, although the period tended to increase to an average of 42 months (Ford *et al.*, 1995, p. 86). However, in *Cheltenham & Gloucester Building Society* v. *Morgan* (1996) 28 HLR 443, the Court of Appeal held that:

> 'the logic and spirit of the legislation require, *especially in cases where the parties are proceeding under arrangements such as those reflected in the CML statement,* that the court should take as its starting point the full term of the mortgage and pose at the outset the question: would it be possible for the mortgagor to maintain payment of the arrears by instalments over that period?' (p. 453; emphasis added)

Thus, the Council of Mortgage Lenders' self-regulation was used to justify a departure from the pre-existing practice. A further reason was that the borrower would have to pay the costs incurred by the lender at some stage and so, if one were to make the most generous arrangement at the outset, then costs would be minimized because lenders would always get possession on a reapplication due to default.

Local Authorities, RSLs and Private Landlords

Various statutes circumscribe the landlords' right to possession. By way of contrast to the lenders' right, it is common for landlords to be required to show that the arrears have arisen *and* that it is reasonable to grant possession. So, there is a double hurdle before a landlord is entitled to possession. For local authority *secure tenants*, the authority must show that 'rent[5] lawfully due has not been paid' (Sch. 2, Ground 1, Housing Act 1985). For tenants granted an *assured tenancy*, the rent lawfully due must have been 'unpaid on the date on which the proceedings for possession are begun' and the tenant was in arrears when notice was served (Sch. 2, Ground 10, Housing Act 1988). Even where there is no rent due when proceedings are begun, if the tenant has 'persistently delayed paying rent', the landlord has a ground for possession of an *assured tenancy* (Ground 11). In all three cases, the landlord must also show that it is reasonable for possession to be granted.

It is said that 'all relevant circumstances' should be taken into account by the judge in determining the reasonableness question (*Cumming* v. *Danson* [1942] 2 All ER 652). However, it appears that the fact that, in all likelihood, the tenant would be excluded from a local authority housing register (because most exclusions relate to rent arrears: Shelter, 1998) and that it would be extremely likely that a tenant evicted for rent arrears will be found intentionally homeless (and thus not entitled to priority on the housing register as well as only having an extremely limited right to accommodation) are irrelevant (*Bristol CC* v. *Mousah* (1998) 30 HLR 32).

There is, however, a further ground under which a landlord of an *assured tenant* can gain possession of the property *without needing to show that it would also be reasonable*. Where rent is payable weekly or fortnightly and eight weeks' rent is overdue at the time of the hearing, or where rent is paid monthly and at least two months' rent is overdue at the time of the hearing, the landlord is entitled to possession (Sch. 2, Ground 8, 1988 Act). These periods were shortened by the Housing Act 1996 on the basis that 'for a private landlord, the majority of whom only have a very small number of properties, having a tenant who does not pay the rent can be financially very difficult (especially, for example if there is a mortgage loan to pay)' (DoE, 1995, para. 2.14). Provided that the landlord can show that the rent is in arrears for the relevant period, the court must grant possession.

For some time, the Housing Corporation required RSLs to contract only to use the discretionary grounds for possession of their assured tenancies (and therefore required them not to use Ground 8). Although this does not appear in the current draft of the Resident's Charter, the Tenant's Guarantee clearly delimited RSLs' rights to possession in this way. There was a clear attempt to increase the security granted to RSL tenants so as to create a 'middle ground' between local authorities and the private sector which would also be acceptable to private lenders. There is some doubt as to the validity of this exclusion (Hughes & Lowe, 1995, pp. 148–9; *cf* Alder & Handy, 1996, p. 141), although it can be argued that these delimitations only apply during the actual contractual term and not after that term has ended (see Scottish Homes, 1997, p. 13; that research found few Scottish RSLs adopting this restriction, p. 36, and for their use of Ground 8, see pp. 43–4).

Procedures and Participation

It is clear from research into adjudicative practices that the procedures used and the participation of the parties in those procedures, particularly through effective representation, are closely correlated with success rates (see, for example, Genn & Genn, 1989; Baldwin *et al.*, 1992). Legal aid is, however, difficult to obtain in housing debt cases – the Green Form scheme covers the first two hours of advice but the Legal Aid Board suggest that this 'should normally be sufficient' in respect of tenant housing debt. For borrowers, however, they are willing to sanction extensions to negotiate with the lender as well as for appearances at court and subsequent advice in certain cases (see Luba *et al.*, 1997, pp. 268–9). These are severe restrictions, particularly affecting tenants. Furthermore, those who use the court procedures frequently ('repeat players'), such as lenders and large landlords, usually fare better than those who make one appearance ('one shotters') (Galanter, 1974).

Possession procedures are *different* for rent and mortgage arrears. In the former, proceedings take place in open court and many cases are 'listed' to take place at the same time – 'at its most extreme 104 cases are all listed for the same time (9.45 am) and intended to be completed by 1pm, that is 1 minute and 51 seconds per case' (Nixon *et al.*, 1996, p. 23). This sort of practice, apparently common in many courts (although not as extreme as this), is antithetical to actual 'real' participation in the proceedings. From a base of 498 possession proceedings in respect of rented property, less than three per cent of tenants were represented at the hearing, with just a further 18 per cent of tenants attending. Yet, the same study found that attendance, and particularly representation, usually resulted in fewer outright possessions being granted to the landlord (Nixon & Hunter, 1996, pp. 430–2). It is believed that tenants do not attend because 'they're frightened' or 'there's nothing that can be done' – often agreements have been made between the parties and the actions simply gives judicial backing to it (so that, if the agreement is broken, the landlord can obtain possession more easily). The following description suggests other problems which are closely linked to this lack of participation:

> 'Because tenants are concerned about missing their 'turn', all defendants and indeed all landlord representatives are usually sat in court as the case is called on. Interviews with tenants showed that they clearly considered the system to be degrading and embarrassing as their personal and financial affairs were aired in public. In addition, tenants became increasingly nervous as they waited in court, anticipating public humiliation.' (Nixon *et al.*, 1996, p. 21)

On this basis, it can be argued that the system is weighted heavily in favour of the landlord.

By way of contrast, mortgage possession actions are generally heard in judges' 'chambers' – that is, in a private room in the court building. Proceedings are less formal than open court because, for example, the panoply of court dress is not used. There is a higher attendance rate (51 per cent for first hearings) and higher rates of representation (about one third) (Ford *et al.*, 1995, p. 84). Ford *et al.* suggest that growing awareness of mortgage debt, and better availability of advice, are prominent reasons for greater attendance (which was higher in their study than earlier ones). However, this does not account for the differences in participation levels between borrowers and tenants and it may well be that the procedures play at least some role in stimulating different levels of attendance. This does not mean that borrowers receive rather more court time than tenants. Indeed, the average hearing seems to be about five minutes long, depending upon the number of actions required to be heard per judge (Nixon *et al.*, 1996, p. 24).

Reasons for Possession Proceedings

Differential results also occur because lenders/landlords may well request non-possessory orders. So, for example, the DoE study of rent arrears found that all the local authorities and RSLs studied, bar three, requested suspended possession orders. Of the other three, absolute possession was only requested in respect of those tenants who had not made contact with the landlord. Even where the landlord took possession proceedings as a punitive, emergency measure, it appears that outright possession orders were not requested. Other than these initial hearings, there are considerable discrepancies between social landlords willingness to evict tenants – the DoE study noted that for local authorities with high levels of arrears, the eviction rate varied between 27 and 1.5 per thousand tenancies (DoE, 1994, para.s 19.63–19.68).In general, it appears that RSLs are more willing to evict than local authorities, the former showing higher levels of eviction per thousand tenancies (Bines *et al.*, 1993). Nevertheless, in Nixon *et al.*'s study of ten county courts, it is instructive to note the differences between different types of tenant debt: local authority tenants range of arrears was from £2–3,826; RSLs from £252–2,370; and private sector from £608–9,100 (1996, p. 15).

Lenders' possession policies are, however, less uniform – a point that is taken by Whitehouse in her argument that borrowers do not get real choice when taking out their mortgage (1998, pp. 136–7). No lender actually publicizes their possessions' policy and as regards the Council of Mortgage Lenders Code of Practice, her evidence is that the CML itself anticipated that lenders would deviate from it in line with their own individual policies: '[w]e hope that [lenders follow the Code] but in detail many wouldn't because they are generalised recommendations and the reality of mortgagees is that they have a different approach and an obvious difference is the speed with which they take repossession' (*ibid*). Her study of lenders' practices found different practices based upon different views of the purpose of court action (from understanding the importance of their obligations to a last resort) (1997, p. 161). Sometimes, lenders take possession proceedings simply to make contact with the borrower and to make an arrangement which can then be given the formal blessing of the court.

Differences in policies and practices in relation to possession proceedings between landlords and lenders also lead to differences in outstanding arrears at the time of the first hearing. Nixon *et al.*'s (perhaps startling) finding was that at the date of first hearing, most borrowers were on average 11–18 months in arrears (although in Gateshead the figure was five months); whereas for tenants, the average outstanding arrears were 8–17 *weeks* (although three areas were outside this at 21, 27 and 31 weeks) (1996, p. 14). This means that average rent and mortgage arrears at the time of hearing are often vastly different. A significant correlation between levels of arrears and types of order was found in the research areas (a perhaps less startling fact).

Judicial Discretion

There is now a substantial body of research that broadly suggests that, in addition to the factors already considered (participation, level of housing debt, request of creditor) judicial discretion is heavily influenced by the particular judge's perceptions of the morality of the actions of both creditor and debtor in possession proceedings. Within this research, there is a distinction between those who believe that judges seek to ensure 'fair play' (Ford, 1997, drawing upon Rock, 1973, and Cain, 1986) and those who believe that commercial interests are the most significant (Nixon & Hunter, 1998). The former argument is grounded in the belief that the exercise of discretion depended upon the structures of mortgage debt:

> 'Perspectives and explanations of the genesis of the current situation were important as was the view that the balance of interests between borrower and lender was unequal, and that with due regard to lender's rights, it was the borrower's position that needed to be safeguarded' (Ford *et al.*, 1995, p. 85).

Judges in this study were closely tuned in to the debate about the 'understanding' between the government and the lenders. In turn, this reflected upon their views of the borrowers (lenders were reported to believe that judges were 'favourably disposed' to borrowers: p. 87).

The converse position suggests that judges have adopted a more fatalistic approach. Granted that there are more suspended orders requested and made, but these are a reflection of what is requested by both lenders and borrowers. Judges exhibited 'a clear awareness of the primacy of economic interests in mortgage actions' (Nixon & Hunter, 1998, p. 96). The law is not seeking to protect the borrower but simply forestalling the time when possession would inevitably have to be handed over:

> 'the approach of judges that has been urged upon them by lenders and which has been internalized in the application of discretion, is one which recognizes that the role of the judge is to defend the commercial property rights of the lender. . . . it is that the predominant ideological framework within which judicial discretion is exercised is premised on the commercial value of the dwelling, and this comes into focus when compared to decisions taken in relation to tenants' (*ibid*)

The point is that, provided borrowers have sufficient equity in the property, there is no reason why lenders should not wish for them to have a further trial period – after all, if the borrower defaults again, then the lender can still recoup their full debt (including arrears and costs).

By contrast, judicial attitudes to *social* landlords in the study meant that orders would be rubber stamped because judges commonly believed the landlord could be trusted. Furthermore, the discretion was structured around facilitating the 'use value' of the dwelling (as opposed to its commercial value). So, 'in rented actions local authorities (as landlords) are not viewed as having any rights which require protecting'. Greater stress was therefore placed upon making affordable arrangements for suspended orders, even when actual repayment of arrears was impossible (Nixon & Hunter, 1998, pp. 98–9).

However, all studies refer to differences in emphases between court areas as well as between judges. What we see, then, is *dissonance* in judicial practice so that general statements become unnecessarily broad. Drawing upon Giddens' theory of structuration, it has been argued that the relationship between societal structures and individual agency is the catalyst for this dissonance (Carlton, 1998). Our attention should focus on the mediating forces between structure and agency (see Sarre *et al.*, 1989). For example, how do judges take on board the current state of the housing market, are they aware of the spatial and temporal aspects to that market, from where does their awareness come, from where do the preconceptions about social and private sector tenants and mortgage borrowers derive? On this basis, both the 'fair play' and commercialism arguments provide only partial explanations and, instead, we should consider the role and experience(s) of each individual actor in the possessions process and the interaction between them (Carlton, 1998). In considering such interactions, it will also be necessary to examine the importance of *power/knowledge* of the actors. Take, for example, the person who consistently appears on behalf of the local authority before the same judge, against the inexperience of individual defendants.

Conclusion

Arrears management is a critical part of the role of the housing provider for different reasons. These differences permeate the different management forms to accommodate arrears strategies. Since the 1980s, all agencies have had to be more aware and adept at managing arrears, and this has impacted upon mortgage lenders (who have been required to accommodate debt counselling), 'social' housing (which has been required to take a more proactive stance on rent arrears), and private landlords (who have been given more considerable powers to evict their tenants on three separate rent arrears grounds). There are doubts and few answers (as usual) about the types of agreements entered into by RSLs, as well as their use of certain grounds for possession. Although we have not considered them in this chapter, local authority introductory tenancies will have a bearing in the future on proactive rent collection policies during the early periods of tenancies.

The main point of this chapter has been to show how, when it comes to housing debt, the responses of government, the courts and landlords/lenders are different in (and within) each tenure. We have shown how the government's principal concern in the early 1990s was with mortgage rescue (in the face of interest rate rises largely of their own making). Little attention was paid to tenants' housing debt. The courts have been structured to deal differentially between tenures, and this is probably furthered by individual judges' responses to different types of landlords or lenders. Landlords and lenders have equally developed their own practices of recovery of housing debt. Social landlords and lenders have been forced to move towards proactive policies because of external pressures, although lenders have probably done this as part of a strategy to protect their commercial interests.

What is surprising is that these differential responses are counter-intuitive, for the available research suggests that housing debt arises for similar reasons across tenures. The responses, then, provide further evidence of the tendency to conceptualize problems on a tenurial basis and also suggest an (un-)natural bias towards home ownership.

Further Reading

The best text on the law of possession proceedings is J. Luba *et al.* (1998), *Defending Possession Proceedings*, London: Legal Action Group (which also has many interesting pointers as to influencing the exercise of discretion). More academic is A. Stewart (1996), *Rethinking Housing Law*, London: Sweet & Maxwell, which covers possession in a broader sweep of socio-legal work on home ownership and consumerism (on which, also L. Whitehouse (1998), 'The home owner: citizen or consumer?', in S. Bright and J. Dewar (eds), *Land Law Themes and Perspectives*, Oxford: Oxford University Press). Commentary on the cases discussed in this chapter can be found in C. Davis (1998), vol 1, *Journal of Housing Law*, 56 (*Krausz*); J. Manning (1998), vol 1, *Journal of Housing Law*, 59 (*Mousah*); A. Kenny (1998) *Conveyancer*, 223.

Other (earlier) studies on housing debt and the legal process include: National Association of Citizens' Advice Bureaux (1990), *Market Failure: Low Income Households and the Private Rented Sector*, London: NACAB; School for Advanced Urban Studies (1986), *Civil Justice Review*, London: Lord Chancellor's Department. On possible changes to the procedure of collection of housing debt through the courts, see the LCD website as well as Lord Woolf's 1996 report on *Access to Justice*, London: LCD, especially Ch. 16, paras 20–30. Reforms to the process of recovery of rent arrears, in particular, are anticipated. For use of the accelerated possession procedure, see D. Levison, J. Barelli and G. Lawton (1998), *The Accelerated Possession Procedure: the Experience of Landlords and Tenants*, Rotherham: DETR

For the impact of relationship breakdown on rent arrears, see J. Bull (1994), *Housing Consequences of Relationship Breakdown*, London: HMSO, pp. 41–2. The following additional articles are worthy of attention: S. Wilcox & J. Ford (1997), 'At your own risk', in S. Wilcox (ed.), *Housing Finance Review 1997/98*, York: Joseph Rowntree Foundation; L. Murphy (1994), 'The downside of home ownership: housing change and mortgage arrears in the republic of Ireland', vol 9, *Housing Studies*, 183; R. Burrows (1998), 'Mortgage indebtedness in England: an epidemiology', vol 13, *Housing Studies*, 5; readers should also consult the literature on negative equity considered in Chapter 12.

Endnotes

1. 'Possession' is used throughout this chapter in order to take advantage of the word's colloquial meaning as well as because it is used throughout most of the research in this way. However, the law defines possession in a particular way, to include not only a person in occupation of property, but also a person in receipt of rents and profits from the property. In this way, both landlords and lenders are effectively in possession of the property from the outset, even before so-called possession proceedings are taken (see s. 205, Law of Property Act 1925).
2. These policies guarantee the difference between the mortgage loan and the current market value of the property, where the former is greater than the latter.
3. Concentration is on the mortgage sector and not the private landlord sector, partly because of the dearth of available material on the latter.
4. In *Halifax BS* v *Clark* [1973] Ch 307, it was held that 'any sums due' referred to all the mortgage debt, both capital and arrears, which significantly reduced the efficacy of the section. The amendment contained in the 1973 Act entitled the court to treat as 'any sums due' 'only such amounts as the mortgagor would have expected to be required to pay if there had been no such provision for earlier payment'.
5. It appears that 'rent' may include those charges which the landlord is collecting on behalf of other agencies, such as for water: *Lambeth LBC* v *Thomas* (1998) 30 HLR 89.

Bibliography

Alder, J. and Handy, C. (1996), *Housing Associations: The Law of Social Landlords*, London: Sweet & Maxwell

Audit Commission (1984), *Bringing Arrears Under Control*, London: HMSO

Audit Commission (1989), *Survey of Local Authority Rent Arrears*, London: HMSO

Baldwin, J., Wikeley, N. and Young, R. (1992), *Judging Social Security*, Oxford: Oxford University Press

Bevan, M., Kemp, P. and Rhodes, D. (1995), *Private Landlords and Housing Benefit*, York: Centre for Housing Policy, University of York

Bines, W., Kemp, P., Pleace, N. and Radley, C. (1993), *Managing Social Housing*, London: HMSO

Birch, J. (1998), 'Shock rise in evictions', November/December, *Roof*, 10

Birch, J. (1999), 'Eviction epidemic', January/February, *Roof*, 23

Bridges, L. and Forbes, D. (1990), *Making the Law Work Against Racial Harassment*, London: LAG

Burchardt, T. and Hills, J. (1997a), 'Mortgage payment protection: Replacing state provision?', Issue 33, *Housing Finance*, 24

Burchardt, T. and Hills, J. (1997b), 'From public to private: the case of mortgage payment insurance in great Britain', vol 13, *Housing Studies*, 311

Cain, M. (1986), 'Who loses out on Paradise Island?' in I. Ramsey (ed.), *Debtors and Creditors*, Ablingdon: Professional Books.

Cameron, S. and Gilroy, R. (1997), 'Managing rent arrears', vol 23, *Local Government Studies*, 32

Carlton, N. (1998), *Structure, Agency and Power in Local Authority Possession Proceedings*, Unpublished PhD thesis, University of Bristol

Centre for Housing Research, University of Glasgow (1989), *The Nature and Effectiveness of Housing Management in England*, London: HMSO

Council of Mortgage Lenders (CML) (1998), *Code of Practice on Mortgage Lending*, London: CML

Department of the Environment (DoE) (1987), *Rent Arrears*, LA Circ 18/87, London: DoE

Department of the Environment (DoE) (1994), *Rent Arrears in Local Authorities and Housing Associations in England*, London: HMSO

Department of the Environment (DoE) (1995), *The Legislative Framework for Private Renting*, Consultation Paper Linked to the Housing White Paper *Our Future Homes*, London: DoE

Department of Social Security (DSS) (1998), *Beating Fraud is Everyone's Business: Securing the Future*, Cm 4012, London: SO

Doling, J. and Ford, J. (1991), 'The changing face of home ownership: building societies and household investment strategies', vol 19, *Policy and Politics*, 109

Doling, J. and Stafford, B. (1989), *Home Ownership: The Diversity of Experience*, Aldershot: Gower

Doling, J. and Wainwright, S. (1989), 'Public and private debt', vol 38, *Housing Review*, 36

Duncan, S. and Kirby, K. (1983), *Preventing Rent Arrears*, London: HMSO

Ford, J. (1989), 'Managing or mismanaging mortgage arrears? The case of the building societies', vol 3, *Housing Studies*, 40

Ford, J. (1994), 'Mortgage possession', vol 8, *Housing Studies*, 227

Ford, J. (1997), 'Mortgage arrears, mortgage possessions and homelessness', in R. Burrows, N. Pleace and D. Quilgars (eds), *Homelessness and Social Policy*, London: Routledge

Ford, J. and Kempson, E. (1997), *Bridging the Gap? Safety-nets for Mortgage Borrowers*, York: Centre for Housing Policy, University of York

Ford, J., Kempson, E. and Wilson, M. (1995), *Mortgage Arrears and Possessions: Perspectives from Borrowers, Lenders and the Courts*, London: HMSO

Ford, J. and Seavers, J. (1998), *Housing Associations and Rent Arrears: Attitudes, Beliefs and Behaviours*, York: Centre for Housing Policy, University of York

Ford, J. and Wilcox, S. (1992), *Reducing Mortgage Arrears and Possessions: An Evaluation of the Initiatives*, York: Joseph Rowntree Foundation

Ford, J. and Wilcox, S. (1998), 'Owner occupation, employment and welfare: the impact of changing relationships on sustainable home ownership', vol 13, *Housing Studies*, 623

Galanter, S (1974), 'Why the 'haves' come out ahead: speculations on the limits of legal change', vol 9, *Law and Society Review*, 95

Genn, H. and Genn, Y. (1989), *The Nature and Effectiveness of Representation at Tribunals*, London: LCD

Gentle, C., Dorling, D. and Cornford, J. (1994), 'Negative equity and British housing in the 1990s: cause and effect', vol 31, *Urban Studies*, 181

Housing Corporation (1997), *Performance Standards and Regulatory Guidance*, London: Housing Corporation

Housing Corporation (1998), *The Assured Periodic Tenant's Charter*, London: Housing Corporation

Hughes, D. and Lowe, S. (1995), *Social Housing Law and Policy*, London: Butterworths

Hunter, T. (1998), 'Upturn in home loan arrears', *The Guardian*, 30 June

Hunter, C. and Nixon, J. (1997), 'Tenure preference, discourse and debt: language's role in tenure stigmatisation', paper given to International Sociological Association Research Committee, Alexandria, Virginia, USA, *Housing in the 21st Century: Looking Forward*, June 1997

Independent Housing Ombudsman (1997), *Annual Report and Digest of Cases 1996–97*, London: Independent Housing Ombudsman

Kemp, P. and McLaverty, P. (1995), *Private Tenants and Restrictions in Rent for Housing Benefit*, York: Centre for Housing Policy, University of York

Lord Chancellor's Department (1998), *Judicial Statistics*, London: LCD

Luba, J., Madge, N. and McConnell, D. (1997), *Defending Possession Proceedings*, London: LAG

National Consumer Council (1992), *Mortgage Arrears: Services to Borrowers in Debt*, London: NCC

Malpass, P., Warburton, M., Bramley, G. and Smart, G. (1993), *Housing Policy in Action*, Bristol: School for Advanced Urban Studies, University of Bristol

Nixon, J. and Hunter, C. (1996), "It was humiliating actually. I wouldn't go again': rent arrears and possession proceedings in the county court', vol 11, *Netherlands Journal of Housing and the Built Environment*, 421

Nixon, J. and Hunter, C. (1998), 'Better a public tenant than a private borrower be: the possession process and threat of eviction', in D. Cowan (ed), *Housing: Participation and Exclusion*, Aldershot: Dartmouth

Nixon, J., Hunter, C., Smith, Y. and Wishart, B. (1996), *Housing Cases in County Courts*, Bristol: Policy Press

Pryce, G. (1998), 'Income Support for mortgage interest and the crowding out of mortgage payment protection insurance', Issue 39, *Housing Finance*, 27

Rock, P. (1973), *Making People Pay*, London: Routledge

Sarre, P., Phillips, D. and Skellington, R. (1989), *Ethnic Minority Housing: Explanations and Policies*, Aldershot: Gower

Scottish Homes (1997), *Tenancy Rights and Repossession Rates: In Theory and Practice*, Research Report 55, Edinburgh: Scottish Homes

Shelter (1998), *Access Denied: The Exclusion of People in Need from Social Housing*, London: Shelter

Whitehouse, L. (1997), 'The right to possession: the need for substantive reform', in P. Jackson and D. Wilde (eds), *The Reform of Property Law*, Aldershot: Gower

Whitehouse, L. (1998), 'The impact of consumerism on the home owner', in D. Cowan (ed.), *Housing: Participation and Exclusion*, Aldershot: Dartmouth

Wikeley, N. (1995), 'Income Support and mortgage interest: the new rules', vol 2, *Journal of Social Security Law*, 168

18 Housing and Crime Control

'Such an assumption seems to me to ignore the central fact about deviance: it is created by society. I do not mean this in the way it is ordinarily understood, in which the causes of deviance are located in the social situation of the deviant or in "social factors" which prompt his action. I mean, rather, that *social groups create deviance by making the rules whose infraction constitutes deviance*, and by applying those rules to particular people and labeling them as outsiders. From this point of view, deviance is *not* a quality of the act the person commits, but rather a consequence of the application by others of rules and sanctions to an "offender".' (Becker, 1963, p. 9)

One of the great successes of the Thatcher governments of the 1980s was the depiction of council housing as 'hard-to-let, high-rise, marginalised estates' (Jacobs & Manzi, 1996, p. 548). These were no-go zones for everybody, including the police and other agents of social control. Major's discussion of the environment of council housing in 1995, and Blair's in 1997 when launching the Social Exclusion Unit, concentrated on its 'otherness' – these estates are 'set apart from the rest of the community' (Major, 1995), or there was 'an underclass of people cut off from society's mainstream, without any sense of shared purpose' (Blair, 1997). Stigmatized and marginalized in this way, council housing has been regarded as criminogenic in itself.

This was a partial picture. Data from the British Crime Survey showed that it was true that certain parts of the sector had higher crime rates than other sectors for burglary and violent crime (see Mirlees-Black *et al.*, 1998, pp. 29–43). However, private renting has a higher incidence of these crimes (*ibid*). What one can say is that the worst council estates have higher crime rates than other areas (which can be shown by ward-level analysis of the data). Drawing on the British Crime Survey dataset, Pantazis has found that the most significant correlating factor in terms of *fear of crime* was *poverty*: '. . . poor people are consistently more likely to feel unsafe when alone on the streets after dark, regardless of the type of neighbourhood they reside in. . . . To this effect, anxiety about crime and victimisation can be seen as part of a long chain of insecurities, which may be more prevalent in the lives of people in poverty' (forthcoming).

The concentration on council housing as 'other' was part of the process of encouraging tenants to exercise their right to buy; to exercise the Thatcherite duologue of 'self-reliance' and 'personal responsibility' by leaving the tenure. The success of the policies to reconstruct 'social housing' have led to a *residualized* and *marginalized* sector. There has been 'a clear and more distinctive channelling of deprived groups into council housing and affluent groups into owner occupation . . . a clear sorting of the population into different tenures much more closely related to their affluence and employment' (Murie, 1997, p. 27). But there are two riders to this significant reshuffling of the pack. The first is that many council housing residents would not recognize the picture painted of them. If all council housing was uniformly poor, and council tenants were all so fearful of crime and desperate to move, then why did many people purchase their council properties? Of course, the truth is that council housing, as with other tenures, is not uniformly anything – it is temporally, spatially, and qualitatively differentiated. To talk of 'it' generically is to fall into the trap laid by unfavourably disposed politicians. What can be said is that, since the 1960s, the sector has housed a larger proportion of marginalized people and the sector now demonstrates considerable levels of economic inactivity and polarization of household types (Lee & Murie, 1997, pp. 9–12).

Second, a concentration on council housing sets a unitenurial base to the debate (why does crime happen on council estates?), as if crime does not happen elsewhere or other tenures have not become economically marginalized. More and more people are being excluded from council housing (because of a lack of supply and other factors, such as their behaviour) (Butler, 1998). Where do they go? The lack of supply of council housing means that, even with those the council *is* willing to house, other tenures will often be used to provide accommodation for the economically marginalized (see Part II of this book). Thus, 'There is a danger that, without balancing the picture of poverty on estates with a picture of poverty elsewhere, there is a tendency to reinforce stereotypes which associate council housing estates generally with low-self-esteem and a downward spiral' (Murie, 1997, p. 31). A belief that only local authorities are landlords of 'difficult-to-let' estates belies the fact that RSLs often manage these estates and occasionally have developed them – Pawson and Kearns estimate from a 1996 survey of RSLs that about 52,500 properties were difficult-to-let and these were differentially distributed within the stock (1998). As I write, this morning's newspaper carries the headline 'Billions wasted on unwanted homes' about RSL developments on 'areas where no one wants to live' (Hetherington, 1998).

Nevertheless, the way the problem is framed by the primary definers (powerful individuals, such as members of the government: see Hall *et al.*, 1978, pp. 57–60) also provides the supposed solution. Thus, it should not surprise us that part of the Conservative government's 'solution' to the problem involved further stigmatizing council housing by giving councils the power to give all their tenants a 'probationary' tenancy – even the colloquial name itself, coined by the government, suggested that these tenancies were part of the system of crime control. Thus, the supposed unitenurial nature of the worst 'problems' was met by unitenurial solutions. When in opposition and power, Jack Straw has focused attention on low-level crimes committed by the tenure-less (the homeless, 'aggressive' beggars, and 'vagrants'). The supposed solution has required concentrated policing on 'cleaning up the streets' through 'zero tolerance' strategies – 'pathologising, containing, and controlling, the marginal groups of the city streets' (Brogden & Nijhar, 1997, p. 19; see also Fooks & Pantazis, 1999).

The message has been that, however marginalized a person is, they still have a choice whether or not to commit crime (a version of the Left Realist brand of criminology: see, for discussion, Brownlee, 1998, pp. 318–21). For many politicians this choice thesis is related to a breakdown of society's *mores* or the loss of community values, particularly amongst the so-called 'underclass', who are characterized in one thesis as 'the new rabble' (Murray, 1990). More broadly, however, crime levels have been linked with the failure of the state to control crime, and the limits of the sovereign state. Crime has become a 'normal, commonplace, aspect of modern society' and the state has appeared powerless to prevent or control it (Garland, 1996, pp. 450–2). A knee-jerk response to that failure has been to argue for more punitive responses (such as Michael Howard's refrain that 'Prison Works!') because such responses are 'act[s] of sovereign might' which enable us to keep faith in the state.

The current *zeitgeist* reflects the ever-narrowing penumbra of responses to this failure of the state. When one punitive response fails, we can only conceive of even more punitive responses – in other words, we are trapped in a downward spiral of punishment. This downward spiral is mirrored by the 'increasingly hysterical' discourse about crime 'which trades in images, archetypes and anxieties, rather than in careful analyses and research findings' (Garland, 1996, p. 461). At the same time, such responses paradoxically heighten the public's concern: 'In addition, by increasing the public's sense of insecurity, this discourse of the predatory other serves to increase the intensity of social reaction to law-breaking' (Brownlee, 1998, 326). No longer are we interested in the causes of crime (although we are 'tough' on them, whatever they may be), we are only interested in the responses to crime (and we are 'tough' here as well).

A classic example of this increasingly hysterical discourse has been the concentration, by media and government, upon the so-called 'neighbours from hell' and, less person-specific, anti-social behaviour. Two television series have concentrated upon them; newspapers have been full of stories about them, their eviction, and their estates; and politicians, the police and other local agents have sought to respond appropriately. Local responses have ranged from the bizarre to the extreme, and sometimes both. So, one television programme concerned the following scenario: '*Armed with the power of eviction*, local housing officer Patrick Collins patrols the streets and enforces a policy of zero tolerance. Get tenants to keep their gardens in good nick (preferably with a few hanging baskets on show), he reckons, and you gradually weed out vandalism, graffiti and crime from the area' (review of *Modern Times*, *The Guardian*, 15 April 1998). Oldham Council's tenants now have a 29-page tenancy agreement, designed by 'a woman at war with neighbours from hell' (Hugill, 1998); Dundee Council had a scheme where 'up to four anti-social families will be forced to live together' in a 'ghetto from hell' (Arlidge, 1996). And the judiciary have got in on the act as well, by rewriting the legislation so that 'problem families' may be more easily evicted (see, for example, *Northampton BC* v *Lovatt*, Unreported, CA, 11 November 1997; *Bristol CC* v *Mousah* (1998) 30 HLR 32).

National responses have focused on the creation of overlapping legislation designed to appeal as much to the thirst for punishment as to being careful responses to analysed problems. Few have stopped to think about the nature, extent, and causes of the problem (for a notable exception, see the important Hunter *et al.*, 1998) because it has been portrayed as an omnipresent, 'we all know it's there, we don't need research to tell us this' type of problem. Yet in the past three years, the following legislation has been passed through Parliament as part of the response to this perceived (or created) problem: Housing Act 1996, Part V; Noise Act 1996; Protection from Harassment Act 1997; Crime and Disorder Act 1998. The rumbling voices of discontent about this litany are simply brushed aside ('After all, they cannot *all* be sent to live next door to nice Professor Ashworth', the Vinerian Professor of English Law, who had dared to suggest that new proposals were far too heavy handed: Bennett, 1998). In short, housing and its management has become a crucial part of the crime control industry; housing departments have become the intermediators in the new criminal justice system (see, further, Cowan & Gilroy, 1998).

Such a response has been characteristic of the current supposed panacea of multi-agency working. The net of those responsible for crime control has been widened. The police cannot control crime single handedly. They need the support of others ('Responsibility for the crime problem . . . is now everyone's': Crawford, 1997, p. 25). Here is the derivation of the ubiquitous, solve-all, catch-all, supposedly unproblematic multi-agency, or partnership, approach; the community must rise, phoenix-like, once more. As Crawford puts it, '[A]ppeals to 'community' and 'partnerships' make up an important element in the recalibration of what constitutes the legitimate responsibilities of individuals, groups and the state' (1997, p. 63). This comes at a time when 'community is the site of fear and blame rather than choice and pride' (Taylor, 1998, p. 822). These strategies of increasing punishment and inclusive crime control, part of which Garland terms 'responsibilization', are both reflected in the most recent legislative contribution, the Crime and Disorder Act 1998. Local authorities and police are now to work in partnership to develop strategies of crime control (ss 5 & 6; see also Home Office, 1998); and the civil–criminal law distinction has been further blurred by the creation of anti-social behaviour orders, the breach of which results in criminal liability.

Taking a step back from this rush to criminalize is not easy. However, it is the central purpose of this chapter to examine how this rush has affected the landscape of housing management. I want to pursue a rather simple proposition. The hysteria generated by the failure to control crime, combined with the rise of the undefined notion of 'anti-social behaviour', has created a more concentrated penal response in relation to social housing as a tenure but *not* to other tenures. Thus, the labelling of social housing has affected the responses of housing management and the criminal justice system. Legalistic solutions have been generated which penalize individual tenants without seeking to solve the broader problems of estates and areas (see Papps, 1998). I do not wish to deny the very real problems on some council estates. The point, though, is that these problems exist in all housing tenures, not just social housing. After all, council estates now play host to a variety of different tenures (after the right to buy and other privatization measures). In considering the response of one council to anti-social behaviour, Papps notes that 'Council tenants, who are the perpetrators of anti-social behaviour face more punitive treatment than other residents who may indulge in the same behaviour. Even if the council enforce by-laws and statutory powers more vigorously the non-council tenants will not be threatened with loss of their home' (1998, p. 651).

The Social Exclusion Unit's (SEU) report on neighbourhood renewal has also identified the fact that 'poor neighbourhoods . . . are not all the same kind of design, they don't all consist of rented or council housing, and they are not all in towns and cities. They aren't all 'estates', or 'worst', nor do the people who live there want them described that way' (SEU, 1998b, para. 1.2). However, if people living in poverty are more likely to be in fear of crime than others (Pantazis, forthcoming) *and* we know that three quarters of those living in social housing are amongst the poorest 40 per cent of the population (SEU, 1998b, para. 1.16), then it is likely that some areas of social housing will have a higher concentration of crime levels than other tenures.

In the first section, we pursue this theme through considering criminological analyses of the creation of 'problem' estates. We trace one criminological theme – the importance of places and spaces to both offences and offenders (Bottoms & Wiles, 1997). This strand of criminology provides an important counterbalance to knee-jerk reactions. It can be (and has been) argued that housing policy and the housing market have been crucial determinants in the dynamic creation of 'residential community crime careers' (a phrase referring to the dynamic, changing spatial distribution of crime within communities) (Bottoms & Wiles, 1986, p. 103). In other words, the processes of housing allocation are key in determining the creation of 'problem' estates. This literature tells us that crime is spatially, temporally, and tenurially distributed on an unequal basis – thus, no two estates or areas are the same. Labelling certain areas of public-sector housing as 'problem estates' has crucial effects on the mechanisms of housing allocation and becomes a self-fulfilling prophecy (less popular areas have shorter waiting lists and are, therefore, the preserve of the most desperate; although *cf* Pawson & Kearns, 1998, in the context of RSLs) (Baldwin, 1979, p. 59). Housing allocation concentrates poorer people in poorer accommodation and, in itself, distributes crime. Not all social housing, therefore, can be regarded as crime-ridden, and the concentration must be on the pockets of deprivation that have occurred. The increasing fragmentation of tenure also provides evidence that housing market processes have subtly altered so that unitenurial solutions systematically penalize the occupants of that tenure. Thus, in one study of racial harassment, it was noted that 'Even when victims and perpetrators live next door to one another, they may no longer share the same landlord' and different methods of enforcement apply in different tenures (Dhooge and Barelli, 1996, para. 13.11).

The second section of this chapter will consider the more specific issue of how anti-social behaviour is defined. This is a crucial question because the way we respond is determined by how we define the issue. There are three specific, linked questions: first, what acts constitute anti-social behaviour; second, who commits these acts; and third, what is its spatial dimension (neighbourhood, locality, community, estate)?. None of these questions are susceptible to easy answers and we can only provide broad links with other debates. Once again, the point that is made is that anti-social behaviour does not only occur in social housing tenure, but perhaps occurs naturally in any built-up area. So, for example, the major complaint found by most studies has related to noise levels which are presumably worst in high density housing estates simply because of proximity.

In the third section, we will consider the ways in which housing management currently, and in the future, polices housing. This is done through developing a rough *ad hoc* taxonomy of responses, by contrasting what was available with what has become available for these purposes: 'traditional' housing management responses, such as evictions (including the role of the courts); innovative housing management 'solutions' proposed by central government (including probationary/introductory tenancies; Noise Act 1996; and the anti-social behaviour orders in the Crime and Disorder Act 1998); and finally policing strategies (in particular, multi-agency working and zero tolerance). I will be arguing that housing management has become a key mediator in the burgeoning regulation of anti-social behaviour deviance. It has been given considerable powers for this purpose, but these powers overlap. With each successive legislative provision, they become more and more reactionary.

Somewhat controversially, I think, it will also be argued that landlords/ lenders have always acted as agents of social control – mediating between property and the accretion of capital – through tenancy agreements or mortgage arrangements. The greater rights you give people in their home, the easier it is to monitor and control them, for your threats are commensurably greater as there is more to be lost (*cf* Smith & George, 1997). This is exemplified by the belief that, if you grant a paedophile a public-sector tenancy, you are better able to monitor them (because they will not want to give up a 'tenancy for life') and control them (because your threats are more pertinent than if they had, say, no security). Rather than stressing the *rights* of tenants, we stress their *responsibilities*. As the DoE suggested in 1995: 'A secure tenancy is a valuable asset, providing a home for life. In the government's view this has to be earned' (DoE, 1995, para. 3.1). The extensions of this social control by the Crime and Disorder Act, and other legislation such as the Noise Act 1996, are natural, if unwarranted, extensions of this element in the matrix of social control. They simply make apparent what before was implicit.

18.1   Environmental Criminology

Environmental criminology relates crime *'first*, to particular *places*, and *secondly*, to the way that individuals and organizations shape their activities *spatially*, and in so doing are in turn influenced by *place-based* or *spatial* factors' (Bottoms & Wiles, 1997, p. 305). It has a long history, although in England, it has benefitted from considerable advances in the past twenty years or so ('the Sheffield research'). This research has shown that areal relationships with crime have a temporal dimension in that they change over periods; that the relationships between place, on the one hand, and offences and offenders, on the other, are critical; and third, that the housing market and housing policy are crucial factors in the explanation of the spatial patterning of crime (Bottoms *et al.*, 1992, pp. 118–120; Bottom & Wiles 1986, p. 105; 1997).

The Sheffield research began by considering the patterns of offending across tenures by Sheffield enumeration district in 1966. It found that, whilst rates of crime were lower in owner-occupied accommodation, higher levels of offending were experienced in private renting and council housing (which could not be completely explained by differential levels of policing and recording of crime). Equally, there were differences *within* tenures – some council housing had low rates of offending, whilst others had high rates; and the same pattern was true of private renting. Furthermore, on any key variable (social class, sex, age, percentage married, percentage unemployed), low-rise estates built at the same time and for the same purposes had radically different crime careers.

Factors commonly taken to be influential associations between estates and crime – such as child densities (see, for example Page, 1993), high rates of residential mobility (supposedly signifying lack of commitment to the area), design (Newman, 1972; Coleman, 1985; referred to by Lund as 'architectural determinism': 1995, p. 127), and the original designation of the estate as being for slum clearance tenants (Herbert, 1980) – were not shown to be relevant in the Sheffield research (Bottoms & Wiles, 1986, esp. p. 50–1). This does not mean that they are irrelevant, just that they did not explain the situation in Sheffield at that time. So, for example, Damer's detailed research explains how a problem estate was created by a combination of factors related to the rehousing of slum dwellers on a new estate which other locals believed was meant for them (1974). A rich picture is painted of political and local media antipathy towards, and stereotyping of, the new residents.

In the Sheffield research, two similar estates with differential crime levels were matched together for the purposes of analysis. The central claims of the researchers from their case studies (which have included matched areas of private renting and tower blocks in addition to the above: Bottoms & Wiles, 1986) have been summarized as follows:

> '[I]n order to understand and explain offending behaviour by residents of particular areas, it is vital to consider who lives in these areas; how they came to live there in the first place; what kind of social life the residents have created; how outsiders (including official agencies) react to them; and why they remain in the areas and have not moved.' (Bottoms *et al.*, 1992, p. 122)

A critical (albeit secondary) role, on this view, relates to processes of *allocation*, and the Sheffield research has argued that there is a close interaction, sometimes unintended, between residential community crime careers and processes of housing allocation. So, for example, the fact that a certain estate has a bad reputation (for whatever reason, as well as being either true or false) means that less people will choose to live there, leaving only those in severe housing need or with pre-existing links to the area to choose it. Thus, there is a close relationship between the reputation of an estate, its status as being 'difficult-to-let', and differential housing allocation procedures (although some problem estates are unpopular, but easy to let, especially in high demand areas: Pawson & Kearns, 1998, p. 396). Processes of 'matching' persons to properties has a similar effect so that those in greatest need are assumed to be willing to accept any sort of accommodation; or those typecast as problem families[1] are allocated properties on problem estates (Bottoms & Xanthos, 1986, pp. 206–8; Bottoms & Wiles, 1997, pp. 333–4). Home Office research suggested that 'the most worrying aspect of [the allocations processes on one accommodation block] was how quickly the concentration and escalation of problems occurred', however unintended this result was (Foster & Hope, 1993, pp. 87–9). This could only escalate once the effects of the post-1989 financial regime for council housing, together with the various performance targets, are felt because ever greater pressure to reduce the level of voids in council housing is applied.

In addition to the allocations processes, other micro factors were considered relevant in the Sheffield research. For example, the negative reputation of an estate may affect the types of person seeking rehousing on the estate; schools may be different; estates may register different crime levels on different parts of the estate; the existence of one or two problem families may be crucial (one factor which may have 'tipped' one of the study areas into becoming a problem area); as well as child socialization processes which are area specific (see Bottoms & Wiles, 1997, pp. 336–8). Hope suggests six 'kinds of concentration effect' are occurring in high crime communities in Britain, which 'ratchet together and amplify each other into a spiral of deterioration': compound social dislocations (i.e. an accumulation of social problems alongside crime); criminal embeddedness of local youth; disorder; repeated localised victimisation; diminishing informal control; criminal networks (1998, p. 53). Murie has similarly argued that, in addition to the self-fulfilling prophecy created by stigmatic reputation, 'the causal links [between the changing role and nature of council housing and crime] are not simple and straightforward. The key elements include the changing social composition of neighbourhoods, the loss of social cohesion associated with changing patterns of work, family and kinship links, and the high turnover of population in some estates' (1997, p. 35). Thus, there appears to be some level of agreement amongst researchers as to the environmental causes of crime.

The Sheffield researchers stress the importance of the changing dynamics of housing policy, including the ever-strengthening move to home ownership (see Bottoms & Wiles, 1986, pp. 108–23) – indeed, their research sought to capitalize on the advances of Rex and Moore's study of housing classes (1967). Yet, the increasing fragmentation of housing tenure that we have spied in earlier parts of this book, and the increasing tenure movements (particularly towards home ownership), as well as cross-tenurial policies (such as the creation of cross-tenurial interests, large-scale movements between tenures, and changing housing management structures), all suggest that the changing picture of housing tenure altered some of the residential crime careers. So, for example, the spatial impact of the right to buy and the creation of economically marginal home owners, as well as our increasing understanding of socio-tenurial polarization, has created a more complex appreciation of tenure mix.

Solutions to the 'problem' estate that concentrate on one dimension of housing – such as management (the Priority Estates Project (PEP)) or design (a move towards 'defensible space')[2] – have commonly been unsuccessful in halting crime (although, in the case of the PEP, this was not its motivation) (Foster & Hope, 1993; Murie, 1997, pp. 31–4). The Home Office review of the PEP suggested that it was not entirely successful in its approach of moving towards estate-based housing management and increased tenant participation (although it was hindered by lack of sympathy towards it by one housing manager in Tower Hamlets: Foster & Hope, 1993, pp. 32–4); furthermore, when compared with similar estates that did not have the benefits of the PEP, the effects were comparable. Hope and Foster's analysis of one PEP estate suggested that allocations pressures meant that the tower blocks were used to house young persons and others with histories of mental illness or alcohol problems. They conclude that:

'This study supports the view that the various causal influences on crime on the problem estate tend to interact with each other. This is likely to occur because their effect is mediated by the internal culture of the estate community. Changes in environmental design, management quality, and social mix appear to work together to encourage the growth of social control or of criminality; . . .' (1992, p. 501)

More broadly, the PEP's focus on housing management practices has not been totally successful in destigmatising many of its estates (see Power & Tunstall, 1995). The current concerns are therefore more holistic, focusing also on the causes of poverty as part of a programme of regeneration (this has been a particular focus, for example, of Housing Action Trusts) (see Taylor, 1995; Gilroy, 1996; 1998). A focus on holistic solutions can be spied in the report of the Social Exclusion Unit into 'a strategy for neighbourhood renewal' (1998b).

18.2 Anti-social Behaviour

So far, we have considered the broad aspects of crime, criminality and the environment. In this section, we narrow our focus to anti-social behaviour, in the context of its environment. Much of the current strain of crime control policies have been related to anti-social behaviour, and this is where much of the current media panic concerning housing and crime is located. The presentation is of an unproblematic consensus in the 'war on', 'battle against', or 'clamping down on' anti-social behaviour. Our gaze has consequently been diverted away from three key questions – what is anti-social behaviour? who commits it? where does it occur? Before we consider the reaction to the supposed problem, we need to know what that problem is – how else are we to evaluate the success of the reaction other than in relation to the problem it is supposed to solve (Hunter *et al.*, 1998, p. 2).

What is Anti-social Behaviour?

Even posing this question is problematic, for it cannot be said with any certainty that 'anti-social behaviour' is what we are concerned with. Section 1 of the Crime and Disorder Act may use the phrase, but this has not been a constant. Others have equated anti-social behaviour with 'nuisance'. So, in a draft supplement to its *Performance Standards* on anti-social behaviour, the Housing Corporation quoted Hilary Armstrong, the Housing Minister, as saying 'All [RSLs] should have appropriate procedures for dealing with complaints about nuisance behaviour, including complaints made by neighbours who are not residents'. The current government's Consultation Paper on the Community Safety Order (the antecedent of the anti-social behaviour order) made the following points:

> 'Anti-social behaviour *causes* distress and misery to innocent, law-abiding people – and undermines the communities in which they live. *Neighbourhood harassment* by individuals or groups, often under the influence of alcohol or drugs, has often reached unacceptable levels, and revealed a serious gap in the ability of the authorities to tackle this social menace. The Government is committed to tackle this problem *to*

allow people to live their lives free from fear and intimidation.' (Home Office, 1997, para. 1; emphasis added)

Quite how one can quantify ('unacceptable levels') an undefined problem is a mystery. After all, just two years earlier, the Labour Party had made the point that there are no nationwide records on the extent of the problem (although a similar effect is subsequently discussed: 'But almost every area of the country suffers from serious anti-social behaviour and much is drug-related.': Labour Party, 1995, p. 3). What we are most concerned about, therefore, are the effects 'it' has around us. This appears to be a common thread running through many governmental Consultation Documents, which are more concerned with appealing to popular consciousness than to rigorous analysis of defined problems (see, for example, DoE, 1992; Home Office, 1991).

The closest that we come to an official definition of 'anti-social behaviour' was in the DoE Consultation Paper on Probationary Tenancies. Having discussed its effects ('misery', 'stigmatised'), we are then treated to the following definition:

'Such behaviour manifests itself *in many different ways and at varying levels of intensity.* This can include vandalism, noise, verbal and physical abuse, threats of violence, racial harassment, damage to property, trespass, nuisance from dogs, car repairs on the street, joyriding, domestic violence, drugs and other criminal activities, such as burglary.' (DoE, 1995, p. 2; emphasis added)

Thus, the only official definition we have is that it can be practically any act (but presumably not an omission to act?). It seems that the most common complaint in social housing relates to the levels of noise (see Hunter *et al.*, 1998, p. 5), which in turn suggests that responsibility lies with poor insulation, and more powerful equipment (Scottish Affairs Committee, 1996). But, in general, many of the acts complained about are already criminal offences ('burglaries, thefts from and of vehicles, and intimidation in the form of threats, abuse, assaults, loud noise or the use of aggressive dogs': Labour Party, 1995, p. 1). Perhaps, therefore, the true focus of complaint should relate to policing failures, and not necessarily be used to stigmatize certain persons further.

This point can be illustrated by considering the particular issue of racial harassment. On any view of 'anti-social behaviour', racial harassment would be included. Since the mid-1980s, councils and the police have been exhorted to take action in these circumstances but little action is taken (see, for example, Home Office, 1989; DoE, 1994). It is commonly said that local authorities should evict those of their tenants who are guilty of racial harassment but 'social landlords are often criticised for what appears to be an extremely high rate of attrition' in the eviction of perpetrators (Dhooge and Barelli, 1996, para. 18.17). In fact, in 1993–4, of 85 landlords who had previously issued notices of seeking possession against perpetrators, just 130 such notices were issued. Many local authorities have strong policy statements on racial harassment[3] but take little action (see, for example, Sibbett, 1997, Ch. 2). In one study in Newham, it was found that victims of racial harassment ended up blaming the council and the police more than the perpetrator (Cooper & Qureshi, 1994).

By contrast, Scott and Parkey argue that anti-social behaviour should be considered along a 'spectrum . . . comprising three distinct (yet potentially interrelated) phenomena, these being: neighbour disputes, neighbourhood problems and crime problems' (1998, 329). Such a spectrum accepts that different people (tenants' landlords) perceive the issue in different ways, depending upon their perspective, and has the added benefit of indicating that a range of agencies 'have a part to play in solutions' (*ibid*). Demystifying the discourse in this thought-provoking way provides an important counterbalance to the increasingly hysterical government/media discourse. However, it does not take us much further. To say that different people perceive different conceptualizations of the 'problem' in different ways does not assist with appropriate responses (after all, we all perceive social problems in different ways). Furthermore, individuals, whether tenants or landlords, home owners or lenders, commonly have diverse reactions to the same 'problem'. Simply because one is (say) an RSL tenant does not mean that reactions will be uniform.

We might conclude that 'it' has become a *leitmotif*, a common thread, and the phrase to which we hark back in creating and justifying our responses. But this hides the fact that its boundaries may be unknown other than in the individual consciousness. In other words, in that familiarly flabby political response, we might say that 'we all know' what it is, who does it, and where it occurs. Nevertheless, the label (the 'it') we use is crucial; in terms similar to Becker's conceptualizing of labelling theory, Hunter *et al.* make the following point:

> 'For some these labels ["neighbour nuisance", "neighbour disputes", "anti-social behaviour"] may be interchangeable. However, for others, the choice of label is important. The expression "anti-social behaviour" has strong negative connotations, and its use generally carries the implication that the behaviour in question is blameworthy. The expression "neighbour disputes" does not suggest that blame is necessarily being attributed. It appears to focus on the fact of there being a dispute. *The choice of label may well reflect a conclusion about the appropriate response: punitive responses to "anti-social behaviour", and attempts to mediate agreement in "neighbour disputes".*' (1998, p. 2; emphasis added)

Who commits 'it'?

We must begin with an additional caveat. It is a commonplace observation that different police districts, and different individual members of the police, operate different policing techniques, criteria to record crime, and different responses to the same situation (all within their discretion). Consequently, crime statistics need to be used with care. Housing management also seems to regard differentially those who commit 'it':

'If management believe that it is listening to the voice of the decent law-abiding majority, its response is likely to be more sympathetic. But the situation may already, at least in part, have been prejudged by management's own contribution to the labelling of "respectable" and "disreputable" tenants' (Popplestone & Paris, 1979, p. 22).

Thus, the categorization of an estate or area as a 'problem' or 'difficult-to-let' may also reflect upon the categorization of the types of tenant/owner who commit 'problems'.

The variable housing management response also has an effect on the tenants: 'As everybody *knew* there were anti-social families in the estate, from whom there was a marginal chance of physical, and a real chance of symbolic violence, but as nobody seemed to know exactly where they lived, there was a generalised suspicion directed at the furthest point from them' (Damer, 1974, p. 238). In other words, the process of labelling affects the way occupants view each other.

Karn *et al.* (1997, Part II) draw upon the work of Felstiner *et al.* (1980–1) to consider the steps that occur before a grievance becomes a complaint – 'naming, blaming, and claiming'. This trilogy provides an important insight into the processes which lead to the formation of a complaint, as well as in the identification of complainant, injury, and person complained about. Broadly, for a grievance to crystallize, a person must recognize their injury (naming), attribute fault to a particular person or agency (blaming), and voice their complaint (claiming). Because individuals experience each aspect in different ways, many potential complaints are not identified and thus only a selective number of persons or agencies are blamed (see below for the effect of external stigmatization). For example, if I hold a rowdy, noisy party and you live three doors down from me, you may not feel that this is sufficient to complain about; you may not even recognize that it is a problem. Damer makes the same point: 'Noise was the main anti-social phenomenon in Wine Alley [his study area, a 'problem' estate], and sometimes it could be very noisy indeed, but I honestly doubt whether it was any noisier than the student area of any large city on a Saturday night' (1974, p. 237).

The consensus appears to be that 'a minority' of households are responsible for most of the complaints about anti-social behaviour (Foster & Hope, 1993, pp. 47–50; Reynolds, 1986), although it is believed by governments (both Conservative and Labour) that the problem is growing (DoE, 1995, para. 1.1), to the extent that 'there are thousands of people whose lives are made a misery' (Labour Party, 1995, p. 1). In the context of racial harassment, Sibbett refers to 'a critical, mutually supportive relationship between the individual perpetrator and the wider community' that is referred to as the *'perpetrator community'* (1997, p. 101). Foster and Hope note that, on one of their study estates, 'there was one particular family who were regarded by tenants and housing staff alike as responsible for the majority of the problems'. This family was stigmatized by the other tenants on the estate 'as much because they were gypsies as the trouble they caused' (1993, pp. 48–9). The stigma was therefore twofold and possibly also mutually dependent. Scott and Parkey note that others commonly stigmatized, such as those involved with drugs or released into the community from hospitals, do not appear to be significant in tenants surveys; nor do problems created by lifestyle differences caused by factors such as age (1998, pp. 331–4). Crucially also,[4] research is unclear on how long the person is a tenant before 'it' occurs: 'the vast majority (86 per cent) of those who said that they were the subject of complaint in the previous year had been tenants for more than three years' (*ibid*, 334; Clapham *et al.*, 1995).

Where does 'it' occur?

There are two related questions here. First, are certain areas more likely to experience 'it'? And second, who is affected by 'it'?

Answering the first question tends to reveal ideological, tenurial preferences. So, for example, the Conservatives began their Probationary Tenancies Consultation with the sentence 'Anti-social behaviour by a small minority of tenants and others *is a growing problem on council estates*' (DoE, 1995, para. 1.1). There is only tentative support for this, which suggests that 'where landlords have polarised estates, there may be a higher proportion of neighbour complaints in more disadvantaged areas' (Scott & Parkey, 1998, p. 331, drawing on Clapham *et al.*, 1995). Possible relevant factors were the proportion of tenants in receipt of Housing Benefit, and the degree of turnover on each estate (further research is needed to test these findings) – although the same factors would also affect private and RSL renting. A factor inhibiting our appreciation of the spatial impact of anti-social behaviour and other crime is the differential recording of crime by the police. This has been particularly prevalent in relation to racial harassment (Sibbett, 1997). But the experience of crime reflects different socialization patterns, and no clear results emerge. Certainly the findings from the Sheffield research do not suggest any such correlations. Probably, it would be better to support the view adopted by the Labour Party that 'plenty of those guilty of criminal anti-social behaviour are private tenants or owner occupiers' (1995, p. 7; see also the Scottish Affairs Committee, 1996). One can, no doubt, link certain types of complaints (such as noise) to high density areas, but these exist in all tenures in all cities. Consequently, there is no evidence to support a tenure-skew, other than the important observation that council housing (and also RSLs) accommodates the most marginalized, poor, long-term unemployed people. So, if poverty and social exclusion is correlated with crime, one might expect to find crime being more prevalent in areas of council housing.

There are no answers either to the second question – who is affected by anti-social behaviour? Government departments have adopted various spatial definitions: 'the communities in which [innocent, law-abiding people] live' (Home Office, 1997, para. 1); 'the people next door, down the street or on the floor above or below' (Labour Party, 1995, p. 1, using the notion of neighbour); 'whole estates' (DoE, 1995, para. 1.1). As Henry LJ put it:

'[The term "neighbours"] is clearly intended to cover *all persons sufficiently close to the source of the conduct complained of to be adversely affected by that conduct.* In these days of amplified music, there is force in GK Chesterton's observation: "Your next door neighbour . . . is not a man; he is an environment".' (*Northampton BC* v *Lovatt*, Unreported, CA, 11 November 1997, Transcript, p. 9 – emphasis added)

18.3 Policing Housing

Various statutory agencies are responsible for the policing of housing – social services departments, probation services, housing departments, and the police. Additionally, communities are also requested to become involved in policing their areas, through vehicles such as neighbourhood watch (see Crawford, 1997). There is, consequently, much scope for duplication. The primary aim of this section, however, is to consider how the management personnel of housing might assist in that policing role.

Concentration in this section is upon *social* housing and the role of housing management in crime control. This is because the primary focus of much of the recent debate about environmental crime has concerned social housing, and this is reflected in the legislative responses. Even when the problems are perceived as being tenure-neutral, such as in the Labour Party's document, the proposed solution has revolved around greater involvement for local authorities (as in the 1998 Act). There is, however, a preliminary issue relating to the *legitimacy* of the housing management role in policing areas/estates which particularly relates to 'social' landlords (see Papps, 1998, pp. 652–3).

The issue has been framed in this way: '. . . why should tenants of social landlords be subject to interventionist tactics by their landlords with regard to questions of behaviour?' (Hughes *et al.*, 1994, p. 221). The authors have some difficulty in answering that question, although it is patent that they believe that social landlords should adopt such techniques because, for example, of the need to promote racial and community harmony, to protect the housing stock from becoming difficult-to-let, or because of obligations owed particularly to vulnerable tenants (pp. 222–5). Subsequently, Hughes has suggested that:

'Authorities have traditionally exercised a number of regulatory functions, but the new legislation is a major departure in giving them a general undifferentiated function as agents of social control. Some might see here room for conflict with an authority's responsibilities to provide and manage housing and to deal with homelessness, and (in many ways) to act as a landlord of last resort for those who are marginalised in society.' (Hughes, 1998)

I suggest, however, that there should be no need for such an ideological debate. The processes of housing, from its design, to its allocation, to its management, and through to individual exclusion are concerned with social control (see Cohen, 1985, Chs 5 & 6). This most particularly applies to social housing because of the greater security of tenure given to its tenants. On this basis, the debate about anti-social behaviour is nothing more than the state flexing its muscle – showing who is the big boss – by showing its power (through legislating and increasing insecurity in the sector). Smith and George argue, by contrast, that the various measures proposed by the Conservatives in 1995 for dealing with council tenure, were a preface for a broader attack on council tenure (1997). I argue that this is an incorrect view.

The power of the state lies in its ability to use this security as the proverbial carrot – you only get hold of it if you behave appropriately but once you have shown yourself capable of behaving appropriately, it is yours unless or until you do not. Thus, social housing is part of the crime control system – it is there to focus our minds on *inclusion* and forms part of the mechanics of 'inclusionary control'. 'Working-class deviant behaviour is segregated away and contained; if the proles become threatening, they can be "subjected like animals by a few simple rules"' (Cohen, 1985, p. 224). For the Conservatives, council housing was anathema – those occupying it were, by the very nature of their occupation, *the deviant other*. Security of tenure is one method of controlling such people; the intentional homelessness provision is another. This can clearly be shown by the importance given by some councils to tenancy agreements, and the need clearly to spell out the tenant's obligations (for 29 pages). Consider the following comment from one housing solicitor closely associated with the moves to greater social control:

'The short-termism of eviction and exclusion is purely fire fighting. . . . Having said that, strong action is very often needed at an early stage. Reclaiming an estate from the cycle of decline through enforcement of tenancy agreements, eviction, crime prevention and joint police and housing initiatives, will remove the criminal and anti-social fraternity from their stronghold. The eviction of one 'problem family' sends shockwaves throughout a whole estate. Do this a few times and the offenders soon get the message.' (Malik, 1998, p. 16; see also Harriott, 1998)

The author is clear that punitive measures of social control against the few sufficiently control the remaining tenants. Use of the law is a critical part of this process – the author subsequently refers to the 'full toolbox' of potential legal actions or procedures. These are the innovative solutions to crime and these also focus the mind on its prevention through local authorities ridding themselves of 'problem' occupants.

By contrast, I argue that the changes to the law over the previous three years are unwarranted. Not only do these changes overlap, but they also change the focus from reliance on due process, to more explicit measures of crime control (to adopt Packer's models: 1968; see also Sanders & Young, 1994, pp. 12–20). This change has resulted in 'the repression of criminal conduct [as being] viewed as by far the most important function to be performed by the criminal process' which, in turn, relies to a considerable degree upon the good practice and faith of the housing managers. For the sake of brevity, as well as showing their extent, they are as follows: injunctions and powers of arrest (Housing Act 1996); injunctions and powers of arrest (Protection from Harassment Act 1997); anti-social behaviour orders and powers of arrest (Crime and Disorder Act 1998); amended grounds of possession for nuisance and criminal acts (Housing Act 1996); introductory, or probationary, tenancy scheme for local authorities with easier possession grounds (Housing Act 1996); powers of RSLs to grant assured shorthold tenancies with minimum rights in certain circumstances (Housing Corporation, 1998); powers to curb excessive noise (defined as being above 35 decibels), creation of and offence for the same, and powers to enter and seize goods (Noise Act 1996); requirement of local authority to work with the police in the development of crime reduction strategies (Crime and Disorder Act 1998, ss. 5 & 6); requirement on local authorities to exercise all their functions 'with due regard to the likely effect of the exercise of those functions on, and the need to do all that it reasonably can to prevent crime and disorder in its area' (Crime and Disorder Act 1998, s. 17). Presumably this means that tenant selection and allocation should also be altered as the environmental criminologists have shown how its effects can contribute to the 'tipping' of estates.

Traditional Measures

Traditionally, social housing managers have adopted the belief that taking steps to evict tenants is an admission of failure. It was consequently a last resort, only to be used in certain cases. Other steps are considered more socially desirable, such as (in the case of racial harassment or other forms of anti-social behaviour) sending warning letters threatening eviction. Indeed, only a tiny minority of evictions are brought on the grounds of anti-social behaviour (although some are dealt with as rent arrears cases because it is easier to succeed on this ground). In one Scottish study of local authorities and RSLs, it was found that, whilst two-thirds of RSLs rarely or never take legal action for neighbour nuisance, this was true for less than one-third of authorities (Mullen *et al.*, 1997, p. 43). It is clear that eviction on the ground of a tenant's, or their friends'/visitors'/other residents', behaviour has become an important part of the 'toolbox'. If not eviction, then *injunctions* against further nuisance have also become regarded as an important device in deviance control (see especially s. 152, Housing Act 1996). Concentration here is on evictions – the most potent form of social control.

Eviction: Scope
Since the creation of security of tenure for public sector tenants, there has been a ground to evict those '. . . guilty of conduct which is a nuisance or annoyance to neighbours, or [where the tenant] has been convicted of using the dwelling-house or allowing it to be used for immoral or illegal purposes' (Housing Act 1985, Sch. 2, Ground 2). In *Northampton BC* v *Lovatt*, the Court of Appeal found that there did not need to be any connection between the nuisance complained of and the dwelling house. Thus, as in that case, where the acts complained of took place on a different part of the estate and were not related to the Lovatt's accommodation, this was held to be sufficient. The point was that, according to Henry LJ , 'All [the acts complained of] would damage the quality of life on the estate. All would increase the cost to the community of attempting to keep the peace on the estate. All were legitimate concerns of the local authority as landlord, . . .' (p. 11; for similar comments from Chadwick LJ, see p. 20). Pill LJ dissented, arguing that it was not legitimate to use the Ground in this way: 'It would not include anti-social behaviour elsewhere which was not conducted in the capacity of tenant or resident. *That would be to use the Housing Act as a general instrument for social control, which was not its purpose*' (at p. 12; emphasis added).

The Ground has now been amended by the Housing Act 1996. It makes it much clearer that it is part of a complex of social control:

'The tenant or a person residing in or visiting the dwelling house
(a)   has been guilty of conduct or likely to cause a nuisance or annoyance to a person residing, visiting or otherwise engaging in a lawful activity in the locality, or
(b)   has been convicted of
(i)   using the dwelling-house or allowing it to be used for immoral or illegal purposes, or
(ii)   an arrestable offence committed in, or in the locality of, the dwelling-house' (s. 144)

Thus, the Ground requires no connection between the property and the act (other than (b)(i)).

The court must also be satisfied that it is 'reasonable' to make the order (s 84(2)(a)). We have seen that all factors are regarded as relevant to the determination of reasonableness (see Ch. 13). In several post-1995 cases, it is plain that the higher courts have considerably altered their approaches and have bent over backwards to find it reasonable that the order should be made (although the order might be suspended, as in *West Kensington HA* v *Davis*, Unreported, CA, 24 June 1998). The Court of Appeal has argued that the relevance of rehousing is only a consideration to be taken into account. But the following statement accurately represents the current sentiments of the judiciary to the issue of 'reasonableness':

'The public interest, in my view, is best served by making it abundantly clear to those who have the advantage of public Housing Benefits that, if they commit serious offences at the premises in breach of condition, *save in exceptional cases*, an order for possession will be made. The order will assist the authority, who, . . ., have the duty to manage the housing stock and have the obligation to manage, regulate and control allocation of the houses, for the benefit of the public. In my view the public interest would best be served by the appellant being able in a case such as this to relet the premises to someone who will not use them for peddling crack cocaine.' *Bristol CC* v *Mousah* (1998) 30 HLR 32 (emphasis added)

Mousah had been diagnosed as a chronic schizophrenic with a volatile temperament; Mousah had not sold drugs at the premises (at the most, he was aware that drugs were being sold there).

It follows that reasonableness is an illusionary obstacle in these cases. Whilst District Judges may well be upholding different standards (which, in turn, reflect their ideological views of social housing), it can hardly be said that, in the current state of the law, 'authorities [have] difficulty in convincing the courts of the serious nature of the nuisance caused by the tenant' (DoE, 1995, para. 2.2).

Eviction: Criticisms
Other criticisms of the law relate to delays in getting cases to courts; inconsistency over what is regarded as acceptable evidence; and witness intimidation (exacerbated by delays) (DoE, 1995, para. 2.2). Many of these problems have been dealt with in the Housing Act 1996. So, for example, witness intimidation has been met by the ability of landlords to use professional witnesses (i.e. 'anyone who witnesses relevant incidents in the course of his or her job': Hunter *et al.*, 1998, p. 23) who are able to prove that certain conduct is 'likely to cause a nuisance or annoyance to a person residing, visiting or otherwise engaging in a lawful activity in the locality'. Hunter *et al.* note that we lack systematic evidence of delay (at p. 18) and, though some cases do take a long time to come to court, other evidence points to the fact that the courts could be used 'more effectively', such as through agreements between local authorities and courts to expedite certain cases. Here again, though, the 1996 Act enabled the notice of seeking possession to be dispensed with, where this is 'just and equitable' (s 147(1)). The point is that paring this down further, as some landlords wish, will interfere with the due process rights of the tenants. It

may be unfashionable to argue that such tenants have rights, particularly when their conduct can have deleterious effects on estates, but the effects of stigma are sufficient to raise the importance of legal defences. On the subject of evidence, Hunter et al. make the similar point that 'We simply do not know how many cases are not proceeded with, withdrawn or lost because of inadequate evidence. Nor do we know in how many cases this is cause for concern rather than an indication that legitimate process values are being respected' (*ibid*, p. 23). In short, then, many of the complaints lack substantive evidence but, in any event, have been given far-reaching solutions in the Housing Act 1996.

Innovations in Housing Management

Whilst eviction has been an ever-present threat in the social control of housing estates, legislation has, more recently, provided an ever-increasing number of 'weapons' in the 'war' against anti-social behaviour. In this section, we will concentrate on three such weapons: the introductory tenancy regime; the Noise Act 1996; and the anti-social behaviour order. Only the first is tenure specific to local authorities, but the others, particularly the anti-social behaviour order have been geared towards local authorities.

Introductory Tenancies

This scheme was brought in, as we have seen, because the Conservatives believed that a council tenancy – a 'home for life' – 'has to be earned' (DoE, 1995, para. 3.1). Furthermore, it 'would give a clear signal to new tenants that anti-social behaviour was unacceptable and that it would result in the loss of their home. It would also give reassurance to existing tenants that their authority would take prompt action to remove any new tenants acting in this way' (para. 3.2). Local authorities can opt to enter an introductory tenancy scheme. Its benefit lies in the fact that the tenancy lasts for one year; during that year, the landlord[5] can seek possession for any reason. The decision to seek possession is subject to an internal review at the request of the introductory tenant, and, thereafter, the court must make an order for possession on the request of the council. This is a potent method of crime control in the hands of local authorities. Apparently, at least 40 authorities have chosen to enter such a scheme, including some large landlords like Manchester CC, Lambeth LBC and Sunderland MBC (SLCNG, 1998).

In the introductory tenancy regime, we can witness the most draconian use of the crime control panic. The benefits of the eviction process are that there are sufficient safeguards built into the legislation to protect the due process rights of tenants. In the introductory tenancy regime legislation, however, such safeguards are non-existent. Indeed, the only due process rights appear in the accompanying Guidance (DoE, 1997), which makes it clear that authorities should ensure that the regime 'can never be used as a weapon against vulnerable individuals and ensure that there are safeguards to protect such tenants' (para. 10). Furthermore, landlords using the tenancies are encouraged to evict tenants only on grounds similar to those they are able to use in the secure tenancy regime (para. 19). The only substantive due process rights that the introductory tenant has lie in the right to request a review of the authority's decision to evict (although, as the Guidance suggests, 'it is for those conducting the review to decide, within the constraints of the regulations, how the questioning should be controlled in order to reach a proper assessment of the decision to evict': para. 23). A Statutory Instrument provides the bare bones of the process but no more (as with the homelessness internal review, for example): SI 1997/72. Such internal review processes have, in other areas, been regarded as being notoriously fickle, subject to the individual perceptions of the reviewer(s), and little used (see Davis *et al.*, 1998, Ch. 5; Baldwin *et al.*, 1992).

Noise Act 1996
Under the Noise Act 1996, local authority environmental health officers (EHOs) are entitled to serve warning notices upon persons where noise above a certain level (35decibels) is 'emitted from the offending dwelling during night hours' (s 2(4)(a)). Any subsequent noise above the permitted level is an offence. The noise-making equipment can also be seized by the EHO (s 10(2)). Of course, noise nuisance is a common complaint, but it is difficult to appreciate why the 1996 Act was required when similar powers (albeit not as draconian) existed in the Environmental Protection Act 1990. One possible explanation lies in the campaign by certain sections of the media, most notably the *Daily Mail* and the *Mail on Sunday*, with which the Conservative Party were closely associated. A survey designed to find out whether councils intended to use their powers in the 1996 Act was conducted by the *Mail on Sunday*. This found that, of 134 local authorities, only 16 intended to use the new legislation: 'An astonishing 49 local authorities say they will not, or are unlikely to, introduce the fines aimed at restoring peace and quiet for thousands of residents whose lives are made a misery by a barrage of noise' (Gordon, 1996).

Anti-social Behaviour Orders
A local authority may apply to a Magistrates' Court for an anti-social behaviour order against any person aged 10 or over. The person must have acted in 'an anti-social manner, that is to say, in a manner that caused or was likely to cause harassment, alarm or distress to one or more persons not of the same household as himself'. Additionally, the order must be 'necessary to protect persons in the local government area . . . from further anti-social acts by him' (s 1(1), 1998 Act). Breach of the order is a criminal offence. It is difficult to see why this order was required. After all, as Hunter *et al.* point out in their powerful attack on the order, it is difficult to see quite how far, if at all, this extends the powers of the local authority to gain injunctions and powers of arrest outside those already granted to them by the Housing Act 1996 and Protection from

Harassment Act 1997 (1998, pp. 45–6). Furthermore they argue that 'It is not clear . . . that the anti-social behaviour order is carefully tailored to address the deficiencies of existing remedies. Further uncertainty arises from a lack of clarity over the relationship between civil and criminal justice, and the changing role of the local authority' (*ibid*, p. 47). Cross-reference should also be made with the material about non-police prosecutions considered in Chapter 15. There, it will be remembered, the surveyed material showed that these prosecutions are rare because organizations with such powers tend to operate 'compliance' strategies for various reasons. It is too early to consider how much use of the order is made, but one might speculate that local authorities will shirk away from using it (*cf* Hunter *et al.*, where it is suggested that 'There may be a danger that local authority action will become a substitute for use of the criminal process in situations that would not be appropriate', p. 477 – there is no extrapolation of what the authors regard as 'inappropriate' situations).

Use of the Magistrates' Courts for these orders is significant because it suggests that the government was more concerned with crime control values than with those of due process. Magistrates' Courts are associated with 'summary justice', staffed with lay persons, and are, in essence 'a speedy procedure, uncluttered with elaborate judicial rituals' (Sanders & Young, 1994, p. 253). The research suggests that Magistrates' Courts provide arenas within which class and race bias issues are played out – most magistrates are white, middle class and middle aged with certain values reflecting the property-owning society (*ibid*, pp. 299–300). On the other hand, there also develops a 'local court culture' through which these and other issues are spewed out through rulings on evidence, legal aid, and guilt. The importance of locality, therefore, suggests that the experience of those authorities that do decide to implement the Act in this respect will be fragmented.

Policing Strategies

In this section, two types of policing strategies are considered with specific relationships to housing: zero tolerance, and multi-agency working.

Zero Tolerance
Zero tolerance policing comes from the USA where it has been developed as part of explicit crime control policies, in which due process plays a walk-on part only. This type of policing derives from the 'broken windows' thesis (Wilson & Kelling, 1982). This thesis suggests that if broken windows are not repaired, this will lead to squatting because it is a sign that the police and local agencies of social control are ineffective; squatting in turn will lead to other deviant acts, such as drug use, prostitution, etc.. Given that it requires several leaps of logic and faith, it has had a remarkable reception in criminal justice agencies in the USA and the UK (although see Brogden and Nijhar's comment that 'Applying the

latest chickenburger of policing without thought of context, is like McDonalds selling beefburgers to Hindus and porkburgers to Muslim countries': 1997, p. 21). There is some support for the thesis (see Skogan, 1986), although many of the claims made are controversial. So, for example, there is evidence that deterrent solutions are inappropriate in the case of vandalism (Clarke, 1978, p. 70). The thesis appeals to our salivating need for greater class-based punishment. Most clearly, the thesis is being applied to the policing of begging, and the government are working towards enabling the police to take a more 'directive approach' (Social Exclusion Unit, 1998a, p. 2; see Fooks & Pantazis, 1999).

All the measures considered in this chapter form part of the zero tolerance approach. Nevertheless, a conscious use of the zero tolerance as part of the policing strategy to housing management will produce rather different effects. It will concentrate on deterrence of low-level housing crime, enforce the Noise Act 1996, evictions policies and anti-social behaviour orders. In other words, it will form part of a coordinated strategy involving enforcement, house inspections, estate inspections, lengthy tenancy agreements setting out the responsibilities of the tenant, refusal to house anti-social tenants, even possibly evictions for not doing the gardening. As Harriott puts it: 'We in housing management need to learn from our colleagues in the police and apply the same techniques to our housing management practices if we are to turn the tide of anti-social behaviour which may begin to threaten some of our estates' (1998, p. 29).

Multi-agency Working

As noted in the introduction to this chapter, one of the consequences of the failure of the state to control crime through traditional methods and agencies has been the perceived need to enjoin the 'community' in crime control. Within this method, the 'community' is taken to mean different things, either of a symbolic or real nature (see Crawford, 1997, pp. 149–68). Nevertheless, there appears to have been a gradual realization that both different arms of central government, on the one hand, and of the local state, on the other, need to 'work together' in all spheres of activity. This is expressed in policies concerned with child abuse (DoH, 1990); assessments of need for the purposes of community care and the Children Act 1989 (see Cowan, 1997); and effective solutions to domestic violence and racial harassment. The list can go on and on. The move is from independence to a growing recognition of *interdependence* (Crawford, 1997, p. 66). This carries its own risks for, from another perspective, what is occurring is a dispersal of agencies of social control within the community (net-widening) – 'an inexorable unfolding of *more* social control' (Crawford, p. 73).

This move to multi-agency working, partnerships, joint working, inter-agency working (whatever you want to call it, you will find a corresponding policy initiative) is not unproblematic. For example, housing, social services, probation, and police operate in overlapping areas, made more complex when the agency decentralizes. In any one area, you may find more than one of each. Sampson *et al.* found 'deep rooted structural oppositions between different state agencies, entailing different tasks, preoccupations, responsibilities and powers' (1988, p. 481). Power is a critical issue, with the police often attempting 'to shape and adapt multi-agency agendas to their own interests and preoccupations', although assumptions of unity of interest within individual state agencies is, in itself, not unproblematic (*ibid*, p. 480 & 482; Crawford, pp. 95–6). Multi-agency working also requires a recalibration of the role of housing management for it implies that they are unable to cope with the problems on their estates, and in their accommodation, on their own. It is, in this sense, threatening.

The Crime and Disorder Act 1998, nevertheless, requires local authorities and the police, in conjunction with other state (probation and health committees) and voluntary organizations, to work together to 'formulate and implement . . . a strategy for the reduction of crime and disorder in the area' (s. 6(1)). Strategies need to include the objectives and performance targets. Weighty guidance is now available, although it might be characterized as naive ('It is our clear collective intention that these partnerships should be just that, and that everyone should come to the table on a broadly equal basis': Home Office, 1998, foreword).

By way of conclusion to this section, all of these initiatives (but particularly those in the 1998 Act) require us to reconsider the role of housing management, both in its narrow sense of managing housing, but also in a broader sense, as being a key agent of social control. The 1998 Act may well necessitate the latter being a key influence on the former. It has already been suggested that allocation of accommodation, a key factor considered by environmental criminologists, may well require reconsideration in this light. Reactive housing management – through which housing managers simply react to issues as they arise – may well give way to a more proactive approach, emphasizing a dynamic relationship. between tenants and managers, residents in an authority area and the authority itself, as well as between the agencies. Of course, the 1998 Act might prove a damp squib, but these processes have been going on for some time now, irrespective of that Act.

Conclusion

In this chapter, we have considered the role of housing as a criminogenic situation. It has been argued that the housing market and the local housing processes have contributed to the development of crime, although they are dynamic and change over time. No single method of turning estates round seems successful, no doubt because of the economic marginalization of the areas. We then turned to look at the development of a specific crime – anti-social behaviour – which is clearly linked to the environment. What is interesting (and important) about this crime is that it lacks a definition. Indeed, the various government consultations and legislation have struggled to define it. It is a label which covers a multitude of criminal and non-criminal acts, although it is difficult to pinpoint them. Whilst it, therefore, lacks objective existence, we can nevertheless point to the people who commit it and the places where it is committed. We argued that this can only be understood through an appreciation of local processes and the ideological preference of government, particularly the Conservative stigmatization of council housing.

In the following section, we considered the way anti-social behaviour has become the justification for a wide range of actions that threaten to create a more apparent culture of crime control in housing management. However, we noted that social control has always been a principal motivation for council housing, exemplified by the grant of security of tenure. We then considered the recent 'advances' and the threats they represent to the due process rights of individuals and the recalibration of housing management. These attacks on council housing can only be understood as an attack on the classes which occupy them. In this sense, we are witnessing a definite return to the concept of housing classes developed by Rex and Moore, although here we are showing zero tolerance to the lowest class – council housing. The remaining question is what happens to those who are excluded, for they are likely to be excluded from social housing allocation processes. It is likely that such people end up in the 'twilight zones' of the private rented sector, which in itself suggests that the problems are being passed on through the tenures without any attempt at grappling with their root causes.

Further Reading

Only a small amount of the environmental criminology literature is referred to in this chapter. A. Bottoms and P. Wiles have sought to draw links between the literature and structuration theory (1992), 'Explanations of crime and place' in D. Evans, N. Fyfe and D. Herbert (eds), *Crime, Policing and Place: Essays in Environmental Criminology*, London: Routledge; for other approaches, see, for example, I. Taylor, P. Walton & J. Young (1973), *The New Criminology: For a Social Theory of deviance*, London; Routledge; J. Lea & J. Young (1993), *What is to be Done about Law and Order?*, London: Pluto; see also, D. Evans (1992), 'Left realism and the spatial study of crime', D. Evans, N. Fyfe and D. Herbert (eds), *Crime, Policing and Place: Essays in Environmental Criminology*, London: Routledge; J. Foster (1990), *Villains: Crime and Community in the Inner City*, London: Routledge; A. Power (1986), 'Housing, community and crime', in D. Downes (ed), *Crime and the City: Essays in Memory of John Barron Mays*, London: Macmillan; D. Cook (1997), *Poverty, Crime and Punishment*, London: CPAG; H. Jones and D. Short (1993), 'The pocketing of crime within the city: evidence from Dundee public-housing estates', in H. Jones (ed.), *Crime and the Urban Environment*, Aldershot: Avebury, a more specifically housing policy oriented approach is given by J. English (1979), 'Access and deprivation in local authority housing', in C. Jones (ed.), *Urban Deprivation and the Inner City*, London: Croom Helm; and M. Jones (1988), 'Utopia and reality: the utopia of public housing and its reality at Broadwater Farm', in N. Teymur, T. Markus & T. Woolley (eds), *Rehumanizing Housing*, London: Butterworths.

On anti-social behaviour, the most important text is C. Hunter, T. Mullen, and S. Scott (1998), *Legal Remedies for Neighbour Nuisance: Comparing Scottish and English Approaches*, York: Joseph Rowntree Foundation; more legalistic is J. Luba, N. Madge and D. McConnell (1997), *Defending Possession Proceedings*, London: LAG; a short, but effective, critique of the recent cases on evictions can be found at J. Manning (1998), 'Reasonableness: a new approach', vol 1, *Journal of Housing Law*, 59. One aspect of the social control of neighbour nuisance not considered here (for space considerations) is the move towards mediation, on which see J. Dignan, A. Sorsby & J. Hibbert (1996), *Neighbour Disputes: Comparing the Cost-Effectiveness of Mediation and Alternative Approaches*, Sheffield: Centre for Criminological and Legal Research, University of Sheffield; V. Karn, R. Lickiss, D. Hughes and J. Crawley (1993), *Neighbour Disputes: Responses by Social Landlords*, Coventry: Institute of Housing; Aldbourne Associates (1993), *Managing Neighbour Complaints in Social Housing*, Aldbourne: Aldbourne Associates.

On racial harassment, to which only brief reference is made in the text, see M. Fitzgerald & C. Hale (1996), *Ethnic Minorities, Victimisation and Racial Harassment*, Home Office Study No 154, London: Home Office; Commission for Racial Equality (1987), *Living in Terror*, London: CRE

For material on the Crime and Disorder Act 1998, the Home Office has a dedicated web page at its site.

Endnotes

1. The notion of a 'problem family' is considered below.
2. 'Defensible space' refers to the creation of spaces which can be monitored and subjected to surveillance, as part of a revival of social control mechanisms.
3. Sibbitt, by contrast, has found that 'It is questionable whether [perpetrator eviction] results in much improvement for the victims. In the case of injunctions of 'perpetrator removals', friends and relatives of the perpetrators, or other members of the community, may continue to victimise them' (1997, p. 2).
4. As part of the critique of the legislation.
5. Local authorities and Housing Action Trusts are entitled to use this scheme. For ease of expression, the accompanying text refers only to local authorities.

Bibliography

Arlidge, J. (1996), '"Ghetto from hell" sparks estate fury', *The Observer*, 27 October

Baldwin, J. (1979), 'Ecological and areal studies in Great Britain and the United States', in N. Morris & M. Tonry (eds), *Crime and Justice (An Annual Review of Research)*, Vol 1, Chicago: Chicago University Press

Baldwin, J., Wikeley, N. and Young, R. (1992), *Judging Social Security*, Oxford: Oxford University Press

Becker, H. (1963), *The Outsiders*, New York: The Free Press

Bennett, C. (1998), 'Hell on the range', *The Guardian*, 7 March

Bottoms, A., Claytor, A. and Wiles, P. (1992), 'Housing markets and residential community crime careers: A case study from Sheffield', in D. Evans, N. Fyfe and D. Herbert (eds), *Crime, Policing and Place: Essays in Environmental Criminology*, London: Routledge

Bottoms, A. and Wiles, P. (1986), 'Housing tenure and residential community crime careers in Britain', in A. Reiss and M. Tonry (eds), *Crime and Justice: A Review of Research – Communities and Crime*, Chicago: University of Chicago Press

Bottoms, A. and Wiles, P. (1997), 'Environmental criminology', in R. Morgan & R. Reiner (eds), *The Oxford Handbook of Criminology*, Oxford: Oxford University Press

Bottoms, A. and Xanthos, P. (1986), 'Housing policy and crime in the British public sector', in P. Brantingham and P. Brantingham (eds), *Environmental Criminology*, Beverly Hills: Sage

Brogden, M. and Nijhar, P. (1997), 'Rediscovering the residuum – zero tolerance and reconstituting the control of the poor', in L. Lundy, M. Adler & S. Wheeler (eds), *In Search of the Underclass*, Belfast: SLSA

Brownlee, I. (1998), 'New Labour – new penology? Punitive rhetoric and the limits of managerialism in criminal justice policy', vol 25, *Journal of Law and Society*, 313

Butler, S. (1998), *Access Denied*, London: Shelter

Clapham, D., Kintrea, K., Malcolm, J., Parkey, H. and Scott, S. (1995), *A Baseline Study of Housing Management in Scotland*, Edinburgh: Scottish Office

Clarke, R. (1978), *Tackling Vandalism*, Home Office Research Study No 47, London: HMSO

Cohen, S. (1985), *Visions of Social Control*, Cambridge: Polity

Coleman, A. (1985), *Utopia on Trial*, London: Hilary Shipman

Cooper, J. and Qureshi, T. (1994), 'Violence, racial harassment and council tenants: reflections on the limits of the disputing process', vol 8, *Housing Studies*, 241

Cowan, D. (1997), *Homelessness: The (in)Appropriate Applicant*, Aldershot: Dartmouth

Cowan, D. and Gilroy, R. (1999), 'The homelessness legislation as a vehicle for marginalization: making an example out of the paedophile', in T. Kennett & A. Marsh (eds), *Homelessness: Exploring the New Terrain*, Bristol: Policy Press

Crawford, A. (1997), *The Local Governance of Crime: Appeals to Community and Partnerships*, Oxford: Clarendon

Damer, D. (1974), 'Wine alley: the sociology of a dreadful enclosure', vol 22, *Sociological Review*, 221

Davis, G., Wikeley, N. and Young, R. (1998), *Child Support in Action*, Oxford: Hart

Department of the Environment (DoE) (1992), *Gypsy Site Policy and Illegal Camping*, London: DoE

Department of the Environment (DoE) (1994), *Racial Incidents in Council Housing: The Local Authority Response*, London: HMSO

Department of the Environment (DoE) (1995), *Anti-social Behaviour on Council Estates: A Consultation Paper on Probationary Tenancies*, London: DoE

Department of the Environment (DoE) (1997), 'Part V of the Housing Act 1996 – Conduct of Tenants', Circular 2/97, London: DoE

Department of Health (DoH) (1990), *Working Together*, London: DoH

Dhooge, Y. and Barelli, J. (1996), *Racial Attacks and Harassment: The Response of Social Landlords*, London: HMSO

Felstiner, W., Abel, R. and Sarat, A. (1980–1), 'The emergence and transformation of disputes: naming, blaming, claiming', vol 15, *Law and Society Review*, 631

Fooks, G. and Pantazis, C. (1999), 'Criminalisation of homelessness, begging and street living', in T. Kennett & A. Marsh (eds), *Homelessness: Exploring the New Terrain*, Bristol: Policy Press

Foster, J. and Hope, T. (1993), *Housing Community and Crime: The Impact of the Priority Estates Project*, Home Office Research Study No 131, London: Home Office

Garland, D. (1996), 'The limits of the sovereign state: strategies of crime control in contemporary society', vol 36, *British Journal of Criminology*, 445

Gilroy, R. (1996), 'Building routes to power: lessons from Cruddas Park', vol 11, *Local Economy*, 248

Gilroy, R. (1998), 'Bringing tenants into decision-making', in D. Cowan (ed), *Housing: Participation and Exclusion*, Aldershot: Dartmouth

Gordon, A. (1996), 'Scandal of councils turning deaf ear to new noise laws', *Mail on Sunday*, 10 November

Hall, S., Critcher, C., Jefferson, T., Clarke, J. and Roberts, B. (1978), *Policing the Crisis: Mugging, the State, and Law and Order*, London: Macmillan

Harriot, S. (1998), 'Zero tolerance in housing', June/July, *Housing Review*, 28

Herbert, D. (1980), *The Geography of Urban Crime*, London: Longman

Hetherington, P. (1998), 'Billions wasted on unwanted homes', *The Guardian*, 3 August

Home Office (1989), *The Response to Racial Attacks and Harassment: Guidance for the Statutory Agencies*, London: Home Office

Home Office (1991), *Squatting: A Consultation Paper*, London: Home Office

Home Office (1997), *Community Safety Orders: A Consultation Paper*, London: Home Office

Home Office (1998), *Guidance on Statutory Crime and Disorder Partnerships*, London: Home Office

Hope, T. (1998), 'Community crime prevention', in P. Goldblatt and C. Lewis (eds), *Reducing Offending: An Assessment of Research Evidence on Ways of Dealing with Offending Behaviour*, Home Office Research Study No 187, London: Home Office

Hope, T. and Foster, J. (1992), 'Conflicting forces: changing the dynamics of crime and community on a 'problem' estate', vol 32, *British Journal of Criminology*, 488

Housing Corporation (1998), *Managing Anti-Social Behaviour by RSL Tenants*, London: Housing Corporation

Hughes, D. (1998), 'The legitimacy of using the powers of local authority landlords as means of social control', paper given to the Socio-Legal Studies Association Annual Conference, Manchester Metropolitan University, April

Hughes, D., Karn, V. and Lickiss, R. (1994), 'Neighbour disputes, social landlords and the law', vol 14, *Journal of Social Welfare and Family Law*, 201

Hugill, B. (1998), 'Clear threat', *The Guardian*, 4 March

Hunter, C., Mullen, T. and Scott, S. (1998), *Legal Remedies for Neighbour Nuisance: Comparing Scottish and English Approaches*, York: Joseph Rowntree Foundation

Jacobs, K. & Manzi, T. (1996), 'Discourse and policy change: the significance of language for housing research', vol 11, *Housing Studies*, 543

Karn, V., Lickiss, R. and Hughes, D. (1997), *Tenants' Complaints and the Reform of Housing Management*, Aldershot: Dartmouth

Labour Party (1995), *A Quiet Life: Tough Action on Criminal Neighbours*, London: Labour Party

Lee, P. and Murie, A. (1997), *Poverty, Housing Tenure and Social Exclusion*, Bristol: Policy Press

Lund, B. (1995), *Housing Problems and Housing Policy*, London: Longman

Malik, N. (1998), 'Nowhere to run', September/October, *Roof*, 16

Major, J. (1995), '*The Future of Cities*', London: Downing Street Press Office

Mirless-Black, C., Budd, T., Partridge, S. and Mayhew, P. (1998), *The 1998 British Crime Survey: England and Wales*, London: Home Office

Mullen, T., Scott, S., Fitzpatrick, S. and Goodlad, R. (1997), *Tenancy Rights and Repossession Rates in Theory and Practice*, Research Report 55, Edinburgh: Scottish Homes

Murie, A. (1997), 'Linking housing changes to crime', vol 31, *Social Policy and Administration*, 22

Murray, C. (1990), *Underclass: The Crisis Deepens*, London: IEA

Newman, O. (1972), *Defensible Space*, London: Architectural Press

Packer, H. (1968), *The Limits of the Criminal Sanction*, California: Stanford University Press

Page, D. (1993), *Building for Communities: A Study of New Housing Association Estates*, York: Joseph Rowntree Foundation

Pantazis, C. (forthcoming), 'Fear of crime: vulnerability and poverty', *British Journal of Criminology*

Papps, P. (1998), 'Anti-social behaviour strategies – individualistic or holistic?', vol 13, *Housing Studies*, 639

Pawson, H. and Kearns, A. (1998), 'Difficult to let housing association stock in England: property, management and context', vol 13, *Housing Studies*, 391

Popplestone, G. and Paris, C. (1979), *Managing Difficult Tenants*, Research Series 30, London: Centre for Environmental Studies

Power, A. and Tunstall, J. (1995), *Swimming Against the Tide: Polarization or Progress on 20 Unpopular Council Estates 1980-1995*, York: Joseph Rowntree Foundation

Rex, J. and Moore, R. (1967), *Race, Community and Conflict*, Oxford: Oxford University Press

Reynolds, F. (1986), *The Problem Estate*, Aldershot: Gower

Sampson, A., Stubbs, P., Smith, D., Pearson, G. and Blagg, H. (1988), 'Crime, localities and the multi-agency approach', vol 28, *British Journal of Criminology*, 478

Sanders, A. and Young, R. (1994), *Criminal Justice*, London: Butterworths

Scott, S. and Parkey, H. (1998), 'Myths and reality: anti-social behaviour in Scotland', vol 13, *Housing Studies*, 325

Scottish Affairs Committee (1996), *Housing and Anti-Social Behaviour*, London: SO

Sibbitt, R. (1997), *The Perpetrators of Racial Harassment and Racial Violence*, Home Office Research Study 176, London: Home Office

Skogan, W. (1986), 'Fear of crime and neighborhood change', in A. Reiss and M. Tonry (eds), *Crime and Justice: A Review of Research – Communities and Crime*, Chicago: University of Chicago Press

Social Exclusion Unit (SEU) (1998a), *Rough Sleeping Report by the Social Exclusion Unit*, Cm 4008, London: SO

Social Exclusion Unit (SEU) (1998b), *Bringing Britain Together: A National Strategy for Neighbourhood Renewal*, Cm 4045, London: SO

Social Landlords Crime and Nuisance Group (SLCNG) (1998), *Introductory Tenancies: Report on Survey of Local Authorities Practice as at 1 May 1998*, Coventry: SLCNG

Smith, N. and George, G. (1997), 'Introductory tenancies: a nuisance too far?', vol 19, *Journal of Social Welfare and Family Law*, 307

Taylor, M. (1995), *Unleashing the Potential*, York: Joseph Rowntree Foundation

Taylor, M. (1998), 'Combating the social exclusion of housing estates', vol 13, *Housing Studies*, 819

Wilson, J. and Kelling, G. (1982), 'Broken windows: the police and neighborhood safety', March, *Atlantic Monthly*, 29

Index